The WORLD ENCYCLOPEDIA OF CONTEMPORARY THEATRE

VOLUME 6

BIBLIOGRAPHY/CUMULATIVE INDEX

The WORLD ENCYCLOPEDIA OF CONTEMPORARY THEATRE

VOLUME 6

BIBLIOGRAPHY/CUMULATIVE INDEX

DON RUBIN

LONDON AND NEW YORK

First published 2000 by Routledge

11 New Fetter Lane, London EC4P 4EE

Simultaneously published in the USA and Canada
by Routledge
29 West 35th Street, New York 10001

Routledge is an imprint of the Taylor & Francis Group

Typeset in Sabon and Optima by MCS Ltd, Wiltshire
Printed and bound in Great Britain by Biddles Ltd, Guildford and King's Lynn

British Library Cataloguing in Publication Data
A catalogue record for this book is available from the British Library.

Library of Congress Cataloging in Publication Data
95–214751

ISBN 0–415–05934–8

The World Encyclopedia of Contemporary Theatre would like to acknowledge with sincere thanks the financial contributions of the following:

REGIONAL SPONSORS

Canadian Department of Communications
Ford Foundation
Japan Foundation (Asia Centre)
Ontario Ministry of Citizenship and Culture
Rockefeller Foundation
Routledge
Social Sciences and Humanities Research
    Council of Canada
Unesco
York University

NATIONAL SPONSORS

Autonomous National University of México
Cameroon National Unesco Commission
Canadian National Unesco Commission
Cheik Anta Diop University, Dakar
Cultural Ministry of France
Department of Foreign Affairs and
    International Trade of Canada
German Centre of the ITI
Higher Institute of Dramatic Arts, Damascus
Mexican National Unesco Commission
Joseph S. Stauffer Foundation
University of Bordeaux
Herman Voaden
Woodlawn Arts Foundation

STATE SPONSORS

Apotex Foundation
Austrian Ministry of Education and the Arts
Samuel and Saidye Bronfman Family
    Foundation
Floyd S. Chalmers
Faculty of Fine Arts, York University
Finnish Ministry of Education
FIRT
Georgian Ministry of Culture
Greek Ministry of Culture
Calouste Gulbenkian Foundation

International Theatre Institute (Paris) and
    National Centres in Bangladesh, Belgium,
    Bulgaria, Canada, Czech Republic,
    Finland, Hungary, India, Netherlands,
    Poland, Romania, Slovak Republic,
    Switzerland, United States and Venezuela
Israeli Ministry of Foreign Affairs, Division of
    Cultural and Scientific Relations
Japan Foundation Cultural Centre, Bangkok
Japan Foundation, Toronto
Henry White Kinnear Foundation
Ministry of the Flemish Community
    (Cultural Affairs)
Moldovan Theatre Union
Organization of American States
Polish Ministry of Culture
Republic of Macedonia Ministry of Culture
K.M. Sarkissian and the Zoryan Institute
Conn Smythe Foundation
Turkish Embassy in Canada

LOCAL SPONSORS

Marion Andre
Arts Development and Promotions
Australian Council
Mariellen Black
Lyle B. Blair
Canadian Theatre Review
Centre de Recherches et de Formation
    Théâtrales en Wallonie
Max Clarkson Foundation
Joy Cohnstaedt
Freda's Originals
H. Ian Macdonald
John H. Moore, FCA
Erminio G. Neglia
Farouk Ohan
Ontario Ministry of Skills Development
Peter Perina
E. Marshall Pollock
Rodolfo A. Ramos
Calvin G. Rand
Lynton Reed Printing
Don Rubin and Patricia Keeney
St Lawrence Centre for the Arts
Storewal International Inc.
Anton Wagner

Special thanks to:

Margrethe Aaby (Norway), Eric Alexander (Netherlands), Ebrahim Alkhazi (India), Ina Andre (Canada), Gaida Barisone (Latvia), Curtis Barlow (Canada), Isabelle Barth (France), Alexei Bartoshevitch (Russia), Shaul Baskind (Israel), Jean Benedetti (United Kingdom), Eric Bentley (United States), Don Berkowitz (Canada), Mariellen Black (Canada), Lyle B. Blair (Canada), Gaston Blais (Canada), Monica Brizzi (Italy), Robert Brustein (United States), John Bury (United Kingdom), Judith Cameron (Canada), Richard Cave (United Kingdom), Katarina Ćirić-Petrović (Serbia), Martin Cloutier (United States), Joy Cohnstaedt (Canada), Martha Coigney (United States), Communications Committee (International Theatre Institute), Leonard W. Conolly (Canada), Robert Crew (Canada), Renée L. Czukar (Canada), Esther A. Dagan (Canada), Gautam Dasgupta (United States), Donna Dawson (Canada), Astad Deboo (India), Susan Frances Dobie (Canada), Francis Ebejer (Malta), Krista Ellis (Canada), John Elsom (United Kingdom), Claes Englund (Sweden), Debebe Eshetu (Ethiopia), Martin Esslin (United Kingdom), Alan Filewod (Canada), Stephen Florian (Malta), Joyce Flynn (United States), Mira Friedlander (Canada), Julia Gabor (Hungary), Bibi Gessner (Switzerland), Madeleine Gobeil (Unesco), Mayte Gómez (Canada), Sevelina Gyorova (Bulgaria), René Hainaux (Belgium), Bartold Halle (Norway), Peter Hay (United States), Ian Herbert (United Kingdom), Nick Herne (United Kingdom), Frank Hoff (Canada), Eleanor Hubbard (Canada), Huang Huilin (China), Djuner Ismail (Macedonia), Jasmine Jaywant (Canada), Stephen Johnson (Canada), Sylvia Karsh (Canada), Naïm Kattan (Canada), Karl George Kayser (Meiningen State Theatre, Germany), Ferenc Kerenyi (Hungary), Myles Kesten (Canada), Valery Khasanov (Russia), William Kilbourn (Canada), Pierre Laville (France), George Lengyel (Hungary), Henri Lopes (Unesco), Meredith Lorden (Canada), Paul Lovejoy (Canada), Margaret Majewska (Poland), Lars af Malmborg (Sweden), Georges Manal (France), Suzanne Marko (Sweden), Bonnie Marranca (New York), Vivian Martínez Tabares (Cuba), Ruth R. Mayleas (United States), Giles R. Meikle (Canada), Paul-Louis Mignon (France), Ian Montagnes (Canada), Mavor Moore (Canada), Richard Mortimer (Canada), Judi Most (United States), Julia Moulden (Canada), Irmeli Niemi (Finland), Farouk Ohan (United Arab Emirates), Louis Patenaude (Canada), Oskar Pausch (Austria), André-Louis Perinetti (International Theatre Institute), Natasha Rapoport (Canada), Donald S. Rickerd (Canada), Roehampton Hotel (Canada), Charles-Antoine Rouyer (Canada), Mr and Mrs Irving Rubin (United States), Marti Russell (Canada), Raimonda Sadauskienė (Lithuania), Suzanne Sato (United States), Willmar Sauter (Sweden), Richard Schechner (United States), Petar Selem (Croatia), Małgorzata Semil (Poland), Mary Ann Shaw (Canada), Neville Shulman (United Kingdom), Mikhail Shvidkoi (Russia), David Silcox (Canada), Phillip Silver (Canada), Singer Travel (United States), Ron Singer (Canada), Mike Smith (Canada), Prince Subhadradis Diskul (Thailand), Anneli Suur-Kujala (Finland), Péter Szaffkó (Hungary), Carlos Tindemans (Belgium), Graham Usher (Canada), Indrassen Vencatchellum (Unesco), Janusz Warminski (Poland), Klaus Wever (Germany), Don B. Wilmeth (American Society for Theatre Research), Claudia Woolgar (United Kingdom), Yoh Suk-Kee (South Korea), Piet Zeeman (Netherlands), Paul Zeleza (Canada).

INTERNATIONAL EDITORIAL BOARD

DEDICATION

This series is dedicated to the memory of Roman Szydłowski of Poland (1918–83), a former President of the International Association of Theatre Critics. His vision for all international theatre organizations was truly world-wide and his tenacity in the service of that vision was genuinely legendary. It was Dr Szydłowski who first proposed the idea for a *World Encyclopedia of Contemporary Theatre*.

CONTENTS

VOLUME SIX • BIBLIOGRAPHY/CUMULATIVE INDEX

Introduction. Cultural Cartography: The making of a theatre map   3
Don Rubin

Bibliography

VOLUME SIX

BIBLIOGRAPHY/ CUMULATIVE INDEX

INTRODUCTION

CULTURAL CARTOGRAPHY:
THE MAKING OF A THEATRE MAP

The *World Encyclopedia of Contemporary Theatre* is essentially a piece of cultural cartography – the first attempt to create a truly inter-cultural and non-colonial world map of theatrical activity. It has tried to avoid value judgements (although that is impossible) in its quest to identify and articulate the theatrical and the performative world-wide. The period covered has essentially been the second half of the twentieth century but in many instances the material ranges much further back in time in an effort to allow the contemporary theatre researcher to draw on related materials giving deeper insight into the period under examination. This particular volume – a bibliography of world theatre and cumulative index – becomes to the five preceding regional volumes a compass of sorts identifying in a somewhat more scientific way specific theatrical rivers and mountains within each land and, on occasion, major roads and topographical landmarks.

How was this map created?

As each national essay was written, we asked our writers and regional editors to include a list of significant books. Augmented by members of our International Editorial Board, these lists of recommended 'Further Reading' were included at the end of each essay, pointing the researcher into other areas of examination. This final volume goes still further and includes not only updated 'Further Reading' lists but also thousands of additional books that were not able to be included in the regional volumes for reasons of space.

The emphasis, once again in this volume, has been on nations and their theatres and many books are listed here for the first time in an internationally-published reference work. Our taxonomy too has been built around the 160 countries and the five geographical regions that make up the *WECT* world, a world which follows United Nations regional guidelines and which has allowed us to further focus this map.

Our approach was, of course, not without its complications. Should we, for example, list a book on Brazilian cultural policy under 'Brazil' or under 'Cultural Policy'? Should we list a book about the Nigerian dramatist Wole Soyinka under 'Nigeria' or under 'Playwriting'? And what if such a book were written in Italian but first published in English in Germany? As well, theatre artists (and the books about them) rarely stay within defined lines. Is Grotowski's work primarily about Poland? Should such books appear in a Polish section? Obviously not. On the other hand, to use a Richard Schechner phrase, Grotowski's work is also 'not not' about Poland. Should Grotowski books then appear under the 'Directing' section in our taxonomy or should they appear under headings such as 'Cultural Anthropology' or 'Philosophy' or 'Manifestos'? We thought of double entries and in a few cases we did double-enter, but with a space limit of about 6,000 titles, we were unable to double- or triple-enter too often. Hard placement decisions had to be made. What we opted for finally was the somewhat amusing notion that we would put books where we thought theatre researchers might actually be most likely to look for them.

The result was a taxonomy that begins with the world (International studies of theatre and drama), moves on to studies of theatre by geographical regions and then on to the expanded 160 national bibliographies. From there the taxonomy widens (or perhaps narrows if you prefer) into categories of continuing interest to this project – puppetry, theatre for young audiences, music and dance theatre, cultural policy and theatre anthropology – while allowing the inclusion of traditional areas such as acting, directing, playwriting, design and theatre space.

It was a hard but practical decision to only include *books*, with a few exceptions, in this bibliography and not journal, magazine or newspaper materials. But even dealing with books alone, space limits were reached quickly and we were again faced with crucial choices. More often than not, we turned back to the notion of 'usefulness' as final arbiter. So a book in Korean about avant-garde British theatre might be dropped in this English-language edition in favour of a book about avant-garde British theatre written by a British writer.

The result is a bibliography not of 'all' or even simply the 'best' theatre books in the world (an impossible concept in any event) but a bibliography identifying those books that have been deemed by our writers and editors to be among the most useful for theatre researchers and professional theatre workers. This, we believe, follows our initial mandate: to create a map for theatre people trying to find their way on the high seas of a rapidly internationalizing theatre globe.

Having said that, it should be pointed out as well that though this is essentially a bibliography for those able to work in English, books in other languages (especially French, German, Spanish and Italian) have been included as have national titles in other less widely spoken languages. The same guidelines have been used for books about particular playwrights, directors, designers and actors, and books about those figures generally appear under their home nations.

The exception in this area are books about theatre figures whose works are known in at least three regions of the world (hence the 'Playwriting' section includes mostly internationally-known figures such as Brecht, Beckett, Ionesco or Albee). It should be noted here too that space limitations also prevented us from including collections of plays. The numbers in this category would have been far too vast and the choices for inclusion far too subjective to be useful.

Even harder to taxonomize were works by some of the major international theatre figures of the period – visionary artists such as England's Peter Brook, Brazil's Augusto Boal, Italy's Eugenio Barba, the US director Robert Wilson and cultural anthropologist Richard Schechner, France's Ariane Mnouchkine, Germany's Pina Bausch, Japan's Terayama Shuji and the aforementioned Jerzy Grotowski. So we invented a category that seemed somewhat

logical – 'Visions, statements and manifestos' – and put at least the core works by these and other theatre visionaries in that section along with *studies* of their groundbreaking ideas.

As for annotation, we began this volume by opting for full annotation but realized that the titles and categorization of most of the volumes already offered researchers sufficient information to make decisions on whether books listed would be useful to them. In those instances where titles and categories provided little information, however, we added in keyword annotation and, in some instances, a fuller sense of the contents.

Over the years of work on this volume, nearly a thousand theatre scholars were involved in various ways. Through the early years of our work, Irving Brown of the Theater Research Data Center at Brooklyn College faithfully set up bibliographical systems and policies for us and in recent years was joined by Rosabel Wang whose technical knowledge in the field and generosity of time was deeply appreciated. The major work – the creation of a data base of more than 15,000 theatre titles – was done between 1997 and 1998 by Natasha Rapoport, a professional theatre bibliographer trained in Moscow and now living in Toronto. This volume would not have been completed without her enormous energy, goodwill and bibliographical skills nor without the added technical data base skills and general understanding of her husband, Vladimir Ploshko.

The final editing and shaping of the volume was done during 1999 thanks to research grants from York University and from York's Faculty of Fine Arts. These grants allowed me to engage the talents of a recent York theatre graduate, Amy May, whose computer skills, sense of detail, and constant smile made the dash to the finish line almost seem pleasurable. As always, my co-visionary in this work, Patricia Keeney, held this bibliography together when it was at its most tenuous. They – along with Leonard Conolly, Calvin Rand, Rolf Rohmer and other members of the *WECT* Board of Directors who fought to complete this work – also need to be acknowledged here.

A final personal word to those who must and will one day in the future refine this map. I wish you good sailing, my friends. May your voyage prove to be as extraordinary as mine. May it also be, for your own good health, not half so rocky.

Don Rubin
Toronto/BelVau
August 1999

BIBLIOGRAPHY

A. International, Regional and National Studies, Theatre and Drama

A1. International Studies

Arnott, Peter. **The theatre in its time**. Boston, MA: Little, Brown, 1981. 566 p.

Aslan, Odette. **L'Art du théâtre**. [The art of theatre]. Verviers: Marabout, 1963. 672 p.

Attisani, Antonio. **Enciclopedia del teatro del '900**. [Theatre encyclopedia of the twentieth century]. Milan: Feltrinelli, 1980. 600 p.

Awad, Louis. **Al masrah al alami**. [World theatre]. Egypt: 1964.

Bailey, Claudia Jean. **A guide to reference and bibliography for theatre research**. 2nd edn. Columbus: Ohio State University Libraries, 1983.

Band-Kuzmany, Karin R. M. **Glossary of the theatre. In English, French, Italian and German**. Amsterdam, New York: Elsevier Pub. Co., 1969. 130 p.

Banham, Martin. **The Cambridge guide to theatre**. Cambridge: Cambridge University Press, 1995. – xiii, 1233 p.: ill. *Notes*: Rev. edn. of **The Cambridge guide to world theatre**. 1988. Includes bibliography. One vol. guide to theatre and drama world-wide including theatre history.

Barfoot, C.C. and Cobi Bordewijk, eds. **Theatre intercontinental: forms, functions, correspondences**. Amsterdam/Atlanta, GA: Rodopi, 1993. 224 p.

Beacham, Walton. **Research guide to biography and criticism: world drama**. Washington, D.C.: Beacham, 1986. – vii, 742 p. *Notes*: Includes a cumulative index. to vols 1 and 2 of **Research guide to biography and criticism**. Dramatists. Biography. Bibliography.

Bharati, Sasi. **Glossary of drama, theatre, and electronic media: English–Hindi**. Delhi: B.R. Pub. Corp., 1996. – 142 p.

Bowman, Walter Parker and Robert Hamilton Ball. **Theatre language; a dictionary of terms in English of the drama and stage from medieval to modern times**. New York: Theatre Arts Books, 1961. – xii, 428 p.

Brauneck, Manfred, and Gerard Schneilin, eds. **Theaterlexikon: Begriffe und Epoche. Bühnen und Ensembles**. [Theatre lexicon: terms and periods. Stages and ensembles]. Hamburg: Rowohlt, 1986. 1,120 p.

Brockett, Oscar G. **History of the theatre**. 6th edn. Boston, MA: Allyn & Bacon, 1990. 680 p.

Brown, Michèle. **The Guinness dictionary of theatrical quotations**. Enfield: Guinness Publishing, 1993. – 222 p.: ill.

Brunius, Niklas. **Teaterord [Theatre words]**. rev. version. Stockholm: Nordiska teaterunionen, 1977. – 207 p.: illus. *Notes*: Theatre terms translated in the five Scandinavian languages, German, English and French. Includes indexes.

Buzo, Alexander. **The young person's guide to the theatre and almost everything else**. Ringwood, Victoria: Penguin, 1988. 164 p.

Campos, Geir. **Glossário de termos técnicos do espetáculo**. Niterói, RJ: Universidade Federal Fluminense, Editora Universitária, 1989. – 161 p. Theatre terms in Portuguese.

Cao, Yu, and Wang, Zuo Ling, eds. **China's great encyclopedia of world theatre and drama**. Beijing/Shanghai: China's Great Encyclopedia Press, 1989. 583 p. In Chinese.

Case, Sue-Ellen and Janelle Reinelt. **The Performance of power: theatrical discourse and politics**. Iowa City: University of Iowa Press, 1991. – xix, 284 p.: ill. *Notes*: Includes bibliographical references. Sexual politics and cultural identity in The masque of blackness/Kim F. Hall – The good soldier Schwejk as dialectical theatre/Sarah Bryant-Bertail – Revolution ... history ... theatre: the politics of the Wooster Group second trilogy/David Savran – Bernard Shaw and the drama of imperialism/J. Ellen Gainor – Constructing Patroclus: the high and low discourses of Renaissance sodomy/Gregory W. Bredbeck – The politics of Metamora/Jeffrey D. Mason – The Eurocolonial reception of Sanskrit poetics/Sue-Ellen Case – The artificial eye: Augustan theater and the empire of the visible/Joseph Roach – The playhouse and the committee/Barry B. Witham – Spectacle as government: Dickens and the working-class audience/Janice Carlisle – Victorian players and sages/Nina Auerbach – Charlie Chaplin, Soviet icon/Spencer Golub – Theorizing utopia: Edward Bond's war plays/Janelle Reinelt – Demographics and the academy/Margaret B. Wilkerson – The challenge to professional training and development/Simon Williams – Integrating instruction, production, and research/Jon Whitmore – Conferring power in the theatre/Gay Gibson Cima – New historicism and American theatre history: toward an interdisciplinary paradigm for scholarship/Bruce A. McConachie – The theory of history/Marvin Carlson.

Cassell companion to theatre. Revised and updated edition. London: Cassell, 1997. – ix, 513 p. General guide.

Cheney, Sheldon. **The theatre; three thousand years of drama, acting, and stagecraft**. Rev. and reset illustrated edn, with a new bibliography. New York: McKay, 1972. – xv, 710 p. illus. *Notes*: Bibliography: p. 677–88.

Corvin, Michel. **Dictionnaire encyclopédique du théâtre**. Paris: Bordas, 1995. – 2 vols. (xiii–1013 p.): ill. *Notes*: Includes bibliographical references (p. 971–83) and indexes. vol. 1. A–K – vol. 2. L–Z. Includes general history plus articles on actors, directors, designers, genres, terms.

Couty, Daniel, and Alan Rey, eds. **Le Théâtre**. [Theatre]. Paris: Bordas, 1980.

D'Amico, Silvio, ed. **Enciclopedia dello spettacolo**. [Encyclopedia of the performing arts]. 11 vols. Rome: Le Maschere, 1954–66.

Dieterich, Genoveva. **Diccionario del teatro**. Madrid: Alianza, 1995. – 307 p. *Notes*: Includes bibliographical references (p. 303–305). In Spanish.

——. **Pequeño diccionario del teatro mundial**. Madrid: Ediciones Istmo, 1974. – 293 p. In Spanish.

Dubuc, Robert. **Vocabulaire bilingue du théâtre: anglais–français, français–anglais**. Montréal: Leméac, 1979. – 174 p. *Notes*: Includes indexes. Bibliography: p. 173–174. In French.

Dumur, Guy, ed. **Histoire des spectacles**. [History of the performing arts]. Coll. Encyclopédie de la Pléiade. Paris: Gallimard, 1965. 2,010 p.

Edwards, Christopher. **The world guide to performing arts periodicals**. London: Published by the British Centre of the ITI for the International Theatre Institute (UNESCO), in association with Rose Bruford College, Sidcup, Kent, 1982. – 66 p. *Notes*: Includes indexes.

Esslin, Martin, ed. **The encyclopedia of world theater**. New York: Scribner, 1977.

Fielding, Eric, gen. ed. **Theatre words: an international vocabulary in nine languages**. Prague: Publication and Information Exchange Commission of OISTAT, 1993.

Fischer-Lichte, Erika and Harald Xander. **Welttheater-Nationaltheater-Lokaltheater?: europäisches Theater am Ende des 20. Jahrhunderts**. [World theatre-national theatre-local theatre?: Europe's theatre at the end of the 20th century]. Tübingen: Francke, 1993. – xiii, 229 p. *Notes*: Contributions to a colloquium held June 6–8, 1991, in Mainz. Includes bibliographical references.

Fletcher, Steve, Norman Jopling, and David Hallam. **The book of 1000 plays**. New York: Facts on File, 1989. – 352 p. *Notes*: Includes index. English language dramatic stories and plots.

Gaino, J. Ellen, ed. **Imperialism and theatre: essays on world theatre, drama and performance**. London and New York: Routledge, 1995.

Gassner, John and Edward Quinn, eds. **The reader's encyclopedia of world drama**. London: Methuen, 1975 1969. – xiii, 1,030 p.: ill. *Notes*: Originally published in New York: Crowell, 1969; London: Methuen, 1970.

Gilbert, Helen and Joanne Tompkins. **Postcolonial theory, practice, politics**. London and New York: Routledge, 1996.

Giteau, Cécile. **Dictionnaire des arts du spectacle: théâtre- cinéma- cirque- danse- radio- marionettes- télévision-documentologie**. [Dictionary of the performing arts: theatre- film- circus- dance- radio- puppetry- television-documentation]. Paris: Dunod, 1970. 430 p. In French, English and German.

Granville, Wilfred. **The theater dictionary; British and American terms in the drama, opera, and ballet**. Westport: Conn.: Greenwood Press, 1970, 1952. – ix, 227 p.

Gregor, Josef, and Margret Dietrich. **Der Schauspielführer: der Inhalt der wichtigsten Theaterstücke aus aller Welt.** [The play guide: Synopses of the most important plays from the whole world]. 14 vols. Stuttgart: Anton Hierseman, 1953–89.

Griffiths, Trevor R. and Carole Woddis. **The back stage theater guide: a theatergoer's companion to the world's best plays and playwrights**. New York: Back Stage Books, 1991. – ix, 466 p.: ill.

Gröning, Karl and Werner Kliess. **Illustrated encyclopaedia of world theatre**. London: Thames & Hudson, 1977. – 320 p., 1 p. of plates: ill. Notes: Original edn published 1969, Friedrich Verlag, Hanover, under title: **Friedrichs Theaterlexikon**. Includes bibliographical references and index. English version co-edited by Martin Esslin.

Hamadah, Ibrahim. **Mu'jam al-mustalahat al-diramiyah wa-al-masrahiyah**. Cairo: Dar al Ma'arif, 1985. 296 p.: ill. Notes: Includes index in Arabic and English. Includes bibliographical references (p. 295–6). Arabic language theatre dictionary.

Harrison, Martin. **The language of theatre**. London and New York: Routledge/Theatre Arts Books, 1998. Notes: Includes bibliographical references and index.

——. **Theatre**. Manchester: Carcanet, 1993. – xi, 316 p. Notes: Bibliography: p. 315–16. Theatre dictionary.

Hartnoll, Phyllis, ed. **The concise companion to the theatre**. New York: Oxford University Press, 1972.

——. **The Oxford companion to the theatre**. 4th edn, repr. with corrections, 1993. Oxford: Oxford University Press, 1993, 1983. – vii, 934 p., 96 p. of plates: ill. Notes: Includes bibliographical references (p. 917–32). One-volume general theatre encyclopedia.

Hawkins-Dady, Mark, Leanda Shrimpton and David Pickering. **International dictionary of theatre**. Chicago: St James Press, 1992, 1996. – 3 vols.: ill. Notes: Includes bibliographical references. 1. plays – 2. playwrights – 3. actors, directors, and designers. Theatre dictionary.

Hay, Peter. **Theatrical anecdotes**. London and New York: Oxford University Press. Notes: Includes index. Bibliography (p. 353–8). Entertainers of Great Britain and the United States.

Herbert, Ian, ed. **Who's who in the theatre: a biographical record of the contemporary stage**. Detroit: Gale Research Co. Notes: Includes indexes. vol. 1. Biographies – vol. 2. Playbills. Covers primarily UK – US and English-language theatre.

Hochman, Stanley. **McGraw-Hill encyclopedia of world drama**. 2nd edn. New York; London: McGraw-Hill, 1984. – 5 vols.: ill. Notes: Previous edn: 1972. Bio-bibliographical study of major world dramatists. Comprehensive.

Hodgson, Terry. **The Batsford dictionary of drama**. London: Batsford, 1988. – 430 p.: ill. Notes: Includes bibliographical references.

Hollertz, Malte. **Litet teaterlexikon**. Stockholm: Natur och Kultur, 1959. – 145 p. illus. Notes: Theatre dictionary. In Swedish.

Hont, Ferenc and Géza Staud. **Színhází kislexikon**. Budapest: Gondolat, 1969. – 535 p. plates. Notes: Includes bibliographies. Theatre dictionary. In Hungarian.

Hoyo, Arturo. **Teatro mundial: 1700 argumentos de obras de teatro antiquo y moderno, nacional y extranjero, con descripciones, listas de personajes, criticas y bibliografia**. 2. edn. Madrid: Aquilar, 1961. – 1272p.; 25cm. Dramatic plots. In Spanish.

Huxley, Mike and Noel Witts, eds. **The twentieth century performance reader**. London and New York: Routledge, 1996. 448 p. Notes: Forty seminal texts from over thirty practitioners and theorists from around the world.

Iijima, Tadashi. **Engeki eiga hoso buyo opera jiten**. Tokyo: Hakusuisha, 1955. – 9, 1070 p.: ill. Notes: Includes bibliographical references (p. 1048–70) and indexes. Theatre, music, dance dictionary in Japanese.

International bibliography of theatre. Brooklyn, N.Y.: Theater Research Data Center, Brooklyn College, City University of New York; Distributed by the Publishing Center for Cultural Resources, 1982. Notes: Serial. Annual.

International Theatre Institute. **World of theatre 1988–1990: essays on theatre seasons around the world**. Moscow: Culture Publishing, 1991. 172 p. Notes: Other editions of these collections of seasonal overviews have been published by various ITI centres through the 1990s.

Jacquot, Jean and Denis Bablet, eds. **Les Voies de la création théâtrale**. Paris: Editions du Centre national de la recherche scientifique, starting 1970. 19 vols.: illus. *Notes*: Includes indexes, bibliographies and filmographies – Vol. 9. La formation du comédien – Vol. 10. Krejca-Brook.– Vol. 11. T. Kantor.– Vol. 12. V. Garcia, R. Wilson, G. Tovstonogov, M. Ulusoy.– Vol. 13. Brook.– Vol. 14. Chéreau.– Vol. 15. Le théâtre dans la ville.– Vol. 16. Strehler.– Vol. 17. Meyerhold.–Vol. 18. T. Kantor (2).– Vol. 19. Langhoff.

Kawatake, Shigetoshi. **Engeki hyakka daijiten**. Tokyo: Heibonsha, 1986 1962. – 6 vols: ill. (some col.). *Notes*: Encyclopedia of theatre arts. Originally published: 1962. Includes indexes in vol. 6. Includes bibliographical references. In Japanese.

Kaye, Phyllis Johnson. **American/Soviet playwrights directory**. Waterford, Conn.: O'Neill Theater Center, 1988. – 140 p.: ill. *Notes*: English and Russian. 'A Project of the American Soviet Theater Initiative (ASTI)'.

Kienzle, Siegfried. **Schauspielführer der Gegenwart. Interpretation zum Schauspiel ab 1945.** [A guide to contemporary plays: an interpretation of plays since 1945]. Stuttgart: Alfred Kroner, 1978. 659 p.

Kott, Jan. **The eating of the gods: an interpretation of Greek tragedy**. Evanston, Ill.: Northwestern University Press, 1987 1973. – xix, 334 p. *Notes*: Reprint. Originally published: New York: Random House, 1973. Includes index. Bibliography: p. 275–324.

Kröjer, P.S. Maxim. **Theater A–Z**. Antwerp: Boekengilde Die Poorte, 1959. – 2 vols. *Notes*: Bibliography: vol. 2, p. 265–301. Dictionary in Flemish.

Kuritz, Paul. **The Making of theatre history**. Englewood Cliffs, NJ: Prentice-Hall, 1988. 468 p.

Lai, Stanley Sheng-Chuan. **Oriental crosscurrents in modern Western theatre**. 1986 1983. – ix, 476 p.: ill. *Notes*: Bibliography: p. 363–93. Thesis (Ph. D.)–University of California, Berkeley, 1983. Photocopy. Ann Arbor, Mich.: University Microfilms International, 1986.

Lee, Sang-Kyong. **West–östliche Begegnungen: Weltwirkung der fernöstlichen Theatertradition**. Darmstadt: Wissenschaftliche Buchgesellschaft, 1993. – viii, 218 p.: ill. *Notes*: Bibliographical references (p. 197–206) and index. Theatre. Asia. Influence/Theatre. Europe.

Lista, Giovanni. **La scène moderne: encyclopédie mondiale des arts du spectacle dans la seconde moitié du XXe siècle: ballet, danse, happening, opéra, performance, scénographie, théâtre, théâtre d'artiste**. Paris: Arles: Editions Carré; Actes sud, 1997. – 858 p.: ill. (some col.). *Notes*: Includes bibliographical references and index.

Londré, Felicia Hardison. **The history of world theater**. 2 vols. New York: Continuum, 1991.

Lugo, Marcela Ruiz. **Glosario de términos del arte teatral**. México: Asociación Nacional de Universidades e Institutos de Ensenanza Superior, 1979. – 307 p. In Spanish.

Luterkort, Ingrid. **Theatre words**. Solna: Entré, 1988. – 156 p.: ill. *Notes*: Czech, English, French, German, Hungarian, Italian, Russian, Spanish, and Swedish. Includes indexes.

Magill, Frank Northen. **Critical survey of drama**. Rev. edn. Pasadena, Calif.: Salem Press, 1994. – 7 vols. (xii, 3107 p.). *Notes*: '[This] Revised edition updates and expands, in seven volumes, the original edition of 1985'. Includes bibliographical references and index. vol. 1. Authors: A–Chi – vol. 2. Chu–Fra – vol. 3. Fri–Jam – vol. 4. Jon–Mil – vol. 5. Mor–Sha – vol. 6. Sha–Z – vol. 7. Essays, Index. Bio-bibliography of Commonwealth and US drama.

Matlaw, Myron. **Modern world drama: an encyclopedia**. New York: Dutton, 1983, 1972. – xxi, 960 p. illus. *Notes*: Includes indexes. Bibliography: p. xi.

McNeil, Barbara, Miranda C. Herbert and Dennis La Beau. **Performing arts biography master index: a consolidated index to over 270,000 biographical sketches of persons living and dead, as they appear in over 100 of the principal biographical dictionaries devoted to the performing arts**. 2nd edn. Detroit, Mich.: Gale Research Company, 1982 1981. – xxiv, 701 p. *Notes*: Rev. edn of: **Theatre, film, and television biographies master index**/edited by Dennis La Beau. 1st edn c1979. Bibliography: p. xix–xxi.

Melchinger, Siegfried. **The concise encyclopedia of modern drama**. London: Vision Press, 1966. – 288 p. illus. (incl. ports.). *Notes*: Bibliography: p. 283–6.

Mitchell, John Dietrich. **The director–actor relationship: essays and articles**. New York: Institute for Advanced Studies in the Theatre Arts Press, 1992. – vi, 170 p.: ill. *Notes*: Applied psychoanalysis in the drama – Applied psychoanalysis in the director–actor relationship – Contemporary American theatre ... a psychologic sounding board – Psychoanalytic approach to Kabuki: a study in personality and culture – The actor's 'method', backstage at the Kabukiza, Tokyo – A psychosocial approach to the Peking Opera – How the Chinese actor trains; interviews with two Peking Opera performers – Two faces of China – East–West understanding through the arts – Discussion – The theatre in India – A Sanskrit classic: Shakuntala – The Sanskrit drama Shakuntala – The theatre of India and Southeast Asia – Theatre of Western Europe – The theatre in Russia – The Moscow Art Theatre in rehearsal – The theatre of Western Europe: some highlights – Brecht's theatre, the Berliner Ensemble – In search of Commedia dell'Arte – André Gide, rebel and conformist – The challenge of directing a neo-classical verse tragedy – Theatre in Mexico moves ahead – Riches from abroad – IASTA, an American innovation in workshop production – The International Amateur Theatre Association – Is the play the thing? Acting/Theatre. Production and direction. China. U.S.A. Japan. India. Russia. Germany. Mexico.

Mobley, Jonnie Patricia. **NTC's dictionary of theatre and drama terms**. Lincolnwood, Ill.: National Textbook Co., 1992. – v, 166 p.

Mokulski, S.S. and P.A. Markov, eds. **Teatralnaia entsiklopedia**. [Theatre encyclopedia]. 6 vols. Moscow: Sovietskaia Entsiklopedia, 1961–7.

Molinari, Cesare. **Teatro**. [Theatre]. Milan: Mondadori, 1972.

——. **Theatre through the ages**. New York: McGraw-Hill, 1975. 324 p.

Mordden, Edlan. **The fireside companion to the theatre**. New York: Simon & Schuster, 1988. 313 p.

Moussa, Fatma, ed. **A dictionary of the theatre**. 5 vols. Cairo: Egyptian Book Organization, 1995–98. In Arabic.

Nagler, A.M. **A sourcebook in theatrical history**. New York: Dover, 1952. 611 p.

Nicoll, Allardyce. **The development of the theatre: a study of theatrical art from the beginnings to the present day**. 5th edn. London: George G. Harrap, 1966. 318 p.

Oliva, Judy Lee. **New theatre vistas: modern movements in international theatre**. New York: Garland Pub., 1996. – xv, 219 p. Notes: Includes bibliographical references. Crossing boundaries: directing gay, lesbian, and working-class theatre in Scotland/Richard Trousdell – Belgian/American theatre exchanges: reflections and bridges/Suzanne Burgoyne – Stanislavsky meets Shepard at the Shchepkin/Bonnie Gould – On the edge: Utrecht, Netherlands 1993/Susan Vaneta Mason – Maybe theatre is born: directing student theatre in communist and post-communist Poland/Kathleen Cioffi – The politics of the professional: connecting the prose with the passion/Dennis Barnett – Vestiges of control: censorship and society in contemporary Egyptian theatre/Kenneth Robbins – Year of improvising in the Balkans/Vivian K. Mason – After the visit, the ruins/Ned Bobkoff – East meets West meets Hamlet: get thee to a noh master/Jonah Salz – Kuando 1991: a new beginning, a ritual pilgrimage/Alexandra B. Bonds – Israel's Rina Yerushalmi and her directorial experiments in spatial interrelations/Yael Nir – Diablomundo and the royal hunt: the shadow and the sun/Judy Lee Oliva.

Ortolani, Benito, ed. **International bibliography of theatre**. 7 vols. New York: Theater Research Data Center, 1985–93.

Packard, William, David Pickering and Charlotte Savidge. **The Facts on File dictionary of the theatre**. New York: Facts on File, 1988. – 556 p. Notes: Drama. Bio-bibliography.

Pandolfi, Vito. **Storia universale del teatro drammatico**. [World history of dramatic art]. 2 vols. Turin: Unione Tipografico-Editrice, 1964. 1, 626 p.

Parker, John, ed. **Who's who in the theatre; a biographical record of the contemporary stage, compiled and edited by John Parker**. 15th edn. London: Pitman, 1972. – viii, 1752 p. Notes: 'First edition 1912 … Fifteenth edition 1972'.

Pavis, Patrice. **Dictionniare du théâtre. Termes et concepts de l'analyse théâtrale** [Dictionary of the theatre: terms and concepts of theatrical analysis]. 2nd edn. Paris: Editions Sociales, 1987.

—— and Anne Ubersfeld. **Dictionnaire du théâtre**. Paris: Dunod, 1996. – xvii, 447 p. Notes: Includes bibliographical references (p. 409–35) and index. French drama dictionaries.

Pickering, David. **Dictionary of the theatre**. London: Sphere, 1988. – 556 p.

——. **International dictionary of theatre: actors, directors and designers**. New York: St James Press, 1996. – xv, 829 p.: ill., facsims., photos.

Pierron, Agnès. **Le Théâtre, ses métiers, son langage: lexique théâtral**. Paris: Hachette, 1994. – 111 p.: ill.

Portillo, Rafael, and Jesús Casado. **Diccionario inglés–espanol, espanol–inglés de terminología teatral** [English–Spanish, Spanish–English dictionary of theatre terms]. Madrid: Editorial Fundamentos, 1986. – 230 p.: ill.

Pronko, Leonard. **Theatre East and West: per-**

spectives toward a total theatre. Berkeley, CA: University of California Press, 1967. 230 p.

Queant, G., ed. Encyclopédie du théâtre contemporain. [Encyclopedia of contemporary theatre]. Paris: Olivier Perrin. 211 p.

Quraishi, Muhammad Aslam and Sayyid Izhar Kazmi. Istilahat-i drama. [Theatre terms]. Islamabad: Muqtadirah Qaumi Zaban, 1984. – 60 p. Theatre dictionary in Urdu.

Rae, Kenneth and Richard Southern. An international vocabulary of technical theatre terms: in eight languages (American, Dutch, English, French, German, Italian, Spanish, Swedish). Brussels: Editions Meddens, 1977. – 139 p.

Rischbieter, Henning. Theater-Lexikon. Rev. Zürich-Schwäbisch Hall: Orell-Füssli, 1983. 484 p.

Roose-Evans, James. Experimental theatre from Stanislavsky to today. New York: Universe Books, 1970. – 160 p. illus. Notes: Stanislavsky's life in art.–The school of realism.–Meyerhold and the Russian avant-garde.–Taïrov and the synthetic theatre.–Vakhtangov's achievement.–Craig and Appia: visionaries.–Copeau: le petit pauvre.–The epic theatre: Piscator, Brecht.–The theatre of ecstasy: Artaud, Okhlopkov, Théâtre Panique.–Grotowski and the poor theatre.–The contribution of the modern dance: Martha Graham and Alwin Nikolais.–Peter Schumann and The Bread and Puppet Theatre.–Further experiment today – in America.–Bibliography (p. 155–6). Experimental theatre.

Rubin, Don, ed. The world encyclopedia of contemporary theatre. London and New York: Routledge, 1994–2000. Notes: Vol. 1 Europe. – 1052 p.: ill. Vol. 2 Americas. 1996. – xii, 626p.: ill.; Vol. 3 Africa. 1997. – 426 p.: ill., map; Vol. 4 The Arab world. 1999. – 311 p.: ill, map.; Vol. 5 Asia. 1998. – 488 p.: ill., map; Vol. 6 Theatre bibliography and index. 2000. World theatre overview, country-by-country, since 1945. National histories, demographics, government policies. Includes playwriting, music/dance theatre, puppetry, theatre for young audiences, design and architecture, training and scholarship.

Schindler, Otto G. Theaterliteratur. Ein Bibliographischer Behelf für das Studium der Theaterwissenschaft. [A bibliographic guide for theatre studies]. 3 vols. Vienna: Institut für Theaterwissenschaft, 1973.

Seddio, Pietro. Dizionario dei termini teatrali. Pavia: G. Iuculano, 1990. – 183 p. Notes: Theatre terms. In Italian.

Segerstedt, Bengt, Bendt Segerstedt, Tyr Martin and Niklas Brunius. Theatre words: an international vocabulary in nine languages. Sweden: Entre/Riksteatern, 1988.

Semil, Malgorzata and Elzbiets Wysinska. Slownik wspólczesnego teatru: twórcy, teatry, teorie. Warsaw: Wydawn. Artystyczne i Filmowe, 1990. – 429 p. Notes: General world theatre encyclopedia in Polish.

Shigetoshi, Kawatake, ed. Engeki Hyakka Daijiten. [Encyclopedia of world theatre]. 6 vols. Tokyo: Heibonsha, 1960–2.

Söderberg, Olle. New theatre words. Amsterdam: Sttf, 1995. – 186 p.: ill. Notes: Dutch, English, French, German, Italian, Japanese, Spanish, and Swedish. Includes indexes.

Solomos, Alexis. Theatre directory – persons and things of the theatre world. Athens: Kedros, 1990.

Stupnikov, Igor. Russko–angliiskii i anglo–russkii slovar' teatral'nykh terminov. Petersburg: Izd-vo Evropeiskogo Doma, 1995. – 127 p. Notes: Russian–English theatre dictionary.

Taylor, John Russell. The Penguin dictionary of the theatre. 3rd edn. London; New York: Penguin, 1993. – 349 p.

Teatralnaya entziklopediya. [Theatre encyclopedia]. 5 vols. Moscow: Sovetskaya entziklopediya, 1961–8.

Thomson, Peter and Gamini Salgado. The Everyman companion to the theatre. London: Dent, 1987, 1985. – 484 p. Notes: Includes index. General theatre guide.

Trapido, Joel, Edward A. Langhans and James R. Brandon. An international dictionary of theatre language. Westport, Conn.: Greenwood Press, 1985. – xxxvi, 1032 p. Notes: Bibliography: p. 985–1032. Includes several Asian languages.

University Microfilms International. Music and the performing arts: citations to 2, 014 doctoral dissertations and masters theses published between 1986 and 1988. Ann Arbor, Mich.: U-M-I, 1989. – 56 p. Notes: Cover title. Includes selected British doctoral dissertations beginning July 1988. Academic. Bibliography.

Vasconcellos, Luiz Paulo. Dicionário de teatro. Porto Alegre: L&PM Editores, 1987. – 231 p. Notes: Includes translations from English, French, German, and Spanish into Portuguese. Bibliography: p. 224–9.

Vaughn, Jack A. Drama A to Z: a handbook. New York: Ungar, 1978. – 239 p. Notes: Bibliography: p. 235–9. General guide.

Veinstein, André and Alfred Golding, eds. **Performing arts libraries and museums of the world/Bibliothèques et musées des arts du spectacle dans le monde**. 4th edn. Paris: Centre National de la Recherche Scientifique, 1992. 773 p.

Verdone, Mario. **Teatro contemporaneo**. Rome: Lucarini, 1981. 2 vols.: ill. *Notes*: Includes bibliographies. vol. 1. Teatro italiano – vol. 2. Teatro europeo e nordamericano. Drama. 20th century. History and criticism.

——. **Teatro contemporaneo. Appendice I, 1983**. Rome: Lucarini, 1983. – 400 p., 80 p. of plates: ill.

——. **Teatro contemporaneo. Appendice II, 1984**. Rome: Lucarini, 1985. – 444 p., 48 p. of plates: ill.

——. **Teatro contemporaneo. Appendice III, 1985**. Rome: Lucarini, 1986. – 410 p., 24 p. of plates: ill.

White, R. Kerry. **An annotated dictionary of technical, historical, and stylistic terms relating to theatre and drama: a handbook of dramaturgy**. Lewiston, N.Y.: E. Mellen Press, 1995. – iii, 254 p.: ill.

Who was who in the theatre, 1912–1976: a biographical dictionary of actors, actresses, directors, playwrights, and producers of the English speaking theatre. Detroit: Gale Research Co., 1978. – 4 vols., 2664 p. *Notes*: Focuses on UK and US.

Winslow, Colin. **The Oberon glossary of theatrical terms: over 1300 technical, back-stage, acting, musical, dance and showbusiness terms in common usage**. London, England: Oberon Books, 1991. – 110 p.

Zamora Guerrero, Juan. **Historia del teatro contemporáneo**. [History of contemporary theatre]. 4 vols. Barcelona: Juan Flors, 1961–2.

A2. Studies of Theatre and Drama by Geographical Regions; Cultural and Linguistic groupings

A2a. EUROPE

Berenguer, Angel. **Teatro europeo de los años 80**. Barcelona: Laia, 1983. – 197 p. *Notes*: Dramatists, European. 20th century. Interviews. History. Playwriting.

Braun, Kazimierz. **Wielka reforma teatru w Europie: ludzie, idee, zdarzenia**. Wroclaw: Zaklad Narodowy im. Ossolinskich, 1984. – 416 p.: ill. *Notes*: Summary in English; table of contents also in English. Includes index.

Bibliography: p. 327–31. Theatre. Europe. History. 20th century.

Ch'en, Shih-hsiung. **Hsien tai Ou Mei hsi chü shih**. [History of modern European and American dramas]. Setzuan, 1994. – 14, 28, 1070 p. *Notes*: Includes bibliographical references and index. Drama. 20th century. History and criticism.

Clark, Barrett H. **European theories of the drama**. New York: Crown, 1965. 628 p.

Docherty, Brian. **Twentieth-century European drama**. New York: St Martin's Press, 1994. – x, 228 p. *Notes*: Includes bibliographical references and index. Introduction: thirteen essays in search of a reader – Female masks: Luigi Pirandello's plays for women – The theatre of Bertolt Brecht: theory and practice – Witkiewicz and the theatre of death – Beckett's stage of deconstruction – Antonin Artaud and the theatre of cruelty – Ionesco's plays: a conspiracy of the mind – The heroic world of Jean Anouilh – Arrabal's theatre of liberation – Artaud and Genet's The Maids: like father, like son? – Weiss/Brook: Marat/Sade – Time, identity and being: the world of Václav Havel – The Germans in Britain – The theatre of Dario Fo and Franca Rame: laughing all the way to the revolution.

Dusigne, Jean-François. **Le Théâtre d'art: aventure européenne du XXe siècle**. Paris: Editions Théâtrales, 1997. – 333 p.: ill. *Notes*: Includes bibliographical references (p. 315–18) and index. Focus on directors.

Fjeldstad, Anton. **Gruppeteater i Norden**. Copenhagen: Samleren, 1981. – 300 p. *Notes*: Bibliography: p. 281–98. Kampen mod rampen/Aage Jørgensen – Gruppteater i Finland/Clas Zilliacus – Gruppeteater i Norge/Anton Fjeldstad – Oktober i Södertälje/Margareta Wirmark. Notes: Experimental theatre. Scandinavia. Political aspects.

Grismer, Raymond Leonard. **Bibliography of the drama of Spain and Spanish America**. Minneapolis: Burgess-Beckwith, 1967. – 2 vols. *Notes*: vol. 1. A–L.–vol. 2. M–Z. Spanish and Spanish American drama. Bibliography.

Hattaway, Michael, Boika Sokolova and Derek Roper. **Shakespeare in the new Europe**. Sheffield, England: Sheffield Academic Press, 1994. – 384 p. *Notes*: Includes bibliographical references and index. Eastern Europe. 20th century.

Mennemeier, Franz Norbert, Erika Fischer-Lichte and Doris Kolesch. **Drama und Theater der europäischen Avantgarde**. Tübingen: Francke, 1994. – xvi, 441 p., [12] p. of plates:

ill. *Notes*: Includes bibliographical references and index. Avant-garde (Aesthetics). Europe.

Molla, Juan and Luis González del Valle. **Teatro español e iberoamericano en Madrid, 1962–1991**. Boulder, Colo.: Society of Spanish and Spanish-American Studies, 1993. – 204 p. *Notes*: Theatre. Spain. Spanish American drama. History and criticism.

Pérez Minik, Domingo. **Teatro europeo contemporáneo: su libertad y compromisos**. Canary Islands: Viceconsejería de Cultura y Deportes del Gobierno de Canarias, 1992. – 548 p. *Notes*: Includes bibliographical references. European drama. 20th century. History and criticism.

Quién es quién en el teatro y el cine español e hispanoamericano. Barcelona: C.I.L.E.H., 1991. – 2 vols (xlv, 922 p.). *Notes*: vol. 1. Abad–Gracia – vol. 2. Graciani–Zurita. Who's who in Spain and the Hispanic world. In Spanish.

Rebello, Luiz Francisco. **Teatro moderno: caminhos e figuras**. 2. edn, rev. e ampliada. Lisbon: Prelo, Sociedade Gráfica Editorial, 1965. – 591 p., 11 p. of plates, 10 fold. p.: ill. *Notes*: First published in 1957. Includes index. Bibliography: p. 559–68. Drama. Theatre. History. 20th century. Major figures.

Scaglione, Massimo. **Il dizionario del teatro: manuale di autori classici e contemporanei, di generi teatrali, di attrezzi, curiosità e aneddoti dello spettacolo, per vivere il teatro in scena e fuori scena**. Leumann: Elledici, 1990. – 237 p.: ill. *Notes*: In Italian. European focus. Biographies.

Sprinchorn, Evert. **The modern Scandinavian drama, 1900–1959**. New York, 1960. – 327 p. *Notes*: 'List of plays and playwrights'. Bibliography: p. 302–27. Thesis–Columbia University. Photocopy. Ann Arbor, Mich.,: University Microfilms, 1970.

Straumanis, Alfred and Joseph Daubenas. **Baltic drama: a handbook and bibliography**. Prospect Heights, Ill.: Waveland Press, 1981. – xiv, 705 p. *Notes*: Includes index.

Tanokura, Minoru. **Engi toshi to shintai: Yoroppa genshiko**. Tokyo: Shobunsha, 1988. – 413 p.: ill. *Notes*: Includes bibliographical references. A Japanese view of European theatre. In Japanese.

Taube, Gerd. **Puppenspiel als kulturhistorisches Phänomen: Vorstudien zu einer 'Sozial- und Kulturgeschichte des Puppenspiels'**. Tübingen: M. Niemeyer, 1995. – x, 233 p. *Notes*: Includes bibliographical references (p. 161–230) and index. Puppet theatre. Europe. History.

Yarrow, Ralph, ed. **European theatre, 1960–1990: cross-cultural perspectives**. London; New York: Routledge, 1992. – x, 255 p.: maps. *Notes*: Includes bibliographical references and index. France: towards création collective/David Jeffery – France:Jérôme Savary, the 'ordinary magician' of French theatre/Martin Sorrell – West Germany/Theo Girshausen – Switzerland/Ralph Yarrow – Austria/Susanne Chambalu – Italy/Christopher Cairns – Spain/Gwynne Edwards – Sweden/Margareta Wirmark – Poland (dead souls under western eyes)/George Hyde – Great Britain/Ralph Yarrow and Anthony Frost.

A2b. THE AMERICAS

Acuna, René. **El teatro popular en Hispanoamérica: una bibliografía anotada**. Mexico City: Universidad Nacional Autónoma de México, Instituto de Investigaciones Filológicas, Centro de Estudios Literarios, 1979. – 114 p. *Notes*: Includes index. Folk drama, Hispanic Bibliography.

Adler, Heidrun. **Politisches Theater in Lateinamerika: von der Mythologie über die Mission zur kollektiven Identität**. [Political theatre in Latin America: from the mission mythology to a collective identity]. Beiträge zur Kulturanthropologie. Berlin: Dietrich Reimer, 1982. 171 p. *Notes*: In German.

——. **Theater in Lateinamerika: ein Handbuch**. Berlin: Dietrich Reimer, 1991. – 463 p. *Notes*: Includes bibliographical references and indexes. Latin American drama. 20th century. History and criticism. In German.

Albuquerque, Severino João Medeiros. **Violent acts: a study of contemporary Latin American theatre**. Detroit: Wayne State University Press, 1991. – 297 p. *Notes*: Includes bibliographical references (p. 279–89) and index. Latin American drama. 20th century. Political aspects.

Alpern, Hymen, ed. **Teatro hispanoamericano**. [Spanish-American theatre]. New York: Odyssey Press, 1956.

Amate Blanco, Juan José and Marina Gálvez Acero. **Poesía y teatro de Hispanoamérica en el siglo XX**. [Spanish-American poetry and theatre of the twentieth century]. Cuadernos de Estudio, Serie Literatura, no. 34. Madrid: Cincel, 1981. 88 p.

Arlt, Mirta and Osvaldo, Pelletieri. **Teatro latinoamericano de los setenta: autoritarismo, cuestionamiento y cambio**. Buenos Aires: Corregidor, 1995. – 317 p. *Notes*: Includes bibliographical references. Theatre and society. Latin America.

Azor, Ileana. **Origen y presencia del teatro en**

nuestra América. [Origin and presence of theatre in our America]. Havana: Letras Cubanas, 1988. 304 p.

——. **Teatro latinoamericano, siglo XX: selección de lecturas**. Havana: Editorial Pueblo y Educación, 1989. – 298 p. *Notes*: Includes bibliographical references. Latin American drama. 20th century.

——. **Variaciones sobre el teatro latinoamericano**. [Developments in Latin American theatre]. Havana: Editorial Pueblo y Educación, 1987. 117 p.

Becco, Horacio Jorge. **Bibliografía general de las artes del espectáculo en América Latina**. Paris: UNESCO, 1977. – 118 p.

Boal, Augusto. **Técnicas latinoamericanas de teatro popular: una revolución copérnica al revés**. [Latin American techniques of popular theatre: a Copernican revolution the other way around]. Buenos Aires: Corregidor, 1975. 212 p.

Bonilla, María and Vladich Stoyan. **Teatro latinoamericano en busca de su identidad cultural**. [Latin American theatre in search of its cultural identity]. San José: Culturart, 1988. 327 p.

Cea, José Roberto. **Teatro en y de una comaraca centroamericana**. [Theatre in and of the Central American region]. San Salvador: Canoa Editores, 1993.

Ch'en, Shih-hsiung. **Hsien tai Ou Mei hsi chü shih**. [History of modern European and American dramas]. Setzuan, 1994. – 14, 28, 1070 p. *Notes*: Includes bibliographical references and index. Drama. 20th century. History and criticism.

Dauster, Frank N. **Ensayos sobre teatro hispanoamericano**. [Essays on Spanish-American theatre]. México City: Secretaría de Educación Pública, Dirección General de Divulgación, 1975. 196 p.

——. **Historia crítica del teatro hispanoamericano contemporáneo: siglos XIX y XX**. [History of Spanish-American contemporary theatre: the nineteenth and twentieth centuries]. 2nd edn. México City: De Andrea, 1973.

——. **Perspectives on contemporary Spanish American theatre**. Lewisburg, Pa.: London: Bucknell University Press; Associated University Presses, 1996. – 157 p. *Notes*: Includes bibliographical references. Theatre. Latin America. History. 20th century.

Eidelberg, Nora. **Teatro experimental hispanoamericano 1960–80: la realidad social como manipulación**. [Latin American experimental theatre 1960–80: Social reality as manipulation]. Series Towards a Social History of Spanish and Luso-Brazilian Literatures. Minneapolis, MN: Institute for the Study of Ideologies and Literature, 1985. 221 p.

Elliott, Norma Jean. **Spanish American contemporary political theatre, 1959–1970**. 1983 1980. – iv, 372 p. *Notes*: Bibliography: 358–72. Thesis (Ph. D.)–Ohio State University, 1980. Photocopy. Ann Arbor, Mich.: University Microfilms International, 1983.

Escenarios de dos mundos: inventario teatral de Iberoamérica. Madrid: Centro de Documentación Teatral, 1988. – 4 vols.: ill. *Notes*: Includes bibliographical references (vol. 4, p. 302–29). vol. 1. De mar a mar, Argentina, Bolivia, Brasil, Colombia, Costa Rica – vol. 2. Cuba, Chile, Ecuador, El Salvador, España, Estados Unidos de América – vol. 3. Guatemala, Honduras, México, Nicaragua, Panamá, Perú – vol. 4. Portugal, Puerto Rico, República Dominicana, Uruguay, Venezuela, bibliografía, quién es quién, agenda. Theatre. Latin America. Including Spain and Portugal.

Finch, Mark Steven. **An annotated bibliography of recent sources on Latin American theatre**. Ann Arbor, MI: University Microfilms International, 1986.

Gálvez Acero, Marina. **El teatro hispanoamericano**. [Spanish-American theatre]. Madrid: Taurus, 1988. 176 p.

Garzón Céspedes, Francisco. **Recopilación de textos sobre el teatro latinoamericano de creación colectiva**. Havana, Cuba: Casa de las Américas, 1978. – 564 p. *Notes*: Bibliography: p. 547–62. Latin America. Collective creation.

Grismer, Raymond Leonard. **Bibliography of the drama of Spain and Spanish America**. Minneapolis: Burgess-Beckwith, 1967. – 2 vols. *Notes*: vol. 1. A–L.–vol. 2. M–Z. Spanish and Spanish American drama. Bibliography.

Gutiérrez, Sonia. **Teatro popular y cambio social en América Latina: panorama de una experiencia**. Ciudad Universitaria Rodrigo Facio, Costa Rica: Editorial Universitaria Centro Americana, 1979. – 487 p. *Notes*: Includes index. Bibliography: p. 467–76. Latin American populist drama. 20th century. History and criticism.

Hacia una nueva crítica y un nuevo teatro latinoamericano. Frankfurt am Main: Vervuert, 1993. – 174 p. *Notes*: Spanish and Portuguese. Includes bibliographical references. El teatro latinoamericano actual: modernidad y tradicion/Fernando de Toro – Cambio de paradigma? El Nuevo teatro latinoamericano: la constitucion de la post-modernidad espectacular/Alfonso de Toro – Transformaciones y permanencias en el sistema teatral uruguayo en la decada del 80 – un cambio de paradigma?/Roger Mirza – Postales argentinas: cambio y tradicion en el sistema teatral argentino/Osvaldo Pellettieri – Nuevo teatro venezolano/Leonardo Azparren Giménez – Macunaima e o teatro brasileiro contemporaneo/Sebastião Milaré – Gerald Thomas: ou de armens, filtros e mortes/Silvia Simone Anspach – Practicas teatrales innovadoras en la escena nacional chilena/Sergio Pereira Poza – Espacio y poetica en Ramon Griffero: Analisis de su trilogia: Historias de un galpon abandonaldo, cinema utopia y 99 la Morgue/Eduardo Guerrero – Nuevas tendencias de la dirección teatral en Mexico/Domingo Adame Hernández, Hilda Gómez González – Yuyachkani: los nuevos cominos en la segunda decada/Hugo Salazar del Alcázar – El Paso de la candelaria: Una consistente indagación teatral en el lenguaje no-verbal/Jorge Manuel Pardo – Nuevas escenificaciones en el teatro puertorriqueño/Rosalina Perales. Latin American drama. 20th century. History and criticism.

Hebblethwaite, Frank P. **A bibliographical guide to the Spanish American theatre**. Washington, DC: Pan American Union, General Secretariat, Organization of American States, 1969.

Hoffman, Herbert H. **Latin American play index**. 2 vols. Metuchen, NJ: Scarecrow Press, 1983–4. 131 p.

Instituto Internacional de Teoría y Crítica de Teatro Latinoamericano. **Reflexiones sobre el teatro latinoamericano del siglo XX**. [Reflections on Latin American theatre of the twentieth century]. Buenos Aires: Galerna, 1989; Frankfurt: Lemcke Verlag, 1989.

Jones, Willis Knapp. **Breve historia del teatro latino americano**. [A short history of Latin American theatre]. México City: De Andrea, 1956. 239 p.

——, ed. **Antología del teatro hispanoamericano**. [Anthology of Spanish-American theatre]. México City: Ediciones de Andrea, 1958.

Luzuriaga, Gerardo. **Introducción a las teorías latinoamericanas del teatro: de 1930 al presente**. Puebla, Pue.: Universidad Autónoma de Puebla, Maestría en Ciencias del Lenguaje, 1990. – 212 p. Notes: Includes bibliographical references. Theatre. Latin America. History. 20th century.

—— and Richard Reeves, eds. **Los clásicos del teatro hispanoamericano**. [The classics of the Spanish American theatre]. México City: Fondo de Cultura Económica, 1975. 905 p.

Lyday, Leon F. and George W. Woodyard. **A bibliography of Latin American theatre criticism, 1940–1974**. Austin: Institute of Latin American Studies, University of Texas at Austin, 1976. – xvii, 243 p. Notes: Includes index.

——. **Dramatists in revolt: the new Latin American theatre**. Austin, TX: University of Texas Press, 1976. 275 p.

Menéndez Quiroa, Leonel. **Hacia un nuevo teatro latinoamericano: teoría y metodología del arte escénico**. [Making a new Latin American theatre]. San Salvador: UCA Editores, 1977. – 767 p.

Molla, Juan and Luis, González del Valle. **Teatro español e iberoamericano en Madrid, 1962–1991**. Boulder, Colo.: Society of Spanish and Spanish-American Studies, 1993. – 204 p. Notes: Theatre. Spain. Spanish American drama. History and criticism.

Monleón, José. **América Latina: teatro y revolución**. [Latin America: theatre and revolution]. Caracas: Editorial Ateneo de Caracas/CELCIT, 1978.

Neglia, Erminio. **El hecho teatral en Latino America**. [The theatre event in Latin America]. Rome: Bulzoni, 1985. 216 p.

—— and Florian Smieja. **Medio siglo de teatro latinoamericano: una bibliografía**. Mississauga, Ont.: Silcan House, 1997. – 139 p. Notes: Text in Spanish; introd. in English and Spanish. Bibliographical references to Latin American drama. 20th century.

—— and Luis Ordaz. **Repertorio selecto del teatro hispanoamericano contemporáneo**. 2. edn. Tempe: Center for Latin American Studies, Arizona State University, 1980. – xix, 110 p. Notes: Includes index. Spanish American drama. 20th century. Bibliography.

Ochsenius, Carlos. **Práctica teatral y expresión popular en América Latina: Argentina, Chile, Perú, Uruguay**. [Theatre practice and popular expression in Latin America: Argentina, Chile, Perú, Uruguay]. Buenos Aires: Paulinas, 1988.

Oliver, William, ed. **Voices of change in Spanish American theatre: an anthology**. Austin, TX: University of Texas Press, 1971.

Perales, Rosalina. **Teatro hispanoamericano contemporáneo, 1967–87**. [Contemporary Spanish-American theatre, 1967–87]. Series Escenología, no. 9. México City: Grupo Editorial Gaceta, 1993.

Pérez Coterillo, Moisés, ed. **Escenarios de dos mundos: inventario teatral de Iberoamérica**.

[Stages of two worlds: a theatre inventory of Iberoamerica]. 4 vols. Madrid: Centro de Documentación Teatral, Ministerio de Cultura, 1989.

Pianca, Marina. **El teatro de nuestra América: un proyecto continental, 1959–1989**. Minneapolis, MN: Institute for the Study of Ideologies and Literature, 1990. – 408 p. *Notes*: Includes bibliographical references (p. 377–408). Theatre. Latin America. History. Theatre and society.

Quién es quién en el teatro y el cine español e hispanoamericano [Who's who in the Spanish and Spanish-American theatre and cinema]. 2 vols. Barcelona: Centro de Investigaciones Literarias Españolas e Hispanoamericanas, 1991.

Ripoll, Carlos and Andrés Valdespino, eds. **Teatro hispanoamericano: antología crítica**. [Spanish American theatre: annotated anthology]. 2 vols. Madrid: Anaya Books, 1973.

Rizk, Beatriz. **El nuevo teatro latinoamericano: una lectura histórica**. [The new Latin American theatre: a historical reading]. Series Towards a Social History of Hispanic and Luso-Brazilian Literatures. Minneapolis, MN: Institute for the Study of Ideologies and Literature/Prisma Institute, 1987. 143 p.

Rodríguez, Franklin Rodríguez Abad. **Poética del teatro latinoamericano y del Caribe**. Quito: Abrapalabra Editores, 1994. – 210 p. *Notes*: Includes bibliographical references (p. 169–205). Theatre. Latin America. History. 20th century. Political aspects.

Roster, Peter and Fernando de Toro. **Bibliografía del teatro hispanoamericano contemporáneo, 1900–80**. [A bibliography of contemporary Spanish-American theatre, 1900–80]. 2 vols. Frankfurt: Vervuert, 1985.

Saz, Sánchez, Agustín del. **Teatro hispanoamericano**. [Spanish-American theatre]. Nueva Colección Labor, no. 57. Barcelona: Labor, 1967. 176 p.

——. **Teatro social hispanoamericano**. [Spanish-American social theatre]. Barcelona: Editorial Labor, 1967. 177 p.

Solórzano, Carlos, ed. **El teatro actual latinoamericano**. [The present theatre of Latin America]. México City: Ediciones de Andrea, 1972.

——. **El teatro hispanoamericano contemporáneo**. [Contemporary Spanish-American theatre]. 2 vols. México City: Fondo de Cultura Económica, 1964.

Suárez Radillo, Carlos Miguel. **Lo social en el teatro hispanoamericano contemporáneo**. Caracas: Equinoccio, 1976. – 395 p. *Notes*: Bibliography: p. 391–5. Theatre and society in Latin America. In Spanish.

Taylor, Diana. **Theatre of crisis: drama and politics in Latin America**. Lexington, Ky.: University Press of Kentucky, 1991. – 277 p. *Notes*: Includes bibliographical references (p. 251–69) and index. 20th century. History and criticism/Politics and literature. Latin America.

—— and Juan Villegas Morales, eds. **Negotiating performance: gender, sexuality, and theatricality in Latin America**. Durham: Duke University Press, 1995. – 356 p.: ill. *Notes*: Includes bibliographical references and index. Opening remarks/Diana Taylor – The Multicultural paradigm: an open letter to the national arts community/Guillermo Gómez-Peña – Art in América con acento/Cherríe Moraga – Looking for the magic: Chicanos in the mainstream/Jorge Huerta – Staging AIDS: what's Latinos got to do with it?/Alberto Sandoval – Border boda or divorce fronterizo?/Marguerite Waller – Seduced and abandoned: Chicanas and lesbians in representation/Sue-Ellen Case – Public art, performance art, and the politics of site/María Teresa Marrero – 'Salvación casita': Puerto Rican performance and vernacular architecture in the South Bronx/Juan Flores – Inventions and transgressions: a fractured narrative on feminist theatre in Mexico/Kirsten F. Nigro – A Touch of evil: Jesusa Rodríguez's subversive church/Jean Franco – Ethnicity, gender, and power: carnival in Santiago de Cuba/Judith Bettelheim – New Mayan theatre in Chiapas: anthropology, literacy, and social drama/Donald H. Frischmann – 'A Woman fell into the river': negotiating female subjects in contemporary Mayan theatre/Cynthia Steele – For carnival, clinic, and camera: Argentina's turn-of-the-century drag culture performs 'woman'/Jorge Salessi and Patrick O'Connor – Performing gender: las madres de la plaza de Mayo/Diana Taylor – Closing remarks/Juan Villegas – Bibliography/Tiffany Ana López and Jacqueline Lazú. Latin America. History/Theatre and society. Hispanic American theater. History.

Thompson, Donald. **Music, theater and dance in Central America and the Caribbean: an annotated bibliography of dissertations and theses**. San Juan, P.R.: Revista/Review Interamericana, 1979. – p. 115–40. *Notes*: 'Special Supplement, Spring 1979'. Music. Caribbean Area.

Toro, Fernando de. **Brecht en el teatro hispanoamericano contemporáneo: acercamiento semiótico al teatro épico en Hispanoamérica**.

Ottawa: Girol Books, 1984. – 253 p.: ill. *Notes*: Bibliography: p. 241–51. Spanish American drama. 20th century. History and criticism/ Semiotics and literature Influence/Brecht, Bertolt, 1898–1956.

—— and Peter Roster. **Bibliografía del teatro hispanoamericano contemporáneo (1900–1980)**. Frankfurt am Main: Verlag Klaus Dieter Vervuert, 1985. – 2 vol. *Notes*: Spanish American drama. 20th century. Bibliography.

A2c. AFRICA

Alphonse, T. **Vérité première du second visage africain**. [Truth first from Africa's second face]. Paris: G.P. Maisonneuve et Larose, 1975. 135 p.

Alston, J.B. **Yoruba drama in English: interpretation and production**. Lewiston: Edwin Mellen, 1989. 192 p.

Anpe, Thomas Uwetpak. **An investigation of John Pepper Clark's drama as an organic interaction of traditional African drama with Western theatre**. Madison: University of Wisconsin, 1985. 367 p.

Awoonor, Kofi. 'The modern drama of Africa'. In **The breast of the earth: a survey of the history, culture, and literature of Africa south of the Sahara**. New York: Doubleday, 1975.

Bame, Kwabena N. **Profiles in African traditional popular culture: consensus and conflict**. New York: Clear Press, 1991.

Banham, Martin and Clive Wake. **African theatre today**. London: Pitman, 1976.

——, Errol Hill and George W. Woodyard, **The Cambridge guide to African and Caribbean theatre**. Cambridge: Cambridge University Press, 1994. – vii, 259 p.: ill. *Notes*: Includes bibliographical references and index.

Banks, Thomas. 'African drama'. In **Critical survey of drama: English language series**, ed. Frank N. McGill, vol. 6, 2,416–23. Englewood Cliffs, NJ: Salem Press, 1985.

Barber, Kevin, Joachim Fiebach and Alain Ricard. **Drama and theatre in Africa**. Bayreuth: Eckhard Breitinger & Reinhard Sander, 1986. 87 p.

Blair, Dorothy S. 'Dramatic literature'. In **African Literature in French: A history of creative writing in French and Equatorial Africa**. Cambridge: Cambridge University Press, 1976.

Breitinger, Eckhard, ed. **Theatre and performance in Africa: intercultural perspectives**. Bayreuth African Studies Series 31. Bayreuth, Germany: University of Bayreuth, 1994. 220 p.

Brink, André. **Aspekte van die nuwe Drama**. [Aspects of the new drama]. Pretoria: Academica, 1986. 268 p.

Cornévin, Robert. **Le Théâtre en Afrique de l'ouest**. [Theatre in West Africa]. Paris: Société d'Histoire du Théâtre.

——. **Le Théâtre en Afrique noire et à Madagascar**. [The Theatre in Black Africa and Madagascar]. Paris: Le livre africain, 1970.

Dathorne, O.R. 'African drama in French and English'. In **The black mind: a history of African literature**, Minneapolis: University of Minnesota Press, 1974.

de Graft, J.C. 'Dramatic questions'. In **Writers in East Africa**, eds. Andrew Gurr and Angus Calder, 33–67. Nairobi: East African Literature Bureau, 1974.

Deldime, Roger. **Foi de théâtre**. [Faith in theatre]. Morlan Welz: Lansman, 1993. 127 p.

Diop, Alioune Oumy. 'Réflexions sur le théâtre africain pré-colonial et contemporain'. [Thoughts on Pre-colonial and Contemporary African Theatre]. In **Quel Théâtre pour le développement en Afrique?** [Which theatre for development in Africa?] Institut Cultural Africain, 1985.

Duerden, Dennis. **African art and literature: the invisible present**. London: Heinemann Educational Books, 1977.

East, N.B. **African theatre: a checklist of critical materials**. New York: Africana Publishing, 1970. 47 p.

Etherton, Michael. **The development of African drama**. London: Hutchinson, 1982. 368 p.

Fiebach, Joachim. **Die Toten als die Macht der Lebenden: zur Theorie und Geschichte von Theater in Afrika**. Wilhelmshaven: Heinrichshofen, 1986. – 447 p., 24 p. of plates: ill. *Notes*: Includes bibliographical references and index. Theatre. Africa. History. 20th century. In German.

Finnegan, Ruth. **Oral literature in Africa**. Oxford: Oxford University Press, 1970. 558 p.

Fletcher, Jill. **The story of the African theatre 1780–1930**. Cape Town: Vlaeberg, 1994.

Gérard, Albert. **Contexts of African literature**. Amsterdam and Atlanta, GA: Rodopi, 1990.

——. **Four African literatures: Xhosa, Sotho, Zulu, Amharic**. Berkeley and Los Angeles: University of California Press, 1971.

Graham-White, Anthony. **The drama of black Africa**. New York: Samuel French, 1974, 220 p.

——. **West African drama: folk, popular, and literary**. 1969. – v, 434 p. *Notes*: Bibliography: p. 243–434. Thesis (Ph. D.)–Dept. of Speech and Drama, Stanford University.

Gray, John. **Black theatre and performance: a pan-African bibliography**. New York: Greenwood Press, 1990. – xv, 414 p. *Notes*: Includes bibliographic references (p. 309–323) and index. Black theatre. Africa and the Caribbean. Bibliography.

Gurr, Andrew and Angus Calder, eds. **Writers in East Africa**. Nairobi: East African Literature Bureau, 1974.

Hourantier, Marie-José. **Du rituel au théâtre-rituel: contribution à une esthétique théâtrale négro-africaine**. [From ritual to ritual-theatre: contribution to the black-African theatre aesthetics]. Paris: l'Harmattan, 1984. 284 p.

——. **Du rituel au théâtre-rituel: Esquisse ethnosociologique d'une esthétique théâtrale négro-africaine**. [From ritual to ritual-theatre. Ethno-sociological approach to black-African theatre aesthetics]. 2 vols. Paris: Université de Paris III, 1983. 439 p. and 785 p.

Irwin, Paul. **Liptako speaks: History from oral tradition in Africa**. Princeton, N.J.: Princeton University Press, 1981.

Jahn, Janheinz and Claus Peter Dressler. **Bibliography of creative African writing**. Nendeln, Liechtenstein: Kraus-Thomson, 1973. 446 p.

Jeyifo, Biodun. **The truthful lie: essays in a sociology of African drama**. London: New Beacon Books, 1985. 122 p.

Kalu, Ogbu. **African cultural development**. Engu: Fourth Dimension, 1980.

Kambu-ki-Lelo. **Tradition et modernité dans le théâtre négro-africain d'expression française**. Bukavu, Zaire: Ceruki, 1989. – 80 p. *Notes*: African drama (French). History and criticism.

Kannemeyer, J.C. **Geskiedenis van die Afrikaanse Literatuur I**. [The history of Afrikaans literature 1]. Pretoria: Academica, 1978.

——. **Geskiedenis van die Afrikaanse Literatuur II**. [The history of Afrikaans literature II]. Pretoria: Academica, 1983.

Kavanagh, Robert Mshengu. **Theatre and cultural struggle in South Africa**. London: Zed Books, 1985. 237 p.

Kesteloot, Lilyan. **Anthologie négro-africaine. Panorama critique des prosateurs, poètes, et dramaturges noirs de XXe siècle**. [Negro-African anthology. A critical panorama of Black prose writers, poets and playwrights of the twentieth century]. Revised edition. Brussels: Marabout, 1987. 480 p.

——. 'Les Thèmes principaux du théâtre africain moderne'. [The Main Themes of Modern African Theatre]. In **Notes, Actes du Colloque sur le théâtre négro-africain**, Paris: Présence Africaine, 1970.

Kihero, D. 'Plays good, bad or crazy: drama in East Africa'. **Uganda Review** I (1980).

Kom, Ambroise, ed. **Dictionnaire des oeuvres littéraires négro-africaines de langue française des origines à 1978**. [A dictionary of black African literary works in French from the beginnings to 1978]. Paris: Agence de Coopération Culturelle et Technique, 1983. 671 p.

Lindfors, Bernth, ed. **Forms of folklore in Africa: narrative, poetic, gnomic, dramatic**. Austin: University of Texas Press, 1977. 281 p.

Liyong, Taban. **Popular culture of East Africa: oral literature**. Nairobi: Longman, 1972, 157 p.

Long, Kathryn Louise. **The past and future with apartheid: the function of temporal elements in eight plays by Athol Fugard**. Ann Arbor: University of Michigan, 1985. 231 p.

Luther, C.M. **South African theatre: aspects of the collaborative**. Leeds: University of Leeds, 1987.

L'vov, Nikolai Ivanovich. **Sovremennyi teatr tropicheskoi Afriki**. [Contemporary theatre of tropical Africa]. Moscow: Nauka, 1977. 247 p.

Magnier, Bernard. **Théâtre d'Afrique noire**. [Theatre in Black Africa]. Paris: Présence Africaine, 1984.

Malan, Charles, ed. **Spel en Spiëel. Besprekings van die moderne Afrikaanse drama en teater**. [Play and mirror. Discussions of the modern Afrikaans drama and theatre]. Johannesburg and Cape Town: Perskor-Uitgewery, 1984. 177 p.

Mbele, Majola, ed. **Viewpoints: essays on literature and drama**. Nairobi: Kenya Literature Bureau, 1980.

Mbughuni, L.A. 'The development of English drama in East Africa: a study of the emergence of new trends of modern theatre and drama'. In **The writing of East and Central Africa**. G.D. Killam, ed., 247–63. London: Heinemann, 1984.

Mda, Zakes. **When people play people: development communication through theatre**. Johannesburg: London: Witwaters and University Press; Zed Books, 1993. – x, 250 p.:

ill. *Notes*: Includes bibliographical references and index. Theatre and society. Africa/Community development.

Melone, Thomas, ed. **Mélanges africains**. [The African mix]. Paris, 1973.

Moore, Gerald. **Seven African writers**. London: Hutchinson, 1980.

Naïndouba, Maoundoé and Protais Asseng. **L'étudiant de Soweto**. Paris: Hatier, 1981. – 159 p. African drama (French).

Ndiaye, P.G. 'La création dramatique, spectaculaire et musicale en Afrique'. [Dramatic, spectacular and musical creation in Africa]. In **Patrimonie et création contemporaine en Afrique et dans le monde Arabe**. Mohamed Aziza, ed. Dakar-Abidjan: Les Nouvelles Editions Africaines, 1977.

Nidzgorski, Denis. **Arts du spectacle africain: contributions du Gabon**. [African theatre arts: the contributions of Gabon]. Bandundu: CEEBA, 1980. 373 p.

Ogunba, Oyin. **The movement of transition**. Ibadan: Ibadan University Press, 1975.

—— and A. Irele, eds. **Theatre in Africa**. Ibadan: Ibadan University Press, 1978. 224 p.

Okagbue, O.A. **Aspects of African and Caribbean theatre: a comparative study**. Leeds: University of Leeds, 1990.

Okpaku, Joseph, ed. **The arts and civilization of black and african peoples**. Lagos: Centre for Black and African Arts and Civilization, 1986. 10 vols.

Okpewho, Isidore. **The epic in Africa: towards a poetics of the oral performance**. New York: Columbia University Press, 1979. 240 p.

Olaniyan, Tejumola. **Scars of conquest/masks of resistance: the invention of cultural identities in African, African-American, and Caribbean drama**. New York: Oxford University Press, 1995. – xii, 196 p. *Notes*: Includes bibliographical references (p. 171–90) and index. Black authors. Criticism and interpretation.

Ongoum, Louis Marie and Célestin, Tcheho. **Littérature orale de l'Afrique contemporaine: Approches théoriques et pratiques**. [African oral literature: theory and practice]. Actes du colloque international. Yaounde: CEPER, 1989.

Plastow, J.E. **The development of theatre in relation to the states and societies of Ethiopia, Tanzania and Zimbabwe**. Manchester: University of Manchester, 1991.

Ricard, Alain. **L'Invention du théâtre: Le Théâtre et les comédiens en Afrique noir**. [The invention of theatre: the theatre and comedians of Black Africa]. Lausanne: L'Age d'Homme, 1986. 134 p.

Roscoe, Adrian H. 'A footnote on drama'. In **Uhuru's fire: African literature east to south**. Cambridge: Cambridge University Press, 1977.

Sandoval, Enrique. **The metaphoric style in politically censored theatre**. Edmonton: Concordia University, 1986.

Scherer, Colette, ed. **Catalogue des pièces de théâtre africain en langue française**. [Catalogue of African plays in French]. Paris: Presses de la Sorbonne Nouvelle, 1996.

Scheub, Harold. **The African storyteller: stories from African oral traditions**. Kendall/Hunt, 1990.

Schipper-De-Leeuw, Mineke. 'Origin and forms of drama in the African context'. In **The East African experience**, ed. Ulla Schild, 55–64. Berlin: Reimer, 1980.

——. **Theatre and society in Africa**. Translated by Ampie Coetzee. Athens: Ohio Univeristy Press, 1982. 170 p.

Sidibe, Valy. **La Critique de pouvoir politique dans le théâtre de Bernard Dadié (1966–1980)**. [Criticism of political power in Bernard Dadié's theatre (1966–1980)]. Paris: Université de Paris III, 1984. 323 p.

Silbert, Rachel. **Southern African drama in English: 1900–1964**. Johannesburg: University of Witwatersrand, 1965.

Smith, Rowland. **Exile and tradition: studies in African and Caribbean literature**. New York: Africana, 1976.

Soyinka, Wole. **Myth, literature and the African world**. Cambridge: Cambridge University Press, 1976.

——. 'Theatre in African traditional culture: survival patterns'. In **African history and culture**, ed. Richard Olaniyan, 237–49. Ikeja: Longman, 1982.

Taiwo, Oladele. **An introduction to West African literature**. London: Thomas Nelson & Sons, 1967.

Traoré, Bakary. **The Black African theatre and its social functions**. Translated and with a preface by Dapo Adelugba. Ibadan: Ibadan University Press, 1972. (Originally published in French as *Le théâtre Négro-africain et ses fonctions sociales*, 1958), 130 p.

——. 'Meaning and function of the traditional Negro-African theatre'. In **Colloquium:**

function and significance of African negro art in the life of the people and for the people, 481–93. Paris: Présence Africaine, 1968.

Theatre and society in Africa. Braamfontein: Ravan Press, 1982. 170 p.

Turchin, N.M., ed. **Puti Razvitiia Teatral 'Nogo Iskusstva Afriki Sbornik Nauchnykh Trudov.** [The paths of development of the theatrical art of Africa: a collection of scientific studies]. Moscow: GITIS, 1981.

Vaz, Carlos. **Para um conhecimento do teatro Africano**. [Towards an understanding of African theatre]. Lisbon: Ulmeiro, 1978. 204 p.

Warren, Lee. **The theatre of Africa: an introduction**. Englewood Cliffs, NJ: Prentice-Hall, 1975. 112 p.

Webb, Jugh. **Drama, society and politics: African impact**. Murdoch, Australia: African Studies Seminar, Murdoch University, 1980. 23 p.

A2d. ARAB WORLD

Abu al-'Ala, Ahmad 'Abd al-Raziq. **al-Khitab al-masrahi: qira'at fi al-masrah al-'Arabi**. Cairo: al-Hay'ah al-'Ammah li-Qusur al-Thaqafah, 1994. – 269 p. *Series*: Kitabat naqdiyah. *Notes*: Includes bibliographical references. Arabic drama. 20th century. History and criticism. Arab countries.

Abul Naga, el-Saïd Atia. **Recherche sur les termes de théâtre et leur traduction en arabe moderne**. Algiers: SNED, 1973. – 301 p. Bibliography: p. 289–301. Terminology/French language to Arabic.

al-Ahmed, Ahmed Sulaimaan. **Diraasaat Fi al-Masrah al-'Arabi al-Mu'aasir**. [Studies on the contemporary Arab theatre]. Damascus: al-Ajyaal (Generations) Publishing House, 1972.

Alra'i, Ali. **Al Masrah fil watan al arabi**. [Theatre in the Arab world]. Kuwait, 1987.

Ardash, Sa'd. **al-Mukhrij fi al-masrah al-mu'asir**. Cairo: al-Hay'ah al-Misriyah al-'Ammah lil-Kitab, 1993. – 394 p. *Notes*: Includes bibliographical references. Arab countries. Theatre. History. 20th century.

'Arsan, 'Ali 'Uqlah. **Waqafat ma'a al-masrah al-'Arabi: dirasah**. Damascus: Ittihad al-Kuttab al-'Arab, 1996. – 258 p. *Notes*: Includes bibliographical references. On the Arabic theater; essays. History and criticism. In Arabic.

Ayyuti, Amin. **Dirasat fi al-masrah**. Cairo: Maktabat al-Anjilu al-Misriyah, 1986. – 198 p. *Notes*: Arabic drama. 20th century. History and criticism.

Aziza, Mohamed. **Regard sur le théâtre arabe contemporain**. [A look at contemporary Arab theatre]. Tunis: Maison tunisiènne de l'edition, 1970.

Bebars, Ahmed Samir. **The Arab theatre in the nineteenth century**. Cairo: Egyptian Book Organization. 1985. In Arabic.

Birshid, 'Abd al-Karim. **Hudud al-Ka'in wa-al-mumkin fi al-masrah al-ihtifali**. al-Dar al-Bayda': Dar al-Thaqafah, 1985. – 223 p. *Notes*: Arabic drama. History and criticism.

Botitsiva, Tamara Alexandra. **Alf 'Aam Wa 'Aam 'Ala l-Masrah al-'Arabi**. [The Arab theatre's thousand and one years] Beirut: al-Faraabi Publishing House, 1981.

Bu Shu'ayr, al-Rashid. **Athar Bertolt Brecht fi masrah al-mashriq al-'Arabi**. al-Tab'ah 1. Damascus: al-Ahali lil-Tiba'ah wa-al-Nashr wa-al-Tawzi', 1996. – 384 p. *Notes*: Includes bibliographical references (p. 363–80). Brecht, Bertolt, 1898–1956, influence in the Arab world. In Arabic.

Dagher, Yousef As'ad. **Mu'jam al-Masrahiyyaat al-'Arabiyya Wa l-Mu'arraba**. [Dictionary of Arabic and Arabicized theatrical plays]. Iraqi Ministry of Culture and Fine Arts, 1978.

Doghman, Saad Al Din. **Al Osool Al Tarekhiyah Lenashaat Al Drama Fee Al Adab Al Araby**. [Historical references for the beginning of drama in Arab literature]. Beirut: Arabic Beirut University, 1973.

Ersan, Ali Akla. **Al Thawaher Al Masraheyah Enda Al Arab**. [The Arab theatrical phenomenon]. Damascus: The Arabic Writers Union, 1981.

Faraj, Alfred. **Adwa' al-masrah al-Gharbi**. Cairo: Dar al-Hilal, 1990. – 287 p.: ill. *Notes*: Arab Theatre. 20th century. History and criticism.

Ghalum, Ibrahim 'Abd Allah. **al-Masrah wa-al-taghayyur al-ijtima'i fi al-khalij al-'Arabi: dirasah fi susyulujiya al-tajribah al-masrahiyah fi al-Kuwayt wa-al-Bahrayn**. [Theatre in Kuwait and Bahrain]. Kuwait: al-Majlis al-Watani lil-Thaqafah wa-al-Funnun wa-al-Adab, 1986. – 400 p. *Notes*: Includes biliographical references (p. 386–92). History and criticism. Theatre; social change; Persian Gulf countries.

Hamadah, Ibrahim. **Min hasad al-dirama wa-al-naqd**. Cairo: al-Hay'ah al-Misriyah al-'Ammah lil-Kitab, 1987. – 240 p. *Notes*: Includes bibliographical references (p. 239–40). Arabic drama. History and criticism. Comparative Western and Arabic drama.

Irsaan, 'Ali 'Uqla. **ath-Thawaahir al-Masrahiyya**

'Ind al-'Arab. [Arab theatrical phenomena]. Tripoli, Libya, 1983.

Jayyusi, Salma Khadra and Roger Allen, eds. **Modern Arabic drama: an anthology**. Indiana: University of Indiana Series in Arab and Islamic Studies, 1995. 480 p.

Khouri, Chaki. **Le Théâtre arabe de l'absurde**. Paris: A.-G. Nizet, 1978. – 190 p. *Notes*: Includes index. Bibliography: p. 185–8. Arabic drama. 20th century. History and criticism.

Landau, Jack M. **Studies in the Arab Theatre and Cinema**. Philadelphia: University of Pennsylvania Press, 1958.

Lindaw, Ya'qoub. **Diraasaat Fi l-Masrah Wa s-Sinema 'Ind al-'Arab**. [Studies about the Arab theatre and cinema]. Translated by Ahmed al-Maghaazi. Cairo: Egyptian Public Book Organization, 1972.

al-Madyouni, Mohammed. 'Ishkalaat Ta'seel al-Masrah al-'Arabi'. [The Problem of establishing the origin of the Arabic theatre]. **Carthage Theatre Studies and Research Series**. Bayt al-Hikma Publications, 1993.

Mahfuz, 'Isam. **Masrahi wa-al-masrah**. Beirut: Lebanon Dar 2002, 1995. – 204 p. *Notes*: Includes bibliographical references. Arabic drama. 20th century. History and criticism.

Manzalaoui, Mahmoud. **Arabic Writing Today**, 2 vols. Cairo: American Research Centre in Egypt, 1968–77.

Al Masrah, Derasat Fe. **Wa Al Cenima Inda Al Arab**. [Studies in Arab cinema]. Cairo: Al Hayaa Al Masreya Al Amah Lel Kotab, 1972.

Mubarak, Khalid. **Arabic Drama: A Critical Introduction**. Khartoum, Sudan: Khartoum University Press, 1986. 95 p.

Mu'tamar as-Sinema Wa th-Thaqaafa al-'Arabiyya. [The cinema and the Arab culture conference]: Roundtable lectures under the auspices and supervision of UNESCO, Arab Liaison Centre for Cinema and Television (Beirut, 11/1963 and 1964).

Naga, Abdul. **Recherche sur les termes de théâtre et leur traduction en arabe moderne**. [Research into theatrical terms and their translations into modern Arabic]. Algiers, 1973.

Nawfal, Yusuf Hasan. **Bina' al-masrahiyah al-'Arabiyah: ru'yah fi al-hiwar**. Cairo: Dar al-Ma'arif, 1995. – 339 p. *Notes*: Includes bibliographical references (p. 325–39). Structure of Arab theatre, an examination of dialogue. History and criticism/Verse drama.

Nigm, Mohamad Yousef. **Al Masraheyah Fe Al Adab Al Araby Al Hadeeth**. [The play in contemporary Arabic literature]. Beirut: Dar Al Thakafa, 1980.

Omotoso, Kole. 'Arabic Drama in North Africa'. In **Theatre in Africa**. Edited by Oyin Ogunba and Abiola Irele. Ibadan: Ibadan University Press, 1978.

Oukla Irsan, Ali. **Al zawaher al masrahia indal'arab**. [Arabic forms of performance]. Damascus, 1981.

Qattaaya, Salmaan. **al-Masrah al-'Arabi Min Ayn Wa Ila Ayn**. [The Arabic theatre from where to where]. Damascus: Federation of Arab Writers, 1972.

Rahumah, Muhammad Mahmud. **al-Nass al-gha'ib: dirasah fi masrah Sa'd Allah Wannous**. Cairo: Maktabat al-Shabab, 1991. – 476 p. *Notes*: Includes bibliographical references (p. 467–76). Wannous, Sa'd Allah. A study of this important Arab dramatist.

Reynolds, Dwight Fletcher. **Heroic poets, poetic heros: the ethnography of performance in Arabic oral tradition**. Ithaca, NY: Cornell University Press, 1995. 243 p.

Sarhan, Samir. **Tajarib jadidah fi al-fann al-masrahi**. Cairo: Maktabat Gharib, 1981. – 219 p. *Notes*: 20th century Arab/world theatre. In Arabic.

Shaoul, Paul. **Al-Masrah al'Arabi al-Hadeeth (1976–1989)**. [The modern Arabic theatre (1976–1989)]. Beirut: Riyaad Najeeb ar-Rayyi Publications, 1989.

Shawul, Bul. **al-Masrah al-'Arabi al-hadith (1976–1989)**. London: Riad El Rayyes, 1989. – 570 p. *Notes*: Includes index. On added t.p.: Arab modern theatre.

Tomiche, Nada and Cherif Khaznadar. **Le Théâtre Arabe**. [The Arab theatre]. Paris: Unesco, 1969. 229 p.

Tu'mah, Salih Jawad. **Bibliyughrafiyat al-adab al-'Arabi al-masrarhi al-hadith. (1945–1965)**. Baghdad: Matba'at al-'Ani, 1969. – 124 p. *Notes*: Added t.p.: A bibliographical survey of Arabic dramatic literature: 1945–65 [by] Salih J. Altoma. Introductions in Arabic and English.

'Utaymash, Muhsin. **al-Sha'ir al-'Arabi al-hadith masrahiyan**. Baghdad: al-Jumhuriyah al-'Iraqiyah, Wizarat al-I'lam, 1977. – 383 p. *Notes*: In Arabic. Bibliography: p. 369–82. 20th century. History and criticism. Arabic poetic plays.

Various. **Al masrah al arabi bainal nakli wal ta'sis**. [Arab theatre: Between limitation and creation]. Kuwait, 1988.

Wannus, Nasir. **al-Maraji' al-masrahiyah al-**

'Arabiyah wa-al-mu'arrabah: bibliyughrafiya wa-shuruhat. Suriyah: Dar Jafra, 1992. – 228 p. *Notes*: Includes bibliographical references. Arabic drama.

Wanous, Sa'dallah. **Bayanaat li-Masrah 'Arabi Jadeed**. [Declarations for a new Arabic theatre]. Beirut: Daar al-Fikr al-Jadeed Publishing, 1988.

A2e. ASIA AND THE PACIFIC

Banham, Martin and James R. Brandon, eds. **The Cambridge guide to Asian theatre**. Cambridge: Cambridge University Press, 1997, 1993. viii, 253 p.: ill. *Notes*: Includes bibliographical references and index. Bangladesh – Burma – Cambodia – China – Hong Kong – India – Indonesia – Japan – Korea – Laos – Malaysia – Nepal – Oceania – Pakistan – Philippines – Singapore – Sri Lanka – Taiwan – Thailand – Vietnam.

Bowers, Faubion. **Theatre in the East; a survey of Asian dance and drama**. Ann Arbor, Michigan: University Microfilms, 1969, 1956. – 374 p.: ill.

Brandon, James R. **The performing arts of Asia**. Paris: Unesco, 1971. 168 p.

——. **Theatre in Southeast Asia**. Honolulu: University Press of Hawaii, 1976.

—— and Elizabeth Wichmann, eds. **Asian theatre: a study guide and annotated bibliography**. Theatre Perspectives no. 1 Washington, DC: American Theater Association, 1980.

Byrski, Maria Krzysztof. **Methodology of the analysis of Sanskrit drama**. Warsaw: Wydawn. Uniwersytetu Warszawskiego, 1979. – 157 p. *Notes*: Bibliography: p. 153–7. Sanskrit drama. History and criticism/Drama. In Polish.

Chua Soo Pong, ed. **Traditional theatre in Southeast Asia**. Singapore: UniPress for SPAFA [and] the Centre for the Arts, National University of Singapore, 1995. 150 p.

Davidson, Clifford and John C. Stroupe, eds. **Early and traditional drama: Africa, Asia and the New World**. Kalamazoo, MI: Medieval Institute Publications, 1994. 165 p.

Dzarylgasinova, R.S. and M.V. Krukov, eds. **Kalendarnyje obycai I obriady narodov Vostocnoj Azii: Nozyj God** [Calendar traditions and rites of the people of East Asia: New Year]. Moscow: Nauka, 1985. 264 p.

Foley, Kathy, ed. **Essays on Southeast Asian performing arts: local manifestations and cross-cultural implications**. Berkeley, CA: International and Area Studies, University of California at Berkeley, 1992. 139 p.

Ghulam Ghulam Sarwar, Yousof. **Dictionary of traditional South-East Asian theatre**. New York: Oxford University Press, 1994. 327 p.: ill. *Series*: Oxford in Asia paperbacks. *Notes*: 'Issued under the auspices of the Institute of Southeast Asian Studies, Singapore'.

——. **Southeast Asian traditional performing arts: a preliminary bibliography**. Singapore: Southeast Asian Studies Program, 1990. – vii, 161 p.

Ichikawa, Miyabi, Ying-che Su and Jiryo Miyao. **Ajia geino kenkyu bunken mokuroku**. Tokyo: Waseda Daigaku Engeki Gakkai, 1984. – vi, 337 p. *Notes*: A Bibliography of Asian performing arts.

Ishikawa, Yasuko and Hideharu Umeda. **Barito no geino shiryo shozo mokuroku**. Tokyo: Kunitachi Ongaku Daigaku Fuzoku Toshokan, 1991. – 151 p.: ill., maps. *Notes*: Japanese, English, German, and Indonesian materials; annotations in Japanese. Includes Indonesia, Bali.

Kim, N. **Narodnoje chudozestvennoje tvorcestvo Sovetskovo Vostoka: ocerki istorii massovovo teatralnova iskusstva Srednej Azii**. [People's art of the Soviet East: Historical essays on popular theatical forms of Middle Asia]. Moscow: Nauka, 1985. 197 p.

Kinderman, Heinz, ed. **Einführung in das ostasiatische Theatre**. [Introduction to the oriental theatre]. Maske und Kothurn, Beiheft 7. Vienna/Cologne/Graz: Bohlau, 1985. 426 p.

Lal, P. **An annotated Mahabharata bibliography**. Calcutta: Writer's Workshop, 1967. 31 p.

Marotti, Ferruccio. **Il volto dell'invisibile. Studi e richerche sui teatri orientali**. [The face of the invisible. Studies and research on oriental theatre]. Rome: Bulzoni, 1984. 180 p.

McLean, Mervyn. **An annotated bibliography of Oceanic Music and Dance**. 2nd edn. Warren, MI: Harmonic Park Press, 1995. 502 p.

Miettinen, Jukka O. **Classical dance and theatre in South-East Asia**. Singapore; New York: Oxford University Press, 1992. – xx, 175 p.: ill. (some col.). *Notes*: Includes bibliographical references (p. 169–71) and index. Theatre. Asia, Southeastern/Puppet theatre. Dance.

Mitchell, John Dietrich. **The director–actor relationship: essays and articles**. New York: Institute for Advanced Studies in the Theatre Arts Press, 1992. – vi, 170 p.: ill. *Notes*: Applied psychoanalysis in the drama – Applied psychoanalysis in the director–actor relationship – Contemporary American theatre... a psychologic sounding board – Psychoanalytic approach to Kabuki: a study in personality and culture –

The actor's 'method', backstage at the Kabuki-za, Tokyo – A psychosocial approach to the Peking Opera – How the Chinese actor trains; interviews with two Peking Opera performers – Two faces of China – East–West understanding through the arts – Discussion – The theatre in India – A Sanskrit classic: Shakuntala – The Sanskrit drama Shakuntala – The theatre of India and Southeast Asia – Theatre of Western Europe – The theatre in Russia – The Moscow Art Theatre in rehearsal – The theatre of Western Europe: some highlights – Brecht's theatre, the Berliner Ensemble – In search of Commedia dell'Arte – André Gide, rebel and conformist – The challenge of directing a neo-classical verse tragedy – Theatre in Mexico moves ahead – Riches from abroad – IASTA, an American innovation in workshop production – The International Amateur Theatre Association – Is the play the thing? Acting/Theatre. Production and direction. China. USA. Japan. India. Russia. Germany. Mexico.

Osman, Mohammad Taib, ed. **Traditional drama and music of Southeast Asia**. Kuala Lumpur: Dewan Bahasa dan Pustaka, 1974.

Ottaviani, Gioia. **L'attore e lo sciamano: esempi d'identità nelle tradizioni dell'Estremo Oriente**. [The actor and the shaman in oriental theatre]. Rome: Bulzoni, 1984. – 173 p. Notes: Includes index. Bibliography: p. 121–72. Focuses on Japan and China. In Italian.

Schechner, Richard. **Performance theory – Southeast Asia**. New York: New York University School of the Arts, 1979. – 126 p.: ill. **The Drama Review** 23, no. 2 (June 1979).

Scott, A.C. **The theatre in Asia**. London: Weidenfeld & Nicolson, 1972. 289 p.

Tilakasiri, J. **The puppet theatre of Asia**. Colombo: Dept. of Cultural Affairs, 1968. – xii, 166 p. illus. (part col.). Notes: Bibliography: p. 159–60. Puppets and puppet-plays. Asia. History.

Wichmann, Elizabeth and James R. Brandon. **Asian theatre: a study guide and annotated bibliography**. American Theatre Association, 1980. – 197 p. Series: Theatre perspectives; no. 1.

Yousof, Ghulam-Sarwar. **Dictionary of traditional South-East Asian theatre**. Kuala Lumpur: Oxford University Press, 1994. 327 p.

A2f. LINGUISTIC GROUPINGS

Acuña, René. **El teatro popular en Hispanoamérica: una bibliografía anotada**. [Popular theatre in Spanish America: an annotated bibliography]. México City: Universidad Nacional Autónoma de Mexico, Instituto de Investigaciones Filológicas, Centro de Estudios Literarios, 1979. 114 p.

Berger, Karl H., ed. **Schauspielführer**. Berlin: Henschel, 1963, 1964. – 3 vols. Notes: vol. 3 has index for vols 1–3. Ancient Italian, Spanish, English, French drama, German drama, Austrian, Swiss, Dutch, Russian and Soviet drama.

Bibliographie des arts du spectacle. Louvain: Cahiers théâtre Louvain, 1986. Notes: 'Ouvrages en langue française'. Performing arts. Bibliography. French-speaking countries.

Blair, Dorothy. **African literature in French**. London: Cambridge University Press, 1976.

Hainaux, René. **Les Arts du spectacle: bibliographie: ouvrages en langue française concernant théâtre, musique, danse, mime, marionnettes, variétés, cirque, radio, télévision, cinéma, publiés dans le monde entre 1900 et 1985**. [Books in French about theatre, music, dance, mime, puppetry, light entertainment, circus, radio, television, cinema published between 1900 and 1965]. Brussels: Editions Labor, 1989. n 268 p. Notes: Includes index. Performing arts. Bibliography. French imprints.

Kesteloot, Lilyan. **Les Ecrivains noirs de langue française: Naissance d'une littérature**. [Black writers in French: the birth of a literature]. 2nd edn. Brussels: Université Libre de Bruxelles, 1965.

King, Bruce Alvin. **Post-colonial English drama: commonwealth drama since 1960**. New York: St Martin's Press, 1992. – x, 275 p. Notes: Includes bibliographical references and index. Decolonization in literature.

Ngandu Nkashama, Pius. **Le Littérature africaine écrite en langue française: la poésie, le roman, le théâtre**. [French African literature: poetry, the novel, theatre]. Issy-les-Moulineaux: Les Classiques Africaines, 1979.

Patterson, Michael. **German theatre today: post-war theatre in West and East Germany, Austria and Northern Switzerland**. London: Pitman, 1976. ix, 129 p. Notes: Includes index. Bibliography: p. 118–19.

Rischbieter, Henning. **Theater-Lexikon**. Zürich: Orell-Füssli, 1983. – 1440 columns: ill. Notes: Includes index. Dictionary of German-speaking countries and Europe. In German.

Salien, François O. **Panorama du théâtre africain d'expression française: historique, analyse, critique, perspectives**. [A panorama of francophone African theatre: history, analysis, criticism, perspectives]. Bandundu: CEEBA, 1983. 218 p.

Scherer, Jacques. **Le Théâtre en Afrique noire francophone**. [Francophone Black African Theatre]. Paris: Presses Universitaires de France, 1992.

Stein, Rita, Friedhelm Rickert and Blandine M. Rickert. **Major modern dramatists**. New York: Ungar, 1984, 1986. – 2 vols. *Notes*: Includes indexes. vol. 1. American, British, Irish, German, Austrian, and Swiss dramatists – vol. 2. Norwegian, Swedish, French, Belgian, Italian, Spanish, Russian, Czech, Hungarian, and Polish dramatists. Drama. History and criticism.

Waters, Harold A. **Black theatre in French. A guide**. Sherbrooke, Quebec: Editions Naaman, 1978. 91 p.

A3. National Studies

A3a1. AFGHANISTAN

Jakimovič, Leonid. 'V centre Kabula'. [In the centre of Kabul] **Teatr M.** (December 1983) 42 (12): 133–8.

Rahel, Shafie. **Cultural policy in Afghanistan**. Paris: UNESCO, 1975.

Wilber, Donald N. **Afghanistan: its people, its society, its culture**. New Haven: Hraf Press, 1962. 320 p.

A3a2. ALBANIA

Fjalor enciklopedik Shqipter. [Albanian encyclopedic dictionary]. Tirana: Akademia e Shkencave e RPSSH, 1985.

Gjini, Miho. **Pas shfaqjes**. [After the spectacle: critical essays]. Tirana: Shtëpia Botuese Naim Frashëri, 1975.

——. **Teatri dhe koha: studime dhe artikuj kritikë**. [Theatre and time]. Tirana: Shtëpia Botuese Naim Frashëri, 1975.

——. **Trokitje në dyert e teatrit**. [Knocking at theatre's door]. Tirana: Shtëpia Botuese Naim Frashëri, 1967.

Historia e muzikës Shqiptare. [A history of Albanian music]. Tirana: Shtëpia Botuese e Librit Shkoller, 1985.

Historia e teatrit Shqiptar. [History of the Albanian theatre], 3 vols. Tirana: Shtëpia Botuese e Librit Shkoller, 1983–5.

Hoxha, Ismail. **Nga jeta në teatër, nga teatri në jetë**. [From life to theatre, from theatre to life]. Tirana: Shtëpia Botuese Naim Frashëri, 1983.

Kosova, Bardhyl. **Aleksandër Moisiu**. Tirana: Shtëpia Botuese Naim Frashëri, 1969.

Mjeshtëria e aktorit. [The art of acting]. Tirana: Shtëpia Botuese e Librit Shkoller, 1985.

Moisiu, Vangjel. **Aleksandër Moisiu**. Tirana: Shtëpia Botuese i Nëntori, 1980.

Papagjoni, Josif. **Teatri dhe aktori**. [Theatre and actor]. Shtëpia Botuese Naim Frashëri, 1980.

Selimi, Skënder. **Arti i koreografisë**. [Choreography as art]. Tirana: Shtëpia Botuese e Librit Shkoller, 1987.

Shita, Vehap. **Kur ndizen dritat**. [In the limelight: critical essays]. Prishtina: Rilindja, 1977.

Shkurtaj, Gjovalin. **Kultura e gjuhës në skenë e në ekran**. [The nature of speech on stage and on screen]. Tirana: Shtëpia Botuese e Librit Shkoller, 1983.

Shllaku, Leo. **Zef Jubani**. Tirana: Shtëpia Botuese Naim Frashëri, 1962.

Velça, Kudret. **Rruga e zhvillimit të dramës sonë të re**. [The process of the new Albanian dramaturgy]. Tirana: Shtëpia Qëndore a Krijimtarisë Popullore, 1972.

Vlashi, Gjergj. **Regjisura në estradë**. [Directing for variety]. Tirana: Shtëpia Qëndore e Krijimtarisë Popullore, 1987.

A3a3. ALGERIA

'Aloula, Adb ul-Qaadir. **An-Nashaat al-Masrahi Fi al-Jazaa'ir**. [Theatrical activity in Algeria]. Damascus: Ittihaad al-Kuttaab al-'Arab bi-Dimashq [The Arab Writers' Union in Damascus], 1982.

Archour, Christian. **Dictionnaire des oeuvres algériennes en langue française** [Dictionary of Algerian works in French]. Paris: l'Harmattan, 1990.

Bachetarzi, Maheddine. **Mémoirs**. 3 vols. vol. 1 (1919–39), Algiers: Éditions Nationales Algériennes, 1968. vol. 2 (1939–51) and vol. 3 (1951–74), Algiers: Entreprise Nationale des Livres, 1968 and 1984.

Baffet, Roselyn. **Tradition théâtrale et modernité en Algérie**. [Modern theatrical tradition in Algeria]. Paris: l'Harmattan, 1985. 223 pp.

Baghli, Sid Ahmed. **Aspects of Algerian Cultural Policy**. Paris: UNESCO, 1978.

Bouzar-Kasbadji, Nadya. **L'Émergence artistique algérienne au XXe siècle: contribution de la musique et du théâtre algérois à la renaissance culturelle et à la prise de conscience nationaliste**. Ben Aknoun, Alger: Office des publications universitaires, 1988.: ill. *Notes*: 'Reflet de la presse coloniale et 'indigène,' 1920–1956'. Includes bibliographical references (p. 201–9). Algeria. History and criticism.

Dejeux, Jean. **Djoh'a, hier et aujourd'hui**. [Djoh'a, yesterday and today]. Sherbrooke: Éditions Naaman, 1978.

——. 'Le Théâtre'. **Maghreb: littératures de langue française**. Paris: Acantère Éditions, 1993.

Djeghloul, Abdelkader. **L'Aurore du théâtre Algérien**. [The dawn of Algerian theatre]. Oran: Université d'Oran Centre de Recherche et d'Information Documentaire en Sciences sociales, 1982.

Guseinova, D. **Alzhirskii teatr: ocherki istorii**. [Algerian theatre: historical essays]. Moscow: Rossiysky In-t Iskusstvoznaniya, 1995. 140 p.

Naylor, Phillip and Alf A. Heggoy. **Historical Dictionary of Algeria**. Metuchen, NJ: Scarecrow Press, 1994. 443 p.

ar-Raa'i, 'Ali. **al-Masrah Fi al-Watan al-'Arabi**. [The theatre in the Arab world]. Kuwait: 'al-Majlis al-Watani lith-Thaqaafa Wa l-Funoun Wa l-Aadaab [National Council for Culture, Arts and Literature], 1980.

Ramadaani, Bou'laam. **al-Masrah al-Jazaa'iri Bayn al-Maadi Wa l-Haadir**. [The Algerian theatre between yesterday and today]. Algeria: al-Mu'assasa al-Wataniyya lil-Kitaab [National Book Establishment], 1984.

Roth, Arlette. **Le Théâtre algérien de langue dialectale, 1926–1954**. [Algerian dialectic theatre, 1926–1954]. Paris: François Maspero, 1967.

A3a4. ANGOLA

Almeida Santos, José. **Paginas esquecidas de Luanda de han cem anos**. [A century of writing from Luanda]. 4 vols. Luanda: Da Camara, 1970.

Altuna, Padre Raul Ruiz Asùa. **Cultura tradicional Banto**. [Banto traditional culture]. Luanda: Secretariado Diocesano de Luanda, 1985.

Bastin, Marie-Louise. 'Ritual masks of the Chokwe'. **African arts** 17, no. 4 (August 1985): 40–4.

Redinha, José. **Etnias de culturas de Angola**. [Ethnic cultures in Angola]. Luanda: Instituto de Investigação, 1974.

Van-Dunem, Domingos. 'Para a história da falta de Teatro em Angola'. [Toward a history of Angola's lack of theatre]. **Revista Noticia** (January 1968).

A3a5. ARGENTINA

Acuña, Manuel. **Teatro de títeres**. [Puppet theatre]. Buenos Aires: 1960. 128 p.

Agilda, Enrique. **El alma del teatro independiente: su trayectoria emocional**. [The soul of the independent theatre: Its emotional evolution]. Buenos Aires: Ediciones Intercoop, 1960. 154 p.

Alfonso, Fausto José. **Una década dramática: apuntes sobre teatro mendocino: 1985–1995**. Argentina: s.n., 1995. 101 p. *Notes*: Includes bibliographical references (p. 87–92) and index.

Arias, Bogdanka Wus. **Estudio de la difusión y recepción crítica del teatro norteamericano en Buenos Aires (1940–1965)**. 1967. 209 p. *Notes*: Includes abstract. Includes bibliographical references (p 205–9). Thesis (Ph. D.)–University of Arkansas, 1967. Microfilm. Ann Arbor, Mich.: University Microfilms International, 1978. 1 microfilm reel; 35 mm.

Azor, Ileana. **El neogrotesco argentino: apuntes para su historia**. Caracas: CELCIT, Centro Latinoamericano de Creación e Investigación Teatral, 1994. – 203 p. *Notes*: Includes bibliographical references (p. 197–203). Argentine drama. 20th century. History and criticism/Theatre of the absurd.

Berenguer Carisomo, Arturo. **Las ideas estéticas en el teatro argentino**. [Aesthetic principles in Argentine theatre]. Buenos Aires: Comisión Nacional de Cultura, Instituto Nacional de Estudios de Teatro, 1947. 438 p.

Bernardo, Mane and Sarah Bianchi. **Cuatro manos y dos manitas: memorias titiriteras**. Buenos Aires, República Argentina: Ediciones Tu Llave, 1987. – 282 p.: ill. *Notes*: Puppet theatre. Argentina. History.

Blanco Amores de Pagella, Angela. **Motivaciones del teatro argentino en el siglo XX**. [Motivations for the Argentine theatre of the twentieth century]. Buenos Aires: Ediciones Culturales Argentinas, 1983.

——. **Nuevos temas en el teatro argentino: la influencia europea**. [New themes in Argentine theatre: The European influence]. Buenos Aires: Editorial Huemul, 1965. 185 p.

Casadevall, Domingo F. **La evolución de la Argentina vista por el teatro nacional**. [Argentina's evolution seen through its National Theatre]. Buenos Aires: Ediciones Culturales Argentinas, Ministerio de Educación y Justicia, 1965. 187 p.

——. **El teatro nacional: sinopsis y perspectivas**. [The National Theatre: Synopsis and Perspectives]. Buenos Aires: Ediciones Culturales, Ministerio de Educación y Justicia, 1961. 63 p.

Castagnino, Raúl. **Circo, teatro gauchesco y tango**. [Circus, gaucho theatre and tango].

Buenos Aires: Instituto Nacional de Estudios de Teatro, 1982.

——. **Literatura dramática argentina 1717–1967**. [Argentine dramatic literature 1717–1967]. Buenos Aires: Pleamar, 1968. 208 p.

——. **Sociología del teatro argentino**. [Sociology of the Argentine theatre]. Compendios Nova de Iniciación Cultural no. 47. Buenos Aires: Editorial Nova, 1963. 192 p.

——. **El teatro en Buenos Aires durante la época de Rosas**. [Theatre in Argentine during the Rosas era]. Buenos Aires: Instituto Nacional de Estudios de Teatro, 1945.

De Toro, Fernando, ed. **Otro Teatro: después de Teatro Abierto**. [Other theatres: After Teatro Abierto]. Buenos Aires: IITCTL. 1991.

Dubatti, Jorge. **Peregrinaciones de Shakespeare en la Argentina: testimonios y lecturas de teatro comparado**. Buenos Aires: Centro Cultural Rector Ricardo Rojas, 1996. 152 pp. *Notes*: Papers from the Primeras Jornadas Nacionales de Teatro Comparado held Nov. 17–18, 1995, organized by the Centro Cultural Rector Ricardo Rojas, Universidad de Buenos Aires, and the Centro de Investigación en Literatura Comparada, Universidad Nacional de Lomas de Zamora. Includes bibliographical references.

Enciclopedia teatral. [Theatre encyclopedia]. 12 vols. Buenos Aires: Editorial Cedal, 1968–9.

Ferdis, Rubén. **Diccionario sobre el origen del teatro argentino**. [A dictionary of Argentine theatre origins]. Buenos Aires: Alberto Kleiner, 1988. 105 p. *Notes*: Includes bibliographical references.

Fidalgo, Andrés F. **El teatro en Jujuy**. Buenos Aires: Libros de Tierra Firme, 1995. 118 p. *Notes*: Includes bibliographical references (p. 117–18). Jujuy (Province).

Foppa, Tito Livio. **Diccionario teatral del Río de la Plata**. Buenos Aires: Argentores: Ediciones del Carro de Tespis, 1962. – 1046 p. *Notes*: Argentine biographies. Bibliography.

Giella, Miguel Angel. **De dramaturgos: teatro latinoamericano actual**. Buenos Aires: Corregidor, 1994. 238 p. *Notes*: Includes bibliographical references. Hispanic Argentine drama.

Graham-Jones, Jean. **Drama and dictatorship: theater in Buenos Aires (1976–1985)**. 1993. xi, 376 p. *Notes*: Vita. Bibliography: p. 354–76. Thesis (Ph. D.)–UCLA, 1993.

Griffith, Osbert Leroy. **Expressionism in the Argentine theatre**. 1982. vi, 253 p. *Notes*: Bibliography: p. 243–53. Thesis (Ph. D.)– University of Toronto, 1982. Microfiche. Ottawa, Canada: National Library of Canada, Collections Development Branch. [1984]. 3 microfiches; 11 × 15 cm. (Canadian theses on microfiche 55752).

Halek, Yvonne Charlotte. **Versuch einer strukturalistischen Analyse des Theaterwesens in Argentinien und Chile unter besonderer Berücksichtigung des Zeitraumes 1980–1982**. 1989. 156 p. *Notes*: Includes bibliographical references. Thesis (doctoral)–Freie Universität Berlin. Microfiche. Berlin. Mikrofilm Center Klein, 1992. 2 microfiches: negative.

Marial, José. **Teatro y país: desde 1810 a Teatro Abierto 1983**. [Theatre and nation: From 1810 to Teatro Abierto 1983]. Buenos Aires: Ediciones AGON, 1984. 194 p. *Notes*: Bibliography: p. 192–94.

Moll, Victor, Jorge Pinus and Mónica Flores. **Las lunas del teatro: los hacedores del teatro independiente cordobés (1950–1990)**. Córdoba: Ediciones del Boulevard, 1996. 251 p.: ill. *Notes*: Córdoba. History. 20th century. Theatrical producers and directors. Argentina. Córdoba. Interviews/Actors.

Morale, Giorgio. **Comuna Baires: storia di vent'anni di teatro 1969–1989, con 20 illustrazioni fuori testo**. Florence: La Casa Usher, 1989. 166 p., 16 p. of plates: ill. *Notes*: Includes bibliographical references. Comuna Baires. History. In Italian.

Naios Najchaus, Teresa. **Conversaciones con el teatro argentino de hoy, 1970–1980**. Buenos Aires: Ediciones Agon, 1981. – 166 p. *Notes*: Interviews/Theatrical producers and directors.

——. **Conversaciones con el teatro argentino de hoy, no. II, 1981–1984**. Buenos Aires: Ediciones Agon, 1984. – 223 p. *Notes*: Interviews/Actors, producers and directors. Argentina.

Ordaz, Luis. **El teatro en el Río de la Plata**. [Theatre in the River Plate region]. Buenos Aires: Ediciones Leviatán, 1957.

Parola, Nora Elena. **Elementos del grotesco y del absurdo en el teatro argentino (1960–1980)**. 1989. x, 248 p. *Notes*: Text in Spanish; abstract and vita in English. Includes bibliographical references (p. 235–248). Thesis (Ph. D.)–University of Texas at Austin, 1989. Theatre of the absurd/Grotesque in literature.

Pellettieri, Osvaldo. **Cien años de teatro argentino, 1886–1990: del Moreira al Teatro Abierto**. [One hundred years of Argentine theatre, 1886–1990: From Moreira to Teatro Abierto]. Buenos Aires: Editorial Galerna, 1991.

——. **De Bertolt Brecht a Ricardo Monti: teatro en lengua alemana y teatro argentino (1900–1994)**. Buenos Aires: Editorial Galerna, 1994. 133. *Notes*: Includes bibliographical references. German influences/Argentine drama.

——. **De Sarah Bernardt a Lavelli: teatro francés y teatro argentino (1890–1990)**. Buenos Aires: Editorial Galerna/Revista Espacio, 1993. 93 p. *Notes*: Includes bibliographical references. Argentine drama. French influences.

——. **El teatro y los días: estudios sobre teatro argentino e iberoamericano**. Buenos Aires: Editorial Galerna: Facultad de Filosofía y Letras (UBA), 1995. 343 p. *Notes*: Includes bibliographical references.

——. **El teatro y su mundo: estudios sobre teatro iberoamericano y argentino**. Buenos Aires: Editorial Galerna: Facultad de Filosofía y Letras (UBA), 1997. 409 p. *Notes*: Papers from the 4th Congreso Internacional de Teatro Iberoamericano y Argentino held in Buenos Aires, Aug. 1996, and sponsored by GETEA. Includes bibliographical references.

—— and Eduardo Rovner. **La Puesta en escena en Latinoamérica: teoría y práctica teatral**. Buenos Aires: Editorial Galerna, 1995. – 141 p.; 23 x. *Notes*: Includes bibliographical references. Production and direction.

——. **Teatro argentino de los '60: polémica, continuidad y ruptura**. [Argentine theatre of the 1960s: Polemics, continuity and splits]. Buenos Aires: Corregidor, 1989. 241 p.

——. **Teatro argentino de los '90**. Buenos Aires: Editorial Galerna: Revista Espacio, 1992. 102 p. *Notes*: Includes bibliographical references.

——. **Una historia interrumpida: teatro argentino moderno (1949–1976)**. Buenos Aires: Editorial Galerna, 1997. 285 p.; 23 x. *Notes*: Originally presented as the author's thesis (Universidad de Buenos Aires, 1996). Includes bibliographical references (p. 263–82).

Ricci, Jorge. **Hacia un teatro salvaje**. Santa Fe, Argentina: Universidad Nacional del Litoral, Secretaría de Asuntos Culturales, Departamento de Extensión Universitaria, Centro de Publicaciones, Impr. de la Universidad, 1986. 80 p. *Notes*: Experimental theatre.

Sagaseta, Julia Elena and Adriana Scheinin. **Un acercamiento al proceso creador en el teatro: como lo hacemos, ciclo 1992**. Buenos Aires: San Martin TMGSM, 1992. 157 p. *Notes*: Production and direction. History and criticism.

Taylor, Diana. **Disappearing acts: spectacles of gender and nationalism in Argentina's 'dirty war'**. Durham: Duke University Press, 1997. xii, 309 p.: ill. *Notes*: Includes bibliographical references (p. 291–303) and index. Disappeared persons. Politics and government. 1955–83.

Tschudi, Lilian. **Teatro argentino actual 1960–72**. [Current Argentine theatre 1960–72.] Colección Estudios Latino Americanos no. 10. Buenos Aires: Fernando García Cambeino, 1974. 145 p.

Woodyard, George W. and Osvaldo Pellettieri. **De Eugene O'Neill al 'Happening': teatro norteamericano y teatro argentino, 1930–1990**. Buenos Aires: Editorial Galerna, 1996. 121 p. *Notes*: Includes bibliographical references. Argentina. American influences. History and criticism.

Zawadzki, Gabriela Margareta. **Shakespeare in Argentinien: Bewältigung der Zeitgeschichte im Vergleich mit den beiden Deutschland**. Bern; New York: P. Lang, 1997. 292 p.

Zayas de Lima, Perla. **Contribución bibliográfica al estudio del teatro argentino**. Buenos Aires: Asociación Argentina de Actores, 1985. – 75 p. *Notes*: Argentina. Bibliography.

——. **Diccionario de autores teatrales argentinos, 1950–1990**. Buenos Aires: Editorial Galerna, 1991. – 295 p. *Notes*: Argentine drama. 20th century. Bio-bibliography. In Spanish.

——. **Diccionario de directores y escenógrafos del teatro argentino**. Buenos Aires: Editorial Galerna, 1990. – 391 p. *Notes*: Includes bibliographical references.

A3a6. ARMENIA

Avagian, K., B. Haroutiounian, Sabir Rizaev, Levon Hakhverdian and L. Khalatian. **History of Soviet Armenian Theatre**. Yerevan, 1967.

Babayan, Ida Arseni. **Varaguyri edevum**. (Za zanavesom). Erevan: Sovetakan Grogh Hratarakch'ut'yun, 1982. 285 p. *Notes*: Armenian S.S.R. Production and direction.

Goyan, Georg. **2000 let armianskovo teatra**. [2000 years of Armenian theatre]. Moscow: Gosudarstvennoe Izdatel'stvo Iskusstvo, 1952.

Gulazyan, Davit'. **Husher, tpavorut'yunner**. Erevan: Hayastan Hratarakch'ut'yun, 1972. 93 p.: ill. *Notes*: History. 19th century, 20th century.

Hakhverdian, Levon. **Taghand ev bnavorut'yun: Vardan Achemyane kyank'um ev arvestum**. Erevan: 'Khorhrdayin grogh', 1989. 293 p.: ill. *Notes*: Armenian S.S.R. History. 20th century.

Harut'yunyan, Babken. **Russkaia dramaturgiia na armianskoi sovetskoi stsene**. Erevan: Izd-vo

AN Armianskoi SSR, 1957. 177 p. illus. *Notes*: Armenia/Russian drama. History and criticism.

Hunanyan, Arts'vi Step'ani. **Dramaturgia ev t'atron**. Erevan: Haykakan T'aterakan Enkerut'yun, 1980. 257 p. *Notes*: Armenia (Republic). Dramaturgy.

——. **Dramaturgnere ev ardiakanut'yune**. (Dramaturgi i sovremennost'). Erevan: Haykakan T'aterakan Enkerut'yun, 1978. 273 p. *Notes*: Drama. Armenian S.S.R.

Kagramanov, Nerses Voskanovich. **Drama-turgiia narodov SSSR na armianskoi stsene: 1876–1976**. [Armenian playwriting: 1876–1976]. Yerevan: Izdo-vo Akademiia nauk Armianskoi SSSR, 1980. 78 p.

Malyan, Davit' Melk'umi. **Demk'er hand-ipumer**. Erevan: Haykakan T'aterakan Enkerut'yun, 1974. 249 p. Armenian S.S.R. Anecdotes/Actors, theatrical producers and directors.

Pahare Payazat, Sergey. **T'aterakan husher**. Erevan: Haypethrat, 1960. 210 p.: ill. *Notes*: Actors. Armenia (Republic). Biography of Pahare, 1895–1968.

Rizaev, Sabir, **History of Armenian directing**. Yerevan, 1963.

——. **Rezhissura v armianskom teatre**. Erevan: Izd-vo AN Armianskoi SSR, 1968. 491 p. *Notes*: At head of title: Akademiia nauk Armianskoi SSR. Institut iskusstv. Added t.p. in Armenian. Includes bibliographical references. O rezhisser-skom iskusstve – Rezhissura v starom armian-skom teatre – Rezhissura v novom armianskom teatre (1668–1861) – Rezhissura v armianskom dorevoliutsionnom professional'nom teatre (1861–1920) – Formirovanie rezhisserskogo iskusstva v armianskom sovetskom teatra – Put' k obrazu cheloveka – Putiami poiskov (1945–1965). Theatre. Armenia. Production and direction. History/Theatre. Armenian S.S.R. Production and direction. History/Theatrical producers and directors.

Step'anyan, Garnik Khach'aturi. **Aknarkner sp'yurk'ahay t'atroni patmut'yan**. Erevan: Haykakan SSH GA Hratarakch'ut'yun, 1982. vol. 1: ill. *Notes*: Armenian drama. 20th century. History and criticism.

Tamrazian, Hrant Smbatovich. **Shirvanzadé, gianka ev kordza**. [Shirvanzadé, his life and work]. Yerevan: Haypethat Press, 1961.

T'erzibashyan, V. **Zhasmen**. Erevan: HT'E Hratarakut'yun, 1959. 97 p.: ill. *Subjects*: Actors. Armenia (Republic). Biography.

——. **The History of Armenian Playwriting**. 2 vols. Yerevan, 1959–64.

Thorossian, H. **Histoire de la littérature arménienne des origines jusqu'à nos jours**. [The history of Armenian literature from its beginning to the present]. Paris, 1951.

Two thousand years of the Armenian theatre. New York: Armenian National Council of America, 1954. 12 p.

Vagharshyan, Vagharsh. **Enkerners, barek-amners, ev es**. Erevan: Haypethrat, 1959: ill. *Notes*: Actors. Armenia (Republic). Biography/ Dramatists.

Zak'oyan, G. **Sabir Rizaev**. Erevan: Haykakan T'aterakan Enkerut'yun, 1981. 76 p., 15 p. of plates. Theatrical producers and directors. Armenian S.S.R. Theatre critics.

Zarian, Rouben. **Shakespeare and the Armenians**. Translated by Haig Voskerchian. Yerevan: Academy of Sciences, 1969.

——. **Theatrical portraits**. Yerevan: 1956.

A3a7. AUSTRALIA

Atkinson, Ann, Lindsay Knight and Margaret McPhee. **The Dictionary of performing arts in Australia**. London: Allen & Unwin, 1996. – xv, 343 p., plates: ports. *Notes*: Index. Theatre, film, radio, television.

Australasian drama studies. Brisbane: University of Queensland Department of English, 1982 to date.

Australian and New Zealand theatre record. A monthly facsimile reproduction of newspaper theatre and dance reviews. Sydney: Australian Theatre Studies Centre, University of New South Wales, 1987–96.

Brisbane Arts Theatre, the first fifty years 1936–1986. Brisbane: Brisbane Arts Theatre, 1987. 84 p.: ill.

Brokensha, Peter and Ann Tonks. **Culture and community: economics and expectations of arts in South Australia**. Wentworth Falls, NSW: Social Science Press, 1986. 162 p.

Burstow, Stephen A. **Modern Australian histori-cal drama 1940–1978**. 1978. 61 p. *Notes*: Includes bibliography. Thesis (B.A.)–University of Queensland.

Carroll, Dennis. **Australian contemporary drama**. Revised edn. Sydney: Currency, 1995.

Chesterman, Colleen and Virginia Baxter. **Playing with time: women writing for perfor-mance**. Playworks, 1995.

Fitzpatrick, Peter. **After the doll: Australian drama since 1955**. Melbourne: Edward Arnold, 1979.

——. **Williamson**. Sydney: Methuen Australian Drama Series, 1987.

Fitzsimmons, Brian Arthur. **The place of David Williamson in the history of Australian Drama: A provisional perspective**. Boulder, CO: University of Colorado, 1982. 364 p.

Fotheringham, Richard, ed. **Community theatre in Australia**. Revised edn. Sydney: Currency, 1992.

——. **Sport in Australian drama**. Cambridge University Press, 1992. 272 p. *Notes*: Cultural studies. Drama studies.

Golder, John, Jean Cooney and Margaret Williams. **Preserving the ephemeral: Katharine Brisbane and Currency Press**. Canberra: Friends of the National Library of Australia, 1995. vi, 25 p.: ill.

A guide to Australian drama and theatre. Sydney: Currency Press, 1984.

Hainsworth, J.D. **Hibberd**. Sydney: Methuen Australian Drama Series, 1987.

Holloway, Peter. **Contemporary Australian drama**. Rev. edn. Sydney: Currency Press, 1987. 628 pp.: ill. *Notes*: Includes index. Bibliography: p. 608–11.

Hutton, Geoffrey. **It won't last a week: the first twenty years of the Melbourne theatre company**. Melbourne: Sun Books, 1975.

Irvin, Eric. **Australian melodrama: eighty years of popular theatre**. Sydney: Hale & Iremonger, 1981. xii, 160 p.: ill. *Notes*: Includes index. Bibliography: p. 147–9.

Jenkins, John and Rainer Linz. **Arias: Recent Australian music theatre**. Melbourne: Redhouse Editions, 1997.

Jones, Liz, Betty Burstall and Helen Garner. **La Mana**. Melbourne: McPhee Gribble/Penguin, 1988.

Kefala, Antigone. **Multiculturalism and the arts**. Sydney: Australia Council, 1986. 69 p.

Kelly, Veronica. **The theatre of Louis Nowra**. Sydney: Currency Press, 1998. 224 p. *Notes*: A study of the life and work of a major man of the theatre.

Love, Harold, ed. **The Australian stage: a documentary history**. Kensington, NSW: New South Wales University Press, 1984. 384 p.

Macdonnell, Justin. **Fifty years in the bush: the Arts Council in New South Wales**. Sydney: Currency, 1997.

McCallum, John. **Buzo**. Sydney: Methuen Australian Drama Series, 1987.

Parsons, Philip and Victoria Chance. **Companion to theatre in Australia**. Sydney: Currency Press in association with Cambridge University Press, 1995. – 704 p.: ill. *Notes*: Includes bibliographical references and index. This authoritative reference work records the major developments and the significant figures in theatre in Australia from 1789 to 1995.

——, gen. eds, adapted. **Concise companion to theatre in Australia**. Sydney: Currency, 1997.

Radic, Leonard. **The state of play: the revolution in the Australian theatre since the 1960s**. Ringwood, Vic., Australia; New York: Penguin Books, 1991. 258 p. *Notes*: Includes bibliographical references (p. 242–6).

Rees, Leslie. **A history of Australian drama**. Sydney: Angus & Robertson, 1978.

Rowse, Tim. **Arguinga: the funding of arts in Australia**. Melbourne: Penguin, 1985.

Rutherford, Anna and James Wieland, eds. **War: Australia's creative response**. Hedben Bridge: Dangaroo Press, 1997.

Shoemaker, Adam. **Swimming in the mainstream**. London: University of London, 1990.

Spinks, Kim, ed. **Australian theatre design**. Sydney: Australian Production Designers' Association, 1992.

Sumner, John. **Recollections at play: a life in Australian theatre**. Carlton, Vic.: Melbourne University Press, 1993. xvi, 398 p.: ill. *Notes*: Includes index. Theatrical producers and directors. Australia. Biography/Theatre. Melbourne Theatre Company. History.

Sydney Theatre Company. **Walking on water: Sydney Theatre Company at the Wharf**. Sydney: Currency, 1994.

Tait, Peta. **Converging realities: feminism in Australian theatre**. Sydney: Currency, 1994.

——. **Original women's theatre: the Melbourne Women's Theatre Group 1974–77**. Melbourne: Artmoves, 1993.

Turcotte, Gerry, ed. **Jack Davis: The maker of history**. Sydney: Angus and Robertson, 1994.

Ward, Peter. **A singular act: twenty-five years of the State Theatre Company of South Australia**. Adelaide: State Theatre Company and Wakefield Press, 1992.

Webby, Elizabeth. **Modern Australian plays**. Sydney University Press in association with Oxford University Press Australia, 1993. ix, 85 p. *Notes*: Includes bibliographical references (p. 83–5). Australian drama. 20th century. History and criticism.

West, John. **Theatre in Australia**. Sydney: Cassell, 1978.

Whiteoak, John and Aline Scott-Maxwell, gen. eds. **Companion to music and dance in Australia**. Sydney: Currency, 1998.

Williams, Margaret. **Dorothy Hewett: The feminine as subversion**. Sydney: Currency, 1992.

A3a8. AUSTRIA

Abele, Hans. **Die Bundestheater in der österreichischen Wirtschaft**. [The federal theatres and their role in the Austrian economy]. Vienna: Bundestheaterverband, 1984.

Alexander, Gerda and Hans Groll, eds. **Tänzerin, Choreographin, Pädagogin Rosalia Chladek**. [Rosalia Chladek: dancer. choreographer, teacher]. Vienna: Bundesverlag, 1980.

Awecker, Maria, Sabine Schmall, Heinz Hischenhuber, Girid Schlögl, Walter Schlögl and Margaret Dietrich. **Theatergeschichte des Burgenlandes von 1921 bis zur Gegenwart**. Vienna: Verlag der Österreichischen Akademie der Wissenschaften, 1995. 559 p.: ill. *Notes*: Includes bibliographical references and index. Theatre. Burgenland. History. 20th century.

Deutsches Bühnenjahrbuch: theatergeschichtliches Jahr- und Adreßbuch. Theater, Film, Funk, Fernsehen. [German stage almanac: theatrical yearbook and address register. Theatre, film, radio, television]. Berlin/Hamburg: Genossenschaft Deutscher Bühnenangehöriger, 57. Jg. 1949–.

Doll, Jürgen. **Theater im Roten Wien: vom sozialdemokratischen Agitprop zum dialektischen Theater Jura Soyfers**. Vienna: Böhlau, 1997. 453 p.: ill. *Notes*: Abridgement of author's doctoral thesis. Includes bibliographical references (p. 415–47) and index. Theatre. Political aspects. Austria. Vienna. History. 20th century/Music-halls (Variety-theatres, cabarets, etc.).

Drese, Claus Helmut. **Im Palast der Gefühle: Erfahrungen und Enthüllungen eines Wiener Operndirektors**. [In the palace of emotions: experiences and revelations of a Viennese opera director]. Munich: Piper, 1993.

Eberstaller, Gerhard. **Ronacher: ein Theater in seiner Zeit**. Vienna: Edition Wien, 1993. 208 p.: ill. *Notes*: Includes bibliographical references (p. 199–202) and index. Theatre. Vienna. History. 20th century.

Fuhrich, Edda, and Gisela Prossnitz, eds. **Die Salzburger Festspiele. Bd 1: 1929–1945. Ihre Geschichte in Daten, Zeitzeugnissen und Bildern**. [The Salzburg Festival. Vol. 1: 1929–45. Facts, memorabilia and images]. Salzburg: Residenz, 1990. 327 p.

Goertz, Harald, ed. **Österreichisches Musikhandbuch. Österreichische Komponisten der Gegenwart**. [Austrian music almanac, contemporary Austrian composers]. Vienna: Döblinger, 1989. 248 p.

Greisenegger, Ingrid and Ilse Hanl. **Animazione: Texte zur Theaterarbeit**. [Animation: texts on theatrical work]. Vienna: Dramatisches Zentrum, 1975. 55 p.

Habecker, S. and A. Hofmann. **Theorien; Texte; Analysen: das deutschsprachige Theater seit 1945, ein Arbeitsbuch für die Sekundarstufe II**. Munich: R. Oldenbourg, 1974. 276 p. *Notes*: Includes bibliographical references. *Subjects*: Austria, Germany, Switzerland. Drama. 20th century. History and criticism.

Hadamovsky, Franz. **Bücherkunde deutschsprachiger Theaterliteratur, Teil 2: 1945–79**. [Bibliography of German-language theatre literature, part 2: 1945–79], Vienna/Cologne: Böhlau, 1982. 407 p.

Hadriga, Franz. **Drama Burgtheaterdirektion: vom Scheitern des Idealisten Anton Wildgans**. Vienna: Herold, 1989. 174 p., 16 p. of plates: ill. *Notes*: Includes bibliographical references (p. 172–4). Biography/Burgtheater (Vienna).

Haider-Pregler, Hilde. **Theater and Schauspielkunst in Österreich**. Vienna: Bundespressedienst, 1970. 228 p. Published in English as **The Theatre in Austria**. Vienna: Federal Press Service, 1970. 202 p.

—— and Beate Reiterer. **Verspielte Zeit: österreichisches Theater der dreissiger Jahre**. Vienna: Picus Verlag, 1997. 384 p. *Notes*: 'Das Symposion "Verspielte Zeit. Österreichisches Theater der dreissiger Jahre" fand im Rahmen der Wiener Festwochen vom 14. bis 16. Juni 1996 im Museumsquartier in Wien statt' – Includes bibliographical references and index.

Judtmann, Fritz. 'Die Baugeschichte des neuen Burgtheaters'. [The construction of the new Burgtheater] in **175 Jahre Burgtheater**. Vienna: 1955.

Kahl, Kurt. **Premierenfieber: das Wiener Sprechtheater nach 1945**. Vienna: Pichler, 1996. 208 p.: ill. (some col.). *Notes*: Includes indexes. Vienna. History. 20th century.

Kinz, Maria. **Raimund Theater**. Vienna: Jugend und Volk, 1985. 86 p., 4 p. of plates: ill. *Notes*: Includes index. Bibliography: p. 86. Raimundtheater (Vienna).

Kisser, Erwin, Gerhard Ruiss and Johannes A. Vyoral. **Gegenkonzepte, Dokumentation eines**

Symposiums der Konfliktkommission Theater am 22. und 23. April 1988 im Theater im Künstlerhaus. Vienna: IG Autoren, 1989. 146 p.: ill. *Notes*: Includes bibliographical references.

Kraus, Gottfried, ed. **Musik in Österreich: eine Chronik in Daten, Dokumenten, Essays und Bildern**. [Music in Austria: a chronicle of data, documents, essays and pictures]. Vienna: Brandstätter, 1989. 518 p.

Landa, Jutta. **Bürgerliches Schocktheater: Entwicklungen im österreichischen Drama der sechziger und siebziger Jahre**. [Shocking the bourgeois: developments in Austrian drama in the 1960s and 1970s]. Frankfurt/Main: Athenäum, 1988. 198 p.

Lederer, Herbert. **Bevor alles verweht–: Wiener Kellertheater 1945 bis 1960**. Vienna: Österreichischer Bundesverlag, 1986. 187 p.: ill.; 21 x. *Notes*: Includes bibliographical references and index. Experimental theatre. Vienna.

——. **Im Alleingang: Bericht über fünfundzwanzig Jahre Arbeit**. Vienna: Österreichischer Bundesverlag, 1984. 208 p.: ill. *Subjects*: Austrian drama. History and criticism.

Mitterer, Felix. **10 Jahre Tiroler Volksschauspiele Telfs: eine Chronik**. Innsbruck: Haymon, 1991. 108 p.: ill. (some col.). *Subjects*: Tiroler Volksschauspiele (Telfs, Austria). History.

Österreichischer Bundestheaterverband Bericht 1992/1993. [1992/93 report by the Austrian Federal Theatre Association]. Vienna: Austrian Federal Theatre Association, 1993.

Patterson, Michael. **German theatre today: post-war theatre in West and East Germany, Austria and Northern Switzerland**. London: Pitman, 1976. ix, 129 p. *Notes*: Includes index. Bibliography: p. 118–19.

Pepper, Hugo. **Lachen auf eigene Gefahr: das Kabarett 'Der Rote Hund' 1946–1951**. Vienna: Europaverlag, 1987. 305 p.: ill. *Notes*: Includes bibliographical references (p. 304–5). Musichalls (Variety-theatres, cabarets, etc.). Vienna. Political satire. Kabarett 'Der Rote Hund'. History.

Prawy, Marcel. **Die Wiener Oper**. [The Vienna Opera]. Munich: Goldman, 1980.

Reiter, Wolfgang. **Wiener Theatergespräche: über den Umgang mit Dramatik und Theater**. Vienna: Falter, 1993. 167 p.: ill. Interviews. History and criticism.

Roessler, Peter and Konstantin Kaiser. **Dramaturgie der Demokratie: Theaterkonzeptionen des österreichischen Exils**. Vienna: Promedia, 1989. 232 p. *Notes*:

Includes bibliographical references. Politics and literature.

Rogowski, Christian. **Implied dramaturgy: Robert Musil and the crisis of modern drama**. Riverside, CA: Ariadne Press, 1993. – xiii, 313 p. *Notes*: Includes bibliographical references (p. 281–301) and index. *Subjects*: Drama. History and criticism.

Rubey, Norbert and Peter Schoenwald. **Venedig in Wien: Theater- und Vergnügungsstadt der Jahrhundertwende**. Vienna: Ueberreuter, 1996. 183 p.: ill. *Notes*: Includes bibliographical references (p. 169) and index. *Subjects*: Theatre. Vienna. Social life and customs.

Schreiner, Evelyn and Ulf Birbaumer. **100 Jahre Volkstheater: Theater, Zeit, Geschichte**. Vienna: J&V, 1989. 404 p.: ill. *Notes*: Includes bibliographical references. History. 20th century/Volkstheater (Vienna).

Seebom, Andrea. **Die Wiener Oper: 350 Jahre Glanz und Tradition**. [The Vienna Opera: 350 years of splendour and tradition]. Vienna: Ueberreuter, 1986; New York: Rizzoli, 1987.

Sinhuber, Wolfgang Franz. **Drama und Zeitgeist in Österreich von 1980 bis 1990**. Vienna: WUV-Universitätsverlag, 1995. 176 p. *Notes*: Includes bibliographical references (p. 169–75) and index. Austrian drama. History and criticism. Political aspects.

'Statistik der österreichischen Theater 1989/90'. [Statistics concerning Austrian theatres in 1989/90]. **Theaterstatistik1989/90**. Cologne: Deutscher Bühnenverein, 1991.

Theater in Österreich. Verzeichnis der Inszenierungen. [Theatre in Austria. Catalogue of productions]. Vienna: Wiener Gesellschaft für Theaterforschung/Institut für Theaterwissenschaft/Universität Wien, 1980–.

Urbach, Reinhard and Achim Benning, eds. **Burgtheater Wien 1776–1986. Ebenbild und Widerspruch, zweihundert und zehn Jahre**. [Vienna Burgtheater 1977–86. Likeness and contradiction. 210 years]. Vienna: Bundesverlag u. Schroll, 1986. 263 p.

Vogelsang, Hans. **Österreichische Dramatik des 20. Jahrhunderts: Spiel mit Welten, Wesen, Worten**. Vienna: W. Braumüller, 1981. xv, 335 p. *Notes*: 'Zweite (ergänzte und wesentlich erweiterte) Auflage'–Pref. Bibliography: p. 303–35. Hofmannsthals poetisches Traumtheater – (Tragi-) Komödien der Worte und Gebärden – Dämonisches Theater – Das religiöse und historische Spiel – Kritische Mitleidsdramatik – Ekstatische und klassizistische Dramatik – Modernes Welt- und Zeittheater –

Experimentelles Antitheater (un)menschlicher Isolation. Austrian drama. History and criticism.

Waechter-Böhm, Lisbeth, ed. **Wien 1945 davor/danach**. [Vienna 1945 before/after]. Exhibition catalogue. Vienna: Brandstätter, 1985.

Wagner, Renate. **Die Löwinger-Bühne: das Burgtheater für den kleinen Mann**. Vienna: Ueberreuter, 1996. 222 p.: ill. *Notes*: Includes index. Löwinger-Bühne (Theatre group). History.

A3a9. AZERBAIJAN

Allakhverdiev, Makhmud. **Alaskar Alakabrov: hajat ve jaradygylygy**. [Alaskar Alakbarov: life and creative journey]. Baku: Azerneshr, 1972. 234 p.

——. **Azerbaijan halq teatry**. [Azerbaijani folk theatre]. Baku: Maarif, 1978. 233 p.

——. **Muasir teatrda an'ana va novatorlug masalalari**. (Problemy traditsii i novatorstva v sovremennom teatre). Baku : Azerbaijan Dovlat Nashriiiaty, 1974. – 98 p. *Notes*: In Azerbaijani. Title in colophon: Problemy traditsii i novatorstva v sovremennom teatre. Includes bibliographical references. Drama. History and criticism.

Djafarov, Djafar. **Azerbaijan dram teatry, 1873–1941**. [Azerbaijani Drama Theatre, 1873–1941]. Baku: Azerbaijani State Publishers, 1959. 417 p.

Ilkham, Ragimli. **Dramaturgija ve teatr**. [Dramaturgy and theatre]. Baku: Ishyg, 1989. 146 p.

Ingilab, Kerimov. **Stanovleniye i razvitiie Azerbaijanskogo teatra (konietz XIX-nachalo XX veka)**. [The genesis and development of Azerbaijani theatre from the nineteenth to the beginning of the twentieth century]. Baku: Elm, 1991. 293 p.

Iskenderova, Z. **Shamsi Badalbeili**. Baku: Ishyg, 1976. – 30 p. *Notes*: Theatrical producers and directors. Badalbeili, Shamsi Badalovich.

Jafarov, Jafar Hashym oghlu. **Iskusstvo rezhissera: o tvorcheskom puti Mekhti Mamedova**. Baku: Azerbaidzhanskoe gos. izdvo, 1969. – 136, v: photos. *Notes*: Includes bibliographical references and index. Theatrical producers and directors. Mamedov, Mekhti, 1918–1985.

Mamedov, Mekhti. **Azeri dramaturqijasynyn estetik problemleri**. [Aesthetic problems of Azerbaijani dramaturgy]. Baku: Azerneshr, 1969. 380 p.

Memedli, Gulam, ed. **Azerbaijan teatryn salmanesi, 1850–1930**. [Chronicles of Azerbaijani theatre, 1850–1930]. 2 vols. Baku: Azerneshr, 1975 and 1983.

Yusifbeili, Tamilla. **Shekspir na Azerbaijanskoi stzene**. [Shakespeare on the Azerbaijani stage]. Baku: Azerneshr, 1974. 273 p.

A3a10. BAHRAIN

Abdulla, Mohammad Hassan. **Al-Masrah Fi'l'Bahrayn Wa'l'Kuwait**. [The theatre in Bahrain and Kuwait]. Kuwait City: Majallat Dirasat Alkhalij Wa' l'-Jazira al'Arabiya, University of Kuwait, 1980.

——. **Saqr ar-Rushud Mubdi'ar Ru'ya ath-Thaniya**. [Saqr ar-Rushud the creator of the second thought]. Kuwait City: Manshurat Majallat Dirasat Alkhalij Wa' l'Jazira al-'Arabiya, 1980.

Bahreèin: fidjeri chants de pêcheurs de perles. [Bahrain: Fidjeri chants of the pearl divers]. [sound recording]. France: Auvidis, 1992.

Ghulum, Ibrahim Abdulla. **Zawahir at-Tajriba al-Masrahiya Fi'l'Bahrayn**. [The phenomenon of the theatre experiment in Bahrain]. Kuwait City: al Rubay'an, 1982.

Haddad, Qasim. **Al-Masrah al Bahrayni: At-Tajriba Wa'l'Ufuq**. [The Bahraini theatre: the experiment and the horizon]. Bahrain: Masrah Awal, 1980.

Izzard, Molly. 'The music of the Arabian Gulf'. In Dilmun, **A Journal of Archaeology and History in Bahrain** 9 (1980): 4–9.

Al-Khattir, Mubarak. **Al-Masrah at-Tarikhi Fi'l'Bahrayn**. [The historical theatre in Bahrain]. Bahrain: Ministry of Information, 1985.

Al-Rai, Ali. 'Arabic drama since the thirties'. In **Modern Arabic Literature** (1992): 402–3.

Slauth, Georg and Sami Zubaida, eds. **Mass Culture, Popular Culture and Social Life in the Middle East**. Boulder, CO: Westview Press, 1987.

Tomiche, Nada and Cherif Khaznadar. **Le Théâtre arabe**. Paris: Unesco, 1969. 229 p.

A3a11. BANGLADESH

Ahmed, S.J. **Hajar Bachor: Bangladesher Natok O Natyakala**. [A thousand years: Drama and theatre art of Bangladesh]. Dhaka: Bangladesh Shilpakala Academy, 1995. 88 p.

——. 'Theatre for Development and Cultural Identity'. Warwick: University of Warwick,

1989. (MA thesis, University of Warwick, 1989).

Al-Deen, Selim. **Madhyajuger Bangla Natya.** [Bengali drama of the middle ages]. Dhaka: Bangala Academy, 1996. 528 p.

Biswas, Sukumar. **Bangladesher Natyacharcha O Nataker Dhara.** [Tradition of drama and theatre of Bangladesh]. Dhaka: Bangla Academy, 1988. 544 p.

Chowdhury, Kabir. **Prasango Natok.** [Concerning theatre]. Dhaka: Bangladesh Shilpakala Academy, 1981. 290 p.

Hyder, A.R.Z. 'A Small House Beside a Highway: A Play for Television With an Essay; Development of Drama and Theatre in East Pakistan'. MFA. Thesis, University of Hawaii, 1968.

Hyder, Zia. **Natya O Natok.** [Dramatics and Drama]. Bengali Academy, 1985. 112 p.

Ibrahim, Neelima. **Bangla Natok: Utsa O Dhara.** [Bengali drama: Evolution and development]. Dhaka: Nawroze Kitabistan, 1972. 524 p.

Majumdar, Ramendu. **Bishoy Natok.** [On theatre]. Dhaka: Muktadhara, 1987. 99 p.

Mamud, Hayat. **Gerasim Stepanovitch Lebedeff.** Bengali Academy, 1985. 464 p.

——, ed. **Bangladesher Natya Charcha.** [Theatre of Bangladesh]. Dhaka: Muktadhara, 1986. 293 p.

Mamun, Muntasir. **Unish Shatake Bangladesher Theatre.** [Theatre of Bangladesh in the nineteenth century]. Dhaka: Suborno, 1986.

——. **Unish Shatake Dhakar Theatre.** [Theatre of Dhaka in the nineteenth century]. Dhaka: Bangladesh Shilpakala Academy, 1979. 139 p.

Mukta nataka. Dhaka: Aranyaka Natyadala, 1983. – 87 p. Notes: In Bengali. Articles on a new form of people's theatre; under the auspices of the Aranyaka Natyadala, a theatre group in Bangladesh. Popular culture.

Nisata, Isarata. **Bikshita thiyetara.** Dhaka: Sagara Pabalisarsa, 1992. 143 pp.: ill. Notes: In Bengali. Articles on Bengali theatre, with reference to Bangladesh.

Rahman, Ataur. **Natya Prabondho Bichitra.** [Articles on theatre]. Dhaka: Bangla Academy, 1995. 108 p.

Saikha, Asakara Ibane. **Bamla manca-natyera pascatbhumi.** Dhaka, Bamladesa: Sataram Prakasani, 1986. – 144 p. Notes: Bibliography: p. 143–4. History of the Bengali theatre and stage plays, with reference to post 1947 development in Bangladesh. In Bengali.

A3a12. BELARUS

Aliahnovich, Frantsishak. **Belaruski theatr.** [Belarussian theatre]. Vilnia, 1924. 114 p.

Barishev, Yuri. **Teatralnai a cultura Belorusii XVIII Stoletia.** [The theatrical culture of Belarus in the eighteenth century]. Minsk: Navuka i Tehnika, 1992. 269 p.

—— and Oleg Sannikov. **Belaruski narodni Teatr 'Batleika'e Iago Uzaiemasuviazi z Ruskim 'Viartepam'e Polskim 'Shopkai'.** [The Belarussian 'batleika' folk theatre and its intercommunication with Russian 'viartep' and Polish 'shopka']. Minsk: V-va Akademii Nauk BSSR, 1963. 42 p.

Bushko, Tamara and Ariadna Borisovna Ladygina. **Belaruski savetski teatr.** [The Belarus Soviet theatre]. Minsk: Belarus, 1974. – 220 p. ill. Notes: Summary in Russian and English. Includes bibliographical references.

Buzuk, Rastsislau Leonidavich. **Teatral'nyia daliahliady: rozdum ab suchasnym belaruskim teatry i hledachu.** Minsk: Navuka i Tehnika, 1990. – 143 p., 26 p. of plates: ill. Notes: Theatre audiences.

Churko, Ulia. **Belaruski Balenti Teatr.** [Belarussian dance theatre]. Minsk: Navuka i Tehnika, 1983. 286 p.

Dashkevich, S.M. and A.V. Sabaleuski. **Belaruski dziarzhauny akademichny teatr imia IAkuba Kolasa.** Minsk: Belarus, 1986. – 72 p., 23 p. of plates: ill. (some col.). Notes: History of Belaruski dziarzhauny akademichny teatr imia IAkuba Kolasa. [Kolasa/Belarus Academic Theatre].

Gistoria Belaruskaga Teatra. [History of Belarussian theatre]. 3 vols. Minsk: Navuka i Tehnika, 1983–7.

Gosudarstvennyi russkii dramaticheskii teatr Belarusi, 60. Minsk: Belarus, 1993. – [16] p.: ill. Notes: Published to commemorate the 60th anniversary of the Russian Drama Theatre.

Hrestamatia pa gistorii Belaruskaga teatra e dramaturgii. [A reader on the history of Belarussian theatre and drama]. 2 vols. Minsk: Visheishaia Shkola, 1975.

Karabanova, L. V. **Dramaturhiia Uladzislava Halubka.** Minsk: Navuka i Tehnika, 1982. – 126 p.: ill. Notes: Includes bibliographical references. Halubok, Uladzislau. Dramatic works.

Kaviazina, Sviatlana Mikalaeuna and A.V. Murauiova. **Stanaulenne i razvitstsio rezhysury u belaruskikh dramatychnykh teatrakh,**

1841–1970 hh.: biiabibliiahrafichny pakaza-l'nik. Minsk: Dziarzh. bibliiateka BSSR, 1989. – 276 p. *Notes*: Includes indexes. Production and directing.

Lisnevskii, Ivan. **Dorogami teatrov: vospominaniia starogo aktera**. Minsk: Navuka i Tehnika, 1987. – 54 p. *Notes*: Includes bibliographical references.

Narodni teatr. [Folk theatre]. Minsk: Navuka i Tehnika, 1983. 512 p.

Nekrashevich, A. **Belaruski Pershi Dziarzauni Teatr**. [The first Belarussian State Theatre]. Minsk: Beldziarzvidavestva, 1930. 28 p.

Niafiod, Uladzimir. **Teatr i zhizn': nekotorye problemy teatral'nogo protsessa v Belorussii 70–80-x godov**. Minsk: Navuka i Tehnika, 1989. – 263 p., 30 p. of plates: ill. *Notes*: Includes bibliographical references. Theatre. History.

Niafiod, Vladimir. **Belaruski Teatr: Naris Gistori**. [The Belarussian theatre: a historical essay]. Minsk: Vidavetsva AN BSSR, 1959. 900 p.

——. **Gistoria Belaruskaga Teatra**. [History of the Belarussian theatre]. Minsk: Visheishaia Shkola, 1982. 543 p.

Obukhovich, Anna. **Polveka na stsene**. Minsk: Belarus, 1987. – 141 p., 17 p. of plates: ill. *Notes*: Actors. Soviet Union. Biography. Obukhovich, Anna, 1908–1986.

Pashkin, Yuri. **Russkii Dramaticheskii Teatr v Belorussii XIX veka**. [Russian drama theatre in Belarus in the nineteenth century]. Minsk: Navuka i Tehnika, 1980. 219 p.

Sabaleuski, A. V. **Belorusskaia dramaturgiia v teatrakh narodov SSSR**. Minsk: Navuka i Tehnika, 1972. – 43 p.: ill., ports. *Notes*: In Cyrillic characters. Bibliography: p. 352–435. Belarusian drama. Soviet Union. History. 20th century.

——. **Belaruskaia Sovetskaia Drama**. [Belarussian Soviet drama]. 2 vols. Minsk: Belarus, 1969. 143 p., and Minsk: Mastatskaia Literatura, 1979. 220 p.

Seduro, Vladimir. **Belarussian theatre and drama**. New York: Research Program on the USSR, 1955. 517 p.

Smolski, Richard. **Paznachana chasam: poshuki suchasnai belaruskai rezhysury**. Minsk: Navuka i Tehnika, 1984. – 86 p. *Notes*: Theatrical producers and directors.

——. **Sotvorenie sud'by: istoricheskaia i geroiko-revoliutsionnaia tema v teatrakh Belorussii 70–80-kh godov**. Minsk: Nauka i Tehnika, 1987. – 220 p.: ill. *Notes*: Includes bibliographical references. History and criticism.

Stelmah, V. **Shliahi Beloruskogo Teatru**. [The ways of Belarussian theatre]. Kiev: Mistetsvo, 1964. 172 p.

Vatatsy, Nina Barysauna. **Belaruskaia dramaturhiia, 1966–1986: bibliiahrafichny davednik**. Minsk: Natsyianal'naia bibliiateka Belarusi, 1993. – 445 p. *Notes*: Belarus drama. 20th century. Bibliography.

Vazniasenski, A. **Drugi Belaruski Dziarzauni Teatr**. [The second Belarussian State Theatre]. Minsk: Beldziarzvidavetstva, 1929. 25 p.

A3a13. BELGIUM

Bauwens, Daan. **Kan iemand ons vermaken?: dokumentaire over teater en samenleving in Vlaanderen**. Ghent: Frans Masereelfonds, 1980. – 294 p. *Notes*: Includes index. Bibliography: p. 286–7. Flemish drama. 20th century. History and criticism.

Bie, Mark de. **Dertig jaar Vlaamse auteurs in de officiële schouwburgen**. Wuustwezel: Vereniging van Vlaamse Toneelauteurs, 1975. – 59 p. *Notes*: Flemish drama. History and criticism.

Castro, Nadine Berthe. **Un moyen-âge contemporain: le théâtre de Michel de Ghelderode**. Lausanne: L'Age d'homme, 1979. – 160 p. *Notes*: Bibliography: p. 159–60. Ghelderode, Michel de, 1898–1962. Criticism and interpretation.

Decorte, Jan. **Portrait de Théâtre, 1985–1990**. Amsterdam: B. Bakker, 1991. – 88 p.

Deldime, Roger, ed. **Le Théâtre belge de langue française**. [French language theatre in Belgium]. Brussels: Éditions de l'Université de Bruxelles, 1983. 282 p.

En scène pour demain: Ou soixante ans de théâtre belge [Stagings for tomorrow: sixty years of Belgian theatre]. Brussels: Libres Images aux Presses de la Bellone, 1988. 204 p.

Erenstein, R.L., Jaak van Schoor and Eva Cossee. **Kwetterende dwergen en andere toneelmakers: reacties op de nieuwste theatertrends**. Westbroek: Harlekijn, 1986. – 151 p.: ill. *Notes*: Theatre. Flanders. History. 20th century.

Hellemans, Dina, Ronald Geerts and Marian van Kerkhoven. **Op de voet gevolgd: twintig jaar Vlaams theater in internationaal perspectief**. Brussels: VUB-Press, 1990. – 351 p. *Notes*: Includes bibliographical references (p. 337–9) and indexes. Flemish drama. History and criticism.

Het Hedendaags toneel in België. Brussels: Belgisch Instituut voor Voorlichting en Documentatie, 1969. – 123 p.: ill. *Notes*: Includes index. History and criticism.

Leclercq, Nicole. **Les Arts du spectacle, Belgique: bibliographie des ouvrages en français publiés en Belgique entre 1960 et 1985, concernant le théâtre, la musique, la danse, le mime, les marionnettes, les spectacles de variétés, le cirque, la radio et la télévision, le cinéma**. Liège: Recherches et formation théâtrales en Wallonie, 1988. – 115 p. *Notes*: French imprints. Belgium. Bibliography.

Lilar, Suzanne. **Soixante ans de théâtre belge** [Sixty years of theatre in Belgium]. Brussels: Renaissance de livre, 1952. 107 p. *Notes*: Also available in English and Dutch.

Louvet, Jean. **Le Fil de l'histoire: pour un théâtre d'aujourd'hui**. Louvain-la-Neuve; Brussels: Presses universitaires de Louvain; Diffusion, A. Ferraton, 1991. – 103 p. *Notes*: Includes bibliographical references (p. 97–103). Political plays. History and criticism.

Morckhoven, Paul Van. **The contemporary theatre in Belgium**. Brussels: Information and Documentation Institute, 1970. 125 p.

Passemiers, Rita. **Twintig jaar Teater Vertikaal**. Ghent: Provinciebestuur Oost-Vlaanderen: te verkrijgen bij de Provinciale Kulturele Dienst, 1981. – 77 p., 24 p. of plates: ill. *Notes*: Includes bibliographical references and index. Teater Vertikaal (Ghent).

Rencontre une communauté du théâtre. Charleroi: Maison de la culture de la region de Charleroi, 1986. – 72 p.: ill. *Notes*: French drama. Belgian authors. Bio-bibliography. Reviews.

Renieu, Lionel. **Histoire des théâtres de Bruxelles, depuis leur origine jusqu'à ce jour**. [A history of the theatres in Brussels: from the beginnings to the present]. Brussels: Culture et civilisation, 1974. 1,200 p.

Theaterjaarboeken voor Vlaanderen. [Flanders theatre yearbooks]. Antwerp: Flemish Belgian Centre of the ITI, 1966–.

Le Théâtre contemporain de Belgique. Brussels: Institut Belge d'Information et de Documentation, 1969. – 123 p.: illus. *Notes*: French and Flemish drama. 20th century. Dramatic writing.

Tindemans, Carlos. **Op de top van de citadel: over Alex van Royen**. Antwerp: Vlaams Theater Instituut: Dedalus, 1989. – 128 p.: ill. *Notes*: Actors. Royen, Alex van. Biography.

Van Schoor, Jaak. 'Il teatro fiammingo prima del 1945'. [Flemish theatre before 1945]. In **Storia del XX Secolo**. [A history of the twentieth century], ed. Tullio Gregory. Rome: Istituto della Enciclopedia Italiana, 1993.

A3a14. BÉNIN

Huannou, Adrien. **La Litterature béninoise de langue française**. [Béninese literature in the French language]. Paris: Karthala ACCT, 1984.

Koudjo, Bienvenu. 'La Pratique théâtrale au Bénin'. [Theatre practice in Bénin]. In **Notre Librarie** 69 (May–July 1983): 72–7.

Midiohouan, Guy Ossito. 'La Pratique théâtrale en République Populaire du Bénin depuis 1945'. [Theatre practice in the People's Republic of Bénin since 1945]. In **Semper aliquid novi: littérature comparée et littérature d'Afrique**. [Always Something New: Comparative Literature and African Literature]. Edited by Janos Riesz and Alain Ricard, 357–68. Tübingen: Gunther Narr Verlag, 1990.

Nevadomsky, Joseph. 'Kingship succession rituals in Benin'. **African Arts** 17, no. 1 (November 1983): 47–54.

Savarolles, François. 'La Troupe théâtrale et folklorique de Bénin: les filles des amazones'. [The theatre and folklore troupes of Bénin: daughters of the Amazons]. **Afrique** 63 (January 1967): 22–5.

A3a15. BHUTAN

Karan, Pradyuman P. **Bhutan: A physical and cultural geography**. Lexington: University of Kentucky Press, 1967.

Miller, Robert and Beatrice Miller. 'Bhutanese New Year's Celebrations'. **American Anthropologist**, no. 158 (February 1956).

Olschak, C. **Bhutan: land of hidden treasures**. New Delhi, Bombay and Calcutta: Oxford and IBN Publishing Company, 1971.

Paro Tsechu Programme. Translated and arranged by Tashi Wangmo. Thimphu: Department of Tourism, Royal Government of Bhutan, 1983. 26 p.

Pommaret, François. **Introduction to Bhutan**. Hong Kong: Odyssey, 1991.

Rahul, Ram. **Royal Bhutan**. New Delhi, 1983.

The royal dancers and musicians from the kingdom of Bhutan. [motion picture] New York: The Asia Society and the S.I. New House School of Public Communications, 1979.

A3a16. BOLIVIA

Alvarez García, Francisco. 'Medio siglo de teatro boliviano'. [Half a century of Bolivian theatre]. **Revista Municipal Khana** 33/34 (July 1959): 327–38.

Díaz Machicago, Porfirio. Foreword to **Antología del teatro boliviano**. [Anthology of Bolivian theatre]. La Paz: Editorial Don Bosco, 1979.

Gómez de Fernández, Dora. 'Notas sobre el teatro boliviano'. [Notes on Bolivian theatre]. **Kollasuyo** 72 (April-June 1970): 97–118.

Muñoz Cadima, Willy Oscar. 'IBART: su historia'. [IBART: Its history]. **Teatro. Revista de estudios teatrales** 2 (1992): 157–65.

——. 'Producción dramática boliviana: las dosúltimas décadas'. [Bolivian dramatic production: The last two decades]. **Diógenes: anuario crítico del teatro Latinoamericano. 1987**. [Diógenes: Critical annual of Latin American theatre, 1987], vol. 3, ed. Marina Pianca, 31–6. Ottawa: Girol Books, 1988.

——. **Teatro boliviano contemporáneo**. [Contemporary Bolivian theatre]. La Paz: Casa Municipal de la Cultura Franz Tamayo, 1981. 214 p.

——. 'Teatro boliviano contemporáneo'. [Contemporary Bolivian theatre]. **Revista Iberoamericana** 52, no. 134 (January–March 1986): 181–94.

——. 'El teatro boliviano en la década de los ochenta'. [Bolivian theatre in the 1980s]. **Latin American theatre review** 25, no. 2 (spring 1992): 13–22.

——. 'Teatro boliviano: la última época, 1967–85'. [The last period of Bolivian theatre, 1967–85]. **Bolivia: 1952–86. Los ensayistas**. Georgia Series on Hispanic Thought, nos. 20–1 (1986): 175–87.

——. 'Teatro de los Andes: en busca de un nuevo teatro boliviano'. [Teatro de los Andes: The search for a new Bolivian theatre]. **Latin American theatre review** 27, no. 1 (fall 1993): 23–7.

Soria, Mario T. **Teatro boliviano en el siglo XX**. 3a edn. La Paz, Bolivia: Ediciones Populares Ultima Hora, 1980. 237 p.: ill. *Notes:* Bibliography: p. 227–37. Bolivian drama. History and criticism.

Suárez Radillo, Carlos Miguel. 'El teatro boliviano: de lo histórico a lo humano contemporáneo'. [Bolivian theatre: From historical themes to contemporary human themes]. **Cuadernos hispanoamericanos**, nos. 263–4 (1972): 339–54.

A3a17. BOSNIA-HERZEGOVINA

Borovčanin, Svetko. **Godišnjak jugoslovenskih pozorišta 1991–2**. [The yearbook of Yugoslav theatre 1991–2]. Novi Sad: Sterijino pozorje, 1992.

Dvadeset godina Narodnog pozorišta u Mostaru. [Two decades of the National Theatre in Mostar]. Mostar, 1967.

Lazarević, Predrag, Josip Lesć and Mladen Sukalo. **Narodno pozorište Bosanske krajine Banja Luka 1930–80**. [The National Theatre of Banja Luka, 1930–80]. Banja Luka, 1980.

Lesić, Josip. **Drama i njene sjenke**. [The drama and its shadows]. 1991.

——. **Grad opsjednut pozorištem**. [A city obsessed with theatre]. Sarajevo, 1969.

——. **Istorija jugoslovenske moderne režije**. [The history of modern Yugoslav directing]. 1986.

——. **Jedan vijek bosansko-hercegovačke drame**. [A century of drama in Bosnia and Herzegovina]. Sarajevo, 1976.

——. **Narodno pozorište Sarajevo 1921–1971**. [Sarajevo theatre]. Sarajevo: Narodno pozoriste, 1972. – xi, 599 p., 43 p. of plates: ill.

——. **Narodno pozorište Zenica**. [The National Theatre of Zenica]. Zagreb, 1978.

——. **Pozorišni život Sarajeva za vrijeme autrougarske uprave**. [The theatre in Sarajevo under the Austro-Hungarian monarchy]. Sarajevo, 1973.

——. **Sarejevsko pozorište izmedju dva rata**. [The Sarajevo theatre between the two world wars]. 1976.

——, ed. **Savremena drama I pozorište u Bosni I Hercegovini**. [The contemporary drama and theatre in Bosnia and Herzegovina]. Novi Sad: Sterijino pozorje, 1984.

A3a18. BRAZIL

Almeida, Maria Inez Barros de. **Panorama visto do Rio: Cia Tonia-Celi-Autran**. [A view of Rio: the Tonia-Celi-Autran Company]. Rio de Janeiro: Min-Inacen, 1987. 114 p.

——. **Panorama visto do Rio: Teatro Calcida Becker**. [A view of Rio: the Calcida Becker Theatre]. Rio de Janeiro: Minc-Inacen, 1987. 186 p.

Araújo, Alcione. **Alcione Araújo**. Rio de Janeiro: Fundação Nacional de Artes Cênicas, CENACEN, 1988. – 39 p.: ill., ports. *Notes:* Araújo, Alcione. Interviews.

Autran, Paulo. **Paulo Autran**. Rio de Janeiro: Instituto Nacional de Artes Cênicas, CENACEN, 1987. – 38 p.: ill. *Notes:* Autran, Paolo, Teatro Brasileiro de Comédia.

Baccarelli, Milton J. **O teatro em Pernambuco (trocando a máscara)**. Recife: Governo do

Estado de Pernambuco, Secretaria de Educação, Cultura e Esportes, Fundação do Patrimônio Histórico e Artístico de Pernambuco: Companhia Editora de Pernambuco, 1994. – 184 p. *Notes*: Pernambuco (State). History. Interviews.

Borba Filho, Hermilo. **Fisionomia e espirito do mamulengo**. Rio de Janeiro: Ministério de Cultura, Instituto Nacional de Artes Cênicas, 1987. – 262 p.: ill. *Notes*: Includes bibliographical references (p. 259–61). Puppet plays. Brazil.

Borges, Geninha da Rosa. **Teatro de Santa Isabel: nascedouro & permanência**. Recife: CEPE, 1992. – 149 p.: ill.; 20 x. *Notes*: Includes bibliographical references (p. 147–9). Teatro Santa Isabel (Recife). History.

Brandão, Ignácio de Loyola. **Teatro Municipal de São Paulo: grandes momentos**. São Paulo: Dórea Books and Art, 1993. – 114, 5 p.: ill. (some col.). *Notes*: Includes bibliographical references (p. 119). Teatro Municipal (São Paulo). History.

Cacciaglia, Mario and Sábato Magaldi. **Pequeña história do teatro no Brasil: quatro séculos de teatro no Brasil**. São Paulo: T.A. Queiroz, Editor: Editora da Universidade de São Paulo, 1986 1980. – xi, 275 p. *Notes*: Translation of: **Quattro secoli di teatro in Brasile**. Bibliography: p. 149–50. 'Panorama bibliográfico do teatro brasileiro': p. 151–275. Brazilian drama.

Carvalheira, Luiz Maurício Britto. **Por um teatro do povo e da terra: Hermilo Borba Filho e o Teatro do Estudante de Pernambuco**. Recife: Secretaria de Turismo, Cultura e Esportes, Fundação do Patrimônio Histórico e Artístico de Pernambuco, Diretoria de Assuntos Culturais, 1986. – 248 p., 30 p. of plates: ill. *Notes*: 'Bibliografia de Hermilo Borba Filho': p. 235–8. Bibliography: p. 239–48. Borba Filho, Hermilo, 1917–76/Teatro do Estudante de Pernambuco (Recife).

Clark, Fred M. and Ana Lúcia Gazolla de García. **Twentieth-century Brazilian theatre: essays**. Chapel Hill, N.C.; Madrid: Estudios de Hispanófila; Distribuido por Editorial Castalia, 1978. – 122 p.: ill. *Notes*: History and criticism.

Costa, Iná Camargo. **A hora do teatro épico no Brasil**. Rio de Janeiro: Graal, 1996. – 233 p. *Notes*: Includes bibliographical references (p. 215–23) and index. Brazilian drama. History and criticism. Teatro de Arena de São Paulo. History.

Damasceno, Leslie Hawkins. **Cultural space and theatrical conventions in the works of**

Oduvaldo Vianna Filho. Detroit: Wayne State University Press, 1996. – 290 p., 17 p. of plates: ill. *Notes*: Originally presented as the author's thesis (doctorate)–UCLA, 1987. Includes bibliographical references (p. 267–79) and index. Literature and society. Vianna Filho, Oduvaldo, 1936–74. Criticism and interpretation.

Dória, Gustavo. **Moderno teatro brasileiro**. [Modern Brazilian theatre]. Rio de Janeiro: Ministério de Educação, Serviço Nacional de Teatro, 1975.

Ellis, Lorena B. **Brecht's reception in Brazil**. New York: P. Lang, 1995. – xii, 196 p.: ill. *Notes*: Includes bibliographical references (p. 169–90) and index. Brazilian drama. History and criticism.

Franco, Aninha. **O teatro na Bahia através da imprensa, século XX**. Salvador: Fundação Casa de Jorge Amado, 1994. – 407 p.: ill.; 21 x. *Notes*: Includes bibliographical references. Bahia (State). Calendars.

García, Silvana. **O teatro da militáncia**. [Militant theatre]. São Paulo: Perspectiva, 1990. 125 p.

George, David Sanderson. **Anthropophagy and the new Brazilian theatre**. 1984, 1981. – xv, 232 p. *Notes*: Bibliography: p. 225–32. Thesis (Ph. D.)–University of Minnesota, 1981. Photocopy. Ann Arbor, Mich.: University Microfilms International, 1984. Andrade, Oswald de, 1890–1954. Macunaíma.

——. **Grupo Macunaíma: carnavalização e mito**. São Paulo: Perspectiva: Editora da Universidade de São Paulo, 1990. – 153 p.: ill. *Notes*: Includes bibliographical references. Grupo Macunaíma.

——. **The modern Brazilian stage**. Austin: University of Texas Press, 1992. – xvii, 176 p.: ill. *Notes*: Includes bibliographical references (p. 163–8) and index. Brazilian drama. 20th century. History and criticism/Rodrigues, Nelson. Dramatic production.

Gonçalves, Augusto de Freitas Lopes. **Dicionario histórico e literário do teatro no Brasil**. Rio de Janeiro: Livraria Editora Cátedra, 1975. *Notes*: Brazilian drama dictionary. In Portuguese.

Guzik, Alberto. **TBC, crônica de um sonho: o Teatro Brasileiro de Comédia, 1948–1964**. São Paulo: Perspectiva, 1986. – 233 p.: ill. *Notes*: Bibliography: p. 229–33. Teatro Brasileiro de Comédia. History.

Kilpp, Suzana. **Os cacos do teatro: Porto Alegre, anos 70**. Porto Alegre: Unidade Editorial Porto Alegre, 1996. – 190 p. *Notes*:

Includes bibliographical references (p. 119–23). Porto Alegre. Chronology.

Kühner, Maria Helena. **A comunicação teatral: de 1980 a 1983**. Rio de Janeiro: Associação Carioca de Empresários Teatrais, 1983. – 112 p., 16 p. of plates: ill.

Lara, Cecília de. **De Pirandello a Piolim: Alcântara Machado e o teatro no modernismo**. Rio de Janeiro: Instituto Nacional de Artes Cênicas, Ministério da Cultura, 1987. – 153 p. *Notes*: Includes bibliographical references. Brazilian drama.

Litto, Frederic M. 'Some notes on Brazil's Black Theatre'. In **The Black Writer in Africa and the Americas**, ed. Lloyd Brown. Los Angeles: Hennessey & Ingalls, 1973.

Magaldi, Sábato. **Nelson Rodrigues: dramaturgia e encenações**. São Paulo: Perspectiva: Editora da Universidade de São Paulo, 1987. – 200 p.: ill. *Notes*: Bibliography: p. 195–200. Rodrigues, Nelson. Dramatic works.

——. **Panorama do teatro brasileiro**. [Overview of Brazilian theatre]. São Paulo: Difusão Européia do Livro, 1962. 276 p.

Michalski, Yan. **O teatro sob pressão: uma frente de resistência**. Rio de Janeiro: J. Zahar Editor, 1985. – 95 p.: ill. *Notes*: Theatre and state. A study by a major Brazilian critic.

——. **Praia do Flamengo, 132**. Rio de Janeiro: Edições Muro, 1980. – 121 p., 8 p. of plates: ill. *Notes*: History/Actors. Brazil. Interviews.

——. **Yan Michalski**. Rio de Janeiro: Ministério da Cultura, Instituto Nacional de Artes Cênicas, Biblioteca Edmundo Moniz, do CENACEN, 1986. – 40 p.: ill. *Notes*: A study of the critic.

—— and Rosyane Trotta. **Teatro e estado: as companhias oficiais de teatro no Brasil: história e polêmica**. São Paulo: Rio de Janeiro: Editora Hucitec; Instituto Brasileiro de Arte e Cultura, 1992. – xii, 235 p.: ill. *Notes*: 'Comédia Brasileira (1940–1945), Companhia Dramática Nacional (1953–1954), Teatro Nacional de Comédia (1956–1967)'.

——, Fernando Peixoto and Johana Albuquerque. **Ziembinski e o teatro brasileiro**. São Paulo and Rio de Janeiro: Editora Hucitec; Ministério da Cultura/FUNARTE, 1995. – 517 p.: ill. *Notes*: Includes bibliographical references and index. Brazil. Biography/Actors. Brazil. Biography of Ziembinski, Zbigniew Marian, 1908–78.

Mostaço, Edélcio. **Teatro e política: arena, oficina e opinião**. São Paulo: Proposta Editorial, 1982. – 196 p. *Notes*: Cover subtitle: Uma interpretação da cultura de esquerda. Bibliography: p. 189–96. Politics and the theatre.

Neves, João das. **João das Neves**. Rio de Janeiro: INACEN, 1987. – 56 p.: ill. *Notes*: Brazilian drama. 20th century. History and criticism.

Peixoto, Fernando. **Teatro em movimento**. [Theatre in movement]. São Paulo: Editora Hucitec, 1985. 244 p.

——. **Teatro em pedaços**. [Theatre in pieces]. São Paulo: Editora Hucitec, 1980. 362 p.

——. **Teatro em questão**. [Theatre in question]. São Paulo: Editora Hucitec, 1989. 263 p.

——. **Teatro oficina (1958–1982): trajetória de uma rebeldia cultural**. São Paulo: Brasiliense, 1982. – 124, 2 p.: ill. *Notes*: Bibliography: p. 125. Teatro Oficina (São Paulo, Brazil).

——. **Um teatro fora do eixo: Porto Alegre, 1953–1963**. São Paulo: Editora Hucitec, 1993. – 362 p.: ill. *Notes*: Porto Alegre. History. 20th century.

Peregrino Júnior, João and Walter Rela. **El teatro de costumbres en el Brazil**. Rio de Janeiro. Ministério da Educação e Cultura: Serviço de Documentação, 1959. – 33 p. *Notes*: Bibliography: p. 29–33. Costumbrista theatre. History. Brazil.

Pontes, Joel. **O teatro moderno em Pernambuco**. Recife: FUNDARPE: Companhia Editora de Pernambuco, 1990. – 151, 13 p. *Notes*: Includes bibliographical references (p. 153–4). Pernambuco (State). History. 20th century.

Prado, Décio de Almeida. **Apresentação do teatro brasileiro moderno: crítica teatral, 1947–55**. [An introduction to modern Brazilian theatre: theatre criticism, 1947–55]. São Paulo: Livraria Martins Editors, 1956. 484 p.

——. **Teatro em progresso: crítica teatral 1955–64**. [Theatre in progress: theatre criticism 1955–64]. São Paulo: Livraria Martins Editors, 1964.

——. **Exercício findo: crítica teatral (1964–1968)**. [A finished exercise: theatre critisism]. São Paulo: Livaria Martins-Editora Perspectiva, 1987. – 289 p. *Notes*: Includes index. 'Obras do autor': p. 288–89. Criticism.

——. **O teatro brasileiro moderno**. [The Modern Brazilian Theatre] São Paulo: Perspectiva: Editora da Universidade de São Paulo, 1988. – 149 p. *Notes*: Includes index. Bibliography: p. 141–3. A study of the modern Brazilian theatre.

——. **Peças, pessoas, personagens: o teatro brasileiro de Procópio Ferreira a Cacilda Becker**. São Paulo: Companhia das Letras, 1993. – 173 p.: ill.

Ratto, Gianni. **A mochila do mascate: fragmentos do diário de bordo de um anônimo do século XX**. São Paulo: Editora Hucitec, 1996. – 382 p.: ill. *Notes*: Includes index. Study of set designer Gianni Ratto (b Italy).

Rela, Walter. **El teatro brasileño**. [Brazilian theatre]. Montevideo: Instituto de Cultura Uruguayo-Brasileño, 1980. 142 p.

Renato, José. **José Renato**. Rio de Janeiro: Instituto Nacional de Artes Cênicas, Biblioteca Edmundo Moniz, do CENACEN, 1987. – 32 p.: ill. *Notes*: Brazilian drama. A study of José Renato.

Roux, Richard. **Le théâtre Arena: São Paulo 1953–1977: du 'théâtre en rond' au 'théâtre populaire'**. Aix-en-Provence: Université de Provence, Service des publications, 1991. – 2 vols: ill. *Notes*: Includes bibliographical references (p. 731–49) and indexes. Interviews. Teatro de Arena de São Paulo. History.

Sartingen, Kathrin. **Mosáicos de Brecht: estudos de recepção literaria**. São Paulo: Editora Arte & Ciencia, 1996. – 149 p. *Notes*: Includes bibliographical references. Brecht, Bertolt, 1898–1956. Stage history. Brazil.

——. **Über Brecht hinaus–: produktive Theaterrezeption in Brasilien am Beispiel von Bertolt Brecht**. Frankfurt am Main: P. Lang, 1994. n 360 p.: ill. *Notes*: Originally presented as the author's thesis (doctoral)–Bonn, 1994. Includes bibliographical references (p. 347–359). Brecht, Bertolt, 1898–1956. Stage history.

Schoenbach, Peter Julian. **Modern Brazilian theatre: art and document**. New Jersey, 1973.

70 años, Teatro Municipal. São Paulo. Secretaria Municipal de Cultura, Departamento de Teatros, 1981. – 237 p.: ill. (some col.)., *Notes*: History. Teatro Municipal (São Paulo).

Sheren, Paul. **The Portuguese and Brazilian theatre: Supplement**. Mottisfont Abbey, Romsey Hants., England: Motley Books, 1975. Bibliography.

Silva, Armando Sérgio da. **Oficina, do teatro ao te-ato**. São Paulo: Perspectiva, 1981. n 255 p.: ill. *Notes*: Originally presented as the author's thesis (master's–Universidade de São Paulo). Bibliography: p. 239–49. Teatro Oficina (São Paulo).

Silva, Erotilde Honório. **O fazer teatral: forma de resistência**. Fortaleza: EUFC, 1992. – 229 p.

Notes: Originally presented as the author's thesis (master's)–Universidade Federal do Ceará, 1991. Includes bibliographical references (p. 223–9). Theatre. Political aspects.

Silva, José Armando Pereira da. **O teatro em Santo André, 1944–1978**. Santo André: Prefeitura Municipal de Santo André, 1991. – 140 p.: ill. *Notes*: Includes bibliographical references (p. 140). Santo André theatre (São Paulo). History.

Silveira, Miroel. **A contribuição italiana ao teatro brasileiro, 1895–1964**. São Paulo: Edições Quíron, 1976. – xvi, 319 p. *Notes*: Bibliography: p. 313–19. Italian theatre influences in Brazil.

Sousa, José Galante de. **Subsídios para uma bio-bibliografia do teatro no Brasil**. Rio de Janeiro, 1960. *Notes*: Brazilian bio-bibliography study. In Portuguese.

Vianna Filho, Oduvaldo. **Vianinha: teatro, televisão, política**. [Vianinha: theatre, television, and politics]. With selection, organization and notes by Fernando Peixoto. São Paulo: Brasiliense, 1983. 224 p.

Vieira, César. **Em busca de um teatro popular**. [In search of popular theatre]. Santos: Confenata, 1981. 250 p.

Zaidan, Michel. **O Palco da história: exercicios de interferência histórico-dramático-literária**. Recife: Editora Universitária UFPE, 1992. – 59 p. *Notes*: Includes bibliographical references. Drama in education. Study and teaching.

A3a19. BRUNEI DARUSSALAM

A. Ahmad Hussin. 'Penulisan Drama dan Kemajuannya'. **Kertaskerja Seminar Sastera anjuran Asterawani**, Bandar Seri Begawan Brunei, 1964.

A. Rahman Yusof. **Kiambang Bertaut**. [Play anthology]. Dewan Bahasa dan Bustaka Brunei, 1991.

Budaya Bangsa. Dewan Bahasa dan Pustaka Brunei, 1989.

Haji Abdul Rahman Mohammed Yusof. **Drama Kemerdekaan: Warisan Sebuah Wasiat**. Jawatankuasa Decil Pementasan Drama dan Hiburan Hari Kemerdekaan, 1983.

Haji Ahmad Mohammed Arshad. 'Penulisan Drama dan Kemajuannya di Brunei'. **Kertaskerja Seminar Sastera anjuran Asterawani**, Bandar Seri Begawan, Brunei, 1964.

Haji Magon Hajo Ghafar, ed. **Sasterawani bangsa: antologi drama**. [Writers' union plays: A drama anthology]. Dewan Bahasa dan Pustaka Brunei, 1993.

Haji Mohammed Hj Serudin. 'Penulisan dan Perkembangan Drama Pentas di Brunei'. In **Ikhtisar Bahasa dan Sastera**, 1983.

Haji Mohammed Yussop bin Bakar. **Adat Perkahwinan Orang Melayu Brunei di Muim Saba**. Dewan Bahasa dan Pustaka Brunei, 1989.

Ikhtisar Bahasa dan Sastera. Dewan Bahasa dan Pustaka Brunei, 1983.

Intisari Debudayaan Brunei. 3rd edn. Dewan Bahasa dan Pustaka Brunei, 1986.

Kamus Bahasa Melayu Brunei. Dewan Bahasa dan Pustaka Brunei, 1991.

Al-Marhum Bengiran Shahbandar Pengiran Md Salleh Ibnu Pengiran Syarmayuda. **Syair Rakis**. Pusat Sejarah Brunei, 1983.

Mas Osman. **Biografi Penulis Brunei**. Dewan Bahasa dan Pustaka Brunei, 1987.

Muhammad Abdul Latiff. **Suatu Pengenalan Sejarah Kesusasteraan Melayu Brunei**. 2nd edn. Dewan Bahasa dan Pustaka Brunei, 1985.

Patani. **Pengiran Indera Mahkota**. Dewan Bahasa dan Pustaka Brunei, 1991.

Pehin Orang Kaya Amar Diraja Dato Seri Utama and Jaji Awang Jamil Al-Sufri. **Liku-liku Perjuangan Pencapaian Kemberdekaan**. Dewan Bahasa dan Pustaka Brunei, 1992.

Pg Haji bin Pg Haji Mohammed Tahir and Mohammed Salleh bin Abdu Latif. **Drama Kanak-kanak: Tabung Pecah**. Dewan Bahasa dan Pustaka Brunei, 1990.

Yahya, M.S. **Asas-Asas Kritik Sastera**. Dewan Bahasa dan Pustaka Brunei, 1983.

A3a20. BULGARIA

Arsova-Dimova, Milena and Temenuzhka Mikhailova, **Teatralnoto delo v gr. Pleven: bibliografski ukazatel**. Pleven: Universalna nauch, 1989. n 101 p. *Notes*: Includes index. Bulgarian theatre bibliography.

Beneva-Nacheva, Dora. **Sreshti s vuzvishenoto: album spomeni**. Sofia: Izd-vo na Otechestveniia front, 1984. – 234 p.: ill., facsims., map. *Notes*: Theatre. Bulgaria. History. 20th century. Actors. Singers.

Boiadzhiev, Atanas. **Teatralniiat protses prezhiviano i razmisul**. Sofia: Nauka i izkustvo, 1985. – 166 p. *Notes*: Theatre. History. 20th century.

Bulgarian Centre of the ITI. **The Bulgarian dramatic art**. Sofia: National Centre of Propaganda and Information, 1979. 68 p.

Danovski, Boian, Vladimir Danovski and Neviana Indzheva. **Krustoputishta**. Sofia: Izd-vo Nauka i izkustvo, 1988. – 416 p., 32 p. of plates: ill. *Notes*: Includes bibliographical references. Biography Boian Danovski.

Dobrev, Chavdar Atanasov. **Dramaturgichni idei i teatralna metodologiia**. Sofia: Izd-vo Nauka i izkustvo, 1984. – 229 p. *Notes*: Bulgarian drama. 20th century. History and criticism.

G'orova, Sevelina Tokova. **Rezhis'orite za svoiata profesiia**. Sofia: Nauka i izkustvo, 1974. – 263 p.: ill. *Notes*: Theatrical directors.

——. **Teatralen triumvirat: razvitie i vzaimodeistvie na dramaturgiiata, rezhisurata i akt'orskoto maistorstvo**. Sofia: Nauka i izkustvo, 1981. – 152 p. *Notes*: Includes bibliographical references. History. 20th century.

——. **Teatralna povest**. Sofia: Partizdat, 1984. – 218 p., 16 p. of plates: ill. *Notes*: Theatre. History. 20th century.

Gradev, Dimitur and Vassil Indjev. **The Bulgarian dramatic theatre**. Sofia: Centre for Publicity, Information, and Press at the Committee for Culture, 1982. – 70 p.: ill.; 21 x.

Guiorova, Sevelina. **Le théâtre dramatique Bulgare**. [Bulgarian dramatic theatre]. Sofia: Septemvri, 1979, 120 p.

Kanushev, Dimitur Marinov. **Stsena i vreme**. Sofia: Narodna mladezh, izd-vo na TSK na DKMS, 1982. – 268 p. *Notes*: History and criticism.

——. **Suvremennost, suvremennost!** Plovdiv: Izd-vo Khristo G. Danov, 1987. – 276 p. *Notes*: History and criticism.

——. **Teatralna kritika: izbrano**. Sofia: Bulgarski pisatel, 1980. – 314 p. *Notes*: Dramatic criticism.

Karakashev, Vladimir. **Drama, stsena, vreme: izbrani proizvedeniia**. [Selections. 1982]. Sofia: Bulgarski pisatel, 1982. – 347 p. ill. *Notes*: Bulgarian drama. History and criticism.

Karakostov, Stefan L. **Bŭlgarskiat teatŭr: osnovi na socialisticheskia realizŭm, 1881, 1891, 1945**. [Bulgarian theatre: fundamentals of socialist-realism, 1881, 1891, 1945]. Sofia: Nauka i Izkustvo, 1982. 570 p.

——. **Bulgarski artisti**. Sofia: Bulgarski pisatel, 1985. n 298 p. *Notes*: Theatre. 20th century.

——. **Revoliutskiia i stsena: sb. statii za sots. realiz'm v dramata i teat'ra**. Sofia: Bulgarski pisatel, 1975. – 418 p. *Notes*: Theatre. Socialist realism.

Manova, Miglena. **Ideal i geroi: kriticheski nabliudeniia vurkhu suvremennata dramaturgiia, teatur i televiziia**. Sofia: Nar. mladezh,

1986. – 176 p. *Notes*: Television plays, Bulgarian. History and criticism.

Masalitinov, Nikolai Osipovich and Tania Masalitinova. **Spomeni, statii, pisma**. Sofia: Nauka i izkustvo, 1987. – 377 p. *Notes*: Includes bibliographical references. Biography of Russian director Nikolai Osipovich Masalitinov, 1880–1961.

Natev, Atanas. **The Bulgarian music, theatre, art**. Sofia: National Centre of Propaganda and Information, 1979. 135 p.

Paunov, Dimitur Khr. **Vladimir Tenev: tvorets i grazhdanin**. Sofia: Izd-vo. na Otechestveniia front, 1973. – 155 p., 16 p. of plates: ill. *Notes*: Includes bibliographical references (p. 155). A study of actor-director Vladimir Tenev.

Saev, Georgi. **Naroden teatur 'Ivan Vazov'**. Sofia: Tsentur za propaganda, informatsiia i pechat pri Komiteta za Kultura, 1982. – 1 vol. (unpaged): ill. *Notes*: Introductory comments by Georgi Saev. Study of Naroden teatur Ivan Vazov.

Shoulov, Iosif. **The Bulgarian theatre**. Translated by Elena Mladenova. Sofia: Foreign Language Press, 1964.

Slavinski, Petur. **Tursachi na svoi putishta**. Sofia: Bulgarski pisatel, 1988. – 289 p. A study of dramatist Petur Slavinski.

Stancheva, Liliana. **Frenskata piesa na stsenata na Narodniia teatur, 1904–1970**. Sofia: Izd-vo na Bulgarskata akademiia na naukite, 1986. – 156 p. *Notes*: Titles on added t.p.: La pièce française sur la scène du Théâtre national, 1904–1970. Summary in French and Russian. Includes bibliographical references. French drama. In Bulgaria.

Stoilov, Bogomil. **Suprichastiia**. Plovdiv: Izd-vo Khristo G. Danov, 1984. – 221 p. *Notes*: Theatre. History. 20th century.

Tenev, Liubomir. **Teatralni sezoni**. Sofia: Nauka i izkustvo, 1984. – 158 p. *Notes*: Theatre. History.

Zidarov, Kamen. **Plamutsi ot izpepeliavashta liubov**. Sofia: Bulgarski pisatel, 1986. – 236 p.: ill. *Notes*: Autobiography. Kamen Zidarov.

A3a21. BURKINA FASO

Benon, B. 'Deux expériences théâtrales: Jean-Pierre Guingané et le Théâtre de la Fraternité, Prosper Kampaoré et l'Atelier Burkinabé'. [Two theatre experiments: Jean-Pierre Guingané and the Théâtre de la Fraternité and Prosper Kampaoré and the Atelier Burkinabé]. **Notre Librairie: La Littérature du Burkina Faso**, 101 (April-June 1990).

Bovin, Mette. 'Provocation anthropology: bartering performance in Africa'. **The Drama Review** 32, no. 1 (spring 1988): 21–41.

Boyarn, F. 'Le Théâtre en Haute-Volta'. [Theatre in Upper Volta]. **Premières Mondiales** 30 (1962).

Cornevin, Robert. 'Théâtre et histoire: légendes et coutumes de la Haute-Volta'. [Theatre and History: legends and customs of Upper Volta]. **France-Eurafrique** 231 (1971): 28–30.

Deffontaines, Thérèse-Marie. 'Théâtre-forum au Burkina Faso et au Mali'. [Forum theatre in Burkina Faso and Mali]. **Notre Librairie**, 102 (July-August 1990).

Guingané, Jean-Pierre. 'Théâtre et développement au Burkina Faso'. [Theatre and development in Burkina Faso]. **Revue d'Histoire du Théâtre** 160 (1988): 361–73.

Pageard, Robert. 'Théâtre africaine à Ouagadougou'. [African theatre in Ouagadougou]. **Présence Africaine** 39 (1961): 250–3.

Pièces Théâtrales du Burkina. [Plays of Burkina]. Ouagadougou: Ministère de l'Information et de la Culture, 1983. 157 p.

Voltz, Michel. 'Voltaic Masks'. **The Drama Review** 26, no. 4 (winter 1982): 38–45.

Zimmer, Wolfgang. **Répertoire du théâtre burkinabé**. Paris: Éditions L'Harmattan, 1992. – 138 p. *Notes*: Index. Burkina Faso. 20th century. Bibliography.

A3a22. CAMBODIA

Brandon, James R., ed. **The Cambridge guide to Asian theatre**, Cambridge: Cambridge University Press, 1993.

Pich Tum Kravel. **Sbek Thom: Khmer shadow theatre**. Phnom Penh: UNESCO and Ithaca, New York: Cornell University Southeast Asia Program, 1995.

Sam, Sam-Ang and Chan Moly Sam. **Khmer folk dance**. Newington, Connecticut: Khmer Studies Institute, 1987.

Shapiro, Toni. 'The Dancer in Angkor'. **Asian Art and Culture** (Winter 1995): 9–23.

A3a23. CAMEROON

Brench, Anthony Cecil. **Writing in French from Senegal to Cameroon**. London: Oxford University Press, 1967. 153 p.

Butake, Bole and Gilbert Doho. **Le Théâtre camerounais/Cameroonian theatre: proceedings of the conference on Cameroon theatre**. Yaoundé: BET & Co., 1987.

Eyoh, Hansel, Ndumbe. **Beyond the theatre,**

interviews with selected popular theatre practitioners. Bonn: DSF., 1992.

——. 'Changing the set: 30 years of Cameroonian drama'. In **Small is beautiful: proceedings of the international federation of theatre research 1990 conference**, eds. Claude Schumacher and Derek Fogg. Glasgow: Theatre Studies Publication, 1991.

——. **Hammocks to bridges: an experience in theatre development**. Yaoundé: BET & Co., 1986.

Hourantier, Marie-José. **Du rituel au théâtre**. [From Ritual to Theatre]. Paris: l'Harmattan, 1984.

——, Wére-Wére Liking and Jacques Scherer. **Du rituel à la scène chez les Bassa du Cameroun**. [From ritual to the stage of the Bassa of Cameroon]. Paris: A.G. Nizet, 1979.

Zimmer, Wolfgang. **Bibliographie de théâtre camerounais**. [Bibliography of Cameroonian theatre]. Sarrebruck: University of the Sarre, 1983. 79 p.

——. **Repertoire du théâtre camerounais**. [Repertory of Cameroonian theatre]. Paris: l'Harmattan, 1985.

A3a24. CANADA

Anthony, Geraldine. **Stage voices: twelve Canadian playwrights talk about their lives and work**. Toronto: Doubleday, 1978. 318 p.

Les Arts du spectacle: Canada: bibliographie des ouvrages en français publiés au Canada entre 1960 et 1985, concernant le théâtre, la musique, la danse, le mime, les marionnettes, les spectacles de variétés, le cirque, la radio et la télévision, le cinéma. Liège, Belgium: Recherches et formation théâtrales en Wallonie, 1986. – 79 p.

Ball, John and Richard Plant. **Bibliography of theatre history in Canada: the beginnings through 1984**. Toronto: ECW Press, 1993. – xxii, 445 p. Notes: Includes some text in French. Includes index.

Benson, Eugene and Leonard W. Conolly, eds. **English-Canadian theatre**. Toronto: Oxford University Press, 1987. 134 p.

——. **The Oxford companion to Canadian theatre**. Toronto: Oxford University Press, 1989. – xviii, 662 p.: ill. Standard reference.

Bessai, Diane. **Playwrights of collective creation**. Toronto: Simon & Pierre, 1992. – 292 p.: ill. Notes: Includes bibliographical references and index. Canadian drama (English). 20th century. History and criticism.

Brask, Per K. **Contemporary issues in Canadian drama**. Winnipeg: Blizzard Publishing, 1995. – 249 p. Notes: Includes bibliographical references. Social issues in literature.

Brookes, Chris. **A public nuisance: a history of the mummers troupe**. St John's, NF: Institute for Social and Economic Research, 1988. 249 p.

Bryden, Ronald and Boyd Neil, eds. **Whittaker's theatre: Herbert Whittaker and theatre in Canada 1944–1975**. Toronto: University of Toronto Press, 1985. 190 pp.

Buller, Edward. **Indigenous performing and ceremonial arts in Canada: an annotated bibliography of Canadian Indian rituals and ceremonies (up to 1976)**. Toronto: Association for Native Development in the Performing and Visual Arts, 1981. 151 p.

Canadian plays. Catalogue 1993–94. Toronto: Playwrights' Union of Canada, 1993. 126 p.

Caron, Louis. **La Vie d'artiste: le cinquantenaire de l'Union des artistes**. Montréal: Boréal, 1987. – 217 p.: ill. History of Quebec's actors' union.

Conolly, Leonard W. and Dorothy A. Hadfield. **Canadian drama and the critics**. Rev. edn. Vancouver: Talonbooks, 1995. – 383 p. Notes: Includes bibliographical references and index. Critical history of major Canadian plays.

Delacroix, Jean-Marie, Maurice David Matisson and Philippe Rouyer. **Théâtres au Canada**. Talence, France: University of Bordeaux, France: CERT, 1980. – 197 p., 12 p. of plates: ill. Notes: Includes bibliographies. Major French study of anglophone theatres.

Edmonstone, Wayne. **Nathan Cohen: the making of a critic**. Toronto: Lester & Orpen, 1977. 286 p.

Filewod, Alan D. **Collective encounters: documentary theatre in English Canada**. Toronto: University of Toronto Press, 1987. – xi, 214 p., 14 p. of plates: ill. Notes: Includes index. Bibliography: p. 199–206. Definitive study of Canadian collective creation from the late 1960s to the 1980s.

Glaap, Albert-Reiner, ed. **Das englisch-kanadische Drama**. [English-Canadian drama]. Düsseldorf: Schwann, 1992. 309 p.

—— and Rolf Althof. **On-stage and off-stage: English Canadian drama in discourse**. St John's, NF.: Breakwater, 1995. Notes: Includes bibliographical references. Revised study in English of Canadian theatre through the modern period by leading Canadian critics. Originally published in German as **Das englisch-kanadische Drama** by Schwann (Düsseldorf, 1992).

Grant, Judith Skelton. **Robertson Davies: the well-tempered critic: one man's view of theatre and letters in Canada**. Toronto: McClelland & Stewart, 1981. – 285 p. *Notes*: One of Canada's great men of letters writing on theatre.

Hall, Amelia and Diane Mew. **Life before Stratford: the memoirs of Amelia Hall**. Toronto; Oxford: Dundurn Press, 1989. – 264 p.: ill. *Notes*: Includes index. Canadian actress recalls early theatres including Canadian Repertory Theatre Society.

Hendry, Tom. **Cultural capital: the care and feeding of Toronto's artistic assets**. Toronto: Toronto Arts Council, 1985. 158 p.

Innes, Christopher. **Politics and the playwright: George Ryga**. Toronto: Simon & Pierre, 1985. – 130 p. *Notes*: Includes index. Bibliography: p. 115–22. History and criticism. Ryga, George. Political and social views.

Johnston, Denis. **Up the mainstream: the rise of Toronto's alternative theatres**. Toronto: University of Toronto Press, 1991. 337 p.

Knowles, Richard Paul, ed. **Theatre in Atlantic Canada**. Sackville, NS: Mount Allison University, 1988. 266 p.

Lane, Harry, ed. **Canada on stage 1982–8**. 2 vols. Toronto: Professional Association of Canadian Theatres, 1989, 1992. See also Rubin, Don: **Canada on stage** (8 vols).

Lee, Betty. **Love and whisky: the story of the Dominion Drama Festival**. Toronto: McClelland & Stewart, 1973 and Toronto: Simon & Pierre, 1982. 335 p.

McCallum, Heather and Ruth Pincoe. **Directory of Canadian theatre archives**. Halifax, NS: Dalhousie University, 1992. 217 p.

Optekamp, Yvonne. **Englisch-kanadische Bühnenstücke als Einblicke in die Geschichte Kanadas: thematische Aspekte und dramaturgische Konzepte**. Trier: Wissenschaftlicher Verlag, 1995. – x, 163 p. *Notes*: Includes bibliographical references. Canadian drama (English). 20th century. History and criticism. In German.

Pelletier, Claude. **Dramaturges québécois: dossier de presse**. Sherbrooke [Québec]: La Bibliothèque, 1981, ill. *Notes*: Comprend du texte en anglais. Dossiers de presse. 'Dépouillement et compilation par Claude Pelletier'. Comprend des références bibliographiques. 1. Jean Barbeau, 1970–80. Jean-Claude Germain, 1969–81 – 2. Marcel Dubé, 1955–86. Gratien Gélinas, 1945–86. Jean-Claude Germain, 1975–82. Françoise Loranger, 1949–77 – 3. Jean Daigle, 1976–85. Robert Gurik, 1965–84. Jean-Pierre Ronfard, 1981–86. Jean-Yves Sauvageau, 1970–78.

Perkyns, Richard. **The Neptune story: twenty-five years in the life of a leading Canadian theatre**. Hantsport, NS: Lancelot Press, 1989. 266 p.

Portman, Jamie and John Pettigrew. **Stratford: the first thirty years**. Toronto: McClelland & Stewart, 1989. 512 p.

Ramsay, Lee, Juta Upshall and Anne Sutherland. **Setting our stages: Toronto theatres inside and out: an exhibition of stage designs and theatre architecture**. Toronto: Arts Dept., Metropolitan Toronto Reference Library, 1990. – 41 p.: ill. *Notes*: Exhibition held at the Metropolitan Toronto Reference Library Gallery, Sep. 29–Nov. 25, 1990. Toronto. History.

Rubin, Don. **Canada on stage: Canadian theatre review yearbook**. 8 vols. Downsview, Ont.: CTR Publications. Vols for 1974–82. Additional volumes through 1986 published through University of Guelph.

——. **Canadian theatre history: selected readings**. Toronto: Copp Clark, 1996. 436 p. *Notes*: Includes bibliography (p. 433–6). History of Canada as seen through published writings about its theatre covering 1750–1990.

Rudakoff, Judith with Rita Much. **Fair play: 12 women speak: conversations with Canadian playwrights**. 2nd edn. Toronto: Simon & Pierre, 1991. – 220 p. Canadian women writers in conversation.

Ryan, Toby Gordon. **Stage left: Canadian theatre in the thirties**. Downsview: CTR Publications, 1981.

Saddlemyer, Ann and Richard Plant. **Later stages: essays in Ontario theatre from the First World War to the 1970s**. Toronto: University of Toronto Press, 1996. – xiii, 496 p.: ill. *Notes*: Includes bibliographical references (p. 437–50) and index. Second volume in a study of Ontario theatre.

Stuart, E. Ross. **The history of prairie theatre**. Toronto: Simon & Pierre, 1984. 292 p.

Twenty-fifth Street House Theatre. **Towards a Canadian cultural policy: an indigenous perspective**. Saskatoon: The Theatre, 1981. – 9, 13 p.: ill. *Notes*: Letter of transmittal and brief to the Federal Cultural Policy Review Committee. Theatre and state. Canada/Federal aid to the theatre.

Usmiani, Renate. **Second stage: the alternative theatre movement in Canada**. Vancouver: University of British Columbia Press, 1983. –

xii, 173 p., 4 p. of plates: ill. *Notes*: Includes index. Bibliography: p. 161–4. Major academic study of Canadian experimental groups.

Wagner, Anton, ed. **The Brock bibliography of published Canadian plays in English 1766–1978.** Toronto: Playwrights Press, 1980. 375 p.

——. **Contemporary Canadian theatre, new world visions: a collection of essays.** Toronto, Canada: Simon & Pierre, 1985. – 411 p.: ill. *Notes*: Includes index. Bibliography: p. 355–75.

——. **Establishing Our Boundaries: English-Canadian theatre criticism.** Toronto: University of Toronto Press, 1999. 416 p. Comprehensive study of English-Canada's major theatre critics and critical trends. 18 essays by Canadian scholars.

Wallace, Robert. **Producing marginality: theatre and criticism in Canada.** Saskatoon, Sask.: Fifth House Publishers, 1990. – 253 p.: ill. *Notes*: Includes bibliographical references and index. Critic and editor Wallace theorizes on contemporary theatre directions.

—— and Cynthia Zimmerman. **The work, conversations with English-Canadian playwrights.** Toronto: Coach House Press, 1982. – 377 p. *Notes*: Includes bibliographies and index. Interviews with major Canadian dramatists.

Whittaker, Herbert. **Whittaker's theatricals.** Toronto: Simon & Pierre, 1993. – 264 p.: ill. *Notes*: Includes index. Bibliographical references: p. 254–5. A leading Canadian critic on the Canadian theatre.

Zimmerman, Cynthia, ed. **Playwriting women: female voices in English Canada.** Toronto: Simon & Pierre, 1994. – 235 p. *Notes*: Includes bibliographical references and index. Carol Bolt: making issues entertaining – Sharon Pollock: the making of warriors – Margaret Hollingsworth: feeling out of context – Erika Ritter and Anne Chislett: only connect – Judith Thompson: voices in the dark.

A3a24a. QUÉBEC

Beaucage, Christian. **Le Théâtre à Québec au début du XXe siècle: une époque flamboyante!** Québec: Nuit blanche, 1996. – 317 p.: ill. *Notes*: Includes bibliographical references (p. 295–303) and indexes. Theatre. History.

Bélair, Michel. **Le nouveau Théâtre québécois.** Montréal: Leméac, 1973. – 205 p. *Notes*: Bibliographie: p. 165–71. Theatre. Quebec (Province)/Canadian drama (French). 20th century. History and criticism.

Béraud, Jean. **350 ans de théâtre au Canada français.** [350 years of theatre in French

Canada]. Collection l'Encyclopédie du Canada français, vol. 1. Montréal: Le Cercle du Livre de France, 1958. 316 p.

Bourassa, André-G and Jean-Marc Larrue. **Les Nuits de la 'Main': cent ans de spectacles sur le boulevard Saint-Laurent (1891–1991).** Montréal: VLB, 1993. – 361 p., 16 p. pl.: ill. *Notes*: Includes bibliography (p. 299–311) and index. Performing arts. Quebec (Province). Montréal. History.

—— and Gilles Lapointe. **Refus Globale et ses environs 1948–1988.** [Refus Globale and its adherents 1948–1988]. Montréal: l'Hexagone, 1988. 184 p.

Brisset, Annie. **A sociocritique of translation: theatre and alterity in Quebec, 1968–1988.** Toronto: University of Toronto Press, 1996. – éxxii, 238 p. *Notes*: Includes bibliographical references (p. 225–32) and index. Translating and interpreting. Québec (Province)/Drama. Translating/Theatre and society. Québec (Province)/Canadian drama (French). Québec (Province). History and criticism/Canadian drama (French).

Camerlain, Lorraine and Diane Pavlovic. **Cent ans de théâtre á Montréal: photographies.** [100 years of theatre in Montréal: photographs]. Montréal: Cahiers de théâtre Jeu, 1988. 160 p.

Compagnie Jean Duceppe. **Duceppe, 20 ans.** Montréal: La Compagnie, 1993. – 56 p.: ill.; 22 x. *Notes*: History and criticism of the Compagnie Jean Duceppe. (Montreal).

Cotnam, Jacques. **Le Théâtre québécois: instrument de contestation sociale et politique** [Québec theatre: instrument of social and political protest]. Collection Études littéraires. Montréal: Fides, 1976. 124 p.

Cusson, Chantale, ed. **Répertoire du Centre d'essai des auteurs dramatiques. Des auteurs, des pièces: portraits de la dramaturgie québécoise** [Repertoire of the Centre d'essai des auteurs dramatiques. The authors, the plays: portraits of Québécois playwriting]. 1989 edn. Edited by Hélène Dumas; 1994 edn. Edited by Daniel Gauthier. Montréal: Centre des auteurs dramatiques, 1984 and 1994. 307 and 406 p.

Dassylva, Martial. **Un théâtre en effervescence: critiques et chroniques 1965–1972.** [An effervescent theatre: criticism and chronicles 1965–1972]. Collection Échanges. Montréal: La Presse, 1975. 283 p.

David, Gilbert. **Répertoire théâtral du Québec 1984.** [Theatre repertoire of Québec 1984]. Montréal: Cahiers de théâtre Jeu, 1984. 504 p.

—— and Pierre Lavoie, eds. **Le Monde de Michel Tremblay: des 'Belles-Soeurs'à 'Marcel poursuivi par les chiens'**. [The world of Michel Tremblay: from 'Les Belles-Soeurs'to 'Marcel Pursued by Hounds']. Montréal/Brussels: Cahiers de théâtre Jeu/Éditions Lansman, 1993. 479 p.

Dorion, Gilles, ed. **Dictionnaire des oeuvres littéraires du Québec**. [Dictionary of Québec's literary works]. Vol. 6: 1976–80. Montréal: Fides, 1994. 1,087 p.

Dumas, Hélène. **Théâtre québécois: ses auteurs, ses pièces: répertoire du Centre d'essai des auteurs dramatiques**. 1990, Éd. Outremont, Québec: VLB, 1989 1985. – xi, 307 p., 24 p. pl.: ill. *Notes*: Publ. en collab. avec: Centre d'essai des auteurs dramatiques. Canadian drama (French). Quebec (Province). Bibliography. History and criticism.

Engelbertz, Monique. **Le théâtre québécois de 1965 à 1980: un théâtre politique**. Tübingen: M. Niemeyer, 1989. – ix, 375 p. *Notes*: Major study of Quebec theatre.

Féral, Josette. **La Culture contre l'art**. [Culture against art]. Sillery, PQ: Presses de l'Université du Québec, 1990. 341 p.

Gaboriau, Linda, ed. **Québec plays in translation: 1994 supplement**. Montréal: Centre des auteurs dramatiques, 1994. 28 p.

Gobin, Pierre. **Le Fou et ses doubles: figures de la dramaturgie québécoise**. [The madman and his doubles: figures of Québécois playwriting]. Collection Lignes québécoises. Montréal: Presses de l'Université de Montréal, 1978. 263 p.

Godin, Jean-Cléo and Laurent Mailhot. **Le Théâtre québécois**. Nouv. éd. Montréal: BQ, 1988. – 2 vols *Notes*: Comprend des bibliogr. et des index. 1. Introduction à dix dramaturges contemporains – 2. Nouveaux auteurs, autres spectacles. Essential study of Quebec dramatists.

Gruslin, Adrien. **Le Théâtre et l'état au Québec**. [Theatre and the state in Québec]. Montréal: VLB éditeur, 1981. 414 p.

Hamelin, Jean. **Le Renouveau du théâtre au Canada français**. [The renewal of theatre in French Canada]. Montréal: Éditions du Jour, 1962. 160 p.

Hébert, Chantal. **Le Burlesque au Québec: un divertissement populaire**. [Burlesque in Québec: a popular entertainment]. Cahiers du Québec, Collection Ethnologie. Montréal: Hurtubise-HMH, 1981. 302 p.

Houyoux, Philippe. **Théâtre québécois: M. Dubé, J. Ferron, G. Gélinas, G. Lamarche, J.** Languirand, A. Laurendeau, F. Leclerc, Y. Thériault: bibliographies de travail. Trois-Rivières, Québec: UQTR, Bibliothèque, Centre bibliographique, 1975. Bibliography.

Lacroix, Jean-Guy. **La condition d'artiste: une injustice**. [The situation of the artist: an injustice]. Montréal: VLB éditeur, 1990. 249 p.

Laflamme, Jean and Rémi Tourangeau. **L'Église et le théâtre au Québec**. [Church and theatre in Québec]. Montréal: Fides, 1979. 356 p.

Lapointe, Claude. **André Brassard: stratégies de mise en scène: essai**. Outremont, Québec: VLB, 1990. – 200 p.: ill. *Notes*: Includes bibliography p. 197–200. Theatrical producers and directors. Québec. Brassard, André, 1946–.

Lavoie, Pierre. **Pour suivre le théâtre au Québec: les resources documentaires**. Québec: Institut québécois de recherche sur la culture, 1985. – 521 p. *Notes*: Includes index. Québec bibliography.

Legris, Renée, Jean-Marc Larrue, André-G. Bourassa and Gilbert David. **Le théâtre au Québec, 1825–1980**. [Theatre in Québec, 1825–1980]. Montréal: VLB éditeur/SHTQ/BNQ, 1988. 208 p.

Lemire, Maurice, ed. **Dictionnaire des oeuvres littéraires du Québec**. [Dictionary of Québec literary works]. Vol. 3: **1940–59**; Vol. 4: **1960–69**; Vol. 5: **1970–75**. Montréal: Fides, 1982, 1984, 1988.

MacDougall, Jill R. **Performing identities on the stages of Quebec**. New York: Peter Lang, 1996. *Notes*: Includes bibliographical references and index. Theatre. Québec (Province). History. 20th century/Theatre. Political aspects. Street theatre. Nationalism.

Nardocchio, Elaine Frances. **Theatre and politics in modern Québec**. Edmonton, Alta.: University of Alberta Press, 1986. – xii, 157 p. *Notes*: Includes index. Bibliography: p. 133–148. History and criticism.

Podbrey, Maurice and Bruce R. Henry. **Half man, half beast: making a life in Canadian theatre**. Montréal: Véhicule Press, 1997. *Notes*: Includes index. Biography of Maurice Podbrey, long-time director of Montreal's Anglophone Centaur Theatre.

Pontaut, Alain. **Dictionnaire critique du théâtre québécois**. Montréal: Leméac, 1972. – 151 p.

Ronfard, Jean-Pierre. **Entretiens avec Jean-Pierre Ronfard**. Montréal: Liber, 1993. – 176 p. *Notes*: Includes index. Interviews/Canadian drama (French). Actors. Acting teachers.

Roy, Irène. **Le Théâtre Repère: du ludique au poétique dans le théâtre de recherche**. Québec:

Nuit blanche, 1993. – 95, 5 p. *Notes*: Includes bibliographical references (p. 93–6). Study of Théâtre Répère.

Sauer, Melanie and Hans-Joachim Lope. **Der Aufbruch des frankokanadischen Dramas im Umfeld der 'révolution tranquille' in den 60er Jahren: am Beispiel der Autoren Michel Tremblay, Anne Hébert, Marcel Dubé und Gratien Gélinas 1**. Frankfurt am Main: P. Lang, 1995. – 148 p.

Sicotte, Anne-Marie. **Gratien Gélinas: la ferveur et le doute**. Montréal: Editions Québec/Amérique, 1995. ill. *Notes*: Includes bibliographical references. French-Canadian. 20th century. Biography. Gélinas, Gratien. Author/actor.

Tembeck, Iro. **Dancing in Montreal: seeds of a choreographic history**. Madison, WI: Society of Dance History Scholars, 1994. – xiii, 146 p.: ill. *Notes*: Translation of: **Danser à Montréal**. Includes bibliographical references (p. 125–40) and index. Montréal. History/Dance companies.

Wyczynski, Paul, Julien Bernard and Hélène Beauchamp, eds. **Le Théâtre canadien-français: evolution, temoignages, bibliographie**. [French-Canadian theatre: evolution, testimonies, bibliography]. Archives des lettres canadiennes, 5. Montréal: Fides, 1976. 1,005 p.

A3a25. CANARY ISLANDS

Lezcano, Ricardo. **Historia del Teatro Insular de Cámara de El Museo Canario, 1956–1968**. Las Palmas de Gran Canaria: Ediciones del Cabildo Insular de Gran Canaria, 1996. – 173 p.: ill. (some col.). *Notes*: Teatro Insular de Cámara (Theatre group: Las Palmas, Canary Islands). History.

A3a26. CHAD

Bebnone Palou, Samuel. **Mbang Gaourang**. Paris: UNESCO.

Djimet, Karl. **Le Crime de la dot**. [Crime of the dowry]. Paris: UNESCO.

Moustapha, Baba. **Achua ou le drame d'une fille-mère**. [Achua or the drama of an unwed mother]. Paris: UNESCO.

——. **Le Commandant Chaka**. [Commander Chaka]. (Monde noir poche, no. 19). Paris: Hatier/CEDA, 1983.

——. **Makari aux épines**. [Makari of the thorns]. Paris: NEA./CLE, 1979.

A3a27. CHILE

Boyle, Catherine M. **Chilean theater, 1973–1985: marginality, power, selfhood**. Rutherford: London; Cranbury, NJ.: Fairleigh Dickinson University Press; Associated University Presses, 1992. – 226 p. *Notes*: Includes bibliographical references (p. 213–21) and index.

Bravo-Elizondo, Pedro. **Raíces del teatro popular en Chile**. Guatemala: Impresos D & M, 1991. – 162 p. *Notes*: Includes bibliographical references (p. 159–62). Political aspects.

Brncic, Zlatko. 'El teatro chileno a través de 50 años: 1900–50'. [Chilean theatre over fifty years: 1900–50]. In **Desarrollo de Chile en la primera mitad del siglo XX**. [Chile's development during the first half of the twentieth century]. Santiago: Editorial Universitaria, 1953.

Cánepa Guzmán, Mario. **Historia del teatro chileno**. [History of Chilean theatre]. Santiago: Editorial Universidad Técnica del Estado, 1974. 232 p.

——. **El teatro en Chile**. [Theatre in Chile]. Santiago: Editorial Arancibia Hermanos, 1966. 135 p.

——. **El teatro obrero y social en Chile**. [Working class and social theatre in Chile]. Santiago: Ediciones Culturales y Publicaciones del Ministerio de Educación, 1971.

Castedo-Ellerman, Elena. **El teatro chileno de mediados del siglo XX**. [Chilean theatre in the 1950s]. Santiago: Editorial Andrés Bello, 1982. 240 p.

Fernández, Teodosio. **El teatro chileno contemporáneo, 1941–1973**. Madrid: Playor, 1982. – 213 p. *Notes*: Bibliography: p. 209–13.

Halek, Yvonne Charlotte. **Versuch einer strukturalistischen Analyse des Theaterwesens in Argentinien und Chile unter besonderer Berücksichtigung des Zeitraumes 1980–1982**. 1989. 156 p. *Notes*: Includes bibliographical references. Thesis (doctoral)–Freie Universität Berlin. Microfiche. Berlin. Mikrofilm Center Klein, 1992. 2 microfiches: negative.

Hurtado, María de la Luz. **Memorias teatrales: el teatro de la Universidad Católica en su cincuentenario, 1978–1993**. Santiago: Pontificia Universidad Católica de Chile, 1993. – 226 p.: ill. *Notes*: Includes bibliographical references.

——. **Sujeto social y proyecto histórico en la dramaturgia chilena actual**. Santiago, Chile: CENECA, 1983. *Notes*: Bibliography: p. 110–11. Constantes y variaciones entre 1960 y 1973. Literature and society.

—— and Carlos Ochsenius. **Diez años de teatro en Chile: sus transformaciones entre 1970 y 1980**. Santiago: Centro de Indagación y

Expresión Cultural y Artística, 1980. 143 p. 24 p. 6 p. of plates: ill. History and criticism.

Morgado, Benjanmín, ed. **Histórica del teatro chileno**. [Historical account of the Chilean theatre]. La Serena: Universidad de La Serena, 1985. 329 p.

Munizaga, Giselle and María de la Luz Hurtado. **Testimonios del teatro: treinta y cinco años de teatro en la Universidad Católica de Chile**. [Theatre testimonies: thirty-five years of theatre at the Catholic University of Chile]. Santiago: Editorial Nueva Universidad, 1980. 186 p.

Muñoz, Diego, Carlos Ochsenius, José Luis Olivari and Hernán Vidal. **Poética de la población marginal: teatro poblacional chileno 1978–85. Antología crítica**. [The poetics of the marginalized: community theatre in Chile 1978–85. A critical anthology]. Minneapolis/Santiago: Prisma Institute/CENECA, 1988. 439 p.

Ochsenius, Carlos. **Teatro y animación de base en Chile 1973–86**. [Grassroots theatre and theatre of animation in Chile 1973–86]. Buenos Aires: Ediciones Paulinas, 1988. 124 p.

——. **Teatros universitarios de Santiago, 1940–1973: el estado en la escena**. Santiago: CENECA, 1982. – 145, 3 p. *Notes*: Bibliography.

Pina, Juan Andres. **Teatro chileno en la decada del 80: desarrollo de un movimiento innovador**. Santiago: Instituto Chileno de Estudios Humanísticos, 1982. – 63, 3 p.

Rela, Walter. **Contribución a la bibliografia del teatro chileno, 1804–1960**. [A contribution to the bibliography of Chilean theatre, 1804–1960]. Montevideo: Universidad de la República, 1960. 51 p.

Rodriguez, Orlando and Domingo Piga. **Teatro chileno: su dimensión social**. [The social dimension of Chilean theatre]. Santiago: Editorial Nacional Quimantú, 1973. 95 p.

Rojo, Grínor. **Muerte y resurrección del teatro chileno, 1973–1983**. Madrid: Ediciones Michay, 1985. – 198 p. *Notes*: Bibliography: p. 191–8. Political aspects.

Rojo, Sara. **La mujer en el teatro chileno: del texto al público**. 1991. – xi, 391 p. *Notes*: Abstract in English. Thesis (Ph. D.)–State University of New York at Stony Brook, 1991. Chilean women's theatre. Interviews.

Vidal, Hernán. **Dictadura militar, trauma social e inauguración de la sociología del teatro en Chile**. Minneapolis, MN: Institute for the Study of Ideologies and Literature, 1991. – 230 p.

Series: Literature and human rights; no. 8. *Notes*: Includes bibliographical references (p. 217–25) and index. Theatre. Political aspects. Chile/Chilean drama.

A3a28. CHINA

Adzhimamudova, Viola Sergeevna. **Tian' Khan': portret na fone epokhi**. Moscow: Nauka, 1993. – 239 p. *Notes*: Includes bibliographical references (p. 237–8). Dramatists, Chinese. 20th century. Biography. T'ien, Han, 1898–1968. In Russian.

Arlington, Lewis Charles. **The Chinese drama from the earliest times until today; a panoramic study of the art in China, tracing its origin and describing its actors (in both male and female roles), their costumes and make-up, superstitions and stage slang, the accompanying music and musical instruments, concluding with synopses of thirty Chinese plays**. Bronx, NY: B. Blom, 1966 1930. – 177, xli p. illus., plates (part col.). *Notes*: First published in 1930. Bibliography: p. xli. Chinese drama/Costume.

Bin, Ru, ed. **Theatre section, collection of Chinese children's literature**. Chong Qing Publishing House, 1994. 347 p.

Brecht and China. Beijing: Chinese Centre of the International Theatre Institute, approx. 1985. 26 p.

Chen, Bai Chen and Dong Jian. **History of modern Chinese theatre**. Beijing: China Theatre Publishing House, 1989. 732 p.

Chen, Jack. **The Chinese theatre**. London: Dobson, 1949. 63 p.

Ch'en, Kuo-fu. **T'ien fu chih hua: Ch'uan chu i shu ch'ien t'an**. [Chinese play: Overview of the arts]. Setzuarn Ch'ung-h'ing, 1983.

The Chinese puppet theatre. Translated by J.T. MacDermott. London: Faber & Faber, 1961. 55 p.

Chinese Research Institute of Children's Theatre, eds. **Collection of essays on research of children's theatre**. Beijing: China Theatre Publishing House, 1987. 398 p.

Chinese Research Institute (Theatre Division). **Collection on stage design**. Beijing: China Theatre Publishing House, 1982. 458 p.

Chinese Theatre Association. **A brief introduction to Chinese theatre**. Beijing: Chinese Centre of the International Theatre Institute, approx. 1983 (undated). 32 p.

Chou, I-pai and Hsieh-yüan Shen. **Chou I-pai hsiao shuo hsi ch'ü lun chi**. Hunan: Ch'i Lu shu she, 1986. – 7, 2, 684 p., 1 p. of plates (some col.) *Notes*: Chinese drama. History and criticism. Folk drama.

Chung-kuo hsi ch'ü yen chiu shu mu t'i yao. Beijing: Chung-kuo hsi chü ch'u pan, 1992. – 2, 4, 481 p. *Notes*: Includes indexes. Chinese drama. History and criticism.

Darrobers, Roger. **Le Théâtre chinois**. [The Chinese theatre]. Paris: Presses Universitaires de France, 1995. 127 p.

Dolby, William A. **A history of Chinese drama**. London: Elek. 1976. 327 p. illus. *Notes*: An outline of Chinese drama from its origins to about 1970.

Du, Wenwei. **From M. Butterfly to Madame Butterfly: a retrospective view of the Chinese presence on Broadway**. 1992. – iii, 374 p. *Notes*: Includes bibliographical references. Thesis (Ph. D.)–Washington University, 1992. Dept. of Asian and Near Eastern Languages and Literatures and Dept. of Comparative Literature.

Fei, Faye Chunfang. **Huang Zuolin: China's man of the theatre**. 1991. – ix, 209 p. *Notes*: Includes bibliographical references (p. 202–9). Thesis (Ph. D.)–City University of New York, 1991. Photocopy. Ann Arbor, Mich.: University Microfilms International, 1994. Theatrical producers and directors. China. Biography of Huang Zuolin.

Fu Hsiao-hang and Hsiu-lien Chang. **Chung-kuo chin tai hsi ch'ü lun chu tsung mu**. Beijing: Wen hua i shu ch'u pan she, 1994. – 973 p. *Notes*: Chinese drama. Bibliography.

Gong, He De. **Research on stage design**. Beijing: China Theatre Publishing House, 1987. 412 p.

Guang, Yu Zhe, ed. **The art of puppet theatre**. Shanghai: Shanghai Cultural Publishing House, 1959. 99 p.

Historical documents on fifty years of spoken drama. 3 vols. Beijing: China Theatre Publishing House, 1958. 910 p.

Howard, Roger. **Le Théâtre chinois contemporain**. [The contemporary Chinese theatre]. Brussels: La Renaissance du Livre, 1978. 106 p.

Hsu, Tao-Ching. **The Chinese conception of the theatre**. Seattle, Washington and London: University of Washington Press, 1985. 685 p.

Hu Jao Mu, ed. **The Chinese encyclopedia: volume on traditional opera including comic dialogues**. Beijing and Shanghai: The Chinese Encyclopedia Publishing House, 1983. 661 p. *Notes*: This set contains more than twenty volumes. This volume deals with Chinese traditional opera. In Chinese.

Huei, Li. **Biographies of modern theatre and film artists in China**. Jiang Xi People's Publishing House, 1981–4. 981 p.

Jia, Ah. **Further studies on the principles of traditional theatre**. Beijing: China Theatre Publishing House, 1991. 347 p.

Jiang, Xinhuei. **Zhongguo eiju shi tanwei**. [Looking for details in history of Chinese drama]. Jinan: Qilu Publishing House, 1985. 363 p.

Jiong, Zhang. **General survey of dramatic literature in the People's Republic of China**. Beijing: China Theatre Publishing House, 1990. 390 p.

Kalvodová, Sís, Vanis. **Chinese theatre**. Translated by Iris Urwin. London: Spring Books, 1959. 38 p.

Ku Feng, Yang Ming, Tai Tan and Li Yin-hou. **Tien chü shih**. Beijing: Chung-kuo hsi chü ch'u pan, 1986 – 7, 3, 391 p., 18 p. of plates: ill. (some col.). *Notes*: Folk drama. Yunnan Province. Bibliography.

Ling, Huang Huei, ed. **Selective history of modern Chinese dramatic literature**. An Heui Publishing House, 1990. 373 p.

Ling, Huang Zhuo. **Words of a Director**. Shanghai: Shanghai Arts and Literature Publishing House, 1979. 294 p.

Lopez, Manuel D. **Chinese drama: an annotated bibliography of commentary, criticism, and plays in English translation**. Metuchen, NJ: Scarecrow Press, 1991. – ix, 525 p. *Notes*: Includes indexes.

Lu Ch'ing, Yang Tsu-yü, Hu Tung-sheng and Chang Hsiu-ling. **Ching chü shih chao**. [A pictorial history of Beijing opera]. Beijing: Pei-ching yen shan ch'u pan she, 1990. – 295 p.: chiefly ill. (some col.). *Notes*: Chinese and English. History and criticism/Operas, Chinese. Biography.

Ma, Wei. **Xiju yuyian**. [Language in drama]. Shanghai: Shanghai Publisher of Art and Literature, 1985. 263 p.

Mackerras, Colin, ed. **Chinese drama: an historical survey**. Beijing: New World Press, 1990. 274 p.

——. **Chinese theatre: from its origins to the present day**. Honolulu: University of Hawaii Press, 1983. 220 p.

——. **The Chinese theatre in modern times: From 1840 to the Present Day**. Amherst: University of Massachusetts Press, 1975. 216 p.

Ming, Yu Ren, ed. **Management of theatre**

companies. Shanghai: East China Normal University Press, 1988, 123 p.

Organizing Office, All-China Stage Design Exhibition, eds. **Art on Chinese stages**. Beijing: China Theatre Publishing House, 1986. 216 p.

Poupeye, Camille. **Le Théâtre chinois**. [The Chinese theatre]. Preface by Georges Sion. Brussels: Labor, 1984. 239 p.

Ran, Li Mo. **Li Mo Ran on the art of acting**. Beijing: China Theatre Publishing House, 1989. 350 p.

Ren, Chuanlu. **The reception of Bertolt Brecht in China from 1955 to 1987**. 1992. – 271 p.: ill. *Notes*: Bibliography: p. 263–71. Thesis (Ph. D. in Comparative Literature)–Vanderbilt University, 1992. History and criticism.

Riley, Jo. **Chinese theatre and the actor in performance**. Cambridge and New York: Cambridge University Press, 1997. – xii, 348 p.: ill. *Notes*: Includes bibliographical references (p. 329–43) and index. Acting Study and teaching China. Chinese opera.

Ru, Cheng Shi. **On children's theatre**. Beijing: China Theatre Publishing House, 1994. 422 p.

——. **Literature and the arts in twentieth century China**. New York: Doubleday Anchor, 1963. 212 p.

Scott, Adolphe Clarence. **Actors are madmen: notebook of a theatregoer in China**. Madison, Wis: University of Wisconsin Press, 1982. –xii, 225 p.: ill. *Notes*: Includes index. 20th century/Chinese drama. History and criticism. Description and travel.

Sheng, Gao Wen, ed. **History of Chinese contemporary dramatic literature**. Nan Ning: Guang Xi People's Publishing House, 1990. 442 p.

Sheng, Hu Miao. **Theatre space filled with signs**. Beijing: China Theatre Publishing House, 1987. 412 p.

Snow, Lois Wheeler. **China on stage**. New York: Random House, 1972. 330 p.

Stalberg, Roberta. **China's puppets**. Introduction by Bettie Erda. San Francisco: China Books, 1984. 125 p.

Sun Sheng-yün, Pan Hsia-feng and Fan Tieh-cheng. **Hsi chü piao yen pa tzu kung chiao tsai**. Pei-ching ti 1 pan. Beijing: Chung-kuo hsi chü ch'u pan she: Hsin hua shu tien Pei-ching fa hsing so fa hsing, 1986. – 4, 2, 4, 518 p.: ill. Stage fencing and hand-to-hand fighting.

Sung, Xin. **Xiqu wugong jiacheng**. [Textbook of physical training in Chinese theatrical perfor-

mance]. Beijing: Chinese Drama Publishing House, 1983. 443 p.

Tai, Yih-jian. **The contemporary Chinese theatre and Soviet influence, 1919–1960**. Carbondale, Ill.: Southern Illinois University, Dept. of Speech in the Graduate School, 1978 1975. – v, 196 p. *Notes*: Photocopy of thesis. Ann Arbor, Mich.: University Microfilms International, 1978. –. Bibliography: p. 184–95. Thesis–Southern Illinois University.

Tung, Constantine and Colin Mackerras. **Drama in the People's Republic of China**. Albany: State University of New York Press, 1987. – viii, 353 p. *Notes*: Selected papers presented at the International Colloquium on Contemporary Chinese Drama and Theater, held at the State University of New York at Buffalo, Oct. 15–19, 1984. Includes bibliographies and index.

Wilkinson, Joseph Norman. **The plays and playwrights of the Chinese Communist theatre**. 1981 1970. – iv, 279 p. *Notes*: Microform reproduction: Ann Arbor, Mich.: University Microfilms International, 1981 1 microfilm. Bibliography: p. 262–79. Thesis (Ph. D.)–University of Michigan, 1970. Chinese drama. 20th century. History and criticism/ Communism and culture.

Wu, Yan Zhe, ed. **History of education of modern spoken drama in China**. Shanghai: East China Normal University Publishing House, 1986. 373 p.

Xu, Wang. **Introduction to the management of performing arts**. Shen Yang: Liao Ning Educational Publishing House, 1990. 361 p.

Yang, Daniel Shih-p'êng. **Ching hsi yen chiu shu mu t'i yao**. [An annotated bibliography of materials for the study of the Peking theatre]. Hong Kong, 1985, 1967. – 55 p.; 22 x. *Notes*: Includes index.

——. **The traditional theatre of China in its contemporary setting: an examination of the patterns of change within the Peking Theatre since 1949**. 1968. – 278 p. *Notes*: Includes bibliographical references (p. 258–78). Thesis (Ph. D.)–University of Wisconsin, 1968. Microfilm. Ann Arbor, Mich.: University Microfilms, 1968. 1 microfilm reel; 35 mm.

Ying, Jiao Ju. **Collection of Jiao Ju Yin's theatrical essays**. Shanghai: Shanghai Arts and Literature Publishing House, 1979. 452 p.

——. **Dire evolution of an actor**. Beijing: China Theatre Publishing House, 1988. 365 p.

——. **Theatre in the People's Republic of China**. Beijing: China Theatre Publishing House, 1990. 316 p.

Ying, Zhang Fa. **History of chinese traditional theatre troupes**. Shen Yang: Shen Yang Publishing House, 1991. 479 pp. 1470. Wu, Ch'ien-hao. **20 shih chi Chung-kuo hsi chü wu t'ai**. Ti 1 pan. Ch'ing-tao shih: Ch'ing-tao ch'u pan she, 1993. – 3, 5, 2, 256 p. Notes: 'Kuo chia "pa wu" chung tien t'u shu'. Chinese drama. 20th century. History and criticism.

Yu, Hui-ching. **The Chinese image in western drama**. Orono: Me., 1993. – 40 p. Notes: Includes vita. Bibliography: p. 35–7. Thesis (M.S.) in Theatre–University of Maine, 1993. American Drama. 20th century. History and criticism. Chinese influences.

Yu, Qiou, Yu. **Aesthetic psychology of theatre**. Setzuan: People's Publishing House, 1985. 401 p.

——. **History of theatre theories**. Shanghai: Shanghai Arts and Literature Publishing House, 1983. 666 p.

Yun-tong, Luk, ed. **Studies in Chinese-Western comparative drama**. Hong Kong: Chinese University Press, 1990. 224 p.

Zhang, Geng. **On the art of theatre**. Beijing: China Theatre Publishing House, 1980. 234 p.

—— and Guo Han Cheng. **General history of Chinese traditional theatre**. Beijing: China Theatre Publishing House, 1980. 1,193 p.

Zhou, Ding Yan. **History of Chinese puppet theatre**. Shanghai: Xue Ling Publishing House, 1991. 159 p.

Zhou, Xun and Chunming Gao. **5,000 years of Chinese costumes**. Shanghai: Chinese Costumes Research Group of the Shanghai School of Traditional Opera, 1987. 256 p.

Zou, Jiping. **Gao Xingjian and Chinese experimental theatre**. 1994. – vi, 204 p. Notes: Vita. Includes bibliographical references (197–203). Thesis (Ph. D.)–University of Illinois at Urbana-Champaign, 1994.

Zung, Cecilia S.L. **Secrets of the Chinese drama: a complete explanatory guide to actions and symbols as seen in the performance of Chinese dramas**. New York: B. Bloom, 1964. –xxv, 299 p. illus. Notes: Costume. Mei Lan-fang, 1894–1961.

A3a28a. TAIWAN

Chiang, Wu-ch'ang. **Hsüan ssu ch'ien tung wan pan ch'ing: T'ai-wan ti k'uei lei hsi**. Taipei: T'ai yüan ch'u pan she: Tsung ching hsiao Wu shih t'u shu kung ssu, 1990. – 141 p.: ill. Notes: Puppet theatre. Taiwan.

Liang, Hsiu-chüan. **Shou-yen-shen-fa-pu: kuo chü tan chüeh chi pen tung tso**. Taipei: Yuan liu ch'u pan shih yeh ku fen yu hsien kung ssu, 1983. – 223 p.: ill. (some col.). Notes: Contains autobiographical sketches. Subtitle translated: Movement method for the female roles of the Chinese theatre. Chinese. Opera.

Ma, Sen. **Hsi ch'ao hsia ti Chung-kuo hsien tai hsi chü**. Taipei: Shu lin ch'u pan ch'u pan yu hsien kung ssu, 1994. – 417 p. Notes: Includes bibliographical references (p. 333–354) and indexes. Theatre. Taiwan and China.

Sun, Hsien-chao. **Kuo chü ku shih su yüan**. Taipei: Cheng chung shu chü, 1976. – 7 vols: ill. (part col.). Notes: Taiwan drama. History and criticism. Chinese drama. Bibliography.

Tan, Dasien. **Jengo min-jien si-jiu ien-jiou**. [Study of Chinese folk theatre]. Taipei: Gu, dziun, 1984. 158 p.

Tang, Wen Pjau. **Dzen-go gu-dai si-dziu-cui gau**. [Study of the origin and evolution of Chinese theatre]. Taipei: Lein-chin, 1984. 278 p.

Wang Chin-shan, Fei P'eng and Chien-ming Chu. **Hsi wen hsü lu**. Taipei: Ts'ai t'uan fa jen, 1993. – 24, 321 p. Notes: Taiwan. Bibliography.

Wu, Ching-chi. **Lan-ling chü fang ti ch'u pu shih yen**. Taipei: Yüan liu ch'u pan shih yeh ku fen yu hsien kung ssu, 1982. 279 p., 8 p. of plates: col. ill. Notes: Includes English prefatory matter. Bibliography: p. 275–6. History. 20th century.

A3a28b. TIBET

Jamyang, Norbu. **Zlos-gar: performing traditions of Tibet**. Dharamsala, H.P., India: Library of Tibetan Works & Archives, 1986. – 146 p., 8 p. of plates: ill. Notes: 'Commemorative issue on the occasion of the 25th anniversary of the founding of Tibetan Institute of Performing Arts (1959–84)'–Cover. Includes bibliographical references. Memories of Shoton/Hugh E. Richardson – Music of the Lhasa minstrels/ Geoffrey Samuel – The life of the child Padma 'od-'bar from the theatre to the painted image/Anne-Marie Blondeau – The Bonpo tradition/Ricardo O. Canzio – Three sacred Bon dances/Samten G. Karmay – Preliminary remarks concerning the use of musical notation in Tibet/Mireille Helffer – Thang-stong Gyalpo, father of the Tibetan drama tradition/Janet Gyatso – The state of research in Tibetan folk music/Peter Crossley-Holland – A note on Vajra-dance choreography in the snow in the early 18th century AD/Heather Stoddard – A preliminary study of Gar, the court dance and music of Tibet/Jamyang Norbu with Tashi Dhondup. History and criticism. Tibetan Institute of Performing Arts (Dharamsala, India).

A3a29. COLOMBIA

Andrade, Renée Ovadia. **El nuevo teatro en Colombia**. 1985 1982. – ix, 216 p. *Notes*: Text in Spanish; abstract in English. Vita. Bibliography: p. 210–16. Thesis (Ph. D.) –University of California, Irvine, 1982. Photocopy. Ann Arbor, Mich.: University Microfilms International, 1985. ix, 216 p. Colombian drama.

Antei, Giorgio. **Las Rutas del teatro: ensayos y diccionario teatral**. Bogotá: Centro Editorial, Universidad Nacional de Colombia, 1989. – 265 p.: ill. *Notes*: Includes bibliographical references. Colombian drama. In Spanish.

Arcila, Gonzalo. **Nuevo teatro en Colombia: actividad creadora, política cultural**. Bogotá: Ediciones CEIS, 1983. – 208 p. *Notes*: Political aspects.

Baycroft, Bernard Kent. **Brecht in Colombia: the rise of the new theatre**. 1986. – vii, 239 p. *Notes*: Includes bibliography references (p. 206–39). Thesis (Ph. D.)–Stanford University, 1986. Photocopy. Ann Arbor, Mich.: UMI Dissertation Services, 1995.

Duque Mesa, Fernando, Fernando Penuela and Jorge Prada. **Investigación y praxis teatral en colombia**. Santafé de Bogotá: Instituto Colombiano de Cultura: Subdirección de Comunicaciones Culturales, División de Publicaciones, 1994. – 220 p.: ill. *Notes*: Includes bibliographical references. History and criticism.

El Teatro comprometido de Gustavo Andrade Rivera; Miguel Angel Asturias, dramaturgo; El teatro en Colombia. Bogotá: Letras Nacionales, 1974. – 99 p.: ill. *Notes*: Criticism and interpretation.

Gonzalez, Patricia. **El nuevo teatro colombiano: 1955–1980**. 1985, 1981. – v, 287, 1 p. *Notes*: Vita. Bibliography: p. 267–87. Thesis (Ph. D.) –University of Texas at Austin, 1981. Photocopy. Ann Arbor, Mich.: University Microfilms International, 1985.

González Cajiao, Fernando. **Historia del teatro en Colombia**. [History of theatre in Colombia]. Bogotá: Instituto Colombiano de Cultura, 1986. 444p.

Jaramillo, María Mercedes. **El nuevo teatro colombiano: arte y política**. Medellín: Editorial Universidad de Antioquia, Departamento de Publicaciones, Universidad de Antioquia, 1992. – 373 p. *Notes*: Includes bibliography (p. 360–73). Colombian drama. History and criticism.

Martínez Arango, Gilberto. **Hacia un teatro dialéctico: ensayo de teoría y práctica del hecho teatral**. 1. edn. Medellín: Revista Teatro, 1979. – 95 p. *Notes*: Bibliography: p. 94–5. Political aspects/Improvisation.

Orjuela, Héctor H. **Bibliografía del teatro colombiano**. Bogotá: Instituto Caro y Cuervo, 1974. – xxvii, 312 p. *Series*: Publicaciones del Instituto Caro y Cuervo. Serie bibliográfica; 10. Latin American documents; reel 573, item 4. *Notes*: Includes index. Microfilm. Cambridge, Mass.: General Microfilm Co., [1965?–]. 1 microfilm reel (various items); 35 mm. (Latin American documents; reel 573, item 4). Colombian drama. Bibliography.

Ortega Ricaurte, José Vicente. **Historia crítica del teatro en Bogotá**. [Critical history of theatre in Bogotá]. Bogotá: Instituto Caro y Cuervo, 1974. 312 p.

Pedero, Paloma. **El Pasamanos**. Madrid: Primer Acto, S.A., 1995. – 144 p.: ill. *Notes*: Colombian drama. History and criticism.

Röttger, Kati. **Kollektives Theater als Spiegel lateinamerikanischer Identität: La Candelaria und das neue kolumbianische Theater**. Frankfurt am Main: Vervuert, 1992. – 219 p. *Notes*: Originally presented as the author's thesis (doctoral)–Berlin, Freie Universität. Includes bibliographical references (p. 207–219). Grupo La Candelaria. History.

Shen, Virginia Shiang-lan. **El nuevo teatro de Colombia: la ideología y la dramaturgia en Enrique Buenaventura, Carlos José Reyes y Jairo Anibal Nino**. 1988. – vii, 232 p. *Notes*: Vita. Bibliography: p. 211–32. Thesis (Ph. D.) –Arizona State University, 1988. Criticism and interpretation.

Torres Cárdenas, Edgar Guillermo. **Praxis artística y vida política del teatro en Colombia, 1955–80**. [Artistic practice and political life in the Colombian theatre, 1955–80]. Nuevas Lecturas de Historia 11. Tunja: Universidad Pedagógica y Tecnológica de Colombia, 1990. 96 p.

TPB, 25 años: Centro de Artes Dramáticas y Audiovisuales, 1968–1993. Santafé de Bogotá: Teatro Popular de Bogotá–Centro de Artes Dramáticas y Audiovisuales, 1993. – 241 p.: ill. *Notes*: Teatro Popular de Bogotá. History.

Vargas Bustamante, Misael, Carlos José Reyes Posada, Giorgio Antei and Juan Monsalve. **El teatro colombiano**. [Colombian theatre]. Bogotá: Ediciones del Alba, 1985. 122 p.

Velasco, María Mercedes de. **El nuevo teatro colombiano y la colonización cultural**. Editorial Memoria, 1987. – 207 p. *Notes*: Bibliography: p. 191–204. Literature and society.

A3a30. COMMONWEALTH CARIBBEAN

Baxter, Ivy. **The arts of an island: the development of the culture and of the folk and creative arts on Jamaica, 1494–1962 (Independence).** Metuchen, NJ: Scarecrow Press, 1970. 407 p.

Carter, Steven R. 'Edgar B. White'. In **Afro-American writers after 1955: dramatists and prose writers** vol. 38, eds. Thadious M. Davis and Trudier Harris, 278–83. Detroit, MI: Gale Research, 1985.

Clark, Vévé. 'Drama and disorder'. In **History of Caribbean literatures in European languages**, ed. A. James Arnold. Charlottesville, VA: University of Virginia Press, 1992.

Corsbie, Ken. **Theatre in the Caribbean.** London: Hodder & Stoughton, 1984 60 p. *Notes*: With a foreword by Trevor Rhone.

Hill, Errol. **The Jamaican stage, 1655–1900: profile of a colonial theatre.** Amherst, MA: University of Massachusetts Press, 1992. 346 p.

Johnston, Robert. **The theatre of Belize.** North Quincy: MA: Christopher Publishing House, 1973. 96 p.

King, Bruce Alvin. **Derek Walcott and West Indian drama: not only a playwright but a company, the Trinidad Theatre Workshop 1959–1993.** Oxford; New York: Clarendon Press; Oxford University, 1995. *Notes*: Includes bibliographical references. Theatre. Trinidad and Tobago. West Indies. In literature. Walcott, Derek, 1930–. Criticism and interpretation. Trinidad Theatre Workshop. History.

Nettleford, Rex. **Caribbean cultural identity: the case of Jamaica. An essay in cultural dynamics.** Los Angeles: University of California Press, 1978. 239 p.

Nunley, John Wallace and Judith Bettelheim. **Caribbean festival arts: each and every bit of difference.** Seattle, WA/London: University of Washington Press/St Louis Art Museum, 1988. 218 p.

Olaniyan, Tejumola. **Scars of conquest/masks of resistance: the invention of cultural identities in African, African-American, and Caribbean drama.** New York: Oxford University Press, 1995. – xii, 196 p. *Notes*: Includes bibliographical references (p. 171–90) and index. Black authors. Criticism and interpretation.

Omotoso, Kole. **The theatrical into theatre: a study of drama and theatre in the English-speaking Caribbean.** London: New Beacon Books, 1982. 173 p.

Ortega, Donna Elisabeth. **Towards a theory of Caribbean drama.** 1988. – ii, 64 p.: ill. *Notes*:

Includes bibliographic references. Thesis (Master's) – University of the West Indies, Mona, Jamaica, 1988.

Pearn, J.C. **Poetry as a performing art in the English-speaking Caribbean.** Sheffield, UK: University of Sheffield, 1986.

Stone, Judy. **Studies in West Indian literature: theatre.** London: Macmillan, 1994. 272 p.

A3a31. COMOROS ISLANDS

Chamanga, Mohamed Ahmed. **Rois, femmes et djinns: contes de l'île Danjouan Comores** [Kings, women and spirits: stories from the Island of Danjouan Comoros]. Paris: Centre de recherche Océan Indien-Inalco, 1988.

Lambek, Michael. **Human spirits: a cultural account of trance in Mayotte.** Cambridge: Cambridge University Press, 1981.

Music of the Comoros Islands. [sound recording]. Recorded by Harriet and Martin Ottenheimer. New York: Folkways, 1982.

Rombi, Marie-Françoise and Mohamed Ahmed Chamanga. **Contes comoriens.** [Comorian tales]. Paris: Conseil International de la langue français and Edicef, 1980. 139 p.

A3a32. CONGO

Chemain, Roger, and Arlette Chemain-Dégrange. 'Un Théâtre militant'. [A militant theatre]. In **Panorama critique de la littérature congolaise contemporaine.** [A Critical Overview of Contemporary Congolese Literature]. p. 105–135. Paris: Présence africaine, 1979.

Jadot, Joseph M. 'Le Théâtre des marionnettes au Congo Belge'. [Marionette theatre in the Belgian Congo]. **Bulletin des Seances** 21, no. 3 (1950): 559–69.

Menga, Guy. 'Quel avenir pour le théâtre en langue française au Congo?' [Which route for French-language theatre in the Congo?] **Culture Française** 3–4, no. 1 (1982–3): 45–8.

'Le Théâtre congolais'. [Congolese theatre]. **Afrique Chrétienne** 7, no. 46 (1967): 17–19.

Tati-Loutard, J.B. 'Itinéraire'. [Itinerary]. **Notre Librairie: La Littérature congolaise** 92–3 (March/May 1988).

'Le Théâtre au Congo'. [Theatre in the Congo]. **Het Toneel** 6 (1956).

A3a33. COSTA RICA

Borges, Fernando. **Teatros de Costa Rica.** [Theatres of Costa Rica]. San José: Editorial Costa Rica, 1980. 116 p.

Cañas, Alberto. 'Teatro costarricense en el teatro costarricense'. [Costa Rican theatre in the

Costa Rican theatre scene]. **Escena Costa Rica** 2 no. 4 (1980): 13–14.

Capella, Segreda, Yolanda. 'El teatro en Costa Rica'. [Theatre in Costa Rica]. **Memoria de la Academia de Geografía e Historia de Costa Rica** 1 no. 3 (June 1949): 11–17.

Fernández, Guido. **Los caminos del teatro en Costa Rica**. [Paths of the Costa Rican theatre]. San José: Editorial Universitaria Centroamericana, 1977. 183 p.

Garrido, Lenín. **La imagen teatral**. [The theatrical image]. San José: Editorial Costa Rica, 1973. 173 p.

Herzfield, Anita and Teresa Cajiao. **El teatro de hoy en Costa Rica: perspectiva crítica y antológica**. [Theatre in Costa Rica today: anthology and critical analysis]. San José: Editorial Costa Rica, 1978. 268 p.

Rovinski, Samuel. **Dramatización de lo inmediato**. [Dramatization of the immediate]. San José: Compañia Nacional de Teatro, 1992.

Sáenz, Andrés. **La comedia es cosa seria**. [Comedy is a serious thing]. San José: Ministerio de Cultura, 1985. 182 p.

Sandoval de Fonseca, Virginia. **Resumen de literatura costarricense**. [An overview of Costa Rican literature]. San José: Editorial Costa Rica, 1978.

A3a34. CÔTE D'IVOIRE

Amon d'Aby, François-Joseph. **Le Théâtre en Côte d'Ivoire des origines à 1960**. [Theatre in the Côte d'Ivoire from its origins to 1960]. Abidjan: CEDA, 1988.

Holas, Bohumil. **Craft and culture in the Ivory Coast**. New York: International Publications Service, 1968.

Kotchy, Barthélémy. **La critique sociale dans l'oeuvre théâtrale de Bernard Dadié**. [Social criticism in the theatrical work of Bernard Dadié]. Paris: l'Harmattan (1984).

Liking, Wéré-Wéré and Marie-José Hourantier. 'Les Vestiges d'un kotéba'. [The Remains of the Kotéba]. **Revue de littérature et d'esthetique négro-africaines**, No. 8. Université d'Abidjan (1981).

Sidibé, Valy. 'L'image de la femme dans le théâtre de Bernard Dadié'. [The image of woman in the theatre of Bernard Dadié]. **Revue de littérature et d'esthétique négro-africaines**, No. 9. Université d'Abidjan (1988).

Vinci Leoni, Nicole. **Comprendre l'oeuvre de Bernard Dadié**. [Understanding the work of Bernard Dadié]. Paris: Saint-Paul, 1986.

A3a35. CROATIA

Batušić, Nikola. **Hrvatska dramska knjizevnost i kazalište od predratnih revolucionarnih previranja do 1955: eseji i grada o hrvatskoj drami i teatru**. Split: Knjizevni krug, 1983. – 412 p., 48 p. of plates: ill. *Notes*: In Serbo-Croatian (Roman). 'Dani Hvarskog kazalista, 1935–1955'–Page preceding t.p. Includes bibliographical references. Literature and war.

——. **Hrvatsko narodno kazalište u Zagrebu: 1840–1860–1992**. Zagreb: Hrvatsko narodno kazaliste: Školska knjiga, 1992. – 215 p.: ill. (some col.). *Notes*: Includes bibliography (p. 199–206). Zagreb. Theatre history.

——. **Povijest hrvatskog kazališta**. [The history of Croatian theatre]. Zagreb: Školska knjiga, 1978. 542 p.

——. **Suvremena hrvatska drama i kazaliste (1955–1975): eseji i grada o hrvatskoj drami i teatru**. Split: Književnih krug, 1984. n 388 p., 48 p. of plates: ill. *Notes*: Croatian drama. 20th century. History and criticism.

Batušić, Slavko. 'Das kroatische Theater'. [The Croatian theatre]. In **Theatergeschichte Europas**. [History of European theatre], vol. 10, p. 242–62. Edited by Heinz Kindermann. Salzburg: Otto Müller, 1974.

Bogner-Saban, Antonija. **Marionete osvajaju Zagreb**. Zagreb: Hrvatsko društvo kazališnih kritičara i teatrologa, 1988. – 210 p., 20 p. of plates: ill. *Notes*: In Serbo-Croatian (Roman). Includes bibliographical references and index. Puppet theatre. Croatia.

——. **Tragom lutke i pricala: povijest meduratnog lutkarstva u Splitu, Susaku, Osijeku i Djecje carstvo**. Zagreb: AGM, 1994. – 277 p.: ill. *Notes*: Includes indexes. Puppet theatre. Croatia/Children's plays.

Cindrić, Pavao and Slavko Batušić, eds. **Hrvatsko narodno kazalište 1894–1969: enciklopedijsko izdanje (Enciklopedija s povijesnim pregledom razvitka HNK)**. [Croatian National Theatre 1894–1969: encyclopedic edition (Encyclopedia and historical survey of the development of the Croatian National Theatre)]. Zagreb: Naprijed, 1969. 721 p.

Dani hvarskog kazališta – eseji i grada o hrvatskoj drami i kazalištu. [Essays on Croatian theatre and drama]. Split: Kjiñevni krug. Vol. 10: **Hrvatska dramska književnost i kazalište od predratnih revolucionarnih previranja do 1955**. [Croatian dramatic literature and theatre from pre-war revolutionary turmoil to 1955], 1983. 412 p. Vol. 11: **Suvremena hrvatska drama i kazalište**.

[Contemporary Croatian drama and theatre], 1984. 374 p.

Dobrila, Tone. **Istarske kazalisne druzine u NOB: grada za povijest**. Rijeka: Otokar Kersovani, 1981. – 577 p., 32 p. of plates: ill. *Notes*: Documents in Italian, Serbo-Croatian (Roman), Slovenian. Bibliography: p. 576. World War, 1939–1945. Theatre and the war. (Croatia and Slovenia).

Durbesic, Tomislav. **Eto tako: kazivanja avan-gardnog konzervativca**. Zagreb: Hrvatsko drustvo kazalisnih kriticara i teatrologa, 1989. – 188 p. *Notes*: History and criticism.

Foretić, Dalibor. **Nova drama – svjedočenje of jugoslavenskim dramatikama i njihovim scenskim refleksima**. [New drama – Yugoslav dramatics and their stage reflection]. Rijeka: Izdavački centar/Novi Sad: Sterijno pozorje, 1988. 423 p.

Hećimović, Branko. **Antologija hrvatske drame**. [Anthology of Croatian drama]. 3 vols. Zagreb: Znanje, 1988. 1,385 p.

——. **Repertoar hrvatskih kazališta 1840–1860–1990**. [Repertoire of Croatian theatres 1840–1860–1990]. 2 vols. Zagreb: Globus i Jugoslavenska akademija znanosti i umjetnosti, 1990. 1,423 p.

——. **Suvremena drama i kazaliste u Hrvatskoj**. Novi Sad: Sterijino pozorje, 1987. – 509 p. *Notes*: Includes indexes. Theatre. Croatia. History. 20th century.

Hergesic, Ivo and Nikola Batusic. **Zapisi o teatru**. Zagreb: Hrvatsko društvo kazališnih kriticara i teatrologa, 1985. – 279 p. *Notes*: Includes bibliography (p. 269–75). History and criticism.

Lederer, Ana. **Dobre slucajnosti**. Zagreb: Meandar, 1994. – 134 p. *Notes*: Includes index. Croatian drama. 20th century. History and criticism.

Lesic, Josip. **Savremena drama i pozoriste u Bosni i Hercegovini**. Novi Sad: Sterijino pozorje, 1984. – 417 p. *Notes*: Includes indexes. Theatre. History. Serbian drama. Bosnia and Hercegovina.

Mastrovic, Tihomil. **Drama i kazaliste hrvatske moderne u Zadru**. Zagreb: Nakladni zavod Matice hrvatske, 1990. – 402 p., 32 p. of plates: ill. *Notes*: Includes bibliography (p. 379–81) and index. Croatian drama. 20th century. History and criticism/Zadar (Croatia).

Mrduljas, Igor. **Ad Hoc Cabaret: Hrvatsko ratno glumiste 1991/92**. Zagreb: AGM, 1995. – 330 p.: ill. *Notes*: Yugoslav War, 1991–2. Theatre and the war/Ad Hoc Cabaret.

Selem, Petar. **Otvoreno kazalište**. [Open theatre]. Zagreb: Hrvatsko društvo književnih kritičara i teatrologa, 1979. 216 p.

Senker, Boris. **Pogled u kazalište**. [A look into theatre]. Zagreb: Hrvatsko društvo kazališnih kritičara i teatrologa, 1990. 272 p.

——. **Sjene i odjeci: kazalisni ogledi i studije**. Zagreb: Znanje, 1984. – 216 p. *Notes*: Includes index. Theatre. Croatia. History.

——. **Zapisi iz zamracenog gledalista: kazal-isne kronike**. Zagreb: Matica hrvatska, 1996. – 225 p. *Notes*: Includes index. Croatia. History. 20th century.

Snajder, Slobodan. **Radosna apokalipsa**. Rijeka: Izdavacki centar Rijeka, 1988. – 187 p. *Notes*: Croatian drama. 20th century. History and criticism.

A3a36. CUBA

Aguilú de Murphy, Raquel. **Los textos dramáticos de Virgilio Pinera y el teatro del absurdo**. Madrid: Editorial Pliegos, 1989. – 190 p. *Notes*: Includes bibliography (p. 183–90). Theatre of the absurd/Pinera, Virgilio, 1912–. Dramatic works.

Arrom, Juan José. **Historia de la literatura dramática cubana**. [History of Cuban dramatic literature]. New Haven, CT: Yale University Press, 1944. 132 p.

Baliño Cedre, Omar. **La aventura del Escambray: notas sobre teatro y sociedad**. [The Escambray adventure: notes on theatre and society]. Havana: Editorial José Martí, 1994. 65 p.

Boudet, Rosa Ileana. **Teatro nuevo: una respuesta**. [New theatre: an answer]. Colección Espiral. Havana: Editorial Letras Cubanas, 1983. 304 p.

Carrió, Raquel. **Dramaturgia cubana contem-poráneo: estudios críticos**. [Contemporary Cuban playwriting: critical essays]. Havana: Pueblo y Educación, 1988. 81 p.

Corcho Morffi, Manuel. **30 años en la cultura cubana: (bibliography)**. Havana: Departamento de Información para la Cultura, Biblioteca Nacional José Martí, Ministerio de Cultura, 1988. – vi, 100 p. *Notes*: 'La presente com-pilación recoge la información aparecida en las publicaciones cubanas pertenecientes al fondo bibliográfico de la Biblioteca Nacional José Marti'–P. v.

Espinosa Domínguez, Carlos. 'Una dramaturgia escindida'. [A theatre divided]. In **Teatro cubano contempráneo: antología**. [Contem-porary Cuban theatre: anthology]: 11–127.

Madrid: Instituto Nacional de Artes Escénicas y Músicas del Ministerio de Cultura de España/Fondo de Cultura Económica, 1992.

Franklin, Lillian. **The image of the Black in the Cuban theater: 1913–1965**. 1982. – v, 343 p. *Notes*: Includes bibliography (p. 320–43). Thesis (Ph. D.)–Ohio State University, 1982. Microfilm. Ann Arbor, Mich.: University Microfilms International, 1986. 1 microfilm reel; 35 mm. *Notes*: Cuban drama. 20th century. History and criticism.

González, Jorge Antonio. **Historia del teatro en La Habana**. [History of the theatre in Havana]. Santa Clara: Dirección de Publicaciones de la Universidad Central de Las Villas, 1961. 163 p.

——. **La composición operística en Cuba**. [Operatic composition in Cuba]. Havana: Editorial Letras Cubanas, 1986. 587 p.

González Cruz, Luis and Francesca Colecchia. **Cuban theatre in the United States: a critical anthology**. Tempe, AZ: Bilingual Press, 1992.

Graupera Arango, Elena. **Bibliografía sobre teatro cubano: libros y folletos**. [A bibliography of Cuban theatre: books and pamphlets]. Havana: Biblioteca Nacional José Martí, Departamento de Información y Documentación de la Cultura, 1981. 27 p.

La investigación como parte de un método de creación teatral. [Research as a form of artistic creation]. Havana: Departamento de Publicaciones y Conservación de la Biblioteca Nacional José Martí/Cuban Centre of the International Theatre Institute, 1981. 101 p.

Leal, Rine. **Breve historia del teatro cubano**. [A short history of Cuban theatre]. Colección Panorama no. 2. Havana: Editorial Letras Cubanas, 1980. 185 p.

——. **En primera persona, 1954–1966**. Havana: Instituto del Libro, 1967. – 369 p. *Notes*: Includes indexes. History and criticism.

——. **La dramaturgia del Escambray**. [The playwriting of Escambray]. Havana: Editorial Letras Cubanas, 1984. 94 p.

——. **La selva oscura**. [The dark forest]. 2 vols. Colección Teatro y Danza. Havana: Editorial Arte y Literatura, 1975–1982.

Martin, Randy. **Socialist ensembles: theater and state in Cuba and Nicaragua**. Minneapolis: University of Minnesota Press, 1994. – xii, 260 p. *Notes*: Includes bibliography (p. 239–55) and index. Theatre. Cuba. History. 20th century/ Theatre. Nicaragua. History. 20th century/ Socialism and theatre.

Martínez Tabares, Vivian. **Didascalias urgentes de una espectadora interesada: (aproxima-** ciones al teatro cubano de hoy). Havana: Editorial Letras Cubanas, 1996. – 85 p. *Notes*: Cuban drama. History and criticism.

Montes Huidobro, Matías. **Persona, vida y máscara en el teatro cubano**. [Persona, life and mask in the Cuban theatre]. Miami, FL: Ediciones Universal, 1973. 458 p.

Muguercia, Magaly. **El teatro cubano en vísperas de la Revolución**. Havana: Editorial Letras Cubanas, 1988. – 257 p. *Notes*: Includes bibliography (p. 253–7). History. 20th century.

——. **Indagaciones sobre el teatro cubano**. Havana: Editorial Pueblo y Educación, 1989. – 97 p. *Notes*: Cuban drama. History and criticism.

——. **Teatro, en busca de una expresión socialista**. Havana: Editorial Letras Cubanas, 1981. – 148 p. *Notes*: 'Recopilación de escritos sobre el teatro cubano realizados en el período 1972–1978'. Socialism and theatre.

Noel, Jesse and Ena Thomas. **Spanish Caribbean theatre: conference papers**. 2nd edn. St Augustine (Trinidad and Tobago): Dept. of French and Spanish Literature, University of the West Indies, 1985. – ii, 216 p. *Notes*: 'Papers read at 2nd Conference on Spanish American Literature, St Augustine campus, July 10–11, 1979'–Cover. Papers in English and Spanish. Includes bibliographies. Puerto Rican drama. Cuban drama.

La obra de Brecht en Cuba. [Brecht's influence in Cuban theatre]. Havana: Departamento de Publicaciones y Conservación de la Biblioteca Nacional José Martí/Cuban Centre of the International Theatre Institute, 1981. 146 p.

Oritz, Fernando. **Los bailes y el teatro de los negros en el folklore de Cuba**. [The dance and theatre of the Negro in Cuban folk traditions]. Havana: Ministerio de Educación, Departamento de Cultura, 1951. 588 p.

Palls, Terry Lee. **The theatre in revolutionary Cuba, 1959–1969**. 1976, 1974. – v, 228 p. *Notes*: Bibliography: p. 211–23. Thesis (Ph. D.) –University of Kansas, 1975. Photocopy. Ann Arbor, Mich., U.S.A.: University Microfilms International, 1976. Cuban drama. 20th century. History and criticism.

Raz, Daniela. **Defiant acts: the revolution on the Cuban stage**. 1994. – 156 p. *Notes*: Thesis (B.A., Honors in Social Studies)–Harvard University, 1994. Theatre. Political aspects.

Séjourné, Laurette. **Teatro Escambray: una experiencia**. [The experience of Theatre Escambray]. Havana: Editorial Ciencias Sociales, 1977. 367 p.

Trives, Toni. **Race, gender, and humanism in Cuba's socialist theater**. 1990. – viii, 260 p. *Notes*: Includes abstract and vita. Bibliography: p. 241–60. Thesis (Ph. D.)–University of California, Los Angeles, 1990. Photocopy. Ann Arbor, Mich.: University Microfilms, 1992. Cuban drama. Black authors.

Vasserot, Christilla. **Théâtres cubains**. Montpellier: Maison Antoine Vitez, 1995. – 186 p.: ill. *Notes*: History since 1945. In French.

A3a37. CYPRUS

Chrysanthěs, Kypros. **Theatrikes apodeltióseis kai dyo monoprakta**. [A theatrical scrapbook and two one-act plays]. Nicosia: Theatriké Syllogé Kai Vivliothéke, 1978. 57 p.

Ersoy, Yiassar. **The Turkish Cypriot theatrical movement**. Nicosia: privately printed, 1975.

Mousteris, Michalis. **Istoria tou Kupriakou Theatrou**. [History of the Cypriot theatre]. Limassol: Fili Press, 1983.

——. **Chronologikh Istoria tou Kupriakou Theatrou**. [Chronological history of Cyprus theatre]. Limassol: Fili Press, 1988. 300 p.

The Theatrical Organization of Cyprus. **Ta Sekachrona tou THOK**. [Ten years of THOK]. Nicosia: Proodos Press, 1982.

A3a38. CZECH REPUBLIC

Bahner, Ota and Karel Cejka. **Tri strázníci: ctení o J. Voskovcovi, J. Werichovi a J. Jezkovi**. Ostrava: Nakladatelství A-Z, 1992. – 117 p.: ill. *Notes*: Theatre. Prague. History. Actors. Biography/Jezek, Jaroslav, 1906–1942/Werich, Jan, 1905–/Voskovec, Jirí, 1905–/Osvobozené divadlo (Prague).

Černý, František. **Měnivá tvář divadla aneb Dvě století s pražskými herci**. [Changeable face of theatre, or two centuries with actors from Prague]. Prague: Mladá fronta, 1978. 319 p.

——, ed. **Dějiny českého divadla**. [History of the Czech theatre], 4 vols. Prague: Academia, 1969–83.

——, ed. **Divadlo v Kotcích. Nejstarši pražské městské divaldo 1739–1783**. [Theatre in Kotce. The oldest Prague Municipal Theatre 1739–83]. Prague: Panorama, 1992.

Císař, Jan. **Divadla, která našla svou dobu**. [Theatres that resonated with their time]. Prague: Orbis, 1966. 126 p.

Etlík, Jaroslav and Jan Schmid. **Ctení o Ypsilonce**. Prague: Studio Ypsilon a Directa, 1993. – 143 p.: ill. *Notes*: History. Studio Ypsilon (Prague).

Fencl, Otakar. **The Czechoslovak theatre today**. Prague: Artia, 1963. 84 p.

Goetz-Stankiewicz, Markéta. **The silenced theatre: Czech playwrights without a stage**. Toronto: University of Toronto Press, 1979.

Hájek, Jiří, Olga Janáčková and Vladimír Just. **Divadlo nové doby 1945–1948**. [Theatre of a new age 1945–8]. Prague: Panorama, 1990.

Herman, Josef. **Vy si mne s nekým pletete–, aneb, Z besed na filosofické fakulte: Jan Werich, Hugo Haas, Zdenek Stepánek, Jirí Suchý, Ivan Vyskocil**. Prague: Divadelní ústav, 1994. – 167 p.: ill. *Notes*: Czech Republic. Actors. Interviews.

Hoffmann, Bohuslav. **České drama a divadlo ve druhé polovine 20. století: ukázky s komentári**. Prague: fi Blug, 1992. – 162 p. *Notes*: Czech Republic. Dramatists.

Just, Vladimír. **Proměny malých scén**. [Changes in the small theatres]. Prague: Mladá fronta, 1984. 344 p.

Klosová, Ljuba and Ludmila Kopácová. **Odkaz ceské divadelní avantgardy**. Prague: Divadelní ústav, 1990. – 220 p. *Notes*: 20th century experimental theatre.

Kolár, Jan. **Petadvacet: 1963–1988**. Prague: Studio Ypsilon, 1988. – 188 p.: chiefly ill. (some col.).

Konečná, Hana, ed. **Čtení o Náradním divadle. Útržky dějin a osudů**. [The National Theatre: on its history and its fate]. Prague: Odeon, 1983. 412 p.

Kopáčova, Ludmila and Jana Paterová, eds. **Ceské divadlo**. [Czech theatre]. Vol. 2, **Divadla studiového typu**. [Studio theatre], by Milan Obst, Jan Kolář, Jan Dvořák, Miroslav Křovák, Vlasta Gallerová amd Vladimír Just. Prague: Divadelní ústav, 1980. 87 p.

Kopáčova, Ludmila, Jana Paterová, Otakar Roubínek and Jonatan Tomeš, eds. **České divadlo**. [Czech theatre]. Vols. 6 and 8, **O současné. české režii**. [About contemporary Czech directing], by Jan Císar, Jan Czech, Michal Lázňovský, *et al*. Prague: Divadelní ústav, 1982–3.

Kraus, Karel. **O divadle 1: 1986–9: [sborník]**. Prague: Lidové noviny, 1990. – 413 p. *Notes*: Selected articles from issues no. 1–5 (1986–9) of the samizdat serial **O divadle**.

Langer, Frantisek and Viktor Kudelka. **Frantisek Langer, divadelníkem z vlastní vule: výbor z prací o divadle a dramatu**. Prague: Divadelní ústav, 1986. – 254 p.: ill. *Notes*: Dramatists, Czech. 20th century. Langer, Frantisek, 1888–1965. Biography.

Nadvornikova, Marie. **Postavy ceskeho divadla: vyberova bibliografie kniznich publikaci a clanku z divadelniho tisku 1945–1980**. [Productions of the Czech theatre: selected bibliography of books on theatrical activities, 1945–1980]. Publikace Statni vedecke knihovny v Olomouci, 4. Olomouc: Statni vedecke knihovny v Olomouci, 1983. 85 p.

Osolsobě, Ivo. **Divadlo, které mluví, zpívá a tančí.** [A theatre which speaks, sings and dances]. Prague: Supraphon, 1974. 242 p.

Planá, Ivana. **Divadlo a divadelnictví na Morave: knihy a clánky 1988–1992, soupis premiér a recenzí**. Olomouc: Státní vedecká knihovna v Olomouci, 1993. – 280 p. *Notes*: Includes indexes. Theatre. Moravia. Bibliography 1988–92.

——. **Divadlo a divadelnictví v Severomoravském kraji: knihy a clánky 1983–1987, soupis premiér a recenzí.** Olomouc: Státní vedecká knihovna v Olomouci, 1988. – 167 p. *Notes*: Czech Republic. Bibliography 1983–7.

Prikrylová, Miroslava. **Knihy o divadle a divadelní hry: soupis kniznich publikací vydaných v Ceskoslovensku v letech 1966–1970.** Prague: Divadelní ústav, 1990. – 488 p. *Notes*: Includes index. Theatre. Czechoslovakia. History. Bibliography.

——. **Knihy o divadle: soupis ceských publikaci 1981–1985.** Prague: Divadelní ústav, 1989. – 122 p. *Notes*: Includes index. Theatre. Czechoslovakia. Bibliography 1981–95.

Procházka, Vladimír, ed. **Národni divadlo a jeho předchůdci.** [The National Theatre and its predecessors]. Prague: Academia, 1988. 623 p.

Schönberg, Michal, Radan Dolejs and Václav Kofron. **Osvobozené.** Prague: Odeon, 1992. – 402 p., 64 p. of plates: ill. *Notes*: Originally presented as the author's thesis (Ph. D.–University of Toronto, 1978. Prague. History. 20th century/Osvobozené divadlo).

Šormová, Eva. **Divadlo v Terezíně 1941–1945.** [Theatre in Theresienstadt, 1941–45]. Theresienstadt: Severočeské nakladatelství, 1973.

Trägrová, Jarmila and Jana Peková. **Severoceské profesionální divadlo, 1945–1982: výberová bibliografie.** Ústí nad Labem: Státní vedecká knihovna Maxima Gorkého v Ústí nad Labem, 1987. – 204 p. *Notes*: Includes index. Czech Republic history. Bibliography.

Trensky, Paul I. **Czech drama since World War II**. White Plains: Sharpe, 1978.

Vostrý, Jaroslav. **Cinoherní klub 1965–1972: dramaturgie v praxi.** Prague: Divadelní ústav: Ve spolupráci s Divadelní fakultou Akademie múzických umení v Praze, 1996. – 207 p., 18 p. of plates: ill. *Notes*: Includes bibliography (p. 201) and index. Cinoherní klub.

A3a39. CZECHOSLOVAKIA

Bruna, Otakar. **Nez se zvedne opona**. Prague: Panorama, 1984. – 255 p.: ill. *Notes*: Biography.

Císar, Jan. **Promeny divadelního jazyka.** Prague: Melantrich, 1986. – 194 p. *Notes*: Theatre and society. History. 20th century.

Dvorák, Antonín. **Trojice nejodváznejsich.** Prague: Mladá fronta, 1988 1961. – 236 p., 24 p. of plates: ill. *Notes*: Biography Honzl, Jindrich, 1894–1953/Frejka, Jirí/Burian, Emil Frantisek.

Dvorák, Jan. **Divadlo v akci.** Prague: Panorama, 1988. – 174 p., 48 p. of plates: ill. *Notes*: Includes bibliography (p. 156–74). History. 20th century.

Frejka, Jirí and Jirí Hájek. **Rezie jako projev prubojného ducha: výbor z teoretických studií a statí.** Prague: Divadelní ústav, 1980. – 166 p. *Notes*: 'Jirí Frejka v datech': p. 161–4. Production and direction. History. 20th century.

Goetz-Stankiewicz, Marketa. **The silenced theatre: Czech playwrights without a stage**. Toronto; Buffalo: University of Toronto Press, 1979. – xii, 319 p., 6 p. of plates: ill. *Notes*: Includes index. Bibliography: p. 301–6. Czech drama. 20th century. History and criticism.

Hájek, Jirí. **Divadlo na rozhraní.** Prague: Panorama, 1989 1988. – 271 p. *Notes*: Includes index. History. 20th century.

—— and Michaela Holznerová. **Divadlo nové doby: 1945–1948.** Prague: Panorama, 1990. – 505 p., 40 p. of plates: ill. *Notes*: Includes index. History. 20th century.

Havel, Václav and Vilém Precan. **Do ruzných stran: eseje a clánky z let 1983–1989.** Vyd. 2. (v CSSR 1). Prague: Lidové noviny, 1990. – 527 p. *Notes*: Bibliography (p. 475–88). Politics, theatre and government. 1968–1989.

Hedvábný, Zdenek. **Divadlo Vetrník.** Prague: Panorama, 1988. – 199 p., plates: ill. *Notes*: History. 20th century.

Jindra, Vladimír. **Soucasná scénografie.** Prague: Odeon, 1982. – 71 p.: ill. (some col.). *Notes*: Includes biographical sketches of artists-scenographers. Set designers. Biography. Czechoslovakia. History. 20th century.

Just, Vladimír. **Promeny malých scén: rozmluvy o vývoji a soucasné podobe ceských autorských divadel malých jevištních forem.** Prague: Mladá fronta, 1984. – 302 p.: ill. *Notes*: Bibliography:

p. 299–302. Actors. Dramatists. History. 20th century.

Nádvorníková, Marie. **Postavy ceského divadla: výberová bibliografie kniznich publikací a clánku z divadelního tisku 1945–1980**. Olomouc: Státní vedecká knihovna v Olomoucí, 1983. – 85 p. *Notes:* Bibliography of Czech theatre 1945–1980.

Ornest, Ota and Marie Valtrová. **Hraje vás tatínek jeste na housle?: rozhovor Marie Valtrové s Otou Ornestem**. Prague: Primus, 1993. – 388 p.: ill. *Notes:* Jews. Czechoslovakia/ Ornest, Ota.

Rampák, Zoltán. **Problémy a osobnosti**. Bratislava: Tatran, 1989. – 304 p. *Notes:* Includes indexes. Slovak drama. 20th century. History and criticism.

Vostrý, Jaroslav. **Drama a dnesek**. Prague: Ceskoslovenský spisovatel, 1990. – 97 p. *Notes:* Czech drama. 20th century. History and criticism.

Zach, Ales. **Knihy o divadle: soupis ceských publikací 1971–1980**. Prague: Divadelní ústav, 1986. – 108 p. *Notes:* Includes index. Czechoslovakia. History. Theatre. Bibliography.

A3a40. DENMARK

Ascani, Karen, ed. **Teatro danese nel novecento**. [Danish theatre in the twentieth century]. Biblioteca teatrale 41. Rome: Bulzoni, 1983. 125 p.

Blum, Jacques. **Teaterliv I København**. [Theatre life in Copenhagen]. Copenhagen: Tiderne skifter, 1989.

Brostrøm, Torben and Jens Kistrup. **Dansk Litteraturhistorie**. [History of Danish literature]. Vol. 6. Copenhagen: Politiken, 1977.

—— and Mette Winge. **Danske digtere i det 20 århundrede**. [Danish writers in the twentieth century]. Copenhagen: Gad, 1982.

Dam, Birgitte and Mads Laursen Vig. **90'ernes teater: tendenser i dansk teater og dramatik**. Halvfemsernes teater. Copenhagen: Dansklærerforeningen: Arte, 1993. – 53 p.: ill. *Notes:* Danish drama. 20th century. History and criticism.

Fazakerley, Susan and Kirsten Sylvest. **Teaterliv i halvfemsernes Danmark**. Åarhus: Klim, 1994. – 124 p.: ill., maps. *Notes:* Includes bibliography references (p. 114–15). History. 20th century.

Harsløf, Olav. **Frihed på gaflen!: teater i Danmark fra 1960'erne til 1980'erne**. Copenhagen: Statens Teaterskole, 1993. – 93 p. History. 20th century.

International Theatre Institute. **Teater i Danmark**. [Theatre in Denmark]. Yearbook. Copenhagen: Danish Centre of the International Theatre Institute, 1965–92.

Jensen, Stig Jarl, Kela Kvam and Ulla Strømberg. **Dansk teater i 60erne og 70erne: en artikelsamling**. Copenhagen: Borgen, 1983. – 214 p.: ill. *Notes:* History. 20th century.

Kistrup, Jens and Hans Bendix. **Teatret**. Copenhagen: Bikubenfonden, 1985. – 143 p.: ill. *Notes:* Theatre reviews.

—— and Niels Birger Wamberg. **Kistrups teater: et udvalg af 40 års teaterbetragtninger**. Copenhagen: Gyldendal, 1985. – 110, 15 p.: ill. *Notes:* Includes index. Reviews/Theatre.

Kragh-Jacobsen, Svend. **Teatermosaik**. [Theatre mosaic]. Copenhagen: Lademann, 1979.

Kvam, Kela, Janne Risum and Jytte Wiingaard, eds. **Dansk theaterhistorie**. [History of Danish theatre]. 2 vols. Copenhagen: Gyldenal, 1992.

Lindorff, Hanne. **Femten års danske kvindelige dramatikere, 1968–1984: fortegnelse over deres produktion**. Copenhagen: Forlaget KVINFO, 1984. – ix, 61 p. *Notes:* Includes index. Danish women dramatists. Bibliography.

Ludvigsen, Chr, Kaj Nissen, Erik Thygesen and Kristen Bjørnkjær. **Dramatiker!: en rapport om teaterarbejde**. Copenhagen: Tiderne skrifter, 1981. 185 p. *Notes:* Dramatists, Danish. 20th century.

Lundqvist, Britta. **Teatret til venstre: politisk teater i Danmark**. Copenhagen: Fremad, 1984. – 87 p.: ill. *Notes:* Includes index. Bibliography: p. 86. Political aspects. Workers' theatre. Agitprop theatre.

Rask, Elin. **Trolden med de tre hovedor: Det Kongelige Teater siden 1870, bygningshistorisk og kulturpolitisk**. [The troll with three heads: the Royal Theatre since 1870]. Copenhagen: Akademisk forlag, 1980.

—— and Leif Tuxen. **Ej blot til lyst – også en arbejdsplads. Det Kongelige Teater foer og efter ombygningen**. [Not only for pleasure – also a working place. The Royal Theatre before and after the rebuilding]. Lyngby: Dansk historisk håndbogsforlag, 1987.

Wamberg, Niels Birger. **Teatret på farten: Det Danske teater 1963–88**. Copenhagen: Danske teater, 1988. – 63 p.: ill. *Notes:* Danske teater (Copenhagen). History.

Wiingaard, Jytte. **Dansk teater efter Artaud: en essaysamling om dansk teater 1975–1995**. Grasten: DRAMA, 1995. – 111 p.: ill. *Notes:* Danish drama after Artaud.

A3a41. DJIBOUTI

Andrzejewski, B.W. 'Modern and traditional aspects of Somali drama'. **Folklore in the modern world** (1987): 87–101.

Bliese, Loren F. 'Afar songs'. **Northeast African studies** 4 no. 3 (1982–3): 51–76.

Morin, Didier. **Contes de Djibouti**. [Tales from Djibouti]. Paris: Edicef, 1980. 170 p.

Moumin, Hassan Sheikh. **Leopard among the women: Shabeelnaagood – a Somali play**. Translated by B.W. Andrzejewski. London: Oxford University Press, 1974. 230 p.

Schraeder, Peter J. **Djibouti: Bibliography**. Oxford: Clio Press, 1991.

A3a42. DOMINICAN REPUBLIC

Aguilera-Malta, Demetrio. 'A propósito del teatro en la República Dominica'. [Theatre in the Dominican Republic]. **Bulletin of the Pan American Union** 81 no. 12 (December 1947): 679–83.

Bonelly de Díaz, Aida. 'El teatro nacional en Santo Domingo'. [The National Theatre in Santa Domingo]. **Bohio Dominicano** 25 (1973): 2–18.

Goico Castro, Manuel de Jesús. **Raíz y trayectoria del teatro en la literatura nacional**. [Roots and evolution of the theatre in national literature]. Santo Domingo: Anales de la Universidad de Santo Domingo, 1945.

Grupo Teatro El Gratey. **Panorama del teatro dominicano**. [Panorama of Dominican theatre]. Santo Domingo: Editorial Corripio, 1984.

Henríquez Ureña, Max. **Panorama histórico de la literatura dominicana**. [Historical panorama of Dominican literature]. 2nd edn. Santo Domingo: Librería Dominicana, 1966.

Lockwood, Jaime A. **Teatro dominicano: pasado y presente**. [Dominican theatre: past and present]. Ciudad Trujillo: Editorial la Nación, 1959.

Molinaza, José. **Historia crítica del teatro dominicano**. [A critical history of Dominican theatre]. 2 vols. Santo Domingo: Editora Universitaria, Universidad Autónoma de Santo Domingo, 1984.

Reyes, Ramón E. 'El tema universal y la libertad en el teatro dominicano actual'. [Freedom and other universal themes in contemporary Dominican theatre]. **Revista Aula** 20 (1972).

Reynolds, Bonnie Hildebrand. 'La semiótica y la supervivencia en **Cordón unbilical** de Arturo Rodríguez Fernández'. [Semiotics and survival in **Umbilical Cord** by Arturo Rodríguez Fernández]. **Gestos** 12 no. 1 (November 1991): 85–95.

Sánchez, Federico. **El teatrodominicano en su historia**. [History of Dominican theatre]. Colección Antológica. Santo Domingo: Nuestra Voz, 1986.

A3a43. ECUADOR

Barrera, Isaac J. **Historia de la Literatura ecuatoriana**. [History of Ecuadoran literature]. Quito: Libresa, 1979. 1, 317 p.

Barriga López, Franklin, and Leonardo Barriga López. **Diccionario de la literatura ecuatoriana**. [A dictionary of Ecuadoran literature]. Quito: Casa de la Cultura Ecuatoriana, 1973. 780 p.

Chávez Franco, Modesto. 'El teatro en Guayaquil'. [Theatre in Guayaquil]. In **Guayaquil '70, Metrópolis Dinámica**. [Guayquil '70: a dynamic metropolis], ed. Demetrio Aguilera Malta. Quito: Imprenta Fray Jadoco Ricke, 1970.

Descalzi, Ricardo. **Historia crítica del teatro ecuatoriano**. [A critical essay of Ecuadorian theatre]. 6 vols. Quito: Casa de la Cultura Ecuatoriana, 1968.

Estrella, Ulises. 'El teatro en el Ecuador'. [Theatre in Ecuador]. **Nivel** 10 (October 1963): 5.

——. 'El teatro obrero en el Ecuador'. [Working-class theatre in Ecuador]. **Conjunto** (October 1969): 117–20.

Luzuriaga, Gerardo. **Bibliografía del teatro ecuatoriano, 1900–1982**. Quito: Edit. Casa de la Cultura Ecuatoriana, 1984. – 131 p. Ecuadorian drama. 20th century. History and criticism. Bibliography.

——. 'La generación del 60 y el teatro'. [The generation of the 1960s and the theatre]. UTIEH/C 34 (1980): 157–70.

A3a44. EGYPT

'Abd al-Qadir, Farouk. **Misahah lil-daw', misahat lil-zilal: a'mal fi al-naqd al-masrahi, 67–77**. Cairo: Dar al-Thaqafah al-Jadidah, 1986. – 370 p. **Notes**: History of Egyptian theatrical criticism.

——. **Ru'á al-waqi'– wa-humum al-thawrah al-muhasarah–: dirasat fi al-masrah al-mu'asir**. Beirut: Dar al-Adab, 1990. – 231 p. **Notes**: Arabic drama. 20th century. History and criticism. Focus on Egypt.

Abdel Wahab, Farouk. **Modern Egyptian drama: an anthology**. Minneapolis: Bibliotheca Islamica, 1974. 493 p.

'Abduh, Ayman Labib. **Muhammad Taymur,**

ra'id al-masrah al-ijtima'i. Cairo: Maktabat al-Adab, 1993. – 109 p. Egyptian dramatist Taymur, Muhammad, 1892–1921.

Abou-Saif, Laila. **A bridge through time: a memoir**. London: Quartet, 1986. – 282 p. *Notes*: Originally published: New York: Summit Books, 1985. Autobiography.

——. **The theatre of Naguib al-Rihaani: the development of comedy in Egypt**. Dissertation, University of Illinois: 1968.

Abu Ghazi, Nadiyah Badr al-Din. **Qadiyat al-hurriyah fi al-masrah al-Misri al-mu'asir, 1952–1967**. Cairo: al-Hay'ah al-Misriyah al-'Ammah lil-Kitab, 1989. – 375 p. *Notes*: Originally presented as the author's thesis (master's)–Jami'at al-Qahirah, 1984. Includes bibliographical references (p. 370–373). Arabic drama. 20th century. History and criticism. Politics and literature.

Abyad, Soad. **George Abyad**. Cairo: Egyptian Book Organization (1970). In Arabic.

el-Alem, Mahmoud Amin. **Tawfiq al-Hakïm: intellect and artist**. Cairo: Egyptian Book Organization, 1982. In Arabic.

el-Alemay, Adel. **The Zar ritual and ritual theatre**. Cairo: Egyptian Book Organization (1993). In Arabic.

Armbrust, Walter. **Mass culture and modernism in Egypt**. Cambridge and New York: Cambridge University Press, 1996. 291 p.

'Ashri, Jalal. **Thaqafat hadha al-'asr**. Cairo: al-Hay'ah al-Misriyah al-'Ammah lil-Kitab, 1987. – 191 p. *Notes*: Essays. Arabic literature. Egypt. History and criticism.

el-Ashry, Ahmed. **The hero in the theatre of the sixties**. Cairo: Egyptian Book Organization, 1992. In Arabic.

el-Ashry, Gala. **Theatre: mother of the arts**. Cairo: Egyptian Book Organization. In Arabic.

'Ashur, Nu'man. **'Alam al-masrah**. Cairo: Jumhuriyat Misr al-'Arabiyah: Dar al-Mawqif al-'Arabi, 1985. – 291 p. Arabic drama. Egypt. History and criticism.

Awad, Ramsis. **Bibliographic encyclopedia of the Egyptian theatre**. Cairo: Egyptian Book Organization. In Arabic.

Awbalhi, Samirah and Zaydan Ibn, 'Abd al-Rahman. **al-Shakhsiyat al-turathiyah fi masrah al-Sayyid Hafiz: wazifatuha al-fanniyah wa-al-fikriyah**. Beirut: al-Iskandariyah: Dar Azal; Markaz al-Watan al-'Arabi, 1990. – 125 p. *Notes*: Includes bibliography (p. 119–22). Sayyid Hafiz. Stage history.

Bedaur, Muhammad Mustafá. **Modern Arabic drama in Egypt**. Cambridge: Cambridge University Press, 1987. – viii, 246 p. *Notes*: Includes index. Bibliography: p. 231–9. History and criticism.

Budayr, Hilmi. **Ru'yat al-waqi' fi al-masrah al-Misri al-hadith, 1850–1970**. Misr al-Jadidah [Cairo]: Kuwin Brint, 1990. – 134 p. *Notes*: Includes bibliography (p. 129–32). Arabic drama. History and criticism.

Dawara, Fouad. **The theatre of Tawfiq al-Hakïm**. Cairo: Egyptian Book Organization. In two volumes (1984 and 1986). In Arabic.

Dawood, Abdel Ghany. **Zaki Tulaymat**. Cairo: Egyptian Book Organization (1997). In Arabic.

Dawwarah, Fu'ad. **al-Masrah al-Misri, 1989**. Cairo: al-Hay'ah al-Misriyah al-'Ammah lil-Kitab, 1992. – 427 p. *Notes*: Theatre. History. 20th century.

Egyptian one-act plays. Translated by Denys Johnson-Davies. Passeggiata Press, 1981.

Ethman, Ahmed. **Classical sources of the theatre of Tawfiq al-Hakïm**. Cairo: Harib, 1978. In Arabic.

Fi masrah al-Sayyid Hafiz: dirasat. Cairo: Maktabat Madbuli, 1988. – 2 vols. *Notes*: Includes bibliography (p. 90–1). Sayyid Hafiz. Stage history.

Ghany, Mostafa Abdel. **Egyptian theatre in the eighties**. Cairo: Egyptian Book Organization, 1984. In Arabic.

al-Hakïm, Tawfiq. **Theatrical form**. Cairo: Egyptian Book Organization, 1968. In Arabic.

Hamada, Ibrahim. **The shadow play and the Ibn Daniel plays**. Cairo: Egyptian Book Organization. 1961.

Hammouda, Abdel Aziz. **The political theatre**. Cairo: Egyptian Book Organization, 1971. In Arabic.

Ibrahim, Munir Muhammad. **Min ruwad al-masrah al-Misri**. Cairo: al-Hay'ah al-Misriyah al-'Ammah lil-Kitab, 1986. – 149 p. *Notes*: Includes bibliography (p. 143–8). Arabic drama. History and criticism. Actors. Biography.

Isma'il, 'Abd al-Mun'im. **Drama and society in contemporary Egypt**. Cairo: Dar al-Katib al-'Arabi lil-Tiba'a wal-Nashr, 1967. – 210 p. *Notes*: Bibliography: p. 204–10. Egypt. 20th century. History and criticism. Arabic drama.

Ismail, Said Ali. **History of the Egyptian theatre in the nineteenth century**. Cairo: Egyptian Book Organization, 1997. In Arabic.

Kader, Farouk Abdul. **The rise and fall of the Egyptian theatre**. Cairo: Egyptian Book Organization. In Arabic.

Khashaba, Samy. **Contemporary theatrical issues**. Cairo: Dar El Maarif. In Arabic.

Landau, Jack M. **Studies in the Arab theatre and cinema**. Cairo: Egyptian Book Organization and Philadelphia: University of Pennsylvania Press, 1958. In English and Arabic.

Lirola Delgado, Pilar. **Aproximación al teatro egipcio moderno**. Granada: Grupo de Investigación Estudios Arabes Contemporáneos, Universidad de Granada, 1990. – 155 p. Notes: Includes bibliographical references (p. 125–43) and indexes. Theatre. Egypt. Arab countries. In Spanish.

Muhammad, Hayat Jasim. **Experimental drama in Egypt, 1960–1970, with reference to Western influence**. 1978. – viii, 328 p. Notes: Vita. Bibliography: p. 303–22. Thesis (Ph. D.) –Indiana University, 1978. Microfilm. Ann Arbor, Mich.: University Microfilms International, 1978. 1 microfilm reel; 35 mm.

Munir, Samy. **The Egyptian theatre after World War II**. Cairo: Egyptian Book Organization, 1978. In Arabic.

Nieuwkerke, Karinvan. **A trade like any other: female singers and dancers in Egypt**. Austin: University of Texas Press, 1995. 226 p.

Raghib, Nabil. **Alfred Faraj's theatre language**. Cairo: Egyptian Book Organization, 1985. In Arabic.

——. **Nu'man 'Ashur's theatre art**. Cairo: Egyptian Book Organization, 1982. In Arabic.

——. **Rashad Rushdie's dramatic art**. Cairo: Egyptian Book Organization, 1987. In Arabic.

——. **The theatre of social transformations**. Cairo: Egyptian Book Organization, 1990. In Arabic.

el-Refai, Mohamed. **Palestine and the Egyptian theatre**. Cairo: Egyptian Book Organization, 1995. In Arabic.

——. **A wagon called theatre**. Cairo: Egyptian Book Organization, 1997. In Arabic.

Sadgrove, Philip. **The Egyptian theatre in the nineteenth century: 1799–1882**. Reading, Berkshire: Centre for Middle Eastern and Islamic Studies, University of Durham, Ithica Press, 1996. 214 p.

Sakhsukh, Ahmed. **Qadaya al-masrah al-Misri al-mu'asir**. Cairo: Hay'ah al-'Ammah li-Qusur al-Thaqafah, 1993. – 225 p. History. 20th century.

——. **al-Masrah al-Misri fi muftaraq al-turuq: ru'yah jadidah**. [Egyptian theatre at the crossroads]. Cairo: Egyptian Book Organization, 1995. – 236 p.: ill. Notes: On the Egyptian theatre, from the 1970s. Drama. History and criticism.

Saqr, Muhammad 'Abd al-Salam Ibrahim. **Fi al-adab al-masrahi al-mu'asir fi Misr**. Cairo: Matba'at al-Amanah, 1991. – 207 p. Notes: Includes bibliographical references (p. 201–5). Arabic drama. 20th century. History and criticism. Theatre. Egypt.

Sarhan, Samir. **al-Masrah al-mu'asir**. Cairo: al-Hay'ah al-Misriyah al-'Ammah lil-Kitab, 1987. – 210 p.: ill. Arabic drama. Egypt. History and criticism.

Soleiha, Nehad. **Egyptian theatre**. Cairo: Egyptian Book Organization, 1993. In Arabic.

——. **Theatre: between art and intellect**. Cairo: Egyptian Book Organization, 1985. In Arabic.

Sulayhah, Nihad. **Egyptian theatre: a diary, 1990–1992**. Cairo: General Egyptian Book Organization Press, 1993. – 361 p. Theatre. Egypt. History. 20th century. In English.

——. **Umsiyat masrahiyah**. Cairo: al-Hay'ah al-Misriyah al-'Ammah lil-Kitab, 1987. – 255 p.: ill. Notes: Theatre. Egypt. History. 20th century.

Ubilhi, Samirah. **al-Shakhsiyat al-turathiyah fi masrah al-Sayyid Hafiz: wazifatuha al-fanniyah wa-al-fikriyah**. Alexandria: Ru'ya, 1988. – 119 p. Notes: Includes bibliographical references (p. 100–4). Theatre. Egypt. History. Sayyid Hafiz.

'Umar, Mustafá 'Ali. **al-Sira' al-siyasi fi al-masrah al-Misri fi marhalat al-sittiniyat, 1960–1969**. Cairo: Dar al-Ma'arif, 1984. – 11, 236 p. Notes: Bibliography: p. 223–9. Arabic drama. Egypt. Politics and government.

Zaki, Ahmed. **The theatre: a face and a mask**. Cairo: Egyptian Book Organization, 1988. In Arabic.

A3a45. EL SALVADOR

Armijo, Roberto. 'El teatro y la lucha de liberación nacional en El Salvado' [Theatre and the struggle for national liberation in El Salvador]. **Conjunto** 52 (April-June 1982): 129–32.

Barbero, Edmundo. 'Breve historia del teatro universitario'. [A short history of university theatre]. **Caracol** 1, no. 1 (August 1974): 23–4.

——, ed. **Panorama del teatro en El Salvado**. [An overview of theatre in El Salvador]. 5 vols. San Salvador: Editorial Universitaria, 1972. 564 p.

Campos, Menjívar, Juan Francisco. **La dominación cultural y su influencia en el teatro** salvadoreño. [Cultural domination and its influence in Salvadoran theatre]. Colección Tesario. San Salvador: Departamento de Letras, Universidad de El Salvado, 1984.

Cea, José Roberto. 'Del teatro en El Salvado: panorama histórico crítico'. [On theatre in El Salvador: a historical and critical view]. **Cuadernos de Investigación Teatral** 6 (1979): 1–14.

Gallegos Valdés, Luis. **El teatro en El Salvador**. [Theatre in El Salvador]. San Salvador: Ediciones Bellas Artes, 1961.

Lindo, Hugo. 'Jóvenes dramaturgos de El Salvador'. [Young Salvadoran playwrights]. **Estudios Centro Americanos** 15, no. 154 (November 1960): 584–91.

——. 'Literatura dramática en El Salvador'. [Dramatic literature in El Salvador]. **Cultura Hispánica** 1, no. 3 (July–September 1967): 3–50.

Menén Desleal, Alvaro. 'Historia del teatro en El Salvador: José Emilio Aragón y Luigi Pirandello, posibilidad de un paralelismo imposible'. [History of theatre in El Salvador: José Emilio Aragón and Luigi Pirandello, the possibility of an impossible similarity]. **Cultura** 35 (January–March 1965): 31–4.

Ministerio de Cultura. **El teatro. Historia informal del mismo a través de lo anecdótico y pintoresco**. [An unofficial history of theatre through anecdotes and the picturesque]. San Salvador: Departamento Editorial del Ministerio de Cultura, 1956. 586 p.

Salomón, Roberto. 'Theatre in El Salvador during the eighties'. **Latin America Theatre Review** 25, no. 2 (spring 1992): 173–80.

A3a46. ESTONIA

Aalak, Ivi, Kiullike Tokhver and L.R. Levina. **Estonskii teatr: annotirovannyi ukazatel' bibliograficheskikh i spravochnykh materialov, 1945–1985**. Tallinn: Gos. tsentr. teatral'naia biblioteka: Gos. biblioteka ESSR im. Fr. R. Kreitsval'da, 1986. – 69 p. Notes: Russian and Estonian. Estonian 20th century theatre. Bibliography.

Adson, Artur. **Das estnische Theater**. [Estonian theatre]. Tartu: Akadeemiline Kooperatiiv, 1933. 64 p.

——. **Teatriraamat**. [Theatre book]. Stockholm: Vaba Eesti, 1958. 230 p.

Einas, H. and Eneken Priks. **Kes lavastavad Eesti teatrites?** Tallinn: Eesti Lavastajate Liit, 1997. – 184 p.: ill. Notes: Theatrical producers and directors.

Haan, Kalju. **Karl Menning ja teater 'Vanemuine'**. Tallinn: Eesti Raamat, 1987. – 286 p. Notes: Tartu. History. Biography/ Menning, Karl, 1874–1941/'Vanemuine' (Theatre). History.

Heinpau, Andres and Rita Hillermaa. **Eesti kirjandus ja teatr XX sajandil**. Tallinn: Eesti Rahvusraamatukogu: Eesti Teatriliit, 1990. Notes: Estonian literature. 20th century. Bibliography.

Järv, Ants. **Väliseestlaste teater ja draama**. [Estonian theatre and drama in exile]. Tartu: Tartu Ülikool, 1991. 198 p.

Kalmet, Leo. **Pool sajandit teatriteed**. Tallinn: Eesti Raamat, 1982. – 285 p., 33 p. of plates: ill. Notes: Includes index. Theatrical producers and directors. Kalmet, Leo. 1900–.

Kask, Karin. **Eesti nõukogude teater 1940–1965: sõnalavastus**. Tallinn: Eesti Raamat, 1987. – 591 p., 80 p. of plates: ill. Notes: Includes bibliographies. Estonia. History. 20th century.

——. **Shakespeare eesti teatris**. [Shakespeare in the Estonian theatre]. Tallinn: Eesti Riiklik Kirjastus, 1964. 274 p.

——. **Teatritegijad, alustajad: Eesti teatrilugu kuni 1917**. [Theatre-makers, initiators: history of Estonian theatre till 1917]. Tallinn: Eesti Raamat, 1970. 264 p.

——, Lea Tormis and Vilma Paalma. **Estonskii teatr**. Moscow: Iskusstvo, 1978. – 277 p., 64 p. of plates: ill. Notes: Includes index. History. 20th century. In Russian.

Kuusberg, Paul. **Tänan tähelepanu eest!** Tallinn: Eesti Raamat, 1988. – 213 p. Notes: Includes bibliographical references (p. 211–12). Interviews.

Matt, Frits. **Eesti teatro lavapilt**. [Stage design in the Estonian theatre]. Tallinn: Kunst, 1969. 180 p.

Paalma, Vilma, Merike Vaitmaa and Uno Heinapuu, eds. **'Estonia' lauluteatri rajajaid**. [Founders of the 'Estonia' Music Theatre]. Talinn: ENSV Teatriühing & Eesti Raamat, 1981. 308 p.

Panso, Voldemar and Endel Link. **Teatriartikleid: –kas see on eilne või tänane laul?** Tallinn: Eesti Raamat, 1980. – 359 p., 32 p. of plates: ill. Notes: Bibliography: p. 348–57.

Semper, Johannes. **Teater iseseisva kunstialana: artikleid ja esseid**. Tallinn: Eesti Raamat, 1992. – 203 p.: ill. Notes: Includes bibliographical references (p. 197–9) and index. Biography. History.

Sikk, Rein. **Viiskümmend aastat Rakvere Teatrit**. Tallinn: Eesti Põllumajanduse Infokeskus, 1990. – 67 p.: ill. *Notes*: Rakvere Teater. History.

Tormis, Lea. **Eesti teater 1920–1940**. [Estonian theatre 1920–40]. Tallinn: Eesti Raamat, 1978. 504 p.

Valgemae, Mardi. **Ikka teatrist mõteldes: esseid, päevikukatkendeid ja arvustusi**. Stockholm: Välis-Eesti & EMP, 1990. – 188 p., 14 p. of plates: ill. *Notes*: 20th century dramatists. History and criticism.

Viiding, Riina and Rein Heinsalu, eds. **Estonian theatre**. Tallinn: Estonian Theatre Union, 1989. 160 p.

A3a47. ETHIOPIA

Aklilu, Amsalu. **Acher Ye Ethiopia Sine-Tsehuf Tarik**. [A short history of Ethiopian culture]. Unpublished. Addis Ababa University, 1976.

Ashagre, Aboneh and Peter Harrop. **A preliminary investigation of dramatic elements within traditional ceremonies among the Anuak, Majenger, Nuer and Shako nationalities of Illubabor Administrative Region, South Western Ethiopia**. Report prepared for the Research and Publication Office of Addis Ababa University. Addis Ababa: Department of Theatre Arts, Addis Ababa University, 1984.

Gebeyehu, Tamirat. **Ye Leb Woled Serawochen Be Tenetenet Sele Makenaber**. [Adapting creative works for the stage]. Unpublished. Theatre Arts Department, Addis Ababa University, 1989.

Gessesse, Tesfaye. **Acher Ye Ethiopia Theatre Tenat: Kemegemeriyaw Eske Kebede Mikael**. [A short study of Ethiopia theatre: from the beginning to Kebede Michael]. Proceedings of the Third International Conference of Ethiopian Studies. Addis Ababa: Institute of Ethiopian Studies, Haile Selassie University (Addis Ababa University), 1996.

Leiris, Michel. **La possessione e i suoi aspetti teatrali tra gli Etiopi di Gondar**. [Possession and its theatrical aspects among the Ethiopians of Gondar]. Milan: Ubulibri, 1988. 86 p.

Levine, Donald. **Wax and gold: tradition and innovation in Ethiopian culture**. Chicago and London: University of Chicago Press, 1965.

Mantel-Nieóko, Joanna. 'Ethiopian Literature in Amharic'. In **Literatures in African languages: theoretical issues and sample surveys**, eds. B.W. Andrzejewski, S. Pilaszewicz and W. Tyloch. Cambridge and New York: Cambridge University Press, 1985. 672 p.

Marcus, Harold. **A History of Ethiopia**. Berkeley, Los Angeles and London: University of California Press, 1994.

Messing, Simon D. 'A modern Ethiopia play: self-finding in culture change'. **Anthropological Quarterly** 33 (1960): 149–57.

Plastow, Jane. **Ethiopia: the creation of a theatre culture**. Manchester: University of Manchester Press, 1989.

Ullendorf, Edward. **The Ethiopians: an introduction to country and people**. Oxford: Oxford University Press, 1960.

Zewde, Bahru. **A history of modern Ethiopia: 1855–1974**. Addis Ababa: Addis Ababa University Press, 1992.

A3a48. FINLAND

Ahlfors, Bengt. **Stigzeliuska rummet: dagbok från Svenska Teatern**. Helsinki: Söderström, 1980. – 189, 1 p. *Notes*: Ahlfors, Bengt. Diaries.

Al'tshuller, A. IA. **Russko-finskie teatral'nye sviazi: sbornik nauchnykh trudov**. Leningrad: LGITMiK, 1989. – 144 p. *Notes*: Summary and table of contents in English. Includes bibliographical references. Theatre. Soviet Union. Finland. History. 20th century.

Bandler, Vivica and Carita Backström. **Adressaten okänd**. Helsinki: Schildt, 1992. – 277 p.: ill. *Notes*: Theatrical directors. Biography. Bandler, Vivica, 1917–.

Commondt, Bjarne. **Roospiggar, Frontteater, Landsteater**. Jakobstad: Jakobstads tryckeri och tidnings AB:s förlag, 1981. – 235 p.: ill. *Notes*: Theatre and the war. Theatrical managers. Biography Commondt, Bjarne, 1911–.

Esittelevä näytelmäluettelo. Helsinki: TNL, 1981. – 124 p. Drama. Stories, plots, etc.

Finnish theatre today. Helsinki: Finnish Centre of the International Theatre Institue, 1971. 71 p.

Heikkilä, Ritva. **Sata vuotts suomalaista teatteria**. [A hundred years of Finnish theatre]. Helsinki: Central Organization of Finnish Theatre Associations, 1972.

Hyvönen, Annikki. **Eino Kalima Tsehov-ohjaajana**. Helsinki: Suomalaisen Kirjallisuuden Seura, 1986. – 188 p., 16 p. of plates: ill. *Notes*: Summary in English. Bibliography: p. 168–79. Chekhov, Anton Pavlovich, 1860–1904. Finnish production history.

Kalemaa, Kalevi. **Tuommoisia ja tämmöisiä: Roineen teatterisuvun vaiheita**. Porvoo: Söderström, 1995. – 455 p.: ill. *Notes*: Includes bibliographical references and index. History. Roine, Eero, 1904–66.

Koski, Pirkko. **Kansan teatteri**. [People's theatre]. 2 vols. Porvoo: Helsingin Teaterisäätiö, 1987.

—— and Kari Salosaari. **Suomalaisen näytelmän- ja teatterintutkimuksen bibliografia vuoteen 1974**. Tampere: Tampereen yliopisto, 1976. – 142 p. *Notes*: Summary in English. Includes index. Finnish drama. History and criticism. Bibliography.

Koskimies, Rafael. **Suomen kansallisteatteri 1902–50**. [The Finnish National Theatre 1902–50]. 2 vols. Helsinki: Otava, 1953, 1972.

Niemi, Irmeli and Raija Ojala. **Suomalainen alueteatteri 1978–82: tausta, toiminta, vaikutus**. Helsinki: Valtion painatuskeskus, 1983. – 3, 505, 41 p.: ill., 12 maps. *Notes*: Bibliography: p. 506–16. *Subjects*: Theatre history.

Orsmaa, Taisto-Bertil. **Teatterimme kääne. Ekspressionismi suomalaisessa teatterissa**. [The turning point of Finnish theatre. Expressionism in the Finnish theatre]. Helsinki: Gaudeamus, 1976.

Paavolainen, Pentti. **Teatteri ja suuri muutto Ohjelmistot sosiaalisen murroksen osana 1959–1971: Suomen Teatterijärjestöjen Kekusliiton 50-vuotisjuhlakirja**. Helsinki: Kustannus Oy Teatteri, 1992. – 324 p.: ill. *Notes*: Includes bibliographical references (p. 273–90) and index. Theatre and society. Drama.

Rantamäki, Leena. **Teatteri- ja tanssitaiteen bibliografia: Suomessa 1975–1991**. [Bibliography of theatre and dance: literature published in Finland, 1975–1991]. Helsinki: Teatterikorkeakoulu, 1993. – 496 p. *Notes*: Preface, foreword, and table of contents also in English and Swedish. Includes indexes.

Savutie, Maija. **Finnish theatre: a northern part of world theatre**. Translated by Philip Binham. Helsinki: Finnish Centre of the International Theatre Institute, 1980.

——. **Kohti elävää teatteria**. [Towards living theatre]. Helsinki: Teatterikorkeakoulu – Valtion painatuskeskus, 1986.

Tiusanen, Timo. **Teatterimme hahmottuu**. [Our theatre takes shape]. Helsinki: Kirjayhtymä, 1969.

A3a49. FRANCE

Abirached, Robert. **La Crise du personnage dans le théâtre moderne**. [The crisis of character in modern drama]. Paris: Grasset, 1978. 400 p.

Adamov, Arthur. **Ici et maintenant**. [Here and now]. Paris: Gallimard, 1964. 250 p.

Arnott, Peter D. **An introduction to the French theatre**. London: Macmillan, 1977. 164 p. *Note*: A history of French theatre practice.

Aslan, Odette. **'Patrice Chéreau': Les Voies de la création théâtrale**, vol. XII. Paris: CNRS, 1986. Amiens: Trois Cailloux/MC Amiens, 1983. 237 p.

——. **Roger Blin**. Cambridge: Cambridge University Press, 1988. – ill. *Series*: Directors in perspective. *Notes*: Includes bibliography and index.

Asor Rosa, Alberto and Roger Pillaudin, eds. **Dialogues franco-italiens**. Paris: France-Culture, 1979. – 297 p. *Notes*: Que peuvent les intellectuels?/Jacques Julliard, Alberto Asor-Rosa – Evolution des valeurs depuis 1968/François Chatelet, Franco Ferrarotti – Les femmes et la créativité/Viviane Forrester, Dacia Maraini – Luttes ouvrières et chômage/Jacques Chereque, Bruno Trentin – Energies nouvelles/Jacques Varet, Felice Ippolito – Théâtre d'acteurs, théâtre d'auteurs/Antoine Vitez, Dario Fo – Psychiatrie et politique/Roger Gentis, Franco Basaglia – Le poids du passé dans nos deux pays/Gérard Vincent, Maria-Antonietta Macciocchi – L'opéra/Bernard Lefort, Paolo Grassi – Le monde catholique dans nos deux pays/Francesco Traniello, Philippe Levillain.

Auclaire-Tamaroff, Elisabeth. **Jean-Marie Serreau, découvreur de théâtres**. Paris: L'Arbre Verdoyant, 1986. – 224 p.: ill. *Notes*: Theatrical producers and directors. Biography. Serreau, Jean-Marie, 1915–73.

Bablet, D. and M.L. Bablet. **Le Théâtre du Soleil ou la quête du bonheur**. [The Théâtre du Soleil or the quest for happiness]. Paris: CNRS, 1979.

—— and J. Jacquot, eds. 'Théâtre du Soleil, Shakespeare, Arden, Beckett'. In **Les Voies de la création théâtrale** (Vol. V). Paris: CNRS, 1977. 456 p.

Balazard, Simone. **Le Guide du théâtre**. Paris: Syros-Alternatives, 1989. – 167 p.: ill. *Notes*: Includes bibliographical references.

Banu, Georges. **Le Théâtre: sortie de secours**. [Theatre: emergency exit]. Paris: Aubier, 1984.

——. **Le Théâtre ou l'instant habité**. [Theatre or the peopled minute]. Paris: L'Herne, 1992.

Barrault, Jean Louis. **Reflections on the theatre**. Hyperion reprint edn. Westport, Conn.: Hyperion Press, 1979, 1951. – xi, 185 p., 4 p. of plates: ill. *Notes*: Translation of **Réflexions sur le théâtre**. Reprint of the 1951 edn. published by Rockliff, London. Includes index. Biography/Barrault, Jean Louis.

Barthes, Roland. **Sur Racine**. Paris: Seuil, 1963.

Bensky, Roger Daniel. **Le Masque foudroyé: lecture traversière du théâtre français actuel**. Saint-Genouph: Librairie Nizet, 1997. – 296 p. *Notes*: Includes bibliographical references. Stage-setting and scenery.

Bishop, Tom. **From the Left Bank: reflections on the modern French theater and novel**. New York; London: New York University Press, 1997. – x, 298 p., 8 p. of ill. *Notes*: Includes index. French drama. 20th century. History and criticism.

Blin, Roger. **Souvenirs et propos**. [Remembrances and proposals]. Paris: Gallimard, 1986.

Bloch-Morhange, Lise and David Alper. **Artiste et métèque à Paris**. Paris: Éditions Buchet-Chastel, 1980. – 372 p.: ill. *Notes*: Interviews with 21 expatriate artists living in Paris. Fernando Arrabal – José Balmès et Gracia Barrios – Tahar Ben Jelloun – Julio Cortazar – Edgardo Cozarinsky – André Elbaz – Léonor Fini – Eugène Ionesco – Izis – Nacer Khemir – Milan Kundera – Jorge Lavelli – David Malkin – Raymond Mason – Henry Miller – Moshe Mizrahi – Roman Polanski – Serge Rezvani – Sidney Sokhona – Iannis Xenakis. Intellectual life/Paris.

Bradby, David. **Modern French drama, 1940–1990**. 2nd edn. Cambridge: Cambridge University Press, 1991. – xiii, 331 p.: ill. *Notes*: Rev. edn. of: **Modern French drama, 1940–1980**. 1984. Includes bibliographical references (p. 281–308) and index. Introduction: the inter-war years – The occupation – The Parisian theatre I: philosophical melodrama – The Parisian theatre II: the new theatre – The decentralized theatre I: the fifties – The decentralized theatre II: Planchon and Adamov – The decentralized theatre III: the sixties – Total theatre – La création collective – Playwrights of the seventies – The eighties. French drama. History.

Brown, Frederick. **Theatre and revolution: The culture of the French stage**. New York: Viking Press, 1980. 490 p.

Busson, Alain. **Le Théâtre en France: contexte socio-économique et choix esthétiques**. Paris: La Documentation française, 1986. – 140 p.: ill. *Notes*: Includes bibliographical references. Economic aspects.

Cadars, Pierre. **Gérard Philipe**. Paris: H. Veyrier, 1984. – 212 p.: ill. *Notes*: Discography: p. 211. Bibliography: p. 212. Biography/Philipe, Gérard, 1922–59.

Caracalla, Jean-Paul. **Lever de rideau: histoire des théâtres privés de Paris**. Paris: Denoël, 1994. – 160 p.: ill. (some col.). *Notes*: Includes bibliographical references (p. 160). Theatres. France. Paris. History. 20th century.

Chiari, Joseph. **The contemporary French theatre; the flight from naturalism**. New York: Gordian Press, 1970 1958. – vii, 242 p. *Notes*: Bibliography: p. 231–6. French drama. History and criticism.

Cohn, Ruby. **From Desire to Godot: pocket theater of postwar Paris**. Berkeley: University of California Press, 1987. – xiv, 204 p.: ill. *Notes*: 'Chronology of performances (with publication data)': p. 193–4. Includes index. Bibliography: p. 181–192. Experimental theatre, history.

Conradie, Pieter Jacobus. **The treatment of Greek myths in modern French drama; a study of the 'classical' plays of Anouilh, Cocteau, Giraudoux, and Sartre**. South Africa, 1963. 100 p. *Notes*: Bibliography: p. 100. French drama. 20th century.

Copfermann, Emile. **Vers un théâtre différent**. [Towards a different theatre]. Paris: F. Maspero, 1976. – 190 p. *Notes*: Includes bibliographical references. Experimental theatre.

Corvin, Michel. **Le Théâtre de boulevard**. Paris: Presses universitaires de France, 1989. – 127 p. *Notes*: Includes bibliographical references (p. 126). French drama. 20th century. History and criticism.

——. **Le Théâtre nouveau en France**. [New French theatre]. 7th revised edn. Paris: Presses universitaires de France, 1995, 1963. – 127 p. *Notes*: Bibliography p. 126–7. French drama. 20th century. History and criticism.

——. **Molière et ses metteurs en scène d'aujourd'hui**. [Molière and his directors today]. Lyon: University of Lyon Press, 1985.

Darcante, Jean. **Théâtre, la grande aventure**. Paris: Editions du Sorbier, 1985. – 315 p., 16 p. of plates: ill. *Notes*: Biography. Long-time Secretary-General of the International Theatre Institute recalls his years in theatre.

Delft, Louis van. **Le Théâtre en feu: le grand jeu du théâtre contemporain**. Tübingen: G. Narr, 1997. – 115 p. *Notes*: Includes bibliographical references. French drama. 20th century.

Deshoulières, Christophe. **Le Théâtre au XXe siècle**. Paris: Bordas, 1990 1989. – 223 p.: ill. *Notes*: French drama. 20th century.

Dort, Bernard. **Le Représentation émancipée**. [Performance comes of age]. Arles: Actes-Sud, 1988. 184 pp

——, *et al*. **Avignon: quarante ans de festival.**

[Avignon: forty years of a festival]. Paris: Hachette/Avignon Festival, 1987. 235 p.

——. **Théâtre réel, 1964–1970**. Paris: Éditions du Seuil, 1971, 1964. – 301 p. *Notes:* 'Extrait de diverses revues et publications, 1964–1970.' Bibliography p. 291–4. One of France's major critics and theatre thinkers observes seasons of change.

——. **Théâtres: essais**. Paris: Editions du Seuil, 1986. – 296 p. *Notes:* 'On trouvera ici, pour l'essentiel, des études reprises de Théâtre public (1967) et de Théâtre réel (1971)'–Cover p. 4. Includes bibliographies.

——. **Le Théâtre française au XXe siècle**. Louvain-la-Neuve: Cahiers théâtre Louvain, 1980. – 143 p.: ill.

Dullin, Charles. **Ce sont des dieux qu'il nous faut**. [Gods are what we need]. Paris: Gallimard, 1969. 240 p.

Durand, J.O. **Tous spectateurs: la belle aventure des amis du Théâtre Populaire**. [Spectators all: the fine adventure of the Friends of Popular Theatre]. La Tour d'Aigues, Ed. de l'Aube, 1992. 203 p.

Duvignaud, Jean. **Sociologie du théâtre: essai sur les ombres collectives**. [Sociology of the theatre: an essay on collective shadows]. Paris: Presses universitaires de France, 1965. 585 p.

Eigenmann, Eric. **La Parole empruntée: Sarraute, Pinget, Vinaver: théâtres du dialogisme**. Paris: L'Arche, 1996. – 255 p. *Notes:* Includes bibliographical references (p. 243–54). French drama. 20th century. History and criticism.

Elstob, Kevin. **The plays of Michel Vinaver: political theatre in France**. New York: P. Lang, 1992. – 215 p. *Notes:* Includes bibliographical references (p. 207–15). Political plays, history and criticism/Vinaver, Michel, 1927–.

Evrard, Franck. **Le Théâtre français du XXe siècle**. Paris: Ellipses, 1995. – 117 p.: ill. *Notes:* Includes bibliographical references (p. 109–11) and index. French drama. History and criticism.

Féral, Josette. **Trajectoires du Soleil autour d'Ariane Mnouchkine**. Paris: Editions Théâtrales, 1998. 288 p.

Foumel, Paul. **L'Histoire véritable de Guignol**. [The true history of Guignol]. Lyon: Federop, 1975. 298 p.

Gallois, Yves and Nicolas Treatt. **La Criée: un théâtre dans la cité**. Editions Jeanne Laffitte, 1992. – 157 p.: ill. (some col.). *Notes:* Theatre. Théâtre national de Marseille. History.

Gatti, Stéphane and Michel Séonnet. **Armand Gatti: journal illustré d'une écriture**. Montreuil: Centre d'action culturelle de Montreuil: Parole errante, 1987. – 255 p.: ill. *Notes:* 'Ouvrage publié à l'occasion de l'exposition "50 ans de théâtre vus par les trois chats d'Armand Gatti." Trois 'Hélicographies' en guise d'introduction – 1946–86: chronique – Lexique parlé pour une exposition – Les personnages de théâtre meurent dans la rue – Interviews cinematographiques illustrés – la création collective est solitaire –Biography. Dramatist, Gatti, Armand.

Gauthier, Roger-François, Jean-Claude Lallias and Jean-Jacques Arnault. **Koltès, combats avec la scène**. Paris: CNDP, 1996. – 200 p.: ill.; 21 × 27 cm. +. 1 sound disc (74 min.: digital; $4\frac{3}{4}$ in.) + 16 slides (col.; 2 × 2 in.) + guide (3 p.) in pocket. *Notes:* Includes bibliographical references (p. 198–200). Koltès, Bernard-Marie. Criticism and interpretation.

Germain, Anne. **Renaud-Barrault: les feux de la rampe et de l'amour**. Paris: Editions du Félin, 1992. – 203 p. *Notes:* Includes bibliographical references. Actors. France. Biography/Barrault, Jean Louis/Renaud, Madeleine. Compagnie Renaud Barrault.

Godard, Colette and Natacha Decan. **Le Théâtre depuis 1968**. Paris: J. C. Lattes, 1980. – 246 p., 6 p. of plates: ill. *Notes:* Includes bibliographical references and index. History and criticism.

Gourdon, Anne-Marie. **Théâtre, public, perception**. Paris: Editions du Centre national de la recherche scientifique, 1982. – 253 p.: ill. *Notes:* Includes index. Bibliography: p. 243–6. Theatre audiences.

Green, Anne Marie. **Un festival de théâtre et ses compagnies: le Off d'Avignon**. [A festival and its companies: Off-Avignon]. Paris: L'Harmattan, 1992. 223 p.

Guicharnaud, Jacques and June Guicharnaud. **Modern French theatre from Giraudoux to Genet**. Revised edn. New Haven; London: Yale University Press, 1975, 1967. – xiii, 383 p. *Series:* Yale Romanic studies. *Notes:* Includes index. Bibliography: p. 355–66. Drama in French, 1900–75. Critical studies.

Hill, Victoria Williams. **Bertolt Brecht and post-war French drama**. Stuttgart: Akademischer Verlag H.-D. Heinz, 1978. – 310 p. *Notes:* Bibliography: p. 287–310. History and criticism.

Hopkins, Patricia and Wendell M. Aycock. **Myths and realities of contemporary French theatre: comparative views**. Lubbock, TX: Texas Technical Publications, 1985. 195 p.

Hubert, Marie-Claude. **L'Esthétique de Jean Genet**. (Paris?): SEDES, 1996. 207 p. *Notes*: Includes bibliographical references (p 199–203). Genet, Jean 1910–1986. Aesthetics.

——. **Eugène Ionesco**. Paris: Seuil, 1990. 284 p.: ill. *Notes*: Dramatists, French. 20th century. Biography. Ionesco, Eugène.

——. **Le Théâtre**. Paris: A. Colin, 1988. 187 p. *Notes*: Includes bibliographical references. French drama. History and criticism.

de Jomaron, Jacqueline, ed. **Le Théâtre en France: de la Révolution à nos jours**. [Theatre in France: from the Revolution to the present day]. Paris: A. Colin, 1989. 614 p.

Jourdheuil, Jean. **Le Théâtre, l'artiste et l'État**. [Theatre, the artist and the state]. Paris: Hachette, 1979.

Jouvet, Louis. **Témoignages sur le théâtre**. [An eye-witness's report on theatre]. Paris: Flammarion, 1952.

Knapp, Bettina. **French theater since 1968**. New York: London: Twayne Publishers; Prentice Hall International, 1995. – xiii, 195 p. *Notes*: Includes bibliographical references (p. 183–7) and index. French drama.

——. **Off-stage voices: interviews with modern French dramatists**. Troy, N.Y.: Whitston Pub. Co., 1975. – iii, 324 p. *Notes*: Includes index. Dramatists.

Knowles, Dorothy. **Armand Gatti in the theatre: wild duck against the wind**. London: Rutherford, NJ.: Athlone Press; Fairleigh Dickinson University Press, 1989. – 300 p., 20 p. of plates: ill. *Notes*: Includes index. Bibliography: p. 291–5.

Lamar, Celita. **Our voices, ourselves: women writing for the French theatre**. New York: P. Lang, 1991. – vii, 213 p. *Notes*: Includes bibliographical references (p. 183–208) and index. History and criticism.

Lang, Jack. **Le Théâtre et l'État**. [The theatre and the state]. Bibliothèque de droit public 78. Paris: Librairie générale de droit et de jurisprudence, 1968. 380 p.

Latour, G. **Petites scènes, grand théâtres: le théâtre de création, 1944–1960**. [Small stages, great theatres: the creative theatre, 1944–60]. Paris: 1986. 303 p.

Lavelli, Jorge and A. Satgé. **Lavelli, opéra et mise à mort**. [Lavelli, opera and its execution]. Paris: Fayard, 1979. 269 p.

Laville, Pierre, ed. **Théâtre: 1991–1992**. Paris: Hachette, 1992. 431 p.

Leroy, Dominique. **Histoire des arts de spectacle en France**. Paris: Editions L'Harmattan, 1990. *Notes*: Bibliography (p. 323–33), indexes, charts, graphs. Economic and political study of the French performing arts from the Renaissance to the 20th century.

Madral, Philippe. **Le Théâtre hors les murs**. [Theatre in the Paris suburbs]. Paris: Seuil, 1969. 254 p.

Maréchal, Marcel. **La Mise en théâtre**. [Staging the theatre]. Paris: UGE, 1974. 232 p.

Méreuze, Didier. **Théâtre ouvert à livre ouvert de 1971 à 1988**. Paris: Rato Diffusion, 1988. – 255 p. *Notes*: Bio-bibliography/Théâtre ouvert (Paris). History.

Mignon, Paul-Louis. **Jacques Copeau, ou, Le mythe du Vieux-Colombier: biographie**. Paris: Julliard, 1993. – 348 p.: ill. *Notes*: Includes bibliographical references (p. 333–8) and index. Copeau, Jacques, 1879–1949. Biography/ Théâtre du Vieux-Colombier (Paris).

——. **Louis Jouvet**. Lyon: La Manufacture, 1988. – 307, 5 p.: ill. *Notes*: Discography: p. 286–7. Includes bibliographical references (p. 288–308). Jouvet, Louis, (1897–1951).

——. **Panorama du théâtre au XXe siècle**. Paris: Gallimard, 1978. – 377 p. *Notes*: 'Anthologie de textes': p. 273–358. Includes bibliographical references and index. Theatre. 20th century/Drama. 20th century. History and criticism.

Miller, Judith. **Theater and revolution in France since 1968**. Lexington, Ky.: French Forum, inc., 1977. – 169 p. *Notes*: Bibliography: p. 155–69. Political aspects.

Murray, Timothy, ed. **Mimesis, masochism, and mime: the politics of theatricality in contemporary French thought**. Ann Arbor: University of Michigan Press, 1997. – viii, 320 p. *Notes*: Includes bibliographical references and index. Introduction: the mise-en-scène of the cultural/Timothy Murray – Hors cadre interview/Hélène Cixous – The theatre of cruelty and the closure of representation/Jacques Derrida – The stage setup/Luce Irigaray – From mimetic desire to the monstrous double/René Girard – The utopic stage/Louis Marin – The psychoanalytic reading of tragedy/André Green – The unconscious as mise-en-scène/Jean-François Lyotard – Theatrum analyticum/Philippe Lacoue-Labarthe – The 'Piccolo teatro': Bertolazzi and Brecht: notes on a materialist theater/Louis Althusser – Theatrum philosophicum/Michel Foucault – One less manifesto/ Gilles Deleuze – Algeria unveiled/Frantz Fanon – Modern theatre does not take (a) place/Julia

Kristeva – The tooth, the palm/Jean-François Lyotard – Performance and theatricality: the subject demystified/Josette Féral – The disposition of the voice/Régis Durand.

Nagavajara, Chetana. **Brecht and France**. Bern and New York: P. Lang, 1994. – 191 p. Notes: Includes bibliographical references (p. 177–82) and index.

Neuschäfer, Anne. **Das 'Théâtre du Soleil': commedia dell'arte und creation collective**. Rheinfelden: Schäuble, 1985. – 251 p. Notes: Includes index. Bibliography: p. 234–49. A history of one of France's most important groups.

O'Connor, Garry. **French theatre today**. London: Pitman, 1975. – x, 118 p. Notes: Includes index. Bibliography: p. 110–15.

Papachristos, Katherine. **Le Théâtre de Tristan Tzara: le passage de l'oralité à l'écriture**. New York: P. Lang, 1998. Notes: Includes bibliographical references. Experimental theatre. France. Tzara, Tristan, 1896–1963. Dramatic works.

Parent, Michel. **Nuits en Bourgogne: un festival au carrefour de la vie culturelle française, 1954–1984**. Paris: Libr. Nizet, 1995. – 366 p., xxxii p. of plates: ill. Notes: Drama festivals. Nuits de Bourgogne (Theatrical company)/Festival des Nuits en Bourgogne.

Porter, Melinda Camber. **Through Parisian eyes: reflections on contemporary French arts and culture**. New York: Da Capo Press, 1993. – xii, 244 p.: ill. Notes: Includes index. François Truffaut – Marcel Ophuls – Costa-Gavras – Jean Anouilh – Jean-Louis Barrault – Eugène Ionesco – Breyten Breytenbach – Michael Lonsdale – Peter Brook – Alain Resnais – Alain Robbe-Grillet – Louis Malle – Eric Rohmer – Marcel Carné – Jean Eustache – Bertrand Tavernier – Marguerite Duras – Delphine Seyrig – Roger Vadim – Monique Wittig – Françoise Giroud – Poets of the hexagon – Edmond Jabès – Phillipe Adrien – Jean-Paul Sartre – Jean-Paul Aron – Olivier Todd – Yves Montand – Bernard-Henri Lévy – Françoise Sagan – Jean-François Revel – André Malraux – Régis Debray. Interviews.

Pronko, Leonard Cabell. **Avant-garde: the experimental theater in France**. Berkeley: University of California Press, 1966. – ix, 225 p. illus. Notes: Bibliography: p. 217–25. Avant-garde (aesthetics).

Puaux, Paul. **Avignon en Festivals**. Paris: Hachette, 1983. 318 p. Notes: Annexes. A history of the Avignon Festival.

Ralite, Jack. **Complicités avec Jean Vilar,**

Antoine Vitez. Paris: Tirésias, 1996. – 133 p., 38 p. of plates: ill. Notes: Includes bibliographical references. Vilar, Jean (1912–71). Vitez, Antoine. (1930–90).

Ryngaert, Jean-Pierre. **Lire le théâtre contemporain**. Paris: Dunod, 1993. – 202 p. Notes: Bibliography. Index. Drama. 20th century. History and criticism.

Sandier, Gilles. **Théâtre en crise: des années 70 à 82**. [Theatre in crisis: from 1970 to 1982]. Paris: La pensée sauvage, 1982. 487 p.

——. **Théâtre et combat**. [Theatre and battle]. Paris: Stock, 1970. 368 p.

Serge, Jean and Jean-François Colosimo. **Le Temps n'est plus de la bohème**. Paris: Stock: Kian, 1991. – 347 p. Notes: Theatrical producers and directors. France. Biography/Journalists.

Simon, Alfred. **Dictionnaire du théâtre français contemporain**. [A dictionary of contemporary French theatre]. Paris: Librairie Larousse, 1973. 255 p.

Souriau, Étienne. **Les Deux cent mille situations dramatiques**. [Two hundred thousand dramatic situations]. Paris: Flammarion, 1950. 250 p.

Stewart, E.R. **The decentralisation of French theatre 1940–1952: The Association Jeune France and the Centres Dramatiques**. Warwick: University of Warwick, 1985.

Sueur, Monique. **Deux siècles au Conservatoire d'art dramatique**. [Two centuries at the National Acting School]. Paris: CNSAD, 1986. 235 p.

Temkine, Raymonde. **Le Théâtre au présent**. [Present-day theatre]. Lectoure: Bouffonneries, 1987. 328 p.

——. **Le Théâtre en l'État**. [The state and/of theatre]. Paris: Editions Théâtrales, 1992. 253 p.

Ubersfeld, Anne. **L'École du spectateur**. [School for theatregoers]. Paris: Editions sociales, 1981. 352 p.

——. **Lire le théâtre**. [Reading theatre]. Paris: Editions sociales, 1977. 280 p.

Vaïs, Michel. **L'Écrivain scénique**. Montréal: Presses de l'Université du Québec, 1978. – viii, 278 p.: ill. Notes: Includes index. Bibliography: p. 261–6. Stage-setting and scenery. France.

Vessillier, Michèle. **La Crise du théâtre privé**. [The crisis in the private theatre]. Paris: Presses universitaires de France, 1973. 227 p.

Vilar, Jean. **Jean Vilar par lui-même**. [Jean Vilar by himself]. Avignon: Maison J. Vilar, 1991. 340 p.

——. **Théâtre, service public et autres textes**. [Theatre is a public utility and other writings]. 2nd edn. Paris: Gallimard, 1986. 556 p.

Vinaver, Michel. **Ecritures dramatiques: essais d'analyse de textes de théâtre**. Arles: Actes sud, 1993. – 922, 9 p.: ill. *Notes*: Includes bibliographical references (p. 921–3). Drama. History and criticism. The nature of the play by a noted French dramatist.

—— and Michelle Henry. **Ecrits sur le théâtre**. [Writings on the theatre]. Lausanne: L'Aire, 1982. – 330 p., 16 p. of plates: 37 ill. *Notes*: Includes bibliographical references. Vinaver, Michel, 1927–. Stage history.

Waters, Harold A. **Théâtre noir: encyclopédie des pièces écrites en français par des auteurs noirs**. 1st edn. Washington, D.C.: Three Continents Press, 1988. – xxxix, 214 p. *Notes*: Text in French: introd. in English and French. Includes indexes. Bibliography.

Whitton, David. **Stage directors in modern France**. Manchester: Manchester University Press, 1987. – x, 307 p. *Notes*: Includes bibliographies and index. France. Theatre. Directing, 1900–85. Critical studies.

Yaari, Nurit. **Contemporary French theatre: 1960–1992**. [Paris: Association française d'action artistique: Entr'Actes], 1995. – 351 p., 32 p. of plates: ill. *Notes*: Includes bibliographical references (p. 337) and index. French drama. 20th century. History and criticism.

Zatlin, Phyllis. **Cross-cultural approaches to theatre: the Spanish-French connection**. Metuchen, N.J.: Scarecrow Press, 1994. – vii, 261 p.: ill. *Notes*: Includes bibliographical references (p. 217–29) and index. French drama. Spanish influences/Spanish drama. French influences.

A3a50. FRENCH CARRIBEAN

Antoine, Régis. **La Tragédie du roi Christophe d'Aimé Césaire**. [Aimé Césaire's **Tragedy of King Christophe**]. Collection Lectoguide Francophonie. Paris: Borduas, 1984. 128 p.

Bailey, Marianne Wichmann. **The ritual theatre of Aimé Césaire: mythic structures of the dramatic imagination**. Tübingen: Gunter Narr, 1992. 256 p.

Blaise, J., L. Farrugia, C. Trébos, and S. Zobdar-Quitman. **Culture et politique en Guadeloupe et Martinique**. [Culture and politics in Guadeloupe and Martinique]. Paris: Karthala/Alizés, 1981. 102 p.

Fauquenoy, M. and Elie Stephenson. **O Mayouri (Théâtre guyanais)** [O Mayouri (Guyanese theatre)]. Paris: L'Harmattan, 1988. 164 p.

Harris, Rodney. **L'Humanisme dans le théâtre d'Aimé Césaire**. [Humanism in the plays of Aimé Césaire]. Sherbrooke, PQ: Naaman, 1973. 170 p.

'Instantanés sur le théâtre en Guadeloupe'. [Snapshots of theatre in Guadeloupe]. **Echo Jeunesse** 27 (1994).

Jeanne, Max. 'Sociologie du théâtre antillais'. [The sociology of theatre in the Antilles]. **CARE (Centre Antillais de Recherches et d'Études)** 6 (May 1980): 7–43.

Jones, Bridget. 'Theatre in the French West Indies'. **Carib** 4 (1986): 35–54.

Laville, Pierre. **Les Voies de la création théâtrale**. [The ways of theatrical creation]. Vol. 2. Paris: CNRS, 1970.

M'Bom, Clément. **Le Théâtre d'Aimé Césaire**. [The theatre of Aimé Césaire]. Paris: Nathan, 1979. 176 p.

A3a51. GEORGIA

Cilaia, Sergi. **Kote Marjanisvili, 1872–1947: saiubileo krebuli**. Tbilisi: Khelovneba, 1948. – 275 p.: ill. *Notes*: Marjanisvili, Konstantin Aleksandrovich, 1872–1933/Georgian theatrical directors, biography.

Djanelidze, Dimitri. **Kartuli teatris istoria udzvelesi droidan XVIII saukunemde**. [History of Georgian theatre]. Tbilisi: Literatura da Khelovneba, 1965. 603 p.

——. **Rustaveli da sakhioba**. [Rustaveli and theatre essays]. Tbilisi: Literatura da Khelovneba, 1958. 302 p.

——. **Sakhoiba** [Theatre essays]. Tbilisi: Literatura de Khelovneba, 1968. 227 p.

Gogolašhvili, Margarita. **Meskhetis teatris**. [The Meshketi theatre]. Tbilisi: Sakartvelos teatraluri sazogadoeba, 1976. 91 p.

Gougoushvili, Eteri. **Budni i prazkniki teatra**. [Working days and holidays of the theatre]. Tbilisi: Literatura da Khelovneba, 1971. 254 p.

——. **Kote Marjanisvili**. Tbilisi: Sakartvelos teatraluri sazogadoeba, 1972. – 543 p., 76 p. of plates: ill. *Notes*: Includes bibliographical references.

——. **Simartlis gzit**. [On the road of truth]. Tbilisi: Sakartvelos teatraluri sazogadoeba, 1985. 292 p.

Gurabanidze, Nobar. **Gamarjvebis gzit**. [On the road to victory]. Tbilisi: Literatura da Khelovneba, 1984. 303 p.

——. **Mravalsakheoba teatrisa**. [The diversity of the theatre]. Tbilisi: Literatura da Khelovneba, 1972. 407 p.

——. **Rejisori, msakhiobi, scena**. [The director, the actor, the stage]. Tbilisi: Literatura da Khelovneba, 1968. 363 p.

Ioseliani, Djaba. **The comic and Georgian mask comedy**. Tbilisi: Ganatleba, 1982. 206 p.

Kiknadze, Vasil. **Sandro Akhmeteli**. Tbilisi: Literatura da Khelovneba, 1977. 431 p.

Shaloutashvili, Nadezhda. **Grusinsko-Ukraukrainskie teatralnie sviazi**. [Georgian-Ukrainian theatrical relationships]. Tbilisi: Literatura de Khelovneba, 1984. 281 p.

——. **Mogobrobis gzebit**. [On the road of friendship]. Tbilisi: Sakartvelos teatraluri sazogadoeba, 1978. 379 p.

——. **Ostrovsky kartul szenaze**. [Ostrovsky's plays on the Georgian stage]. Tbilisi: 1958. 208 p.

Shvangiradze, Nino. **Tamar Chavchavadze**. Tbilisi: Literatura da Khelovneba, 1973. 470 p.

——. **Teatraluri etiudebi**. [Theatrical essays]. Tbilisi: Literatura da Khelovneba, 1964. 197 p.

Tumanishvili, Mihail. **Osnem repetisia daitzskeba**. [Until the rehearsal has begun]. Tbilisi: Sakartvelos teatraluri sazogadoeba, 1977. 283 p.

A3a52. GERMANY

Arnold, Heinz Ludwig and Theo Buck, eds. **Positionen des Dramas. Analysen und Theorien zur deutschen Gegenwartsliteratur**. [Views of the drama: analyses and theories of contemporary German literature]. Munich: C.H. Beck, 1977. 287 p.

Balk, Claudia. **Theaterfotografie: eine Darstellung ihrer Geschichte anhand der Sammlung des Deutschen Theatermuseums**. Munich: Hirmer, 1989. – 231 p.: ill. *Notes:* Catalogue of an exhibition held at the Deutsches Theatermuseum from December 8, 1989, to March 5, 1990. 'Herausgegeben vom Deutschen Theatermuseum' –Dust jacket. Includes bibliographical references (p. 229–30) and index. Stage photography. Exhibitions/Deutsches Theatermuseum.

Becker, Joachim. **Theater für Pforzheim**. Germany: Oktogon, 1990. – 104 p. ill., plans. *Notes:* Theatre architecture. Designs and plans. Buildings, structures, etc/Stadttheater Pforzheim.

Beckmann, Heinz. **Nach dem Spiel: Theaterkritiken 1950–1962**. Munich: A. Langen, G. Müller, 1963. – 398 p. *Notes:*

Includes index. Drama. 20th century. History and criticism.

Bodek, Richard. **Proletarian performance in Weimar Berlin: Agitprop, chorus, and Brecht**. Columbia, SC, USA: Camden House, 1997. – xiv, 184 p.: ill. *Notes:* Includes bibliographical references (p. 163–79) and index. Agitprop theatre. Berlin/Workers' theatre. History. Political aspects. Brecht, Bertolt, 1898–1956. Criticism and interpretation.

Brauneck, Manfred and Gérard. **Theaterlexikon: Begriffe und Epochen, Bühnen und Ensembles**. 3., vollständig überarb. u. erw. Neuausg. Reinbek bei Hamburg: Rowohlt, 1992. 1137 pp.: ill. *Notes:* Bibliography: p. 1133–7. Theatre dictionary. In German.

Brüster, Birgit. **Das Finale der Agonie: Funktionen des 'Metadramas' im deutschsprachigen Drama der 80er Jahre**. Frankfurt am Main; New York: P. Lang, 1993. – 398 p. *Notes:* Includes bibliographical references (p. 373–98). German drama. History. 20th century.

Burwell, Michael. **Theater der Zeit as a mirror of GDR drama, with a focus on Baierl, Kerndl, Braun, and Müller**. 1980. – 2 v. (ii, 546 p.). *Notes:* Bibliography: p. 542–6. Thesis (Ph. D.) –University of Minnesota, 1980. Microfilm. Ann Arbor, Mich.: University Microfilms International, 1980. 1 reel; 35 mm. German drama. History and criticism. Volker Braun/Helmut Baierl/Rainer Kerndl/Heiner Müller/**Theater der Zeit** (journal).

Buscher, Barbara. **Wirklichkeitstheater, Straßentheater, freies Theater. Entstehung und Entwicklung freier Gruppen in der Bundesrepublik Deutschland 1968–1976**. [Political theatre, street theatre, free theatre: the creation and development of independent companies in the Federal Republic of Germany 1968–76]. Frankfurt/New York: Peter Lang, 1987. 506 p.

Calandra, Denis. **New German dramatists: a study of Peter Handke, Franz Xaver Kroetz, Rainer Werner Fassbinder, Heiner Müller, Thomas Brasch, Thomas Bernhard and Botho Strauss**. London: Macmillan, 1983. – ix, 190 p., [8] p. of plates: ill. *Notes:* Includes index. Bibliography: p. 177–86.

Daiber, Hans. **Deutsches Theater seit 1945**. [German theatre since 1945]. Stuttgart: Reclam, 1976. 428 p.

——. **Schaufenster der Diktatur: Theater im Machtbereich Hitlers**. Stuttgart: Neske, 1995. – 405 p.: ill. *Notes:* Includes indexes. Theatre and state. History. National socialism.

Davies, Cecil William. **Theatre for the People:**

The Story of the Volksbühne. Manchester: Manchester University Press, 1977. 181 p.

Deutscher Bühnenverein, ed. **Theaterstatistik**. [Theatre statistics]. Cologne: DBV, annually.

——. **Was spielten die Theater? Bilanz der Spielpläne in der Bundesrepublik Deutschland 1947–1975**. [What did the theatres produce? A listing of the repertoire in the Federal Republic of Germany, 1947–75]. Cologne: DBV, 1978. 112 p.

——. **Was spielten die Theater? Werkstatistik**. [What did theatres produce? Repertoire statistics]. Cologne: DBV, 1992.

——. **Wer spielte was? Werkstatistik**. [Who played what? Repertoire statistics]. Cologne: DBV, 1992.

Deutsches Bühnenjahrbuch. Das große Adreßbuch für Bühne, Film, Funk und Fernsehen. [German stage yearbook: directory for stage, film, radio and television]. Hamburg: Genossenschaft Deutscher Bühnen-Angehörigen im Verlag der Bühnenschriften-Vertriebs-GmbH, annually.

Dieckmann, Friedrich, ed. **Ensembles der Deutschen Demokratischen Republik: Theater, Ensembles, Schulen, Institutionen**. [Ensembles of the German Democratic Republic: theatres, ensembles, schools, institutions]. Berlin: Henschel, 1973–89.

Doll, Hans Peter. **Stuttgarter Theaterarbeit 1972–1985**. Stuttgart: Württembergisches Staatstheater, 1985. – 256 p.: ill. (some col.). *Notes*: Theater. Stuttgart. History. 20th century.

Elfe, Wolfgang and James N. Hardin. **Twentieth-century German dramatists, 1919–1992**. Detroit: Gale Research, 1992. – xv, 567 p.: ill. *Notes*: Includes bibliographical references (p. 479–85) and index. Bibliography.

Faber, Monica and Loni Weizert. **–dann spielten sie wieder: das Bayerische Staatsschauspiel 1946–1986**. Munich: Bruckmann, 1986. – 272 p.: ill. *Notes*: Includes indexes. Munich. History. 20th century/Bayerisches Staatsschauspiel.

Fetting, Hugo. **Von der Freien Bühne zum politischen Theater: Drama und Theater im Spiegel der Kritik**. 1. Aufl. Leipzig: Reclam, 1987. – 2 vols. *Notes*: Includes bibliographical references and indexes. Berlin. Revues. History.

Funke, Christoph, Daniel Hoffmann-Ostwald and Hans-Gerald Otto, eds. **Theater-Bilanz 1945 bis 1969. Eine Bild-dokumentation über die Bühnen der Deutschen Demokratischen Republik**. [Theatre survey 1945 to 1969: a visual documentation of the stages of the German Democratic Republic]. Berlin: Henschel, 1971. 392 p.

Funke, Christoph and Wolfgang Jansen. **Theater am Schiffbauerdamm: die Geschichte einer Berliner Bühne**. Berlin: Ch. Links, 1992. – 254 p.: ill. *Notes*: Includes bibliographical references (p. 241–5) and index. Theater am Schiffbauerdamm (Berlin). History.

Gadberry, Glen W. **Theatre in the Third Reich, the prewar years: essays on theater in Nazi Germany**. Westport, Conn.: Greenwood Press, 1995. – viii, 187 p. *Notes*: Includes bibliographical references (p. 167–78) and index.

Garten, Hugh Frederick. **Modern German drama**. 2nd edn. London: Methuen, 1964. – 272 p. plates. *Notes*: German drama. 20th century. History and criticism.

Grau, Dieter and Anton Strambowski. **Bund der Theatergemeinden**. Düsseldorf: Droste Verlag, 1996. – 89 p. *Notes*: Bibliography of works by the Bund der Theatergemeinden: p. 78–84. Directories/Bund der Theatergemeinden.

Guntner, J. Lawrence and Andrew M. McLean. **Redefining Shakespeare: literary theory and theater practice in the German Democratic Republic**. Newark: University of Delaware Press, 1997. *Notes*: Includes bibliographical references and index. English drama. History and criticism. Germany (East). Shakespeare, William, 1564–1616. Stage history.

Hasche, Christa, Traute Schölling, Joachim Fiebach and Ralph Hammerthaler. **Theater in der DDR: Chronik und Positionen**. Berlin: Henschel, 1994. – 285 p. *Notes*: Includes bibliographical references (p. 262–73) and index. Chronology/Theatre. Germany (East).

Hayman, Ronald, ed. **The German theatre. A symposium**. London: Oswald Wolff, 1975. 287 p.

Herzfeld-Sander, Margaret, ed. **Essays on German theatre**. New York: Continuum, 1985. 356 p.

Hoffmann, Christel. **Theater für junge Zuschauer. Sowjetische Erfahrungen – sozialistische deutsche Traditionen – Geschichte in der DDR**. [Theatre for young audiences: Soviet experiences – German socialist traditions – history in the GDR]. Berlin: Akademie-Verlag, 1976. 252 p.

Hoffmeister, Donna L. **The theater of confinement: language and survival in the milieu plays of Marieluise Fleisser and Franz Xaver Kroetz**. 1st edn. Columbia, S.C.: Camden House, 1983. – 176 p. *Notes*: Revision of the author's thesis (Ph. D.)–Brown University,

1979. Includes index. Bibliography: p. [167]–73. *Subjects*: German drama. 20th century. History and criticism/Communication in literature/Fleisser, Marieluise, 1901–74. Criticism and interpretation/Kroetz, Franz Xaver, 1946–.

Hörburger, Christian. **Nihilisten, Pazifisten, Nestbeschmutzer.** Tübingen: Verein für Friedenspädagogik, 1993. – 299 p.: ill. *Notes*: Includes bibliographical references (p. 297–5). Music-halls (Variety-theatres, cabarets, etc.). Theatre and society.

Hortmann, Wilhelm and Michael Hamburger. **Shakespeare on the German stage: the twentieth century.** Cambridge: Cambridge University Press, 1998. *Notes*: Includes bibliographical references and index. English influences/Shakespeare, William, 1564–1616. Stage history.

Iden, Peter. **Theater als Widerspruch: Plädoyer für die zeitgenössische Bühne: am Beispiel neuerer Aufführungen der Regisseure Luc Bondy** ... Munich: Kindler, 1984. – 251 p.: ill. *Notes*: Includes index.

Innes, C.D. **Erwin Piscator's political theatre; the development of modern German drama.** Cambridge: Cambridge University Press, 1972. – 248 p. *Notes*: Bibliography: p. 227–34. Piscator, Erwin, 1893–1966.

——. **Modern German drama: a study in form.** Cambridge: Cambridge University Press, 1979. – 297 p.: ill. *Notes*: Includes index. Bibliography: p. 288–90. German drama. 20th century. History and criticism.

Jacobs, Montague. **Deutsche Schauspielkunst: Zeugnisse zur Bühnengeschichte klassischer Rollen.** [German acting: testimony to the history of classic roles]. Berlin: Henschel, 1954. 539 p.

Jansen, Wolfgang. **Glanzrevuen der zwanziger Jahre.** Berlin: Edition Hentrich, 1987. – 207 p.: ill. (some col.). *Notes*: Includes index. Bibliography: p. 182–7. 'Discographie der Berliner Ausstattungs-Revuen': p. 188–203. Music-halls (Variety-theatres, cabarets, etc.). Berlin.

Kässens, Wend, Jörg Werner Gronius and Luc Bondy. **Theatermacher: Gespräche mit Luc Bondy, Jürgen Flimm, Hansgünther Heyme, Hans Neuenfels, Peter Palitzsch, Claus Peymann, Frank-Patrick Steckel, George Tabori, Peter Zadek.** Frankfurt am Main: Hain, 1990 1987. – 211 p. Interviews. Directors. Germany (West).

Kim, Kisôn. **Theater und Ferner Osten: Untersuchungen zur deutschen Literatur im ersten Viertel des 20. Jahrhunderts.** Frankfurt am Main: Lang, 1982. – 318 p. *Notes*: Bibliography: p. 291–318. Asia. Influence/German drama.

Klunker, Heinz. **Zeitstücke, Zeitgenossen. Gegenwartstheater in der DDR.** [Contemporary theatre, plays and artists in the GDR]. Hannover: Fackelträger-Verlag, 1972. 235 p.

Kranz, Dieter. **Berliner Theater: 100 Aufführungen aus drei Jahrzehnten.** [Theatre in Berlin: 100 productions from three decades]. Berlin: Henschel, 1990. 518 p.

Kreuzer, Helmut, ed. **Deutsche Dramaturgie der sechziger Jahre.** [German drama and theatre in the 1960s]. Tübingen: Niemeyer, 1974. 182 p.

Kuhns, David F. **German expressionist theatre: the actor and the stage.** Cambridge; New York: Cambridge University Press, 1997. – x, 311 p. *Notes*: Includes bibliographical references (p. 293–8) and index.

Lange, Wigand. **Theater in Deutschland nach 1945: zur Theaterpolitik d. amerikanischen Besatzungsbehörden.** Frankfurt am Main; Bern; Cirencester/U.K.: Lang, 1980. – x, 775 p. *Notes*: Revision of thesis (Ph. D.)–University of Wisconsin–Madison, 1979. Includes index. Bibliography: p. 699–729. Theatre. Censorship. Germany (West). German drama. American influences. Reconstruction (1939–1951).

Lennartz, Knut. **Vom Aufbruch zur Wende: Theater in der DDR.** Seelze: Erhard Friedrich, 1992. – 110 p.: ill. *Notes*: Theatre. East Germany.

Linke, Manfred, ed. **Theater/Theatre 1967–1892.** Berlin: Zentrum Bundesrepublik Deutschland des ITI, 1983. 352 p.

Material zum Theater. Beiträge zur Theorie und Praxis des sozialistischen Theaters. [Material for the theatre: contributions to the theory and practice of socialist theatre]. Berlin: Verband der Theaterschaffenden der DDR, 1972–89. 222 issues.

Mittenzwei, Werner. **Der Realismus-Streit um Brecht: Grundriss der Brecht-Rezeption in der DDR, 1945–1975.** Berlin: Aufbau-Verlag, 1978. – 209 p. *Notes*: A revision and expansion of an essay published in the journal **Sinn und Form**. Includes bibliographical references and index.

——, ed. **Theater in der Zeitenwende. Zur Geschichte des Dramas und des Schauspieltheaters in der Deutschen Demokratischen Republik 1945–68.** [Theatre in changing times: history of the drama and of performance in the German Democratic Republic 1945–68]. 2 vols. Berlin: Henschel, 1972. 396 + 482 p.

Mück, Hans-Dieter. **Schau-Bühne: Schillers Dramen 1945–1984: eine Ausstellung des Deutschen Literaturarchivs und des Theatermuseums der Universität zu Köln.** Marbach am Neckar: Deutsche Schillergesellschaft, 1984. 707 p.: ill. (some col.). *Notes*: Discography: p. 455–63. Filmography: p. 464–502. Includes bibliographical references and index. Schiller, Friedrich, 1759–1805. Stage history.

Nagel, Ivan. **Kortner, Zadek, Stein.** Munich: Hanser, 1989. – 86 p. *Notes*: Theatrical directors. History. 20th century. Fritz Kortner, Peter Zadek and Peter Stein.

Nossig, Manfred, ed. **Die Schauspieltheater in der DDR und dessen Erbe (1970–74).** [Stage performances in the GDR and their legacy (1970–74)]. Berlin: Akademie-Verlag, 1976. 264 p.

Patterson, Michael. **German theatre: a bibliography: from the beginning to 1995.** Leicester: Motley, 1996. – 887 p. *Notes*: Includes index.

Pforte, Dietger. **Freie Volksbühne Berlin, 1890–1990: Beiträge zur Geschichte der Volksbühnenbewegung in Berlin.** Berlin: Argon, 1990. – 274 p.: ill. *Notes*: Includes bibliographical references and index. Freie Volksbühne Berlin. History.

Profitlich, Ulrich, ed. **Dramatik der DDR.** Frankfurt am Main: Suhrkamp, 1987. – 472 p.: ill. *Notes*: Bibliography: p. 399–473. Die Tage des Büsching: Brechts Garbe – ein deutsches Lehrstück/Stephan Bock – Aspekte der Bewältigungsdramatik in den vierziger und fünfziger Jahren/Karl-Heinz Hartmann – Vorbilder, Verräter und andere Intellektuelle: DDR–Friedensdramatik 1950/1/Helmut Peitsch – Agitproptheater in der DDR: Auseinandersetzung mit einer Tradition/David Bathrick – Auseinandersetzung mit der Gegenwart: Fernsehdramatik in den sechziger Jahren/Knut Hickethier – Das Ich und die Gleichen: Versuch über Stefan Schütz/Marlies Janz – Theater der Blicke: Zu Heiner Müllers Bildbeschreibung/Hans-Thies Lehmann – Eine passende Mütze für die achtziger Jahre?: Kabarettistische Repertoirestücke als theatralische Mischform/Manfred Jäger. Antike Mythen auf dem Theater der DDR: Geschichte und Poesie, Vernunft und Terror/Wolfgang Emmerich – Fridericus Rex: Das schwarze Preussen im Drama der DDR/Jost Hermand – Beim Menschen geht der Umbau langsamer: Der 'neue Mensch' im Drama der DDR/Ulrich Profitlich – Baal, Fätzer: und Fondrak: Die Figur des Asozialen bei Brecht und Müller/Theo Girshausen – 'Zweiter Clown im kommunistischen Frühling: Peter Hacks und die Geschichte der komischen Figur im Drama der DDR/Bernhard Greiner – 'Der freundliche Blick

auf Widersprüche …': Volksstücktradition und Realismus im DDR-Drama/Klaus Siebenhaar. German drama. 20th century. History and criticism. Germany (East).

Reichel, Peter. **Resüme mit Trendmarkierungen: Autor, Werk, Wirkung: die DDR-Dramatik in der Mitte der 80er Jahre.** Berlin: Verband der Theaterschaffenden der DDR, 1987. – 124 p. *Notes*: Includes bibliographical references (p. 117–20). (East) German drama. History and criticism.

Robinson, David W. **No man's land: East German drama after the Wall.** Netherlands: Harwood Academic Pub., 1995. – 220 p.: ill. *Notes*: Includes bibliographical references and index. German drama. Germany (East). History and criticism.

Rühle, Günther. **Theater in unserer Zeit.** [Contemporary theatre]. 3 vols. Frankfurt: Suhrkamp, 1976–92.

Sautter, Siegfried, Renate Laur and Otfried Laur. **Berliner Theater Club, 1967–1987: Berlins grosse Besucherorganisation: Festschrift.** Berlin: Der Club, 1987. – 496 p.: ill. (some col.). *Notes*: Contains lists of plays performed, photographs of productions, posters, etc., from the theatres in Berlin.

Schneider, Rolf. **Theater in einem besiegten Land: Dramaturgie der deutschen Nachkriegszeit 1945–1949.** Frankfurt/M; Berlin: Ullstein, 1989. – 144 p., 16 p. of plates: ill. *Notes*: German postwar drama.

Schulze-Reimpell, Werner. **Development and structure of the theatre in the Federal Republic of Germany.** Translated by Patricia Crampton. Cologne: Deutscher Bühnenverein and Bonn-Bad Godesberg: Inter Nationes, 1979.

Schwab-Felisch, Hans. **75 Jahre Düsseldorfer Schauspielhaus 1905–1980.** Düsseldorf: Econ, 1980. – 124 p.: ill. *Notes*: Bibliography: p. 48. Includes list of plays presented at the theatre 1945–1980. Düsseldorfer Schauspielhaus. History.

Sebald, Winfried Georg, ed. **A radical stage: theatre in Germany in the 1970's and 1980's.** Oxford: Berg; New York: St Martin's Press, 1988. – 244 p. *Notes*: Includes index. Critical studies.

Sieg, Katrin. **Exiles, eccentrics, activists: women in contemporary German theater.** Ann Arbor: University of Michigan Press, 1994. – viii, 239 p.: ill. *Notes*: Includes bibliographical references and index. History and criticism. Political and social views.

Strauss, Botho. **Versuch, ästhetische und poli-**

tische Ereignisse zusammenzudenken: Texte über Theater, 1967–1986. Frankfurt am Main: Verlag der Autoren, 1987. – 270 p. *Notes*: Includes bibliographical references and index. History and criticism.

Sucher, C. Bernd, Christine Dössel and Jean-Claude Kuner. **Theaterlexikon**. Munich: Deutscher Taschenbucherlag, 1995 1996. – 2 vols. *Notes*: Includes bibliographical references. Vol. 1 German writers, directors, actors, dramaturgs, critics; periods, ensembles. Vol. 2 Genres, theory. In German.

Theaterarbeit in der DDR. [Documentation of GDR theatre performances]. 19 vols. Berlin: Verband der Theaterschaffenden der DDR, 1976–90.

Treusch, Hermann, Rüdiger Mangel and Günther Rühle. **Spiel auf Zeit: Theater der Freien Volksbühne 1963–1992**. Berlin: Edition Hentrich, 1992. – 237 p.: ill. *Notes*: Includes bibliographical references and indexes. Freie Volksbühne Berlin. History.

Trilse-Finkelstein, Ch Jochanan and Klaus Hammer. **Lexikon: Theater international**. Berlin: Henschel, 1995. – 1024 p. *Notes*: Includes biographies.

Ullrich, Renate. **Mein Kapital bin ich selber: Gespräche mit Theaterfrauen in Berlin-O, 1990–1991**. Berlin: Zentrum für Theaterdokumentation und -information, 1991. – 195 p. *Notes*: Women in the theatre. History. 20th century. Interviews.

Völker, Klaus. **Bertelsmann Schauspielführer**. Munich: Bertelsmann Lexikon Verlag, 1992. – 576 p.: ill. *Notes*: Includes index. Play guide in German.

——. **Elisabeth Bergner: das Leben einer Schauspielerin: ganz und doch immer unvollendet**. Berlin: Edition Hentrich, 1990. – 413 p.: ill. (some col.). *Notes*: Includes material by E. Bergner. Includes bibliographical references (p. 412). Biography/Bergner, Elisabeth, 1897–1986.

——. **Fritz Kortner: Schauspieler und Regisseur**. Berlin: Edition Hentrich, 1993 1987. – 442 p.: ill. *Notes*: Bibliography: p. 417. Biography/Theatrical producers and directors. Kortner, Fritz.

Wekwerth, Manfred. **Theater in Diskussion: Notate, Gespräche, Polemiken**. Berlin: Henschel, 1982. – 342 p. *Notes*: 2nd edn. Previous edn: Bristol: Enuanom, 1994.

Zadek, Peter and Laszlo Kornitzer. **Das wilde Ufer: ein Theaterbuch**. Cologne: Kiepenheuer & Witsch, 1994. – 350 p.: ill. *Notes*: Includes index. Theatrical producers and directors. Germany. Biography. Zadek, Peter.

A3a53. GHANA

Agovi, Kofi. 'The origin of literary theatre in colonial Ghana, 1920–1957'. **Research Review** 6, no. 1 (1990): 1–23.

——. 'The philosophy of communication in traditional Ghanaian society: the literary and dramatic evidence'. **Research Review** 5, no. 2 (1989).

——. 'Sharing creativity: group performance of Nzema Ayabomo Maiden Songs'. **The Literary Griot: International Journal of Black Oral and Literary Studies** 1, no. 2 (1989).

Angmor, Charles. 'Drama in Ghana'. In **Theatre in Africa**, Oyin Ogunba and Abiola Irele, eds, 55–72. Ibadan: Ibadan University Press, 1978.

Bame, Kwabena N. **Come to laugh: a study of African traditional theatre in Ghana**. Legon: Institute of African Studies; New York: Lilian Barber, 1985. 102 p.

——. 'Comic play in Ghana'. **African Arts/Arts d'Afrique** 1, no. 4 (1968): 30–4, 101.

——. 'Popular theatre in Ghana'. **Institute of African Studies Research Review** 3, no. 2 (1967): 34–8.

Collins, John. **Highlife Time**. Accra: Anansesem Publications, 1994.

——. 'Life on the road – modern African minstrels: the Jaguar Jokers'. In **West African Popular Roots**. Philadelphia: Temple University Press, 1992.

Gibbs, James. **Ghanaian theatre: a bibliography: a work in progress**. Llangynidr: Nolisment, 1995. – 57 p. *Notes*: 2nd edn. Previous edn.: Bristol: Enuanom, 1994.

Kadjani, John. 'Observations on spectator–performer arrangements of some traditional Ghanaian performances'. **Institute of African Studies Research Review** 2, no. 3 (1966): 61–6.

Nketia, J.H. Kwabena. **A calendar of Ghana festivals**. Legon: Institute of African Studies, 1964. 13 p.

——. **Ghana – music, dance and drama**. Legon: Institute of African Studies, 1965.

A3a54. GREECE

Bakounakis, Nicos. **Norma's Spectre**. Athens: Kastaniotis, 1991.

Chrysostomidis, Alekos. **Popular Theatre**. Athens: Smirniotakis, 1989.

——. **To laiko theatro: chroniko, historiko, anamneseis: anekdota, he noutike komodia ...** Athens: Smirniotakis, 1987. – 192 p.: ill. *Notes*: Bibliography: p. 6. History.

Evangelatos, Spiros. **Again About Erotokritos: an attempt to identify the poet.** Athens: Kastaniotis, 1989.

Fotopoulos, Dionysis. **Tales beyond the façade.** Athens: Kastaniotis, 1990.

Grammatas, Theodore. **Modern Greek theatre and society.** Athens: S.D. Vassilopoulos, 1990.

Gressler, Thomas H. **Greek theatre in the 1980s.** Jefferson, N.C.: McFarland, 1989. – xiii, 191 p.: ill. *Notes*: Includes index. Bibliography: p. 183–5.

Halls, Aliki Bacopoulou. **Modern Greek theatre: roots and blossoms.** Athens: Diogenis, 1982.

Hatzipandazis, Thodoros and Lila Maraka, eds. **Athenian Epitheorisi.** 3 vols. Athens: Ekdotiki Hermes, 1977.

Kaimi, Julio. **Karagiozis or the ancient comedy in the soul of the shadow theatre.** Translated by K. Mekkas and T. Milias. Athens: Gavriilidis, 1990.

Kallerges, Lykourgos. **Synkomide ideon agathon.** Athens: Ekdoseis Dodone, 1995. – 276 p.: ill. *Notes*: History.

Kaphtantzes, Giorgos. **Theatro sta vouna tes D. Makedonias ton kairo tes Katoches.** Thessalonika: Ekdose Periodikou Giati, 1990. – 155 p.: ill. *Notes*: Theatre. Greece/Macedonia. History.

Koun, Karolos. **Social position and aesthetic policy of the Art Theatre.** Athens: Glaros, 1943.

——. **We make theatre for our soul.** Athens: Kastaniotis, 1987.

Michaelides, George. **Modern Greek Playwrights.** Athens: Kaktos, 1975.

Minotis, Alexis. **Makrines philies.** Athens: Kaktos, 1981. – 155 p.: ill. *Notes*: Theatrical producers and directors. Greece. Autobiography/Minotis, Alexis.

——. **Poreuesthai kata techne.** Athens: Ekdoseis Kastaniote, 1988. – 237 p.: ill. *Notes*: Greek drama, Modern. 20th century. History and criticism.

Myrsiades, Linda S. **The Karagiozis heroic performance in Greek shadow theatre.** Translated by K. Myrsiades. Hannover: Hannover University Press, 1988.

Pallantios, Menelaos. **Prosopo/prosopeio Katina Paxinou – Alexis Minotis: times kai agapes epicheirema.** Athens: Tetradia Euthynes, 1993. – 137 p.: ill. *Notes*: Includes bibliographical references. Biography of Greece's directors. Katina Paxinou and Alexis Minotis.

Paxinou, Katina and Alexis Minotis. **Long journey to Ithaca.** Athens: Epikerotita, 1989.

Pontani, F.M. **Teatro Neoellenico.** Milan: 1962.

Puchner, Walter. **Greek drama theory – twelve studies.** Athens: 1988.

——. **Laiko theatro sten Hellada: synkritike melete.** Athens: Ekdoseis Patake, 1989. – 402 p. *Notes*: Includes bibliographical references (p. 255–351) and indexes. Folk drama, Greek (modern). Balkan peninsula. History.

——. **Philologika kai theatrologika analekta: pente meletemata.** Athens: Ekdoseis Kastaniote, 1995. – 469 p. *Notes*: Includes bibliographical references (p. 11–12) and indexes. History and criticism/Theatre.

Regional Theatre of Larissa. **15 years of theatre in Thessaly.** Larissa: Regional Theatre of Larissa, 1991.

Regional Theatre of Patras. **The first three years.** Patras: Regional Theatre of Patras, 1991.

Rotas, Vasiles. **Theatro kai antistase.** Athens: Kentro Marxistikon Ereunon ('Synchrone Epoche'), 1981. – 84 p.: ill. *Notes*: 20th century. History and criticism/Theatre. Political aspects.

——. **Theatro kai glossa, 1925–1977.** Athens: Epikairoteta, 1986. – 2 vols. Greek drama, Modern. History and criticism.

Sakellariou, Haris. **The theatre of the resistance.** Athens: Thema, 1989.

Sideris, Yannis. **He historia tou Neo hellenikou theatrou kai to Theatriko Mouseio.** Athens: Kallitechniko Pneumatiko Kentro Hora, 1972. – 70 p.: ill.; 19 x. *Notes*: Greece. Theatre. History. Bibliography. In Greek.

——. **History of modern Greek Theatre.** Athens: Kastaniotis, 1990. In English.

——, *et al.* **The modern Greek Theatre: a concise history.** Translated by L. Vassardaki. Athens: 1957.

Solomos, Alexis. **Theatriko lexiko: prosopa kai pragmata sto pankosmio theatro.** Athens: Kedros, 1989. – 399 p., 12 p. of plates: ill. (some col.). *Notes*: Encyclopedia of modern Greek theatre.

——. **Vios kai paignion: skene, proskenio, paraskenia.** Athens: Dodone, 1980. – 182 p., 8 p. of plates: ill. *Notes*: Includes index. Directors. Autobiography.

Techni Experimental Stage. **1979–90: eleven years of theatre in Thessaloniki**. Thessaloniki: 1990.

Tsouchlou, Demetra and Asantour Bacharian. **He skenographia sto neoelleniko theatro**. Athens: Apopse, 1985. – 399 p.: ill. (some col.). *Notes*: Includes bibliographies. Stage-setting and scenery. 20th century.

Varveres, Giannes. **He krise tou theatrou: keimena theatrikes kritikes**. Athens: Ekdoseis Kastaniote, 1985 1991. – 2 vols. *Notes*: Includes index. 1. 1976–84 – 2. 1984–9. 20th century.

Vitti, Mario. **Function of ideology in Greek ethographia**. Athens: Keirmena, 1974.

Walton, J. Michael. **Living Greek theatre: a handbook of Classical performance and modern production**. New York: Greenwood Press, 1987.

A3a55. GUATEMALA

Acuña, René. **Introducción al estudio del Rabinal Achí**. [Introduction to the study of Rabinal Achí]. México City: Universidad Nacional Autónoma de México, Centro de Estudios Mayas, 1975.

——. 'Una década de teatro guatemalteco 1962–1973'. [A decade of Guatemalan theatre, 1962–1973]. **Latin American Theatre Review** 8, no. 2 (September 1975): 59–74.

Albizurez, Palma, Francisco Barrios y Barrios and Catalina Barrios y Barrios. 'Literatura dramática guatemalteca'. [Guatemalan dramatic literature]. In **Historia de la literatura guatemalteca**. [History of Guatemalan literature]. Guatemalan City: Universidad de San Carlos, 1987.

Batres Jáuregui, Antonio. **Memorias de antaño, con una historia del teatro en Guatemala**. [Old memories, and a history of the Guatemalan theatre]. Oakland, CA: Pacific Press, 1986.

Bravo-Elizondo, Pedro. 'Guatemala: VII temporada de teatro departamental, Mayo 19–21 [Departmental Theatre, May 19–21], 1989'. **Latin American Theatre Review** 23, no. 2 (spring 1990): 111–114.

Carrera, Mario Alberto. **Ideas políticas en el teatro de Manuel Galich**. [Political ideas in the theatre of Manuel Galich]. Guatemalan City: Facultad de Humanidades, Universidad de San Carlos, 1966.

Carrillo, Hugo. 'Orígenes y desarollo del teatro guatemalteco'. [Origins and development of Guatemalan theatre]. **Conjunto**, 20 (April–June 1974): 72–80.

Fernández Molina, Manuel. **Dos estudios históricos sobre el teatro en Guatemala: el teatro en la ciudad de Guatemala en la época de la independencia y la incidencia de los terremotos en el teatro quatemalteco**. [Two historical studies on Guatemalan theatre: theatre in Guatemala City during independence and the influence of earthquakes in Guatemalan theatre]. Guatemala City: Dirección General de Bellas Artes, 1982.

García Mejía, René. **Raíces del teatro guatemalteco**. [Roots of Guatemalan theatre]. Guatemala City: Tipografía Nacional, 1972.

Herrera, Ubico and Ana Sivia. **El teatro en Guatemala en el siglo XX: contribución de Luis Herrera al surgimiento de un quehacer teatral**. [Theatre in Guatemala in the twentieth century: Luis Herrera's contribution to the theatre profession]. Guatemala City: Serviprensa Centroamericana, 1980.

——. 'La escenificación teatral en Guatemala en la segunda mitad del siglo XX: dos décadas de teatro 1950–70'. [Theatre in Guatemala in the second half of the twentieth century: two decades of theatre 1950–70]. In **Historia general de Guatemala**. [A general history of Guatemala].

Klein, Maxine. 'A country of cruelty and its theatre'. **Drama Survey** 7, nos. 1–2 (winter 1968–spring 1969): 164–70.

Solóranzo, Carlos. **Teatro guatemalteco contemporáneo**. [Contemporary Guatemalan theatre]. Madrid: Aguilar, 1973.

A3a56. GUINEA

Cornevin, Robert. **Le Théâtre en Afrique noire et à Madagascar**. [Theatre in Black Africa and Madagascar]. Paris: Le livre Africain, 1970. 334 p.

Fodeba, Keita. **Le Théâtre de Keita Fodeba**. [The Theatre of Keita Fodeba]. Paris: P. Seghers, 1950.

Touré, J.M. 'Mobiliser, informer, éduquer; un instrument efficace: le théâtre'. [To mobilize, to inform, to educate; an effective instrument: the theatre]. **Notre Librairie: La Littérature Guinéenne**. 88–9 (July–September 1987).

A3a57. GUINEA-BISSAU

Crowley, Daniel J. 'The Carnival of Guinea-Bissau'. **The Drama Review: A Journal of Performance Studies** 33, no. 2 (summer 1989): 74–86.

Vaz, Carlos. **Para um conhecimento do teatro Africano**. [Toward understanding African theatre]. Lisbon: Ulmeiro, 1978. 204 p.

A3a58. HAÏTI

Clark, Vèvè. 'Haiti's Tragic Overture: (Mis)Representations of the Haitian Revolution in World Drama (1796–1975)'. In **Representing revolution: essays on reflections of the French Revolution in literature, historiography and art**, ed. James Heffernan. Hannover, NH: University Press of New England, 1991.

Cornevin, Robert. **Le Théâtre haïtien des origines à nos jours**. [Haïtian theatre from its beginnings to the present]. Collection Caraïbes. Montréal: Leméac, 1973. 301 p.

Fouchard, Jean. **Le Théâtre à Saint-Domingue** [Theatre in Saint-Domingue]. Port-au-Prince: Editions Henri Deschamps, 1988. 294 p.

Fouché, Franck. **Vodou et théâtre: pour un nouveau théâtre populaire**. [Voodoo and theatre: towards a new popular theatre]. Montréal: Editions Nouvelle Politique, 1976. 125 p.

Gouraige, Ghislain. **Histoire de la littérature haïtienne de l'indépendance à nos jours**. [History of Haïtain literature from independence to the present]. Port-au-Prince: N.A. Théodore, 1960.

Louis-Jean, Antonio. **La Crise de possession et la possession dramatique**. [The convulsion of possession and dramatic possession]. Montréal: Leméac, 1970.

University of the West Indies (Mona, Jamaica). Library. **Haiti, the visual and performing arts: a select list of material from the collections of the Library, UWI (Mona)**. Kingston, Jamaica: The Library, University of the West Indies (Mona), 1990. – 7 p. *Notes*: Prepared for the exhibition 'Vive la difference', Haitian art and craft. Bibliography.

Viatte, Auguste. **Histoire littéraire de l'Amérique française, des origines à 1950**. [Literary history of French America from its origins to 1950]. Québec/Paris: PUL/PUF, 1959.

A3a59. HONDURAS

Ardón, Víctor F. 'La producción dramática en Honduras'. [Dramatic production in Honduras]. **Humanismo** 6, nos. 48–9 (March–June 1958): 116–26.

Caballero, Alma and Francisco Salvador. **Teatro en Honduras**. [Theatre in Honduras]. 2 vols. Tegucigalpa: SECTIN, 1977.

Durand, Jorge Fidel. 'Sobre el teatro en Honduras'. [On theatre in Honduras]. **Honduras Rotaria** 17 no. 183 (June 1958): 12–13.

——. 'Teatro en Honduras'. [Theatre in Honduras]. **Boletín de la Academia Hondureña de la Lengua** 10 no. 11 (November 1965): 55–9.

Fernández, Mauro. 'El teatro en Honduras'. [Theatre in Honduras]. **Repertorio Latino Americano** 2 no. 18 (September 1976): 18.

Reyes, Candelario. **Método de la basura: una manera de hacer teatro campesino**. Honduras: Centro Cultural Hibueras, 1992. – 51 p. *Notes*: Method (Acting) in Honduras.

——. 'El movimiento teatral hondureño'. [The Hondurian theatre movement]. **Conjunto** (March 1991): 85–6.

A3a60. HUNGARY

Alpar, Agnes. **A fővárosi kabarék mősora 1945–1980**. [The programme of Budapest cabarets 1945–1980]. Budapest: MSZI, 1981.

Antal, Gábor. **Színházmuvészetünkrol**. Budapest: Kossuth, 1983. – 446 p. *Notes*: History. 20th century.

Benedek, András. **Színhází muhelytitkok: tanulmányok**. Budapest: Magveto, 1985. – 514 p. *Notes*: History. 20th century/Theatre. Production and direction.

Borsa, Miklós and Pál Tolny. **Az ismeretlen Operaház**. [The unknown opera house]. Budapest: Mdszaki, 1984.

Buchmuller, Eva and Anna Koós. **Squat Theatre**. New York: Artists Space, 1996. – xviii, 229 p.: ill. *Notes*: Catalogue accompanying the exhibition 'Mr. Dead & Mrs. Free, a history of Squat Theatre' held at Artists Space, March 30–May 25, 1996. Includes bibliographical references (p. 203). Squat Theatre (group). History. Experimental theatre.

Csillag, Ilona, ed. **A százéves színésziskola**. [The one-hundred-year-old acting school]. Budapest: Magvető, 1964.

Dénes, Tibor. **Le Décor de théâtre en Hongrie: passé-present**. [Hungarian stage design: past and present]. Munich: Danubia, 1973.

Gábor, Éva. A. **Thália Társaság, 1904–08**. [The Thália Society, 1904–08]. With a summary in English. Budapest: Hungarian Theatre Institute, 1988.

Hont, Ferenc, ed. **Magyar Színháztörténet**. [Hungarian theatre history]. Budapest: Gondolat, 1962.

Hungarian theatre, 1982–1984. Budapest: Hungarian Centre of the International Theatre Institute, 1985. – 95 p.: ill.

Kerényi, Ferenc, ed. **A Nemzeti Színház 150 éve**.

[150 years of the National Theatre]. Budapest: Gondolat, 1987.

Kocsis, Rózsa. **Igen és nem; a magyar avantgard színjáték története**. Budapest: Magveto Kiadó, 1974 1973. – 654 p. illus. Notes: Includes bibliographical references. Experimental theatre. History.

Koltai, Tamás. **Cselekvo színház: kritikák, esszék, tanulmányok**. Budapest: Magveto, 1980. – 479 p. Notes: Reviews. Essays.

——. **Négy kritikus év: színikritikák, 1990–1993**. Budapest: Meszprint Kft., 1994. – 300 p. Notes: Reviews. Essays.

——. **Színházváltás, 1986–1991: kritikák, portrék, interjúk**. Budapest: Meszprint, 1991. – 316 p. Notes: Theatre. Reviews. Essays.

Kósa, Károly. **A Szolnoki Szigligeti Színház adattára és bibliográfiája, 1978–1985**. Szolnok: Készült a Verseghy Ferenc Megyei Könyvtár Sokszorosítójában, 1987. – 193 p.: ill. Notes: Includes indexes. Hungary. 20th century. Bibliography.

Kun, Éva. **Die Theaterarbeit von Sándor Hevesi: Ungarns Beitrag zur Reform des europäischen Theaters im 20. Jahrhundert**. [Sándor Hevesi's work in the theatre: the contribution of Hungary to the twentieth-century reform of European theatre]. Munich: Kitzinger, 1978.

Lengyel, György and Erzsébet Bereczky. **The Hungarian theatre today**. Budapest: Hungarian Centre of the International Theatre Institute, 1983. – 252 p.: ill. Notes: Performing arts. Drama. 20th century.

Mályusz-Császár and Judit Szántó, eds. **A magyar színháztörténet rövid vázlata**. [A brief outline of Hungarian theatre history]. Budapest: Hungarian Theatre Institute, 1979.

Matulef, Gizelle Beke. **Hungarian grotesque-absurd drama: contacts and parallels with Western theatre of the absurd to 1972**. 1983. – 241 p.: ill. Notes: Vita. Bibliography: p. 203–19. Thesis (Ph. D.)–Indiana University, 1983. Hungarian drama. History and criticism.

Mihályi, Gábor. **Színházról vitázva: tanulmányok, kritikák**. Budapest: Népmuvelési Propaganda Iroda, 1976. – 391 p., 22 p. plates: ill. Notes: Includes index. Bibliography: p. 375–7. Theatre. History. 20th century.

Nagy, Péter. **Le Théâtre classique français en Hongrie**. [French classical theatre in Hungary]. Budapest: Akadémiai, 1969.

——. **Zsöllyére ítélve: színikritikák**. Budapest: Gondolat, 1981. – 397 p. Notes: Includes index. Hungarian drama.

Némethné Fertsek, Ilona. **A kortárs magyar dráma színmuvészetünkben, 1957–1982: bibliográfia**. Budapest: Országos Színháztörténeti Múzeum és Intézet, 1990 1991. – 2 vols. Notes: 1. A–K – 2. L–Z. Hungarian drama. 20th century. Bibliography.

Siklós, Olga. **A magyar drámairodalom útja 1945-től 1957-ig**. [Hungarian dramatic literature from 1945 to 1957]. Budapest: Magvető, 1970.

Staud, Géza. **Adelstheater in Ungarn**. [Theatres of the nobility in Hungary]. Vienna: Verlag der Österreichischen Akademie der Wissenschaften, 1977. 393 p.

——. 'La Formation du nouveau public des théâtres en Hongrie après la IIe guerre mondiale'. [The development of new theatre audiences in Hungary after World War II]. In **Das Theater und sein Publikum**, ed. Heinz Kindermann. Vienna: Verlag der Österreichischen Akademie der Wissenschaften, 1977. 421 p.

——. **Magyar Színháztörténeti bibliográfia**. [Bibliography of Hungarian theatre history], 2 vols. Budapest: Magyar Színházi Intézet, 1976.

——, ed. **A Budapesti Operaház száz éve**. [One hundred years of the Budapest Opera House]. Budapest: Zeműkiadó, 1984.

Székely, György. **Magyar színházmuvészeti lexikon**. Budapest: Akadémiai Kiadó, 1994. – 882 p.: map, ports. Notes: Hungarian theatre encyclopedia. In Hungarian.

Sziládi, János. **Tapsrend: válogatott írások a színházról: tanulmányok, kritikák**. Budapest: Gondolat, 1982. – 240 p. Notes: Hungarian drama. History and criticism.

A3a61. ICELAND

Brynja Benediktsdóttir. **Brynja og Erlingur fyrir opnum tjöldum**. Reykjavík: Mál og menning, 1994. – 287 p., 16 p. of plates: ill. Notes: Includes indexes. Actors, producers and directors. Biography.

Einarsson, Sveinn. **Theatre in Iceland 1971–1975**. Reykjavík: Union of Icelandic Actors, 1976. – 43 p.: ill. Notes: Icelandic drama. History. 20th century.

——. **Theatre in Iceland, 1975–1980**. Reykjavík: Published by Association of Icelandic Actors: Icelandic Centre of the ITI: Icelandic Theatre Board, 1982. – 52 p.: ill. Notes: Icelandic drama. History.

——. **Íslensk leiklist**. Reykjavík: Bókaútgáfa Menningarsjóðs, 1991 1996. – 2 vols.: ill.

Notes: Vol. 2 published by: Hið íslenska bókmenntafélag. Includes bibliographical references and indexes. 1. Ræturnar – 2. Listin. Acting. History.

Friis, Erik J., ed. **Modern Nordic Plays – Iceland**. New York: Twayne, 1973.

Halldórsson, Baldvin. **Theatre in Iceland 1980–85: a yearbook**. Reykjavík: Union of Icelandic Actors, Icelandic Centre of ITI, Icelandic Theatre Board, 1985. – 72 p.: ill. *Notes*: Icelandic drama. History.

Haugen, Einar, ed. **Fire and ice: three Icelandic plays**. Reykjavík, 1967.

Janzon, Leif, ed. **Nordisk teater**. [Nordic theatre]. Stockholm, 1988.

Magnússon, Sigurdur A. **Icelandic Crucible**, Reykjavík, 1985.

Páll, Baldvin Baldvinsson and Martin S. Regal. **Theatre in Iceland 1992–1994**. Reykjavík: The Icelandic Centre of ITI: Icelandic Theatre Board: Union of Icelandic Actors, 1994. (unpaged): ill. *Notes*: Icelandic drama. History.

A3a62. INDIA

Ambras, Tewia. 'Tamasha: People's Theatre of Maharashtra State'. Ph.D. dissertation, Michigan State University, 1974.

Anand, Mulkraj. **The Indian Theatre**. New York: Roy Publications, 1951.

Bajwa, Joginder Singh and R.R. Gupta. **Bibliography of Panjabi drama**. Patiala: Modern Library Prakashan, 1982. – 95 p.: ports. *Notes*: English and Panjabi. Includes indexes.

Bandyopadhyaya, Biresvara. **Pathanatakera katha**. Calcutta: Moma: Paribesaka Pustaka Bipani, 1987. 82 pp. *Notes*: In Bengali. On the street theatre of West Bengal.

Bhanawat, Mahendra. **Lok Rangmanch**. [Folk theatre]. Jaipur: Bhartiya Lok Kala Mandal, 1971.

Bharucha, Rustom. **Chandralekha: woman/dance/resistance**. New Delhi: HarperCollins, 1993.

——. **The theatre of Kanhaiyalal: Pebet and memoirs of Africa**. Calcutta: Seagull Books, 1992.

——. **Theatre and the world: performance and the politics of culture**. London and New York: Routledge, 1993.

Bhat, G.K. **Theatrical aspects of Sanskrit drama**. Pune: Bhandarkar Oriental Research Institute, 1983.

Bhayani, Utpala. **Tarjanisanketa: rangabhumi para prastuta Gujarati ane itara bhashanam natakoni samiksha, 1984–85 thi 1990–91**. Mumbai: Amadavada: Srimati Nathibai Damodara Thakarasi Mahila Vidyapitha; Mukhya vikreta Navabharata Sahitya Mandira, 1992. 328 pp. *Notes*: In Gujarati. Includes index. Critical articles on Gujarati, Hindi, Marathi, and English theatre, 1984–1991.

Candresvara. **Bharata mem jana-natya andolana**. Ilahabada: Sabdapitha, 1994. 103 pp. *Notes*: In Hindi. On People's Theatre Movement in India since 1943.

Chaterjee, Sunit Kumar. **Indian drama**. Delhi: Publication Division, Ministry of Information and Broadcasting, Government of India, 1981.

Chattopadhyay, Rita. **Modern Sanskrit dramas of Bengal: 20th century AD**. Calcutta: Sanskrit Pustak Bhandar, 1992. ii, 283 p.

Chopra, P.N., ed. **Folk entertainment In India**. Delhi: Ministry of Education and Culture, 1981.

Contemporary Indian theatre: interviews with playwrights and directors. New Delhi: Sangeet Natak Akademi, 1989. – 192 p.: ill. *Notes*: Includes bibliographical references. Dramatists. India. Producers and directors. Interviews.

Dasgupta, H.N. **The Indian Theatre**. Delhi: Gian Publishing House, 1988.

——. **Indian Stage Vol. I–IV**. Calcutta: Metropolitan Publishing House, 1944.

Dass, Veena Noble. **Modern Indian drama in English translation**. Hyderabad: V.N. Dass, 1988. v, 238 p., 3 p. of plates: ill. *Notes*: Studies on the plays of Mohan Rakesh, Badal Sircar, Vijay Tendulkar, and Girish Karnad. Includes index. Bibliography: p. 217–30.

Desai, S.D. **Happenings: theatre in Gujarat in the eighties**. Gandhinagar: Gujarat Sahitya Akademi, 1990. x, 505 pp. *Notes*: Includes indexes. Reviews.

Devaliya, Visvabhavana. **Natya prastutikarana, svarupa aura prakriya**. 1. samskarana. Delhi: Surya-Prakasana, 1986. 288 p., 24 p. of plates: ill. *Notes*: In Hindi. Bibliography: p. 281–8. Aspects of 20th century Hindi theatre. History and criticism.

Frasca, Richard Armand. 'The Terukkuttu: Ritual Theatre of Tamilnadu'. Berkeley: University of California, 1984. 430 p. (Ph. D. Dissertation University of California, 1984).

——. **The Theatre of the Mahabharata: Terukuttu Performance in South India**. Honolulu: Hawaii Press, 1990.

Gargi, Balwant. **Folk Theatre of India**. Calcutta: Rupa, 1991. 217 pp.

——. **Theatre in India**. New York: Theatre Arts, 1962.

Ghosh, Manmohan. **The Natyashastra ascribed to Bharat Muni**. Calcutta: Granthalaya Pvt., 1967.

Ghosha, Ajitakumara. **Bamla natyabhinayera itihasa**. Calcutta: Pascimabanga Rajya Pustaka Parshada, 1985. 10, 461 pp., 24 p. of plates: ill. *Notes*: In Bengali. Includes indexes. Bibliography: p. 433–5. Historical study on the art of Bengali acting.

Ghosha, Karttika Kumara. **Odisara rangamanca o mora nata-jibana**. Calcutta: Odisa Buk Shtora, 1977. iii, v, iv, 223 p. *Notes*: In Oriya. On Oriya drama and theatre, 1921 to date; narratives of an Oriya dramatist and actor.

Gupta, Somnath. **Parsi Theatre: Udhabhau Aur Vikas**. [Parsi theatre: origin and development]. Allahabad: Lokbharati Prakashan, 1981.

Hansen, Kathryn. **Grounds for play: the Nautanki theatre of North India**. Berkeley: University of California Press, 1992. – xvii, 367 p.: ill., music. *Notes*: Includes bibliographical references (p. 337–50) and index. Nautanki/Folk drama, Hindi. History and criticism.

Hawkes, S.J. 'Forms of Chhau: An Investigation of an Indian Theatre'. Exeter, UK: University of Exeter, 1983. (Ph. D. Dissertation University of Exeter, 1983).

Jain, N.C., ed. **Adhunik Hindi Natak Aur Rangmanch**. [Modern Hindi drama and theatre]. Delhi: Macmillan Company of India, 1978.

——. **Indian theatre: tradition, continuity and change**. New Delhi: Vikas, 1992. 98 p.

——. **Rang Darsham**. [Theatre view]. Delhi: Macmillan Company of India.

Janaki, S.S. **Sanskrit drama in theory and practice**. New Delhi: Rashtriya Sanskrit Sansthan, 1995. – viii, 77 p. *Notes*: Includes bibliographical references.

Kale, Pramod. **The theatric universe**. Delhi: Popular Publications, 1974.

Kotovskaja, M.P. **Sintez iskusstv: Zreliscnyje iskusstva Indil**. [Synthesis of the arts: Performing arts of India]. Moscow: Nauka, 1982. 255 p.

Krishna Bhatta, S. **Indian English drama: a critical study**. London: Oriental University Press, 1987. – viii, 252 p. *Notes*: Revision of the author's thesis (Ph. D.)–Karnatak University, 1982. Includes index. Bibliography: p. 204–46.

Kulakarni, Raghunatha Purushottama. **The theatre according to the Natyasastra of Bharata**. Delhi: Kanishka Publishers, 1994. – 132 p.: ill. *Notes*: Includes bibliographical references (p. 53–4) and index. Stage-setting and scenery/Bharata Muni. Natyasastra.

Kulkarni, Govind Malhar. **Marathi natyasrshti**. Pune: Mehata Pablisinga Hausa, 1993. 167 p. *Notes*: In Marathi. Includes bibliographical references. Articles on Marathi theater. Theatre. India. Maharashtra. History. 20th century/Marathi drama. 20th century. History and criticism.

Lal, Lakshmi Narayan. **Parsi-Hindi Rangmach**. [Parsi-Hindi theatre]. Delhi: Rajpal & Sons, 1973.

Madhur, Shivkumar. **Bharat Ke Loknatya**. [Indian folk theatre]. Delhi: Vani Prakashan, 1980.

Mahanty, Kamalalochana and Durgacarana Kuamra. **Kamalalocana parikrama**. Calcutta: Odisa Buk Shtora, 1989. 216 p. *Notes*: In Oriya. Survey, chiefly on plays, of Kamalalochana Mahanty and his contribution to theatre in Orissa; articles and reminiscences.

Mainkar, Trimbak Govind. **Sanskrit theory of drama and dramaturgy: The theory of the samdhis and the samdhyangas in Bharata's Natyasastra**. 3rd edn. Delhi: Ajanta Publications, 1985, 1978. – 6, 192 p. *Notes*: English and Sanskrit. Published in 1978 as **The theory of the samdhis and the samdhyangas**. Includes index. Bibliography: 5th prelim. page.

Mathur, J.C. **Drama in rural India**. Delhi: ICCR Publications, 1967.

Mehta, Tarla. **Sanskrit play production in ancient India**. 1st edn. Delhi: Motilal Banarsidass Publishers, 1995. xxxii, 446 p.: ill. (some col.). *Notes*: Originally presented as the author's thesis (Ph. D.–Bombay University, 1982) under the title: 'The production techniques of Sanskrit dramas in ancient India'. Includes bibliographical references (p. 429–42) and index.

Mukherjee, Sushil Kumar. **The story of the Calcutta theatres: 1753–1980**. Calcutta: K.P. Bagchi and Company, 1982.

Mukhopadhyay, Das Gupta, ed. **Lesser known forms of performing arts in India**. Delhi: Sterling Publishers, 1978.

Nadiya Simha, Taurambama. **Manipuri nrtya**. Calcutta: Sribhumi Pabalisim Kompani, 1992. –5, 77, 1 p.: ill. *Notes*: In Bengali; includes songs with music in letter notation for the rhythm of the dance. Includes bibliographical references (p. 78). On Manipuri dance.

Naidu, V. **Ramayana and Mahabharata: contemporary theatrical experiments in English with Indic oral traditions of storytelling**. Leeds: University of Leeds, 1994. (Ph. D. Dissertation University of Leeds, 1994).

Narayan, Birendra. **Hindi drama and stage**. Delhi: Bansal Company, 1981.

Narayanapilla, Ke. Es. **Drsyavedi**. Kottayam: Di. Si. Buks: Distributors, Current Books, 1985. 195 p. *Notes*: In Malayalam. Articles on the Malayalam theatre and dance in Kerala.

Neog, Maheswar. **Bhaona, the ritual play of Assam**. New Delhi: Sangeet Natak Akademi, 1984. 65 pp.: ill. *Notes*: Bibliography: p. 65. Popular culture. Assam.

Nisata, Isarata. **Bikshita thiyetara**. Dhaka: Sagara Pabalisarsa, 1992. 143 p.: ill. *Notes*: In Bengali. Articles on Bengali theatre, with reference to Bangladesh.

Ojha, Dasaratha. **Hindi nataka-kosa: [san 1325 se 1970 taka ke Hindi-natakom ka adhikarika adhyayana]**. Delhi: Nesanala, 1975. – 22, 654 p. *Notes*: Hindi drama.

——. **Hindi Natak Udhbhau Aur Vikas**. [Hindi drama: Its origin and development]. Delhi: Rajpal & Sons, 1954.

Panchal, Goverdhan. **Bhavai and its typical aharya: costume, make-up, and props in bhavai, the traditional dramatic form of Gujarat**. Ahmedabad: Darpana Academy of the Performing Arts, 1983. – 32 p.: ill. *Notes*: Cover title. Includes bibliographical references. Gujarat/Costume. India.

——. **The theatres of Bharata and some aspects of Sanskrit play-production**. New Delhi: Munshiram Manoharlal Publishers, 1996. – xix, 162 p.: ill. *Notes*: Includes bibliographical references (p. 150–4) and index. Stage-setting and scenery. Sanskrit drama. History and criticism.

Pande, Anupa. **A historical and cultural study of the Natyasastra of Bharata**. Jodhpur: Kusumanjali Prakashan: 1991. vii, 340 pp. *Notes*: Based on the author's thesis (D. Phil.–University of Allahabad, 1987). Classical work on Indic dramaturgy and histrionics; a critical study. Includes index. Includes bibliographical references (p. 328–33). Sanskrit drama. Music, Karnatic. Philosophy and aesthetics.

Parmar, Shaym. **Traditional folk media**. Delhi: Communication Publishers, 1977.

Patil, Anand. **Western influence on Marathi drama: a case study**. Panaji, Goa: P. Bhide, Rajhauns Vitaran, 1993. xii, 326 pp.: ill. *Notes*:

Includes bibliographical references (p. 299–318) and index.

Pilla, En. En. **Natakam veno natakam**. Kottayam: Di. Si. Buks: Distributors, Current Books, 1994. 134 p. *Notes*: In Malayalam; includes passages in English. Viewpoints of a Malayalam playwright on contemporary Malayalam drama and theatre.

Piretti Santangelo, Laura. **Il teatro indiano antico. Aspetti e problemi**. [Ancient Indian theatre: Aspects and problems]. Bologna: Clueb, 1982. 133 pp.

Pradhana, Sudhi. **Gana-naba-sat-goshthi natyakatha**. Calcutta: Pustaka Bipani, 1992. 12, 191 p. *Notes*: In Bengali. Includes index. Articles on 20th century theatre movement in West Bengal, India. *Subjects*: Theatre. India. West Bengal. History. 20th century/Bengali drama. India. West Bengal. 20th century. History and criticism.

Purna Chandra Rao, P.V. **To the rural masses through street play**. Secunderabad: Cultural Forum, Rural Development Advisory Service, 1984. 47 p.

Rabindranath Tagore – a centennial volume (1861–1961). Sahitya Akadmi. 1961.

Rahu, Kironmoy. **Bengali theatre**. New Delhi: National Book Trust, 1978.

Ramakrishna Rau, Abburi. **Living theatre: articles in English and Telugu collected from 'Abburi samsmarana' and 'Abburi satajayamti samputi'**. Hyderabad: Abburi Trust, 1996. – 68 p. *Notes*: Articles, chiefly on contemporary Telugu drama. *Subject*: Telugu drama. 20th century. History and criticism.

Rang yatra: twenty-five years of the National School of Drama Repertory Company. New Delhi: National School of Drama, 1992. 284 pp.: ill. (some col.).

Rangacharya, Adya. **The Indian theatre**. Delhi: National Book Trust, 1980.

Rangnath, H.K. **The Karnataka theatre**. Dharvad: Karnataka University, 1960.

Richmond, Farley P., Darius L. Swann, Phillip Zarilli, eds. **Indian theatre: traditions of performance**. University of Hawaii Press, 1990.

Saha, Kanika. **Adhunika Bamla kabyanatya, udbhaba o bikasa**. Calcutta: Praptisthana Debi Pustakalaya, 1994. 11, 258 p. *Notes*: In Bengali. Modern Bengali poetic drama, origin and development. Includes bibliographical references (p. 243–52) and index.

Sanadhya, Devarshi. **Bharatiya Natya sastra tatha Hindi-natya-vidhana**. New Delhi: Esa.

Canda, 1981. – x, 854 p. *Notes*: In Hindi. Includes index. Bibliography: p. 813–19. Hindi drama. History and criticism.

Sankarappilla, Ji. **Natakadarsanam**. Kottayam: Di. Si. Buks: Distributors, Current Books, 1990. 504 p. *Notes*: In Malayalam. Articles, most on the Malayalam theater, 1964–88, and 20th century Malayalam drama. Includes bibliographical references.

Sarat Babu, Manchi. **Indian drama today: a study in the theme of cultural deformity**. New Delhi: Prestige, 1997. 158 p. *Notes*: Includes bibliographical references (p. 154–8) and index.

Sarma, Madana Mohana. **Svatantryottarayugina pariprekshya aura nukkara nataka: eka mulyankana**. Ahmedabad: Parsva Prakasana, 1992. 244 p. *Notes*: In Hindi. Includes bibliographical references. Post-independence Hindi street play; a study.

Sarma, Omaprakasa. **Svatantryottara Hindi rangamanca**. Kanapura: Atula Prakasana, 1994. 440 pp. *Notes*: In Hindi. Includes bibliographical references (p. 435–40). Study of the post 1947 Hindi theatre.

Schechner, Richard. **Performative circumstances from the Avant Garde to the Rāmlilā**. Calcutta: Seagull Books, 1983.

Shah, Anuparna and Uma Joshi. **Puppetry and folk dramas: for non-formal education**. New Delhi: Sterling, 1992. 174 p.

Singh, R.S.P. **Nataka-samalocana-sandarbha: Hindi nataka se sambandhita samalocanatmaka granthom ki visleshanatmaka grantha-sandarbha-suci**. Patana: Janaki Prakasana, 1979. – xxii, 420 p. *Notes*: In Hindi. Includes index. Hindi drama. History and criticism. Bibliography.

Sirkar, Badal. **The third theatre**. Calcutta: Badal Sirkar, 1978.

Srampickal, J.J. **Popular theatre as a medium for conscientization and development in India**. Leeds: University of Leeds, 1989. (Ph.D. Dissertation University of Leeds).

Subodha, Madhuri. **Hamari ranga asmita**. New Delhi: Intaranesanala Pablisarsa (Indiya), 1994. 128 p. *Notes*: In Hindi. Includes bibliographical references. Theatre in India; its history and development with special reference to Hindi theatre in modern times.

——. **Hindi rangamanca aura aitihasika nataka**. Delhi: Prakasana Vibhaga, Dilli Visvavidyalaya, 1995. xiv, 369 p.: ill. *Notes*: Includes bibliographical references (p. 359–69). Historical plays by Hindi authors and their theatrical aspects; covers the period, early 20th century to contemporary times.

Taneja, Jai Dev. **Adhunika Bharatiya rangaparidrsya**. New Delhi: Takshasila Prakasana, 1992. 224 p. *Notes*: In Hindi. Includes bibliographical references. Study of the history and development of theatre in India.

——. **Hindi rangakarma: dasa aura disa**. New Delhi: Takshasila Prakasana, 1988. 357 p. *Notes*: In Hindi. On contemporary Hindi drama and theatre.

Thompson, Edward. **Tagore: poet and dramatist**, 1948.

Tombi Simha, Nommaithema. **Manipuri sahityada anauba mityem ama**. Imphala: Bhi. Ai. Pablikesansa, 1985. v, xii, 247 p. *Notes*: In Manipuri. Includes indexes. Articles on modern Manipuri literature and theatre.

Tourlet, Christiane and Jacques Scherer. **Quand le Dieu Rama joue à Benarès**. [When the god Rama plays in Benares]. Cahiers Théâtre Louvain 68–9. Louvain-la-Neuve, Cahiers Théâtre Louvain, 1990. 203 p.

Varadpande, M.L. **Krishna theatre in India**. Atlantic Highlands, NJ: Humanities Press, 1982. 145 p.

——. **Traditions of Indian theatre**. New Delhi: Abhinau Prakashan, 1978.

—— and Sunil Subhedar, eds. **The critic of Indian theatre**. Atlantic Highlands, NJ: Humanities Press, 1982. 203 p.

Vasishtha, Suresa. **Hindi nataka aura rangamanca: Brekhta ka prabhava**. Delhi: Prema Prakasana Mandira, 1995. 195 p. *Notes*: Includes bibliographical references (p. 187–95). Influence of Bertolt Brecht, 1898–1956, on Hindi drama and theatre, chiefly of 20th century; a study.

Vatsyayan, Kapila. **Traditional Indian theatre: multiple streams**. Delhi: National Book Trust, 1980.

Venu, G. and Nirmala Paniker. **Mohiniyattam: Attaprakaram with notation of mudras and postures**. Trivandrum: By the Author, 204 p.

Venu, Ji. **Production of a play in Kutiyattam**. Irinjalakuda, Trichur District, Kerala, S. India: Natanakairali, 1989. viii, 104, 1 p., 12 p. of plates: ill. *Notes*: Documentation of Kutiyattam with the kramadipika (production manual) and the attaprakaram (acting manual) from the Sanskrit drama tradition of Kerala. Includes bibliographical references (p. 105).

Wade, Bonnie C. **Performing arts in India: essays on music, dance and drama**. University of California Center for South and Southeast Asia Studies Monograph Series 21. Berkeley and Lanham, MD: Centre for South and Southeast Asia Studies, University of California and UP of America, 1983. 270 p.

Yajnik, Y.K. **The Indian theatre**. London: George Allen & Unwin, 1933.

Yakshagana dance drama of South India: make-up and costuming in Yakshagana. Washington, D.C.: Japan Foundation, 1981. – 1 videocassette (21 min.): sd., col.; $\frac{3}{4}$ in. Series: Video documentation series. Make-up and costuming in Asian performing arts. Notes: Title on container: Make-up and costuming in Yakshagana. U-matic. Shows actors preparing for performance in Yakshagana; explaining what various pieces of costume signify as well as how make-up is applied and what it signifies. Differences in costuming female and male characters is also shown. Directors, Toru Itaya, Hitoshi Matushita, Hiroto Murasawa. India.

Zarrilli, Phillip B. **The Kathakali complex: actor, performance and structure**. New Delhi: Abhinav Publications, 1984. 406 p.

A3a63. INDONESIA

Anderson, B. Sutton. **Mythology and tolerance of the Javanese**. Ithaca: Cornell University Press, 1965.

Asih, S. **Daftar drama: koleksi Pusat Dokumentasi Sastra H.B. Jassin**. Jakarta: Pusat Dokumentasi Sastra H.B. Jassin, 1986. – vol. 1. Notes: Bibliography of Indonesian drama.

Buurman, Peter. **Wayang Golek: the entrancing world of classical Javanese Puppet Theatre**. Oxford: Oxford University Press, 1991. 152 p.

Cazzola, Gabriele. **L'attore di Dio: conversazioni balinesi**. [God's actor: Conversation in Bali]. Biblioteca di cultura 56. Rome: Bulzoni, 1990. 127 p.

Citra manusia dalam drama Indonesia modern, 1920–1960. Jakarta: Pusat Pembinaan dan Pengembangan Bahasa, 1993. xi, 188 p. Notes: Includes bibliographical references (p. 184–8). Aspects of human life in Indonesian. History and criticism.

Coudrin, Gildas-Louis. **Wayang Golek: tradition vivant**. [Wayang golek: A living tradition]. La Gaubretière: CEPMA, 1986. 155 p.

Giava-Bali rito e spettacolo. [Java-Bali, rite and performance]. Biblioteca Teatrale 46. Rome: Bulzoni, 1985. 348 p.

Groenendael, Victoria M. Clara van. **Wayang theatre in Indonesia: an annotated bibliography**. Dordrecht, Holland; Providence, R.I.:

Foris, 1987. 221 p. Notes: Includes indexes. Puppet theaters. Indonesia. Bibliography.

Harun, Chairul. **Kesenian randai di Minangkabau**. Jakarta: Department Pendidikan dan Kebudayaan, 1991. v, 135 p.: ill. Notes: Includes bibliographical references (p. 134–5). History of randai, a traditional theatre of Minangkabau ethnic group, and its relation with Minangkabau customs.

Keeler, Ward. **Javanese shadow plays, Javanese selves**. Princeton: Princeton University Press, 1987. 282 p.

Long, Roger. **Javanese Shadow Theatre: movement and characterization in ngayogyakarta wayang kulit**. Ann Arbor: UMO Research Press, 1982. 195 p.

Nalan, Arthur S., ed. **Aspek manusia dalam seni pertunjukan**. Bandung: STSI Press, 1996.

Peacock, James L. **Rites of modernization: symbolic and social aspects of Indonesian proletarian drama**. Chicago: University of Chicago Press, 1968.

Riantiarno, Nano. **Teguh Karya & Teater Populer, 1968–1993**. Jakarta: Pustaka Sinar Harapan, 1993. – 184 p., 11 p. of plates: ill. Notes: Includes bibliographical references (p. 88). Teguh Karya, b. 1937, Indonesian film director and his Jakarta-based Teater Populer, 1968–93.

Saini, K.M. **Beberapa gagasan teater**. [Some ideas on theatre]. Jakarta: Nur Cahaya, 1981.

——. **Dramawan dan karyanya**. [Dramatists and their works]. Jakarta: Angkasa, 1983.

——. **Peristiwa teater**. [The theatrical event]. Bandung: ITB Press, 1995.

——. **Teater Indonesia dan beberapa masalatinya**. [Indonesian theatre and its problems]. Jakarta: Binacipta, 1988.

Siregar, Ahmad Samin, Razali Kasim and Z. Pangaduan Lubis. **Kamus istilah seni drama**. Jakarta: Pusat Pembinaan dan Pengembangan Bahasa, Departemen Pendidikan dan Kebudayaan, 1985. – vi, 65 p. Indonesian theatre encyclopedia.

Sitanggang, S.R.H., Zainal Hakim and Agus Sri Danardhana. **Struktur drama Indonesia modern, 1980–1990**. Jakarta: Pusat Pembinaan dan Pengembangan Bahasa, 1995. x, 164 pp.: ill. Notes: Includes bibliographical references (p. 163–4). Literary criticism on modern Indonesian drama, 1980–90.

Soedarsono. **Wayang Wong. The state ritual dance of the Court of Yogjakarta**. Gajah Mada University Press, 1984.

Sri Muljono. 'Performance of Wayang Purwa Kulit'. In **Traditional drama music of South East Asia**. Kuala Lumpur: Dewan Bahasa dan Pustaka, 1974.

Sumardjo, Jakob. **Perkembangan teater modern dan sastra drama Indonesia**. [The development of modern Indonesian theatre and dramatic literature]. Jakarta: Citra Aditya Bhakti, 1992. 396 p.

Widyawan, Rosa. **Modern Indonesian drama. a select bibliography**. Sydney: Bibliographic Information on Southeast Asia, 1986. – 3 microfiches: negative. *Series*: BISA special projects. *Notes*: Title from separate label. Indonesian drama. Bibliography.

Zurbechen, Mary Sabina. **The language of Balinese shadow theatre**. Princeton: Princeton University Press, 1987. 291 p.

A3a64. IRAN

Armaghani, Ahmad. **Kitabshinasi-i namayishi: pizhuhish va tadvin az Ahmad Armaghani**. Chap-i 2. Mashhad: Guruh-i Ti'atr-i Rudaki, 1975. 69 p. *Notes*: Includes bibliographical references (p. 60) and index. Iranian drama. Bibliography.

Beeman, William O. **Culture, performance and communication in Iran**. Tokyo: ILCAA, 1982. 223 p.

Beyza'i, Bahram. **Namayesh dar Iran**. [Theatre in Iran]. Tehran: Kaivan, 1965. 242 p.

Chelkowski, Peter J., ed. **Ta'ziyeh and ritual and drama in Iran**. New York: New York University Press and Soroush, 1979. 288 p.

Chodko, Alexandre. **Jong-i Shadat, an anthology of martyrdom**. 4 vols. Tehran: Soroush, 1977–1979.

——. **Théâtre persan: choix de téazies ou drames**. [Persian theatre. A choice: ta'ziyeh or drama]. Paris, 1878.

Elwell-Sutton, L.P., ed. **Bibliographical guide to Iran**. Brighton, Sussex: Harvester Press; Totowa, NJ: Barnes & Noble, 1983: p. 341–7.

Emami, Karim, ed. **Shiraz Festival of Arts – the first ten years (1967–76), An Illustrated Album**. Tehran: Soroush, 1976. 145 p.

Enjavi-Shirazi and Said Abolqasem. **Bazi-ha-ye namayeshi**. [Theatrical games]. Tehran: Amir Kabir, 1973.

Gaffary, Farrokh. 'Déguisement et cortèges en Iran'. [Disguising and masquerade in Iran]. In **Carnavals et mascarades** [Carnivals and masquerades], ed. Giovanni Pier d'Ayala and Martin Boiteux. Paris: Bordas/Spectacle, 1988.

——. 'Iranian Secular Theatre', In **McGraw-Hill encyclopedia of world drama**, (vol. 3), ed. by Stanley Hochman, New York: McGraw-Hill, 1984.

——. 'Baqqal-bazi' [The play of grocer]. In **Encyclopaedia Iranica**, vol. 3, New York: pub. in association with Columbia University [n.d.].

——. 'Dalqak' [The Jester]. In **Encyclopaedia Iranica**, vol 4, New York: pub. in association with Columbia University [n.d.].

Ghanoonparvar, M.R. and John Green. **Iranian drama – an anthology**. Costa Mesa, Cal: Mazda, 1989. 302 p.

Gobineau. **Religions et philosophies dans l'Asie Centrale**. [Religion and philosophy in central Asia]. Paris: Gallimard, 1957. 484 p.

Haery, Mahmoud M. **Ru-howzi: the Iranian traditional improvisatory theatre**. 1982. – x, 165 p.: ill. *Notes*: Bibliography: p. 158–65. Thesis (Ph. D.)–New York University, 1982. Photocopy. Ann Arbor, Mich.; University Microfilms International, 1986. x, 165 p.

Jennati, A'tai Abolqasem. **Bonyadeh namayesh dar Iran**. [The foundation of theatre in Iran]. Tehran: Saffi Ali Shah, 1955.

Kapuscinski, Gisele. **Modern Persian drama – an anthology**. New York, London: University Press of America, 1987. 227 p.

Khodayar, Naser and Johari Mansour, eds. **Anahita**. Tehran: Anahita Theatre Publications, 1960–3.

Khojasteh Kia. **Shahnameh-e Ferdowsi va trajedi-e Atheni**. [Shahnameh Ferdowsi and the Athenian tragedy]. Tehran: Sherkateh entesharat-e elmi va farhangi [Scientific & Cultural Publications Company], 1990. 111 p.

——. **Qaremanan-e badpa dar qesse-ha va namayesh-ha ye Irani**. [The whirlwind heroes in Iranian stories and plays]. Tehran: Nashr-e Markaz, 1996. 207 p.

Krymski, Agatangel. **Perskij teatr**. [Persian theatre]. Kiev. 1925.

Male, Andrea Ritzel-Moosavi. **Komödiantische Volkstheatertraditionen in Iran und die Entstehung des iranischen Berufstheaters nach europäischem Vorbild von der Jahrhundertwende bis 1978**. Frankfurt am Main; New York: P. Lang, 1993. ix, 167 pp.: 2 ill. *Notes*: Originally presented as the author's thesis (doctoral)–Ludwig-Maximilians-Universität in Munich, 1990. Includes bibliographical references (p. 154–67). History. 20th century.

Malekpour, Jamshid. **'Adabiyat-e namayeshi**

dar Iran. [Drama in Iran]. 2 vols. Tehran: Toos, 1983. 532 pp. and 524 p.

——. **Seyr-e tahavol-e mazamin dar shabih khani ta'ziyeh**. [Persian passion plays]. Tehran: Jahad-daneshgahi, 1987. 280 p.

——. **Guzidah'i az tarikh-i namayish dar jahan**. Tehran: Sazman-i Intisharat-i Kayhan, 1985. – 13, 572 p.: ill. *Notes*: In Persian. Title on added t.p.: The selected history of world theatre. Includes indexes. Bibliography: p. 533–5. Stage setting and scenery. History.

Mamian, Arsen, ed. **Iranahai verjin 50-amiya tatroni vastakavorner**. [Fifty years of Armenian theatre in Iran]. Tehran: Alik, 1985. 190 p.

Mamnoun, Parviz. **Seyri dar tatr-e mardomi-e Isfahan**. [A reflection on popular theatre in Isfahan]. Tehran, 1977.

Marouffi, Abbas, ed. **The First International Puppet Theatre Festival**. Tehran: The Centre of Dramatic Arts (CDA), 1989. 206 p.

Massoudieh, Mohammad. **Taghi Mucighi-e mazhabi-e Iran: musighi-e ta'ziyah**. [The religious music of Iran: music of ta'ziyeh].Tehran: Soroush, 1989. 242 p.

Mir Khadivi, Asghar. **Khatirat-i si sal pusht-i sahnah-i ti'atr**. Mashhad: Intisharat-i Tamaddun (Bastan-i sabiq), 1993. 336 p.: ill. *Notes*: History. 20th century.

Muntaziri, 'Ali. **Sayah'ha-yi mandigar**. Tehran: Intisharat-i Barg, 1988. 3 v.: ill. *Notes*: Includes indexes. History. 20th century.

Nushin, 'Abdol-Hosseyn. **Honar-e teatr**. [The art of theatre]. Tehran, 1952.

Papazian, Vahram. **Hetadartz haiatzk**. [A reflection on the past]. 2 vols. Yerevan: 1956–7. Vol II, from p. 382.

Pelly, L.S. **Miracle plays of Hasan and Hussein** London, 1879. *Notes*: Contains a translation of thirty-seven plays.

Rezvani, Medjid. **Le Théâtre et la danse en Iran**. [Theatre and dance in Iran]. Paris: G.P. Maisonneuve et Larose, 1962. 299 p.

Rossi, Ettore and Alessio Bombaci. **Elenco di drammi religiosi persiani**. Vatican, 1961. *Notes*: A descriptive catalogue of Enrico Cerulli's collection of 1,055 *ta'ziyeh* manuscripts.

Sayyad, Parviz. **Theater of the diaspora**. Costa Mesa, Cal.: Mazda, 1992. 187 p.

Shahriyari, Khusraw. **Kitab-i namayish: farhang-i vazhahha, istilahha, sabkha va jarayanha-yi namayishi**. Tehran: Amir-i Kabir, 1986. – 2 v. (606 p., 94 p. of plates): ill. *Notes*: Indexes. Persian language drama dictionary.

Smith, A.C.H. **Orghast at Persepolis, an international experiment in theatre**. London, New York: Eyre Methuen/The Viking Press, 1972. 246 p.

Taghian, Laleh. **Dar bareyeh Ta'ziyeh va tatr dar Iran**. [On ta'ziyeh and theatre]. Tehran: Nashr-e Markaz, 1995. 240 p.

——. **Ketabshenassi-e teatr**. [Bibliography of theatre]. Tehran: Namayesh, 1992. 315 p.

Yarshater, Ehsan. 'Persia'. **The reader's encyclopedia of world drama**, John Gassner and Edward Quinn, eds. 647–652. London: Methuen & Co. Ltd., 1970–5.

A3a65. IRAQ

Abbaas, 'Ali Muzaahim. **Salaaman Ayyuha l-Masrahiyyoun**. [Greetings, oh dramatists]. Baghdad: Wa'i l-'Ummaal Press, 1985.

'Abd Allah, 'Ali. **al-Masrah al-musiqi fi al-'Iraq**. Baghdad: Dar al-Shu'un al-Thaqafiyah al-'Ammah, Wizarat al-Thaqafah wa-al-I'lam, 1995. – 159 p. *Notes*: Includes bibliographical references. Musical theatre. History/Arabic drama. Iraq.

Alsenad, Abedalmutalab Abood. **Professional production of Shakespeare in Iraq: an exploration of cultural adaptation**. 1988 1989. – ix, 196 p. *Notes*: Includes bibliographical references. Thesis (Ph. D.)–University of Colorado. Microfiche. Ann Arbor, Mi.: University Microfilms International, 1988. 3 microfiches.

Fareed, Badri Hassoun. **al-Masrah al-'Iraaqi Fi 'Aam 1967**. [The Iraqi theatre in the year 1967]. Baghdad: 1968.

Hasan, Khidr Jum'a. **Hisaad al-Masrah Fi Ninewa1880–1971**. [The theatrical harvest in Nineveh 1880–1971]. al-Mawsil: al-Jumhour Press, 1972.

al-Jaadir,'Abd al-Mun'im. **Min Tareekh an-Nahda l-Fanniyya Fi l-'Iraaq al-Hadeeth**. [From the history of the modern artistic renaissance in Iraq] Baghdad: Baghdad Press, 1950.

Mafraji, Ahmad Fayadah, ed. **A view of children's theatre in Iraq**. Baghdad: State Organization for Theatre and Cinema, 1978.

——. **Haqqi ash-Shibli Raa'id al-Masrah al-'Iraaqi**. [Haqqi ash-Shibli the Iraqi theatre pioneer]. Baghdad: Twaini Press, 1985.

——. **al-Haraka al-Masrahiyya Fi l-'Iraaq**. [The theatrical movement in Iraq] Baghdad: ash-Sha'b Press, 1965.

——. **Masaadir Diraasat al-Masrah Fi l-'Iraaq**. [Sources for studying the theatre in Iraq]. Baghdad, 1979.

——. **Masrah Fi l-'Iraaq**. [The theatre in Iraq]. Baghdad, 1987.

Nasir, Yasin. **Buq'at daw', buq'at zill: maqalat fi al-masrah al-'Iraqi al-mu'asir**. Baghdad: Dar al-Shu'un al-Thaqafiyah al-'Ammah 'Afaq 'Arabiyah', 1989. – 325 p.: ill. *Notes*: Includes bibliographical references. Arabic drama. Criticism.

——. **Wajhan li-Wajh**. [Face to face]. Baghdad: Daar as-Saa'a Press, 1967.

al-Taalib, 'Umar. **al-Masrahiyya al-'Arabiyya Fi l-'Iraaq 'Aam**. [The Arabic stage play in Iraq] Baghdad: an-Nu'maan Press, 1971.

Tharwat, Yusuf 'Abd al-Masih. **Tariq wa-al-hudud: maqalat fi al-adab wa-al-masrah wa-al-fann**. Baghdad: al-Jumhuriyah al-'Iraqiyah, Wizarat al-I'lam:Tawzi' al-Dar al-Wataniyah lil-Nashr wa-al-Tawzi' wa-al-I'lan, 1977. – 315 p.; 25 cm. *Series*: Silsilat 'dirasat' – Wizarat al-I'lam, al-Jumhuriyah al-'Iraqiyah; 118. Silsilat dirasat (Iraq. Wizarat al-I'lam); 118. *Notes*: Includes bibliographies. *Subjects*: Literature, Modern. 20th century. History and criticism/Arabic drama. Iraq. History and criticism.

at-Tu'ma, Saaleh Jawaad. **Bibliografia al-Adab al-Masrahi al-'Arabi al-Hadeeth**. [Bibliography of modern Arabic theatre literature]. Baghdad 1969.

az-Zubaydi, 'Ali. **al-Masrahiyya al-'Arabiyya Fi l-'Iraaq**. [The Arabic play in Iraq]. Cairo: Arab Research and Studies Institute and the Arab League, 1966.

A3a66. IRELAND

Barbour, Sheena, ed. **Irish performing arts yearbook 1992**. London: Rhinegold, 1992. 97 p.

Bell, Sam Hanna. **The theatre in Ulster; a survey of the dramatic movement in Ulster from 1902 until the present day**. Totowa: N.J.: Rowman and Littlefield, 1972. – xi, 147 p. *Notes*: Includes bibliographical references.

Bort, Eberhard. **The state of play: Irish theatre in the 'nineties**. Trier: Wissenschaftlicher Verlag, 1996. *Notes*: 'Papers given at an international conference on contemporary Irish theatre at the University of Tübingen'–back cover. Includes bibliographical references and index. Preface: 'There's a buzz …'/Eberhard Bort – A place called Tübingen/Ivy Bannister – The state of play: Irish theatre in the 'nineties/Christopher Murray – National theatre: the state of the Abbey/Karin McCully – Reclaiming performance: the contemporary Irish independent theatre sector/Anna McMullan – Deevy's leap: Teresa Deevy remembered in the 1990s/Cathy Leeney – Commitment and risk in Anne Devlin's Ourselves alone and After Easter/Brendan MacGurk – A hard act: Stewart Parker's Pentecost/Gerald Dawe – Beyond Field day: Brian Friel's Dancing at Lughnasa/Robert F. Garratt – 'Come on you boys in green': Irish football, Irish theatre, and the 'Irish diaspora'/Eberhard Bort – Reinventing women: Charabanc Theatre Company/Claudia W. Harris – Between a Bible and a flute band: community theatre in the Shankill and in Long Kesh/Tom Magill – The experience of understanding Belfast: the adventure of translating Graham Reid/Beate Richter – The Northern Irish troubles: a problem of representation/Stuart Marlow – Beyond the Theatre review: the Arts Council and regional developments in Irish theatre/Mary Cloake – Local arts centres and Irish theatre/Paul O'Hanrahan.

Etherton, Michael. **Contemporary Irish dramatists**. New York: St. Martin's Press, 1989. – xvi, 253 p., [8] p. of plates: ill. *Notes*: Includes index. Bibliography: p. 239–49. Northern Ireland in literature. History and criticism.

Fitz-Simon, Christopher. **The Irish theatre**. London: Thames & Hudson, 1982. 208 p.

Fox, Ian. **100 nights at the opera: an anthology to celebrate the 40th anniversary of Wexford Opera Festival**. Dublin: Townhouse and Country House, 1991. 151 p.

Frazier, Adrian. **Behind the scenes at the Abbey**. London/Berkeley, CA: University of California Press, 1990. 258 p.

Harrington, John P. **The Irish play on the New York stage, 1874–1966**. Lexington, Ky.: University Press of Kentucky, 1997. – 192 p.: ill. *Notes*: Includes bibliographical references (p. 166–79) and index.

——. **Modern Irish drama**. 1st edn. New York: Norton, 1991. – xiv, 577 p. *Notes*: Includes bibliographical references (p. [574]–577). Cathleen ni Houlihan; On Baile's strand; Purgatory/W.B. Yeats – Spreading the news; The rising of the moon/Lady Gregory – Riders to the sea; The playboy of the western world/J.M. Synge – John Bull's other island/Bernard Shaw – Juno and the paycock/Sean O'Casey – The quare fellow/Brendan Behan – Krapp's last tape/Samuel Beckett – Translations/Brian Friel – Backgrounds and criticism.

Hogan, Robert and Michael O'Neill, eds. **Joseph Holloway's Irish theatre**. 3 vols. Dixon, CA: Proscenium Press, 1968–70.

Hunt, Hugh. **The Abbey: Ireland's national theatre, 1904–1978**. Dublin; New York: Gill and Macmillan, 1979. – 306 p., 8 p. of plates: ill. *Notes*: Includes bibliographical references and indexes.

Hynes, Jerome. **Druid: the first ten years**. Galway: Druid Performing Arts and Galway Arts Festival, 1985. – 79 p.: ill. History. Druid Theatre Company.

King, Kimball. **Ten modern Irish playwrights: a comprehensive annotated bibliography**. New York: Garland Pub., 1979. – xiii, 111 p. *Notes*: Includes index. Brendan Behan–John Boyd–James Douglas–Brian Friel–John B. Keane–Thomas Kilroy–Hugh Leonard–James McKenna–Thomas Murphy–Edna O'Brien.

Maxwell, D.E.S. **A critical history of modern Irish drama, 1891–1980**. Cambridge; New York: Cambridge University Press, 1984. – xvii, 250 p.: ill. *Notes*: Includes index. Bibliography: p. 225–39.

Mikhail, E.H. **An annotated bibliography of modern Anglo-Irish drama**. Troy, NY: Whitston, 1981.

——. **A research guide to modern Irish dramatists**. Troy, N.Y.: Whitston Pub. Co., 1979. – vii, 104 p. *Notes*: Includes index.

O'Driscoll, Robert, ed. **Theatre and nationalism in twentieth-century Ireland**. London: Oxford University Press, 1971. – 216 p., 4 plates. illus. *Notes*: Includes bibliographical references.

O'Hagan, John W., Christopher Duffy and T. Duffy. **The performing arts and the public purse: an economic analysis**. Dublin: Arts Council, 1987. 89 p.

O'Malley, Conor. **A poets' theatre**. Dublin, Ireland: Elo Press, 1988. – 168 p.: ill. (some col.). *Notes*: Includes bibliographical references (p. 161–4) and index. Lyric Players Theatre, history.

Pine, Richard. **Brian Friel and Ireland's drama**. London: Routledge, 1991. 256 p.

—— and Richard Cave. **The Dublin Gate Theatre, 1928–1978**. Cambridge/Teaneck, NJ: Chadwyck-Healey, 1984. 124 p.

Richtarik, Marilynn J. **Acting between the lines: the Field Day Theatre Company and Irish cultural politics, 1980–1984**. Oxford: Clarendon Press, Oxford University Press, 1994. – 356 p. *Notes*: Includes bibliographical references. Political aspects. Northern Ireland/Field Day Theatre Company.

Rollins, Ronald Gene. **Divided Ireland: bifocal vision in modern Irish drama**. London: University Press of America, 1987. – 116 p. *Notes*: Includes bibliography. Irish writers, 1900–.

Schrank, Bernice and William W. Demastes. **Irish playwrights, 1880–1995: a research and production sourcebook**. Westport, Conn.: Greenwood Press, 1997. – xii, 454 p. *Notes*: Includes bibliographical references (p. 419–23) and indexes.

Sekine, Masaru. **Irish writers and the theatre**. Gerrards Cross: Smythe, 1986. – viii, 246 p. *Notes*: Includes index. Theatre, 1891–1980.

Shaughnessy, Edward L. **Eugene O'Neill in Ireland: the critical reception**. New York: Greenwood Press, 1988. – xv, 221 p.: ill. *Notes*: Includes index. Bibliography: p. 129–33. O'Neill, Eugene, 1888–1953. Stage history.

Stagecast: Irish stage and screen directory. Monkstown: Stagecast, 1992. 144 p.

Swift, Carolyn. **Stage by stage**. Swords, Co. Dublin, Ireland: Poolbeg, 1985. – 312 p., 16 p. of plates: ill. *Notes*: Includes index. Theatre. Censorship. Pike theatre.

Taylor, Richard. **The drama of W. B. Yeats: Irish myth and the Japanese No**. New Haven: Yale University Press, 1976. – xiii, 247 p. *Notes*: Includes index. Bibliography: (p. 227–36). Verse drama. Critical studies.

Worth, Katharine. **The Irish drama of Europe from Yeats to Beckett**. Atlantic Highlands, NJ: Humanities Press, 1978.

A3a67. ISRAEL

Abramson, Glenda. **Modern Hebrew drama**, London: Weidenfeld & Nicolson, 1979. 232 p.

Altshuler, Mordechai. **ha-Te'atron ha-Yehudi bi-Verit ha-Mo'atsot: mehkarim, 'iyunim, te'udot**. [Jewish theater in the Soviet Union]. Jerusalem: ha-Merkaz le-heker ule-te'ud Yahadut Mizrah Eropah, ha-Universitah ha-'Ivrit bi-Yershalayim, 1996. – 335 p.: ill. *Notes*: Includes bibliographical references and index. History/Theatre, Yiddish. Soviet Union. Biography/Mikhoels, Solomon Mikhailovich, 1890–1948.

Barzel, Hillel. **Deramah shel matsavim kitsoniyim: milhamah ve-Sho'ah**. [Drama of extreme situations: war and Holocaust]. Tel-Aviv: Sifriyat po'alim, 1995. – 383 p.

Ben-Zvi, Linda. **Theatre in Israel**. Ann Arbor: University of Michigan Press, 1996. – xxi, 450 p., 8 p. of plates: ill. *Notes*: Includes bibliographical references and index. Israeli drama. History and criticism. Arabic drama. History and criticism.

Bernstein-Cohen, Miriam. **Ke-tipah ba-yam**. [A drop in the sea]. Ramat Gan, 1971. 253 p.

Contemporary Hebrew drama. New York, NY: The Foundation, 1980, 1989, – 30 p.

Ephrat, Gideon. **Israeli drama**. Tel Aviv, 1975. 328 p.

Feingold, Ben-Ami. **The Holocaust in Hebrew drama**. Tel Aviv, 1990. 143 p.

Finkel, Simon. **Stage and wings**. Jerusalem: Israel University Press, 1969. 306 p.

Friedman, Maurice, ed. **Martin Buber and the theatre**. New York: Funk & Wagnalls. 1969. 170 p. *Notes*: Study of the philosopher's views on art.

Gershoni, Gershon K. **The Hebrew theatre**. Jerusalem: Israel Digest, 1963.

Kohansky, Mendel. **The Hebrew theatre: its first fifty years**. Pref. by Tyrone Guthrie. Jerusalem: Israel Universities Press, 1969. *Notes*: Valuable study by the long-time critic of the *Jerusalem Post*. Includes list of productions by the major theatre.

Lahad, Ezra. **Original Hebrew plays presented in Israel, 1948–1970**. Jerusalem: Centre for Public Libraries, 1971. – 46 p. *Notes*: 'Appeared originally in Hebrew as an appendix to … [ha-Mahazeh ha-'Ivri be-makor uve-targum] by E. Lahad.'

Lery, Emanuel. **The Habima – Israel's national theatre 1917–77: A study of cultural nationalism**. New York: Columbia University Press, 1979. 346 p. *Notes*: Includes bibliography (p. 329–36) and index.

Manor, Giora. **ha-Tov ba-zemanim, ha-ra' ba-zemanim: pirke otobiyografyah**. [Best of times, the worst of times]. [Israel]: Tag, 1996. – 176 p.: ill. *Notes*: Theatrical directors. Israel. Autobiography/Dance and theatre critics.

Ofrat, Gideon. **ha-Te'atron ha-radikali: ha-te'atron he-hadash shel sof shenot ha-shishim**. [Avant-garde theatre]. Jerusalem: ha-Universitah ha-'Ivrit, ha-Fakultah le-mada'e ha-ruah, ha-Hug le-toldot ha-te'atron, 1977. – 235 p.

Ohed, Michael. **Raphael Klatzkin**. Tel Aviv, 1989. 263 p.

Orion, Dan. **From test to play**. Tel Aviv, 1988. 171 p.

Richetti, Giorgio and Giorgio Romano. **Teatro in Israele**. [Theatre in Israel]. Bologna: Cappelli, 1960. 131 p.

Rosenfeld, Lulla. **Bright star of exile: Jacob Adler and the Yiddish theatre**. New York: Crowell, 1977. 368 p.

Shako, Zara. **The theatre in Israel**. New York: Herzl Press, 1963. 143 p.

Shoham, Haim. **Challenge and reality in Israeli drama**. Ramat Gan, 1975. 247 p.

——. **Theatre and drama in search of an audience**. Tel Aviv, 1989. 159 p.

Zusman, Ezra. **After the première**. Tel Aviv, 1981. 336 p.

A3a68. ITALY

Alonge, Roberto. **Pirandello e il teatro**. Palermo: Palumbo, 1985. – 482 p. *Notes*: Photographic reprints of essays previously published in various works, under the direction of the Centro nazionale di studi pirandelliani, between 1975 and 1984. Includes bibliographical references. Pirandello, Luigi, 1867–1936. Stage history.

Amoia, Alba della Fazia. **The Italian theatre today: twelve interviews**. Troy, N.Y.: Whitston Pub. Co., 1977. – xiii, 136 p. *Notes*: Includes index. History and criticism.

Angelini, Franca. 'Teatri moderni'. [Modern theatre]. Chap. in **Letteratura Italiana**. [Italian literature], vol. 6. Turin: Einaudi, 1986.

——. **Il teatro del Novecento da Pirandello a Fo**. [Italian theatre of the twentieth century from Pirandello to Fo]. Bari: Laterza, 1976.

——, ed. **Scrivere il teatro**. [Writing for the theatre]. Rome: Bulzoni, 1990.

Apollonio, Mario. **Storia del teatro italiano**. [History of the Italian theatre]. 2 vols. Series Civiltà europea. Florence: Sansoni, 1981.

Artese, Erminia and Alberto Arbasino. **Il Teatro italiano oggi**. [Cosenza]: Lerici, 1980. – 244 p. *Notes*: Includes bibliographical references. History and criticism.

Asor Rosa, Alberto and Roger Pillaudin. **Dialogues franco-italiens**. [Paris]: France-Culture, 1979. – 297 p. *Notes*: Que peuvent les intellectuels?/Jacques Julliard, Alberto Asor-Rosa – Evolution des valeurs depuis 1968/François Chatelet, Franco Ferrarotti – Les femmes et la créativité/Viviane Forrester, Dacia Maraini – Luttes ouvrières et chômage/Jacques Chereque, Bruno Trentin – Energies nouvelles/Jacques Varet, Felice Ippolito – Théâtre d'acteurs, théâtre d'auteurs/Antoine Vitez, Dario Fo – Psychiatrie et politique/Roger Gentis, Franco Basaglia – Le poids du passé dans nos deux pays/Gérard Vincent, Maria-Antonietta Macciocchi – L'opéra/Bernard Lefort, Paolo Grassi – Le monde catholique dans nos deux pays/Francesco Traniello, Philippe Levillain.

Barsotti, Anna. **Futurismo e avanguardie nel teatro italiano fra le due guerre**. Rome: Bulzoni, 1990. – 240 p. *Notes*: Includes bibliographical references and index. Avant-garde (aesthetics).

Bartolucci, Giuseppe. **Teatro italiano**. Salerno: 10/17, 1983. – 2 vols: ill. *Notes*: Bibliography: vol. 2, p. 65–6. [1] Tradizione, moderno, contemporaneo – [2] Postavanguardia. 20th century.

Bentley, Eric. ed. **The genius of the Italian theater**. New York. New American Library, 1964. – 584 p. *Notes*: Seven plays, and five essays on the Italian theatre and playwrights. Bibliography: p. 564–7.

Bernard, Enrico. **Autori e drammaturgie: prima enciclopedia del teatro italiano del dopoguerra (1950–1992)**. 3rd revised edn. Rome: E & A, 1993. – 365 p. *Notes*: Italian post-war drama. Bio-bibliography.

Brown, Kenneth H. **Post-war Italian theatre: special issue**. New Orleans: New York: Tulane Drama Review; distributed by Hill and Wang, 1964. – 260 p.: ill.;. *Notes*: Issued as Vol. 8, no. 3 of the *Tulane Drama Review*. Includes bibliographical references. Does the Italian theatre exist?/Luciano Codignola – Sixteen years of the Piccolo Theatre/Giorgio Strehler and Paolo Grassi – Essays, correspondence, notes/Ugo Betti – Italian theatre since the war/Vito Pandolfi – Reading De Filippo/Luciano Codignola – Oh, these ghosts (TDR play)/ Eduardo De Filippo – Shakespeare with tears.

Calcagno, Paolo. **Eduardo: la vita è dispari: conversazione con Paolo Calcagno**. Naples: T. Pironti, 1985. 117 p.: chiefly ill. *Note*: Actors. Italy. Biography. De Filippo, Eduardo. Interviews. Pictorial works.

Cappelletti, D. **La sperimentazione teatrale in Italia tra norma e devianza**. [Theatrical experimentation in Italy from the normal to abnormal]. Rome: ERI, 1986.

——. **Teatro in piazza: ipotesi sul teatro popolare e la scena sperimentale in Italia**. Rome: Bulzoni, 1980. – 285 p. *Notes*: Includes bibliographies and index. Street theatre. Popular culture.

Carriglio, Pietro and Giorgio Strehler. **Teatro italiano**. Rome: Laterza, 1993. – vol. 1: ill. *Notes*: Includes bibliographical references. History and criticism.

Colomba, Sergio. **Assolutamente moderni: figure, temi e incontri nello spettacolo del Novecento**. Bologna: Nuova Alfa Editoriale, 1993. – 236 p. *Notes*: Includes indexes. Theatre. History. 20th century.

Cruciani, F. **Teatro nel Novecento. Registi, pedagoghi e comunità teatrali nel XX secolo.** [Theatre in the twentieth century: directors, teachers and the theatre community]. Florence: Il Mulino, 1989.

—— and C. Falletti. **Civiltà teatrale nel XX secolo.** [Theatre civilization in the twentieth century]. Bologna: Il Mulino, 1986.

—— and N. Savarese, eds. **Guida bibliografica al Teatro.** [Bibliographic guide to theatre]. Milan: Garzanti, 1991.

D'Amico, Silvio. **Storia del teatro drammatico.** [History of theatre]. 8 vols. 5th edn. Rome: Bulzoni, 1991.

Davico Bonino, Guido. **Il teatro del '900.** [Theatre in the twentieth century]. Turin: Einaudi, 1991.

——. Identikit dell'attore italiano. [The identity of Italian actors]. Turin: Rosenberg e Sellier, 1990.

De Filippo, Isabella and Sergio Martin. **Eduardo De Filippo: vita e opere, 1900–1984.** Milan: A. Mondadori, 1986. 192 p.:ill. (Some col.). Actors. Biography.

De Marinis, M. **Capire il teatro. Lineamenti di una nuova teatralogia.** [Understanding theatre: outline of a new theatre theory]. Florence: Casa Usher, 1988.

De Matteis, Stefano. **Lo specchio della vita: Napoli, antropologia della città del teatro.** Bologna: Il Mulino, 1991. – 318 p. *Notes*: Includes bibliographical references and index. Theatre. Naples. History. 20th century. De Filippo, Eduardo, 1900–. Criticism and interpretation.

Duecento anni alla Scala. [Two hundred years of La Scala]. Milan: Electra, 1978.

Duse, V. **Per una storia della musica del Novecento.** [On the history of music in the twentieth century]. Turin: EDT, 1990.

Ferrari, Franco. **Guida al teatro italiano contemporaneo.** Milano: Gammalibri, 1980. – 139 p. *Notes*: Bibliography: p. 126–39.

Galli, Quirino. **La drammaturgia popolare nell'Italia contemporanea.** Rome: EdUP, 1997. – 188 p.: ill. *Notes*: Includes bibliographical references. Italian drama. History and criticism.

Grande, Maurizio. **La riscossa di Lucifero: ideologie e prassi del teatro di sperimentazione in Italia (1976–1984).** Rome: Bulzoni, 1985. – 246 p. *Notes*: Includes bibliographical references and index. Experimental theatre.

Guazzotti, G. **Teoria e realtà del Piccolo Teatro di Milano.** [Myths and realities of Milan's Piccolo Teatro]. Turin: Einaudi, 1986.

Guerrieri, Gerardo and Stefania, Chinzari. **Il teatro in contropiede: cronache e scritti teatrali 1974–1981**. Rome: Bulzoni, 1993. – xlix, 769 p. *Notes*: 'Archivio Gerardo Guerrieri'–Ser. t.p. Includes bibliographical references and index.

Günsberg, Maggie. **Patriarchal representations: gender and discourse in Pirandello's theatre**. Oxford; Providence: Berg, 1994. – xvii, 228 p.: ill. *Notes*: Includes bibliographical references (p. 208–17) and index. *Subjects*: Sex roles in literature/Patriarchy. Italy. History and criticism.

Hirst, David. **Dario Fo and Franca Rame**. New York: St. Martin's Press, 1989. – x, 218 p., 8 p. of plates: ill. *Notes*: Bibliography: p. 211–15. Criticism and interpretation. Study of Italy's first family of actor/writers.

Jacobbi, Ruggero. **Teatro da ieri a domani**. [Theatre from yesterday to tomorrow]. Florence: Nuova Italia, 1972.

Livio, G. **La scena italiana**. [The Italian stage]. Milan: Mursia, 1989.

——. **Il teatro in rivolta**. [Theatre in revolt]. Milan: Mursia, 1976.

Lo spazio, il luogo, l'ambito, da Scenografie del Teatro alla Scala 1947–1983. [The space, the place, the environment: the scene designs of La Scala, 1947–1983]. Milan: Silvana, Cinisello Balsamo, 1983.

Lunari, Luigi. **Cento trame del teatro italiano**. [A hundred plots from the Italian theatre]. Milan: Pirroe, 1993.

Mango, Achille. **La morte della partecipazione. Cinque studi sul teatro**. [The death of participation: five studies on theatre]. Rome: Bulzoni, 1980.

——. **Verso una sociologia del teatro**. [Towards a sociology of theatre]. Trapani: Celebes, 1978.

McLeod, Addison. **Plays and players in modern Italy; being a study of the Italian stage as affected by the political and social life, manners, and character of to-day**. Port Washington: N.Y.: Kennikat Press, 1970 1912. – 355 p. illus. *Notes*: Reprint of the 1912 edn. History and criticism.

Meldolesi, Claudio. **Fondamenti del teatro italiano: la generazione dei registi**. Florence: Sansoni, 1984. – 577 p. *Notes*: Includes bibliographical references and index. The Italian director's theatre.

Nuzzaci, Antonella. **Il teatro futurista: genesi, linguaggi, tecniche**. Rome: Edizioni Nuova Cultura, 1995. – 177 p. *Notes*: Includes bibliographical references (p. 169–77). History and criticism/Futurism.

Pandolfi, Vito. **Il teatro italiano contemporaneo**. [Contemporary Italian theatre]. Milan: Schwarz, 1959.

Ponte di Pino, Oliviero. **Il nuovo teatro italiano, 1975–1988: la ricerca dei gruppi, materiali e documenti**. Florence: La Casa Usher: Distribuzione, PDE, 1988. – 215 p. *Notes*: Experimental theatre. Collective theatre.

Prosperi, Giorgio. **Autori e drammaturgie: prima enciclopedia del teatro italiano del dopoguerra**. Roma: E & A: Distribuzione C.I.D.S., 1988. – 185 p. Dramatists, Italian. 20th century.

Puppa, Paolo. **Teatro e spettacolo nel secondo Novecento**. Roma: Laterza, 1990. – 341 p. *Notes*: History. 20th century.

Quadri, Franco. **L'Avanguardia teatrale in Italia: (materiali 1960–1976)**. 2. edn. Turin: Einaudi, 1977. – 2 vols. (ix, vii, 826 p.): ill. *Notes*: Bibliography: p. 741–821. Theatre. History. Experimental theatre.

——. **La politica del regista: teatro 1967–1979**. Milan: Il formichiere, 1980. – 2 vols. (xvii, 668 p.). *Notes*: Includes indexes. [1] A–M – [2] N–Z. Theatrical directors of Italy.

——. **Il teatro degli anni Settanta**. [Theatre in the 1970s]. 2 vols. Turin: Einaudi.

Rigotti, Domenico. **Vent'anni di teatro milanese, 1960–1980**. Milan: Pan, 1981. – 169 p. *Notes*: Includes bibliographical references and index. Milan. History.

Ripellino, A.M. **Siate buffi. Cronache di teatro, circo e altre arti (1969–1977)**. [A chronicle of theatre, circus and other arts (1969–1977)]. Rome: Bulzoni, 1989.

Sanguanini, Bruno. **Il pubblico all'italiana: formazione del pubblico e politiche culturali tra Stato e teatro**. Milan: F. Angeli, 1989. – 346 p. *Notes*: Includes bibliographical references. Theatre and society. Theatre audiences.

Scarlini, Luca. **Un altro giorno felice: la fortuna dell'opera teatrale di Samuel Beckett in Italia: 1953–1996**. Florence: Maschietto & Musolino, 1996. – 79 p.: ill. *Notes*: Includes bibliographical references (p. 76–9). Beckett, Samuel, 1906–1989. Productions.

Seren Gay, Domenico. **Teatro popolare dialettale: indagine-enciclopedia sul teatro piemontese**. Ivrea: Priuli & Verlucca, 1977. – 339 p.: ill. *Series*: Collana Ricerche 2. *Notes*: Theatre. Italy. Piedmont. Dictionaries/Actors. Portraits/Popular culture. Dictionaries and encyclopedias/Italian language. Dialects.

Strehler, Giorgio. **Il Piccolo teatro d'arte: quar-ant'anni di lavoro teatrale, 1949–1987**. Milan: Electa, 1988. – 115 p.: ill. *Notes*: Exhibition held in Milan in 1988. Piccolo teatro in Milan. History.

Taviani, Ferdinando. **Uomini di scena, uomini di libro: introduzione alla letteratura teatrale italiana del Novecento**. Bologna: Il Mulino, 1995. – 254 p. *Notes*: Includes bibliographical references and index. History and criticism.

Tessari, Roberto. **Pinocchio: 'summa atheolog-ica' di Carmelo Bene**. Florence: Liberoscambio, 1982. – 121 p.: ill. *Notes*: Bibliography: p. 91–4. Pinocchio/Bene, Carmelo. Stage history.

Tinterri, Alessandro. **Il Teatro italiano dal natu-ralismo a Pirandello**. Bologna: Il Mulino, 1990. – 411 p. *Notes*: Includes bibliographical refer-ences (p. 407–11). Naturalism in literature and Pirandello, Luigi, 1867–1936.

Torresani, Sergio. **Il teatro italiano negli ultimi vent'anni (1945–1965)**. Cremona: G. Mangiorotti: Distribuzione Editrice 'Padus', 1965. – 366p. 21cm. *Notes*: Bibliography: p. 351–4. Post-war period.

Vallauri, Carlo. 'Per una Sociologia del teatro politico'. [Towards a sociology of political theatre]. In **Fantasia e sovversione**. Milan: Angeli, 1979.

Verdone, Mario. **Teatro del Novecento**. Brescia: Editrice La Scuola, 1981. – 208 p. *Notes*: Includes index. Bibliography: p. 195–197. History and criticism.

——. **Teatro del tempo futurista**. 2nd edn. Rome: Bulzoni, 1988. – 462 p., [38] p. of plates: ill. *Notes*: Includes bibliographical references (p. 441–5) and index. Futurism.

A3a69. JAPAN

Ashihara, Eiryo. **Watashi no han jijoden**. Tokyo: Shinjuku Shobo, 1983. – 290 p., 2 p. of plates: ill. Japanese arts critics. Biographies.

Goodman, David G. **Japanese drama and culture in the 1960's: the return of the gods**. Armonk, N.Y.: M.E. Sharpe, 1988. – xii, 363 p., [8] p. of plates: ill. *Notes*: Includes biblio-graphies. Find Hakamadare!/Fukuda Yoshiyuki – Kaison, the priest of Hitachi/Akimoto Matsuyo – My beatles/Satoh Makoto – John Silver/Kara Juro – The dance of angels who burn their own wings/Satoh Makoto.. [et al.]. Japanese drama. History and criticism.

Kan, Takayuki. **Sengo engeki: shingeki wa norikoerareta ka**. Tokyo: Asahi Shinbunsha, 1981. – 271 p.: ill. *Notes*: History of Shingeki.

Kato, Takeshi. **Machi no nioi gei no tsuya**.

Shohan. Tokyo: Atarashii Geino Kenkyushitsu, 1993. – 277 p.: ill. *Notes*: A collection of Kabuki anecdotes.

Kawatake, Shigetoshi. **Geino Jiten**. [An encyclo-pedia of Japanese theatrical art]. Tokyo: Tokyodo, 1961. – 794 p. ill., fold. maps.

Kinoshita, Junji. **Ikiru koto to tsukuru koto to: engeki mondo**. Shohan. Kyoto-shi: Jinbun Shoin, 1994. – 218 p.: ill. *Notes*: Japanese modern drama.

Miyagishi, Yasuharu. **Dorama ga mieru toki**. Shohan. Tokyo: Kage Shobo, 1992. – 227 p.: ill. *Notes*: Japanese drama. History and criticism.

Nakayama, Mikio. **Dento engeki to kindai**. Shohan. Tokyo: Kobundo Shuppansha, 1995. – 170 p.: ill. *Notes*: Includes bibliographical references. Kabuki plays. History and criticism.

Nihon koten engeki kinsei bunken mokuroku: 1994-nenban. Shohan. Osaka-shi: Izumi Shoin, 1995. – 605 p. *Notes*: 'Chikamatsu Kenkyujo kiyo bessatsu' – Colophon.

Nishido, Kojin. **Shogekijo wa shimetsushita ka: gendai engeki no seiza**. Tokyo: Renga Shobo Shinsha, 1996. – 269 p. *Notes*: Japanese drama. History and criticism.

Nomura, Takashi. **Gikyoku to butai**. Tokyo: Riburo Poto, 1995. – 581 p. *Notes*: Japanese drama. History and criticism.

Ooka, Kinji. **Kansai shingekishi**. Osaka-shi: Toho Shuppan, 1991. – 722 p., 16 p. of plates: ill. *Notes*: Includes bibliographical references (p. 693) and index. Kansai Region.

Ortolani, Benito. **The Japanese theatre: from shamanistic ritual to contemporary pluralism**. Leiden, Netherlands; New York: E.J. Brill, 1990. – xix, 352 p., 16 p. of plates: ill. *Notes*: Includes bibliographical references (p. 309–36) and index. The beginnings – Kagura – Gigaku – Bugaku – Theatrical arts from the ninth to the thirteenth century – Nogaku – Kabuki – The puppet theatre – The modern theatre: shimpa – Shingeki: the new drama – Modern music and dance theatre – History of western research on the Japanese theatre.

Ozaki, Hirotsugu. **Nihon no shingeki: shashin-shu**. Tokyo: Noberu Shobo, 1990. – 258 p. *Notes*: Includes bibliographical references. Pictorial of the theatre.

Ozasa, Yoshio. **Gendai engeki no mori**. Tokyo: Kodansha, 1993. – 443 p.: ill. *Notes*: Japanese drama. History and criticism.

——. **Nihon gendai engekishi. Showa senchu hen**. Tokyo: Hakusuisha, 1993, 1994. – 2 vols:

ill., ports. *Notes*: Includes indexes. Theatre. History and criticism.

Pronko, Leonard C. **Guide to Japanese drama**. 2nd edn. Boston: G.K. Hall, 1984. – xviii, 149 p. *Notes*: Includes index. Japanese drama. History and criticism.

Sakka, shosetsuka jinmei jiten. Tokyo: Nichigai Asoshietsu: Hatsubaimoto Kinokuniya Shoten, 1990. – 649 p. *Notes*: Novelists and dramatists in Japan. Biographies. Criticism.

Senda, Akihiko. **Gekiteki runessansu: gendai engeki wa kataru**. Shohan. Tokyo: Riburopoto, 1983. – 498 p.: ill. *Notes*: One of Japan's leading theatre critics interviews major directors and other theatre artists.

———. **Gendai engeki no kokai**. Tokyo: Riburo Poto, 1988. – 489, v p.: ill. *Notes*: Japanese drama. 20th century. History and criticism.

———. **Metamorphoses in contemporary Japanese theatre, life-size and more-than-life-size**. Tokyo, Japan: Japan Foundation, 1986. – 16 p.: ill. *Notes*: History. 20th century.

———. **Nihon no gendai engeki**. Tokyo: Iwanami Shoten, 1995. – viii, 246, 5 p.: ill. *Notes*: Includes bibliographical references (p. 1–5). History. 20th century.

———. **Trends in contemporary Japanese theatre**. Tokyo: Japan Foundation, 1990 1995, – 28 p.: ill. *Notes*: Japanese drama. History and criticism.

———. **The voyage of contemporary Japanese theatre**. [English translation of **Gendai engeki no kokai**]. Honolulu: University of Hawaii Press, 1997. – xix, 306 p.: ill. *Notes*: Includes bibliographical references (p. 297–8) and index. Japanese theatre. 20th century. History and criticism.

Senda, Koreya and Fujio Fujita. **Gekihaku Senda Koreya**. Tokyo: Orijin Shuppan Senta, 1995. – 216 p.: ill. *Notes*: Includes bibliographical references (p. 165). Chronological list of author's works: p. 171–211. Japan. Senda, Koreya, 1904–. Interviews. Haiyuza. History.

Shinbashi to Enbujo no 70-nen. Tokyo: Shinbashi Enbujo, 1996. – 764 p., 12 p. of plates: ill. (some col.). *Notes*: Includes bibliographical references (p. 764). Shinbashi Enbujo. History.

Soma, Hiroshi and Kiyonobu Torii. **Kabuki costumes and make-up**. Tokyo: Kodansha. – 172 p. col. plates. *Notes*: Text entirely in Japanese. Accompanied by 'Supplement' in English. Illustrated t.p. and end papers.

Suwa, Haruo and Yukio Sugai. **Kindai no engeki**. Shohan. Tokyo: Benseisha, 1996 1997.

– 2 vols. *Notes*: Includes bibliographical references. History and criticism.

Taisho no engeki to toshi. Shohan. Kokubunji-shi: Musashino Shobo, 1991. – 300 p.: ill. *Notes*: Includes bibliographical references. Theatre. History. 20th century.

Taku, Shoichi. **Kaiso no puroretaria engeki**. Tokyo: Miraisha, 1983. – 189 p. *Notes*: Socialism and theatre.

Tamaribuchi, Leslie L. **The Shôgekijô paradigm: 'wild and agile' contemporary Japanese theater**. 1990. – ix, 106 p. ill. (some col.). *Notes*: Includes bibliographical references (p. 102–6). Thesis (A.B., Honors in East Asian Languages and Civilizations)–Harvard University, 1990.

Thornbury, Barbara E. **Behind the mask: community and performance in Japan's folk performing arts**. 1995. *Notes*: Awaji puppets, Mibu kyogen, Kurokawa no, and Hayachime kagura are discussed. Includes bibliographical references (p. 161–3). Bugaku/Dengaku.

Tschudin, Jean Jacques. **La Ligue du théâtre prolétarien japonais**. Paris: L'Harmattan, 1989. – 351 p. *Notes*: Includes bibliographical references (p. 336–44) and index. Theatre. History. 20th century/Nihon Puroretaria Gejiko Domei.

Tsuboike, Eiko and Hideo Mori. **Theater Japan: a who's who guide to theater and dance in Japan**. 2nd edn. Tokyo, Japan: Japan Foundation, 1993. 463 p.: ill. Biography.

Yamanouchi, Tomio. **Gendai engeki no rinen. The idea of a modern theatre**. Tokyo: Miraisha, 1968. – 328 p. *Notes*: In Japanese. Includes bibliographical references. Drama. 20th century. History and criticism.

A3a70. JORDAN

Badr, Mahmud Isma'il. **Masrah al-thamaninat al-Urduni: dirasah naqdiyah tatbiqiyah mu'asirah**. al-Tab'ah 1. 'Amman: Wizarat al-Thaqafah, 1990. – 267 p. *Notes*: Arabic drama. Jordan. History and criticism.

Document on the first national conference of culture. Amman: University of Jordan, 1985.

The Fawness Theatre: al-Bayan at-Ta'sisi. [Founding manifesto]. Amman, 1984.

Hawamidah, Mufid. **al-Masrah fi al-Urdun**. Amman: Lajnat Tarikh al-Urdun, 1993. – 59 p. *Notes*: Includes bibliographical references (p. 51–52). Arabic drama. Jordan. History and criticism.

———. **Juhud al-masrahiyin al-Urduniyin**. Irbid: Markaz al-Dirasat al-Urduniyah, Jami'at al-Yarmuk, 1988. – 147 p.: ill. *Notes*: Theatre. Jordan. Statistics. Directories.

—— and Jibril Shaykh. **Bahth 'an al-masrah: dirasat fi al-masrah al-Urduni; ma'a nass kamil li-masrahiyat Jibril al-Shaykh (Taghribat Zarif al-Tul)**. Irbid: Dar al-Amal, 1985. – 240 p. *Notes*: Includes bibliographical references. Theatre. Jordan. History. 20th century.

Hawari, Bashir. **Dirasat**. [Studies]. Amman: Jordianian Book League, 1980.

Musa, Mahmud 'Isá. **Hamlit al-mu'akas: qira'at fi al-masrah al-Urduni**. [Contrary Hamlet: readings in the Jordanian theatre]. Amman: Wizarat al Thaqafah, 1995. – 290 p. *Notes*: Includes bibliographical references. Arabic drama. Jordan. History and criticism.

Shamma, Abdullateef and Ahmad Shequem. **Al-Masrah fil-Urdan**. [Theatre in Jordan]. Amman: Jordanian Theatre Professionals Association, 1981.

Al-'Uzaizi, Rox. **Funun**. [Arts magazine]. Amman: Ministry of Youth and Culture, 1978.

Zuyudi, Makhlad. **al-Mukhrij fi al-masrah al-Urduni**. Amman: Dar al-Yanabi', 1993. *Notes*: Includes bibliographical references. Arabic drama. Jordan. History and criticism.

A3a71. KAZAKHSTAN

Bogatenkova, Liudmila. **Uslyshat' i poniat' cheloveka**. Alma-Ata: 'Oner', 1987. – 302 p., 24 p. of plates: ill. *Notes*: Includes bibliographical references. Theatre. Kazakstan. History. 20th century.

Kadyrov, Akhmedzhan Nasyrovich. **Teatr ham vaqit**. Almuta: Qazaqstan, 1988. – 229 p.: ill. *Notes*: Includes bibliographical references. Musical theatre. Kazakstan.

Shostak, Irina. **Rezhisser Mambetov: spektakli raznykh let**. Alma-Ata: Oner, 1989. – 142 p., 16 p. of plates: ill. *Notes*: Includes bibliographical references. Directors. Soviet Union. Biography. Kazakstan. History. Mambetov, A.

A3a72. KENYA

Björkman, Ingrid. **'Mother, sing for me': people's theatre in Kenya**. London: Zed Books, 1989. 107 p.

Brown, David M. 'The form of protest in Kenya: drama or the novel'. **Critical Arts** 1, no. 3 (1980): 47–58.

Fiebach, Joachím. 'On the social functions of modern African theatre and Brecht'. **Darlite** 4, no. 2 (1970).

Kidd, Ross. 'Popular theatre in Kenya: working with peasants and workers in the struggle against poverty and oppression'. **Fuse** 12, no. 6 (Spring 1984): 259–64.

——. 'Popular theatre and popular struggle in Kenya: the story of the Kamiriithu Community Educational and Cultural Centre'. **Cultures in Contention**, Douglas Kahn and Dianne Neumaier, eds., 50–61. Seattle: Real Comet Press, 1985.

Killam, G.D. **An introduction to the writing of Ngugi**. London: Heinemann, 1980. 122 p.

Mwangi, Meja. **The Cockroach Dance**. Nairobi: Longman, 1979, 383 p.

Ngugi wa Thiong'o. **The barrel of a pen: resistance to repression in neo-colonial Kenya**. Trenton, N.J.: African World Press, 1983.

——. **Detained: a writer's prison diary**. London: Heinemann, 1981.

——. **Homecoming: essays**. London: Heinemann, 1982. 155 pp.

——. 'Women in cultural work: the fate of Kamiriithu People's Theatre in Kenya'. **Development Dialogue** 1–2 (1982): 115–33.

——. **Writers in politics: essays**. London: Heinemann, 1981. 142 p.

Nwankwo, Chimalum. 'Women in Ngugi's plays'. **Ufahamu** 14, no. 3 (1985): 85–92.

Pio, Zirimu. **Black aesthetics**. Nairobi: East Africa Literature Bureau, 1973.

Ruganda, J. **Telling the truth laughingly**. Nairobi: East African Education Press, 1992. 204 p.

Senorga-Zake, George W. **Folk music of Kenya**. Nairobi: Uzima Press, 1986. 188 p.

Umeasiegbu, Rems Nna. **Words are sweet: Lgbo oral literature**. Nairobi: East Africa Publishing House, 1980, 137 p.

A3a73. KOREA

Chang, Han-Gi. **Hanguk Yonkuksa**. [History of Korean theatre]. Seoul: Dongguk University, 1986. 360 p.

Cho, Dong-Il. **Talchumui-youksawa-wonli**. [History and theory of mask theatre]. Seoul: Hongik-SA, 1987. 406 p.

Cho, Oh-Kon. **Korean puppet theatre: kkoktu kaksi**. East Lansing: Asian Studies Center, Michigan State University, 1979. – 188 p.: ill. *Notes*: Bibliography: p. 187–8. Plays: Kkoktu Kaksi; translated from the text in Kim Chaechul's Chosun younkugsa.–Pak Cheomji's daughters; translated from the text in Kwon Taek-mu's Chosun Mingankug.–The script of the play of Kkoktu kaksi; translated from the text in Lee Tu-hyon's Hankuk kamyonkug. Puppets and puppet-plays. Korea/Folk drama, Korean.

——. **Traditional Korean theatre**. Studies in Korean Religions and Culture 2. Berkeley: Asian Humanities Program, 1988. 364 p.

Ch'oe, Ung, T'ae-su Yu and Tae-bom Yi. **Han'guk ui kuk yesul**. Seoul: Ch'ongmun'gak, 1996. ix, 580 pp., 7 p. of plates: ill. (some col.). *Notes*: Includes bibliographical references (p. 563–8) and index. Drama. History and criticism.

Han, Sang-ch'ol. **Han'guk yon'guk ui chaengchom kwa pansong: Han Sang-ch'ol yon'guk p'yongnonjip**. Seoul: Hyondae Mihaksa, 1992. 327 p. *Notes*: Theatre. History. 20th century.

Ho, Kyu. **Minjok kuk kwa chont'ong yesul: yon'guk 30-yon yonch'ul chagop**. Seoul: Munhak Segyesa, 1991. 395 pp.: ill. *Notes*: Folk drama. History and criticism. Theatre. Korea (South). Reviews.

Ho, Yong. **Pujori yon'guk**. [The theatre of the absurd]. Seoul: Hansin Munhwasa, 1982. – 417 p.: ill. *Notes*: In Korean. Includes index. Bibliography: p. 393–9.

——. **Yon'gungnon**. [The theory of the theatre]. Seoul: Hansin Munhwasa, 1990. – 854 p.: ill. *Notes*: In Korean. Includes bibliographical references (p. 805–23).

ITI Korean Centre. **The Korean Theatre**. Seoul, 1981. 90 p.

Jang, Han-ki. **Minsock Gug Gua Dongyang Yungug**. [Korean traditional theatre and oriental theatre]. Seoul: Young-Guy Kim, 1983. 272 p.

Jo, Hung Yun. **Hangugui Mu**. [Korean ritual performance]. Seoul: Dong Sick Choi, 1983. 151 p.

Kaehwagi, Yunkeuk Sahwesa. **A social history of theatre in the Enlightenment period**. Seoul: Saemun-sa, 1987. 271 p.

Kang, Chin. **Urisik kukchakpop**. [P'yongyang]: Munye Ch'ulp'ansa, 1990. – 434 p. *Notes*: North Korean drama. History and criticism. Cultural policy.

Kardoss, John. **An outline history of Korean drama**. New York: Long Island Univ. Press, 1966. 33 p.

Kim, Mi-do. **Han'guk kundae kuk ui chae chomyong**. Seoul: Hyondae Mihaksa, 1995. 420 p. *Notes*: Includes bibliographical references and index. Korean drama. 20th century. History and criticism.

Kim, U-t'ak. **Han'guk chont'ong yon'guk kwa ku koyu mudae**. Seoul: Songgyun'gwan Taehakkyo Ch'ulp'anbu, 1986. – 209 p.: ill. *Notes*: Summary in English with caption title: A study on the stage-structure proper to the Korean national drama, Changguk. Includes bibliographical references (p. 207–9). Stagesetting and scenery.

Korean Culture and Arts Foundation. **Moonye Yungam**. [Annual survey of culture and arts]. Seoul, published since 1976.

Korean National Commission for Unesco. **Korean dance, theatre and cinema**. Seoul: Si-sa-vong-o-sa, 1983.

Kuktan Arirang 10-chunyon kinyom huigokchip. Seoul: Konggan Midio, 1996. – vol. 1: ill. *Notes*: Korean drama. 20th century. Kuktan Arirang. History.

Lee, Du Hyun. **Hankuk Sinkeuksa Yongu**. [A study of modern Korean theatre]. Seoul: Seoul National University Press, 1966. 331 p.

—— *et al.* **Kuklip Keukchang Samsipnyon**. [Thirty years of Korean national theatre]. Seoul: Korean National Theatre, 1980. 914 p.

Lee, Sa Hyun. **Hanguk yonkuksa**. [History of Korean theatre]. 2nd edn. Seoul: Hakyonsa, 1987. 374 p.

Lee, Sang Il. **Chukjaewa Madangkeuk**. [Festival and madang-keuk]. Seoul: Chosun-Ilbo-sa, 1986. 311 p.

——. **Hankuk Yunkeuksa**. [A history of Korean theatre]. Seoul: Minjung-sugwan, 1973. 310 p.

Myung, Inn Seo and Chun-ho, Ch'oe. **O T'aesok ui yon'guk segye**. Seoul: Hyondae Mihaksa, 1995. 255 p.: ill. *Notes*: Includes bibliographical references. Criticism and interpretation.

Park, Jin Tae. **Hanguk kamyunkuk yongu**. [Study of Korean mask theatre]. Seoul: Saemun-sa, 1985. 220 p.

Pukhan ui kaguk yon'guk 40-yon. Seoul: Sinwon Munhwasa, 1990. – 358 p. *Notes*: Musical theatre. Korea (North).

Seoul Drama Critics Circle. **Hankuk Yunkeukkwa Cholmun Uisik**. [Korean theatre and young consciousness]. Seoul: Minum-sa, 1979.

Sin, Chong-ok. **Han'guk sin'guk kwa soyang yon'guk**. Seoul: Saemun-sa, 1994. 496 p. *Notes*: Includes bibliographical references (p. 459–84) and index. 20th century. History and criticism.

Son, Sok-chu. **Yon'guk sajon**. Seoul: Han'guk Munhwa Yesul Chinungwon, 1981. –396 p.: ill. *Notes*: Korean language theatre encyclopedia.

Suh Yun-Ho. **Hankuk Kundai Hikoksa Yungu**. [A study of modern Korean drama]. Seoul: Korean Cultural Research Center, 1982. 368 p.

——. **Hankuk Yunkeukron**. [A treatise on Korean theatre]. Seoul: Samilgak, 1975. 254 p.

Sung, Kyung-Lin. **Hangukui mooyong**. [Korean traditional dance]. Seoul: Kyoyang Guksa, 1976. 217 p.

Swortzell, Lowell, ed. **International guide to children's theatre and educational theatre**. New York and Westport: Greenwood Press, 1990. *Note*: Section on Korea.

Uri Nuri. **Yong**. [Yon'guk yonhwa rul pinnaen kugyesulga]. Seoul: Ujin Ch'ulp'an, 1994. – 205 p.: ill. *Notes*: 'Han'guk Adong Munhagin Hyophoe ch'uch'on toso'–Cover. Theatrical producers and directors. Biography.

Yang, Sung-guk. **Han'guk kundae yon'guk pip'yjongsa yon'gu**. Seoul: T'aehaksa, 1996. 542 p. *Notes*: Includes bibliographical references (p. 517–522) and index. Theatre and society.

——. **Han'guk yon'guk ui hyonsil**. Seoul: T'aehaksa, 1994. 424 p. *Notes*: Korean drama. History and criticism.

Yi, Kang-nyol. **Han'guk sahoejuui yon'guk undongsa**. Seoul: Tongmunson, 1992. 326 p.: ill. (some col.). *Notes*: Includes bibliographical references (p. 324–6). Theatre. Korea (North). History. Socialism and theatre.

Yi, Kwang-nae. **Hyondae huigongnon**. Seoul: Iu Ch'ulp'ansa, 1983. – 446 p. *Notes*: Includes bibliographical references. Korean drama. 20th century. History and criticism. Bibliography.

Yi, Mi-won. **P'osut'umodon sidae wa Han'guk yon'guk**. Seoul: Hyondae Mihaksa, 1996. 381 p. *Notes*: Includes bibliographical references and index. Korea (South). History. 20th century. Postmodernism.

Yi, Sang-u. **Yon'guk sok ui sesang ilkki**. Seoul: Naeil ul Yonun Ch'aek, 1995. 360 pp.: ill. *Notes*: Includes bibliographical references. Dramatic criticism. Korea (South).

Yi, T'ae-ju. **Segye yon'guk ui mihak. Yi T'ae-ju cho**. Seoul: Tandae Ch'ulp'anbu, 1983. 409 p. Korean drama. 20th century. History and criticism. Addresses, essays, lectures.

Yoh, Suk Kee. **Hankuk Yunkeuke Hyonsil**. [Present state of Korean theatre]. Seoul: Tonghwa-chulpan-kongsa, 1974. 360 p.

——. **Tongsoe Yunkeuke Pigyo Yungu**. [A comparative study of theatre east and west]. Seoul University Press, 295 p.

Yu, Min-yong. **Hankuk Yunkeuk Sango**. [Miscellanies on Korean theatre]. Seoul: Moonye-pipyung-sa, 1978. 391 p.

——. **Hankuk Hyundai Higoksa**. [A history of modern Korean drama]. Seoul: Hongsung-sa, 1982. 616 p.

——. **Kaehwagi yon'guk sahoesa**. Seoul: Saemun-sa, 1987. 271 p. *Notes*: Includes index. Bibliography: p. 255–9. Theatre and society. History.

——. **Chont'ongguk kwa hyondaeguk**. Seoul: Tan'guk Taehakkyo Ch'ulp'anbu, 1992. 521 p. *Notes*: One article in Japanese. Korean drama. 20th century. History and criticism.

——. **Han'guk kundae yon'guksa**. Seoul: Tan'guk Taehakkyo Ch'ulp'anbu, 1996. x, 987 p.: ill. *Notes*: Includes bibliographical references and index. History. 20th century.

A3a74. KUWAIT

Dasgupta, Gautam. 'The eyes of war'. **Performing arts journal** 13 (1991).

Davis, Eric and Nicolas Gavrielides. 'Statecraft, historical memory and popular culture in Iraq and Kuwait'. In **Statecraft in the Middle East: oil, historical memory and popular culture**. Miami: Florida International University Press, 1991. 274 p.

Dukhi, Yusuf Farhan. **Al-aghani al-kuwaytiya** [Kuwaiti songs]. Qatar: Arab Gulf States Folklore Centre, 1984. 503 p.

Gharib, Salih. **Safahat tawthiqywah lil-harakah al-masrahiyah fi al-Kuwayt**. Kuwait: S. al-Gharib, 1988. – vol. 1: ill. *Notes*: Includes bibliographical references (v. 1, p. 290). Theatre. History. 20th century. Sources.

Grösel, B. and H. Gube. 'Das Kuwait Conference Centre'. [The Kuwait Conference Centre]. **Bühnentechnische Rundschau** 83 (1989): 13–17.

Kamal, Safwat. **Madkhal fi-dirasat al-fulklur al-kuwayti**. [An introduction to the study of Kuwait folklore]. Kuwait City: Ministry of Information, 1973.

al-Najjar, Muhammead Rajab, ed. **al-ghatawi aw al-alghaz al-sha'biya fi-l-kuwayt wa usuluha fi-l-turath al-sha'bi**. [al-Ghatawi or Kuwaiti oral folk riddles and their origins in folk culture]. Kuwait City: al-Rubay'an, 1985.

——. **Mu'jam al-alghaz al-sha'biya fi-l-kuwayt**. [The encyclopedia of Kuwaiti folk riddles]. Qatar: Arab Gulf Folklore Centre, 1985.

al-Nuri, Abdallah. **al-'amthal al-darija fi-l-kwayt**. [Common proverbs in Kuwait]. 2 vols. Beirut: Qalfat Press, 1976.

Scarce, Jennifer M. **The evolution of culture in Kuwait**. Edinburgh: Her Majesty's Stationery Office, 1985.

al-Shamlan, Sayf Marzuq. **al-al'ab al-sha'biya al-kuwaytiya**. [Kuwaiti folk games]. Beirut: Dar I'lam al-Fikr, 1970.

A3a75. KYRGYZSTAN

Istoriya sovetskogo dramaticheskogo teatra. [History of Soviet dramatic theatre]. 6 vols. Moscow: Nauka, 1966–71.

Kazmina, N. 'Smotrite, kto k nam prishel!'. [Look who is coming to us!]. **Teatr** 3 (1989).

Levikova, E. 'Chetviortyi tour'. [The fourth tour]. **Teatr** 3 (1987).

Zhunushov, Abrasul. **Sakhna cheberleri: makalalar zhyinagy**. Frunze, 1988. 179 p.: ill. Notes: In Kyrgyz. History. 20th century.

A3a76. LAOS

Bowers, Faubion. **Theatre in the East: Asian dance and drama**. New York: Thomas Nelson & Sons, 1956. 374 p.

Brandon, James. **The Cambridge guide to Asian theatre**. Cambridge: Cambridge University Press, 1993. 253 p.

Caitlin, Amy. 'Laos'. **International encyclopedia of dance**, 1988.

Ratnam, Perala, ed. **Laos and its culture**. New Delhi: Tulsi, 1982.

Visages du Laos. [Faces of Laos, sound recording]. Le Chant du Monde, 1960s.

A3a77. LATVIA

Akurātere, Livija. **Aktiermāksla latviešu teātri**. [The art of acting in the Latvian theatre]. Riga: Zinātne, 1983. – 295 p., 32 p. of plates: ill. Notes: Includes index. Bibliography: p. 275–6. Theatre. History. 20th century.

——. **Rizhskii teatr russkoi dramy, 1940–1983: ocherk istorii**. Riga: Zinātne, 1983. – 357 p., 80 p. of plates: ill. Notes: Includes bibliographical references and index. Theatre. Latvia. Riga. History. 20th century/Russian drama.

——, Lilija Dzene, Valentīna Freimane and Viktors Hausmanis. **Latviešu padomju teātra vēsture (1940–70)**. [Soviet Latvian theatre history (1940–70)]. 2 vols. Riga: Zinātne, 1974. 500 p.

——, Ligita Bērziua, Lilija Dzene, and Silvija Radzobe. **Rīgas Krievu drāmas teātris (Krievu val)**. [The Riga Russian Dramatic Theatre (in Russian) 1940–83]. Riga: Zinātne, 1983. 359 p.

Augstkalna, Maija. **Arnolds Burovs un vina lelles**. Riga: 'Liesma', 1986. – 135, 5 p., 32 p. of plates: ill. (some col.). Notes: Puppet theatre. Latvia. Criticism and interpretation.

Bērziņa, Ligita and Janīna Brance. **Latviešu teātra bronika: 1913–17**. [A chronicle ot the Latvian theatre: 1913–17]. Riga: Zinātne, 1991. 351 p.

—— and Guna Zeltiņa. **Latviešu teātra hronika: 1909–12**. [A chronicle of the Latvian theatre: 1909–12]. Riga: Zinātne, 1988. 510 p.

Bibers, Gunars. **Latviešu padomju dramaturģija**. [Soviet Latvian drama]. Riga: Zvaigzne, 1976. 231 p.

Cielava, Skaidrite. **Janis Kuga**. Riga: Zinātne, 1992. – 173 p.: ill. (some col.). Notes: Includes bibliographical references (p. 161–9). Scene design. Kuga, Janis, 1878–1969.

Dzene, Lilija. **Drāmas teātris**. [The Drama Theatre]. Riga: Zinātne, 1979. 380 p.

——. **Mūsu paaudzes aktieri**. [Actors of our generation]. 2nd edn. Riga: Latvijas Valsts izdevniecba, 1964. 408 p.

Freinberga, Silvija. **Impresija un ekspresija**. Riga: Liesma, 1984. – 213 p.: ill. Notes: Latvian drama. History and criticism.

——. **Pauls Putniņš un latviešu drāmas divi gadu desmiti**. [Pauls Putniņš and twenty years of Latvian drama]. Riga: Liesma, 1989. 287 p.

Grēviņš, Māris. **Dailes teātris**. [Daile Theatre]. Riga: Liesma, 1971. 240 p.

Hausmanis, Viktors. **Dramaturgs Hariis Gulbis**. [Playwright Harijis Gulbis]. Riga: Liesma, 1980. 151 p.

——. **Rainis mūasdienu teātrĪ: 1965–1990**. [Rainis in modern theatre]. Riga: Liesma, 1990. – 109 p.: ill. Notes: Rainis, Janis, 1865–1929. Stage history.

——. **Rainis un teātris**. [Rainis and the theatre]. Riga: Liesma, 1965. 240 p.

Kundziņš, Kārlis. **Latviešu teātra hronika: 1901–08**. [A chronicle of the Latvian theatre: 1901–08]. Riga: Zinātne, 1977. 228 p.

——. **Latviešu teātra repertuārs līdz 1940 gadam**. [Latvian theatre repertoire to 1940]. Riga: LPSR Zinātņu akadēmijas izdevnieĪba, 1955. 288 p.

——. **Latviešu teātra vēsture: 1. sēj**. [Latvian theatre history: volume I]. Riga: Liesma, 1968. 400 p.

——. **Latviešu teātra vēsture: 2. sēj**. [Latvian theatre history: volume 2]. Riga: Liesma, 1972. 438 p.

Pētersons, Pēteris. **DarbĪbas māksla. Rakstu krājums par teātri**. [The art of activity: essays on the theatre]. Riga: Liesma, 1978. 296 p.

——. **Drāma kā kritērijs: apceres**. Riga: Liesma, 1987. – 340 p., 18 p. of plates: ill. *Notes*: Includes bibliographical references. Theatre. Latvia. History. 20th century.

Radzobe, Silvija. **Cilvēks un laiks Gunāra Priedes lugās**. [People and time in the plays of Gunars Priede). Riga: Zinātne, 1982. 287 p.

——, Edite Tisheizere, Edite and Guna Zeltina. **Latvijas teatris: 80. gadi**. Riga: Preses Nams, 1995. – 472 p.: ill. *Notes*: Includes bibliographical references and index. Theatre. History. 20th century.

Sapiro, Adolfs. **Starp-bridis: pirms izrades, luga, ar makslinieku, lomu dalisana, ar aktieri, pec izrades**. Riga: Liesma, 1991. – 204 p.: ill. *Notes*: Theatre. Production and direction. History. 20th century.

Skatuves makslas meistari. Riga: Liesma, 1980. – 246 p. *Notes*: Evalds Valters – Karlis Pabriks – Martins Verdins – Elvira Bramberga – Antonija Jansone – Vilis Verners – Hermanis Vazdiks – Luijs Smits – Arturs Kalejs – Amalija Jaunvalka – Malvine Ustube – Elza Barune – Irma Laiva – Olga Krumina. Theatre. Latvia. History. 20th century. Biographies.

Stepiņš, Laimonis. **Henriks Ibsens latviešu teātri**. [Henrik Ibsen in the Latvian theatre]. Riga: Liesma, 1978. 210 p.

Vilsons, Alfons, Biruta Gudriķe, Ingrīda Kiršentāle and Viktors Hausmanis. **Šekspšrs latviesu teĺtrĺ**. [Shakespeare in the Latvian theatre]. Riga: Latvijas Valsts izdevniecĺba, 1964. 168 p.

Vintere, M.Em. **Jaunako dramaturgijas darbu bibliografisks raditajs–anotacijas**. Riga: Em. Melngaila Tautas makslas nams, 1976. – 31 p. *Notes*: Latvian drama. Bibliography.

Zake, Ina. **Teatry Rigi**. Riga: Liesma, 1977. – 45 p.: ill. *Notes*: Theatre. Riga. History. 20th century.

A3a78. LEBANON

Abdel-Nour, Jabbour. **Etude sur la poésie dialectale au Liban**. [Studies in the dialectic poetry of Lebanon]. The Lebanese University, 1996.

Abu Murad, Nabil. **al-Akhawaan Rahbaani, Hayaat Wa Marsah, Khasaa'is al-Kitaaba ad-Draamiyya**. [The Rahbaani brothers, life and theatre, attributes of writing for drama]. Beirut: Amjaad Publishing House, 1990.

——. **al-Masrah Fi Lubnaan: Maraahilahu, Anwaa'ahu, Qadaayaah (1975–1990)**. [The theatre in Lebanon: Its phases, types and issues (1975–1990)]. Beirut: 1997.

Mahfouth, 'Isaam. **Masrahi Wa l-Masrah**. [A dramatist and the theatre]. Beirut: 2002 Publishing House, 1966.

Al-Masrah Fi Lubnaan. [The theatre in Lebanon]: a documentary publication. Ministry of Culture and Higher Education in Lebanon, [n.d.].

Najm, Mohammed Yousef. **Najeeb Haddaad. Beirut: ath-Thaqaafa**. Publishing House, 1966.

Salaamé, Ghassane. **Le Théâtre politique au Liban(1968–1973)**. [Political theatre in Lebanon (1968–1973)]. Beirut: Dar al-Mashreq, 1986.

As-Sawda, Yousef. **Taareekh Lubnaan al-Hadaari**. [The history of the Lebanese civilization]. Beirut: an-Nahaar Publishing House, 1972.

A3a79. LIBERIA

Best, Kenneth Y. **Cultural policy in Liberia**. Paris: UNESCO, 1974. 59 p.

Dempster, Roland T., Bai T. Moore and H. Carey Thomas. **Echoes from the valley: Being Odes and other poems**. Robertsport, Liberia: Douglas Muir Press, 1947. 73 p.

Dorsinville, Roger. 'Rediscovering our cultural values'. In **Black people and their culture**, 130–7. Washington: Smithsonian Institute, 1976.

Gale, Steven H. 'Liberian drama'. **Liberian studies journal** 9, no. 2. (1980–1): 69–74.

Henries, A. and Doris Banks. **A survey of Liberian literature**. Tübingen, Germany: Horst Erdmann Verlag, 1970.

Johnson, S. and M. Jangaba. **The Warrior King Sao Boso: Liberian writing**. Tübingen, Germany: Horst Erdmann Verlag, 1970.

Martin, Carlos. 'Blamadon: the bud of Liberian theatre'. **Liberia: political, economic and social monthly** 23–4 (1976): 28–32.

Moore, Bai T. **Categories of Liberian indigenous songs**. Chicago: African Studies Centre, Depaul University, 1970.

——. **Tribes of the Western province and Dewoin people**. Monrovia: Departmentof Interior Folkway Series, 1955.

A3a80. LIBYA

El-Giernazi, Fawzi. **The Tawarig people and folk dances of Southern Libya**. Ottawa: Jerusalem International Publishing House, 1984. 72 p.

Kashlaf, Sulayman. **Ba'da an yurfa' al-sitar: kitabat 'an al-masrah al-Libi**. al-Jamahiriyah al-'Arabiyah al-Libiyah al-Sha'biyah al-

Ishtirakiyah: al-Munsha'ah al-Sha'biyah lil-Nashr wa-al-Tawzi' wa-al-I'lan wa-al-Matabi', 1981. – 130 p. *Notes*: Includes bibliographical references. Theatre. Libya. History. 20th century.

A3a81. LITHUANIA

Aleksaite, Irena and Valentinas Didzgalvis. **Teatras: vaidybos problemos**. Vilnius: Mintis, 1983. – 98 p., 8 p. of plates: ill. *Notes*: Summary in English and Russian. Includes bibliographical references. Theatre. Lithuania. History. 20th century.

Aleksienė, Grazžina. **Truikys Liudas**. Exhibition catalogue. Vilnius: Lietuvos TSR dailės muziejus, 1979. 32 p.

Bieliauskas, Feliksas, Egidijus Banionis and Aleksandras Guobys. **Teatras, 1940–1960: dokumentai ir medziaga**. Vilnius: LTSR Mokslu akademijos Istorijos institutas, 1986. – 298 p. *Notes*: 1940–60. Includes indexes. Lithuania. Documents.

Gaizutis, Algirdas. **Lietuviu tarybinis dramos teatras, 1957–1970**. Vilnius: Vaga, 1987. – 381 p., 32 p. of plates: ill. *Notes*: Includes bibliographical references and index. Lithuanian drama.

Jansonas, Egmontas. **Etiudai apie teatra**. [Sketches about theatre]. Vilnius: Vaga, 1988. 245 p.

Kuleshova, Vera. **Stasys Ušinskas**. Moscow: Sovietskiý khudozhnik, 1973. 159 p.

Lankutis, Jonas. **Lietuvių dramaturgijos raida**. [Development of Lithuanian drama]. Vilnius: Vaga, 1988. 454 p.

Mackonis, Jonas and G. Aleksiene. **Lietuvos scenografija. Lithuanian scenography**. Vilnius: Vaga, 1968. – 149 p. illus. *Notes*: Summary in Russian, English, French and German; title and list of illustrations also in Russian, English, French and German.

Maknys, Vytautas. **Lietuvių teatro raidos bruožai 1570–1940**. [Features in the development of Lithuanian theatre 1570–1940]. 2 vols. Vilnius: Mintis, 1972, 1979. 554 p.

Petuchauskas, Markas. **Teatro akimirkos**. [Theatre moments]. Vilnius: Mintis, 1977. 136 p.

——, ed. **Lietuvių tarybinis teatras 1940–1956**. [Lithuanian Soviet drama theatre 1940–56]. Vilnius: Mintis, 1979. 387 p.

Rutkutė, Dana. **Aktorius teatro veidrodyie**. [The actor in the looking-glass of theatre]. Vilnius: Vaga, 1989. 192 p.

Sabalis, Kristina, Balys Sruoga and Sapiega Kazimieras. **Balys Sruoga: Lithuanian drama, theory and practice**. 1978. – 194 p. *Notes*: Vita. 'Kazimieras Sapiega, by Balys Srouga, an historical chronicle in four acts, nine scenes, translated from the Lithuanian by Kristina Sabalis': p. 49–194. Bibliography: p. 45–7. History and criticism. Sruoga, Balys, 1896–1947.

Sakalauskas, Tomas. **Monologai**. Vilnius: Mintis, 1981. 230 p.

Samulionis, Algis. **Balys Sruoga**. Vilnius: Vaga, 1986. 428 p.

——, ed. **Neramios šviesos pasauliai**. [Worlds of restless light]. Vilnius: Vaga, 1976. 246 p.

Saviciunaite, Vida. **Kauno Valstybinis akademinis dramos teatras: 1920–1990**. [The Kaunas State Drama Theatre: 1920–1990]. Kaunas: Sviesa, 1990. – 198 p.: ill. (some col.). *Notes*: Lithuanian, English, German, and Russian. 20th century/Kauno Valstybinis akademinis dramos teatras. History.

Siupsinskiene, Klara. **Pjeses; bibliografine rodykle (1945–1970)**. Vilnius, 1972. – 179 p. *Notes*: Lithuanian drama. Bibliography.

——. **Pjeses: bibliografine rodykle, 1971–1985**. Vilnius: Lietuvos TSR Valstybine respublikine biblioteka, 1986. – 115 p. *Notes*: An annotated bibliography of all dramas published 1971–1985 in the Lithuanian language in the USSR. Includes index.

Sruoga, Balys. 'Mūsų teatro raida'. [Development of our theatre]. In **Lietuva 1918–1938**. Kaunas: Šviesa, 1990. 368 p.

Tanana, Mariia. **Russkii dramaticheskii teatr Litvy: 1946–1996**. Vilnius: Ruskij dramaticeskij teatr Litvy, 1996. – 123 p.: ill. *Notes*: Theatre. Lithuania. History. 20th century/ Gosudarstvennyi russkii dramaticheskii teatr.

Vasiliauskas, Valdas. **Teatras be iliuzijy**. [Theatre without illusions]. Vilnius: Vaga, 1989. 252 p.

Vengris, Antanas. **Kastantas Glinskis**. Vilnius: Mintis, 1965. 131 p.

——. **Nemuno mergaitė**. [Maid of Nemunas]. Vilnius: Vaga, 1990. 140 p.

——, ed. **Lietuvių tarybinis dramos teatras 1957–1970**. [Lithuanian Soviet drama theatre 1957–70]. Vilnius: Vaga, 1987. 383 p.

——, ed. **Teatrinės minties pėdsakais**. [The world and Lithuanian directors and actors]. 2 vols. Vilnius: Mintis, 1969, 1982. 688 p.

——, Vytautas Mažeika and Žilvinas Dautartas. **Lietuvių teatras 1918–1929**. [Lithuanian theatre, 1918–29]. Vilnius: Mintis, 1984. 336 p.

A3a82. LUXEMBOURG

20 saisons-passions du Théâtre du Centaure. Luxembourg: Esch-sur-Alzette, 1993. – 1 v. (unpaged): ill. Notes: 'Plaquette accompagnant la rétrospective photographique organisée en collaboration avec le Théâtre d'Esch et la Banque et caisse d'Epargne de l'Etat.' Théâtre du Centaure.

A3a83. MACEDONIA

Aleksiev, Aleksandar. Founders of Macedonian drama. Skopje: Misla, 1972.

——. Ilinden i makedonskata dramska literatura. Skopje: Makedonska kniga, 1983. – 157 p. Notes: Includes bibliographical references. Macedonian drama. 20th century.

Georgievski, Ljubiša. Ontology of the theatre. Skopje: Misla, 1985.

——. World dream. Skopje: Studentski zbor. 1979.

Hećimović, Branko. Suvremene makedonske drame. [Contemporary Macedonian drama]. Zagreb: Znanje, 1982.

Ivanov, Blagoja. Suvremena drama i pozorište u Makedoniji. [Contemporary drama and theatre in Macedonia]. Novi Sad: Sterijino pozorje, 1982. – 372 p. Notes: Articles translated from the Macedonian into Serbo-Croatian. Includes indexes. Macedonian drama. 20th century. History and criticism.

Ivanovski, Ivan. On its own soil. Skopje: Jultura, 1983.

——. Paraleli i meridijani: teatarski sintezi. Bitola: Misirkov, 1990. – 246 p. Notes: Includes bibliographical references. Theatre. Macedonia (Republic). History. 20th century.

Matevski, Mateja. Drama i teatar: ogledi, kritiki i prikazi. Jubilejno izd. Skopje: Misla, 1987. – 428 p. Theatre. Macedonia (Republic)/ Macedonian drama. 20th century. History and criticism.

Siljan, Rade. Macedonian drama: the nineteenth and twentieth centuries. Skopje: Makedonska kniga, 1990.

——. 100 years of Macedonian drama. Skopje: Matica Makedonska, 1992.

Stefanovski, Risto. The theatre in Macedonia. Skopje: Misla, 1990.

A3a84. MADAGASCAR

Andrianjafy, Danielle Nivo. 'Le Théâtre'. [The Theatre]. Notre Librairie Madagascar: La Littérature d'Expression Française 110 (July–September 1992). 7 p.

Andriatsila, Niarivo. 'Le Théâtre Malgache'. [The Malagasy Theatre]. La Revue de Madagascar 26 (July 1946).

Artistic Department, Ministry of Art and Culture. Fantaro ny teatra. [Know the theatre]. Antananarivo: Artistic Department, Ministry of Art and Culture, 1982.

——. 'The Hira Gasy'. [Malagasy Song]. News of the Ministry of Art and Culture. Antananarivo: Ministry of Art and Culture, 1984.

Ary, Michel Francis Robin. 'Le Théâtre à Madagascar'. [Theatre in Madagascar]. Bulletin of Madagascar 72 (January 1953).

Bertrana, G. 'Une Expérience théâtrale à Madagascar'. [A theatrical experience in Madagascar]. Education et Théâtre 8 (1952).

Gerard, A. 'La Naissance du théâtre à Madagascar'. [The birth of theatre in Madagascar]. Université de Liège Bulletin d'Information 8 (1967): 28–35.

Haring, Lee. 'Funeral Oratory: Living and Dead'. In Verbal arts in Madagascar: performance in historical perspective. Philadelphia: University of Pennsylvania Press, 1992. 242 p.

Ramiandrasoa, Jean Irénée. 'Le Théâtre Malgache Classique'. [Malagasy classical theatre]. Notre Librairie: Madagascar, La Littérature d'Expression Malgache 109 (April–June 1992). 9 p.

Ravaloson, Charles. Ny Teatra Tany Am-pita Sy Eto Madagasikara. [Theatre from abroad and that of Madagascar]. Antananarivo, 1962–3.

Ravaloson, Rajohnson Andriambatosoa. Ny Teatra sy ny fampandrosoana. [Theatre and Development]. Antananarivo, 1986.

A3a85. MALAYSIA

Aveling, Harry. Moths. Kuala Lumpur: Dewan Bahasa dan Pustaka, 1974.

Beng, Tan Sooi. Bangsawan: a social and stylistic history of popular Malay Opera. Singapore: Oxford University Press, 1993.

Bhasi, Matavur and Es Guptannayar. Malayala natakasarvvasvam. Tiruvanantapuram: Caitanya Pablikkesans, 1990. – xx, 637 p., 12 p. of plates: ill. Notes: In Malay. Encyclopedia of Malay drama, incorporating who's who of authors.

Ishak, Solehah. Histrionics of development: a study of three contemporary Malay playwrights. Kuala Lumpur: Dewan Bahasa dan Pustaka, 1987.

——. Pengalaman Menonton Teater. [The

experience of attending theatre]. Kuala Lumpur: Dewan Bahasa dan Pustaka, 1992.

——. **Protest: modern Malaysian drama: an anthology of six plays**. Kuala Lumpur: Dewan Bahasa dan Pustaka, 1992.

Istilah drama dan teater, bahasa Inggeris-bahasa Malaysia, bahasa Malaysia-bahasa Inggeris. Kuala Lumpur: Dewan Bahasa dan Pustaka, Kementerian Pendidikan Malaysia, 1987. – xiii, 81 p.; 14 x. *Notes*: Terms and phrases from English and Malay.

Jit, Krishen. **Membesar Bersama Teater**. [Growing with theatre]. Translated by Nor Azmah Shehidan. Kuala Lumpur: Dewan Bahasa dan Pustaka, 1986.

Johari, Roselina Khir. **The role of the play-wright in contemporary Malaysian theatre**. 1977. – 101 I. *Notes*: Vita. Thesis (A.M.)–Indiana University, 1977.

Mana, Sikana. **Di sekitar perikiran drama moden**. [Thinking about modern drama]. Kuala Lumpur: Dewan Bahasa dan Pustaka, 1989.

——. **Drama moden Malaysia: perkembangan dan perubahan**. [Modern Malaysian drama: Development and change]. Kuala Lumpur: Dewan Bahasa dan Pustaka, 1987.

Matusky, Patricia. **Malaysian shadow play and music: continuity of an oral tradition**. Kuala Lumpur: Oxford University Press, 1993.

Mohammed, Anis Mohd. Nor. **Zapin: folk dance of the Malay world**. Singapore: Oxford University Press, 1993.

Mohammed, Ghouse Nasuruddin. **The Malay traditional music**. Kuala Lumpur: Dewan Bahasa dan Pustaka, 1992.

Mohammed, Safian Hussain, Tahani Ahmad and Johan Jaaffar, eds. **Sejarah Kesusasteraan Melayu: Jilid 1**. [The history of Malay literature: Volume 1]. Kuala Lumpur: Dewan Bahasa dan Pustaka, 1974.

Mustapha, Kamil Yassin. 'The Malay Bangsawan'. In **Traditional drama and music of Southeast Asia**. Kuala Lumpur: Dewa Bahasa dan Pustaka, 1974.

Nanney, Nancy Kathleen. **An analysis of modern Malaysian drama**. 1983. – viii, 374 p. *Notes*: Bibliography: p. 365–74. (Ph. D.) Thesis. University of Hawaii, 1983. Microfilm. Ann Arbor, Michigan: University Microfilms International, 1984. 1 microfilm reel; 35 mm.

Nur, Nina Zuhra. **An analysis of modern Malay drama**. Shah Alam: Biroteks, MARA Institute of Technology, 1992. xiii, 244 pp.: ill. *Notes*: Based on the author's thesis (Ph. D. University

of Hawaii, 1983) under title: An analysis of modern Malaysian drama. Includes bibliographical references (p. 237–44). Malay drama. 20th century. History and criticism.

Pillai, Janet. 'Malaysia'. In **International guide to children's theatre and educational theatre: a historical and geographical source book**. Edited by Lowell Swortzell. New York: Greenwood Press, 1990.

Rahmah, Bujang. **Boria: a form of Malay theatre**. Institute of Southeast Asian Studies, 1987.

——. **Seni Persembahan Bangsawan**. [The art of the bangsawan in Malaysia and Singapore]. Kuala Lumpur: Dewan Bahasa dan Pustaka, 1975.

——. **Sejarah Perkembangan Drama Bangsawan di Tanah Melayu dan Singapura**. [The history of the development of bangsawan in Malaysia and Singapore]. Kuala Lumpur: Dewan Bahasa dan Pustaka, 1975.

Sarmma, Vi.Es. **Malayala natakam, 1880–1980**. Trivandrum: Kottayam: Vi.Es. Sarmma; Vitaranam, Nasanal Bukk Stal, 1983. – 170 p. *Notes*: In Malayalam. Chronological bibliography of Malayalam plays, 1880–1980.

Sarwar, Ghulam. **Panggung Semar: aspects of traditional Malay theatre**. Petaling Jaya: Tempo Publishing, 1992.

Sheppard, Mubin. **Royal pleasure ground: Malay decorative arts and pastimes**. Singapore: Oxford University Press, 1986.

Sweeney, Amin. **The Ramayana and the Malay shadow play**. Bangi: Universiti Kebangsaan Malaysia, 1972.

——. **Malay word music: a celebration of oral creativity**. Kuala Lumpur: Dewan Bangsawan dan Pustaka, 1994.

Tan, Sooi Beng. **Ko-tai, a new form of Chinese urban street theatre in Malaysia**. Singapore: Institute of Southeast Asian Studies, 1984. – v, 69 p., 1 p. of plates: ill. *Notes*: Includes bibliographical references. Musical theatre. Malaysia/Popular music. History and criticism.

——. **A social and stylistic history of popular Malay opera**. Singapore: Oxford University Press, 1993.

A3a86. MALI

Arnoldi, Mary Jo. **Bamana and Bozo puppetry of the Ségou region youth societies**. Lafayette, Indiana: University of Indiana Press, 1977.

——. 'The conceptual meaning of theatre among the Beledugu Bamana: an ethnographic overview'. In **Discourse in ethnomusic-ology II: A tribute to Alan P. Merriam**. Caroline Card, ed. p. 67–82. Bloomington: Archives of Traditional Music, Indiana University, 1981.

——. 'Performance, style and the assertion of identity in Malian puppet drama'. **Journal of Folklore** Research 25, no. 1–2 (January–August 1988): 87–100.

——. 'Playing the puppets: Innovation and Rivalry in Bamana youth theatre of Mali'. **The Drama Review** 32, no. 2 (summer 1988): 65–82.

——. **Playing with time: art and performance in central Mali**. Bloomington: Indiana University Press, 1995. – xx, 227 p., 8 p. of plates: ill. (some col.). Notes: Includes bibliographical references (p. 213–20) and index. Bambara Rites and ceremonies. Social life and customs/Puppet theatre. Mali. Ségou (Region).

Decock, Jean. 'Pre-Théâtre et rituel: National Folk Troupe of Mali'. **African Arts/Arts d'Afrique** 1, no. 3 (1968): 31–7.

Diabaté, Massa Makan. **Première anthologie de la musique malienne**. [First anthology of Malian music]. Recording. Edition Barenreiter, 1983.

Diallo, Mamadou. **Essai sur la musique tradi-tionelle au Mali**. [An essay on traditional music in Mali]. Paris: ACCT, 1983.

Diawara, Gaoussou. **Panorama Critique du théâtre malien dans son évolution**. [Critical overview of the Malian theatre in its evolution]. Dakar: Sankoré, 1981. 109 p.

Hopkins, Nicholas S. 'Le Théâtre moderne au Mali'. [Modern theatre in Mali]. **Présence Africaine** 25, no. 53 (March 1965): 162–93.

Maiga, M. 'Le kotéba'. **La Littérature malienne** (July–October 1984): 75–6.

Messaillou. 'La farce villageoise à la ville, le kotéba de Bamako'. [The village farce in the city, the Koteba of Bamako]. **Présence africaine** (Nov. 1964), 55 p.

A3a87. MALTA

Blouet, Brian. **The story of Malta**. London: Faber & Faber, 1967.

Calleja, Oreste. **4 Drammi**. [4 plays]. Blata l-Baijda: Union Press, 1972.

——. **Ghasfur tac-comb, Haz Zabbar**. Gutenberg Press, 1993.

Cassar Pullicino, Guze. **Guze Muscat Azzopardi: studju**. [Guze Muscat Azzopardi: a study]. Pieta: Indipendenza, 1991.

——. **Il folklore malti**. [Maltese folklore]. Msida: Malta University Press, 1975.

Ebejer, Francis. **The bilingual writer as Janus**. Valletta: Foundation for International Studies, 1989.

Eynaud, Joseph. **Il teatro italiano a Malta (1630–1830)**. [Italian theatre in Malta (1630–1830)]. Sta Venera: Lux Press, 1979.

Friggieri, Oliver. **Kittieba ta' Zmienna**. [Contemporary authors]. Valletta: A.C. Aquilina, 1976.

Ganado, H. **Rajt Malta Tinbidel**. [I saw Malta change]. Malta: 1977.

Kirkpatrick, O.L., ed. 'Francis Ebejer' in **Contemporary dramatists**. London: St James Press, 1986.

Kissaun, Michael. 'Post-war Amateur Theatre (1944–51)'. **Malta yearbook 1956**. Sliema: De la Salle Brothers, 1958.

Luttrell, Anthony. **Approaches to medieval Malta**. London: British School at Rome, 1975.

Mompalao Depiro, Joseph C. **The MADC Story 1910–85**. Sta Venera: Imprint, 1985.

Schiavone, Michael, ed. **Il-Purcissjonijiet tal-Gimgha l-KbirafMalta w Ghawdex**. [The Good Friday processions in Malta and Gozo]. Blata l-Bajda: Indipendenza, 1992.

Wettinger, Godfrey and M. Fsadni. **L-Ghanja ta' Pietru Caxaru**. [The singing of Pietru Caxaru]. Fgura: Printwell, 1983.

A3a88. MAURITANIA

Anthologie de musique maure. [Anthology of Mauritanian music]. [sound recording]. Paris: Ocora, 1982.

Belvaude, Catherine. **Ouverture sur la littérature en Mauritanie: tradition orale, écriture, témoignages**. [Introduction to litera-ture in Mauritania: oral, written and testimonial traditions]. Paris: L'Harmattan, 1989. 152 p.

Ould Hamody, Mohamed Said. **Bibliographie générale de la Mauritanie**. [General biblio-graphy of Mauritania]. Nouakchott: Centre culturel français de Nouakchott and Paris: Sepia, 1995. 580 p.

A3a89. MAURITIUS

Decotter, A. André. **Le Plaza, un demi-siècle de vie théâtrale**. [The Plaza Theatre: a half-century of theatre life]. Port Louis: Precigraph, 1983.

Gordon-Gentil, Alain. **Le Théâtre de Port Louis**. [The Theatre of Port Louis]. Port Louis: Editions Vizavi. 1994.

Morna, Colin Lowe. **Mauritius: twenty-five years of independence**. Port Louis: Institutional Investor. 1989.

A3a90. MEXICO

Alcaraz, José Antonio. **Suave teatro, 1984**. Azcapotzalco: Universidad Autónoma Metropolitana, 1985. – 215 p. *Notes*: Theatre. Mexico. History. 20th century.

Alcocer, Alfonso. **Teatro Juárez**. Guanajuato, 1984. – 148 p.: ill. (some col.).

Argudín, Yolanda. **Historia del teatro en México**. [History of theatre in México]. México City: Editorial Panorama, 1986. 221 p.

Artaud, Antonin. **México et le voyage à la Tarahumaras**. [México and the trip to the land of the Tarahumaras]. Complete works. Paris: Gallimard, 1956–65.

Azar, Héctor. **Cómo acercarse al teatro**. México City: Plaza y Valdés, 1988. – 115 p.: ill. *Notes*: Theatre and society. Mexico. History. 20th century.

——. **Funciones teatrales**. 1. edn. México City: SEP/CADAC, 1982. – 524 p. *Notes*: Includes bibliographical references (p. 519–24). Theatre. Mexico. History. 20th century.

Beardsell, Peter R. **A theatre for cannibals: Rodolfo Usigli and the Mexican stage**. Rutherford [N.J.]: London: Fairleigh Dickinson University Press; Associated University Presses, 1992. – 242 p. *Notes*: Includes bibliographical references (p. 232–8) and index. Rodolfo Usigli. Criticism and interpretation.

Bello Paredes, Guadalupe. **Así pasen cincuenta años: historia del teatro experimental en Mérida, 1942–1992**. Mérida, Yucatán: Universidad Autónoma de Yucatán, Dirección General de Extensión, Departamento Editorial, 1994. – 287 p.: ill. *Notes*: Includes bibliographical references (p. 285). Experimental theatre. Mérida. History.

Burgess, Ronald D. **Mexican theatre: the generation of 1969**. 1982 1980. – 166 p. *Notes*: Bibliography: p. 164–6. Thesis (Ph. D.)–University of Kansas, 1980. Photocopy. Ann Arbor, Mich.: University Microfilms International, 1982. Mexican drama. History and criticism. Theatre and society.

——. **The new dramatists of México, 1967–85**. Lexington, KY: University Press of Kentucky, 1991. 166 p.

Careaga, Gabriel. **Sociedad y teatro moderno en México**. México City: Editorial J. Mortiz, 1994. – 255 p. *Notes*: Includes bibliographical references. Theatre and society.

Ceballos, Edgar. **Diccionario enciclopédico básico de teatro mexicano**. [Encyclopedia dictionary of Mexican theatre]. Mexico: Siglo XX, 1996. 545 pp.: ill.

Cervera, Andrade and Alejandro Cervera. **El teatro regional de Yucatán**. [Theatre in Yucatán]. Mérida: Imprenta Guerra, 1947. 98 p.

Cucuel, Madeleine. **Le Théâtre mexicain contemporain**. Rouen: Université de Rouen, 1987. – 133 p. *Notes*: Includes bibliographical references. Introduction/Emilio Carballido – Les recherches théâtrales au Mexique (1923–47)/ Madeleine Cucuel – Luigi Pirandello et le théâtre mexicain contemporain 1930–1950: une aventure idéologique– La difusión y recepción del teatro mexicano en Francia/Osvaldo Obregón – L'endroit: Orinoco d'Emilio Carballido – Los viejos y la dramaturga mexicana/Guilherm Schmidhuber dela Mora. History and criticism.

Díaz Plaja, Guillermo Monterde and Francisco Monterde. 'Historia de la literatura española e historia de la literatura mexicana' [History of Spanish literature and history of Mexican literature]. **Enciclopedia del arte escénico** [Encyclopedia of performing arts], ed. Porrúa. México City: 1966.

Foster, David William. **Estudios sobre teatro mexicano contemporáneo: semiología de la competencia teatral**. [Studies on contemporary Mexican theatre: Semiology of theatre]. Utah Studies in Literature no. 25. New York: Peter Lang, 1984. 149 p.

Frischmann, Donald H. **El nuevo teatro popular en México**. México City: INBA, 1990. – 310 p.: ill. *Notes*: Includes bibliographical references (p. 301–10). Theatre. History. 20th century.

Geirola, Gustavo. **Teatralidad latinoamericana de la utopia experimentación teatral**. 1995. – 2 vols. (xi, 526 p.): ill. *Notes*: Bibliography: p. 504–26. Thesis (Ph. D.)–Arizona State University, 1995. Mexican American authors. History and criticism. Theatre. Political aspects.

Gorostiza, Celestino, ed. **Teatro mexicano del siglo XX**. [Mexican theatre of the twentieth century], vol. III, 7–57. México City: Fondo de Cultura Económica.

Horcasitas, Hernándo. **El teatro Nahuatl**. [Nahuatl theatre]. México City: Universidad Nacional Autónoma de México, 1974. 647 p.

Huerta, Jorge A. **A bibliography of Chicano and Mexican dance, drama and music**. Oxnard, Calif.: Colegio Quetzalcoatl, 1972 1993. – iii, 59 p.: ill. *Notes*: Dance music. Mexico. History and criticism. Bibliography.

Jiménez, Sergio and Edgar Ceballos, eds. **Teoría y prática del teatro en México: compilación de textos de Usigli, Novo, Seki Sano, Wagner, Moreau, Azar, Mendoza, Sarrás, Gurrola, Castillo, Tavira y Sabido**. [Theory and practice of theatre in México: a compilation of texts by Usigli, Novo, Seki Sano, Wagner, Moreau, Azar, Mendoza, Sarrás, Gurrola, Castillo, Tavira and Sabido]. México City: Gaceta, 1982. 369 p.

Lambs, Ruth Stanton. **Mexican theatre of the twentieth century: bibliography and study**. Claremont, Calif.: Ocelot Press, 1975. – 143 p.

Layera, Ramón. **Usigli en el teatro: testimonios de sus contemporáneos, sucesores y discípulos**. México City: Instituto Nacional de Bellas Artes, CITRU, 1996. – 282 p. *Notes*: Usigli, Rodolfo. Criticism and interpretation.

Leñero, Vicente. **Vivir del teatro**. [Living by the theatre]. Colección Contrapuntos. México City: Joaquín Mortiz, 1982. 252 p.

—— and Fernando de Ita. **El Teatro de los Insurgentes, 1953–1993**. México City: Ediciones de Milagro, 1993. – 193 p.: ill. (some col.). *Notes*: Musical theatre. Teatro de los Insurgentes (Mexico City). History.

Magaña-Esquivel, Antonio, ed. **Medio siglo de teatro mexicano**. [Half a century of Mexican theatre]. México City: Instituto Nacional de Bellas Artes, 1964. 173 p.

——. **El teatro: contrapunto**. [Theatre: counterpoint]. Colección: Presencia de México no. 12. México City: Fondo de Cultura Económica, 1970. 111 p.

María y Campos, Armando de. **Entre cómicos de ayer**. [Among yesterday's comedians]. México City: Arriba el Telón, 1950. 204 p.

——. **Informe sobre el teatro social de los siglos XIX y XX: testimonios y comentarios**. [A report on social theatre of the nineteenth and twentieth centuries: testimonies and commentaries]. México City: Confederación de Trabajadores de México, 1959. 150 p.

——. **La Vírgen frente a las candilejas o el teatro Guadalupano**. [The Virgin Mary in the footlights of theatre in Guadaloupe]. México City: Ediciones Populares, 1954. 148 p.

Mendoza Gutiérrez, Alfredo. **Nuestro teatro campesino**. [Our peasant theatre]. 2nd edn. Colección del Instituto Nacional de Capacitación del Magisterio no. 31. México City: Secretaría de Educación Pública, 1964. 292 p.

Mendoza López, Margarita. **Primeros renovadores del teatro en México 1928–41: vivencias y documentos**. [Renewers of Mexican theatre 1928–41: documents and personal experiences]. México City: Instituto Mexicano del Seguro Social, Coordinación de Teatros, 1985. 174 p.

Monterde, Francisco. **Bibliografía del teatro en México**. [Bibliography of theatre in México]. Introduction by Rodolfo Usigli. New York: Burt Franklin, 1970. 649 p.

——. **Teatro mexicano del siglo XX**. [Mexican theatre in the twentieth century]. México City: Fondo de Cultura Económica, 1956.

Mora, Juan Miguel de. **Panorama del teatro en México**. [Overview of theatre in Mexico]. México City: Latinoamericana, 1970. 292 p.

Moreau, Andrade. **Entre bastidores**. [In the wings]. México City: Arana, 1965. 308 p.

Rabell, Malkah. **Luz y sombra del antiteatro**. [Lights and shadows of the anti-theatre]. México City: Universidad Nacional Autónoma de México, 1970.

Reyes de la Maza, Luis. **Cien años de teatro en México** [One hundred years of theatre in México]. Sepsetentas no. 61. México City: Secretaría de Educación Pública, 1972. 161 p.

——. **En el nombre de Dios hablo de teatros**. México City: Universidad Nacional Autónoma de México, 1984. – 387 p., [12] p. of plates: ill. *Notes*: Includes bibliographical references and index. Mexican drama. History and criticism.

Río, Marcela del. **Perfil del teatro de la Revolución Mexicana**. New York: P. Lang, 1993. – xiii, 278 p. Includes bibliographical references (p. 267–73) and index. Mexican drama. History and criticism.

Royaard, Rense and Christine Boom. **Mexican drama**. Amsterdam: International Theatre Bookshop, 1992. – 109 p.: ill., maps. *Notes*: Translated from Dutch. Includes bibliographical references (p. 106–7). Mexican drama. 20th century. History. Drama.

Solórzano, Carlos. **Testimonios teatrales de México**. [Theatrical testimonies of México]. México City: Universidad Nacional Autónoma de México, 1973. 240 p.

Sten, María. **Vida y muerte del teatro Nahuatl**. [The life and death of Nahuatl theatre]. Sepsetentas. México City: Secretaría de Educación Pública, 1974. 208 p.

Usigli, Rodolfo. **Itinerario del autor dramático. ¿Qué pasa con el teatro en México?** [The playwright's itinerary. What is happening to theatre in México?]. México City: Imprenta Mondial, 1940. 217 p.

——. **Teatro completo** [Complete theatre].

3 vols. México City: Fondo de Cultura Económica, 1963–6.

A3a91. MOLDOVA

Bryžinky, V.S. **Narodnyj teatr mordvy**. [Popular theatre in Moldova]. Saransk: Moldovian Publishing House, 1985. 168 p.

Lat'eva, Lidiia V. **Litso I maska**. Chişinău: Lit-ra artistikă, 1980. 212 p.

A3a92. MONGOLIA

Cultural policy in the Mongolian People's Republic: a study. Paris: UNESCO, 1982. 49 p.

Dix-huit chants et poémes Mongols. [Eighteen Mongolian chants and poems]. Paris: Librairie Orientaliste Paul Geuthner, 1937. 28p.

Haslund-Christensen, Henning. **The music of the Mongols: Eastern Mongolia**. New York: Da Capo Press, 1971. 97 p.

Metternich, Hilary Roe, ed. **Mongolian folktales**. Boulder, CO: Avery Press; Seattle: University of Washington Press, 1996. 130 p.

A3a93. MOROCCO

'Azzam, Muhammad. **al-Masrah al-Maghribi: dirasah**. Damascus: Ittihad al-Kuttab al-'Arab, 1987. – 244 p. *Notes*: Includes bibliographical references (p. 233–9). Arabic drama. Morocco. History and criticism.

Badawi, 'Abd al Qadir. **Difa'an 'an al-masrah al-Maghribi**. al-Dar al-Bayda': Manshurat al-Badawi, 1996. – 356 p.: ill. (some col.). *Notes*: Arabic drama. Morocco. History and criticism.

Ben Zeidan, Abd-El-Rahman. 'As'elat al-Masrah al-Araby'. [Some questions of the arabic theatre]. In **Selselat al-Derasat al-Naqdeia** 7 (Critical Studies 7) Casablanca: Dar al-Thaqafa (The Culture House) 1987.

——. **Nahwo Kitaba Jadida Ala al-Kitaba al-Masraheya al-Maghrebeia**. [Towards a new form of Moroccan theatre writing]. n.d.

Ibn Zaydan, 'Abd al-Rahman. **Kitabat al-takris wa-al-taghyir fi al-masrah al-Maghribi**. Al-Dat al-Bayda': Ifriqiya al-Sharq, 1985. – 131 p. *Notes*: Arabic drama. Morocco. History and criticism.

al-Ka'aak, Osman. **Mahrajan al-Masrah al-Arabi al-Motanaqqell**. [The itinerant theatre festival in the Arab world]. Rabat, 1984.

Kapchan, Deborah A. **Gender on the market: Moroccan women and the revoicing of tradition**. Philadelphia: University of Pennsylvania Press, 1996.

Landau, Rom. **Moroccan drama, 1900–1955**. San Francisco: American Academy of Asian Studies, 1956. – 430 p.: map. *Notes*: Includes bibliographical references and index.

Louassini, Zouhir. **La identidad del teatro Marroqui**. [The identity of Moroccan theatre]. Granada: Grupo de Investigaçion Estudios Arabes Contemporaneos, 1992.

al-Mani'ee, Hasan. **Abhath Fi al-Masrah al-Maghraby**. [Research in the Moroccan theatre]. Rabat: Matba'aa Sawt Meknas [The Voice of Meknas Printing House], n.d.

al-Oafy, Najib. **Jadal al-Quera** [Literary debates] **Contemporary Moroccan innovation**, Rabat: Dar al-Nashr al-Maghrabeia, n.d.

Ouzri, Abdelwahed. **Le Théâtre au Maroc: structures et tendances**. [The theatre in Morocco: structures and trends]. Casablanca: Les Éditions Toubkal, 1997.

al-Sellawy, Muhammad Adeeb. 'al-Ehtifaleya Fi al-Masrah al-Maghraby al-Hadith'. [Celebration in the new Moroccan theatre]. In **al-Mawsoo'aa al-Saghira** [The Compact Encyclopaedia]. Baghdad, n.d.

al-Torris, Abd-El-Khaleq. **Entesar al-Haqq Be El-Batel**. [The victory of truth by falsehood]. Tetouan: al-Matba'aa al-Mahdeya [The Mahdeya Print House], 1933.

A3a94. MOZAMBIQUE

Fresu, Anna and Mendes de Oliveira. 'Reflexão sobre teatro popular: origins do teatro em Mozambique e sua evolucão'. [Reflections on popular theatre: the theatre in Mozambique from its origins to its evolutionary phase]. **Tempo** (7 October 1979): 55–7.

Gorodnov, Andrej. 'Mozambik – novaja žizn tradicii'. [Mozambique – new life to the tradition]. **Teatr** 46, no. 9 (September 1983): 139–44.

Hamilton, R.G. **Literatura Africa Literature Necessária**. [African Literature, Necessary Literature]. 2 vols. Lisbon: 1981, 1984.

Mankell, Henning. 'Om att arbeta med teater i Mocambique'. [On working with theatre in Mozambique]. **Entre** 16, no. 3 (1989): 10–29.

Salutin, Rick. 'Theatre, language and song in Mozambique'. **This Magazine** 13, no. 1 (1979): 26–30.

A3a95. MYANMAR

Aung, Maung Hin. **Burmese drama**. London: Oxford University Press, 1937 (reissued 1947 and 1967).

——. **Towards Peace and Democracy in Burma**. Rangoon: 1949.

Becker, A.L. 'Journey through the night: some reflections on Burmese traditional theatre', In **Traditional drama and music of Southeast Asia**, ed. M. Osman, Kuala Lumpur: 1974.

Bowers, Faubian. **Theatre in the East: survey of drama and dance**. New York: Thomas Nelson & Sons, 1956.

Brandon, James R. **Theatre in Southeast Asia**. Cambridge: Harvard University Press, 1967.

Hla Pe. **Kaonmara Pya Zat** 1. [Popular Burmese modern drama]. London, 1952.

Khyac' Cam Van' ". **Ya ne' Mran' ma' rup' se" sabhan'**. Rangoon: Pan' " Myui" Ta ra Ca pe, 1989. – 283, 13 p. Notes: In Burmese. Puppet theatre in Burma. Includes bibliographical references (p. 284–96). History.

Kyo' Chan' ". **Sa bhan' sac'**. Rangoon: Ca pe Biman', 1989. – 199 p.: ill. Notes: In Burmese. On the Burmese theatre. Includes bibliographical references (p. 198–9). Burmese drama. 20th century. History and criticism.

Lha Samin'. **Mran' ma' rup' se' sabhan'**. Rangoon: Loka 'a mran' Ca pe phran' khyi re', 1968. – 339 p.: ill. Notes: Includes glossary on puppetry and bibliographical references. Puppets. Burma.

Ma Thanegi. **The imitation of life: Burmese puppets**. Bangkok: Tamarind Press. [n.d.].

Sein, Kenneth. **The great Po Sein: a chronicle of the Burmese theatre**. Westport, Conn: Greenwood Press, 1976. 170 p.

Singer, N. **Burmese dance and theatre**. Singapore, Oxford University Press, 1995.

——. **Burmese puppets**. Singapore: Oxford University Press, 1992. 98 pp.

So' Jan', U. **Pra jat' sa muin'-**. Rangoon: Ca pe lo ka, 1965. – 240 p. Notes: In Burmese. History/Theatre and state. Burma.

Tinker, Hugh. **The union of Burma: a study of the first years of independence**. London: Oxford University Press, 1961.

U Nu. **Saturday's Son**. New Haven: Yale University Press, 1975.

Zagrski, Ulrich. **Burma: unknown paradise**. Tokyo: Kodansha, 1972.

A3a96. NAMIBIA

Levinson, Olga. **Our first thirty years: the history of the South African Arts Association**. Windhoek: 1977. Notes: Includes Namibia.

O'Callaghan, Marion. **Namibia: the effects of apartheid on culture and education**. Paris: UNESCO, 1977. 169 p.

A3a97. NEPAL

Amatya, Shaphalya. **Some aspects of cultural policy in Nepal**. Paris: UNESCO, 1983. 63 p.

Anderson, Mary M. **The festivals of Nepal**. London: George Allen & Unwin, 1977. 288 p.

Coomaraswami, A.K., ed. **Natya Darpan**. Cambridge: Cambridge University Press, 1917.

Karan, P.P. and W.M. Jenkins. **A cultural and physical geography of Nepal**. Kentucky: University of Kentucky Press, 1960.

Lall, Kesar. **Lores and legends of Nepal**. Kathmandu: Ratnat Postak Bhandar: 1978.

Manupuria, Trilok Chandra and Indra Majupuria. **The complete guide to Nepal**. India: Smt. M.D. Gupta, Lalitpur Colony, Laskkar (Gwalior), 1986. 341 p.

Pradhan, Mrigendra ManSingh. **Avinaya Darpan**. Kathmandu: Tribhuvan University, 1976.

——. **Nepali Niritya Kala**. Kathmandu: Krishna Pradhan, 1996.

——. **Niritya Kala**. Kathmandu: Sajha Prakashan, 1980.

——. **Niritya Tatha Nirityakar**. Kathmandu: Pradhan Natya Mandal, 1994.

——. **Pancha Buddha and dance**. Kathmandu: Royal Nepal Academy, 1996.

Sakya, Karna. **Tales of Kathmandu**. Brisbane, 1980.

Slusser, Mary Shephard. **Nepal mandal: a cultural study of the Kathmandu Valley**. 2 vols. Princeton, NJ: Princeton University Press, 1982.

A3a98. NETHERLANDS

Abbing, H. **Een economie van de kunsten: Beschouwingen over kunst en kunstbeleid**. [The economics of the arts: views on art and arts policy]. Groningen: Historische uitgeverij, 1989. 273 p.

Alkema, Hanny and Christine Boer. **Poppen-, object-, en beeldend theater in Nederland**. [Puppet, object and pictorial theatre in the Netherlands]. Amsterdam: Dutch Theatre Institute, 1991. 157 p.

Alphenaars, Carel. **De Goden van het theater: 22 Nederlandse en Vlaamse toneelschrijvers aan het woord**. Westbroek: Harlekijn, 1983. – 239 p.: ill. Subjects: Dutch drama. 20th century. History and criticism. Interviews. Playwriting.

Austen, Steve, ed. **10 jaar margetheater in Nederland**. [Ten years of Dutch fringe theatre]. Utrecht/Antwerp: Spectrum, 1980. 160 p.

Baal: vijftien jaar toneelhistorie 1973–1988. Amsterdam: International Theatre Bookshop, 1988. – 179 p.: ill. History. Baal (Theatre group).

Baart, Jan. Mime in Nederland. Amsterdam: Meulenhoff Informatief, 1982. – 144 p.: ill. Notes: Cover title. Dutch and English. Bibliography: p. 144. Mime.

Bruyne, Paul de. 1984 voorbij: over theater, traditie, rugzak en rode pruik. Westbroek: Harlekijn, 1984. – 185 p. Notes: Includes bibliographies. Theatre. History. 20th century. History and criticism.

Coffeng, Joh M. Lexicon van Nederlandse tonelisten. Amsterdam: Polak & Van Gennep, 1965 1964. – 232 p. illus., ports. Notes: Theatre dictionary. In Dutch.

Deddes, Ingrid, ed. Tomaat documentation: een documentair verslag van een actie, 9 oktober 1969–28 februari 1970. [Tomato documentation: a documentary account of a protest, 9 October 1969–28 February 1970]. Amsterdam: Instituut voor Theateronderzoek/Holland Festival, 1979. 333 p.

De Voogd, G.J. Facetten van vijftig jaar Nederlands toneel 1920–70. [Facets of Dutch theatre from 1920 to 1970]. Amsterdam: Moussault, 1970. 236 p.

Dieho, Bart. Theater op de bres. Vormingstheater in Nederland en Vlaanderen. [Theatre in the breach. Socio-developmental theatre in the Netherlands and Flanders]. Amsterdam: Dutch Theatre Institute, 1979. 96 p.

Een cultuur van verandering: advies cultuurnota, 1997–2000. The Hague: Raad voor Cultuur, 1996. – 15 vols. Notes: 1. Beeldende kunst, bouwkunst en vormgeving – 2. Musea – 3. Monumenten en archeologie – 4. Archieven – 5. Letteren – 6. Bibliotheken – 7. Media – 8. Film – 9. Theater – 10. Muziek en muziektheater – 11. Dans – 12. Amateurkunst en kunsteducatie – 13. Festivals – 14. Bovensectoraal – [15]. Algemeen. Subjects: Netherlands. Cultural policy.

Erenstein, Robert and Joost Sternheim, eds. Baal: 15 jaar toneelhistorie, 1973–88. [Baal: 15 years of theatre history, 1973–88]. Amsterdam: International Theatre Bookshop, 1988. 179 p.

Frey, Martin. Kreatieve Marge: die Entwicklung des niederländischen Off-Theaters. [The creative fringe: the development of Dutch Off-Theatre]. Vienna: Bohlau, 1991. 166 p.

Gieling, Lia. Toneelbeeld: vanaf 1945 in Nederland. [The stage set in the Netherlands since 1945]. Amsterdam/The Hague: SDU, 1990. 176 p.

Heteren, Lucia van. Laten we gaan: de opvoeringsgeschiedenis van Samuel Beckett in Nederland tot 1992. Amsterdam: Nederlands Theater Instituut: International Theatre & Film Books, 1992. – 138 p.: ill. Notes: Includes bibliographical references (p. 123–5) and index. Beckett, Samuel, 1906–1989. Stage history. Netherlands.

Kassies, J. Op zoek naar cultuur. [In search of culture]. SUN-schrift, Nijmegen: SUN, 1980. 376 p.

Leeuwe, Hans H. J. de, Abraham Haak and Hans Mulder. Van tooneel tot tejater: opstellen voor Prof. Dr. H.H.J. de Leeuwe. Zutphen: Walburg Pers, 1983. – 128 p.: ill. Notes: Summaries in English. Bibliography of works by De Leeuwe: p. 106–12. De Turkse violist/Hans Mulder – Enige 19de-eeuwse beschouwingen over toneelvernieuwing/A.C. Haak – Melodrama, genre of kwalificatie?/Louis Houët – Circensisch theater/Karel Hupperetz – Nederlands televisiedrama/Sonja de Leeuw – Manus de Snorder/J.P.M. Mannens – Zij moet van het tooneel af/Hans Mulder – Theater en vrede tussen fatum en utopie/Els Wiertz-Boudewijn – Vormingstheater/Gemma van Zeventer. Dutch drama.

Maanen, Hans van. Het Nederlandse toneelbestel van 1945 tot 1995. Amsterdam: Amsterdam University Press, 1997. – 422 p.: ill. Notes: Includes bibliographical references (p. 353–66) and index. History. 20th century.

Ogden, Dunbar H. Performance dynamics and the Amsterdam Werkteater. Berkeley: University of California Press, 1987. – xxii, 261 p.: ill. Notes: Includes bibliographical references and index. Experimental theatre. Werkteater (Amsterdam).

——. Das 'Werkteater' von Amsterdam: Geschichte, Inszenierungen, Spieldynamik. [The Amsterdam Werktheater: history, stagings, performance dynamics]. Würzburg: Königshausen und Neuman, 1993. 290 p.

Perkins, Elizabeth. The plays of Alma De Groen. Amsterdam/Atlanta: Rodpi, 1994. 183 p.

Roseboom, Koos and Marleen Sikker, eds. Een oneindig circuit: de theaterzucht in Nederland. [A never-ending circuit: the craving for theatre in the Netherlands]. Amsterdam: Alligator/Instituut voor Theateronderzoek, 1986. 79 p.

Rutten, André. Haagse Comedie: Haagse Comedie 40 jaar. The Hague: Haagse Comedie, 1987. – 148 p.: ill. (some col.). Notes: Summary in English. Includes indexes. History. Haagse Comedie (Theatre company).

Stroman, B. **De nederlandse toneelschrijfkunst: verklaring van een gemis**. [Dutch playwriting: an explanation of an absence]. Amsterdam: Moussault, 1973. 240 p.

A3a99. NETHERLANDS ANTILLES AND ARUBA

Gordijn, W. **Culturele kroniek '48–'68**. [Cultural chronicle '48–'68]. Amsterdam: Stichting voor Culturele Samenwerking, 1970.

Heuvel, Pim and Freek van Wel. **Met eigen stem: herkenningspunten in de letterkunde van de Nederlandse Antillen en Aruba**. [A voice of their own: points of reference in literary writing of the Netherlands Antilles and Aruba]. Assen/Maastricht: Van Gorcum, 1989.

Palm, Jules Ph. De, ed. **Encyclopedie van de Nederlandse Antillen**. [Encyclopedia of the Netherlands Antilles]. 2nd edn. Zutphen: de Walburg Pers, 1985. S.v. 'Literatuur' [Literature] and 'Toneel' [Drama].

A3a100. NEW ZEALAND

Atkinson, Laurie, Pat Hawthorne and Judy Russell, eds. **Playmarket 1973–1994**. Wellington: Playmarket, 1995. 38 p.

Harcourt, Peter. **A dramatic appearance: New Zealand theatre 1920–1970**. Wellington: Methuen, 1978. 177 p.

Lane, Dorothy F. **The island as site of resistance: an examination of Caribbean and New Zealand texts**. New York: Peter Lang, 1995. 181 p.

Marsh, Ngaio. **Black beech and honeydew: an autobiography**. Rev. and enl. edn. Auckland: Collins, 1981, 1965. – 310 p., 16 p. of plates: ill. *Subjects*: Women authors, New Zealand. 20th century. Biography/Women theatrical producers and directors. Stage history.

Mason, Bruce. **Every kind of weather**, ed. David Dowling. Auckland: Reed Methuen, 1986. 306 p.

McNaughton, Howard Douglas. **New Zealand drama: a bibliographical guide**. Christchurch: University of Canterbury, 1974. – 112 p. *Notes*: Includes indexes. New Zealand drama. Bibliography.

——. **New Zealand drama**. Boston: Twayne, 1981. 168 p.

New Zealand cultural statistics: Nga Tatauranga Whakapuaki Tuakiri o Aotearoa. Wellington: Statistics New Zealand: Te Tari Tatau and Ministry of Cultural Affairs: Te Manatu Tikanga-a-Iwi, 1995.

New Zealand performing arts touring directory. Wellington: Creative New Zealand, 1996. 75 p.

Performance: a handbook of the performing arts in New Zealand. Wellington: Association of Community Theatres, 1980 [for 1979 and 1980], 1983 [for 1981 and 1982], 1985 [for 1983 and 1984]. 33, 37, 62 p.

Playmarket directory of New Zealand plays and playwrights. Wellington: Playmarket, 1992. 228 p.

Robinson, Roger and Nelson Wattie, eds. **The Oxford companion to New Zealand literature**. Auckland: Oxford University Press, forthcoming.

Scotts, Neil, Lewis Holden and Jenny Neale. **Arts facts: a statistical profile on the arts in New Zealand**. Wellington: Department of Internal Affairs, 1987. 140 p.

Simpson, Adrienne. **Opera's farthest frontier: a history of professional opera in New Zealand**. Auckland: Reed, 1996. 288 p.

Simpson, E.C. **A survey of the arts in New Zealand**. Wellington: Wellington Chamber Music Society, 1961. 181 p.

Smyth, Bernard W. and Hilary Howorth. **Books and pamphlets relating to culture and the arts in New Zealand: a bibliography including works published to the end of the year 1977**. Christchurch: University of Canterbury Dept. of Extension Studies in association with UNESCO and Department of Internal Affairs, 1978. 103 p.

Tait, David. **New Zealanders and the arts: results from a survey of attendance and interest patterns in the performing and visual arts**. Wellington: Queen Elizabeth II Arts Council of New Zealand and Department of Internal Affairs, 1983. 64 p.

Thompson, Mervyn. **All my lives**. Christchurch: Whitcoulls, 1980. 185 p.

Thomson, John. **New Zealand drama 1930–1980: an illustrated history**. Auckland: Oxford University Press, 1984. 108 p.

——. 'Bibliography: Drama', In **The Oxford history of New Zealand literature in English**, ed. Terry Sturm. Auckland: Oxford University Press, 1991: 621–623.

Von Antropoff, Rurik, Klaus Peter Müller and Albert-Reiner Glaap. **Dramatic voices from England, Canada and New Zealand: Festschrift für Albert-Reiner Glaap**. Berlin: Cornelsen, 1989. – 256 p.: 1 port. *Notes*: Text in English, with foreword in English and German. Includes bibliographic references. Canadian drama

(English). 20th century/English drama. New Zealand drama.

A3a101. NICARAGUA

Arellano, Jorge Eduardo. 'Teatro'. [Theatre]. In **Panorama de la literaturia nicaragüense** [An overview of Nicaraguan literature]. Managua: Editorial Nueva Nicaragua, 1986.

——. **Un siglo de teatro en Nicaragua**. Managua: Instituto Nicaragüense de Cultura, 1993, 1988. – 34 p.: ill. *Notes*: Reprint. Originally published: Escenarios de dos mundos. Madrid: Centro de Documentación Teatral, 1988, t. 3, p. 189–217. With new final ch. by Consuelo Pérez Díaz. 'Bienal de Teatro, 1993'. Includes bibliographical references. History. 20th century.

Bolt, Alan. 'Magic Theatre. Political Theatre'. **Communications from the International Brecht Society** 15, no. 2 (April 1986): 48–51.

——. 'Teatro en Nicaragua: arquetipos y símbolos'. [Theatre in Nicaragua: archetypes and symbols]. **Conjunto** 94 (1993): 43–53.

——. 'El teatro estudiantil universitario'. [University student theatre]. **Conjunto** 45 (1980): 5–13.

Brookes, Chris. **Now we know the difference**. Vancouver: NC Press, 1983. 140 p.

——. 'Notes on Nicaragua: two theatres'. **Theatrework** 2, no. 3 (March 1982): 18–20.

Caballero, Attilio. 'Semana Santa en Nicaragua: rito, tradición y contemporaneidad'. [Holy week in Nicaragua: ritual, tradition and contemporaneity]. **Conjunto** 77 (1988): 92–6.

Craven, David. 'Art in contemporary Nicaragua'. **Oxford Art Journal** 11, no. 1 (1988): 51–63.

Cuadra, Pablo Antonio. 'Breve nota sobre el teatro nicaragüense'. [Brief notes on Nicaraguan theatre]. In **Tres obras de teatro nuevo** [Three plays from the new theatre]. Ediciones de la Academia Nicaragüense de la Lengua, 1957.

Gómez, Mayte. 'No more black sheep: a women's theatre collective in Nicaragua/No más ovejas negras: colectivo de teatro de mujeres en Nicaragua'. **Aquelarre** 2, no. 4 (winter 1990): 20–24.

Kaiser-Lenoir, Claudia. 'Arte y prática social: el nuevo teatro en Nicaragua'. [Art and social practice: the new theatre in Nicaragua]. **Conjunto** 78 (January–April 1989): 75–9.

——. 'Nicaragua: theatre in a new society'. **Theatre Research International** 14, no. 2 (1989): 122–130.

Kidd, Ross. 'Testimony from Nicaragua: an interview with Nidia Bustos'. **Theatrework** 2, no. 6 (September–October 1982): 32–40.

Martin, Randy. 'Country and city: theatre in revolution'. **The Drama Review** 31, no. 4 (winter 1987): 58–76.

Morton, Carlos. 'The Nicaraguan drama: theatre of testimony'. **Latin American Theatre Review** 17, no. 2 (spring 1984): 89–93.

Pérez Estrada, Francisco. **Teatro folklore nicaragüense**. [Nicaraguan folklore theatre]. Managua: Editorial Nuevos Horizontes, 1946.

Rapp, Siegfried. **'Wir erinnern uns an die Zukunft': das 'Teatro Popular' in Nicaragua, oder, Der mühevolle Weg eines Entwicklungslandes zu authentischem Theater**. Egelsbach; New York: Hänsel-Hohenhausen, 1992. – 111 p.: ill. *Notes*: Includes bibliographical references (p. 108–11). Theatrical companies. Nicaragua.

Ruf, Elizabeth. 'Teatro del pueblo, por el pueblo y para el pueblo'. [Theatre of the people, for the people and by the people]: An interview with Alan Bolt'. **The Drama Review** 31, no. 4 (winter 1987): 77–90.

Sáenz, Faustino. 'Revalorización de nuestra Comedia Maestra'. [A re-evaluation of our national play]. **Ventana** 23 (January 1988): 7.

Weiss, Judith. 'Teyocoyani and the Nicaraguan popular theatre'. **Latin American Theatre Review** 23, no. 1 (fall 1989): 71–79.

A3a102. NIGER

Abdoulaye, Mamadou. 'Le théâtre au Niger'. [Theatre in Niger]. MA Thesis, University of Abidjan.

Beik, Janet. **Hausa theatre in Nigeria: a contemporary oral art**. New York: Garland, 1987. 327 p.

——. 'National development as theme in current Hausa drama in Niger'. **Research in African Literature** 15, no. 1 (spring 1984): 1–24.

Bovin, Mette. 'Ethnic performances in rural Niger: An aspect of ethnic boundary maintenance'. **Folk** 16–17 (1974–5): 459–74.

Dan-Inna, Chaibou. 'La Théâtralité en pays hausa'. [Theatricality in Hausa country]. MA thesis, University of Abidjan, 1979.

Galadima, Dodo Idi. **Le Théâtre moderne nigérien: naissance et évolution**. [Modern theatre in Niger: birth and evolution]. Thesis. University of Niamey, 1987.

Harding, Frances. 'Continuity and Creativity in Tiv Theatre'. Ph.D. dissertation, University of Exeter, 1988.

Illo, Bija. 'La Critique sociale dans l'oeuvre dramatique de Djibo Mayaki'. [Social Criticism in the Dramatic Works of Djibo Mayaki]. MA Thesis. University of Niamey, 1994.

A3a103. NIGERIA

Aboada, Fola. **Fola Aboada in interview with Dapo Adelugba**. Ibadan, Nigeria: Dept. of Theatre Arts, University of Ibadan, 1985. – ii, 43 p. *Notes*: 'July 20, 1985'. Theatre. History. 20th century.

Adelugba, Dapo. **Wole Soyinka, a birthday letter, and other essays**. Ibadan, Nigeria: University of Ibadan, Department of Theatre Arts, 1984. – 151 p. *Notes*: Theatre. History. 20th century.

Alston, Johnny Baxter. **Yoruba drama in English: clarification for productions**. Iowa City: University of Iowa, 1985. 226 p.

——. **Yoruba drama in English: interpretation and production**. Lewiston, N.Y.: E. Mellen Press, 1989. – 192 p. *Notes*: Includes index. Bibliography: Nigerian drama (English). Yoruba authors. History and criticism.

Art and culture in Nigeria and the diaspora. Studies in Third World Societies Series. Williamsburg: William and Mary College, 1991.

Axworthy, Geoffrey, Martin Banham, Michael Etherton and Chris Nwamuo. **The faces of Nigerian theatre**. [Calabar]: Centaur Publishers, 1990. – viii, 76 p. *Notes*: Includes bibliographical references. History. 20th century.

Badejo, Diedre Lorraine Gomez. **Yoruba theater: a case study in continuity and change**. 1988 1985. – x, 243 p.: ill. (some col.). *Notes*: Bibliography: p. 236–43. Thesis (Ph. D.) –UCLA, 1985. Photocopy. Ann Arbor, Mich.: University Microfilms International, 1988. x, 243 p. *Subjects*: Yoruba drama. 20th century. History and criticism.

Brooks, Christopher. **Duro Ladipo and the Moremi legend. the socio-historical development of the Yoruba music drama and its political ramifications**. 1989. – xii, 274 p. ill. *Notes*: Includes bibliographical references (p. 262–74). Thesis (Ph. D.)–University of Texas at Austin, 1989. Vita. Microfilm. Ann Arbor, Mich.: University Microfilms International, 1990. 1 microfilm reel; 35 mm. Yoruba drama. History and criticism. Music and mythology. Politics and government. To 1960.

Clark, Ebun. **Hubert Ogunde: the making of Nigerian theatre**. Oxford and New York: Oxford University Press, 1980 1979. – xix, 170 p., 8 p. of plates: ill. *Notes*: Revision of the author's thesis (M. Phil.)–University of Leeds,

1974. Includes index. Bibliography: p. 163–6. Nigeria. History/Theatre. Political aspects. Biography.

Cole, Herbert M. and Chike C. Aniokor. **Ibo arts: community and cosmos**. Los Angeles: Museum of Cultural History, 1984. 256 p.

Dunton, Chris. **Make man talk true: Nigerian drama in English since 1970**. London; New York: Hans Zell Publishers, 1992. – 215 p. *Notes* : Includes bibliographical references (p. 193–209) and index. Ola Rotimi – Zulu Sofola – Kole Omotoso – Bode Sowande – Femi Osofisan – Tess Onwueme – Olu Obafemi and Tunde Fatunde – Akanji Nasiru and Segun Oyekunle. Nigerian drama (English). History and criticism. Politics and literature.

——. **Nigerian theatre in English: a critical bibliography**. London; New Providence, NJ: Hans Zell Publishers, 1998. *Notes*: Includes index. Nigerian drama (English). History and criticism.

Götrick, Kacke. **The actor, the art of acting and liminality**. 1993. [no publisher listed]. *Notes*: On Yoruba Apidan Theatre, Egungun masking and professional acting troupes. Includes bibliographical references.

——. **Apidan theatre and modern drama: a study in a traditional Yoruba theatre and its influence on modern drama by Yoruba playwrights**. Stockholm, Sweden: Almqvist & Wiksell International, 1984. – 271 p., 8 p. of plates: ill. (some col.). *Notes*: Includes index. Bibliography: p. 256–65. Performing arts. Nigeria.

Jeyifo, Abiodun. **The Yoruba popular travelling theatre of Nigeria**. Lagos: Ministry of Social Development, Youth, Sports and Culture, 1984. 213 p.

Laurence, Margaret. **Long drums and cannons: Nigerian dramatists and novelists**. New York: Frederick A. Praeger, 1969.

Malomo, Jide and Dapo Adelugba. **Jide Malomo in interview with Dapo Adelugba**. Ibadan, Nigeria: Dept. of Theatre Arts, University of Ibadan, 1985. – ii, 71 p. *Notes*: 'Aug. 4, 1985.' Theatre management. Malomo, Jide. Interviews.

Nwamuo, Chris. **Essays in theatre administration in Nigeria**. Owerri, Nigeria: Totan Publishers, 1986. – v. <1>: ill. *Notes*: Bibliography: p. 99–101. Theatre management.

Nzewi, Meki. **The drama scene in Nigeria**. Enugu: Fourth Dimension, 1985. 240 p.

Obiechina, Q. **An African popular theatre: a study of Onitsha market pamphlets**. Cambridge: Cambridge University Press, 1973.

Oduneye, Bayo and Dapo Adelugba. **Bayo Oduneye reflects on Stanislavsky today.** Ibadan, Nigeria: Dept. of Theatre Arts, University of Ibadan, 1990. *Notes*: 'September 3, 1990'. Theatre. History. Stanislavsky.

Ogonna, Nnabuenyi. **Mmonwu: a dramatic tradition of the Ibo.** Lagos: Lagos University Press, 1984. 226 p.

Ogunbiyi, Yemi, ed. **Drama and theatre in Nigeria: a critical sourcebook.** Lagos: Nigeria Magazine Publishing, 1981. 522 p.

Otokunefor, Henrietta C. and Obiageli C. Nwodo. **Nigerian female writers: a critical perspective.** Lagos: Malthouse Press, 1989. – xii, 160 p. *Notes*: Includes bibliographical references and index. Positivism and the female crisis: the novels of Buchi Emecheta/Helen Chukwuma – The works of Flora Nwapa/Yemi I. Mojola – The writings of Ifeoma Okoye/Charles Nnolim – The novels of Adaora Ulasi/Yemi I. Mojola – The ascetic feminist vision of Zaynab Alkali/Seiyifa Koroye – The Nigerian woman as a dramatist: the instance of Tess Onwueme/Chidi Amuta – Zulu Sofola's theatre/Olu Obafemi – Zulu Sofola: her writings and their undermeanings/Ayo Akinwale – Female voices in poetry: Catherine Acholonu and Onolara Ogundipe-Leslie as poets/Obi Maduakor – Junior African literature series by Remi Adedeji/Willfred F. Feuser – Audrey Ajose in children's fiction/Obiageli C. Nwodo – The writings of Teresa Meniru/Charles E. Nnolim – The fiction of Martina Nwakoby/Juliet Okonkwo – Helen Ofurum's A welcome for Chijioke/Henrietta C. Otokunefor – Mary Okoye on juvenile detective story/Obiageli C. Nwodo – Mabel Segun: critical review/Funso Aiyejina – Rosina Umelo and Nigerian juvenilia/Helen Chukwuma – The works of Rosemary Uwemedino:a critical review/Chidi Ikonne.

Ukpokodu, Iremkokiokha Peter. **Socio-political theatre in Nigeria since Independence.** San Francisco: Mellen Research University Press, 1992. 300 p.

Wren, Robert M. **J.P. Clark.** Boston: Twayne, 1984. 181 p.

A3a104. NORWAY

Aarseth, Asbjørn. **Den Nationale Scene 1901–31.** [The National Stage 1901–31]. Oslo: Gyldendal Norsk Forlag, 1969. 499 p.

Alme, Gunnar. **Theatre in Norway 1979.** [Oslo]: Norsk Teaterunion, 1979. – 58 p.: ill. *Notes*: Cover title. Performing arts. History. 20th century.

Anker, Øyvind. **Scenetunsten i Norge fra fortid til nutid.** [Theatrical art in Norway from the beginning to the present]. Oslo: Studier i Norge, 1968. 123 p.

Arntzen, Knut Ove and Siren Leirvåg, eds. **Vestlandsmodernismen i norsk teater.** [Western modernism and its influence on Norwegian theatre]. **Teatervitenskapelige Studier** no. 3. Bergen: University of Bergen, 1992. 113 p.

Bringsværd, Tor Åge and Halldis Hoaas, eds. **Norsk teaterårbok 1975.** [Norwegian theatre yearbook 1975]. Oslo: Aschehboug, 1976.

Broch, Kirsten. **Komedianter og kremmere: det Dramatiske selskab i Bergen, 1794–1994.** Bergen: Alma mater, 1994. – 124 p.: ill. *Notes*: Includes bibliographical references (p. 122) and index. Theatre. Dramatiske selskab (Bergen). History.

Grøndahl, Carl Henrik. **Teater mot teater.** [Oslo]: Dyade Forlag, 1985. – 134 p. *Notes*: Theatre. History. 20th century.

Hagnell, Viveka. **Norsk teater 1900–1990: repertoarpolitik och samhällstematik.** [Oslo]: Rådet for humanistisk forskning, NAVF: Universitetsforlaget, 1991. – 258 p.: ill. *Notes*: Summary in English. Includes bibliographical references (p. 241–5). Norwegian drama. 20th century. History and criticism.

Just, Carl. **Litteratur om norsk teater.** Oslo: N. W. Damm, 1953. – 31 p. *Notes*: Theatre. Norway. Bibliography.

Mæhle, Leif. **Det Norske Teatret 75 år, 1963–1988.** Oslo: Norske Teatret, 1988. – 468 p.: ill. (some col.). *Notes*: Includes index. History. 20th century/Norske teatret.

Næss, Trine. **Mellomkrigstidens teater i den norske hovedstaden: forholdet til det ikke-realistiske utenlandske teater.** Oslo: Solum, 1994. – 425 p.: ill. *Notes*: Includes bibliographical references (p. 408–16). History. 20th century.

Nordic Theatre Studies: Yearbook for Theatre Research in Scandinavia, 5 vols. Copenhagen: Munksgaard, 1989–.

Nygaard, Knut and Eiliv Eide. **Den Nationale Scene 1931–1976.** [The National Stage 1931–1976]. Oslo: Gyldendal Norsk Forlag, 1977. 518 p.

Olsen, Arne Thomas and Else Martinsen. **Studioteatret: frihet og fornyelse.** Oslo: Universitetsforlaget, 1995. – 172 p.: ill. *Notes*: Studioteatret (Theatre group: Oslo). History.

På norske scener. [On Norwegian stages]. Annual yearbook. Oslo: Det Norske Teatres Forening, 1987–.

Parmer, Vidar. **Teater: pantomime, linedans,**

ekvilibristikk, menasjeri, vokskabinett, kos-morama etc. på Fredrikshald. Halden (Norway): Halden Kommune, 1967. – 317 p.: ill. *Notes*: Includes index. Theatre. History/Halden Kommune.

Rønneberg, Anton. **Nationaltheatret gjennom femti år**. [The National Theatre: through fifty years]. Oslo: Gyldendal Norsk (Kirstes bok-trykkeri), 1949. – 514 p.: ill. *Notes*: Includes index. Oslo. Nationaltheatret. History.

———. **Nationaltheatret 1949–1974**. [The National Theatre 1949–74]. Oslo: Gyldendal Norsk Forlag, 1974. 339 p.

Sletbak, Nils, ed. **Det Norske Teatret 50 År: 1913–1963**. [The Norwegian Theatre: 50 years: 1913–1963]. Oslo: Det Norske Samlaget, 1963. 487 p.

Wiik, Steinar. **I storm og stille: Riksteatret 1949–1989**. Oslo: Riksteatret, 1990. – 224 p.: ill. (some col.). *Notes*: Summary in English. Includes bibliographical references and index. History.

A3a105. OMAN

Anthony, John D. **Historical and cultural dictio-nary of the Sultanate of Oman and the Emirates of Eastern Arabia**. Metuchen, NJ: Scarecrow Press, 1976.

Excerpts from Omani history. Oman: Ministry of Education, Training and Youth, 1985.

Johnstone, Thomas Muir, 'Folklore and Folk Literature in Oman and Socrata'. **Arabian Studies** 1 (1974): 7–23.

———. 'Folk tales and Folklore of Dhofar'. **Journal of Omani Studies** 6 (1983): 123–6.

Oman: arts traditionels du sultanat d'Oman. [Oman: traditional arts of the Sultanate of Oman]. [sound recording]. Ivry, France: Auvidis, 1993.

Shawqi, Yusuf. **Dictionary of traditional music in Oman**. Translated and expanded by Dieter Christensen. Wilhelmshaven: F. Noetzel, 1994. 224 p.

Theatre in the Domestic Club. Oman: Domestic Club, 1977.

A3a106. PAKISTAN

'Abdulhamid and Hamid Shakir. **Thetar kahani, 'Abdulhamid artist ki zabani**. Faisalabad: Qartas, 1994. 288 pp.: ill. *Notes*: Autobiographical narration by a theatre artist from Punjab, Pakistan; includes biographical sketches of famous stage artists, producers, directors and dramatists. Urdu drama. History and criticism.

Erven, Eugene Van. **The playful revolution: theatre and liberation in Asia**. Bloomington: Indiana University Press, 1992.

Hussain, Mohammad Shahid. **Folk tradition and Urdu theatre** (in Urdu). New Delhi: Husnain Publications, 1992.

Javaid, Inam-ul-Haq. **Punjabi drama** (in Urdu). Islamabad: Idara-e-Saqafat, 1986.

Sohail, Ahmed. **Jadeed theatre**. [Contemporary theatre]. Islamabad: Idara-e-Saqafat, 1984.

A3a107. PALESTINE

Abd Raouf Mahammid, Muhammad. **Ma-sirt el-Haraka al-Masrahiya fi Adfa il Gharbiya 1967–87**. [History of the theatrical movement in the West Bank 1967–87]. Im il Fahem, Israel: Markaz al-Thourath al-Arabiy-al-Taieba, 1989.

Anees, Mohamad. **Al Harakah Al Masrahiah Fee Al Manatek Al Mohtala**. [The Palestinian theatrical movement in the occupied territories]. Jerusalem, 1979.

Asadi, Jawad. **al-Masrah wa-al-Filastini alladhi fina**. Damascus: Tunis: al-Ahali lil-Tiba'ah wa-al-Nashr wa-al-Tawzi'; Da'irat al-Thaqafah, Munazzamat al-Tahrir al-Filastiniyah, 1992. – 162 p.: ill. *Notes*: Theatre. History. 20th century.

Beidas, Khalil. **Masareh Al Athhan**. [The theatre of the mind]. Beirut: Palestinian Union of Journalist writers, 1978.

Bisouson, Moeen. **Al Aamal Al Masrahiya**. [The theatrical works]. Beirut: Dra Al Awdah, 1979.

Butitsiefa, Tamara Alexandrovna. **Alf Mil Am wa-Am ala Al Masrah Al-Arab**. [A thousand and one nights of Arabic theatre]. Beirut: Dar il Farbi, 1981.

Habibi, Emile. **The secret life of said the pessoptimist**. London: Zed Books, 1987.

Haddad, 'Abir Zibaq and Nayif Khuir. **al-Masrah al-Filastini fi al-Khalil: bahth wa-tahlil**. [Palestinian-Arab theatre in Galilee]. Nazareth: Wizarat al-Ma'arif wa-al-Thaqafah, Da'irat al-Thaqafah al-'Arabiyah, 1994. – 139, 4 p.: ill. *Notes*: English summary. Originally presented as the author's thesis (masters). Includes biblio-graphical references. *Subjects*: Theater. West Bank. Hebron. History/Arabic drama.

Jawzi, Nasri. **Tarikh al-masrah al-Filastini, 1918–1948**. Nicosia: Sharq Briss, 1990. – 186 p.: ill. *Notes*: Title on p. facing t.p.: History of Palestinian theatre.

Al-Jouzy, Nasry. **Falasteen Lan Nansaki**. [Palestine, we won't forget you]. Damascus: Tarbeen, 1971.

Kanafany, Ghassan. **Al Athar Al Kamelah**. [The complete works, part 3]. Beirut: The Organization of Ghassan Kanafany, Dar Al Taleeah, 1978.

Khadra Jayyusi, Salma, ed. **Anthology of modern Palestinian literature**. New York: Columbia University Press, 1992.

Khory Yousef Q. **Al Sahafa Al Arabiah Fee Falasteen 1876–1948**. [The Arabic journal in Palestine 1876–1948]. Beirut: Moassassat Al Derasat Al Falasteniyah, 1976.

Laâbi, Abdellatif, ed. **Anthologie de la poésie Palestinienne contemporaine**. [Anthology of contemporary Palestinian poetry]. Paris: Messidor, 1990.

Lustick, Ian. **Arabs in the Jewish state: Israel's control of national minority**. Austin: University of Texas Press, 1980.

Mhamid, Muhamad. **Masirat al-harakah al-masrahiyah fi al-Diffah al-Gharbiyah, 1967–1987**. al-Tayyibah: Markaz Ihya' al-Turath al-'Arabi, 1989. – 188 p.: ill. *Notes*: Includes bibliographical references (p. 165–75). Palestinian theatre. West Bank. History.

Said, Edward W. **Culture and imperialism**. London: Chatto & Windus, 1993.

Sanbar, E., S. Hadidi, *et al*, eds. **Palestine: l'Enjeu culturel**. [Palestine: The cultural game of chance]. Paris: Circé/Institut du Monde Arabe, 1997.

al-Sawahry, Khalil. **Zaman Al Ihtelal**. [The time of occupation]. Damascus: The Union of Arabic Writers, 1979.

Sharif, Maher al-, ed. **La Patrimoine culturel palestinien**. [Palestinian cultural heritage] Paris: Sycomore, 1980.

Yaghi, Abd al-Rahman. **Hayat Al Adab Al Falasteny Al Hadeeth: Min Awal Al Nahda Hata Al Nakba**. [Modern Palestinian literature from the revolution until the disaster]. Beirut: Dar Al Afak al-Gadedah, 1981.

Ziad, Rawfeek. **An Al Adab, Al Adab Al Shaby Fee Falasteen**. [The folk literature of Palestine: Literature in Palestine]. Beirut: Dar Alawda, 1970.

A3a108. PANAMÁ

Avila C., José. **El teatro panameño**. [Panamanian theatre]. Bogotá: Instituto Caro y Cuero, 1972.

Calvo, Alberto. 'El Teatro Nacional y algo de su historia'. [The National Theatre and its history]. **Lotería** 3 no. 35 (October 1958): 57–60.

Domínguez, Daniel. 'El teatro en Panamá: entre problemas, excepciones y esperanzas'. [Panamanian theatre: between problems, circumstances and hopes]. **Latin American Theatre Review** 25 no. 1 (1992): 123–7.

López, Ana Lucía. 'Teatro panameña contemporánea'. [Contemporary Panamanian theatre]. **UCR/AEC** (1976): 369–73.

Rodríguez C., Héctor. 'La dramaturgia panameña contemporánea'. [Contemporary Panamanian dramaturgy]. **Revista Nacional de Cultura** 26 (1994): 171–178.

——. 'Génesis del teatro panameño. [The development of modern Panamanian theatre]. **Universidad** 4, no. 46 (1992): 77–90.

——. **Primera historia del teatro panameño**. [The first history of Panamanian theatre]. Panamá City: National Institute of Culture, 1984.

A3a109. PAPUA NEW GUINEA

Beir, Ulli, ed. **Introduction to five New Guinea plays**. Milton: Jacaranda Press, 1971.

Eri, Vincent. **The crocodile**. Brisbane: Jacaranda Press, 1970.

Gillison, Gillian. 'Living Theatre In New Guinea's Highlands'. **National geographic** August 1983, p. 146–69.

——. **Between culture and fantasy: a New Guinea highlands mythology**. Chicago: Chicago University Press, 1993.

Goroka's travelling players. Theatre Raun Raun, Report to the National Cultural Council April 1975–June 1976.

Hannet, Leo. 'Em rod bilong kago'. **Kovave** (pilot issue; June 1969): 47–51.

Holmes, John H. **In primitive New Guinea**. London: Seeley & Service, 1924.

Kaniku, John Wills. 'Cry of the Cassowary; and Turuk, Wabei, Kulabob'. In **Two plays from New Guinea**. Melbourne: Heinemann Educational, 1970.

Kiki, Albert Maori. **Kiki: ten thousand years in a lifetime**. Melbourne: F.W. Cheshire, 1968.

Murphy, Greg. 'Kainantu Farces and Raun Raun Theatre'. **Gigibori** 4 no. 1 (February 1978): 28–39.

——. 'Nema Namba: A Dance Drama by the Raun Raun Theatre'. **Gigibori** 3 no. 2 (April 1977): 13–18.

Paradise: in flight with air niugini. Port Moresby: Morauta and Associates (March–April 1997).

Schwimmer, Erik. 'Aesthetics of the Aika'. In **Exploring the visual art of Oceania** (1979): 287–92.

Williams, F.E. **Drama of the Orokolo: the social and ceremonial life of the Elema**. Oxford: Clarendon Press, 1940.

——. **Orokaiva society**. Territory of Papua, Anthropology Report, 10. Oxford: Clarendon Press, 1930.

A3a110. PARAGUAY

Benítez, Luis. 'Teatro'. [Theatre]. In **Historia de la cultura del Paraguay**. [History of Paraguayan culture]. Asunción: Comuneros. [n.d.].

——. **El teatro paraguayo**. [Paraguayan theatre]. Lima: Servicio de Publicaciones del Teatro Universitario de San Marcos, 1971.

Bogada, Víctor. '1980–90: un decenio de teatro en el Paraguay'. [1980–90: a decade of theatre in Paraguay]. **Latin American Theatre Review** 25, no. 2 (spring 1992).

Cardozo, Efraín. 'El teatro'. [The theatre]. In **Apuntes de historia cultural del Paraguay** [Notes on Paraguay's cultural history]. Asunción: Biblioteca de Estudios Paraguayos, 1985.

Carmona, Antonio and Edda de los Ríos. 'Paraguay'. **Diógenes. Anuario crítico del teatro latinoamericano**, vol. 2, 107–12. 1986.

Centurión, Carlos. 'Teatro'. [Theatre]. In **Historia de la cultura paraguaya** [History of Paraguayan culture]. Asunción: Biblioteca Ortíz Guerrero, 1961.

de los Ríos, Edda. 'El teatro Municipal de Asunción, Paraguay: historia y reflexion'. [Municipal theatre of Asunción, Paraguay: history and reflection]. **Latin American Theatre Review** 21, no. 1 (fall 1987): 109–14.

Novoa, Bruce and C. May Gamboa. 'Tiempoovillo: Paraguayan Experimental Theatre'. **Latin American Theatre Review** 8, no. 2 (spring 1975): 75–83.

Plá, Josefina. **Cuatro siglos de teatro en el Paraguay**. [Four centuries of theatre in Paraguay]. Colección Teatro. Asunción: Universidad Católica, 1990. 225 p.

Rodríguez Medina, Carlos. 'El teatro en el Paraguay'. [Theatre in Paraguay]. In **Teatro y cine: aproximaciones** [Approaches to theatre and film]. 7th edn. Asunción: FVD.

Vallejos, Roque. 'El teatro en el Paraguay'. [Theatre in Paraguay]. In **La literatura paraguaya como expresión de la realidad nacional**. [Paraguayan literature as an expression of national reality]. Asunción: Don Bosco, 1971.

Velázquez, Rafael Eladio. 'El teatro'. [The theatre]. In **Breve historia de la cultura en Paraguay** [An outline of cultural development in Paraguay]. 2nd edn. Asunción: Comuneros, 1982.

A3a111. PERU

Boggs, Bruce Alan. **Experimental techniques in three plays by Gregor Díaz**. 1989. – iii, 60 p. *Notes*: Includes bibliographical references (p. 59–60). Thesis (M.A.)–Texas Tech University, 1989. Experimental theatre. 20th century. Criticism and interpretation.

Cotto-Escalera, Brenda Luz. **Crupo Cultural Yuyachkani: group work and collective creation in contemporary Latin American theatre**. 1995. – viii, 213 p. *Notes*: Vita. Includes bibliographical references (p. 194–212). Thesis (Ph. D.)–University of Texas at Austin, 1995. Peru/Theatre. Political aspects. Latin America/Grupo Cultural Yuyachkani.

Hesse Murge, José. 'El teatro en el Perú'. [Theatre in Perú]. In **Teatro peruano contemporàneo** [Contemporary Peruvian theatre]. Madrid: Aguilar, 1963.

Mego, Alberto. **El teatro popular y de aficionados en Lima 1970–80: características y perspectivas. Plan de teatros pilotos**. [Popular and amateur theatre in Lima 1970–80: definitions and perspectives. Pilot theatres]. Lima. [n.d.].

Morris, Robert J. **The contemporary Peruvian theatre**. Lubbock, TX: 1977.

——. **The Peruvian theatre, 1946–1966**. 1972, 1968. – iv, 306 p. *Notes*: Vita. Bibliography: 285–9. Thesis (Ph. D.)–University of Kentucky, 1968. Photocopy. Ann Arbor, Mich.: University Microfilms International, 1972. *Notes*: Peruvian drama. 20th century. History and criticism.

Natella, Arthur A. **The new theatre of Peru**. New York: Senda Nueva de Ediciones, 1982. – 130 p. *Notes*: English and Spanish. Bibliography: p. 113–30. Peruvian drama. 20th century. History and criticism/Salazar Bondy. Solari Swayne, Enrique. Ríos, Juan. Criticism and interpretation.

Pérez Luna, Edgardo. **Los treinta años de Guillermo Ugarte Chamorro**. [Thirty years of Guillermo Ugarte Chamorro]. **Estudios de teatro peruano** no. 43. Lima: Servicio de Publicaciones del Teatro Universitario de San Marcos, 1965.

Salazar del Alcázar, Hugo. **Teatro y violencia: una aproximación al teatro peruano de los 80'**. 1st edn. Lima, Perú: Centro de Documentación y Video Teatral: Jaime Campodónico, 1990. – 52 p.: ill. *Notes*: Includes bibliographical references. Peruvian drama. 20th century. History and criticism.

Sotomayor Roggero, Carmela. **Panorama y tendencias del teatro peruano**. Lima: Herrera Editores, 1990. – 120 p.: ill. *Notes*: Includes bibliographical references. Peruvian drama. History and criticism.

Teatro Universitario de San Marcos. [San Marcos University theatre]. **Actividades del Teatro Universitario** 34. Lima: Servicio de Publicaciones del Teatro Universitario de San Marcos, 1972.

A3a112. PHILIPPINES

Aguila, Reuel Molina. **Ligalig at Iba Pang Dula**. Manila: Kalikasan Press, 1989.

Buenaventura, Cristina L. **The theatre in Manila: 1846–1946**. Manila: De La Salle University Press, 1994.

Chua, Soo Pong, ed. **Traditional theatre in Southeast Asia**. Singapore: SPAFA and Centre for the Arts of the National University of Singapore, 1995.

Cruz, Isagani R. ed. **A short history of theater in the Philippines**. n.p., 1971. – viii, 330 p. *Notes*: Prologue, by I.R. Marcos.–Foreword, by I.R. Cruz.–The roots of Philippine theater in the pre-Spanish period, by E. David.–Filipino drama during the Spanish period, by D. Salazar.–The Moro-Moro, by F. Mendoze.–The zarzuela in the Philippines, by I.R. Cruz.–Colonial theater, by I.R. Cruz.–The period of stageless drama, by E. Florentino.–Contemporary Philippine theater, by I.R. Cruz.–Appendix A: Some theaters in Greater Manila, by M.L. Jacob.–Appendix B: Questionnaire on the theater history of the Philippines, by the PETA Research and Information Center.–Appendix C: The Philippine Educational Theater Association, by M.L. Jacob.–Appendix D: A checklist of Philippine plays from 1900–1946.–Seventy years of Philippine theater: a bibliography of critical works, 1900–1970, by F.S. Dizon and I.R. Cruz (p. 307–27).

Fernandez, Doreen G., ed. **Contemporary Theatre Arts: Asia and the United States**. Quezon City: New Day Publishers, 1984.

——. **The Iloilo Zarzuela 1903–1930**. Quezon City: Ateneo de Manila University Press, 1978.

——. **In performance**. Quezon City: Vera-Reyes Inc., 1981.

——. **Palabas, essays on Philippine theatre history**. Quezon City: Anteneo de Manila University Press, 1996.

Florentino, Alberto Z. **The world is an apple and other prize plays**. Manila: Cultural Publishers, 1959.

Guerrero, Wilfrido Ma. **My favourite 11 plays**. Manila: New Day Publishers, 1976.

Hiblang Abo, Tong Perez's **On North Diversion Road** and Malou Jacob's **Juan Tamban**. Manila: ASEAN COCI, 1992.

Joaquin, Nick. **A portrait of the artist as Filipino**. Manila: Alberto S. Florentino, 1966.

Lapeña-Bonifacio, Amelia. **Ang Bundok at Iba Pang Dula**. Manila: De La Salle University Press, 1994.

Lumbera, Bienvenido and Pacita Gavino. **Tanghal: towards a Filipino stage design**. [Philippines]: Coordinating Center for Production Design and Cultural Promotions Division, 1990. – 37 p.: ill.; 16 x. Stage-setting and scenery.

Manlapaz, Edna Zapanta. **Aurelio Tolentino: selected writings**. Quezon City: University of the Philippines Press, 1975.

Mojares, Resil B. **Theatre in society, society in theatre (social history of a Cebuano village 1840–1940)**. Quezon City: Ateneo de Manila University Press, 1985.

Noriega Jr, Bienvenido M. **Bayan-Bayanan at Iba Pang Dula**. Manila: National Book Store Inc., 1982.

Philippine drama: twelve plays in six Philippine languages. Quezon City: NSTA-Assisted UPS Integrated Research Progress 'A', 1987.

Ramas, Wilhelmina Q. **Sugbuanon theatre from Sotto to Rodriguez and Kabahar: an introduction to pre-war Sugbuanon drama**. Quezon City: Published for the Asian Center [by] University of the Philippines Press, 1982. xii, 369 pp. *Notes*: Contains plays in Cebuano and English. History and criticism/Cebuano drama. 20th century. Translations into English. Cebu (Province). History.

Riggs, Arthur Stanley. **The Filipino drama [1903]**. Manila: Intramoros Administration, 1981.

Salanga, Alfredo Navarro. **Kamao: dula ng protesta, 1970–1986**. Manila: Center for Literature, Cultural Center of the Philippines, 1987. – 218 p. *Notes*: In Tagalog. Moses, Moses/Rogelio Sikat – Welga/Panday-Sining at Bonifacio Ilagan – Pagsambang bayan/Bonifacio Ilagan – May isang sundalo/Rene O. Villanueva – Ang mga unang araw sa buha ng bagong iskolar ng bayan/Richie Valencia Buenaventura at Edgar Vencio – Buwan at baril/Chris Millado – Nukleyar II/Al Santos – Radio play para sa boykot sa U.P. Diliman/Peryante. Philippine drama. 20th century/Popular culture. Political aspects.

Sebastian, Federico. **Ang Dulang Tagalog**. Manila: BBS Silangan Publishing House, 1955.

Sikat, Regelio *et al*. **Tatio sa Tanghalau**. Manila: Kalikasan Press, 1990.

Tiongson, Nicanor G. **Kasaysayan at Estetika ng Sinakulo at Ibang Dulang Panrelihiyon sa Malolos**. Quezon City: Ateneo de Manila University Press, 1975.

——. **Kasaysayan ng Komedya sa Pilipinas: 1706–1982**. Manila: De La Salle University Press, 1982.

——. **Philippines Circa 1907**. Quezon City: Philippine Educational Theatre Association, 1985.

——. **What is Philippine drama?** Theatre Studies 1: Quezon City: Philippine Educational Theatre Association, 1983.

——, ed. **Modern ASEAN plays: Philippines**. With scripts in English translation of Al Santos' The system of Professor Tuko, Rene O. Villanueva's Strands of Gray, Tony Perez's North Diversion Road and Malou Leviste Jacob's Juan Tamban. Published by the ASEAN Committee on Culture and Information and the ASEAN Department of Foreign Affairs, Manila, 1992, 236 p.

A3a113. POLAND

Adamski, Jerzy. **Teatr z bliska: pamietnik teatralny z lat 1971–1981**. Warsaw: Ludowa Spóldzielnia Wydawnicza, 1985. – 268 p. *Notes*: Includes index. Theatre. History. 20th century/Adamski, Jerzy.

Axer, Erwin. **Cwiczenia pamieci**. Warsaw: Panstwowy Instytut Wydawniczy, 1984. – 265 p., 25 p. of plates: ill. *Notes*: Includes index. Bibliography: p. 247–8. Biography.

Banu, Georges. **Ryszard Cieslak, acteur-emblème des années soixante**. [Arles, France]: Actes sud, 1992. – 125 p.: ill. *Notes*: Portions translated from Polish, English and Italian. Includes bibliographical references. Biography. Cieslak, Ryszard, 1937–90.

Beres, Stanislaw and Kazimierz Braun. **Rozdarta kurtyna: rozwazania nie tylko o teatrze**. London: ANEKS, 1993. – 247 p.: ill. *Notes*: Polish drama.

Braun, Kazimierz. **A history of Polish theater, 1939–1989: spheres of captivity and freedom**. Westport, CT: Greenwood Press, 1996. – xii, 233 p. *Notes*: Includes bibliographical references (p. 185–208) and indexes. 20th century/ Theatre. Political aspects. Transl. of **Teatr Polski: 1939–1989** – obszary wolnosci – obszary znewolenia (Warsaw: Semper, 1994).

Bujanski, Jerzy Ronard. **Starego Teatru druga mlodosc**. Kraków: Wydawn. Literackie, 1985. – 248 p., 16 p. of plates: ill. *Notes*: Includes bibliographical references and index. Stary Teatr. History and biography.

Bukowska, Miloslawa. **Odmiany konwencji w teatrze współczesnym na przykladzie inscen-izacji 'Wyzwolenia' Stanislawa Wyspianskiego**. Wroclaw: Zaklad Narodowy im. Ossolinskich, 1981. – 288 p., 96 p. of plates: ill. *Notes*: Includes bibliographical references and index. Wyspianski, Stanislaw, 1869–1907. Stage history. Polish drama.

Cegiela, Anna. **Polski slownik terminologii i gwary teatralnej**. Wroclaw: 'Wiedza o Kulturze', 1992. *Notes*: Includes bibliographical references. Dictionary. In Polish.

Ciechowicz, Jan. **Dom opowiesci: ze studiów nad Teatrem Rapsodycznym Mieczyslawa Kotlarczyka**. Gdansk: Uniwersytet Gdanski, 1992. – 240 p.: ill. *Notes*: Summary in English. Includes bibliographical references and index. Kotlarczyk, Mieczyslaw/Teatr Rapsodyczny. History. Biography.

Ciesielski, Zenon. **Od Fredry do Rózewicza: dramat i teatr polski w Szwecji w latach 1835–1976**. Gdansk: Wydawn. Morskie, 1986. – 397 p., 40 p. of plates: ill. *Notes*: Summary in English. Includes index. Bibliography: p. 349–63. Polish drama. Swedish/Polish drama. Relations.

Cioffi, Kathleen M. **Alternative theatre in Poland, 1954–1989**. Amsterdam, Netherlands: Harwood Academic Publishers, 1996. – viii, 258 p.: ill. *Notes*: Includes index. Bibliography p. 233–47.

Csató, Edward. **Dwie strony rampy**. [Warsaw]: Czytelnik, 1956. – 352 p. Polish drama. 20th century. History and criticism.

——. **The Polish Theatre**. Translated by Christina Cenkalska. Warsaw: Interpress, 1968. 191 p.

Czerwinski, Edward Joseph. **Contemporary Polish theater and drama (1956–1984)**. New York: Greenwood Press, 1988. – xix, 155 p. *Notes*: Includes index. Bibliography: p. 131–44. Polish drama. 20th century. History and criticism.

——. **The contemporary theater in Poland and its impact in other Slavic countries in the light of the history and program of 'Dialog'**. 1981 1965. – iv, 293 p. *Notes*: Bibliography:

p. 231–93. Thesis (Ph. D.)– University of Wisconsin, 1965. Photocopy. Ann Arbor: University Microfilms International, 1981. Theatre history as seen through the journal **Dialog**.

——. 'The Polish Theatre of the Absurd'. In **Studies in Polish Civilization: Selected Papers Presented at the First Congress of the Polish Institute of Arts and Sciences in America**, ed. Damian S. Wandycz, 199–213. New York: Institute on East Central Europe, Columbia University and the Polish Institute of Arts and Sciences in America, 1971.

Drozdowski, Bohdan and Catherine Itzin. **Twentieth century Polish theatre**. London: J. Calder, 1980. – 249 p.: ill. *Notes*: Bibliography: p. 233–49. Drama in Polish.

Dziewulska, Malgorzata. **Teatr zdradzonego przymierza**. Warsaw: Panstwowy Instytut Wydawniczy, 1985. – 149 p. History. 20th century.

Fik, Marta. **Przeciw, czyli za**. Warsaw: Czytelnik, 1983. – 421 p. *Notes*: Includes indexes. Theatre. Poland. Reviews.

——. **Trzydzieści pięć sezonów: teatry dramatyczne w Polsce w latach 1944–1979**. Warsaw: Wydawnictwa Artystyczne i Filmowe, 1981. – 524 p., 64 p. of plates: ill. *Notes*: Includes indexes. Bibliography: p. 470–8. History. 20th century.

Filipowicz, Halina. **The theatre of Tadeusz Rózewicz**. 1979. – 310 p. *Notes*: Bibliography: p. 287–310. Thesis (Ph. D.)–University of Kansas, 1979. Microfilm. Ann Arbor, Mich.: University Microfilms, 1979. 1 microfilm reel; 35 mm. Polish drama. Criticism and interpretation.

Filler, Witold. **Contemporary Polish Theatre**. Translated by Krystyna Deplicz. Warsaw: Interpress, 1977. 147 p.

Findlay, Robert R., Philip George Hill and Béla Királyfálvi. **Contemporary Russian and Polish theater and drama**. Washington, D.C.: University and College Theatre Association, 1982. – 86 p.: ill. *Notes*: 'The essays, interviews, reports of conversations and the like that appear here grew from the work of participants in a National Endowment for the Humanities-funded institute that met for six weeks in June and July 1980 at the Graduate Center of the City University of New York'.

Gąssowski, Szczepan. **Współcześni dramatopisarze polssy**. [Contemporary Polish playwrights]. Warsaw: Wydawnictwa Artystyczne I Filmowe, 1979.

Gerould, Daniel. **Twentieth century Polish avant-garde drama: plays, scenarios, critical documents**. Ithaca and London: Cornell University Press, 287 p. Intro III. *Notes*: Bibliography (p. 281–7). Valuable study of modern Polish theatre.

——, Bolesław Taborski, Steven Hart and Michał Kobiałka. **Polish plays in translation: an annotated bibliography**. New York: City University of New York, 1983.

Goldfarb, Jeffrey C. **The persistence of freedom: the sociological implications of Polish student theatre**. Boulder: Westview, 1980. 159 p. *Notes*: Bibliography (p. 151–9).

Grodzicki, August. **Polish theatre directors**. Warsaw: 'Interpress'. RSW 'PKR', 1979. – 185 p.: ill. *Notes*: Translation of **Rezyserzy polskiego teatru**. A study of Poland's major directors from Axer to Grotowski.

——. **W teatrze zycia: wspomnienia z lat 1920–1980**. Warsaw: Panstwowy Instytut Wydawniczy, 1984. – 308 p., 16 p. of plates: ill. *Notes*: Includes index. History and criticism.

—— and Roman Szydłowski. **Teatr w polsce ludowej**. [Theatre in people's Poland]. Warsaw, 1975.

Hartmann, Karl. **Das polische Theater nach dem zweiten Weltkrieg**. [Polish theatre after the Second World War]. Marburg, 1964.

Itzin, Catherine. **Special double Polish theatre issue**. London: J. Calder, 1979. – 249 p.: ill. *Notes*: Special issue of: **Gambit**, v. 9, no. 33–4. Bibliography: p. 233–49. The dead class/ Tadeusz Kantor – The cuttlefish, or The hyrcanian worldview/Stanislaw Ignacy Witkiewicz – Ninety-three/Stanislawa Przybyszewska – Hamlet 70/Bohdan Drozdowski. *Subjects*: Polish drama. 20th century/Polish drama. 20th century. History and criticism.

Kaminska, Ida. **My life, my theatre**. New York: MacMillan, 1973. 310 p.: illus. *Notes*: The leading lady of Poland's Yiddish theatre tells her story.

Karpinski, Maciej. **Teatr Andrzeja Wajdy**. Warsaw: Wydawnictwa Artystyczne i Filmowe, 1991. – 209 p.: ill. *Subjects*: Wajda, Andrzej, 1926–. Criticism and interpretation. Director's study.

Kelera, Józef. **Panorama dramatu: studia i szkice**. Wroclaw: Wydawn. Dolnoslaskie, 1989. – 225 p. *Notes*: Includes bibliographical references and index. Polish drama. 20th century. History and criticism.

Kiec, Izolda, Dobrochna Ratajczak and Jacek Wachowski. **Teatr i dramat polskiej emigracji 1939–1989: praca zbiorowa**. Poznan: Wydawn.

Acarus, 1994. – 291 p.: ill. (some col.). *Notes*: Includes bibliographical references and index. Polish drama. Foreign countries. History and criticism.

Kłossowicz, Jan. **Tadeusz Kantor. Teatr.** Warsaw: Państwowy Instytut Wydawniczy, 1991.

Kott, Jan. **Jak wam sie podoba: spotkanie pierwsze.** Warsaw: Panstwowy Instytut Wydawniczy, 1955 1962. – 3 vols. *Notes*: 2. Poskromienie zlosników – 3. Miarka za miarke. *Subjects*: Polish drama. 20th century. History and criticism.

——. **Still alive: an autobiographical essay.** New Haven: Yale University Press, 1994. – xi, 291 p. *Notes*: Poland. History. 1945–80. Kott, Jan, 1914–. Literature. Criticism/Poland.

Krajewska, Anna. **Dramat i teatr absurdu w Polsce.** Poznan: Wydawn. Nauk. UAM, 1996. – 274 p., 26 p. of plates: ill. *Notes*: Includes bibliographical references and index. Theatre of the absurd. Poland. 20th century. History and criticism.

Kuchtówna, Lidia and Barabara Lasocka. **Leon Schiller–w stulecie urodzin 1887–1987.** Warsaw: Panstwowe Wydawn. Nauk., 1990. – 290 p.: ill. *Notes*: Includes bibliographical references and index. Schiller, Leon, 1887–1954. Criticism and interpretation. Director's study.

Kuharski, Allen James. **The theatre of Witold Gombrowicz.** 1991. – iv, 442 p. *Notes*: Includes bibliographical references (p. 301–27). Thesis (Ph. D.)–University of California, Berkeley, 1991. Microfilm. Ann Arbor, Mich.: University Microfilms International, 1992. 1 reel; 35 mm. *Notes*: Gombrowicz, Witold. Criticism and interpretation. Playwright's study.

Lewkowski, Kazimierz A. **Miedzy dramatem a teatrem.** Lódz: PWSFTiT, 1992. – 143 p., 22 p. of plates: ill. *Notes*: Includes bibliographical references. History and criticism.

Magala, Slawomir. **Polski teatr studencki jako element kontrkultury.** Warsaw: Mlodziezowa Agencja Wydawnicza, 1988. – 179 p., 12 p. of plates: ill. *Notes*: Includes bibliographical references. *Subjects*: Student theatre. Alternative theatre.

Majchrowski, Zbigniew. **Gombrowicz i cien Wieszcza: oraz inne eseje o dramacie i teatrze.** Wyd. 1. Gdansk: Wydawn. Uniwersytetu Gdanskiego, 1995. – 181 p.: ill. *Notes*: Includes bibliographical references (p. 173) and index. History and criticism/Gombrowicz, Witold. Dramatic production.

Marczak-Oborski, Stanisław. **Teatr czasu wodry.** [Theatre during the war]. Warsaw: Panstwowy Instytut Wydawniczy, 1967.

—— and Barbara Król-Kaczorowska. **Teatr polski w latach 1918–1965: teatry dramatyczne.** Warsaw: Panstwowe Wydawn. Nauk., 1985. – 558 p.: ill. *Notes*: Summary in French. Bibliography: p. 433–4. Theatre. History. 20th century.

Misiołek, Edmund. **Bibliographie théâtrale polonaise, 1964–1972.** [Polish theatre bibliography, 1964–1972]. Warsaw: Polish Centre of the ITI, 1974. 154 p.

Morawiec, Elzbieta. **Powidoki teatru: swiadomosc teatralna w polskim teatrze powojennym.** Kraków: Wydawn. Literackie, 1991. – 371 p. *Notes*: Includes bibliographical references. Theatrical producers and directors. 1945–89.

Niziolek, Grzegorz. **Sobowtór i utopia: teatr Krystiana Lupy.** Kraków: Universitas, 1997. – 235 p., 46 p. of plates: ill. *Notes*: Includes bibliographical references. Lupa, Krystian, 1943–. Criticism and interpretation.

Opalski, Józef. **Rozmowy o Konradzie Swinarskim i Hamlecie.** Kraków: Wydawn. Literackie, 1988. – 278 p., 32 p. of plates: ill. *Notes*: Includes bibliographical references (p. 243–4). Stage history. Swinarski, Konrad. Interviews. Hamlet.

Osterloff, Barbara, Magdalena Raszewska and Franciszek Sielicki. **Leksykon teatralny.** Warsaw: Twój Styl, 1996. – 283, [2] p. *Notes*: Includes bibliographical references (p. 285). Polish theatre encyclopedia.

Plesniarowicz, Krzysztof. **Teatr nie-ludzkiej formy.** Kraków: Tow. Autorów i Wydawców Prac Naukowych Universitas, 1994. – 135 p. *Notes*: Includes bibliographical references (p. 129) and index. History. 20th century.

Popiel, Jacek. **Dramat a teatr polski dwudziestolecia miedzywojennego.** Kraków: Universitas, 1995. – 255 p.: ill. (some col.). *Notes*: Includes bibliographical references and index. Polish drama. History and criticism.

——. **Dramat i teatr po roku 1945.** Wroclaw: Wiedza o Kulturze, 1994. – 303 p. *Notes*: Includes bibliographical references and index. Polish drama. History and criticism.

Puzyna, Konstanty. **Burzliwa pogoda.** [Stormy weather]. Warsaw: Panstwowy Instytut Wydawniczy, 1971.

Raszewski, Zbigniew. **Raptularz 1965–1967.** Warsaw: Wyd. Znak, 1996. – 268 p.: ill. *Subjects*: Theatre and state. Teatr Narodowy.

Rogacki, Henryk. **Leon Schiller: czlowiek i**

teatr. Lódz: Wydawn. lódzkie, 1995. – 176 p., 32 p. of plates: ill. *Subjects*: Biography/Schiller, Leon.

——. **Warszawskim szlakiem Leona Schillera**. Warsaw: Wydawn. PTTK Kra', 1990. – 113 p.: ill., map. *Notes*: Includes bibliographical references. Schiller, Leon, 1887–1954. Criticism and interpretation.

Ronikier, Joanna and Kazimierz Wisniak. **Piwnica pod Baranami, czyli, Koncert ambitnych samouków**. Warsaw: Wydawn. Tenten, 1994. – 341 p.: ill. (some col.). *Notes*: Includes index. Music-halls (Variety-theaters, cabarets, etc.). History.

Rudnicki, Adolf. **Teatr zawsze grany**. Warsaw: Czytelnik, 1987. – 127 p. Jewish theatre. Poland. History. 20th century.

Segel, Harold B. **Polish romantic drama**. Ithaca and London: Cornell University Press, 1977, illus. Intro. Plays by Mickiewicz, Krasinski and Slowacki with a valuable introduction by the editor.

Sławinska, Irena. **The Slavic Contribution to the Great Reform**. Warsaw, 1972.

—— and Wojciech Kaczmarek. **Wokól wspólczesnego dramatu i teatru religijnego w Polsce, 1979–1989**. Wroclaw: Wiedza o kulturze, 1993. – 321 p. *Notes*: Includes bibliographical references (p. 297–99) and index. Christian drama. History and criticism.

Sugiera, Malgorzata. **Miedzy tradycja i awangarda: teatr Jerzego Grzegorzewskiego**. Kraków: Towarzystwo Autorów i Wydawców Prac Naukowych 'Universitas', 1993. – 212 p., 16 p.: ill. *Notes*: Summary in English. Includes bibliographical references. Theatrical producers and directors. Stage setting and scenery. Grzegorzewski, Jerzy.

Szydłowski, Roman, **The theatre in Poland**. Warsaw: Interpress, 1972. 176 p.: illus. *Notes*: General study of theatre in Poland, directors, designers, actors, television/radio drama and criticism by the long-time drama critic for the communist daily **Trybuna Ludu**.

Tomczyk-Watrak, Zofia. **Józef Szajna i jego teatr**. Warsaw: Panstwowy Instytut Wydawniczy, 1985. – 145 p.: ill. Szajna, Józef.

Udalska, Eleonora. **Teatr polski konca XX wieku**. Kielce: Szumacher, 1997. – 44, 1 p. *Notes*: Includes bibliographical references (p. 43–5). Polish drama. 20th century. History and criticism.

Wolicki, Krzysztof. **Gdzie jest teatre?** [Where is theatre?]. Krakow: Wydawnictwo Literackie, 1978.

Zelwerowicz, Aleksander. **O sztuce teatralnej: artykuly, wspomnienia, wywiady z lat 1908–1954**. Wroclaw: Wiedza o Kulturze, 1993. – 356 p.: ill. *Notes*: Includes bibliographical references (p. 284–317) and index. History. 20th century.

A3a114. PORTUGAL

Barbosa, Pedro. **Teoria do Teatro Moderno, axiomas e teoremas**. [Theory of the modern theatre, axioms and theorems]. Oporto: EdiSoes Afrontamento, 1982.

Cruz, Duarte Ivo. **Introdução ao Teatro Portuguesa do Século XX**. [An introduction to the Portuguese theatre of the twentieth century]. Lisbon: Espiral, 1969.

França, José-Augusto. **Notícia duma Morfologia Dramática**. [Notes on a dramatic morphology]. Lisbon: Confluencia, 1953.

Karimi, Kian-Harald. **Das portugiesische Gegenwartsdrama unter der politischen Zensur, 1960–1974: auf der Suche nach dem verlorenen Theater**. Frankfurt am Main; New York: P. Lang, 1991. – xvii, 416 p.: ill. *Notes* : Includes bibliographical references (p. 397–408) and index. Theatre. Censorship. History. 20th century. Portuguese drama.

Mendonça, Fernando. **Para o Estudo do Teatro em Portugal**. [Towards a study of theatre in Portugal]. Rio de Janeiro: Assis, 1971.

Pedro, António. **Pequeño Tratado de Encenação**. [A short treatise on the scene]. Lisbon: Confluência, 1962.

Picchio, Luciana. **Storia del Teatro Portoghese**. [History of the Portuguese theatre]. Rome: Edizioni dell'Ateneo, 1964. Republished in Portuguese, Lisbon: Portugália, 1969.

Porto, Carlos. **Em busca do Teatro Perdido**. [In search of the lost theatre]. 2 vols. Lisbon: Platano Editora, 1973.

——. **10 años de teatro em Portugal**. [10 years of theatre in Portugal]. Lisbon: Caminho, 1985.

——. **O TEP e o teatro em Portugal: histórias e imagens**. Porto: Fundação Eng. António de Almeida, 1997. – 367 p.: ill. *Notes*: Includes bibliographical references (p. 361–3). Círculo de Cultura Teatral/Teatro Experimental do Porto. History.

Rebello, Luiz Francisco. **100 Años de Teatro Português**. [100 years of Portuguese theatre]. Oporto: Brasília, 1984.

——. **Combate por um teatro de combate**. [The struggle for a theatre of struggle]. Lisbon: Seara Nova, 1977. 233 p.

——. **Dicionário do teatro português**. Lisbon: Prelo Editora, 1970. – ill. *Notes*: In Portuguese.

——. **História do Teatro Português**. [History of the Portuguese theatre). Lisbon: Publicaçoes Europa-America, 1967. 141 p.

——. **História do teatro de revista em Portugal**. Lisbon: Publicações Dom Quixote: Distribuição, Diglivro, 1984 1985. – 2 vols.: ill. (some col.). *Notes*: Includes bibliographies and indexes. v. 1. Da regeneração à República – 2. Da República até hoje. Portugal. The musical revue. History.

——. **History of theatre**. Translated by Candida Cadavez. Europalia '91 series 'Synthesis of Portuguese Culture'. Lisbon: Imprensa Nacional-Casa da Moeda, 1991. 112 p.

——. **Teatro moderno: caminhos e figuras**. [Modern theatre: trends and personalities], 2nd edn. Lisbon: Prelo, 1964.

Redondo, Junlor. **Panorama do teatro moderno**. [An overview of modern theatre]. Lisbon: Arcádia, 1961.

Ribas, Tomaz. **O Teatro da Trindade: 125 anos de vida**. Porto: Lello & Irmão Editores, 1993. – 96 p.: ill. (some col.). *Notes*: Includes bibliographical references (p. 96). Lisbon. History. Teatro da Trindade.

Saviotti, Gino. **Filosofia do teatro**. [Philosophy of the theatre]. Lisbon: In Quérito, 1945.

Sena, Jorge de and Francisco Rebello. **Do teatro em Portugal**. Lisbon: Edições 70, 1989 1988. – 447 p. *Notes*: A collections of essays and reviews published in various periodicals on the theatre during 1946–1960. Includes bibliographical references and index. History and criticism.

Sheren, Paul. **The Portuguese and Brazilian theatre: supplement**. Mottisfont Abbey, Romsey Hants., England: Motley Books, 1975. – v. Bibliography.

Soares, Fernando Luso. **Teatro, vanguarda, revolução e seguança**. [Theatre, vanguard, revolution and bourgeois security]. Lisbon: Afrodite, 1973.

Tabucchi, António. **Il teatro portoghese del dopoguerra**. [Portuguese theatre since World War II). Rome: Abete, 1976. 124 p.

A3a115. PUERTO RICO

Antush, John. **Recent Puerto Rican theatre**. Houston, TX: Arte Público, 1991.

Arriví, Francisco. **Conciencia puertorriqueña del teatro contemporáneo: 1937–56**. [Puerto Rican conscience in the contemporary theatre: 1937–56]. San Juan: Instituto de Cultura Puertorriqueña, 1967. 207 p.

——. 'Evolución del autor dramático puertoriqueño a partir de 1938'. [Evolution of the Puerto Rican playwright from 1938]. In **Areyto Mayor**. San Juan: Instituto de Cultura Puertorriqueña, 1966.

Braschi, Wilfredo. **Apuntes sobre el teatro puertorriqueño**. [Notes on Puerto Rican theatre]. San Juan: Coqui, 1970. 111 p.

Collins, J.A. **Contemporary theater in Puerto Rico: the decade of the seventies**. Río Piedras, P.R.: Editorial Universitaria, Universidad de Puerto Rico, 1982. – xxiii, 261 p.: ill. *Notes*: Includes bibliographical references. Puerto Rican drama. History and criticism.

Dávila López, Grace Yvette. **Diversidad y pluralidad en el teatro puertorriqueño contemporáneo, 1965–1985**. 1989. – xiii, 318 p. *Notes*: Abstract in Spanish and English. Vita. Includes bibliographical references (p. 303–18). Thesis (Ph. D.)–University of California, Irvine, 1989. Photocopy. Ann Arbor, Mich.: University Microfilms International, 1992. Theatre and society.

Figueroa Chapel, Ramón. **Crítica de teatro (1977–1979)**. Río Piedras: Editorial Edil, 1982. – 319 p. *Notes*: Includes index. Reviews.

García del Toro, Antonio. **Mujer y patria en la dramaturgia puertorriqueña: (proyecciones del sentimiento patrio en la figura de la mujer como protagonista de la dramaturgia puertorriquena)**. Madrid: Playor, 1987. – 267 p. *Notes*: Bibliography: p. 246–67. Women and nationalism.

González, Nilda. **Bibliografía de teatro puertorriqueño: siglos XIX y XX**. Río Piedras, P.R.: Editorial Universitaria, Universidad de Puerto Rico, 1979. – xix, 223 p. *Notes*: Includes indexes. Puerto Rican drama. Bibliography.

Historia crítica de un siglo de teatro puertorriqueño. [Critical history of a century of Puerto Rican theatre]. San Juan: Instituto de Cultura Puertorriqueño, 1980. 569 p.

Márquez, Rosa Luisa, Antonio Martorell and Miguel Villafane. **Brincos y saltos: el juego como disciplina teatral: ensayos y manual de teatreros ambulantes**. [Cayey, P.R.]: Ediciones Cuicaloca con el co-auspicio del Colegio Universitario de Cayey, 1992. – 266 p.: ill. *Notes*: Includes bibliographical references (p. 264–5). Street theatre. Puerto Rico.

Matilla Jimeno, Alfredo and Alfredo Matilla Rivas. **De teatro: artículos periodísticos de Alfredo Matilla Jimeno**. San Juan, PR: Instituto de Cultura Puertorriqueña, 1993. – 327 p. *Notes*: Includes bibliographical references and index. Reviews.

Montes Huidobro, Matías. **Persona: vida y máscara del teatro puertorriqueño** [Persona: life and image of the Puerto Rican theatre]. San Juan: Instituto de Cultura Puertorriqueña, 1986. 631 p.

Morfi, Angelina. 'El teatro en Puerto Rico'. [Theatre in Puerto Rico]. **La gran enciclopedia de Puerto Rico**. Vol. 6: **Teatro/Religión**. San Juan: Ediciones R, 1976.

Navarra, Gilda. **Polimnia: taller de histriones, 1971–1985**. [Polimnia: Players' Workshop, 1971–85]. Barcelona: 1988. 200 p.

Pasarell, Emilio J. **Orígenes y desarrollo de la pasión teatral en Puerto Rico**. [Origins and development of theatrcial passion in Puerto Rico]. 2 vols. Río Piedras: Editorial Universitaria, 1967.

Quiles Ferrer, Edgar Heriberto. **Teatro puertorriqueño en acción: (dramaturgia y escenificación): 1982–1989**. San Juan, P.R.: Ateneo Puertorriqueño, 1990. – 299 p.

Ramos Perea, Roberto. **Perspectivas de la nueva dramaturgia puertorriqueña: ensayos sobre el nuevo teatro nacional**. [Perspectives on the new Puerto Rican drama: essays on the new national theatre]. Cuadernos del Ateneo Collection, Theatre Series no. 1. San Juan: Ateneo Puertorriqueño, 1989. 93 p.

Saez, Antonia. **El teatro en Puerto Rico: notas para su historia** [Notes for the history of Puerto Rican theatre]. 2nd edn. San Juan: Editorial Universitaria, 1972. 134 p.

Sosa Ramos, Lydia Esther. **Desarrollo del teatro nacional en Puerto Rico**. Carolina, P.R.: First Book Publishing, 1994. – 251 p.: ill. *Notes*: Includes bibliographical references (p. 243–7). History.

Witte, Ann Barbara. **The image of the United States in Puerto Rican theater: a portrait of cultural conflict**. 1986. – vi, 172 p. *Notes*: Vita. Bibliography: p. 169–72. Thesis (M.A.)–University of Texas at Austin, 1986.

A3a116. QATAR

'Atwan, Hassan. **al-Hayah al-masrahiyah fi Qatar: dirasah susyulujiyah wa-tawthiq**. [Qatar?]: H. 'Atwan, 1987. – 447 p.: ill. *Notes*: In Arabic. Theatre. Qatar/Arabic drama.

Kutayyib 'An al-Masrah al-'Aalami. [A booklet on the world theatre]. Doha: Culture and Arts Administration, March 1981.

Mohammed Qaafoud, **al-Adab al-Qatari al-Hadeeth**. [Modern Qatari Literature].

Othmann al-Hamaamsi, **Taqreer al-Majlis al-A'ala l'Ri'aayat ash-Shabaab**. [The Supreme Council for Youth Welfare report], 1983.

Taqreer 'An at-Tarbiya al-Masrahiyya Fi Dawlat Qatar. [A report on theatrical education in Qatar], 1981.

See also occasional theatre articles in various issues of the following magazines: **Doha, Covenant Iraqi Writers Magazine, New Gulf Magazine** and **Education Magazine**.

A3a117. ROMANIA

Alterescu, Simion, ed. **An abridged history of Romanian theatre**. Bucharest: Academiei Republicii Socialiste România, 1983. 192 p.

——, ed. **Istoria teatrului in România**. [History of theatre in Romania]. 3 vols. Bucharest: Academiei Republicii Socialiste Romania, 1965, 1971, 1973.

—— and Ion Zamfirescu, eds. **Teatrul românesc contemporan 1944–1974**. [Contemporary Romanian theatre: 1944–1974]. Bucharest: Meridiane, 1975. 332 p.

Association of Theatre and Music Artists. **Aspects du théâtre roumain contemporain**. [Aspects of contemporary Romanian theatre]. 2 vols. Bucharest: Arta Grafica, 1967 and 1971.

Baleanu, Andrei. **Arta transfigurarii**. Bucharest: Editura Eminescu, 1983. – 211 p. *Notes*: Includes bibliographical references. Romanian drama. History and criticism.

Barbuta, Margareta. **Demnitatea teatrului**. Bucharest: Editura Eminescu, 1984. – 207 p. *Notes*: Includes bibliographical references. Romanian drama. History and criticism.

Berlogea, Ileana. **Teatrul românesc, teatrul universal**. [Romanian theatre, universal theatre]. Confluenţe, Iaşi: Junimea, 1983. 230 p.

——. **Teatrul şi societatea contemporană**. [Theatre in contemporary society]. Bucharest: Meridiane, 1985. 340 p.

Brădăţeanu, Virgil. **Istoria dramaturgiei româneşti şi a artei spectacolutuu**. [History Romanian playwriting and the performing arts]. 3 vols. Bucharest: Didactică şi Pedagogică, 1966, 1979, 1982.

Deleanu, Horia. **Elogiu regizorului**. Bucharest: Meridiane, 1985. – 299 p., 12 p. of plates: ill. *Notes*: Includes bibliographical references. History. 20th century. Theatrical producers and directors. Romania.

——. **Elogiu scenei**. Bucharest: Meridiane, 1988. – 285 p., 12 p. of plates: ill. *Notes*: Includes bibliographical references. History. 20th century.

——. **Întâlniri memorabile**. Bucharest: Editura

Hasefer, 1995. – 189 p.: ill. *Notes*: Romanian drama. 20th century. History and criticism.

Duicu, Serafim. **Dictionar de personaje dramatice**. Bucharest: Editura Iriana, 1994. – 205 p. *Notes*: Characters and characteristics in Romanian dramatic literature.

Ghitulescu, Mircea. **O panoramă a iiteraturii dramatice române contemporane: 1944–1984**. [An overview of contemporary Romanian dramatic literature: 1944–1984]. Cluj-Napoca: Dacia, 1984. 316 p.

Ionescu, Miruna. **Teatrul ca lume**. Bucharest: Editura Eminescu, 1994. – 281 p. *Notes*: History and criticism.

Iosif, Mira. **Teatrul nostru cel de toate serile: interpretari scenice 1967–1977**. Bucharest: Editura Eminescu, 1979. – 313 p. *Notes*: Reviews. History.

Măciucă, Constantin. **Motive şi structuri dramatice**. [Dramatic motifs and structures]. Bucharest: Eminescu, 1986. 278 p.

——. **Viziuni şi forme teatrale**. Bucharest: Meridiane, 1983. – 269, 3 p., 12 p. of plates: ill. *Notes*: Bibliography: p. 263–70. Romanian drama. History and criticism.

Masek, Victor Ernest. **Literatură şi existenă dramatică**. [Literature and dramatic existence]. Bucharest: Meridiane, 1983. 212 p.

Massoff, Ioan. **Teatrul românesc. Privire Istorisă**. [Romanian theatre: a historical review]. 8 vols. Bucharest: Editura Minerva, 1961–81.

Popescu, Marian. **Chei pentru labirint**. [Key for the labyrinth]. Bucharest: Cartea Românească, 1986. 252 p.

——. **Teatrul ca literatură**. [Theatre as literature]. Bucharest: Eminescu, 1987. 230 p.

Râpeanu, Valeriu. **O Antologie a dramaturgiei româneşti: 1944–1977**. [An anthology of Romanian plays: 1944–1977]. 2 vols. Bucharest: Eminescu, 1978.

Saceanu, Amza. **Clasicii nu vor sa îmbatrîneasca: J.L. Caragiale, Camil Petrescu, V.I. Popa, G.M. Zamfirescu si teatrul contemporan**. Bucharest: Meridiane, 1983. – 357, 2 p., 24 p. of plates: ill. *Notes*: Bibliography: p. 356–8. History.

——. **Teatrul ca lume**. Bucharest: Meridiane, 1985. – 356 p., 24 p. of plates: ill. *Notes*: Dramatists. Interviews.

Sava, Ion and Virgil Petrovici. **Teatralitatea teatrului**. Bucharest: Editura Eminescu, 1981. – 442 p., 64 p. of plates: ill. *Notes*: Includes bibliographical references. History. 20th century.

Savinescu, Vasile. **Privitor la aceeasi scena: cronici, interviuri, studii, comentarii, însemnari si note teatrale**. Bucharest: Editura Afirmarea, 1994. – 310 p. *Notes*: Teatrul de Nord (Satu Mare, Romania). History.

Sever, Alexandru. **Iraclide. Esseuri despre teatru si dramaturgie**. [Essays on theatre and drama]. Bucharest: Eminescu, 1988. 170 p.

Silvestru, Valentin. **Jurnal de drum al unui critic teatral: 1944–1984**. Bucharest: Editura Meridiane, 1992. – v. <1>: ill. Romanian drama. History and criticism. Biography. Silvestru, Valentin.

——. **Ora 19.30: studii critice asupra teatrului dramatic din deceniul opt al secolului douazeci**. Bucharest: Meridiane, 1983. – 495 p., 24 p. of plates: ill. *Notes*: Includes index. History. 20th century.

——. **Un deceniu teatral: studii de critica si istorie**. Bucharest: Editura Eminescu, 1984. – 282 p. *Notes*: Romanian drama. 20th century. History and criticism.

Tutungiu, Paul. **Dialoguri despre teatru**. Iasi: 'Junimea', 1980. – 180 p. *Notes*: Eighteen interviews. Romanian drama.

Zamfirescu, Ion. **Drama istorică universală şi natională**. [Universal and national historical drama]. Bucharest: Eminescu, 1976. 279 p.

A3a118. RUSSIA

Agamerzians Ruben. **Vremya. Teatr. Rezhisser**. [Time. Theatre. Directors]. Leningrad: Iskusstvo, 1987.

Akimov, Nikolai. **Teatralroye naslediye**. [Theatre legacy]. 2 vols. Moscow/Leningrad: Iskusstvo, 1976.

Alianskii, IUrii Lazarevich. **Teatr v kvadrate obstrela**. Leningrad: Iskusstvo, 1985. – 189 p., 32 p. of plates: ill. *Notes*: Russia (Federation). Saint Petersburg. History. World War, 1939–45. Theatre and the war.

Al'tshuller, A.IA, T.D. Ismagulova and N.V. Kudriasheva. **Voprosy teatrovedeniia: sbornik nauchnykh trudov**. St. Peterburg: Vserossiiskii nauchno-issl. in-t iskusstvoznaniia, 1991. – 212 p. *Notes*: Includes bibliographical references. Russia (Federation). History. 20th century.

Anastasiov, Arkady, Grigori Boyadzhiov, Anna Obraztsova and Konstantin Rudnitski. **Novatorstvo sovetskogo teatra**. [Novatorship in Soviet theatre]. Moscow: Iskusstvo, 1963.

Babayan, Mariam, E. I. Zernitskaia and L.R. Levina. **Armianskii dramaticheskii teatr: annotirovannyi ukazatel' bibliograficheskikh i spravochnykh materialov, 1920–1980**.

Moscow: Gos. biblioteka Armianskoi SSR im. V.F. Miasnikia, 1983. – 140 p. *Notes*: Russian drama. History and criticism. Bibliography.

Bartoshevich, Aleksei Vadimovich, T.V. Butrova and Tatiana Konstantinovna Shakh-Azizova. **Dialog kultur: problema vzaimodeistviia russkogo i mirovogo teatra XX veka: sbornik statei**. St. Petersburg: Dmitrii Bulanin, 1997. – 263 p. *Notes*: Includes bibliographical references. Russia (Federation). History. 20th century.

—— and Boris Isaakovich Zingerman. **Zapadnoe iskusstvo: XX vek: klassicheskoe nasledie i sovremennost'**. Moscow: 'Nauka', 1992. – 266 p. *Notes*: Includes bibliographical references. 20th century. History.

Benedetti, Jean. **The Moscow Art Theatre letters**. London: Methuen Drama, 1991. – xv, 377 p. *Notes*: Includes index. Correspondence.

Boiadzhiev, Grigorii. **Poeziia teatra**. Moscow: Iskusstvo, 1960. – 460 p. illus. *Notes*: Poetic drama. History.

Bol'shakova, Y.B. and Y.A. Pokrovskaia. **Zhizn' stseny i kontraktnyi mir: sbornik**. Moscow: GITIS, 1994. – 197 p. *Notes*: Includes bibliographical references. History and criticism.

Bushueva, Svetlana. **Russkoe akterskoe iskusstvo XX veka**. [Russian acting art in the twentieth century]. St. Petersburg: Rossiiskii in-t istorii iskusstv, 1992. *Notes*: Summaries in English; table of contents also in English. Includes bibliographical references.

——. **Vzaimosviazi: teatr v kontekste kul'tury: sbornik nauchnykh trudov**. Leningrad: VNII isskustvoznaniia, 1991. – 153 p. *Notes*: Includes bibliographical references. History. 20th century. Performing arts.

Chagall, Marc. **Marc Chagall and the Jewish theater**. New York: Guggenheim Museum, 1992. – xv, 207 p.: ill. (some col.). *Notes*: Exhibition held at Solomon R. Guggenheim Museum, September 23, 1992–January 17, 1993 and the Art Institute of Chicago, January 30–May 7, 1993. Includes bibliographical references (p. 200–4). Jewish theatre. Russia (Federation). History.

Dal, Oleg. **Vospominaniya. Materialy iz arkbiva**. [Memories. Materials from an archive]. Moscow: Arts Publishing Culture Editorial Complex, 1992.

Davidov, Mike. **People's Theatre from box office to the stage**. Moscow: Progress, 1977.

Edwards, Christine. **Stanislavsky heritage: its contribution to the Russian and American theatre**. New York: New York University Press, 1965. 346 p.

Efros, Anatoly. **Prodolzbeniye teatralnogo romana**. [Continuation of the theatre romance]. Moscow: Iskusstvo, 1985.

Gaevski, Vadim. **Divertisment**. [Divertissement]. Moscow: Iskusstvo, 1981.

Golub, Spencer. **The recurrence of fate: theatre and memory in twentieth-century Russia**. Iowa City: University of Iowa Press, 1994. – xiii, 277 p.: ill. *Notes*: Includes bibliographical references (p. 201–62) and index. Russian drama. 20th century. History and criticism.

Gorchakov, Nikolai Mikhailovich and William-Alan Landes. **The art of stage: for the director and actor**. Studio City, Calif.: Players Press, 1995. Biography. Vakhtangov, Evgenii, 1883–1922.

Green, Michael. **The Russian Symbolist Theatre: an anthology of plays and critical texts**. Ann Arbor, MI: Ardis, 1986.

Houghton, Norris. **Moscow rehearsals: an account of methods of production in the Soviet theatre**. New York: Octagon Books, 1975.

Iofiov, Moisei. **Profili iskusstva**. [Arts' profiles]. Moscow: Iskusstvo, 1963.

Iskusstvo teatra. Sverdlovsk: Izd-vo Ural'skogo universiteta, 1987. – v. *Notes*: Theatre audiences. Russia (Federation). Ural Mountains Region.

Istoriya russkogo sovetskogo dramaticheskogo teatra. [History of Russian Soviet dramatic theatre]. 2 vols. Moscow: Prosvestcheniye, 1984–7.

Istoriya sovetskogo aramattchestogo teatra. [History of Soviet dramatic theatre]. 6 vols. Moscow: Nauka, 1966–71.

Ivanov, Oleg Konstantinovich and Kim Krivitskii. **Vakhtangov i vakhtangovtsy**. [Vakhtangov and vakhtangovism]. Moscow: Moskovskii rabochii, 1984. – 155 p., 32 p. of plates: ill. *Notes*: Biography.

Kaidalova, N. and T. Gorshunova. **Teatr na IUgo-Zapade: spektakli, aktory, roli** [Theatre of the South-West: plays, actors, roles]. Moscow: Teatr, 1992. – 1 v. (unpaged): ill. (some col.). *Notes*: Russia (Federation). Teatr na IUgo-Zapade (Moscow). History.

Kalish, Victor. **Teatralnaya vertikal**. [Theatre vertical]. Moscow: Union of Theatre Workers of Russian Federative Socialist Republic, 1991.

Kholodov, Yefim. **Piesy i gody**. [Plays and years]. Moscow: Sovetsky pisatel, 1967.

Knebel, Maria. **Poeziya pedagogiki**. [Poetry of pedagogics]. Moscow: All-Union Theatre Society, 1984.

Komissarzhevski, Viktor. **Moscow theatres**. Translated by Vic Schneierson and W. Perelman. Moscow: Foreign Languages Publishing House, 1959.

Kotovskaia, Melitina and S.A. Isaeva. **Mir iskusstv**. Moscow: GITIS. 1991. – 493 p. *Notes*: Includes bibliographical references. History. 20th century.

Krymova, Natalia. **Imena**. Moscow: Iskusstvo, 1971.

——. **Stanislavskii–rezhisser**. Moscow: Iskusstvo, 1984. – 144 p. *Notes*: Includes bibliographical references. Stanislavsky, Konstantin, 1863–1938.

Lemâitre, Maurice. **Le Théâtre futuriste italien et russe**. [Italian and Russian futurist theatre]. Paris: Centre de Créativité, 1967.

Liubimov, Nikolai. **Byloe leto: iz vospominanii zritelia**. Moscow: Iskusstvo, 1982. – 204 p., 48 p. *Notes*: Includes bibliographical references. Moscow. History. 20th century.

Macleod, Joseph Todd Gordon. **The New Soviet Theatre**. London: George Allen & Unwin, 1943.

Mnemozina: dokumenty i fakty iz istorii russkogo teatra XX veka. Moscow: GITIS, 1996. – 286 p. *Notes*: Includes bibliographical references. Russia (Federation). History. Sources.

Moscow Art Theatre: past, present, future. Louisville: Ky.; Actors Theatre of Louisville, 1989. – 100 p.: ill. *Notes*: 'A monograph from the 1989 Classics in Context Festival, Louisville, Kentucky USA'. Backdrop for Art: a chronology of events during the lives of Stanislavsky, Chekhov and Gorky/Sonja Kuftinec – Chekhov, Gorky, and the identity of the Moscow Art Theatre/Laurence Senelick – Anton, himself/Karen Sunde – Remembering the future/Anatoly Smelyansky – Visionary sons of Stanislavsky/Paul Schmidt – The theatrical Faith of Oleg Yefremov/Mikhail Shvydkoi – Contemporary playwrights of the Moscow Art Theatre/Mikhail Shvydkoi – Cinzano (Italian vermouth without intermission)/Liudmila Petrushevskaya – The First 90 years: a production chronology of the Moscow Art Theatre 1898–1988/Felicia Hardison Londré – The Actors Theatre of Louisville 1989 Classics in Context Festival: a record.

Nemirovich-Danchenko, Vladimir Ivanovich. **My life in the Russian theatre**. With an introduction by Joshua Logan and a chronology by Elizabeth Reynolds Hapgood. London: Bles, 1968. – xxv, 365 p. 12 plates, illus. *Notes*: Translation of **Iz proshlogo**. Autobiography of Nemirovich-Danchenko, Vladimir Ivanovich, 1858–1943.

Obraztsova, Anna Georgievna. **Dramaturgicheskii metod Bernard Shaw**. Moscow: Nauka, 1965. – 313 p. Includes index. Bibliography: p. 305–8. Russia's leading Shaw expert analyses the dramatist from a socialist viewpoint.

——. **Sovremennaia angliiskaia stsena: (na rubezhe 70-kh godov)**. Moscow: Izd. Nauka, 1977. – 245 p.: ill., ports. Great Britain/English drama. 20th century. History and criticism.

——, Boris Aleksandrovich Smirnov, E. Khaichenko and Melitina Petrovna Kotovskaia. **Teatral'noe iskusstvo Vostoka: osobennosti razvitiia: sbornik nauchnykh trudov**. Moscow: Gos. in-t teatral'nogo iskusstva im. A.V. Lunacharskogo, 1984. – 128 p. Includes bibliographical references. Asia. History and criticism.

Okhlopkov, Nikolai Pavlovich, E.I. Zotova, Tatiana Lukina and S.K. Nikulin. **N.P. Okhlopkov: stat'i, vospominaniia**. Moscow: VTO, 1986. – 367 p., 112 p. of plates: ill. *Notes*: Bibliography: p. 359–66. Biography of director Okhlopkov, Nikolai Pavlovich.

Otcherki istorii russkoi sovetskoi dramaturgii. [Essays on the history of Russian Soviet dramaturgy]. 3 vols. Leningrad/Moscow: Iskusstvo, 1963–8.

Pyžova, O.V. **Fragmenty teatral'noj sud'by**. [Fragments of a theatrical destiny]. Moscow: Soviet Russia, 1986. 336 p.

Raphael, Jay Elliot. **An annotated and critical bibliography of the works written in English since 1900 on the pre- and post-revolutionary Russian theatre**. 1980 1971. – iii, 246 leaves. *Notes*: Includes indexes. Thesis–Michigan State University. Photocopy. Ann Arbor, Mich.: University Microfilms International, 1980.

Rudnitski, Konstantin. **Spektakli raznykh let**. [Shows of different years]. Moscow: Iskusstvo, 1974.

——. **Teatralnye siuzbety**. [Theatre plots]. Moscow, 1990.

Rühle, Jürgen. **Das gefesselte Theater: von Revolutionstheater zum sozialistischen Realismus**. [The enchained theatre: from theatre of the revolution to socialist-realism]. Cologne: Kiepenheuer & Witsch, 1957.

Russell, Robert. **Russian drama of the revolutionary period**. Basingstoke: Macmillan, 1988.

—— and Andrew Barrat, eds. **Russian theatre in**

the age of modernism. Basingstoke: Macmillan, 1990.

Shcherbakov, Konstantin. **S zhelan'em istiny: ob odnom pokolenii v iskusstve**. Moscow: Sov. pisatel', 1988. – 398 p. *Subjects*: Russian history and criticism.

Shvidkoi, Mikhail. **Sekrety odinokikh komediantov: zametki o zarubezhnom teatre vtoroi poloviny XX veka**. Moscow: Tekst, 1992. – 384 p.: ill. *Notes*: Russian theatre.

Simonov, Ruben. **Stanislavski's Protégé: Eugene Vakhtangov**. Adapted and translated by Miriam Goldina. New York: Drama Book Specialists, 1969. 243 p.

——. **Tvorcheskoye naslediye**. [Creative legacy]. Moscow: All-Union Theatre Society, 1981.

Slonim, Mark L'ovich. **Russian theatre from the Empire to the Soviets**. Cleveland, OH: World, 1961.

Smeliansky, Anatoly. **Cambridge studies in modern theatre: the Russian theatre after Stalin**. Great Britain: Cambridge University Press, 1999. 265 p.: ill. *Notes*: Contains a chronology and glossary of names.

——. **Oleg Yefremov**. Moscow: Novosti, 1988. 106 p.: ill. *Notes*: 'Translated from the Russian by Mikhail Nikolsky'. Biography/Efremov, Oleg. Director of the Moscow Art Theatre.

Smirnova, Natalia Ilinichna. **Teatr Sergeia Obraztsova**. [Sergei Obraztsov's theatre]. Moscow: Izdatelstvo-Navka, 1971.

Smith, Alan. **The dramatic works of Aleksej Arbuzov**. 1981. – 386 p. *Notes*: Vita. Bibliography: p. 373–86. Thesis (Ph. D.)–Indiana University, 1981. Russian drama. 20th century. Arbuzov, Aleksei. Criticism and interpretation.

Soloveva, O. **Podvig aktera. [Sbornik]**. Moscow, 1970. – 234 p.: ill. *Notes*: World War, 1939–1945. Correspondence, reminiscences, etc.

Sovetskii teatr. [Soviet theatre]. Moscow: Iskusstvo, 1967.

Stenberg, Douglas. **From Stanislavsky to Gorbachev: the theatre-studios of Leningrad**. New York: P. Lang, 1995. – 248 p.: ill. *Notes*: Includes bibliographical references (p. 245–6). Interviews.

Svobodin, Alexander. **Teatralnaya Plostchad**. [Theatre square]. Moscow: Iskusstvo, 1981.

Tovstonogov, Giorgi. **Zerkalo stzeny**. [Mirror of the stage]. 2 vols. Leningrad: Iskusstvo, 1980.

Vilenkin, Vitalii. **Vospominaniia s kommentari-iami**. Moscow: Iskusstvo, 1991. – 495 p.: ill. *Notes*: Includes bibliographical references. Soviet Union/Authors. 20th century.

Worrall, Nick. **The Moscow Art Theatre**. London; New York: Routledge, 1996. – xi, 243 p. *Notes*: Includes bibliographical references (p. 226–31) and index. History.

Zakharov, M. **Kontakty na raznykh urovniakh**. Moscow: Iskusstvo, 1988. – 267 p., 32 p. of plates: ill. *Notes*: Biography/Theatrical producers and directors. Zakharov, M. In Russian.

Zingerman, Boris Isaakovich. **Obraz cheloveka i individual'nost' khudozhnika v zapadnom iskusstve XX veka**. Moscow: Izd-vo Nauka, 1984. – 214 p.: ill. *Notes*: Includes bibliographical references. Artists. Psychology/Individuality.

——. **Sovremennoe zapadnoe iskusstvo: XX vek: problemy kompleksnogo izucheniia**. Moscow: Nauka, 1988. – 277 p. Includes bibliographical references. 20th century/Western art.

—— and Aleksandr Abramovich Anikst. **Teatr Chekhova i ego mirovoe znachenie**. Literaturno-khudozh. izd. Moscow: Nauka, 1988. – 382 p. *Notes*: Includes bibliographical references. Chekhov, Anton Pavlovich, 1860–1904. Dramatic works.

Zolotnitskii, David. **V sporakh o teatre: sbornik nauchnykh trudov**. St. Petersburg: Rossiiskii in-t istorii iskusstv, 1992. – 153 p. *Notes* : Includes bibliographical references and index. Shakespeare, William, 1564–1616. Stage history. Russia (Federation).

A3a119. RWANDA

Houdeau, Serge. **Panorama de la littérature rwandaise: bilan, bibliographie, choix de textes en français**. [An overview of Rwandan literature: assessment, bibliography and selected French texts]. Butare: 1979. 209 p.

Jadot, J.M. **Les écrivains du Congo belge et du Ruanda-Urundi: Une histoire, un bilan, des problèmes**. [Writers of the Belgian Congo and Ruanda-Urundi: a history, an assessment and some issues]. Brussels: ARSC, 1959. 167 p.

Kabasha, Théobald. **Aspects historiques, dramaturgiques et thématiques du théâtre rwandais**. [Historical, dramaturgical and thematic aspects of Rwandan theatre]. Butare: Université Nationale du Rwanda. Master's Thesis. 1981. 156 p.

Munyarugerero, François-Xavier. **La Littérature rwandaise: bilan, problèmes et perspectives**. [Rwandan literature: assessment, issues and perspectives]. Ruhengeri: Université Nationale du Rwanda. Master's Thesis. 1982. 244 p.

Rugamba, Cyprien, Damien Rwegera and Médard Mwumvaneza. **Théâtre et enseignement**. [Theatre and education]. Kigali.

A3a120. SAN MARINO

Casali, Augusto. **Filodrammatica– che passione: il Piccolo teatro Arnaldo Martelli**. Repubblica di San Marino: AIEP, 1992. – 310 p.: ill. Piccolo teatro Arnaldo Martelli. History.

A3a121. SAUDI ARABIA

Abd Allah, Malhah. **Athar al-badawah 'ala almasrah fi al-Saudiya**. [The impact of Bedouin lifestyle on Saudi theatre]. Cairo: Matba'at Nasr al-Islam, 1994. 185 p.

El-Azma, Nazeer. **The Saudi theatre: a critical study**. Riyadh: Literary Club, 1992.

Eberhard, Frank. 'Bühnewagen für das KFCC in Riyadh'. [Revolving platform for the KFCC in Riyadh]. **Bühnentechnische Rundschau** 84 no. 4 (1990): 44–5.

Al-Khatib, Nasir. 'Madkhal Ila Dirasat Al-Masrah'. [An introduction to the study of theatre in Saudi Arabia]. Diploma thesis, Higher Institute of Theatrical Arts, Cairo, 1984. 148 p.

Al-Malibari, Muhammad Abdu'llah. **The first theatre in Saudi Arabia** [in Arabic]. Mecca: Majallat Quraysh, 1960.

Al-Molla, Jasim. **Annual report on student theatrical activity at King Saud University**. Riyadh: King Saud University. Reports began 1983.

A3a122. SÉNÉGAL

Diahkaté, Lamine. Préface à **Nder en flamme**. [Preface to **Nder in Flames**] by Alioune Badara Beye. Dakar: Nouvelles Editions Africaines, 1990.

——. 'Le Théâtre sénégalais, saison 1992–1993, 1993–1994'. [Senegalese theatre for the 1992–1993 and 1993–1994 Seasons]. In **Le Monde du Théâtre**. [The World of Theatre]. Tunis: I.T.I., 1995.

Diop, Alioune Oumy. **Le Théâtre traditionnel au Sénégal**. [Traditional theatre in Senegal]. Dakar: N.E.A., 1990.

Fall, Marouba. 'Le Théâtre sénégalais face aux exigences du public'. [Senegalese theatre and the demands of the public]. **Ethiopiques** II, no. 2–3 (1984).

Harris, Jessica. 'Toward a New Senegalese Theatre'. **The Drama Review: African Performance Issue** 25, no. 4 (winter 1981): 13–18.

Hermantier, Raymond. 'Art dramatique et animation culturelle au Sénégal'. [Dramatic Art and Cultural Animation in Senegal]. In **Notes,**

Actes du Colloque sur le théâtre négro-africain. [Notes, Colloquium on Black African theatre]. Paris: Présence Africaine, 1970.

Kum'a Ndumbe, Alexandre III. 'Le Théâtre senegalaise'. [The Senegalese theatre]. **Cameroun Littéraire** 2 (1983): 44–52.

Lemoine, Lucien. **Douta Seck ou la tragédie du roi Christophe**. [Douta Seck or The Tragedy of King Christophe]. Paris: Présence Africaine, 1993.

Répertoire culturel: le Sénégal, Inventaire des activités, ressources et infrastructures culturelles des pays membres de l'Agence de Coopération culturelle et technique (l'ACCT). [Cultural repertory: Senegal, Inventory of the Activities, Resources and Cultural Infrastructures of the Member Countries of the Agency for Cultural and Technical Cooperation, France]. Paris: Gamma Pair, 1982.

Senghor, Léopold Sédar. 'Le Groupe *Yewu* de Ousmane Cissé et les Frères du théâtre de Samb: meilleures troupes pour 1969'. [Ousmane Cissé's *Yewu* Group and Samb's Brothers of the Theatre: Best Troupes of 1969]. **Mali Magazine** no. 2 (August 1969).

——. 'Poésie et théâtre'. [Poetry and Theatre]. **Ethiopiques** (nouvelle série) 2, no. 2–3 (1984).

——, and Hossman. 'Situation du théâtre Sénégalais'. [The situation of Senegalese theatre]. **Afrique** (1965).

Traoré, Bakary. **L'Exil d' Albouri et La Décision**. [Preface to The Exile of Albouri and The Decision] by Cheik Aliou Ndao. Paris: Honfleur, 1967.

A3a123. SERBIA/MONTENEGRO

Cvetković, Sava V., ed. **Repertoar narodnog pozorita u beogradu 1868–1965**. [Repertoire of the National Theatre in Belgrade 1868–1965]. Belgrade, 172 p.

Drašković, Boro. **Paradoks o reditelju**. [The paradox of the director]. Novi Sad: Sterijino pozorje, 1988. 247 p.

Finci, Eli. **Posle predstave: savremena domaca drama na sceni (1948–1975)**. Novi Sad: Sterijino pozorje, 1978. – 284 p. *Notes*: In Serbo-Croatian (Roman). Includes bibliographical references and indexes. Serbian drama. History and criticism.

——. **Više i manje od života I-V**. [More and less than life I-V]. Belgrade: Prosveta, 1955–77.

Het, Ognjanka. **Medu kulisama**. Nis: Prosveta: Narodno Pozoriste, 1992. – 166 p.: ill. *Notes*: Actors. Belgrade. Biography.

Hristić, Jovan. **Pozorište, pozorište I-n.** [Theatre, theatre I-II]. 2 vols. Belgrade: Prosveta, 1977–82. 332 and 340 p.

——. **Pozorišni referati. Pozorište, pozorište III.** [Theatre essays. Theatre, theatre III]. Belgrade: Nolit, 1992. 332 p.

Lešić, Josip. **Istorija jugoslovenske moderne režije.** [The history of modern Yugoslav directing]. Novi Sad: Sterijino pozorje & IRO Dnevnik, 1986. 470 p.

Marjanovic, Petar. **Ocima dramaturga: ogledi i clanci iz istorije srpske drame i pozorista.** Novi Sad: Srpska citaonica i knjiznica Irig, 1979. – 215 p. *Notes*: In Serbo-Croatian (Roman). Includes bibliographical references and index. Serbian drama. History and criticism.

Miočinović, Mirjana. **Eseji o drami.** [Essays on drama]. Belgrade: Vuk Karadžić, 1975.

Misailović, Milenko. **Dramaturgija scenskog prostora.** [The dramaturgy of stage space]. Novi Sad: Sterijino pozorje & IRO Dnevnik, 1988. 457 p.

Perović, Sreten. **Darovi scene. Studije i kritike I. Pozorišne kritike II.** [Gifts of the stage: studies and criticism I, drama reviews II]. 2 vols. Titograd: Leksikografski zavod Crne Gore, 1986. 467 and 367 p.

—— and Radoslav Rotkovic. **Savremena drama i pozoriste u Crnoj Gori.** Novi Sad: Sterijino pozorje, 1987. – 311 p. *Notes*: In Serbo-Croatian (Roman). Includes indexes. Montenegro. History. Reviews.

Selenić, Slobodan, ed. **Antologija savremene srpske drame.** [An anthology of contemporary Serbian drama]. Belgrade: Srpska književna zadruga, 1977. 722 p.

Stamenković, Vladimir. **Kraljevstvo eksperimenta. Dvadeset godina BITEF-a.** [The kingdom of experiment. Twenty years of BITEF]. Belgrade: Nova knjiga, 1987. 272 p.

Stojković, Borivoje S. **Istorija srpskog pozorišta od Srednjeg veka do modernog doba. Drama i opera.** [The history of the Serbian theatre from the Middle Ages to modern times. Drama and opera]. Belgrade: Muzej pozorišne umetnosti SR Srbije, 1979. 1,031 p.

Volk, Petar. **Beogradske scene: pozorisni zivot Belgrada 1944–1974.** Beograd: Muzej pozorisne umetnosti SR Srbije, 1978. – 780 p. *Notes*: In Serbo-Croatian (Roman). Includes index. Belgrade (Serbia). History.

——. **Pozorišni život u Srbiji 1944–1986.** [Theatre life in Serbia 1944–86]. Belgrade: Fakultet dramskih umetnosti, 1990. 1,416 p.

A3a124. SEYCHELLES

Gordon, A.N. **Mauritius: records of private and public life.** Edinburgh: R. and R. Clark, 1894. 231 p.

Kochelin, Bernard. **Les Seychelles et l'océan indien.** [Seychelles and the Indian Ocean]. Paris: L'Harmattan, 1985.

Lionnet, Guy. **Regard sur la culture seychelloise.** [A look at Seychelles culture]. Lagazet: Ministry of Information, Culture and Sports. 8 p.

Paccioni, Fabio. **Animation théâtrale.** [Theatrical animation]. Paris: UNESCO, 1983. 13 p.

Skerrett, A. and D. Skerrett. **Spectrum guide to Seychelles.** Nairobi: Camerapix, 1991. 65 p.

A3a125. SIERRA LEONE

Akar, John. 'The arts in Sierra Leone'. **African forum** 1, no. 2 (fall 1965): 87–91.

Dele Charley, Raymond. 'A theatre for my country'. MA thesis, London Drama Board, 1981.

Graham-White, Anthony. 'African drama: a renaissance?'. **Ba Shiru** 5, no. 1 (1973): 78–83.

Palmer, Eustace. 'The development of Sierra Leone writing'. In **A celebration of black and African writing**, eds. Bruce King and K. Ogungbesan, 245–57. Oxford: Oxford University Press, 1975.

——. 'The plays of Sarif Easmon'. **Journal of the New African Literature and the Arts** 8 (1973): 242–64.

Porter, Abioseh Michael. 'Krio literature: the most popular literature in Sierra Leone'. In **Signs and Signals: popular culture in Africa.** Ed. Raol Granquist. Stockholm: Umea University Press, 1990.

Rowe, Sylvester E. 'Sierra Leone's newly born theatre'. **African Arts** 9, no. 1 (October 1975): 56–9.

Spencer, Julius. 'A historical background to the contemporary theatre in Sierra Leone'. **International Journal of Sierra Leone Studies**, no. 1 (1988): 26–35.

Warritay, Batilloi I. 'Cultural misdirection and the Sierra Leone theatre'. **Afriscope** 5, no. 8 (1975): 50–3.

A3a126. SINGAPORE

Birch, David. 'The life and times of Singapore English drama: loosening the chains, 1958–63'. **Performing Arts** 3 no. 1 (1986): 28–32.

——. 'The 1981 Singapore Drama Festival'. **Commentary** 5, nos. 3–4 (August–September 1982): 100–3.

Hung, Yu-ho. **Tsou tsai hsi chü kuo tao shang.** Singapore: Chün feng ch'i yeh, 1994. – 229 p. *Notes*: On the development of various aspects of drama in Singapore.

Le Blond, M. 'Drama in Singapore: towards an English language theatre'. In **Discharging the canon: cross-cultural readings in literature**, ed. Peter Hyland, 112–25. Singapore: Singapore University Press, 1986.

Lim Chor Pee. 'Is drama non-existent in Singapore?'. **Tumasek** 1 (January 1964): 42–4.

Seet Khiam Keong. 'Waiting in the wings: a critical look at Singapore's playscripts from the 1960s to 1980, Part 1'. **Commentary** 5, nos. 3–4 (August–September 1982): 47–55.

Traditional drama. Singapore: National Library, 1988. – 25 p. *Notes*: 'Compiled in conjunction with the Singapore Heritage Week, 8–15 Sept. 1988.'

Yeo, Robert. 'Towards an English language Singaporean theatre'. **Southeast Asian review of English** 4 (July 1982): 59–73.

A3a127. SLOVAKIA

Bagar, Andrej. **O veciach divadla.** Bratislava: Tatran, 1980. – 278 p. *Notes*: Includes bibliographical references and index. History. 20th century.

Boor, Ján. **Dialektika dejín divadla.** [Dialectic of the history of theatre]. Bratislava: Tatran, 1977. 196 p.

Cahojová, Bozena. **Katalóg slovenských hier, 1971–1983.** Bratislava: LITA, 1984. – 108 p. *Notes*: Includes index. Slovak drama. 20th century. Bibliography.

Ćávojský, Ladislav and Vladimír Śtefko. **Slovenske ochotnxcke divadlo 1839–1980.** [Slovak amateur theatre 1839–1980]. Bratislava: Obzor, 1983. 508 p.

Encyklopédia dramatických umení Slovenska. [Slovak encyclopedia of dramatic art]. Bratislava: Veda, 1989. 700 p.

Jaborník, Ján. **Slovenské divadlá v sezóne 1983–1984.** Bratislava: Tatran, 1985. – 246 p., 96 p. of plates: ill. *Notes*: Includes index. History. 20th century.

Karvǎs, Peter. **Priestory v divadle a divadlo v priestore.** [Space in theatre and theatre in space]. Bratislava: Tatran, 1984. 587 p.

——. **K problematike estetickej kategórie komiücna.** [Towards the problematic of the aesthetic category of the comic]. Bratislava: Výskumný ústav kultúry, 1980. 166 p.

——. **Reštrutturacia umeleck Úých potrieb a premeny dramatických umení.** [The restructuring of artistic needs and changes in dramatic art]. Bratislava: Výskumný ústav kultúry, 1982. 170 p.

——. **Úvod do základných problémov divadla.** [Introduction to the basic problems of theatre]. Bratislava: Ústredie slovenských ochotníckych divadiel, 1948. 236 p.

——. **Zamyšlení nad dramatem.** [Reflections on the drama]. Prague: Ćs. spisovatel, 1964. 136 p.

——. **Zamyšlení nad dramaturgií.** [Reflections on dramaturgy]. Prague: Ćs. spisovatel, 1969. 138 p.

Kret, Anton, Jaroslav Blaho, Dagmar Hubová and Ladislav Lajcha. **Slovenské národné divadlo.** [The Slovak National Theatre]. Bratislava: Tatran, 1990. 158 p.

Mittelmann-Dedinský, Móric and Ladislav Lajcha. **Pohlady z parteru.** Bratislava: Tatran, 1986. – 305 p. *Notes*: Includes indexes. History. 20th century.

Pamätnica Slovenského národného divadla, Slovenské vydavateľstvo Krásnej literatúry. [The scrapbook of the Slovak National Theatre]. Bratislava: Vydavateùstvo Krasnej literatury, 1960. 522 p.

Pašteka, Július. **Estetické paralely umenia.** [The aesthetic parallels of art]. Bratislava: Veda, 1976. 432 p.

Rampák, Zoltán. **Dráma, divadlo, spoločnost.** [Drama, theatre, society]. Bratislava: Tatran, 1976. 438 p.

——. **Cesta drámy.** [The path of drama]. Bratislava: Tatran, 1984. 344 p.

Siskocá, Hela. **Martinské divadlo v tlaci, 1983–1993: bibliografia: výber clánkov zo slovenskej tlace.** Martin: Okresná kniznica, 1994. *Notes*: Includes index. Reviews. Bibliograpy. Theatre. Slovakia.

A3a128. SLOVENIA

Berger, Ales. **Ogledi in pogledi.** Ljubljana: Mestno gledalisce ljubljansko, 1984. – 312 p. *Notes*: Includes bibliographical references and index. History. 20th century.

Erjavec, Aleš, and Marina Gržinić, eds. **Ljubljana, Ljubljana.** Ljubljana: Mladinska knjiga, 1991. 156 p.

Filipic, Lojze. **Ziva dramaturgija 1952–1975.** *Notes*: Ljubljani: Cankarjeva Zalozba, 1977. –

564 p. *Notes*: Ljubljana/Theatre. History. 20th century.

Hečimović, Branko. **Izabrane slovenske drame**. [Selected Slove plays]. Zagreb: Znanje, 1982. 345 p.

Inkret, Andrej. **Drama in gledališče**. [Drama and theatre]. Ljubljana: Državna založba Slovenije, 1986. 133 pp.

——. **Milo za drago**. [Measure for measure]. Ljubliana: Knjižnnica Mesmega gledališča Ijubljanskega, 1978. 527 p.

Jovanovic, Dusan. **Paberki**. Ljubljana: Mestno gledalisce ljubljansko, 1996. – 220 p. Slovenian drama. History and criticism.

Kalan, Filip. **Essais sur le théâtre**. [Essays on theatre]. Ljubliana: Edition de l'Academie d'art dramatique, 1961. 252 pp.

——. **Hvalnica igri**. Ljubljana: Cankarjeva zalozba, 1980. – 304 p., 48 p. of plates: ill. *Notes*: Includes bibliographical references and index. History. 20th century.

——. **Odmevi z ekrana**. [Echoes from the screen]. Maribor: Obzorja, 1969. 181 p.

Kralj, Vladimir. **Dramaturški vademekum**. [Theory of drama, a vade-mecum]. Ljubliana: Mladinska knjiga, 1984. 197 p.

——. **Pogledi na dramo**. [Aspects of drama]. Ljubljana: Cankarjeva založba, 1963. 412 p.

Mahnic, Mirko. **Slovo**. Ljubljana: Slovenska matica, 1986. – 250 p. *Notes*: History and criticism.

Moravec, Dušan. **Temelji slovenske teatrologije**. [Elements of Slovene theatre studies]. Ljubljana: Cankarjeva založba, 1990. 237 p.

Petan, Zarko and Tone Partljic. **Oder 57: pricevanja**. Ljubljana: Mestno gledalisce ljubljansko, 1988. – 238 p., 8 p. of plates: ill. *Notes*: History. 20th century.

Pibernik, France. **Razmerja v sodobni slovenski dramatiki: pogovori, dopisovanja razmisljanja**. Ljubljana: Mestno gledalisce ljubljansko, 1992. – 323 p. *Notes*: Drama. Slovenia. 20th century.

Predan, Vasja. **Kritikovo gledalisce**. Ljubljana: Slovenska matica, 1990. – 278 p. *Notes*: Includes index. Slovenian drama. History and criticism.

——. **Po premieri**. Ljubljana: Drzavna zalozba Slovenije, 1981. – 479 p. *Notes*: Includes bibliographical references and indexes. History and criticism.

——. **Savremena drama i pozoriste u Sloveniji**. Novi Sad: Sterijino pozorje, 1986. – 491 p.

Notes: In Serbo-Croatian (Roman). Translated from the Slovenian. Includes bibliographical references. Slovenian drama. History and criticism.

——. **Sled odrskih senc: gledaliski dnevnik**. Ljubljana: Mihelac, 1995. – 375 p. *Notes*: Includes index. Predan, Vasja. Diaries.

——. **Theatralia**. Ljubljana: Mestno gledalisce ljubljansko, 1991. – 211 p. Biography.

Repertoar slovenskih gledališč 1867. [Repertoire of Slovene theatres since 1867]. 6 vols. Ljubljana: Slovenski gledališki muzej, 1967–93.

Tomše, Dušan, ed. **Živo gledališče. Pogledi na slovensko gledališče v letih 1945–70**. [Live theatre. Aspects of Slovene theatre 1945–70]. 3 vols. Ljubljana: Knjiznica Mesmega gledališča Ijubljanskega, 1975.

—— and Vasja Predan. **Mali gledaliski imenik**. Ljubljana. 1969. – 186, [2] p. *Notes*: Bibliography: p. 187. Dramatic plots and biographies. In Slovenian.

Vidmar, Josip. **Gledališke kritike**. [Theatre reviews]. Ljubljana: Cankarjeva založba, 1968. 361 p.

Zinaić, Milan and NK, eds. **Neue Slowenische Kunst**. [New Slovenian art]. Los Angeles: AMOK Books, 1991. 283 p.

A3a129. SOMALIA

Luterkort, Ingrid. 'Finding a theatre for Somalia'. **Theatre International** 9 (1983): 17–23.

Moumin, Hassan Sheikh. **Leopard among the women: Shabeelnaagood – a Somali play**. Translated by B.W. Andrzejewski. London: Oxford University Press, 1974. 230 p.

Sheik-Abdi, Abdi. **Tales of Punt: Somali folktales**. Macomb, IL: Dr Leisure, 1993. 135 p.

Younis, Mohammed Abdulmuniem. **The Somalia nation and people**. Cairo: Dar Al-Nahdha al-Masriyah [Egyptian Nahdha Centre], 1962.

Al-Zahaer Hamdi. **The story of Somalia**. Dar al-Shaab Bil-Qahirah [The People's Centre in Cairo], 1977.

A3a130. SOUTH AFRICA

Astbury, Brian. **The space**. Cape Town: Moira and Azriel Fine, 1979.

Barrow, Brian and Yvonne Williams-Short, eds. **Theatre alive! The Baxter story 1977–1987**. Cape Town: The Baxter Theatre, 1988.

Blecher, Hilary. 'Goal oriented theatre in the Winterveld'. **Critical Arts** 1 no. 3 (1980): 23–39.

Bosman, F.C.L. **Drama en Toneel in Suid-Afrika, Deel I: 1652–1855**. [Drama and theatre in South Africa from 1652–1855]. Amsterdam/Pretoria: J.H. de Bussy, 1928. Volume II: 1855–1916. Pretoria: J.L. van Schaik, 1980.

Brink, André P. **Aspekte van die Nuwe Drama**. (Aspects of the new drama). Pretoria: Academica, 1986.

Brooke, Brian. **My own personal star: an autobiography**. Johannesburg: Limelight Press, 1978. – 262 p.: ill. Notes: Theatrical producers and directors. Autobiography/Brooke, Brian.

Brown, Duncan and Bruno van Dyk, eds. **Exchanges: South African writing in transition**. Pietermaritzburg: University of Natal Press, 1991. 125 p.

Campschreur, Willem and Joost Divendal. **Culture in another South Africa**. New York: Olive Branch Press, 1989. – 288 p.: ill. (some col.). Notes: Summary in Afrikaans, etc. Contributions from the Culture in Another South Africa Festival and Conference, Amsterdam, Dec. 1987. Includes bibliographical references. Now we enter history: introduction/Mongane Wally Serote. The last bastion of freedom under siege: a reflection on theater/Anthony Akerman. Ntyilo-ntyilo: song/Miriam Makeba – In the name of art: a reflection on fine art/Steven Sack – Restrictions on the media: a reflection on journalism/Mono Badela and David. Towards a survey: a reflection on poetry/Cosmo Pieterse – The aloe and the wild rose: song/Abdullah Ibrahim (Dollar Brand) – The melody of freedom: a reflection on music/Jonas Gwangwa and Fulco van Aurich. The struggle against cultural racism: a reflection on ruling class culture in South Africa/Patrick Fitzgerald – Towards new cultural relations: a reflection on the cultural boycott/Conny Braam and Fons Geerlings.

Chapman, Michael, Colin Gardner and Es'kia Mphahlele, eds. **Perspectives on South African English Literature**. Johannesburg: Ad Donker, 1992.

Coplan, David B. **In township tonight! South Africa's black city music and theatre**. Johannesburg: Ravan Press, 1985.

Davis, Geoffrey V. and Anne Fuchs. **Theatre and change in South Africa**. Amsterdam, Netherlands: Harwood Academic Publishers, 1996. – xiii, 336 p.: ill. Notes: Includes bibliographical references and index. 'A truly living moment': acting and the Statements plays/Brian Crow – 'The many individual wills.' From Crossroads to Survival. The work of Experimental Theatre Workshop '71/Robert McLaren – Whose popular theatre and performance?/Martin Orkin – The performance aesthetics of township theatre: frames and codes/Christopher Balme – Theatre for export: the commercialization of the Black people's struggle in South African export musicals/Jerry Mofokeng – Theatre in exile/Anthony Ackerman – My life in the theatre of war: the development of an alternative consciousness/Matthew Krouse – What is a tribal dress? the 'Imbongi' (Praise-singer) and the 'People's poet.' Reactivization of a tradition in the liberation struggle/Peter Horn – The workers' theatre in Natal/Ari Sitas – 'An interest in the making of things.' An interview with William Kentridge/Geoff V. Davis and Anne Fuchs – Tooth and nail. Rethinking form for the South African theatre/Malcolm Purkey – Physical images in the South African theatre/Mark Fleishman – 'I will remain an African.' An interview with Maishe Maponya/Geoff V. Davis and Anne Fuchs – Politics and the theatre: current trends in South Africa/Zakes Mda – Theatre: the political weapon in South Africa/Doreen Mazibuko – 'This compost heap of a country.' An interview with Barney Simon/Geoff V. Davis and Anne Fuchs – So what's new? The story behind the play/Fatima Dike – PACT: can the leopard change its spots?/Carol Steinberg – The future of the performing arts councils in a new South Africa/Arnold Blumer – 'It's time to have a South African culture.' An interview with Ramolao Makhene/Geoff V. Davis and Anne Fuchs.

Daymond, M.J., J.U. Jacobs and M. Lenta, eds. **Momentum. On recent South African writing**. Pietermaritzburg: University of Natal Press, 1984.

Du Toit, P.J. **Amateurtoneel in Suid-Afrika**. [Amateur theatre in South Africa.] Pretoria: Academica, 1988.

Fuchs, Anne. **Playing the Market: the Market Theatre, Johannesburg, 1976–1986**. Chur, Switzerland; New York: Harwood Academic Publishers, 1990. – 183 p.: ill. Notes: Includes bibliographical references (p. 170–6) and index. Market Theatre (Johannesburg). History.

Glasser, Mona. **King Kong: a venture in the theatre**. Cape Town: Norman Howell, 1960.

Gray, Stephen. **Southern African literature: an introduction**. London: David Philip, 1979.

Gunner, Liz, ed. **Politics and performance: theatre, poetry and song in South Africa**. Johannesburg: Witwatersrand University Press, 1994.

Hauptfleisch, Temple, ed. **The Breytie Book: a**

collection of articles on South African Theatre. Johannesburg: The Limelight Press, 1985.

—— and Ian Steadman, eds. **South African theatre: four plays and an introduction**. Pretoria: HAUM Educational, 1984.

Jones, Laura. **Nothing except ourselves: the harsh times and bold theater of South Africa's Mbongeni Ngema**. New York, N.Y., USA: Viking, 1994. – xii, 207 p.: ill., 8 p. of plates. *Notes*: Includes bibliographical references (p. 193–5) index. Dramatists. Biography. Ngema, Mbongeni.

Kavanagh, Robert, ed. **South African people's plays**. London: Heinemann, 1981.

——. **Theatre and cultural struggle in South Africa**. London: Zed Books, 1985.

Larlham, Peter. **Black theatre, dance, and ritual in South Africa**. Ann Arbor: UMI Research Press, 1985.

Ndlovu, Duma, ed. **Woza Afrika! An anthology of South African plays**. New York: George Braziller, 1986.

Orkin, Martin. **Drama and the South African state**. Johannesburg: Witwatersrand University Press, 1991.

——. **Shakespeare against apartheid**. Johannesburg: Ad Donker, 1987.

Schach, Leonard. **The flag is flying: a very personal history of theatre in the old South Africa**. Cape Town: Human & Rousseau, 1996. – 191 p.: ill. *Notes*: Includes bibliographical references (p. 179–80) and index.

Scheub, Harald. **The Xhosa 'Ntsomi'**. Oxford: Clarendon Press, 1975.

Schwartz, Pat. **The best company: the story of Johannesburg's Market Theatre**. Johannesburg: Ad Donker, 1988. 280 p.

Sher, Antony and Gregory Doran. **Woza Shakespeare!: Titus Andronicus in South Africa**. London: Methuen Drama, 1996. – xii, 302 p.: ill. *Notes*: 20th century/Shakespeare, William, 1564–1616. Dramatic production.

Steadman, Ian. **Popular culture and performance in South Africa**. Durban: Contemporary Cultural Studies Unit, 1986. 76 p.

Storrar, Patricia. **Beginners please: a history of children's theatre in South Africa**. Johannesburg, 1988.

Visser, Nick and Tim Couzens, eds. **Dhlomo, H.I.E.: Collected Works**. Johannesburg: Ravan, 1985.

White, Landeg and Tim Couzens. **Literature and society in South Africa**. Cape Town: Maskew Miller Longman, 1984.

Woolfson, Malcolm. **But the melody lingers on: the 'inside story' of the Johannesburg Operatic and Dramatic Society – its shows, personalities, triumphs, and tribulations**. Johannesburg: Perskor, 1992. – 280 p.: ill. (some col.). *Notes*: Includes index. Musical theatre. History. Johannesburg Operatic and Dramatic Society.

A3a131. SOUTH PACIFIC

Dorras, Jo and Peter Walker. (Vanuatu) **The old stories: a play about the history of Vanuatu**. Port Vila, Vanuatu: n.p. [Wan Smolbag Theatre], n.d [1993].

Hereniko, Vilsoni Tausie. (Fiji) **A child for Iva: a three-act play**. Auckland: Heinemann, 1981.

——. **The monster and other plays**. Suva: Mana Publications, 1989.

——. **Two plays** [A Child for Iva and Sera's Choice]. Introduction by Andrew Horn. Suva: Mana Publications, 1987.

—— and Teresia Teaiwa. **The last virgin in paradise: a serious comedy**. Suva: Institute for Pacific Studies, 1993.

Nacola, Jo. (Fiji) 'A Few To Go'. In **I Native no more: three drama sketches**. Suva: Mana, 1976.

Thomas, Larry. (Fiji) **Just another day: a play**. Suva: Fiji Centre, University of the South Pacific, 1989.

——. 'Outcasts', 'Yours dearly', 'Men, women and insanity'. In **3 plays**. Suva: University of the South Pacific, 1991. Revised edition 1995.

Tjibaou, J[ean-] M[arie]. (New Caledonia) **Kanaké. See kanaké: the Melanesian way**. Translated by Christopher Plant. Papeete, Tahiti, French Polynesia: Les Editions du Pacifique, 1978.

Veramu, Joseph C. (Fiji) **Killers of Turukawa**. N.p [Suva]: South Pacific Creative Arts Society, n.d. [1980s].

Wan Smolbag Theatre. (Vanuatu) **George and Sheila**. Video. Port Vila, Vanuatu: Wan Smolbag Theatre 1994.

——. **Kasis Road**. Video. Port Vila, Vanuatu: Wan Smolbag Theatre, 1996.

——. **Like any other lovers**. Video. Port Vila, Vanuatu: Wan Smolbag Theatre, 1992.

——. **On the reef**. Video. Port Vila, Vanuatu: Wan Smolbag Theatre, Handspan Theatre (Melbourne, Australia) and Pasifika Communications (Fiji), 1995.

——. **Pacific star**. Video. Port Vila, Vanuatu: Wan Smolbag Theatre and Pasifika Communications (Fiji), 1993.

——. **Storian blong Angela** [Angela's story]. Video. Port Vila, Vanuatu: Wan Smolbag Theatre, 1993.

——. 'The Tale of Mighty Hawk and Magic Fish'. In **Sacred Earth Dramas**. London: Faber, 1993.

——. **Things we don't talk about**. Video. Port Vila, Vanuatu: Wan Smolbag Theatre, 1996.

——. **Three plays for the Pacific**. 'The Tale of Mighty Hawk and Magic Fish', 'The Invasion of the Litter Creatures', 'On the Reef'. Port Vila, Vanuatu: Wan Smolbag theatre, n.d. [1994].

A3a132. SPAIN

Alonso, José Luis, Juan Antonio Hormigón, Inmaculada Alvear, Carlos Rodríguez and María Jesús Valdés. **Teatro de cada día: escritos sobre teatro**. Madrid: Publicaciones de la Asociación de Directores de Escena, 1991. – 670 p.: ill. *Notes*: Includes bibliographical references. Spanish drama. Criticism and interpretation.

Alvar López, Manuel. **El teatro y su crítica: Reunión de Málaga de 1973**. [Theatre and criticism: the Málaga Conference, 1973]. Málaga: Diputación Provincial de Málaga, 1975. 520 p.

Alvaro, Francisco. **El espectador y la crítica: el teatro en Espana en 1985**. Valladolid: F. Alvaro, 1986. – 335 p.: ill. *Notes*: Includes indexes. History and criticism. Annual series. Volumes back to 1958.

Amorós, Andrés, Marina Mayoral and Francisco Nieva. **Análisis de cinco comedias: teatro español de post-guerra**. [Analysis of five comedies: post-war Spanish theatre]. Colección Literatura y Sociedad. Madrid: Castalia, 1977. 218 p.

Arias de Cassío, Ana María. **Dos siglos de escenografía en Madrid**. [Two centuries of set design in Madrid]. Madrid: Mondadori, 1991.

Bartomeus, Antoni. **Els autors de teatre català: testimoni d'una marginació**. Barcelona: Curial, 1976. – 396 p., 6 p. of plates: ill. *Notes*: Dramatists, Catalan. Interviews.

Berenguer, Angel. **Teoría y Crítica del teatro. Estudios sobre teoría y crítica teatral**. [Essays on the theory and criticism of theatre]. Alcalá de Henares: Universidad de Alcalá, 1991.

Bernal, Francisca and César Oliva. **El teatro público en España, 1939–1978**. Madrid: Ediciones J. García Verdugo, 1996. – 138 p. *Notes*: Includes bibliographical references (p. 119–20). History. 20th century.

Borel, Jean Paul. **El teatro de lo imposible: Ensayo sobre una de las dimensiones fundamentales del teatro español contemporáneo**. [Theatre of the impossible: essays on one of the fundamental dimensions of twentieth-century Spanish theatre]. Translated by Gonzalo Torrente Ballester. Colección Guadarrama de Crítica y Ensayo. Madrid: Ediciones Guadarrama, 1966. 304 p.

Bryan, T. Avril. **Censorship and social conflict in the Spanish theatre: the case of Alfonso Sastre**. Washington, D.C.: University Press of America, 1982. – x, 145 p. *Notes*: Bibliography: p. 133–42. Literature and society. Censorship. Sastre, Alfonso. Political and social views.

Buero Vallejo, Antonio. **Teatro español actual**. [Spanish theatre today]. Madrid: Fundación Juan March, 1977. 297 p.

Byrd, Suzanne Wade. **García Lorca: 'La Barraca' and the Spanish national theater**. New York: Abra Ediciones, 1975. – 142 p.: ill. *Notes*: Bibliography: p. 137–42. Theatre and state. Biography/García Lorca, Federico, 1898–1936. Barraca (Theatrical troupe). History.

Cabal, Fermín. **La situación del teatro en España**. [The Spanish theatre now]. Madrid: Asociación de Autores de Teatro, 1994. – 62 p.: ill. *Notes*: Includes bibliographical references. Theatre and society.

——, Alonso de Santos and José Luis. **Teatro español de los 80**. [Spanish theatre in the 80s]. Madrid: Fundamentos, 1985. – 265 p. Interviews.

Cantalapiedra Erostarbe, Fernando. **El teatro español de 1960 a 1975: estudio socioeconómico**. Kassel: Reichenberger, 1991. – viii, 227 p. *Notes*: Includes bibliographical references (p. 221–4).

Cobo, Angel. **José Martín Recuerda: génesis y evolución de un autor dramatico**. Granada: Diputación Provincial de Granada, 1993. – 184 p.: ill. *Notes*: Includes bibliographical references (p. 183–185). Martín Recuerda, José. Biography.

The contemporary Spanish theatre: a collection of critical essays. Lanham, MD: University Press of America, 1988. 261 p.

Cuadernos de bibliografía de las artes escénicas. Madrid: Centro de Documentación Teatral, Instituto Nacional de las Artes Escénicas y de la Música, Ministerio de la Cultura, 1994. – v. *Notes*: Serial. Theatre. Spain. Bibliography.

Dona i teatre: ara i aquí. Barcelona: Institut Català de la Dona, ICD: Generalitat de

Catalunya, 1994. – 187 p. *Notes*: Includes bibliographical references. Women in the theatre. Catalan drama. History and criticism.

Dougherty, Dru and María Francisca Vilches de Frutos. **El teatro en España entre la tradición y la vanguardia**. [Theatre in Spain between tradition and the avant-garde]. Madrid: Consejo Superior de Investigaciones Cientificas/ Fundación García Lorca, 1992.

Edwards, Gwynne. **Dramatists in perspective: Spanish theatre in the twentieth century**. Cardiff: University of Wales Press, 1985. – 269 p. *Notes*: Includes bibliography and index. Spanish drama. History and criticism.

La escritura teatral a debate: nuevas tendencias escénicas. [Playwriting under debate: new stage trends]. Madrid: Ministerio de Cultura, Direccion General de Musica y Teatro, Centro Nacional de Nuevas Tendencias Escenicas, 1986. 275 p.

Estudis escènics: gener de 1985. Barcelona: Edicions 62, 1985. – 142 p. *Notes*: Includes bibliographical references. Catalonia. History and criticism.

Fàbregas, Xavier and Ricard Salvat. **Homenatge a Xavier Fàbregas: Universitat de Paris-Sorbonne, Centre de'etudes catalanes, 16 de novembre de 1993**. Barcelona: Publicacions de l'Abadia de Montserrat, 1996. – 85 p. *Notes*: Includes bibliographical references. Catalonia. History. 20th century. Fàbregas, Xavier, 1931–.

Fernández Torres, Alberto. **Documentos sobre el teatro independiente español**. [Madrid]: Centro Nacional NTE: Ministero de Cultura, Instituto Nacional de las Artes Escénicas y de la Música, 1987. – 442 p.: ill. *Notes*: Includes bibliographical references. History. 20th century.

Ferreras, Juan Ignacio. **El teatro en el siglo XX: desde 1936**. [Theatre in the twentieth century: since 1936]. Madrid: Taurus, 1988. 144 p.

Floeck, Wilfried. **Spanisches Gegenwartstheater**. Tübingen: Francke, 1997. – 2 vols. *Notes*: Spanish drama. History, criticism.

Forys, Marsha. **Antonio Buero Vallejo and Alfonso Sastre: an annotated bibliography**. Metuchen, N.J.: Scarecrow Press, 1988. – xiii, 209 p. *Notes*: Includes index. Drama in Spanish. Buero Vallejo, Sastre, Alfonso – Bibliographies.

Gallén, Enric. **El teatre a la ciutat de Barcelona durant el règim franquista (1939–1954)**. Barcelona: Publicacions de l'Institut del Teatre de la Diputació de Barcelona: Edicions 62, 1985. – 440 p. *Notes*: Bibliography: p. 431–40.

Barcelona. History. 20th century. Theatre and state.

——. **Estudios sobre teatro español clásico y contemporáneo**. [Studies in classical and contemporary Spanish theatre]. Madrid: Fundación Juan March, 1978. 252 p.

García, Crisógono. **Teatro, hoy**. [Theatre today]. Madrid: Editorial Religión y Cultura, 1981. – 285 p.: ill. *Notes*: Spanish drama. History and criticism.

García Lorenzo, Luciano, ed. **Documentos sobre el teatro español contemporáneo**. [Documents on the contemporary Spanish theatre]. Colección Temas no. 17. Alcobendas, Madrid: Sociedad General Española de Librería, 1980. 449 p.

George, David J. and John London. **Contemporary Catalan theatre: an introduction**. [Sheffield]: Anglo-Catalan Society, 1996. – 136 p. *Notes*: Catalan drama. 20th century. History and criticism.

Giuliano, William. **Buero Vallejo, Sastre, y el teatro de su tiempo**. [Buero Vallejo, Sastre and the theatre of their time]. New York: Las Americas S.A., 1971. 264 p.

Gómez González, Juan. **Teatro español en democrracía: nuestra realizada con motivo de la Semana Teatro Español en Rio de Janeiro**. Madrid: Ministerio de Cultura, Dirección General del Libro y Bibliotecas, Centro de las Letras Españoleas, 1995, 1993. – 43 p. *Notes*: Spanish drama. 20th century. Bibliography.

Gordon, José. **Teatro experimental español: antología e historia**. [Spanish experimental theatre: an anthology and history]. Madrid: Escelicer, 1965. 211 p.

Halsey, Martha T. and Phyllis Zatlin. **The Contemporary Spanish theater: a collection of critical essays**. Lanham, MD: University Press of America, 1988. – xi, 261 p.: ill. *Notes*: Includes index. Bibliography: p. 225–48. History. 20th century.

Holt, Marion. **The contemporary Spanish theater (1949–1972)**. Boston: Twayne Publishers, 1975. – 189 p. *Notes*: Bibliography: p. 177–80. Spanish drama. 20th century. History and criticism.

Hormigón, Juan Antonio. **Comienzo de la era del hierro; He conocido a Zaubrek**. Madrid: Asociación de Directores de Escena de Espāna, 1994. 279 p.: ill. History. 20th century.

——. **Teatro, realismo y cultura de masas**. [Theatre, realism and mass culture]. Edición de Bolsillo, Literatura y Ensayo no. 340. Madrid: Cuadernos para el Diálogo, 1974.

——, ed. **Teatro de cada día de José Luis Alonso**. [The everyday theatre of Jose Luis Alonso]. Madrid: Asociación de Directores de Escena, 1991.

Huerta Calvo, Javier. **El teatro en el siglo XX**. [Theatre in the twentieth-century]. Colección Lectura Crítica de la Literatura española. Madrid: Playor, 1985. 140 p.

Isasi Angulo, Armando C. **Diálogos del teatro español de la post-guerra: entrevistas**. [Conversations about post-war Spanish theatre: a collection of interviews]. Madrid: Ayuso, 1974. 547 p.

Lamartina-Lens, Iride. **Literary, historical and social myths in contemporary Spanish theater. a feminist interpretation**. 1986. – vi, 178 p. Thesis (Ph. D.)–Rutger, 1986. Microfilm. Ann Arbor, MI: University Microfilms International, 1986. 1 microfilm reel; 35 mm. *Notes*: Vita. Includes bibliographical references (p. 171–7). Spanish drama. 20th century. Sexism and literature.

Marcus, Maury Hal. **Freedom and tyranny in the theater of late Franco Spain**. 1981. – v, 362 p. Thesis (Ph. D.)–Southern Illinois University, 1981. Microfilm. Ann Arbor, Mich.: University Microfilms International, 1981. 1 microfilm reel; 35 mm. *Notes*: Vita. 'Synopses of selected plays': p. 323–61. Bibliography: p. 305–22. Spanish drama. 20th century. History and criticism/Theater. Spain. History and criticism. Politics and government. 1939–75.

Mariscal, Ana [Ana Arroyo]. **Cincuenta años de teatro en Madrid**. [Fifty years of theatre in Madrid]. Madrid: El Avapiés, 1984. 146 p.

Martinez Thomas, Monique. **Valle-Inclan, père mythique: le théâtre espagnol des années 60 face à l'esperpento**. Toulouse (France): Presses universitaires du Mirail, 1993. – 268 p. *Notes*: Includes bibliographical references (p. 257–64) and index. *Subjects*: Spanish drama. 20th century. History and criticism. Valle Inclan, Ramon del (1869–1936).

Medina Vicario, Miguel Angel. **El teatro español en el banquillo**. [Spanish theatre on the stand]. Valencia: Fernando Torres, S.A., 1976. 483 p.

Miralles, Alberto. **Aproximación al teatro alternativo**. [Madrid]: Asociación de Autores de Teatro, 1994. – 76 p. *Notes*: Experimental theatre. History.

Molinari, Andrés. **Pequeño diccionario de teatro andaluz**. [Encyclopedia of Andalusian theatre]. Seville: Alfar, 1994. – 297 p.: ill. *Notes*: Includes biographical and bibliographical references (p. 295–7).

Monleón, José. **Cuatro autores críticos: J.M. Rodríguez Méndez, J. Martín Recuerda, Francisco Nieva y Jesús Campos**. [Four critical authors: J.M. Rodríguez Méndez, J. Martín Recuerda, Francisco Nieva and Jesús Campos]. Granada: Secretariado de Extensión Universitaria, Gabinete de Teatro, 1976. 162 p.

——. **Treinta años del teatro de la derecha**. [Thirty years of right-wing theatre]. Barcelona: Tusquets, 1971. 155 p.

Moreno, Pastora. **Esperpento: el tren de una utopía: teoría y práctica de una propuesta comunicativa**. Seville: Editorial Guadalmena, 1992. – 250 p.: ill. *Notes*: Includes bibliographical references (p. 241–4). Esperpento (Theatre company). History.

Oliva, César. **Cuatro dramaturgos 'realistas' en la escena de hoy: sus contradicciones estéticas. Carlos Muñiz, Lauro Olmo, Rodríguez Méndez, Martín Recuerda**. [Four 'realist' dramatists today: their aesthetic differences]. Murcia: Universidad de Murcia, Departamento de Literatura Española, 1978. 172 p.

——. **Teatro desde 1936**. [Theatre since 1936]. Colección Estudios, no. 42. Madrid: Alhambra, 1989. 496 p.

Pérez de Olaguer, Gonzalo. **Teatre Independent a Catalunya**. [Independent theatre in Catalonia] Barcelona: Bruguera, 1970.

Pérez-Stansfield, María Pilar. **Direcciones del teatro español de post-guerra**. [Directions in post-war Spanish theatre]. 1st edn. Colección Ensayos. Madrid: Porrúa Turanzas, 1983. 361 p.

Portillo, Rafael and Jesús Casado, **Abecedario del teatro**. 2nd edn. Seville: Productora Andaluza de Programas: Centro Andaluz de Teatro: Padilla Libros Editorial, 1992. – 205 p.: ill.

El Público, quién, cómo, cuándo, dónde. [The theatre public, who, how, when, where?] Madrid: Centro de Documentación Teatral, 1985. – 72 p.: ill. *Notes*: Theatre audiences.

Rabassó, Carlos A. **Pedrolo, Nieva, Arrabal: teatrilogía del vanguardismo dramático: aproximaciones hermenéutico-fenomenológicas al teatro español contemporáneo**. Barcelona: Editorial Vosgos, 1993. – 132 p. *Notes*: Includes bibliographical references (p. 117–124). Spanish drama. History and criticism. Arrabal, Fernando. Nieva, Francisco. Pedrolo, Manuel de, 1918–91.

Ragué Arias, María José. **El teatro de fin de milenio en España: de 1975 hasta hoy**. Barcelona: Editorial Ariel, 1996. – 365 p. *Notes*: Includes bibliographical references (p. 265–339) and index. Spanish drama. History and criticism.

Rodríguez Lloveras, J. **Treinta y cinco años de teatro tras la cortina**. [Thirty-five years of theatre behind the curtain]. Barcelona: By the author, 1970. 306 p.

Rodríguez Méndez, José María. **Comentarios impertinentes sobre el teatro español**. [Some impertinent comments on Spanish theatre]. Barcelona: Peninsula, 1972. 216 p.

——. **La incultura teatral en España**. [Theatre illiteracy in Spain]. Barcelona: Laia, 1974. 215 p.

Rubio Jiménez, Jesús. **El teatro poético en España: del modernismo a las vanguardias**. Murcia: Universidad de Murcia, 1993. – 156 p. History and criticism.

Ruíz Ramón, Francisco. **Historia del teatro español. Siglo XX**. [History of the Spanish theatre. Twentieth-century]. 8th edn. Madrid: Cátedra, 1989. 576 p.

Salvat, Ricard. **El teatro como texto, como espectáculo**. [Theatre as text and as spectacle]. Biblioteca de Divulgación Temática no. 17. Barcelona: Montesinos, 1984. 152 p.

Sastre, Alfonso. **Drama y sociedad**. Hondarribia, Gipuzkoa: Argitaletxe Hiru, 1994. – 213 p. Notes: Includes bibliographical references. History and criticism. Theatre and society.

Valdivieso, L. Teresa. **España, bibliografía de un teatro silenciado**. Manhattan, Kan.: Society of Spanish and Spanish-American Studies, 1979. – xiii, 120 p. Notes: Includes indexes. Spanish underground literature. Spain. Bibliography.

Villegas, Juan. **Ideología y discurso crítico sobre el teatro de España y América Latina**. [Ideology and critical discourse in the theatre of Spain and Latin America]. Minneapolis: Prisma Institute, 1988.

Wellwarth, George E. **Spanish underground drama**. University Park: Pennsylvania University Press, 1972. 169 p.

Zatlin, Phyllis. **Cross-cultural approaches to theatre: the Spanish-French connection**. Metuchen, N.J.: Scarecrow Press, 1994. – vii, 261 p.: ill. Notes: Includes bibliographical references (p. 217–29) and index. French drama. Spanish influences/Spanish drama. French influences.

A3a133. SRI LANKA

Alwis, Anton. **Tavar Hol nava udava** [Tavar Mantapattin putija elucci – Re-awakening of Tower Hall] Colombo: Kolamba Nagarikaya, 1978. 52 p., 2 p. of plates: ill. Notes: Sinhalese drama. 20th century. History/Tower Hall.

Fernando, Michael. **Die singhalesische Bühne und Bertolt Brecht**. Berlin: Brecht-Zentrum der DDR, 1984. 242 p. Notes: Originally presented as the author's thesis (doctoral)–Humboldt Universität zu Berlin, 1982. Bibliography: p. 235–42. Political aspects. History and criticism/Brecht, Bertolt, 1898–1956.

Goonethillaka, M.H. **Kolam Nataka Sahitya**. [Kolam: A traditional drama]. Colombo: Ratna Publishers. 165 p.

——. **Nadagam**. New Delhi: Satguru, 1991. 93 p.

Hapuarachchi, D.V. **Sinhala Natya Itihasaya**. [A history of Sinhala drama]. Colombo: Lakehouse Publishing, 1983. 220 p.

Kariyawasam, Tissa. **Gan Madu Puranaya**. [Community rituals]. Colombo: Library Services Board, 1985. 220 p.

——. **Sinhala Natakaye Vikashanaya 1867–1911**. [A history of Sinhala drama 1867–1911]. Colombo: Pradeepa, 1979. 260 p.

——. **Visi Vasaraka Natya Ha Ranga Kalava 1912–1931**. [Twenty years of Sinhala drama and theatre 1912–1931]. Colombo: S. Godage and Bros., 1981. 178 p.

——. **Visipas Vasaraka Natya Ha Ranga Kalava 1932–1956**. [Twenty-five years of Sinhala drama and theatre 1932–1956]. Colombo: S. Godage and Bros., 1983. 200 p.

——. **Vishva idyala Natya Vamsaya 1921–1981**. [A history of university drama 1921–1981]. Colombo: S. Godage and Bros., 1983. 104 p.

——. **Yak Thovil Ha Inhala Samajaya**. [Demon rituals in Sinhala society]. Colombo: Ministry of Cultural Affairs, 1975. 172 p.

Manoratna, Jayalat and Ranjit Dharmakirti. **Simhala natya kalave haraskadak: tunveni sinuva Jayalat Manoratna natya ulela nimitten nukut karini**. [Colombo]: As. Godage saha Sahodarayo, 1992. 79 pp. Notes: In Sinhalese. Scholarly articles on contemporary Sinhala drama and theatre. Sinhalese drama. 20th century. History and criticism.

Sarachchandra, Ediriweera. **The folk drama of Ceylon**. Colombo: The Government Press, 1952; reprint edn, 1968; reissued 1992. 180 p.

Subashinghe, Somalatha. 'Sri Lanka'. In **International guide to children's theatre and educational theatre: a historical and geographical source book**, p. 290–6. Lowell

Swortzell, ed. Westport: Greenwood Press, 1990.

A3a134. SUDAN

Ali Ibrahim, Abdullahi. **An introduction to his plays**. Khartoum, 1986.

Ali Al-Waki, Ithman and Saad Yusuf. **Al Haraka Al Masrahiyya Fi Assoudan**. Khartoum, 1979.

Filewod, Alan. 'Underdeveloped alliance'. **Canadian Theatre Review** 53 (winter 1987): 39–42.

Hussain, M. Rida. **Al Drama Lil Huwat**. Khartoum, 1979.

Al-Mubarak Mustafa, Khalid. **Arabic drama: a critical introduction**. Khartoum: Khartoum University Press, 1986.

——. **Harf Wa Nuqt'a**. Khartoum, 1980. 158 p.

Al-Nisairi, Uthman Jaafar. **Al Masrah Fi Al Soudan 1905–1915**. [Theatre in Sudan 1905–1915]. Khartoum, 1969. 15 p.

Al-Tayed, Ahmed. **Tarikh Al Fann Al Masrahi**. Ed. Uthman Hassan. Khartoum, 1984. 41 p.

'Uthman, al-Fatih Mubarak. **Masrah Firqat al-Asdiqa': bayna al-qawl al-yawmi wa-al-qawl al-masrahi, al-dahik wa-ma'zaq al-marji'iyah: masrahiyat Bayan raqm namudhhan**. [The Asdiqaa' theatrical company: between what is said daily and what is said on the stage, laughter and the authority's predicament: the stage play proclamation of an exemplary number]. Khartoum: Nadi al-Masrah al-Sudani, 1989. – 23 p Sudan. History and criticism.

A3a135. SWEDEN

Anderman, Gunilla M. **Contemporary Swedish drama**. Lampeter, Wales: Swedish-English Literary Translators Association, 1987. – 59 p.: ill. Notes: Carl-Johan Seth – Translating drama/G.M. Anderman – It all started in the sixties – Social reform and the emergence of feminism – Two comedies – Community theatre – Into the eighties – Theatre for children of all ages. History and criticism.

Anderson, Margareta. **Fiasko- och succépjäser: delstudier rörande pjäser med låga publiksiffror på svenska teatrar 1945–68**. [Hits and flops at Swedish theatres 1945–68]. Lund, Sweden: Institute for Research in the Dramatic Arts, 1969. – 2 vols.: ill. Notes: Bibliography: vol. 2, p. 141. Theatre audiences.

Bergman, Gösta M., ed. **Svensk teater. Strutturförändringar och organisation 1900–1970**. [Swedish theatre. Structural

changes and organization 1900–70]. Uppsala: Almqvist & Wiksell, 1970. 125 p.

Dahlström, Gil, et al., eds. **Kungliga Dramatiska Teatern 1788–1988. Jubileumsföreställning fyra akter**. [The Royal Dramatic Theatre 1788–1988. Jubilee performance in four acts]. Höganäs: Bra Bok, 1988. 280 p.

Ek, Sverker R. **Spelplatsens magi. Alf Sjöbergs regikonst**. [The magic of the playground. Alf Sjöberg's art of directing]. Stockholm: Gidlunds, 1988. 390 p.

Eklund, Hans, Barbro Stribolt and Bengt Wittströn. **Från Humlan till Intiman: Stockholms privatteatrar**. Lund: Signum, 1990. – 248 p.: ill. (some col.). Notes: Includes bibliographical references (p. 235–6) and index. Stockholm. History. 20th century.

Engel, Ann Mari. **Teater i folkets park 1905–1980: arbetarrörelsen, folkparkerna och den folkliga teatern: en kulturpolitiske studie**. Stockholm: Akademilitteratur, 1982. – 222 p.: ill. Notes: Summary in English. Includes index. Bibliography: p. 209–16. Thesis (doctoral)– Stockholms universitet, 1982. Popular culture. Socialism and theatre.

Engel, P.G., and Leif Janzon. **Sju decennier. Svensk teater under 1900-talet**. [Seven decades. Swedish theatre in the twentieth century]. Lund: Forum, 1974. 212 p.

Englund, Claes, ed. **Teaterårsboken**. [Theatre yearbook]. Stockholm: Entré, annually from 1982.

Hammergren, Lena, Karin Helander and Willmar Sauter. **Svenska teaterhändelser: 1946–1996**. Stockholm: Natur och kultur, 1996. – 446 p.: ill. Notes: Includes bibliographical references (p. 401–28) and index. Performing arts. History and criticism.

Knuttgen, Birgitta Dahlgren. **Experiments in modern Swedish drama: the radical theatre movement in Sweden in the 1960s and 1970s**. Thesis (Ph. D.)–Harvard University, 1984. 298 p. Notes: Bibliography: p. 284–98. History and criticism/Theatre and society.

Liljenberg, Bengt. **Svenska stycken efter Strindberg. Anteckningar kring den suenska scendramatiken och dess författare 1910–1960**. [Swedish plays after Strindberg. Notations on the Swedish stage drama and its authors 1910–1960]. Stockholm: Carlssons, 1990. 271 p.

Marker, Lise-Lone and Frederick Marker. **Ingmar Bergman: a life in the theatre**. Revised edition. Cambridge: Cambridge University Press, 1992. 262 p.

Näslund, Erik. **Birgit Cullberg**. Stockholm: Norstedt, 1978. 369 p.

Ödeen, Mats. **Skådespelarna tar makten: om teatern och den nya klassen under två decennier**. Stockholm: Carlsson, 1993. – 380 p. *Notes*: Includes bibliographical references (p. 370–1) and index. Theatre. Political aspects.

Osten, Suzanne. **Unga Klara: Young Klara work and theories**. [Stockholm: s.n.], 1990. – 49 p.: ill. *Notes*: Unga Klara, Suzanne Osten's youth theatre, is examined by Osten herself.

Qvarström, Birgit and Eric Lindqvist. **Riksteatern 50 år: kavalkad i text och bild**. Solna: Entre/Riksteatern, 1983. – 141 p.: ill. *Notes*: History. Svenska riksteatern.

Ralf, Klas, ed. **Operan 200 år. Jubelboken**. [The Royal Opera's 200 years. The Jubilee book]. Stockholm: Prisma, 1973. 252 p.

Ringby, Per. **Avantgardeteater och modernitet: Pistolteatern och det svenska teaterlivet från 1950-tal till 60-tal**. Gideå: Vildros, 1995. – 416 p.: ill. *Notes*: Includes bibliographical references (p. 398–403) and index. Experimental theater. (Theatre group). History.

Sauter, Willmar, Curt Isaksson and Lisbeth Jansson. **Teaterögon: publiken möter föreställningen upplevelse-utbud-vanor**. Stockholm: Liber, 1986. – 508 p.: ill. *Notes*: Summary in English. Bibliography: p. 498–504. Theatre audiences.

Sjögren, Henrik. **Ingmar Bergman på teatern**. [Ingmar Bergman in the theatre]. Stockholm: Almqvist & Wiksell, 1968. 316 p.

——. **Stage and society in Sweden: aspects of Swedish theatre since 1945**. Uddevalla, Sweden: The Swedish Institute, 1979. – 181 p.: ill. *Notes*: Theatre and society.

——. **Teater i Sverige efter andra världskriget**. Stockholm: Natur och kultur, 1982. – 170 p.: ill. *Notes*: Includes index. Bibliography: p. 166–7. History. 20th century.

Teater i Göteborg. [Theatre in Göteborg]. 3 vols. Umeå: Acta Universitatis Umensis, 1978.

Teater i Stockholm 1910–1970. Stockholm: Almqvist & Wiksell international, 1982. – 3 vols. in 4: ill. *Notes*: Summaries in English. Includes bibliographies and indexes. I:1. Teaterliv i helbild och närbild/med bidrag av Lennart Forslund. [*et al.*] – I:2. Teater i förvandling/Sverker R. Ek – II. Repertoar – III. Register. History. 20th century.

Ullberg, Hans. **Riksteater i krig och fred: några drag ur teaterns utveckling i Sverige 1940–1958**. Norsborg: Entré, 1994. – 181 p.:

ill. *Notes*: Includes bibliographical references (p. 178) and index. Svenska riksteatern. History.

Värnlund, Holger. **Kulturen, möten och mödor: bidrag till studiet av kulturens villkor**. Stockholm: Carlsson, 1995. – 309 p. *Notes*: Cultural policy.

Wingren, G. **Dramatik tryckt på svenska 1914–1962**. [Utg. av] Avdelningen för dramaforskning [vid Litteraturvetenskapliga institutionen i Uppsala]. Uppsala: Utgivaren, 1970. – xi, 575 p. *Notes*: Continuation of **Svensk dramatisk litteratur underåren 1840–1913** by G. Wingren. Swedish drama. Bibliography.

A3a136. SWITZERLAND

Arnold, Peter. **Auf den Spuren des 'anderen' Theaters, oder, der Beitrag der Claque Baden zur Zukunft des Theaters in der Schweiz: ein Bericht**. Zürich: Limmat, 1987. – 325, [1] p.: ill. Originally presented as the author's thesis (doctoral)–Freie Universität Berlin, 1986. *Notes*: Bibliography: p. 319–26. Experimental theatre.

Ausgangspunkt Schweiz – Nachwirkungen des Exiltheaters: Schweizer Theaterjahrbuch 50. [Switzerland as starting point – the influence of political exiles on the theatre: Swiss theatre yearbook no. 50]. Willisau: SGTK, 1989.

Bachmann, Dieter and Rolf Schneider. **Das verschonte Haus: das Zürcher Schauspielhaus im Zweiten Weltkrieg**. Zürich: Ammann, 1987. – 263 p. *Subjects*: Schauspielhaus (Zurich, Switzerland). History.

Besson, Benno, Christa Neubert-Herwig and Ulrike Jauslin-Simon. **Jahre mit Brecht**. Willisau: Theaterkultur-Verlag, 1990. – 256 p.: ill. *Notes*: Includes bibliographical references (p. 253–6). Theatrical producers and directors. Besson speaks of his years working with Brecht.

Biner, Pierre. **Aperçu de la situation théâtrale et inventaire des salles dans 61 localités de Suisse romande: mission exploratoire 1978**. Lausanne: Conseil suisse romand du théâtre dramatique, 1979. – 477 p.: ill. *Notes*: Includes index. French-speaking theatres. Inventory of groups.

Blubacher, Thomas. **Befreiung von der Wirklichkeit?: das Schauspiel am Stadttheater Basel 1933–1945**. Basel: Editions Theaterkultur Verlag, 1995. – 411 p.: ill. *Notes*: Includes bibliographical references (p. 371–91) and index. Stadttheater Basel. History.

Dürrenmatt, Friedrich. **Writings on theatre and drama**. London: J. Cape, 1976. – 183 p. *Notes*: These essays are taken from F. Dürrenmatt's 2 volume work **Theater-Schriften und Reden** and

Dramaturgisches und Kritisches. Bibliography: p. 18–19. In place of a portrait: from the beginning.–Writing as an occupation.–Something on the art of writing plays.–Writing and the stage.–The lady's not for burning: comedy by C. Fry.–The taming of the shrew.–Shakespeare twice: on two performances in the framework of the June festival plays.–On Ronald Searle.–Note on comedy.–Theatre problems.–Thoughts before a new performance.–Friedrich Schiller.–American and European drama.–Chat about criticism in front of the press.–Concerning the freedom of the theatre (fragment).–Dramatic theory about the audience.–Dramaturgical considerations about The Anabaptists.–Principles of adaptation (epilogue to the book edition of King John.–Notes on Titus Andronicus.–Aspects of dramaturgical thinking (fragment).–On the theory of dramatic art in Switzerland (fragment). Words from the noted Swiss dramatist.

Fries, Othmar. **Das Theater, unsere Welt: das Schweizer Theater, 1970–1980**. Lucerne: Raeber, 1980. – 303 p.: numerous ill. (some col.). *Notes*: Contributions chiefly in German, with 3 in French and 1 in Italian. Includes index. Bibliography: p. 290–1. History. 20th century.

Fues, Wolfram Malte. **Theater am Neumarkt 1983–1989**. Zürich: Theater am Neumarkt, 1989. – 140 p.: ill. *Notes*: 'Eine Dokumentation mit Beiträgen von Wolfram Malte Fues. [*et al.*].'–P. 1. Theater am Neumarkt (Zürich).

15 Thesen zu einer Schweizerischen Theaterpolitik. Über Situation und Zukunft des Theaters in der Schweiz. [Fifteen proposals for a Swiss theatre policy: on the situation and future of theatre in Switzerland]. Berne: Swiss Centre of the International Theatre Institute, 1985.

Habecker, S. and A. Hofmann. **Theorien; Texte; Analysen: das deutschsprachige Theater seit 1945, ein Arbeitsbuch für die Sekundarstufe II**. 1st edn. München: R. Oldenbourg, 1974. 276 p. *Notes*: Includes bibliographical references. Austria, Germany, Switzerland. Drama. 20th century. History and criticism.

Hoehne, Verena and Christian Jauslin. **Dramatiker-Förderung: Dokumente zum schweizer Dramatiker-Förderungsmodell**. Bonstetten: Theaterkultur-Verlag, 1986. – 240 p.: ill. *Notes*: French and German. Federal aid to the theatre. History. 20th century.

—— and Peter Zeindler. **Zwei Theater unterwegs: Théâtre populaire romand (La Chaux-de-Fonds) und Theater für den Kanton Zürich (Winterthur)**. Bonstetten: Theaterkultur-Verlag, 1981. – 167 p.: ill. *Notes*: Théâtre populaire romand/Theater für den Kanton Zürich. History.

Kachler, Karl Gotthilf and Gustava Iselin-Haeger. **Lebendiges Theater in schwieriger Zeit: ein Kapitel Basler Theatergeschichte 1936–1946: Charaktere in Maske und Darstellung vor Ausbruch und während des Zweiten Weltkrieges**. Basel: Buchverlag Basler Zeitung, 1982. – 120 p.: ill. *Notes*: Basel. History. 20th century.

——, Silvia Maurer, Martin Dreier and Lydia Benz-Burger. **Schweizerische Theatersammlung, 1927–1985: beharrlicher Aufbau von ihren Anfängen bis heute**. [Swiss theatre 1927–1985]. Bonstetten: Theaterkultur-Verlag, 1985. – 252 p., [1] folded leaf of plates: ill. (some col.). *Notes*: Sponsored by the Schweizerische Gesellschaft für Theaterkultur. Preface also in French, Italian, and Spanish. Includes bibliographical references and index. History. 20th century.

Keiser, César. **Herrliche Zeiten 1916–1976: 60 Jahre Cabaret in der Schweiz**. [The glorious years 1916–76: sixty years of cabaret in Switzerland]. Berne: Benteli Verlag, 1976.

Der Kritiker als Theater und Kulturpolitiker. [Theatre critics as politicians for the arts]. Boswil: Stiftung Künstlerhaus, 1985.

Lendenmann, Fritz. **Eine grosse Zeit: das Schauspielhaus Zürich in der Ära Wälterlin, 1938/39–1960/61**. Zürich: Orell Füssli, 1995. – 176 p.: ill. *Notes*: Includes index. Pictorial works/Wälterlin, Oskar, 1895–1961/Schauspielhaus (Zurich). History.

Liègme, Bernard and Claude Vallon. **Le feu du théâtre**. Lausanne: Editions de l'Aire, 1980. – 135 p., 7 p. of plates: ill. *Notes*: Bibliography: p. 133–5. Dramatists. Interviews. Liègme, Bernard.

Maurer, Roland. **Die Schweizer Theaterszene**. [Theatre in Switzerland]. Zürich: Schweizer Kulturstiftung Pro Helvetia, 1983. 86 p.

——. **The Swiss theatre scene: a survey**. Zurich: Swiss Council for the Arts Pro Helvetia, 1984. – 89 p.: ill., col. map. *Notes*: Translation of: **Schweizer Theaterszene**. Col. map of Switzerland inserted. Bibliography: p. 83–5. Performing arts. Switzerland.

May, Glado von. **Stadttheater St. Gallen 1980 bis 1992**. St. Gallen: Stadttheater St. Gallen, 1991. – 226 p.: ill. (some col.). *Notes*: Stadttheater St. Gallen. History.

Meier, Peter. **Schlagt ihn tot, den Hund! Es ist ein Rezensent: Theater- und Literaturkritik**. Bern: Zytglogge, 1987. – 143 p. *Notes*:

Criticism. Europe, German-speaking. History and criticism.

Müller, Eugen. **Schweizer Theatergeschichte**. [History of the Swiss theatre]. Zurich: Oprecht Verlag, 1944.

Pastori, Jean Pierre. **Le Théâtre de Lausanne: de la scène à la ville, 1869–1989**. Lausanne: Payot, 1989. – 156 p.: ill. *Notes*: Includes bibliographical references and index. Lausanne. History.

Schweizer Theaterbuch. [Swiss theatre book]. Zürich: SBV, 1964.

Stücklin, Umberto. **Baseldytschi Bihni: e Basler Läggerli wiird 100, 1892–1992**. Basel: GS-Verlag, 1991. – 127 p.: ill.; 22 x. *Notes*: Basler Heimatschütz-Theater (Basel). History.

Szene Schweiz/Scène Suisse/Scena Svizzera: Eine Dokumentation des Theaterlebens in der Schweiz. [Swiss stage: a yearbook of Swiss theatre life]. Zürich: SGTK, annually since 1973.

Das Theater – unsere Welt/Le Théâtre – notre monde. Das Schweizer Theater/Le Théâtre suisse 1970–80. [The theatre, our world: Swiss theatre 1970–80]. Lucerne: SBV, 1980. 303 p.

Voser, Irma. **Theater kritisch gespiegelt**. Zürich: Ammann, 1985. – 293 p.: ill. *Notes*: Includes index. Zurich. History. 20th century. Criticism.

A3a137. SYRIA

Aadel, Abu Shanab. **Masrah 'Arabi Qadeem, karagūz** [An old Arabic theatre, karagūz]. Damascus: Ministry of Culture, n.d.

Abu Hayf, 'Abd Allah. **al-Injaz wa-al-mu'anah: hadir al-masrah al-'Arabi fi Suriyah: dirasah**. Damascus: Ittihad al-Kuttab al-'Arab, 1988. – 430 p. *Notes*: Includes bibliographical references. History. Arabic drama. Syria.

Aliksan, Jan. **al-Masrah al-Qawmi wa-al-masarih al-radifah fi al-qutr al-'Arabi al-Suri, 1959–1989: tajribah ra'idah fi masirat al-masrah al-'Arabi al-hadith**. Damascus: Wizarat al-Thaqafah fi al-Jumhuriyah al-'Arabiyah al-Suriyah, 1988. – 269 p.: ill. *Notes*: Includes bibliographical references (p. 247–51). Masrah al-Qawmi (Syria). History.

al-Baaroud i, Fakhri. **Muthakkaraat al-Baaroudi** (al-Baaroudi's Memoirs). Beirut and Damascus: al-Hayaat, 1951.

al-Bahra, Nasr ud-Deen. **Ahaadeeth Wa Tajaarib Masrahiyya**. [Theatrical discussions and experiences]. Damascus: Federation of Arab Writers, 1977.

al-Jindi, Adham. **A'laam al-Adab Wa al-Fann**. [Noted personalities in art and literature]. Damascus, n.d.

al-Kisaan, Jaan. **al-Wilaada ath-Thaaniya lil-Masrah Fi Souriyya**. [The Second birth of the theatre in Syria]. Damascus: Federation of Arab Writers. 1983.

Muhammad, Nadim Ma'alla. **Maqalat naqdiyah fi al-'ard al-masrahi**. Beirut (Lebanon): Dar al-Fikr al-Jadid, 1990. – 280 p. *Notes*: Syria. Arab countries. History. 20th century.

Najm, Mohammed Yousef. **al-Masrahiyya Fi al-Adab al-'Arabi**. [The stage play in Arabic literature], Damascus: Daar ath-Thaqaafa Press, n.d.

al-Qaasimi, Mohammed Sa'eed, Jamaal ud-Deen al-Qaasimi and Khaleel al-'Athm. **Qaamous as- Sina'aat ash-Shamiyya**. [Directory of Syrian Industries]. Damascus: Daar Tallaas Publishing, 1988.

Qatayah, Salman. **Hayat al-fannan Salim Qatayah**. Aleppo: S. Qatayah, ? 1900, 1989 – 86 p.: ill. *Subjects*: Theatrical producers and directors. Syria/Qatayah, Salim.

Thureel, 'Adnaan Bin. **al-Masrah as-Souri Munthu Abi Khaleel al-Qabbaani Ila l-Yawm**. [The Syrian theatre from Abi Khaleel Al-qabbaani to today]. Damascus: Damascus Distribution Office, 1971.

A3a138. TAJIKISTAN

Istoriya sovetskogo dramaticheskogo teatra. [History of Soviet dramatic theatre]. 6 vols. Moscow: Nauka, 1966–71.

Nurdzanov, N.H. **Istoriya tadzikskogo sovetskogo teatra**. [The history of Tadzik soviet theatre]. Dushanbe: Donish, 1990. 408 p.

Nurjonov, Nizom and Olga Kaidalova. **Istoriia tadzhikskogo sovetskogo teatra, 1941–1957**. Dushanbe: Donish, 1990. 404 p.: ill. *Notes*: Includes bibliographical references (p. 370–7) and index. Tajikistan. History. 20th century.

Rahmatulloev, Hojiqul. **Zuhuri ishqi sahna**. Dushanbe: Adib, 1987. – 122 p., 16 p. of plates: ill. *Notes*: In Tajik. Summary in Russian. History. 20th century.

Rashid, Ahmed. **The Resurgence of Central Asia**. London and New Jersey: Oxford University Press, 1994.

Rozanova, Evgenia. 'Pod krylom kuliabskoy lastochki'. [Under the wing of Kuliab swallow]. **Teatr** 10 (1991).

Sharopov, Mardon and Nizom Nurjonov.

Komediia na tadzhikskoi stsene. Dushanbe: Donish, 1978. – 49 p. *Notes*: Includes bibliographical references. Tajik drama (comedy). History and criticism.

A3a139. TANZANIA

Balisidya, N. **Fasihi ya Kiswahili: Wakati Ukuta**. [Time is like a wall]. Dar es Salaam: Mulika, 1970.

Etherton, Michael. **The development of African drama**. London: Hutchinson, 1982.

Fiebach, Joachim. 'On the social function of modern African literature and Brecht'. **Darlite**, Vol. 4, No. 2, 1970.

Kazooba, B. 'The art of heroic recitations at a Bahaya king's court', University of Dar es Salaam, 1977. Unpublished.

Leshoai, Bob. 'Tanzania Socialist Theatre'. **New Theatre Magazine** 12, no. 2, 1972.

Lihamba, Amandina. 'Theatre and political struggle in East Africa'. In **Between state and civil society in Africa: perspectives on development**, ed. Eghosa Osaghae. Dakar: Codesria, 1994. 281 p.

Makoye, Herbert. 'Modification and use of traditional dances in Tanzania plays'. Unpublished, 1993.

Masanja, John. 'Production technique and contemporary dance troupes in Tanzania', University of Dar es Salaam. Unpublished, 1984.

Mbughuni, L.A. **The cultural policy of the United Republic of Tanzania**. Paris: UNESCO, 1974.

——. 'Old and new drama from East Africa: A review of the works of four contemporary dramatists, Rebeca Njau, Ebrahim Hussein, Penina Muhando and Ngugi', In **African Literature Today**, No. 8, London, 1976.

Mbwana, Ali. 'The contribution of modern dance troupes towards the development of traditional African theatre'. Unpublished, University of Dar es Salaam, 1984.

Mlama, P. 'African theatre, the case of Tanzania', University of Dar es Salaam, 1981. Unpublished.

——. 'Digubi, a Tanzanian indigenous theatre form', **The Drama Review**, 25, no. 4 (1981): 3–12.

——. **Culture and Development: The Popular Theatre Approach in Africa**. Uppsala: Nordiska Afrikainstitutet [The Scandinavian Institute of African Studies], 1991. 219 p.

——. 'Reinforcing existing indigenous communication skills: the use of dance in Tanzania'. In **Women in grassroots communication: furthering social change**. Pilar Riaño, ed. Thousand Oaks, California: Sage, 1994. 315 p.

A3a140. THAILAND

Association of Southeast Asian Nations. **The cultural traditional media of Asia**. Manila, 1986.

Brandon, James. **Theater in Southeast Asia**. Cambridge: Harvard University Press, 1967.

Dhanit Yupho. **The preliminary course of training in Thai theatrical art**. Bangkok: The Thai Farmers Bank Limited, 1954. – 64 p.: ill. (some col.), music. *Notes*: Published in 1952 under title: Preliminary course of training in Siamese theatrical art.

Kullman, C.H. and W.C. Young, eds. 'Thailand'. In **Theater companies of the world**. Westport, Conn.: Greenwood Press, 1986.

Mattani Mojdara Rutnin. **The humanities and education for development in Thailand: the development of theatre studies at the university level**. Bangkok: Thai Khadi Research Institute, Thammasat University, 1980. 43 p. *Notes*: Bibliography: p. 43. Study and teaching (Higher). Performing arts. History. 20th century.

Rutnin, Mattani Mojdara. **Modern Thai literature**. Bangkok: Thammasat University Press, 1988.

——. **The Siamese theatre**. Bangkok: The Sompong Press, 1975.

Virulrak, Surapone. 'Theatre in Thailand today'. **Asian theatre journal** (Spring 1990): 95–104.

Yupho, Dhanit. **Khon masks**. Bangkok: Fine Arts Department, 1989.

A3a141. TOGO

Apedo-Amah, Ayayi Togoata. 'Le Concert-party: une pédagogie pour les opprimés'. [The concert party: instruction for the oppressed]. **Peuples noirs, peuples africains** 8, no. 44 (1985): 61–72.

Larrier, Renée Brenda. **La Scène togolaise: langues, coutumes, costumes: entrevue avec Sénouvo Agbota Zinsou**. 1990. *Notes*: Published in special issue of **Contemporary French civilization** 14 (2), summer–fall 1990.

Messa, Abotsi Fo. 'Les Promesses togolaises'. [The Togolese promises]. **Bingo** (November 1978): 65–7.

Reisner, Gena. 'Three ceremonies in Togo'. **The**

drama review: African performance issue 25, no. 4 (winter 1981): 51–8.

Ricard, Alain. 'Concours et concert: théâtre scolaire et théâtre populaire au Togo'. [Contest and concert: scholarly theatre and popular theatre in Togo]. **Revue d'Histoire du Théâtre** 1 (January–March 1975): 44–86.

——. 'Concert party as genre: the happy stars of Lomé'. **Research in African Literatures** 5 (fall 1974): 165–79.

——. 'Reflexions sur le théâtre à Lomé: la dramaturgie du concert-party'. [Reflections on the theatre in Lomé: concert party dramaturgy]. **Recherche, Pedagogie et Culture** 57 (1982): 63–70.

Zinsou, Senouvo Agbota. 'La Naissance de théâtre togolais modern'. [The birth of modern Togolese theatre]. **Culture Française** 31–2 (1982–3): 49–57.

A3a142. TUNISIA

Aziza, Mohamed. **Les Formes traditionnelles du spéctacle**. [Traditional forms of theatre]. Tunis: Société Tunisienne de Diffusion, 1975.

Bahr, Mohamed. **Le Chant et la musique dans le théâtre arabe en Tunisie**. [Song and music in Arab theatre of Tunisia]. Paris: Université de Paris III, 1984. 104 p.

B'chir, Badra. **Elements du fait théâtral en Tunisie**. [Elements of Theatrical Activity in Tunisia]. Tunis: Cahiers du CERES [Centre d'Etude, et de Recherche, Economique et Social], 1993. 218 p.

——. 'Contre le social, famille et théâtre'. [Against the social, the family and the theatre] In **Des relations interpersonnelles dans la famille Maghrebine**. [Interpersonal relations in the Maghreb family]. Tunis: Cahiers du CERES [Centre d'Etude, et de Recherche, Economique et Social], 1988.

——. 'Evolution des formes de créativité et dynamique sociale: l'apport de la comédienne tunisienne au théâtre en Tunisie'. [The evolution of creative styles and social dynamics: The contribution of the actress in Tunisian theatre]. In **Théâtre et changement social**. [Theatre and social change]. Tunis, 1995.

Ben Halima, Hamadi. **Nisf Qarn Min al-Masrah al-'Arabi bil-Bilaad at-Tounisiyya (1907–1957)**. [A half-century of the Arab theatre in Tunisia (1907–1957)]. Tunis: Tunis University Publications, 1974.

Ben at-Tajani, Hamda. **Hayati al-Masrahiyya**. [My theatrical life]. Tunis: The City of Tunis Press, 1981.

Ben Salim, Omar. **ar-Rasid al-Masrahi bi-Wizarat ath-Thaqaafa**. [Theatrical assets in the Ministry of Culture], In **Literary Series**, 8th issue, publications of the Tunis University Social and Economic Studies and Research Centre. Tunis: Tunis Press, 1993. – 271 p. *Notes*: Includes bibliographical references (p. 267–9). Theatre. Tunisia. History.

Bin Salim, 'Umar. **al-Rasid al-masrahi bi-Wizarat al-Thaqafah**. Tunis: Markaz al-Dirasat wa-al-Abhath al-Iqtisadiyah wa-al-Ijtima'iyah, 1993.

Charfeedine, Moncef. (al-Moncef). **Taareekh al-Masrah at-Tounisi Munthu Nash'atihi Ila Nihaayat al-Harb al-'Aalamiyya al-'Oula**. [The history of the Tunisian theatre from its inception to the end of the First World War]. Tunis, 1972.

Un demi-siècle de théâtre Arabe en Tunisie (1907–1957). [A half-century of Arabic theatre in Tunisia (1907–1957)]. Tunis, 1974.

González Rebolledo, María Victoria. **Una panorámica del teatro tunecino contemporáneo, 1900–1975**. Granada: Grupo de Investigación Estudios Arabes Contemporáneos, Universidad de Granada, 1991. – 166. *Notes*: Includes bibliographical references (p. 151–9) and indexes. Tunisia. Arabic drama. History and criticism.

El Houssi, Majid. **Pour une histoire du théâtre Tunisien**. [A history of Tunisian theatre] Padua: Francisci Editore, 1982.

Idris, Muhammad Mas'ud. **Bibliyughrafiyat al-masrah al-Tunisi, 1881–1956**. Tunis: Dar Sahar lil-Nashr, 1993. – v. *Notes*: Includes indexes.Tunisia. History. Bibliography.

Karrou, Ab l-Qasim Mohammed. 'Abd ar-Razzaq Karabaka'. In **Distinguished personalities of the Arab Maghreb** *Series*, Tunis: Tunis Press, 1965.

'Littérature et arts du spectacle à Tunis: 1966–1967'. [Literature and the performing arts in Tunis]. **Institut des Belles-Lettres Arabes Revue** 120 (1968).

Madani, Izziddine. 'al-Masrah at-Tounisi'. [The Tunisian theatre]. In **Encyclopedia of the theatre**, Michel Corvin, ed. Paris: Bordas Press, 1991. In French.

—— and Mohammed as-Saqanji. **Ruwwaad at-Ta'leef al-Masrahi Fi Tunis**. [Pioneering playwrights in Tunisia]. Tunis: Tunisian Distribution Company, 1986.

al-Madyouni, Mohammed. **Masrah Izziddine al-Madani Wa at-Turaath**. [The Izziddine al-Madani theatre and heritage]. Tunis: Daar Rasm Tunis, 1983.

Majiri, Mahmud. **Dirasat fi al-masrah al-Tunisi.** Tunis: Majallat al-Hayah al-Thaqafiyah, 1993. – 170 p.: ill. *Notes:* Includes bibliographical references. Production and direction.

Maquoi, Azza. **Karakouz i el culte a la negativitat.** [Karagoz and the cult of the negation]. Translated into Catalan by Montserrat Benet. Barcelona: Institute del Teatre, 1984. 192 pp.

Massaoud, Mohammed Idris. **Dirasaat Fi Tarikh al-Masrah at-Tounisi 1881–1956.** [Studies on the history of Tunisian theatre 1881–1956]. Tunis: Higher Institute of Theatre Arts, issued by Daar Sahar Publishing Company, 1993.

Mediouni, Mohamed. 'Theatre phenomenon in Tunisia in the twentieth century: A reading of the Tunisian theatre process'. In **Aspects of Tunisian civilization in the twentieth century.** Tunis: La Faculté des Lettres Manouba, 1996.

al-Mizzi, Hamadi. **at-Tansheet al-Masrahi al-Madrasi Fi Tounis.** [Stimulation of school theatres in Tunisia]. Tunis: Daar ar-Riyaah al-Arba' Press, 1985.

Mohammed, Yahya. **Fi ad-Darb al-Masrahi.** [On the theatrical path]. Tunis: Tunis Press, 1988.

Muzughi, Hasin, Jamal Bin Hamadah, Ahmad al-Bukhari Gharib and Juma'ah Shaykhah. **Fahrisat al-masrah al-Tunisi: bibliyughrafiya tahliliyah 'addat khissisan bi-munasibat al-dawrah al-dawliyah al-sabi'ah li-Ayyam Qartaj al-Masrahiyah.** [Tunisian theatre: an analytical bibliography]. Tunis: al-Jumhuriyah al Tunisiyah, 1995. – 73, 32 p.: ill. *Notes:* Includes indexes.

Rebolledo, Maria Victoria Gonzalez. **Una panoramica del teatro Tunecino contemporaneo (1900–1975).** [Survey of contemporary Tunisian theatre (1900–1975)]. Universidad de Granada, Grupo de Investigacion Estudios Arabes Contemporaneos, 1991.

as-Samlaali, al-Haadi. **Thikrayaat Fannaan.** [Memories of an artist]. Tunis: Tunis Press, 1982.

Saqanji, Mohammed. **Firqat Médina Tounis lil-Masrah – Safha Mushriqa Min Hayaat al-Masrah al-'Arabi Fi Bilaadina.** [The city of Tunis theatrical company – A shining page out of the life story of the Arabic theatre in our country]. Tunis: Kahiya Company, 1988.

Thiry, Jacques. 'Pour une approche du théâtre tunisien contemporain'. [An approach to contemporary Tunisian theatre]. In **Théâtre de toujours, d'Aristote à Kalisky.** [Theatre Today: From Aristotle to Kalisky]. Gilbert Debusscher and Alain van Crugten, eds. Brussels: Editions de l'Université de Bruxelles, 1983.

A3a143. TURKEY

Akı, Niyazi. **Çağdaş Türk Tiyatrosuna Toplu Baktiş, 1923–1967.** [A general survey of the contemporary Turkish theatre, 1923–1967]. Ankara: Atatürk Üniversitesi Yayınları, 1968.

And, Metin. **Culture, performance and communication in Turkey.** Tokyo: Institute for the Study of Language and Cultures of Asia and Africa, 1987.

——. **Cumhuriyet dönemi Türk tiyatrosu, 1923–1983.** Ankara: Türkiye Is Bankasi Kültür Yayinlari, 1983. – 699 p.: ill. *Notes:* Updated edn. of: 50 yilin Türk tiyatrosu. 1973. Bibliography: p. 696–9. Turkish drama. 20th century. History and criticism.

——. **Drama at the crossroads.** İstanbul: Isis Press, 1991.

——. **50 yilin Türk tiyatrosu.** Istanbul. 1973. – 703 p. illus. *Notes:* Bibliography: p. 701–3. Turkish drama. 20th century. History and criticism.

——. **Geleneksel Türk Tiyatrosu.** [Traditional Turkish theatre]. Ankara: Bilgi Yayınevi, 1969.

——. **A History of theatre and popular entertainment in Turkey.** Ankara: Forum Yaymlarl, 1963–4.

——. **Karagöz: théâtre d'ombres turc.** [Karagöz: Turkish shadow theatre]. Ankara: Dost Yayınevi, 1977.

——. **Türk Tiyatrosunun Evreleri.** [The phases of Turkish theatre]. Ankara: Turhan Kitabevi, 1983.

Ayvaz, H. **Rejisör Muhsin Ertugrul: hayati ve eserleri.** Istanbul: Kültür Matbaasi, 1943. – 28, 4 p.: ill. *Notes:* Biography/Motion picture actors and actresses. Directors. Ertugrul, Muhsin.

Çalislar, Aziz. **Tiyatro kavramlari sözlügü.** Istanbul: Boyut, 1992. 231 pp. *Notes:* Theatre dictionaries. In Turkish.

Ertugrul, Muhsin. **Benden sonra tufan olmasin!: anilar.** Istanbul: Dr. Nejat F. Eczacibasi Vakfi Yayinlari, 1989. – 669 p., 16 p. of plates: ill. *Notes:* Includes index. History. 20th century. Biography/Ertugrul, Muhsin, b. 1892.

—— and Özdemir Nutku. **Gerçeklerin düsleri: tiyatro düsünceleri.** Levent, Istanbul: Dr. Nejat F. Eczacibasi Vakfi Yayinlari, 1993. – 849 p. *Notes:* Includes bibliographical references (p. 745–64) and indexes. History. 20th century.

Halman, Talât Sait. **Modern Turkish drama**. Chicago: Bibliotecha Islamica, 1976.

Landau, J.M. **Shadow plays in the Near East**. Jerusalem: Palestine Institute of Folklore and Ethnology, 1948.

——. **Studies in the Arab theatre and cinema**. Philadelphia: University of Pennsylvania Press, 1958.

Martinovitch, N.N. **The Turkish theatre**. New York: B. Blom, 1968.

Nekimken, Albert Lee. **The impact of Bertolt Brecht on society and the development of political theater in Turkey**. Riverside: Calif., 1978. – xi, 1, 607 p. Notes: Bibliography: p. 584–607. Bibliography of Brecht in Turkey (1955–77): p. 482–514. Thesis (Ph. D.)–University of California, Riverside. Turkish drama. 20th century. History and criticism.

Nutku, Özdemir. **Darülbedayi'nin Eılı Yılı**. [Fifty years of darülbedayi]. Ankara: Ankara Üniversitesi, Dil ve Tarih Coğrafya Fakültesi Yayınları, 1969.

——. **Meddahlık ve Meddah Hikâyeleri**. [Meddah and medah stories]. Ankara: Türkiye ış Bankası Kültür Yayıları, 1976.

——. 'The Transformation of Turkish Culture'. In **A panorama of the Turkish republic under the leadership of Atatürk. A collection of essays**, eds. Gülsen Renda and C. Max Kortpeter, 165–78. Princeton, NJ: Kingston Press, 1986.

Ofluoglu, Mücap. **Aglamakla gulmek arasinda**. Istanbul: Mitos Yayinlari, 1993. – 238 p., 16 p. of plates: ill. Subjects: Actors. Biography. Ofluoglu, Mücap.

Özgű, Meláhat. 'L'influenza dell'oriente e dell'occidente sul concetto turco di teatro'. [The influence of east and west on the Turkish concept of theatre]. In **Teatro Oriente/Occidente**, ed. Antonella Ottai, 415–20. Rome: Bulzoni, 1986.

Özön, Mustafa Nihat and Baha Dürder. **Türk tiyatrosu ansiklopedisi**. Istanbul: Remzi Kitabevi, 1967. – 494 p. Notes: Turkish theatre encyclopedia.

Sakiroglu, Mahmut and Talât Sait Halman. **Prof. Dr. Metin And bibliyografyasi**. Kizilay, Ankara: Turhan Kitabevi, 1993. – 65 p., [6] p. of plates: col. ill., facsims. Notes: Includes index. Folk drama. Theatre. Turkey. Bibliography. And, Metin, 1927–.

Sener, Sevda. 'Contemporary Turkish Drama'. In **A panorama of the Turkish republic under the leadership of Atatürk. A collection of essays**, eds. Gülsen Renda and C. Max Kortpeter, 249–66. Princeton, NJ: Kingston Press, 1986.

——. **Cağdas Türk Tiyatrosunda İnsan 1923–1972**. [Man in contemporary Turkish theatre, 1923–1972]. Ankara: Ankara Üniversitesi Dil ve Tarih Coğrafya Fakültesi Yayınarı, 1972. – 159 p. Notes: Bibliography: p. 147–53. Turkish drama. 20th century. History and criticism.

Sevinçli, Efdal. **Görüsleriyle uygulamalariyla bir tiyatro adami olarak Muhsin Ertugrul**. Istanbul: ARBA, 1990. – 325 p. Notes: Includes bibliographical references (p. 281–325). History. 20th century.

——. **Izmir'de tiyatro**. Izmir: Ege Yayincilik, 1994. – 109 p.: ill. Notes: Includes bibliographical references. Izmir. History.

Siyavusgil, S. Esat. **Karagöz: its history, its characters, its mystic and satiric spirit**. İstanbul: Turkish Press Broadcasting and Tourist Department, 1961.

Sokullu, Sevinç. **Türk Komedyasmen Evrimi**. [The evolution of Turkish comedy]. Ankara: Kultur Bakanlığı Yayınları, 1979.

Yüksel, Ayşegül. **Haldun Taner Tiyatrosu**. [The theatre of Haldun Taner]. Ankara: Bilgi Yayınevı, 1986.

A3a144. TURKMENISTAN

Aboukova, FA. **Turkmenskaja opera: puti formirovanija, Ozanrovaja tipoligija**. [Turkmenian opera: Its paths of formation, genre typology]. Aschabad: Ylym, 1987. 162 p.

Istoriya sovetskogo dramaticheskogo teatra. [History of Soviet dramatic theatre]. 6 vols. Moscow: Nauka, 1966–71.

Ivanovskaya, Polina. 'Staroye i novoye'. [Old and New]. **Teatr** 3 (1981).

——. 'Zhiviot takoy tiuz'. [Such Tiuz Lives]. **Teatr** 7 (1978).

Miagkova, I. 'Da ne pokochnetsia dom vash!' [May your home not totter!]. **Teatr** 6 (1992).

Rashid, Ahmed. **The resurgence of Central Asia**. London and New Jersey: Oxford University Press, Zed Books, 1994.

A3a145. UGANDA

Breitinger, Eckhard. 'Popular urban culture in Uganda'. **New Theatre Quarterly**, Vol. 8 (1992).

——. 'Theatre and political mobilisation: case studies from Uganda'. In **Southern African Writing: Voyages and Explorations**, ed.

Geoffrey V. Davis. Amsterdam and Atlanta: Rodopi, 1994. 226 p.

Carpenter, Peter. 'East and West: a brief review of theatre in Ghana and Uganda since 1960'. **Makerere Theatre Journal** 8 (1963): 35–9.

Cook, David. 'Theatre goes to the people: a report'. **Transition** 25, no. 2 (1966): 23–33.

Frank, Marion. **AIDS: education through theatre: case studies from Uganda**. Bayreuth: African Studies Series 35. University of Bayreuth. 205 p.

Horn, Andrew. 'Uganda's theatres: the exiled and the dead'. **Index on Censorship** 8, no. 5 (September–October 1979): 12–15.

——. 'Uhuru to Amin: The Golden Decade of Theatre in Uganda'. In **Essays in African Literature**, ed. H.H. Anniah Gowda, 22–49. Mysore, India: Centre for Commonwealth Literature and Research, 1978.

Mbowa, Rose. **Artists under siege: theatre and the dictatorial regimes in Uganda**. Kampala: Makerere University, 1994. *Notes*: Serumaga, Robert. Political aspects. Theatre and state.

——. 'Cultural Dualism in Ugandan Theatre Since Colonialism'. In **Contemporary Drama in English: Centres and Margins**, Vol. 2., ed. Bernhard Reitz, 163–73. Trier: Wissenschaft Verlag, 1994.

Senotongo, Nuwa. 'The role of theatre in adult education on Uganda'. **Makerere Adult Education Journal** 1, no. 1 (1977): 24–32.

A3a146. UKRAINE

Berezkin, Viktor. **Daniil Lider**. [Danylo Lider]. Kiev: Mystetstvo, 1988. 199 p.

Boboshko, Yuri. **Hnat Yura**. Kiev: Mystetstvo, 1980. 186 p.

——. **Rezhyser Les Kurbas**. Kiev: Mystetstvo, 1987. – 197 p., 24 p. of plates: ill. *Notes*: Includes bibliographical references. Theatrical and directors. Biography. Kurbas, Les, 1887–1942.

Chabanenko, Ivan. **Zapysky teatral'noho pedahoha: zbirnyk statei**. [Notebooks of the theatrical pedagogue: a collection of essays]. Kiev: Mystetstvo, 1980. 189 p.

Ciszkewycz, Ihor. **Transformation–a discovered form: Berezil theater, 1922–1934**. Thesis (Ph. D.)–Southern Illinois University at Carbondale, 1988. Photocopy. Ann Arbor, Mich.: University Microfilms, 1989. – viii, 329 p.: ill. *Notes*: Includes abstract and vita. Bibliography: p. 245–53. Ukrainian drama.

Kurbas, Les, 1887–1942. Criticism and interpretation.

Fialko, Valerii. **Rezhissura i stsenografiia: puti vzaimodeistviia**. Kiev: Mystetstvo, 1989. – 143 p.: ill. (some col.). *Notes*: Stage design. History. 20th century.

Grinshpun, Izakin. **O druz'iakh moikh i uchiteliakh**. Kiev: Mystetstvo, 1986. – 167 p. *Notes*: Includes bibliographical references. Theatrical producers and directors. Biography. Grinshpun, Izakin Abramovich.

Horbachov, Dmytro. **A.H. Petrytskyi. Radianskyi kbudozhnyk**. [A.H. Petrytskyi. Soviet artist]. Kiev: 1971. 152 p.

Kornienko, Nelli. **Teatr sohodni – Teatr zavtra**. [Theatre today – theatre tomorrow]. Kiev: Mystetstvo, 1986. 221 p.

Kovalenko, Georgiy. **Khudozhnyk teatra Daniil Lider**. [Theatre artist Danylo Lider]. Moscow: Iskusstvo, 1980. 199 p.

Kulish, Mykola. **Tvory v 2-x tomakh**. [Works in two volumes]. Kiev: Dnipro, 1990. Vol. 1, 508 p. Vol. 2, 874 p.

Kurbas, Les. **Les Kurbas: Staty i vospominaniia o. L. Kurbase. Literaturnoe nasledie**. [Les Kurbas: Articles and memoirs about L. Kurbas. Literary heritage]. Edited by Mykola Labinskyi and Les Taniuk. Foreword by Natalia Kuziakina. Moscow: Iskusstvo, 1987. 462 p.

——. **Les Kurbas: U teatralnii diialnosti, u otsinkakh suchasnykiv – documenty**. [Les Kurbas: Articles on theatre, essays by his contemporaries – documents]. Edited by Valerian Revutskyi. Compiled by Osyp Zinkewych. Baltimore, MD: Smoloskyp Publishers, 1989. 1,026 p.

——, Mykola Labins'kyi and IU Kosenko. **Molodyi teatr: heneza, zavdannia, shliakhy**. Kiev: Mystetstvo, 1991. – 316 p., 40 p. of plates: ill. *Notes*: Includes bibliographical references (p. 289–306) and index. Theatrical producers and directors. Kurbas, Les, 1887–1932. Molodyi teatr (Kiev, Ukraine). Writings of Kurbas and a study.

Kuziakina, Natalia. **Stanovlenie ukrainskoi sovetskoi rezhissury**. [The beginnings of Ukrainian Soviet theatre directing]. Leningrad: Leningradskii gosud. institut teatra, muzyki kinematograhii, 1984. 79 p.

——. **Ukrainska dramaturhiia pochatku 20 stolittia. Shliakhy onoalennia**. [Ukrainian dramaturgy in the beginning of the twentieth century. Directions of renewal]. Leningrad: Leningradskii gosud. institut teatra, muzyki I kinematograhii, 1984. 79 p.

Kyselov, Yosyp. **Dramaturhy Ukrainy**. [Play-wrights of Ukraine]. Kiev: Dnipro, 1967. 378 p.

Kysil, Oleksandr. **Ukrainsky teatr**. [Ukrainian theatre]. Edited by Pavlo Perepelytsia and Rostyslav Pylypchuk. Kiev: Mystetstvo, 1968. 258 p.

Onyshkevych, Larissa. **Existentialism in modern Ukrainian drama**. 1973. Thesis–University of Pennsylvania. Microfilm. Ann Arbor, Mich.: University Microfilms, 1974. 1 microfilm reel; 35 mm. – 154 p. *Notes*: Includes bibliographical references. Ukrainian drama. History and criticism.

Ostapenko, S.M. **Ukrains'kyi dramatychnyi teatr: rekomendatsiinyi bibliohrafichnyi pokazhchyk**. Kiev: DRBK, 1988. – 43 p. Ukraine. Bibliography.

Revutsky, Valerian and Osyp Zinkevych. **Les Kurbas: u teatral'nii diial'nosti, v otsinkakh suchasnykiv–dokumenty**. Baltimore: Ukr. vyd-vo Smoloskyp im. V. Symonenka, 1989. – 1026 p.: ill. *Notes*: Includes bibliographical references (p. 925–76). History. 20th century. Kurbas, Les, 1887–1942. Archives/Berezil' (Theatre).

Rulin, Petro. **Na shliakhakh revoliutsiinoho teatru**. [The direction of revolutionary theatre]. Edited by Pavlo Perepelytsia. Kiev: Mystetstvo, 1972. 354 p.

Shliakhy i problemy rozvythu ukrainskoho radianskoho teatru. [The directions and problems of the development of Ukrainian Soviet theatre]. Edited by M.K. Yosypenko. Kiev: Mystetstvo, 1970. 344 p.

Stanishevskyi, Yuri. **Baletnyi teatr Radianskoi Ukrainy**. [Ballet theatre of Soviet Ukraine]. Kiev: Muzychna Ukraina, 1986. 236 p.

——. **Internatsional'nyi pafos ukrains'koho radians'koho muzychnoho teatru: ohliad vystav za tvoramy kompozytoriv bratnikh respublik URSR**. [International pathos of the Ukrainian Soviet Musical Theatre: an overview of performances of works by composers from other Soviet Republics]. Kiev: Muzychna Ukraina, 1979. 156 p.

Taniuk, Les. **Marian Krushelnytskyi**. Moscow: Iskusstvo, 1974. 223 p.

——. **Monolohy: teatr, kultura, polityka**. Kharkov: Folio, 1994. – 382 p. *Notes*: Includes bibliographical references (p. 379–81). Theatre and society. Politics and government. 1917–.

Ukrainskyi dramatychnyi teatr. [Ukrainian dramatic theatre]. 2 vols. Vol. 1 Kiev: Naukova dumka, 1967. 518 p. Vol. 2 Kiev: Vydavnytstvo Akademii nauk URSR, 1959. 648 p.

Ukrajinska Avangarda 1910–1930. [Ukrainian avant-garde 1910–1930]. Exhibition catalogue. Zagreb, 1991. 144 p.

Verykivska, Iryna. **Stanovlennia ukraïns'koï radianskoï stsenohrafiï**. Kiev: Nauk. dumka, 1981. – 205 p.: ill. (some col.). *Notes*: Includes index. Bibliography: p. 198–201. Design. 20th century.

Volyts'ka, Iryna Vasylivna. **Teatral'na iunist' Lesia Kurbasa: (problema formuvannia tvorchoï osobystosti)**. L'viv: Instytut narodoznavstva NAN Ukraïny, 1995. – 149, [2] p.: ill. *Notes*: Theatrical producers and directors. Biography/Kurbas, Les', 1887–1942.

A3a147. UNITED ARAB EMIRATES

'Abd ul-Qadir, 'Abd ul-Ilah. **Al-Masrah Fi-l-Imaraat: Ru'ya Naqdiyya**. [The theatre in the Emirates: a critical examination]. Abu Dhabi: Far' Bin Dasmal Press, 1985. 160 p.

——. **Tarikh al-harakah al-masrahiyah fi Dawlat al-Imarat, 1960–1986**. al-Shariqah: Ittihad Kuttab wa-Udaba' al-Imarat, 1989. – 298 p.: ill. *Notes*: Includes bibliographical references. Arabic drama. 20th century. History and criticism. United Arab Emirates.

Duwaib, Rif'at Mohammed. **Kitaah Aghaani al-A'raas Min Dawlat al'Imaraat al'Arabiyyah al'Muttahida**. [Wedding songs from the United Arab Emirates]. Abu Dhabi: Ministry of Information and Culture, Kathim Press, 1982. 200 p.

George, Jose. 'The arrest and trial of Malay Indians in the United Arab Emirates'. **TDR** 38 no. 2 (1994): 138–49.

Jumm'a, Dha'in. **Karraas An al-Masrah al-Madrasi**. [School theatre in the UAE]. Abu Dhabi: National Press, 1985. 16 p.

Majallat Kulliyat al-Adaab Li Jami'at al-Imaraat. [Literature in the Emirates]. Dubai: 'al-Bayaan' Commercial Press for Emirates University. Since 1985.

Muhadaraat Al-Mawsam Ath-Thaqaafi Li Wizarat Al-I'laam Wa Th-Thaqaafa Munthu'l Aam 1971 Hatta Al-Aan. [Cultural lectures sponsored by the Ministry of Information and Culture since 1971]. Abu Dhabi: Ministry of Culture. Annual series.

An-Nuwais, Abdullah. **Kitaab al-I'laam Wa-t-Tanmiya**. [Cultural information and development in the UAE]. Abu Dhabi: Union Institute for Journalism, Publishing and Distribution, 1981.

Ohan, Farouk. 'Al-Ihtifaal al-Masrahi Fi Taqaleed Ar-Raqs Ash-Sha'bi: Raqsat al-Alayalah Fi al-Imaraat al-Arabiyyah al

Muttahida'. [Theatrical festivities in the traditions of popular dances: the 'ayala' dance in the United Arab Emirates]. **Majallat al Ma'thouraat as-Sha'biyya**. [Popular Legacies Magazine]. (January 1988): 41–61.

Taboor, Abdullah. **Al-Arabiyyah al-Muttahidah Bi-Imarat Ra's al-Khaimah**. [The theatrical movement in Ras al-Khaimah]. Ras al-Khaimah: Nakheel Press, 1985.

Thani, Ahmad Rashid. **Al-Masrah fi al-Imarat: al-hadir as-al-mustaqbal** [al-Shariqah]: Da'irat al-Thaqafah wa-al-I'lam, Hukumat al-Shariqah, Dawlat al-Imarat al-'Arabiyah al-Muttahidah, 1994. 213 p.

A3a148. UNITED KINGDOM

Acheson, James. **British and Irish drama since 1960**. New York: St. Martin's Press, 1993. – x, 230 p. *Notes*: Includes bibliographical references and index. 'The absolute absence of the absolute': the theory and practice of Samuel Beckett's drama/James Acheson – Pinter and the pinteresque/John Fletcher – Revitalised ritual and theatrical flair: the plays of Peter Shaffer/William Hutchings – Mirrors of Utopia: Caryl Churchill and Joint Stock/Frances Gray – Casting the audience: theatricality in the stage plays of Peter Nichols/Andrew Parkin – Translations of history: story-telling in Brian Friel's theatre/Katharine Worth – Tom Murphy: acts of faith in a godless world/Richard Allen Cave – Edward Bond: a political education/Anthony Jenkins – Stoppard's theatre of unknowing/Mary A. Doll – Making history: the plays of Howard Brenton/Hersh Zeifman – Forgiving history and making new worlds: Timberlake Wertenbaker's recent drama/Ann Wilson – Freedom and form in David Hare's drama/James Gindin – Honouring the audience: the theatre of Howard Barker/Robert Wilcher – The plays of Pam Gems: personal/ political/personal/Katherine H. Burkman – Postmodern classics: the verse drama of Tony Harrison/Romana Huk. English and Irish drama.

Aldgate, Anthony. **Censorship and the permissive society: British cinema and theatre, 1955–1965**. Oxford and New York: Oxford University Press, 1995. – viii, 171 p.: ill. *Notes*: Includes bibliographical references (p. 157–68) and index. Theatre censorship.

Ansorge, Peter. **Disrupting the spectacle: five years of experimental and fringe theatre in Britain**. London: Pitman, 1975. 87 p.

Banks, Morwenna and Amanda Swift. **The joke's on us: women in comedy from music hall to the present day**. London: Pandora, 1987. – ix, 294 p.: ill. *Notes*: Includes bibliographical references (p. 281–5) and index. Women in the theatre. 1850–1986.

Barnes, Philip. **Companion to post-war British theatre**. London: Croom Helm, 1986. 288 p.

Bate, Jonathan and Russell Jackson. **Shakespeare: an illustrated stage history**. Oxford and New York: Oxford University Press, 1996. – xiii, 253 p.: ill. *Notes*: Includes bibliographical references (p. 231–45) and index. Shakespeare's Elizabethan stages/R.A. Foakes – The king's men and after/Martin Wiggins – Improving on the original: actresses and adaptations/Michael Dobson – The age of Garrick/Peter Holland – The Romantic stage/Jonathan Bate – Actor-managers and the spectacular/Russell Jackson – European cross-currents: Ibsen and Brecht/Inga-Stina Ewbank – From the Old Vic to Gielgud and Olivier/Anthony Davies – Shakespeare and the public purse/Peter Thomson – Director's Shakespeare/Robert Smallwood – A career in Shakespeare/Judi Dench – Shakespeare in opposition: from the 1950s to the 1990s/Russell Jackson.

Belsey, Catherine. **Critical practice**. London: Methuen, 1980.

Bergan, Ronald. **The great theatres of London: an illustrated companion**. San Francisco: Chronicle Books, 1988. 200 p.: ill. (chiefly col.). *Notes*: Includes index. London (England). History.

Bigsby, C.W.E. **Contemporary English drama**. New York: Holmes & Meier, 1981. – 192 p. *Notes*: Includes bibliographical references and index. The language of crisis in British theatre/C.W.E. Bigsby – Whatever happened to John Osborne?/Arnold P. Hinchliffe – Articulacy and awareness: the modulation of familiar themes in Wesker's plays of the 70s/Glenda Leeming – Harold Pinter's idiom of lies/Guido Almansi – Joe Orton: the comedy of (ill) manners/Martin Esslin – Tom Stoppard: light drama and dirges in marriage/Ruby Cohn – Edward Bond's Dramatic strategies/Jenny S. Spencer – The Court and its favours/Julian Hilton – Three socialist playwrights: John McGrath, Caryl Churchill, Trevor Griffiths/Christian W. Thomsen – Art and commerce: the new drama in the West End marketplace/John Russell Taylor. History and criticism.

Billington, Michael. **One night stands: a critic's view of modern British theatre**. London: Nick Hern, 1995, 1993. – xv, 382 p. *Notes*: Includes index.

——. **Peggy Ashcroft**. London: Mandarin, 1989, 1988. – 324 p.: ill. *Notes*: Originally published: London: Murray, 1988. Includes index. Biography. Ashcroft, Peggy.

Branagh, Kenneth. **Beginning**. London: Chatto & Windus, 1989. – x, 244 p.: ill. *Notes*: Autobiography/Branagh, Kenneth/Renaissance Theatre Company.

Brown, John Russell. **Modern British dramatists, new perspectives**. Englewood Cliffs, N.J.: Prentice-Hall, 1984. – 186 p. *Notes*: Includes index. Bibliography: p. 181–3. Drama in English, 1945–78 – Critical studies.

Bull, John. **New British political dramatists: Howard Brenton, David Hare, Trevor Griffiths, and David Edgar**. London: Macmillan, 1991 1984. – xix, 244 p., 12 p. of plates: ill. *Notes*: Includes index. Bibliography: p. 232–8. History and criticism.

——. **Stage right: crisis and recovery in British contemporary mainstream theatre**. New York: St. Martin's Press, 1994. – xx, 251 p. *Notes*: Includes bibliographical references (p. 227–42) and index. English drama.

Cabochel, L. **Le Théâtre en Grande-Bretagne pendant la seconde guerre mondiale**. [Theatre in Britain during World War II]. Paris: Didier, 1969. 409 p.

Cavanagh, John P. **British theatre: a bibliography, 1901 to 1985**. Mottisfont, Hampshire, England: Motley Press, 1989. – 510 p. *Notes*: Includes indexes. English drama.

Cave, Richard Allen. **New British drama in performance on the London stage, 1970 to 1985**. New York: St. Martin's Press, 1988. – xii, 322 p. *Notes*: Includes index. Bibliography: p. 315–16. History and criticism.

Chambers, Colin. **Other spaces**. London: Methuen, 1980.

Colby, Douglas. **As the curtain rises: on contemporary British drama, 1966–1976**. Rutherford, N.J.: Fairleigh Dickinson University Press, 1978. – 103 p.: ill. *Notes*: Bibliography: p. 100–3. Stoppard, Tom. Hampton, Christopher. Pinter, Harold.

Cook, Judith. **Directors' theatre: sixteen leading directors on the state of theatre in Britain today**. London: Hodder and Stoughton, 1989. – 157 p.

Coveney, Michael. **The Citz: 21 years of the Glasgow Citizens Theatre**. London: Nick Hern Books, 1990. – xi, 308 p.: ill. *Notes*: Includes bibliographical references (p. 297–8) and index. Citizens' Theatre (Glasgow). History.

Craig, Sandy. **Dreams and deconstructions: alternative theatre in Britain**. Ambergate, Derbyshire: Amber Lane Press, 1980. – 192 p.: ill. *Notes*: Includes index. Bibliography: p. 187.

20th century/Experimental theatre. Great Britain.

Davies, Andrew. **Other theatres**. London: Methuen, 1987.

De Jongh, Nicholas. **Not in front of the audience: homosexuality on stage**. London; New York: Routledge, 1992. – xiv, 214 p., [8] p. of plates: ill. *Notes*: Includes bibliographical references (p. 201–4) and index. Theatre. History/London and New York.

Demastes, William W. **British playwrights, 1956–1995: a research and production sourcebook**. Westport, Conn.: Greenwood Press, 1996. – xi, 502 p. *Notes*: Includes bibliographical references (p. 461–3) and indexes. English drama. History and criticism.

Devlin, Vivien. **Kings, queens, and people's palaces: an oral history of the Scottish variety theatre, 1920–1970**. Edinburgh: Polygon, 1991. – 233 p.: ill. *Notes*: Includes bibliographical references (p. 204). Music-halls (Variety-theatres, cabarets, etc.). Interviews.

DiCenzo, Maria. **The politics of alternative theatre in Britain, 1968–1990: the case of 7:84 (Scotland)**. Cambridge; New York: Cambridge University Press, 1996. – xiv, 247 p.: ill. *Notes*: Includes bibliographical references (p. 228–37) and index. History.

Eddershaw, Margaret. **Performing Brecht**. New York: Routledge, 1996. – x, 188 p. *Notes*: Includes bibliographical references (p. 178–80) and index. Stage history. Great Britain.

Elsom, John. **Cold War theatre**. London: Routledge, 1992.

——. **Post-war British theatre**. Revised paperback edn. London: Routledge & Kegan Paul, 1979. – viii, 232 p., 4 p. of plates: ill. *Notes*: Includes index. History and criticism.

——. **Post-war British theatre criticism**. London: Routledge & Kegan Paul, 1978.

——, and Nicholas Tomalin. **The history of the National Theatre**. London: Cape, 1978.

Findlater, R. **Banned: a review of theatrical censorship in Britain**. London: MacGibbon & Kee, 1967. 238 p.

Havergal, Giles. **Choosing a play: the conditions of artistic choice at the Citizens' Theatre, Glasgow, 1969–1985**. Dundee: Lochee, 1987. – 20 p. *Notes*: Citizens' Theatre. History.

Hayman, Ronald. **British drama since 1970: an introductory bibliography**. London: British Council, 1990. – 14 p.; 21cm. *Notes*: English drama. 20th century.

Hinchliffe, Arnold. **British theatre, 1950–1970**. Oxford: Basil Blackwell, 1974. 205 p.

Holland, Peter. **English Shakespeares: Shakespeare on the English stage in the 1990's**. Cambridge: Cambridge University Press, 1997. – xv, 295 p.: ill. *Notes*: Includes bibliographical references and index. Stage history.

Hunt, H., K. Richards, and J.R. Taylor. **The Revels history of drama in English**. Vol. II: 1880 to the Present Day. London: Methuen, 1978. 297 p.

Innes, C.D. **Modern British drama, 1890–1990**. Cambridge [England]; New York: Cambridge University Press, 1992. – xxiii, 484 p.: ill. *Notes*: Includes bibliographical references and index. Defining British drama – Patterns of development and organizing principles – Critical treatment – Arthur Pinero: the problem play versus the new realism – Reinterpretation of Ibsen – Refurbishing nineteenth-century styles – Thesis drama and metaphysical comedy – Symbolism and politics – Shavian influences and the question of censorship – Intellectual drama versus public theatre: Granville-Barker and John Galsworthy – Realism versus Agitprop: D.H. Lawrence and the Workers' Theatre Movement – Sean O'Casey: expressive realism and the imagery of politics– Terence Rattigan: updating the well-made play – John Osborne: the rhetoric of social alienation – Arnold Wesker: utopian realism – Brechtian influences: epic stagecraft and British equivalents. John Arden: the popular tradition and epic alternatives – Edward Bond: rationalism, realism and radical solutions – David Edgar: from Agitprop to socialist realism – Howard Brenton and David Hare: utopian perspectives on modern history – Oscar Wilde: paradoxical fantasy and moral subversion – John Synge: satiric artifice and critical realism – Somerset Maugham: popular comedy versus social criticism – Noel Coward: comedy as social image – Ben Travers: society as farce – Joe Orton: farce as confrontation – Harold Pinter: power plays and the trap of comedy – Politics and comedy: Peter Barnes and Trevor Griffiths – Traditionalism and theatricality: Alan Ayckbourn and Michael Frayn – Tom Stoppard: theatricality and the comedy of ideas – Rejection of society: J.M. Barrie versus Wilde's Salomé – W.B. Yeats: theatre of the mind – J.B. Priestley: temporal dislocation and transcendence – Expressionistic archetypes: W.H. Auden and Christopher Isherwood. T.S. Eliot: the drama of conversion – Appealing to the popular imagination: Christopher Fry and Peter Shaffer – Apocalyptic visions and Artaudian theatre: John Whiting and David Rudkin – Samuel Beckett: interior space and play as image – Early groups and feminist principles – Pam Gems: reinterpreting the stereotype – Caryl Churchill: theatre as a model for change.

Itzin, Catherine. **Stages in the revolution: political theatre in Britain since 1968**. London: Eyre Methuen, 1980. – xv, 399 p. *Notes*: Includes index. Bibliography: p. 390–92. Political and avant-garde theatre by a former editor of *Theatre Quarterly*.

Kershaw, Baz. **The politics of performance: radical theatre as cultural intervention**. London; New York: Routledge, 1992. – 281 p. *Notes*: Includes bibliographical references (p. 259–65) and index. Political aspects. Theatre and society.

King, Kimball. **Twenty modern British playwrights: a bibliography, 1956–1976**. New York: Garland Publishing, Inc., 1977. – [i–xiv], 1–289 [1] p.; 21.5 cm. *Notes*: Arden.–Alan Ayckbourn.–Peter Barnes.–Robert Bolt.–Edward Bond.–Simon Gray.–Christopher Hampton.–Ann Jellicoe.–Peter Nichols.–Joe Orton.–John Osborne.–Harold Pinter.–Anthony Shaffer.–Peter Shaffer.–N.F. Simpson.–Tom Stoppard.–David Storey.–Arnold Wesker.–Heathcote Williams.–Charles Wood.

Klein, Dennis A. **Peter and Anthony Shaffer, a reference guide**. Boston, MA: G.K. Hall, 1982. – xi, 110 p. *Notes*: Includes indexes. Shaffer, Peter, 1926–. Shaffer, A. (Anthony), 1926–. Bibliography.

Lacey, Stephen. **British realist theatre: the new wave in its context 1956–1965**. London; New York: Routledge, 1995. – ix, 206 p. *Notes*: Includes bibliographical references (p. 192–201) and index.

Lamb, Charles. **Howard Barkers's theatre of seduction**. Netherlands: Harwood Academic Publishers, 1997. – xii, 153 p.: ill. *Notes*: Includes bibliographical references (p. 145–8) and index. English drama. Criticism and interpretation.

Lawson, Robb. **The story of the Scots Stage**. New York: B. Blom, 1971. 303 p.

Lewis, Peter. **The National: a dream made concrete**. London: Methuen, 1990. – 245 p.: ill. *Notes*: Includes bibliographical references (p. 234–5) and index. History of the National Theatre.

Lloyd Evans, Gareth and Barbara Lloyd. **Plays in review, 1956–1980: British drama and the critics**. London: Batsford Academic and Educational, 1985. – 257 p. *Notes*: Reviews.

MacLennan, Elizabeth. **The moon belongs to everyone: making theatre with 7:84**. London:

Methuen, 1990. – viii, 214 p.: ill. *Notes*: Includes index. Company. History/7:84 Scotland.

Marowitz, Charles. **Burnt bridges: a souvenir of the swinging sixties and beyond**. London: Hodder & Stoughton, 1990. – 245 p.: ill. *Notes*: Includes index. Autobiography. American director recalls his years in England and his experiments at the Open Space.

—— and Simon Trussler. **Theatre at work: playwrights and productions in the modern British theatre: a collection of interviews and essays**. London: Methuen, 1967. – 191 p. English drama. History and criticism.

McGrath, John. **A good night out: popular theatre: audience, class, and form**. 2nd edn. London: Nick Hern Books, 1996. – xvi, 126 p. Theatre and society. Political aspects.

Meyer, Michael. **Not Prince Hamlet: literary and theatrical memoirs**. London: Secker & Warburg, 1989. – xii, 291 p., 16 p. of plates: ill. *Notes*: Includes index. Meyer, Michael, 1921–. Translator of Ibsen and Strindberg recalls his life in art.

Mikhail, E.H. **Contemporary British drama 1950–1976: an annotated critical bibliography**. Totowa, NJ: Rowman & Littlefield, 1977.

Miles, Patrick. **Chekhov on the British stage**. New York, NY: Cambridge Univ. Press, 1993. – xii, 258 p.: ill. *Notes*: Includes index. Chekhov on the British stage: differences/John Russell Brown – The 'inevitability' of Chekhov: Anglo-Russian theatrical contacts in the 1910s/Aleksey Bartoshevich – Chekhov, naturalism and the drama of dissent: productions of Chekhov's plays in Britain before 1914/Jan McDonald – Bernard Shaw's dialogue with Chekhov/Anna Obraztsova – Coping with the outlandish: the English response to Chekhov's plays 1911–1926/Stephen le Fleming – Komisarjevsky's 1926 Three sisters/Robert Tracy – Peggy Ashcroft and Chekhov/Gordon McVay – Far from the West End: Chekhov and the Welsh language stage 1924–1991/W. Gareth Jones – Chekhov re-viewed: the Moscow Art Theatre's visits to Britain in 1958, 1964, and 1970/Cynthia Marsh – A path to Chekhov/Oleg Yefremov – Subsequent performances: Chekhov/Jonathan Miller – The 'dwindling scale': the politics of British Chekhov/Vera Gottlieb. The cherry orchard: a new English version by Trevor Griffiths/David Allen – Changes of direction: Mike Alfreds' methods with Chekhov/Stuart Young – Chekhov and the company problem in the British theatre/Patrick Miles – Design for Chekhov/Arnold Aronson – My search for standards as a translator of Chekhov's plays/Ariadne Nicolaeff – Chekhov into English: the case of The seagull/Richard Peace – English translations of Chekhov's plays: a Russian view/Valentina Ryapolova – Appendix: A chronology of British professional productions of Chekhov's plays 1909–91/Patrick Miles and Stuart Young.

Moore-Gilbert, B.J. **The Arts in the 1970s: cultural closure?** London; New York: Routledge, 1994. – viii, 312 p. *Notes*: Includes bibliographical references and index. Introduction: cultural closure or post-avantgardism?/Bart Moore-Gilbert – The politics of culture: institutional change in the 1970s/Stuart Laing – The impact of radical theory on Britain in the 1970s/Antony Easthope – Cultural devolution? Representing Scotland in the 1970s/Willy Maley – Finding a voice: feminism and theatre in the 1970s/Elaine Aston – Artifice and the everyday world: poetry in the 1970s/Robert Sheppard – Apocalypse now? The novel in the 1970s/Bart Moore-Gilbert – Boxed in: television in the 1970s/Garry Whannel – Stepping out of line: British 'new dance' in the 1970s/Judith Mackrell – A diversity of film practices: renewing British cinema in the 1970s/Andrew Higson – Blood on the tracks: popular music in the 1970s/Dave Harker – 'Is it possible for me to do nothing as my contribution?' Visual art in the 1970s/Stuart Sillars – Up against the wall: drama in the 1970s/Martin Priestman. Arts and society. Great Britain.

Morley, Sheridan. **Shooting stars: plays and players 1975–1983**. London; New York: Quartet Books, 1983. – xv, 383 p.: ill. *Notes*: Includes index.

Mulryne, J.R. and Margaret Shewring. **Making space for theatre: British architecture and theatre since 1958**. Stratford-upon-Avon: Mulryne and Shewring, 1995. – 192 p.: ill. (some col.); 24 x. *Notes*: Conservation and restoration.

Page, Adrian. **The death of the playwright?: modern British drama and literary theory**. Houndmills, Basingstoke: Macmillan, 1992. – x, 212 p. *Notes*: Includes bibliographical references (p. 208–9) and index. Word made flesh: women and theatre – Popular drama and realism: the case of television – Shelagh Delaney's A Taste of honey as serious text: a semiotic reading – Eye of judgment: Samuel Beckett's Later drama – Bakhtin, Foucault, Beckett, Pinter – Forms of dissent in contemporary drama and contemporary theory – Age of surfaces: Joe Orton's Drama and postmodernism – Plays of Caryl Churchill: essays in refusal – Staging the other.

Palmer, Richard H. **The contemporary British**

history play. Westport, Conn: Greenwood Press, 1998. 272 p. *Notes*: Includes bibliographical references and index. Historical drama.

Peacock, D. Keith. **Harold Pinter and the new British theatre**. Westport, Conn.; London: Greenwood Press, 1997. – xvi, 227 p.: ill.; 24cm. *Notes*: Includes index. Bibliography: p. 215–19. Pinter, Harold, 1930–. Criticism and interpretation.

——. **Radical stages: alternative history in modern British drama**. New York: Greenwood Press, 1991. – 202 p. *Notes*: Includes bibliographical references (p. 192–8) and index. Historical drama, English.

Rabey, David Ian. **British and Irish political drama in the twentieth century: implicating the audience**. New York: St. Martin's Press, 1986. – x, 237 p. *Notes*: Includes index. Bibliography: p. 216–32. History and criticism.

Roberts, Peter and Donald Cooper. **The Best of Plays and Players, 1968–1986**. London: Methuen; HEB, Inc., 1989. – 272 p.: ill. *Notes*: Includes index. Essays and other material from the popular theatre monthly.

Roberts, Peter and Zoë Dominic. **The Best of Plays and Players, 1953–1968**. London: Methuen, 1988. – 253 p.: ill. *Notes*: Includes index.

Rosenfeld, Sybil Marion. **A short history of scene design in Great Britain**. Oxford: Blackwell, 1973. – xviii, 214 p.: ill. *Notes*: Includes index. Bibliography: p. 198–205.

Sanderson, Michael. **From Irving to Olivier: a social history of the acting profession in England, 1880–1983**. London: New York: Athlone Press; St. Martin's Press, 1984. – xii, 375 p., 8 p. of plates: ill. *Notes*: Includes index. Bibliography: p. 336–51.

Shank, Theodore. **Contemporary British theatre**. New York: St. Martin's Press, 1993. – xi, 243 p.: ill. *Notes*: Includes index. The multiplicity of British theatre/Theodore Shank – Sated, starved or satisfied: the languages of theatre in Britain today/Tony Dunn – Digging the Greeks: new versions of old classics/Ruby Cohn – Cultural transformations/Jatinder Verma – Edward Bond and the Royal National Theatre/Ian Stuart – Spread a little happiness: West End musicals/Sheridan Morley – Breaking the boundaries: The People Show, Lumiere & Son and Hesitate and Demonstrate/Lynn Sobieski – Diverse assembly: some trends in recent performance/Tim Etchells – Experimental theatre in Scotland/Alasdair Cameron – The Welsh National Theatre: the Avant-garde in the Diaspora/David Hughes – LIFTing the theatre: the London International Festival of Theatre/Claire Armitstead – The electronic media and British drama/Martin Esslin – The playwriting profession: setting out and the journey/Theodore Shank – Directors: the new generation/Jane Edwardes – Recent tendencies in design/Matt Wolf.

Southern, Richard. **Changeable scenery: its origin and development in the British theatre**. London: Faber & Faber, 1982, 1952. – 411 p., 36 p. of plates: ill. *Notes*: Includes bibliographical references and index. Stage-setting and scenery.

Steinberg, Micheline. **Flashback: a pictorial history, 1879–1979: one hundred years of Stratford-upon Avon and the Royal Shakespeare Company**. Stratford-upon-Avon: RSC Publications, 1985. – 126 p.: chiefly ill. (some col.), 21 x. *Notes*: Includes index. Royal Shakespeare Company. History.

Stevenson, Randall and Gavin Wallace. **Scottish theatre since the seventies**. Edinburgh: Edinburgh University Press, 1996. – vi, 240 p. *Notes*: Includes bibliographical references and index.

Stoll, Karl-Heinz. **The new British drama: a bibliography with particular reference to Arden, Bond, Osborne, Pinter, Wesker**. Bern and Frankfurt/M.: Lang, 1975. – 94 p.

Stuart, Ian. **Politics in performance: the production work of Edward Bond, 1978–1990**. New York: P. Lang, 1996. – 191 p. *Notes*: Includes bibliographical references (p. 177–85) and index. History and criticism. Stage history.

Taylor, John Russell. **Anger and after: a guide to the new British drama**. London: Eyre Methuen, 1977. – 391 p. 8 p. of plates: ill. *Notes*: Includes index. History and criticism.

——. **The second wave**. London: Methuen, 1971. 236 p.

Thorpe, Matilda. **Stage struck**. London: Hodder & Stoughton, 1990.

Trussler, Simon. **The Cambridge illustrated history of British theatre**. Cambridge and New York: Cambridge University Press, 1994. – xii, 404 p.: ill. *Notes*: Includes bibliographical references (p. 396–9) and index. Roman Britain and the early Middle Ages 44–950 – The high Middle Ages 950–1300 – The later Middle Ages 1300–1485 – The shaping of a professional theatre 1485–1572 – The era of the outdoor playhouses 1572–1603 – The Jacobean theatre 1603–1625 – The Caroline and Commonwealth theatre 1625–1660 – The Restoration theatre 1660–1682 – The birth of a bourgeois theatre

1682–1707 – The actors ascendant 1707–1728 – Opposition and oppression 1728–1741 – The Garrick years 1741–1776 – From manners to melodrama 1776–1814 – The end of the monopoly 1814–1843 – Towards a respectable theatre 1843–1871 – The speculative theatre 1871–1891 – Romance and realism 1891–1914 – The war and the long weekend 1914–1939 – The utility theatre 1939–1956 – Anger and affluence 1956–1968 – Alternative theatres 1968–1979 – Theatre and the marketplace 1979–1990.

——. **New theatre voices of the seventies: sixteen interviews from Theatre Quarterly, 1970–1980**. London; New York: Methuen, 1986 1981. – xvi, 200 p. *Notes:* Reprint. Originally pubished: London: Eyre Methuen, 1981. Includes index. Dramatists. Directors.

——, ed. **Political developments on the British stage in the sixties and seventies: symposium of September 17/18, 1976 at the University of Rostock**. Rostock: Wilhelm-Pieck-University, 1977. 135 p.

Tushingham, David. **Food for the soul: a new generation of British theatremakers**. London: Methuen, 1994. – 136 p. *Notes:* Theatrical producers and directors.

Tynan, Kenneth. **The life of Kenneth Tynan**. London: Phoenix, 1995 1987. – x, 467 p., 24 p. of plates: ill. *Notes:* Originally published: London: Weidenfeld & Nicolson, 1987. Includes index. Tynan, Kenneth, 1927–80. Biography.

——. **He that plays the king; a view of the theatre**. London, New York: Longmans, Green, 1950. – 256 p. *Notes:* Drama criticism.

——. **A view of the English stage, 1944–1965**. London: Methuen, 1984 1975. – 386 p. *Notes:* Originally published: London: Davis-Poynter, 1975. Includes index. Performances, 1944–63.

Vinson, James, ed. **Contemporary dramatists**. London: Macmillan, 1982.

Wardle, Irving. **The theatres of George Devine**. London: Eyre Methuen, 1979. – xvi, 295 p., 4 p. of plates: ill. *Notes:* Includes index. Bibliography: p. 287. Theatrical producers and directors. Biography/Devine, George, 1910–1966/ English Stage Company.

Weintraub, Stanley. **British dramatists since World War II**. Detroit, Mich.: Gale Research Co., 1982. – 2 vols.: ill. v. pt. 1. A–L – pt. 2. M–Z.

Wike, Jonathan. **John Arden and Margaretta D'Arcy: a casebook**. New York: Garland, 1995. – xvi, 264 p. *Notes:* Includes bibliographical references (p. 245–51) and index. English drama. History and criticism.

Wilmeth, Don B. **American and English popular entertainment: a guide to information sources**. Detroit: Gale Research Co., 1980. – xviii, 465 p. *Notes:* Includes indexes. United States. Great Britain. Popular culture. Bibliography.

Wilson, Sheila. **The theatre of the fifties**. London: Library Association, 1963.

Woddis, Carole and Trevor Griffiths. **Bloomsbury theatre guide**. London: Bloomsbury, 1988.

Zeifman, Hersh and Cynthia Zimmerman. **Contemporary British drama, 1970–90: essays from Modern Drama**. Toronto: University of Toronto Press, 1993. – xiii, 348 p. *Notes:* Includes bibliographical references (p. 338–43) and index.

A3a149. UNITED STATES OF AMERICA

Adler, Thomas P. **American drama, 1940–1960: a critical history**. New York: Twayne Publishers, 1994. – xii, 251 p.: ill. *Notes:* Includes bibliographical references (p. 228–42) and index. Setting the stage: America at war and at peace – Eugene O'Neill: 'Faithful realism' with a poet's touch – Lillian Hellman: The conscience of the culture – Arthur Miller: Fathers and sons, society and the self – William Inge: The terms of diminishment – Other voices of the '50's: Marching to different drummers – Tennessee Williams in the 1940's and 1950's: Artist of the fugitive kind – Tennessee Williams in the 1960's and 1970's: Death and the artist – Lorraine Hansberry: Exploring dreams, explosive drama – From the margins: Edward Albee and the avant-garde.

The American actor. New Haven, Conn.: Yale School of Drama, 1977. – 177 p.: ill. A special issue of the journal **Yale/Theatre** (vol. 8, nos 2 and 3).

American Federation of Arts. **The ideal theatre: eight concepts**. New York: American Federation of Arts, 1962. 142 p.

Appelbaum, Stanley. **Great actors and actresses of the American stage in historic photographs: 332 portraits from 1850 to 1950**. New York: Dover Publications, 1983. 136 p.: ill. *Notes:* Includes index.

Atkinson, Brooks. **Broadway**. New York: Limelight Editions, 1990, 1974. – ix, 564 p.: ill. *Notes:* Includes index. Story of Broadway by the former critic of the **New York Times**.

Auslander, Philip. **Presence and resistance: postmodernism and cultural politics in contemporary American performance**. Ann Arbor:

University of Michigan Press, 1994. – viii, 206 p.: ill. *Notes*: Includes bibliographical references (p. 175–97) and index. Performance art. Arts and society.

Bentley, Eric. **Are you now or have you ever been; the investigation of show business by the Un-American Activities Committee, 1947–1958**. New York: Harper & Row, 1972. – xix, 160 p. *Notes*: Dramatization of selections from the Hearings of the Committee. Black-listing of entertainers.

——. **The dramatic event, an American chronicle**. London: D. Dobson, 1956, 1954. 278 p. Drama. History and criticism.

——. **What is theatre?: incorporating The dramatic event, and other reviews**. New York: Limelight Editions, 1984, 1968. – xvi, 491 p. *Notes*: Originally published: New York: Atheneum, 1968. Includes index. Reviews.

Berkowitz, Gerald M. **New Broadways: theater across America: approaching a new millennium**. New York: Applause, 1997. – ix, 269 p.: ill. *Notes*: Includes bibliographical references (p. 243–9) and index. Regional theatres.

Berney, Kathryn Ann and N.G. Templeton. **Contemporary American dramatists**. London and Detroit: St. James Press, 1994. – xxvi, 771 p.

Bigsby, C.W.E. **Confrontation and commitment: a study of contemporary American drama 1959–66**. London: MacGibbon & Kee, 1967. 187 p.

——. **A critical introduction to twentieth-century American drama**. Cambridge and New York: Cambridge University Press, 1982 1985. – 3 vols: ill. *Notes*: Includes bibliographies and indexes. 1. 1900–1940 – 2. Tennessee Williams, Arthur Miller, Edward Albee – 3. Beyond Broadway. History and criticism.

——. **Modern American drama, 1945–1990**. Cambridge and New York: Cambridge University Press, 1994 1992. – ix, 362 p. *Notes*: Includes bibliographical references (p. 342–54) and index. The absent voice: American drama and the critic – Eugene O'Neill's Endgame – Tennessee Williams: the theatricalising self – Arthur Miller: the moral imperative – Edward Albee: journey to apocalypse – A Broadway interlude – Sam Shepard: imagining America – David Mamet: all true stories – The performing self – Redefining the centre: politics, race, gender. History and criticism.

Biner, Pierre. **The living theater**. New York: Avon, 1972. 256 p.

Bloom, Thomas Alan. **Kenneth Macgowan and the aesthetic paradigm for the new stagecraft in America**. New York: P. Lang, 1996. – xii, 184 p.: ill. *Notes*: Includes bibliographical references (p. 171–7) and index. Experimental theatre. Macgowan, Kenneth, 1888–1963.

Bordman, Gerald Martin. **The Oxford companion to American theatre**. 2nd edn. New York: Oxford University Press, 1992. viii, 735 p.

Branch, William. **Black thunder**. New York: Mento, 1992. 520 p.

Brecht, Stefan. **The original theater of the City of New York: from the mid-60s to the mid-70s**. New York: Suhrkamp, 1978. – 2 vols.: ill. *Notes*: v. 1 The theatre of visions: Robert Wilson – v. 2. Queer theatre. History and criticism. **Queer Theatre** subsequently published by Methuen, 1986. – 178 p.: ill.

Brockett, Oscar. **The essential theater**. 4th edn. New York: Holt, Rinehart & Winston, 1988. – 447 p., 8 p. of plates: ill. (some col.). *Notes*: Includes index. Bibliography: p. 419–30. Theatre. History.

Brown-Guillory, Elizabeth. **Their place on the stage: Black women playwrights in America**. New York: Praeger, 1990. – xiv, 163 p. *Notes*: Includes bibliographical references (153–8) and index. Afro-American authors. History and criticism.

Brustein, Robert. **Dumbocracy in America: studies in the theater of guilt, 1987–1994**. Chicago: Dee, 1995. – 276 p. *Notes*: Includes index. History and criticism.

——. **Making scenes: a personal history of the turbulent years at Yale, 1966–1979**. New York: Limelight Editions, 1984 1981. – viii, 341 p., [16] p. of plates: ill. *Notes*: Reprint. Originally published in New York: Random House, 1981. Includes index. American theatre criticism by the former Dean of the Yale Drama school.

——. **Reimagining American theater**. Chicago: I.R. Dee, 1992 1991. – xi, 307 p. *Notes*: Originally published: New York: Hill & Wang, 1991. Includes index. History and criticism.

——. **Who needs theater: dramatic opinions**. New York: Atlantic Monthly Press, 1987. 320 p.

Clum, John M. **Acting gay: male homosexuality in modern drama**. New York: Columbia University Press, 1994. – xxii, 381 p.: ill. *Notes*: Includes bibliographical references (p. 361–71) and index. History and criticism.

Clurman, Harold. **The fervent years**. New York: Hill & Wang, 1957. 304 p.

Cohn, Ruby. **Dialogue in American drama**.

Bloomington, IN: Indiana University Press, 1971. 340 p.

———. **New American dramatists, 1960–1990**. New York: St. Martin's Press, 1991. – ix, 184 p.: ill. *Notes*: Looking forward – Broadway bound: Simon, Kopit, McNally, Wilson – Roaming around: Ribman, Rabe, Guare, Hwang – Ladies' day: Owens, Howe, Henley, Norman – Actor-activated: Gelber, Horovitz, van Itallie, Terry, Fornes – Agit-prop and political purpose: the Becks, Holden, Valdez, Nelson – Black on black: Childress, Baraka, Bullins, Kennedy – From gay to ridiculous: Duberman, Patrick, Tavel, Bernard, Ludlam – Visuals and visions: Foreman, Breuer – Eloquent energies: Mamet, Shepard.

Elam, Harry. **Taking it to the streets: the social protest theater of Luis Valdez and Amiri Baraka**. Ann Arbor: University of Michigan Press, 1997. – xi, 187 p.: ill. *Notes*: Includes bibliographical references (p. 167–75) and index. Workers' theater. California/Mexican American theater. Baraka, Imamu Amiri, 1934–. Criticism and interpretation/Teatro Camposino.

Elder, Eldon. **Will it make a theater?**. New York: American Council for the Arts, 1993. 248 p.

Epstein, Helen. **Joe Papp: an American life**. New York: Da Capo, 1996 1994. – vi, 554 p.: ill. *Notes*: Originally published: Boston: Little, Brown, c1994. Includes bibliographical references (p. 479–97) and index. Biographical study of a major American director.

Ewen, David. **Complete book of the American musical theater; a guide to more than 300 productions of the American musical theater from The black crook (1866) to the present**. New York: Holt, Rinehart & Winston, 1968, 1959. – 447 p. illus. *Notes*: United States/Musicals. Stories, plots, etc.

Falk, Doris V. **Lillian Hellman**. New York: Ungar, 1978. – ix, 180 p. *Notes*: Includes index. Bibliography: p. 166–70. Hellman, Lillian, 1907–84. Critical studies.

Feinsod, Arthur. **The simple stage: its origins in the modern American theater**. New York: Greenwood Press, 1992. – xxi, 243 p.: ill. *Notes*: Includes bibliographical references (p. 223–33) and index. Stage design.

Gavin, Christy. **American women playwrights, 1964–1989: a research guide and annotated bibliography**. New York: Garland Pub., 1993. – v, 493 p. *Notes*: Includes indexes.

Gohdes, Clarence Louis Frank. **Literature and theater of the States and regions of the USA: an historical bibliography**. Durham, NC: Duke University Press, 1997 1967. – ix, 276 p.

Goldberg, RoseLee. **Performance art**. New York: Abrams, 1988. 216 p.

Gottfried, Martin. **Opening nights; theater criticism of the sixties**. New York: Putnam, 1969. – 384 p. *Notes*: US reviewer responds to theatre.

———. **A theatre divided**. Boston, MA: Little, Brown, 1967. 330 p.

Harburg, Ernest and Bernard Rosenberg. **The Broadway musical: collaboration in commerce and art**. New York: New York University Press, 1993. 356 p.

Harris, Andrew Bennett. **Broadway theatre**. London; New York: Routledge, 1994. – xiii, 180 p., 12 p. of plates: ill. *Notes*: Includes bibliographical references (p. 160–5) and index. History and criticism.

Henri, Adrian. **Total art: environments, happenings and performance**. Oxford and New York: Oxford University Press, 1974. 216 p.

Hirsch, Foster. **The boys from Syracuse: the Shuberts' theatrical empire**. Carbondale, Ill.: Southern Illinois University Press, 1997. *Notes*: Includes bibliographical references and index. Biography/Shubert, Lee, 1873?–1953/Shubert, Sam S., 1875–1905/Shubert, Jacob J., 1878?–1963/Schubert family/Shubert Organization. History.

———. **A method to their madness: the history of the actors studio**. New York: Da Capo, 1984. 367 p.

Hischak, Thomas. **The theatergoer's almanac: a collection of lists, people, history, and commentary on the American theater**. Westport, Conn.: Greenwood Press, 1997. – x, 287 p. *Notes*: Includes index. Bibliography: p. 239–244.

Houseman, John. **Final dress: a memoir**. New York N.Y.: Simon & Schuster, 1984, 1983. – 559 p., 32 p. of plates: ill. *Notes*: Includes index. Theatrical producers and directors. United States. Autobiography/Houseman, John.

———. **Front and center**. New York: Simon & Schuster, 1979. – 512 p., 24 p. of plates: ill. *Notes*: Continued by: **Final dress**. Includes bibliographical references and index. Autobiography/Houseman, John.

Hyman, Colette A. **Staging strikes: workers' theater and the American labor movement**. Philadelphia: Temple University Press, 1997. – xi, 209 p.: ill. *Notes*: Includes bibliographical references (p. 171–99) and index.

Jain, Naresh Kumar. **Love in modern American**

drama. New Delhi: Manohar Publications, 1991. – 173 p. *Notes*: Includes index. Includes bibliographical references (p. 152–68).

Kerr, Walter. **Pieces at eight**. New York: Dutton, 1968. – viii, 244 p. *Notes*: American drama. 20th century. History and criticism. Reviews.

King, Bruce Alvin. **Contemporary American theater**. New York: St. Martin's Press, 1991. – xii, 289 p.: ill. *Notes*: Includes bibliographical references and index. Women playwrights on Broadway: Henley, Howe, Norman and Wasserstein/Barbara Kachur – Not-quite mainstream male playwrights: Guare, Durang and Rabe/Dennis Carroll – New realism: Mamet, Mann and Nelson/David Savran – Black theatre into the mainstream/Holly Hill – The sound of a voice: David Hwang/Gerald Rabkin – Elizabeth LeCompte and the Wooster Group/Alexis Greene – Lee Breuer and Mabou Mines/S.E. Gontarski – Beyond the Broadway musical: crossovers, confusions and crisis/by Glenn Loney – Once upon a time in performance art/Lenora Champagne – Performance artist/art performer: Laurie Anderson/Mel Gordon – Contemporary American dance theatre: Clarke, Goode and Mann/Theodore Shank – From C-R to PR: feminist theatre in America/Alisa Solomon – Poets of Bohemia and suburbia: the post-literary dramaturgies of Farabough, Harrington and Shank/Jim Carmody – Not either/or but and: fragmentation and consolidation in the post-modern theatre of Peter Sellars/Don Shewey.

King, Christine E. and Brenda Coven. **Joseph Papp and the New York Shakespeare Festival: an annotated bibliography**. New York: Garland Pub., 1988. – xxxii, 369 p. *Notes*: Includes indexes. New York Shakespeare Festival. Bibliography.

King, Kimball. **Ten modern American playwrights: an annotated bibliography**. New York: Garland Pub., 1982. – xv, 251 p. *Notes*: Includes index. Edward Albee – Amiri Baraka – Ed Bullins – Jack Gelber – Arthur Kopit– David Mamet – David Rabe – Sam Shepard – Neil Simon – Lanford Wilson.

Kolin, Philip C. **American playwrights since 1945: a guide to scholarship, criticism, and performance**. New York: Greenwood Press, 1989. – xiii, 595 p. *Notes*: Includes bibliographies and indexes.

——. **Studies in American drama, 1945– present. Volume 4, 1989**. Erie, PA: P.C. Kolin and C.H. Kullman, 1989. – 290 p.: ill. History and criticism.

—— and Colby H. Kullman. **Speaking on stage:**

interviews with contemporary American playwrights. Tuscaloosa: University of Alabama Press, 1996. – x, 425 p.: ill. *Notes*: Includes bibliographical references and index. 20th century. History and criticism. Interviews. United States.

Lahr, John. **Acting out America; essays on modern theatre**. [Harmondsworth: Eng.]. Penguin Books, 1972. – 203 p. *Notes*: Drama. 20th century.

——. **Up against the fourth wall, essays on modern theater**. New York: Grove Press, 1970. – 305 p. *Notes*: Includes bibliographical references. History and criticism.

Larson, Gary. **The reluctant patron: the United States government and the arts, 1943–1965**. Philadelphia, PA: University of Pennsylvannia Press, 1983. 314 p.

Leiter, Samuel L. **The encyclopedia of the New York stage, 1940–1950**. Westport, Conn: Greenwood Press, 1992. – xlvii, 946 p. *Notes*: Continues **The Encyclopedia of the New York stage, 1930–1940**. Includes bibliographical references (p. 843–52) and indexes.

——. **Ten seasons: New York theater in the seventies**. New York: Greenwood Press, 1986. – xii, 245 p. *Notes*: Includes index. Bibliography: p. 217–19. New York Theatre, 1970–80.

Levine, Ira. **Left-wing dramatic theory in the American theatre**. Ann Arbor, Mich.: UMI Research Press, 1985. – xvi, 233 p.: ill. *Notes*: Includes index. Bibliography: p. 215–24. History and criticism.

The Living book of the Living Theater. With an introductory essay by Richard Schechner. Greenwich: Conn.: New York Graphic Society [1971], (unpaged) chiefly illus.

MacNicholas, John. **Twentieth-century American dramatists**. Detroit, Mich.: Gale Research Co., 1981. – 2 vols: ill. Includes index. bibliography: pt. 2, p. 457–462. *Subjects*: American drama. 20th century. Biobibliography.

Malpede, Karen, ed. **Three works by the Open Theater**. [New York]. Drama Book Specialists, 1974. – 191 p. illus. *Notes*: Malpede, K. Introduction.–Chaikin, J. Notes on acting time and repetition.–Terminal.–Waldman, M. Terminal portfolio.–The mutation show.– Mark, M.E. The Mutation show portfolio.–Nightwalk.–Morath, I. Nightwalk portfolio.–Chronology.–Gildzen, A. The Open Theater: a beginning bibliography. An early view of Joseph Chaikin's experimental US company.

Marowitz, Charles. **Alarums and excursions: our theaters in the nineties**. New York: Applause, 1996. – xii, 306 p. *Notes*: Includes index. History and criticism.

Marranca, Bonnie. **Theatre writings**. New York: Performing Arts Journal Publications, 1984.

—— and Gautam Dasgupta. **American playwrights, a critical survey**. New York: Drama Book Specialists, 1981. *Notes*: History and criticism.

Maufort, Marc. **Staging difference: cultural pluralism in American theater and drama**. New York: P. Lang, 1995. – x, 396 p.: ill. *Notes*: Includes bibliographical references (p. 375–87) and index. American drama. 20th century. History and criticism. Social aspects.

McCarthy, Mary. **Mary McCarthy's theater chronicles, 1937–1962**. New York: Greenwood Press, 1987. 348 p.

McNamara, Brooks. **The Shuberts of Broadway: a history drawn from the collections of the Shubert Archive**. Oxford and New York: Oxford University Press, 1990. – xxvi, 230 p.: ill. *Notes*: Includes bibliographical references (p. 221–3) and index. Theatrical producers. United States. Biography. Shubert (Family).

Miller, Arthur. **'Salesman' in Beijing**. London: Methuen, 1984. – 254 p.: ill. *Subjects*: Theater. China. Miller directs his own play in China.

Mordden, Ethan. **The American theatre**. New York: Oxford University Press, 1981. 365 p.

——. **The fireside companion to the theater**. New York: Simon & Schuster, 1988. – 312 p.: ill. *Notes*: 'Featuring photographs from the Lincoln Center Library of the Performing Arts' Theatre Collection, New York Public Library'. Includes index.

Nannes, Caspar Harold. **Politics in the American drama**. Ann Arbor: University Microfilms International, 1993 1960. – 256 p.

Napier, Valantyne. **Glossary of terms used in variety, vaudeville, revue and pantomime, 1880–1960**. Westbury: Badger Press, 1996. – 62 p.: ill., ports.; 22cm.

Nightingale, Benedict. **Fifth row center: a critic's year on and off Broadway**. New York: Times Books, 1986. – 346 p. *Notes*: Includes index. Diaries. American drama.

Novick, Julius. **Beyond Broadway**. New York: Hill & Wang, 1968. 393 p. *Notes*: Seminal study of US regional theatre.

Parker, Dorothy. **Essays on modern American drama: Williams, Miller, Albee, and Shepard**.

Toronto: University of Toronto Press, 1987. – xiii, 216 p. *Notes*: Originally published in **Modern drama, 1967–1984**. History and criticism.

Pereira, John W. **Opening nights: 25 years of the Manhattan Theater Club**. New York: P. Lang, 1996. – x, 480 p.: ill. *Notes*: Includes indexes.

Performing arts books, 1876–1981: including an international index of current serial publications. New York: R.R. Bowker Co., 1981. – xviii, 1656 p. *Notes*: Includes indexes. Bibliography. United States. Imprints.

Probst, Gerhard F. **Erwin Piscator and the American theater**. New York: P. Lang, 1991. – xiii, 211 p.: ill. *Notes*: Includes bibliographical references (p. 143–50) and index. Political aspects. Piscator, Erwin, 1893–1966. Criticism and interpretation.

Robinson, Alice M., Vera Mowry Roberts and Milly S. Barranger. **Notable women in the American theater: a biographical dictionary**. New York: Greenwood Press, 1989. – xv, 993 p.

Robinson, Marc. **The other American drama**. Cambridge; New York, NY, USA: Cambridge University Press, 1994. – viii, 216 p. *Notes*: Includes bibliographical references (p. 206–11) and index. Gertrude Stein – Tennessee Williams – Sam Shepard – Maria Irene Fornes – Adrienne Kennedy – Richard Foreman. Experimental drama. History and criticism.

Rood, Karen Lane. **American culture after World War II**. Detroit: Gale Research, 1994. – xxx, 393 p.: ill. *Series*: Dictionary of twentieth-century culture. *Notes*: Includes index. Art – Literature – Drama and film – Music and dance – Radio and television.

Roudané, Matthew Charles, ed. **Public issues, private tensions: contemporary American drama**. Atlanta: Dept. of English, Georgia State University, 1988. – 134 p. *Notes*: Special issue: **Studies in the literary imagination**, vol. 21, no. 2, fall 1988. Hysteria, crabs, gospel, and random access: ring around the audience/ Herbert Blau – 'Dead! and never called me Mother!': the missing dimension in American drama/Martin Esslin – Of course, it's only my private opinion/Gerald Weales – Judy Grahn's gynopoetics: The queen of swords/Sue-Ellen Case – Sam Shepard's pornographic visions/ Lynda Hart – Arthur Miller: public issues, private tensions/Robert A. Martin – Public faces, private graces: apocalypse postponed in Arthur Kopit's End of the world/Thomas P. Adler – The comic vision of Lanford Wilson/Martin J. Jacobi. History and criticism.

——. **American dramatists**. Detroit, Mich.: Gale Research, 1989. – xvii, 484 p. *Notes*: Includes bio-bibliographies and indexes.

Sainer, Arthur. **The new radical theater notebook**. New York: Applause, 1997. – xv, 493 p. *Notes*: Includes index. Experimental theatre.

Schanke, Robert A. **Ibsen in America: a century of change**. Metuchen, N.J.: Scarecrow Press, 1988. – xix, 322 p., 24 p. of plates: ill. *Notes*: Includes index. Bibliography: p. 281–309. Interviews/Women in literature. Stage history. Characters. Women.

Schechter, Joel, ed. **Special issue on contemporary American playwriting**. [New Haven, Conn.]: **Theater**, 1978. – 156 p.: ill. Notes: Published as the Spring 1979 (v. 9, no. 2) issue of **Theater**. 'Who's on first': contemporary American playwriting/The editors – Time/Sam Shepard – Richard Foreman and some uses of cinema/James Leverett – Hotel Universe: playwriting and the San Francisco Mime Troupe/ William Kleb – The Crack in the Chimney: reflections on contemporary American playwriting/Robert Brustein – The basic training of American playwrights: theater and the Vietnam War/Robert Asahina – New playwrights in America: an outsider's view/Martin Esslin – Fifteen years of reading new plays: reflections on the closing of the Office of Advanced Drama Research/Arthur Ballet – Jack Gelber talks about surviving in the theater/Albert Bermel – On black theater/Amiri Baraka. Plays: A fragment of The Agamemnon – An Evening with Dead Essex/Adrienne Kennedy – Book of Splendors: Part II (Book of Levers) Action at a Distance/Richard Foreman – Notes on the $ Value of Man/Cindy Lubar – The $ Value of Man/Robert Wilson and Christopher Knowles – Scenes from Dressed Like an Egg.

Seller, Maxine Schwartz, ed. **Ethnic theater in the United States**. Westport, CT: Greenwood Press, 1983. 606 p.

Shank, Theodore. **American alternative theater**. New York: St. Martin's Press, 1983, 1982. *Notes*: Includes index. Bibliography: Experimental theatre.

Sheehy, Helen. **Margo: the life and theater of Margo Jones**. Dallas: Southern Methodist University Press, 1989. – 316 p., 32 p. of plates: ill. *Notes*: Includes bibliographical references (p. 277–302). Biography/Jones, Margo.

Shuman, Robert Baird. **American drama, 1918–1960: an annotated bibliography**. Pasadena, Calif.: Salem Press, 1992. – xiv, 177 p. *Notes*: Includes index.

Silvester, Robert. **United States theatre: a bibli-ography, from the beginning to 1990**. New York: Romsey, England: G.K. Hall; Motley Press, 1993. – 400 p.

Speck, Frank, Leonard Broom and Will Long. **Cherokee dance and drama**. Norman, OK: University of Oklahoma Press, 1983. 112 p.

Sponberg, Arvid F. **Broadway talks: what professionals think about commercial theater in America**. New York: Greenwood Press, 1991. – xxx, 224 p. *Notes*: Includes bibliographical references (p. 209–13) and index. Interviews. Theatrical producers and directors.

Stasio, Marilyn. **Broadway's beautiful losers**. New York: Delacorte, 1985 1972. – xxii, 425 p.: ill. *Notes*: Look: we've come through/H. Wheeler – The beauty part/S.J. Perelman – The last analysis/S. Bellow – Xmas in Las Vegas/J. Richardson – Johnny No-Trump/M. Mercier. American drama. 20th century. History and criticism. Plays that closed the first time around.

Stratman, Carl Joseph. **American theatrical periodicals, 1798–1967: a bibliographical guide**. Durham, N.C.: Duke University Press, 1997 1970. – xxii, 133 p. *Notes*: Includes index. Bibliography: p. 89–91. Photocopy. Ann Arbor, MI.: UMI Books on Demand, 1997.

Szilassy, Zoltán. **American theater of the 1960s**. Carbondale: Southern Illinois University Press, 1986. – xiii, 113 p. *Notes*: Includes bibliographical references and index. 20th century/ Experimental theatre.

Taylor, Thomas James. **American theater history: an annotated bibliography**. Pasadena, Calif.: Salem Press, 1992. – xi, 162 p. *Notes*: Includes index.

Thomas, Lundeana. **Barbara Ann Teer and the National Black Theater: transformational forces in Harlem**. New York: Garland Pub., 1997. – xxvi, 190 p.: ill. *Notes*: Includes bibliographical references (p. 176–83) and index. History.

The Vandamm Collection. Theatre photographs from the studios of Florence Vandamm and Francis Joseph Bruguiere from 1915 to 1960 in the New York Public Library, Library and Museum of the Performing Arts. Teaneck, N.J.: Cambridge, England: Somerset House, 1980. – 877 microfiches. *Notes*: Micro-reproduction of theatrical photographs taken by F. Vandamm and others, housed in the New York Public Library, Library and Museum of the Performing Arts; includes card catalogues which serve as indexes to the collection.

Vaughn, Robert Francis. **A historical study of the influence of the House Committee on Un-American Activities on the American theater,**

1938–1958. Thesis–University of Southern California, 1970. – iv, 591 p. *Notes*: Microfilm. Ann Arbor, Mich.: Xerox University Microfilms, 1978. – 1 reel; 35 mm. Bibliography: p. 573–91. Theatre and state. United States. House Committee on Un-American Activities.

Weales, Gerald. **American drama since World War II**. New York: Harcourt, Brace & World, 1962. 246 p.

Weinberg, Mark S. **Challenging the hierarchy: collective theater in the United States**. New York: Greenwood Press, 1992. – x, 267 p. Includes bibliographical references (p. 249–61) and index. Collective creation.

Wilmeth, Don B. **American and English popular entertainment: a guide to information sources**. Detroit: Gale Research Co., 1980. – xviii, 465 p. *Notes*: Includes indexes. United States. Great Britain. Popular culture. Bibliography.

—— and Tice L. Miller. **Cambridge guide to American theatre**. Cambridge and New York: Cambridge University Press, 1996. – xiii, 463 p. *Notes*: Includes bibliographical references (p. 419–30) and index. United States theatre spinoff of Cambridge Guide to Theatre.

Woll, Allen L. **Dictionary of the Black theater: Broadway, off-Broadway, and selected Harlem theater**. Westport, Conn.: Greenwood Press, 1983. – xvi, 359 p.

Young, William C. **Famous actors and actresses on the American stage: documents of American theater history**. New York and London: Bowker, 1975. – 2 v. (xxi, 1298 p.). *Notes*: Includes index. Bibliography: p. 1215–27. Readings from contemporary sources.

Ziegler, Joseph. **Regional theater: the revolutionary stage**. New York: Da Capo, 1977. 283 p.

A3a149a. Black Theatre (Afro-American)

Abramson, Doris E. **Negro playwrights in the American theater**. New York: Columbia University Press, 1969. 335 p.

Anadolu-Okur, Nilgun. **Contemporary African American theater: Afrocentricity in the works of Larry Neal, Amiri Baraka, and Charles Fuller**. New York: Garland Pub., 1997. – xxxv, 199 p. *Notes*: Includes bibliographical references (p. 179–185) and index. History and criticism. Neal, Larry, 1937–. Baraka, Imamu Amiri, 1934–. Fuller, Charles. Criticism and interpretation.

Asante, K.W. 'African and African-American Dance, Music and Theater'. **Journal of Black Studies** 15 (June 1985): 355–479.

Brown-Guillory, Elizabeth. **Their place on the stage: black women playwrights in America**. New York: Greenwood Press, 1988. 163 p.

California State College, San Bernardino. Library. **Black and Brown bibliography: a selected list of books relating to the history of Afro-Americans and Mexican-Americans**. San Bernardino: California State College, 1970. – 3 vols. *Notes*: v. 1. History.–v. 2. Literature, art, music, theatre.–v. 3. Philosophy, social sciences, political science, education.

Craig, Evelyn Quita. **Black drama of the Federal theater era: beyond the formal horizons**. Amherst: University of Massachusetts Press, 1980. – x, 239 p. *Notes*: Includes index. Bibliography: p. 222–30. History and criticism. Federal Theater Project.

Davis, Thadious and Trudier Harris, eds. **Afro-American writers after 1955: dramatists and prose writers**. Detroit, MI: Gale Research Company, 1985. 390 p.

Flowers, H.D. **Blacks in American theater history: images, realities, potential**. Edina, Mn.: Burgess International Group, 1992 1993. – ix, 208 p.: ill. *Notes*: Includes bibliographical references and index. Afro-Americans in the performing arts.

Hay, Samuel A. **African American theater: an historical and critical analysis**. New York: Cambridge University Press, 1994. 300 p.

Hill, Errol. **Shakespeare in sable: a history of black Shakespearean actors**. First paperback printed 1986. Amherst: University of Massachusetts Press, 1986. – xxviii, 216 p.: ill. *Notes*: Includes index. Bibliography: p. 203–5. Afro-American actors. Biography.

——. **The theatre of Black Americans: a collection of critical essays**. New York, NY: Applause, 1987. – viii, 363 p. *Notes*: Bibliography: p. 359–63. Roots and rituals – The image makers – The presenters – The participators. History and criticism.

Isaacs, Edith Juliet Rich. **The negro in the American theater**. New York: Theatre Arts, 1968 1947. – 142 p. ill. *Notes*: Photocopy. Ann Arbor Mich.: University Microfilms, 1968. *Subjects*: Afro-American actors.

Mayfield, William. **Playwrighting for Black theater**. Pittsburgh, Pa.: W.F. Mayfield, 1990. – 134 p.: ill. *Notes*: Afro-American authors. History and criticism. Playwriting.

Mitchell, Loften. **Black drama**. New York: Hawthorne Press, 1967. 248 p.

——. **Voices of the black theater**. Clifton, N.J.: J.T. White, 1975. – ix, 238 p.: ill. *Notes*:

Contains taped individual recollections of Black theatrical figures with introductory essays and comments by L. Mitchell. Includes index. The words of Eddie Hunter.–The words of Regina M. Andrews.–The words of Dick Campbell.–The words of Abram Hill.–Interlude: Paul Robeson.–The words of Frederick O'Neal.–The words of Vinnette Carroll.–The words of Ruby Dee. Afro-American actors. Afro-American authors. History and criticism.

Molette, Carlton and Barbara Carlton. **Black theater: premise and presentation**. Bristol, IN: Wyndham Hall Press. 1986. 166 p.

Muse, Daphne. **The Drama Review: Black Theater issue**. Vol. 16 No. 4. New York: New York University, 1972. – 135 p.: ill.

Olaniyan, Tejumola. **Scars of conquest/masks of resistance: the invention of cultural identities in African, African-American, and Caribbean drama**. New York: Oxford University Press, 1995. – xii, 196 p. *Notes*: Includes bibliographical references (p. 171–90) and index. Black authors. Criticism and interpretation.

Patterson, Lindsay, comp. **Anthology of the American Negro in the theater; a critical approach**. [2nd edn, rev.]. New York: Publishers Co, 1970. – xiv, 306 p. illus. *Notes*: Bibliography: p. 293–4. Moral and social conditions.

Perkins, Kathy. **Female black playwrights**. Bloomington, IN: University of Indiana, 1989. 288 p.

Peterson Jr., Bernard, ed. **A century of musical in black and white: an encyclopedia of musical stage works by, about, or involing African Americans**. Westport, CT: Greenwood Press, 1993. 529 p.

Sanders, Leslie Catherine. **The development of Black theater in America: from shadow to substance**. Baton Rouge, LA/London: Louisiana State University Press, 1988. 252 p.

Tanner, Jo A. **Dusky maidens. the odyssey of the early black dramatic actress**. Westport, Conn.: Greenwood Press, 1992. – xiii, 171 p.: ill. *Notes*: Includes bibliographical references (p. 159–60) and index. *Subjects*: Afro-American actresses. Biography.

Washington, Rhonnie Lynn. **Dissertations concerning Black theater**. 3rd edn Detroit, Mich.: The Network, 1994. – iv, 91 p. *Notes*: Includes bibliographical references.

Waters, Harold A. **Théâtre noir: encyclopédie des pièces écrites en français par des auteurs noirs**. [Black theatre: encyclopedia of plays written in French by black authors]. Washington, DC: Three Continents Press, 1988. 269 p.

Williams, Mance. **Black theater in the 1960s and 1970s: a historical-critical analysis of the movement**. Westport, Conn.: Greenwood Press, 1985. – 188 p. *Series*: Contributions in Afro-American and African studies, 0069–0624; no. 87. *Notes*: Includes index. Bibliography: p. 165–75. History. American drama.

A3a149b. US HISPANIC THEATRE

Allen, Richard. **Teatro hispanoamericano: una bibliografía anotada**. [Spanish-American theatre: an annotated bibliography]. Boston, MA: G.K. Hall & Co., 1987.

Broyles-González, Yolanda. **El Teatro Campesino: theater in the Chicano movement**. Austin: University of Texas Press, 1994. – xviii, 286 p.: ill. *Notes*: Includes bibliographical references (p. 255–65) and index. El Teatro Campesino and the Mexican popular performance tradition – Theater of the sphere: Toward the formulation of a native performance theory and practice – Toward a re-vision of Chicana/o theater history: The roles of women in El Teatro Campesino – El Teatro Campesino: From alternative theater to mainstream. Workers' theater.

De Costa, Elena. **Collaborative Latin American popular theater: from theory to form, from text to stage**. New York: P. Lang, 1991. – xii, 175 p.: ill. *Notes*: Includes bibliographical references (p. 169–75). Theatre and society. Political aspects.

De la Roche, Elisa. **Teatro hispano!: three major New York companies**. New York: Garland, 1995. – ix, 211 p. *Notes*: Includes bibliographical references (p. 191–207) and index. Theatrical companies. New York. History/INTAR. Puerto Rican Traveling Theater. Repertorio Español. History.

Feyder, Linda, ed. **Shattering the myth: plays by Hispanic women**. Houston, YX: Arte Público, 1992. 255 p.

Garza, Roberto, ed. **Contemporary Chicano theater**. Notre Dame, IN: University of Notre Dame Press, 1976. 248 p.

González-Cruz, Luis and Francesca Colecchia. 'Introduction'. **Cuban theater in the United States**, 7–17. Tempe, AZ: Bilingual Press, 1992.

Huerta, Jorge A. **Chicano theater: themes and forms**. Ypsilanti, MI: Bilingual Press, 1982. 274 p.

Kanellos, Nicolás. **Mexican American theater: legacy and reality**. Houston, TX: Arte Público, 1987. 120 p.

——, ed. **Hispanic theater in the United States**. Houston, TX: Arte Público, 1984.

——, ed. **Mexican American theater: then and now**. Houston, TX: Arte Público, 1983. 120 p.

Pottlitzer, Joanne. **Hispanic theater in the United States and Puerto Rico**. New York: Ford Foundation, 1988. 85 p.

Zalacaín, Daniel. **Teatro absurdista hispano-americano**. Valencia; Chapel Hill: Albatros Hispanófila, 1985. – 198 p. *Notes*: Bibliography: p. 193–8. Hispanic drama. 20th century. History and criticism/Theatre of the absurd.

Zalacaín, Joseph. **Regional theater: the revolutionary stage**. New York: Da Capo, 1977. 283 p.

A3a150. UNION OF SOVIET SOCIALIST REPUBLICS

Alianskii, Iurii. **Azbuka teatra: 50 malen'kikh rasskazov o teatre**. Leningrad: Detskaia lit-ra, 1986. – 142 p.: ill. *Notes*: History. 20th century.

Alpers, Boris and N.S. Todriia. **Iskaniia novoi stseny**. Moscow: Iskusstvo, 1985. – 398 p. *Notes*: Includes bibliographical references and indexes. History. 20th century.

Anastasev, Arkadii. **Pomecheno vremenem**. Moscow: Iskusstvo, 1977. – 197 p. *Notes*: Reviews/Russian drama. 20th century. History and criticism.

Anninskii, Lev. **Bilet v rai: razmyshleniia u teatral'nykh pod"ezdov**. Moscow: Iskusstvo, 1989. – 190 p. *Notes*: Soviet Union. History. 20th century.

Autant-Mathieu, Marie-Christine. **Le Théâtre soviétique durant le Dégel, 1953–1964**. Paris: CNRS, 1993. – 368 p.: ill. (some col.). *Notes*: Includes bibliographical references (p. 331–40) and index. Soviet Union. History. 20th century.

Barboi, IU.M. **Struktura deistviia i sovremennyi spektakl'**. Leningrad: LGITMiK, 1988. – 200, 1 p. *Notes*: Includes bibliographical references (p. 193–201). Soviet Union. History. 20th century.

Barshay, Deborah Lynda. **Tovstonogov's classics at the Gorki Theatre, 1957–1968**. Thesis (Ph. D.)–Brown University, 1981. Photocopy. Ann Arbor, Mich.: University Microfilms International, 1983. – vii, 171 p.: ill. *Notes*: Vita. Bibliography: p. 144–54. Production and direction/Tovstonogov, Georgii Aleksandrovich/Bolshoi dramaticheskii teatr imeni M. Gorkogo (Leningrad).

Bocharov, M.D. and IAkov IAvchunovskii. **Revoliutsiia, dramaturgiia, teatr**. Rostov: Izd-vo Rostovskogo universiteta, 1984. – 205, 3 p. *Notes*: Bibliography: p. 190–206. Russian drama. 20th century. History and criticism/Socialist realism in literature.

Braun, Edward. **Meyerhold: a revolution in theatre**. Iowa City: University of Iowa Press, 1995. – 347 p.: ill. *Notes*: Rev. edn. of: **Theatre of Meyerhold**. London: Methuen, 1979. Includes bibliographical references (p. 334–8) and index. Biography. History. 20th century. Meyerhold, Vsevelod Emilovich.

——, ed. **Meyerhold on theatre**. Rev. edn. London: Methuen Drama, 1991. – 336 p.: ill. *Notes*: Includes bibliographical references (p. 325–[7]) and index. A valuable collection of Meyerhold's own writings with useful introductions.

Bugrov, Boris Semenovich. **Geroi prinimaet reshenie: dvizhenie dramy ot 50-kh godov**. Moscow: Sov. pisatel', 1987. – 364 p. *Notes*: Includes bibliographical references. Russian drama. History and criticism.

Carnicke, Sharon Marie. **The theatrical instinct: Nikolai Evreinov and the Russian theater of the early twentieth century**. New York: P. Lang, 1989. – xii, 247 p.: ill. Includes bibliographical references (p. 225–42) and index. Evreinov, N.N. (Nikolai Nikolaevich), 1879–1953.

Davidow, Mike. **People's theater: from the box office to the stage**. Moscow: Progress Publishers, 1977. – 248 p., 32 p. of plates: ill. *Notes*: Soviet Union. History. 20th century.

Donat, Branimir. **Sovjetska kazalisna avangarda**. Zagreb: Cekade, 1985. – 351 p., xxiv p. of plates: ill. *Notes*: In Serbo-Croatian (Roman). Includes bibliographical references. Soviet Union. History. Experimental theatre.

Dugin, Yevgeni. **Perestroika and development of culture: literature, theatre, and cinema**. New Delhi: Sterling Publishers, 1989. – vi, 194 p. *Notes*: Articles and speeches. Perestroika/Russian literature. History and criticism.

Efros, Anatolii. **Anatolii Efros**. [Works. 1993]. Moscow: Fond Russkii teatr, Izd-vo Panas, 1993. – 4 vols. *Notes*: Repetitsiia–liubov' moia (izd. 2-e) – vol. 2. Professiia–rezhisser (izd. 2-e) – vol. 3. Prodolzhenie teatral'nogo romana (izd. 2-e) – vol. 4. Miscellaneous. Collected works of one of the USSR's most distinguished directors.

Franz, Norbert. **Das sowjetrussische Theaterwesen unter Gorbacev: Versuche einer Neuorganisation (1985–1987)**. Cologne: Bundesinstitut für Ostwissenschaftliche und Internationale Studien, 1988. – 68 p. *Notes*: Summary in English and German. Includes bibliographical references (p. 55–63). Theatre management. Soviet Union. Perestroika/Soviet Union. Intellectual life. 1970–91.

Fridshtein, IUrii Germanovich. **Anatolii Efros–poet teatra**. Moscow: Teatr Antona Chekhova AO 'Mezhdunarodnyi kommercheskii soiuz', 1992. – 154 p.: ill. *Notes*: Directors. History. Efros, Anatolii. Biography.

Gaevskii, Vadim. **Fleita Gamleta: obrazy sovremennogo teatra**. Moscow: V/O 'Soiuzteatr' STD SSSR, Glav. red. teatral'noi lit-ry, 1990. – 349 p.: ill. *Notes*: Includes bibliographical references (p. 349). History. 20th century.

Gottlieb, Vera. **Chekhov in performance in Russia and Soviet Russia**. New York: Clearwater Pub. Co., 1984. – 90 p. *Notes*: Originally published in Cambridge by Chadwyck-Healey, in association with the Consortium for Drama and Media in Higher Education. Accompanies the slide set: Chekhov in performance in Russia and Soviet Russia. Bibliography: p. 83–4. Chekhov, Anton Pavlovich, 1860–1904. Stage history.

Gugushvili, Eteri and Boris Nikolaevich Liubimov. **Teatralnaia pravda: sbornik statei**. Tbilisi: Teatralnoe obshchestvo Gruzii, 1981. – 490 p. *Notes*: Includes bibliographical references. Actors.

Hoover, Marjorie L. **Meyerhold and his set designers**. New York: P. Lang, 1988. – x, 258 p., 14 p. of plates: ill. *Notes*: Includes index. Bibliography: p. 233–5. Stage-setting and scenery. History.

IUzovskii, IU. **O teatre i drame: v dvukh tomakh**. Moscow: Iskusstvo, 1982. – 2 vols: ill. *Notes*: v. 1. Stat'i, ocherki, fel'etony – v. 2. Iz kriticheskogo dnevnika. Reviews/Shakespeare, William, 1564–1616. Stage history.

Karimullin, Abrar Gibadullovich. **Tatarskaia stsena. ukazatel 'literatury, 1917–1967**. Kazan': IIaLI im. G. Ibragimova KFAN SSSR, 1979. – 331 p. *Notes*: Foreword in Russian and Tatar. Includes indexes. Master microform held by: MH. Microform master no.: 10,585. Microfilm, master negative of a copy in the Library of the Academy of Sciences of the USSR at Harvard University, 1 reel; 35 mm. Bibliography of Tatar (USSR) copy books.

Kolakowski, Tadeusz. **Dramat radziecki na scenach polskich w dwudziestoleciu miedzywojennym**. Warsaw: Wydawnictwa Uniwersytetu Warszawskiego, 1982. – 230 p.: ill. *Notes*: Summary in English and Russian. Includes bibliographical references and indexes. History. 20th century.

Kornienko, N.N. **Teatr segodnia–teatr zavtra: sotsioesteticheskie zametki o drame, stsene i zritele 70–80-kh godov**. Kiev: Mystetstvo,

1986. – 220 p. *Notes*: Bibliography: p. 212–18. Russian drama. 20th century. History and criticism.

Kudriavtsev, Sergei. **Terentévskii sbornik, 1996**. Moscow: 'Gileia', 1996. – 318 p.: ill. *Notes*: Includes bibliographical references and index. 20th century. History and criticism. Experimental theatre. Criticism and interpretation.

Liubomudrov, Mark Nikolaevich. **Protivostoianie: teatr, vek XX: traditsii–avangard**. Moscow: Molodaia gvardiia, 1991. – 316 p. *Notes*: Romanized record. History. 20th century.

Makarevich, Irina. **Soviet theatre: new ideas**. Moscow: Novosti Press Agency Pub. House, 1981. – 90 p., 32 p. of plates: ill. *Notes*: History. 20th century.

Markov, Pavel. **O teatre**. Moscow: Iskusstvo, 1974. – v.: ill. *Notes*: Includes bibliographical references and indexes. History.

——. **The Soviet theater**. Westport, Conn.: Greenwood Press, 1978 1934. – 176 p., 36 leaves of plates: ill. *Notes*: Reprint of the 1934 edn. published by V. Gollancz, London, which was issued as no. 3 of the New Soviet library. Includes index.

——. **Teatral'naia entsiklopediia. Dopolneniia. Ukazatel'**. Moscow: Sov. entsiklopediia, 1967. – 296 columns. illus., ports. *Notes*: National theatre encyclopeia. In 5 vols.

Matskin, Aleksandr. **Obrazy vremeni; stat'i v literature i teatre. Stat'i raznykh let**. Moscow: Sovetskii pisatel', 1959. – 406 p. *Notes*: 20th century/Theatre. Soviet Union.

Naumova, E.A. and V.M. Kanaeva. **Letopis' raboty frontovykh brigad teatrov Vserossiiskogo teatral'nogo obshchestva vo vremia Velikoi Otechestvennoi Voiny**. Moscow: Soiuz teatral'nykh deiatelei Rossiiskoi Federatsii, 1992. – 152 p. *Notes*: Soviet Union. History. World War, 1939–1945. Theatre and the war.

Nosova, Elena Andreevna and L.R. Levina. **Mezhdunarodnaia tema v sovremennoi sovetskoi dramaturgii i teatre: rekomendatel'nyi bibliograficheskii spisok**. Moscow: [Gos. teatral'naia biblioteka], 1985. – 22 p. *Notes*: Soviet theatre bibliography.

Pliatt, Rostislav. **Bez epiloga**. Moscow: 'Iskusstvo', 1992. – 172 p., 81 p. of plates: ill. *Notes*: Actors. Soviet Union. Biography.

Proskurnikova, Tatiana and Galina Makarova. **Teatr absurda: sbornik statei i publikatsii**. Moscow: Gos. in-t iskusstvoznaniia, 1995. –

215 p. *Notes*: Theatre of the absurd. History and criticism.

Radishcheva, Olga Aleksandrovna. **Stanislavskii i Nemirovich-Danchenko: istoriia teatral'nykh otnoshenii: 1897–1908**. Moscow: Izd-vo 'Artist. Rezhisser. Teatr', 1997. – 460, 1 p. *Notes*: Includes index. *Subjects*: Theatrical producers and directors. Soviet Union. Biography/ Stanislavsky, Konstantin, 1863–1938/ Nemirovich-Danchenko, Vladimir I., 1858–1943/Moscow Art Theatre.

Rudnitski, Konstantin. **Proza i stsena**. Moscow: Izd-vo Znanie, 1981. – 111 p., 8 p. of plates: ill. *Notes*: Bibliography: p. 110. History.

——. **Real'nost' i obraznost': problemy sovet-skoi rezhissury 30–40-kh godov**. Moscow: Izd-vo Nauka, 1984. – 303 p. *Notes*: Includes bibliographical references. Soviet Union. History.

——. **Spektakli raznykh let**. Moscow: Iskusstvo, 1974. – 341 p. *Notes*: Includes bibliographical references. Production and direction.

——. **Teatral'nye siuzhety**. Moscow: Iskusstvo, 1990. – 463 p., 80 p. of plates: ill. *Notes*: Soviet theatre in the 1970s and 1980s.

——. **Théâtre russe et sovietique**. Paris: Editions du Regard, 1988. – 319 p.: ill. (some col.). *Notes*: Translation of the English version of the Russian original, **Russian and Soviet theater, 1905–1932**. Includes index. Includes bibliographical references (p. 307–12). Experimental theatre. History. In French.

Russian issue [of the Drama review]. New York: School of the Arts, New York University, 1973. – 141 p.: ill. *Series*: **The Drama review**; 17, no. 1 (T-57). *Notes*: Essays by various authors on twentieth century Russian drama. Soviet Union. 20th century.

Sabaleuski, A.V. **Belorusskaia dramaturgiia v teatrakh narodov SSSR**. Minsk: Nauka i tekhnika, 1972. – 43 p.: ill., ports. *Notes*: Bibliography: p. 352–435. Belarusian drama. Soviet Union. History. 20th century.

Shaland, Irene. **Tennessee Williams on the Soviet stage**. Lanham; London: University Press of America, 1987. – 100 p. *Notes*: Williams, Tennessee, 1911–83. Stage history. Soviet Union.

Shostak, Irina. **Rezhisser Mambetov: spektakli raznykh let**. Alma-Ata: Oner, 1989. – 142 p., 16 p. of plates: ill. *Notes*: Includes bibliographical references. Directors. Soviet Union. Biography. Kazakstan. History. Mambetov, A.

Shvyidkoi, Mikhail. **Dramaturgiia, teatr, zhizn'**. Moscow: Znanie, 1987. – 54, 1 p.: ill. *Notes*:

Includes bibliographical references (p. 55). Soviet Union. History. 20th century.

Smelianskii, Anatolii M. **Klassika i sovremen-nost': problemy sovetskoi rezhissury 60–70-kh godov**. Moscow: Nauka, 1987. – 368 p. *Notes*: Includes bibliographies. History. 20th century. Production and direction.

——. **The Soviet theatre: problems and principal trends in Soviet Theatre**. Moscow: Novosti Press Agency Pub. House, 1986. – 87 p.: ill. *Notes*: Translation of: **Sovetskii teatr**. History. 20th century.

—— and M. Shvydkoi. **Teatr–vremia peremen**. Moscow: Iskusstvo, 1987. – 222 p. *Notes*: Includes bibliographical references. Production and direction.

Smirnov, Sergei Rostislavovich. **Sovetskaia dramaturgiia, 1955–1985**. Irkutsk: Izd-vo Irkutskogo universiteta, 1988. – 171 p. *Notes*: Includes index. Russian drama. 20th century. History and criticism. Bibliography.

Solov'eva, Inna Natanovna. **Nemirovich-Danchenko**. Moscow: Iskusstvo, 1979. – 408 p., 25 leaves of plates: ill. *Notes*: Includes bibliographical references. Theatrical producers and directors. Soviet Union. Biography/Nemirovich-Danchenko, Vladimir Ivanovich, 1858–1943. Moscow Art Theatre (MKAT).

—— and Vera Vasilevna Shitova. **K.S. Stanislavskii**. Moscow: Iskusstvo, 1986. – 166 p.: ill. (some col.). *Notes*: Biography of Stanislavsky, Konstantin, 1863–1938.

Sosin, Gene. **Children's theater and drama in the Soviet Union (1917–1953)**. New York, 1958. – 387. *Notes*: Photocopy. Ann Arbor, Michigan, University Microfilms, 1972. Bibliography: l. 369–87. Thesis, Columbia University. *Subjects*: Children's plays, Russian. History and criticism.

Tovstonogov, Georgi. **Stat'i; Zapisi repetitsii**. [Selections. 1984]. Leningrad: Iskusstvo, Leningradskoe otd-nie, 1984. – 367 p., 9 p. of plates: ill. *Notes*: 'Literaturnye raboty G.A. Tovstonogova': p. 353–367. Production and direction. History. 20th century.

Vakhtangov, Evgeni, Liubov Vendrovskaia and Galina Kaptereva. **Evgenii Vakhtangov**. Moscow: Vseros. teatral'noe ob-vo, 1984. – 583 p., 64 p. of plates: ill. (some col.). *Notes*: Includes index. Biography. Vakhtangov, Evgenii Bagrationovich, 1883–1922.

Vladimirov, Sergei. **Drama, rezhisser, spektakl'**. Leningrad: Iskusstvo, 1976. – 219 p. *Notes*: Bibliographical references. V.V. Maiakovskii.– S. IA. Marshak.–A.M. Volodin.–Teatral'nye razmyshleniia.–O tvorcheskoi rezhissure.–Segodnia, seichas, zdes'…–Iz teatral'nogo dnevnika. History and criticism.

Worrall, Nick. **Modernism to realism on the Soviet stage: Tairov-Vakhtangov-Okhlopkov.** Cambridge and New York: Cambridge University Press, 1989. – xviii, 238 p.: ill. *Notes:* Includes index. Bibliography: p. 224–5. Tairov, Aleksandr IAkovlevich, 1885–1950. Vakhtangov, Evgenii Bagrationovich, 1883–1922. Okhlopkov, Nikolai Pavlovich. Criticism and interpretation. Part of Directors in Perspective series.

Zingerman, Boris Isaakovich. **Teatralnye stranitsy 1969.** Moscow: 1969. – 539 p. illus. (part col.). *Notes:* Bibliographical footnotes. History.

A3a151. URUGUAY

Ayestarán. Lauro. **El cenetario del Teatro Solís.** [Centenary of the Solís Theatre]. Montevideo: Comisión de Teatros Municipales, 1956.

Calvetti, Jaime. **Apuntes monográficos.** Montevideo: Edición Libro Uruguayo de Teatro, 1993. – 58 p.: ill. *Notes:* 'Incluyendo: algunos aspectos de acercamiento a la completud del sistema de categorías en formaciones del teatro uruguayo bajo la dictadura 1973–1984'. Bibliographical references (p. 55–8). History. 20th century.

Castillo, Andrés and A. Queirolo de la Sovera. **Il teatro indipendiente.** [Independent theatre]. Italy: Centro Di Azione Latina, 1964.

Dibarboure, José Alberto. **Proceso del teatro uruguayo.** [The evolution of Uruguayan theatre]. Montevideo: Editorial Claudio García, 1940.

Diverzo, G. and E. Filgueiras. **Montevideo en carnaval.** [Montevideo in Carnival]. Montevideo: Editorial Monte Sexto, 1990.

Fontana, Roberto. **Memoria en dos actos: mi testimonio sobre el Teatro Independiente de Montevideo.** Montevideo: ARCA, 1988. – 120 p.: ill. *Notes:* Includes index. Teatro Independiente de Montevideo. History.

El Galpón: un teatro independiente uruguayo y su función en el exilio. [El Galpón: an independent Uruguayan theatre and its role in exile]. México City: Cuadernos de Difusión Cultural de la Institución Teatral El Galpón, 1983. 55 p.

Ganduglia, Néstor. **15 años de teatro barrial y una canción desesperada.** Montevideo, Uruguay: YOEA: Multiversidad Franciscana de América Latina, 1996. – 197 p.: ill. *Notes:* Includes bibliographical references (p. 195–6). Community theatre. History. Workers' theatre. Street theatre.

Landó, Cristina. **Cuarenta años: comedia nacional.** [Forty years: Comedia Nacional]. Montevideo: Departamento de Cultura de la Intendencia Municipal de Montevideo, 1987. 28 p.

Legido, Juan Carlos. **El teatro uruguayo.** [Uruguayan theatre]. Montevideo: Ediciones Tauro, 1968. 160 p.

Literatura uruguaya del medio siglo. [Uruguayan literature of the mid-century]. Montevideo: Alfa, 1966.

Mibelli, Américo and Wilson Armas. **Las dependencias del teatro independiente, 1937–52.** [Dependencies of the independent theatre, 1937–52]. La Paz/Canelones: Talleres Gráficos Vanguardia, 1960.

Mirza, Roger, ed. **Teatro uruguayo contemporáneo: antología.** [Contemporary Uruguayan theatre: an anthology]. Madrid: Ministerio de Cultura/Fondo de Cultura Económica, 1992. 1, 112 p.

Montero Zorrilla, Pablo. **Montevideo y sus teatros.** [Montevideo and its theatres]. Montevideo: Asociación de Teatros del Interior, 1993.

Ostuni, Omar. **Por los teatros del interior: crónicas y hechos que revelan histórias desconocidas del teatro uruguayo.** Montevideo: Asociación de Teatros del Interior, 1993. – 178 p. *Notes:* Includes bibliographical references. History. 20th century.

Pignataro Calero, Jorge. **Directores teatrales del Uruguay: 50 retratos.** Montevideo: Editorial Proyección, 1994. – 250 p.: ill. *Notes:* Includes bibliographical references. Uruguayan directors.

——. **El teatro independiente uruguayo.** [Uruguayan independent theatre]. Montevideo: Editorial Arca, 1968. 134 p.

Rela, Walter. **Historia del teatro uruguayo, 1808–1979.** [History of the Uruguayan theatre, 1808–1979]. Montevideo: Editorial Alianza Cultural Uruguay-EEUU, 1980.

——. **Repertorio bibliográfico del teatro uruguayo, 1816–1964.** Montevideo: Editorial Síntesis, 1965. – 35 p. facsim. *Notes:* Uruguayan drama. Bibliography

——. **Teatro uruguayo, 1808–1994: historia.** [Montevideo]: Academia Uruguaya de Letras, 1994. – 347 p. *Notes:* Includes bibliographical references (p. 325–42) and index. Uruguayan drama. History and criticism.

Scoseria, Cyro. **Un panorama del teatro uruguayo.** [Overview of the theatre in Uruguay]. Montevideo: Publicaciones AGADU, 1963.

Silva Valdés, Fernán, ed. **Teatro uruguayo**. [Uruguayan theatre]. Madrid: Aguilar, 1966.

Vanrell Delgado, Juan María. **La historia de la Comedia Nacional**. [History of the Comedia Nacional]. Montevideo: Intendencia Municipal de Montevideo, 1987. 249 p.

A3a152. UZBEKISTAN

Abdullaeva, Salomat, ed. **Abror Hidoyatov**. Tashkent: Gafur Gulyam Literature and Art Publishing House, 1985.

Allanazarov, Toresh. **Nekotorye voprosy istorii karakalpakskoi sovetskoi dramaturgii**. Nukus: Karakalpakstan, 1987. 265 p. *Notes*: Includes bibliographical references (p. 259–64). Kara-Kalpak drama. History and criticism.

Allworth, Edward A. **The modern Uzbeks: from the fourteenth century to the present: a cultural history**. Hoover Institution Press, 1990.

Avdeev, Boris. **Povest' o tantsovshchitse**. [Legend of a dancer]. Tashkent: Gafur Gulyam Literature and Art Publishing House, 1987.

Avdeeva, Liubov Aleksandrovna. **Tanets Makarram Turganbaeva**. [The dances of Mukarram Turganbaeva]. Tashkent: Gafur Gulyam Literature and Art Publishing House, 1989.

Karimova, Rozia. **Buhkarskii tanets**. [Bukharan dance]. Tashkent: Gafur Gulyam Literature and Art Publishing House, 1978.

——. **Ferghanskii tanets**. [Ferghana dance]. Tashkent: Gafur Gulyam Literature and Art Publishing House, 1973.

——. **Khorezmskii tanets**. [Khorezm dance]. Tashkent: Gafur Gulyam Literature and Art Publishing House, 1975.

——. **Tantsy ensemblya 'Bakhor'**. [Dances of the Bakhor ensemble]. Tashkent, Khamza Hakim-zade Niyazi Institute of Fine Art Studies, 1979.

——. **Tanovar**. Tashkent, 1993.

——. **Uzbekskie tantsy v postanovke Isakhara Akilova**. [Uzbek dances staged by Isakhar Akilov]. Tashkent: Gafur Gulyam Literature and Art Publishing House, 1987.

Khamidova, Marfua. **Akterckoe iskusstvo uzbekskoi musikal'noi dramy**. [Actor's art of Uzbek musical drama]. Tashkent: Khamza Hakim-zade Niyazi Institute of Fine Arts Studies, 1987.

Levin, Theodore. **The one hundred thousand fools of God: musical travels in Central Asia (and Queens, New York)**. Indiana: Indiana University Press, 1996.

Mirchazhdarova, Z.M. **Muyzka v dramatickom teatre Uzbekistana**. [Music in the dramatic theatre of Uzbekistan]. Tashkent: Izdetelstvo literatury i iskusstba im. G. Guljama, 1986. 102 p.

Miunts, Marionella and Alla Sosnovskaia. **Khudozhniki teatra i kino**. [Theatre and cinema design]. Tashkent: Gafur Gulyam Literature and Art Publishing House, 1982. 149 p.: ill. (some col.). *Notes*: English and Russian. Scene painting. History. 20th century.

Mukhtarov, Il dar Askadovich. **Teatr i ego aktery: tendentsii razvitiia uzbekskogo stsenicheskogo iskusstva 50–70-kh godov: na materiale Teatra imeni Khamzy**. Tashkent: Izd-vo Fan Uzbekskoi SSR, 1989. 144 p. *Notes*: Includes bibliographical references. History. 20th century/Hamza teatri.

——. **Teatr i klassika: klassika na stsene sovremennogo uzbekskogo teatra**. Nauchno-populiarnoe izd. Tashkent: Gafur Gulyam Literature and Art Publishing House, 1988. 174 p.: ill. *Notes*: Includes bibliographical references. History. 20th century.

Qodirov, Muhsin. **Sahnamiz lochinlari**. Tashkent: Ghafur Ghulom nomidagi Adabiët va sanat nashriëti, 1986. 203 p.: ill. *Notes*: Bibliographical references. History. 20th century.

Shirokaya, O.I. **Al'bom Tamara Khanum**. [Album of Tamara Khanum]. Tashkent: Gafur Gulyam Literature and Art Publishing House, 1973.

Sosnovskaya, Alla Georgievna. **Puti razbitiya teatral'no-dekopatsionnovo iskusstva Uzbekistana**. [The path of development of the art of theatrical decoration in Uzbekistan]. Tashkent: Khamza Hakim-zade Niyazi Institute of fine Art Studies, 1989.

Tuliakhodzhaeva, Mukhabbat Turabovna; IUldashev, Takhir Ismailovich. **Uzbekskaia dramaturgiia na stsene teatra: (60–80-gody)**. Tashkent: Izd-vo Fan Uzbekskoi SSR, 1990. 132 p. *Notes*: At head of title: Ministerstvo kul'tury Uzbekskoi SSR. Ordena druzhby narodov Institut iskusstvoznaniia im. Khamzy. Errata slip inserted. Includes bibliographical references. *Subjects*: Uzbek drama. 1960–1980 History and criticism.

Tursunov, Tashpulat. **Oktiabrskaia revoliutsiia i uzbekskii teatr**. Tashkent: Izd-vo Fan Uzbekskoi SSR, 1983. 192 p. *Notes*: Includes bibliographical references. Theatre and state. Uzbekistan/Communism and culture.

A3a153. VENEZUELA

Acevedo Donis, Mibelis. **Horacio Peterson: memoria de un sueño**. Caracas: FUNDARTE,

Alcaldía de Caracas, Dirección de Artes Escénicas, Cátedra Popular de Teatro Horacio Peterson, 1993. – 80 p.: ill. *Notes*: Theatrical producers and directors. Biography.

Azparren Giménez, Leonardo. **La máscara y la realidad: comportamientos del teatro venezolano contemporáneo**. Caracas: FUNDARTE, Alcaldía de Caracas, 1994. – 109 p. *Notes*: Includes bibliographical references (p. 107–8). History. 20th century.

——. **Teatro en crisis**. [Theatre in crisis]. Caracas: Fundarte, 1987. – 104 p. *Notes*: Includes bibliographical references. History. 20th century.

——. **El teatro venezoloano**. [Venezuelan theatre]. Caracas: Departamento de Literatura del Instituto Nacional de Cultura y Bellas Artes, 1967.

——. **El teatro venezolano y otros teatros**. [Venezuelan and other theatres]. Caracas: Monte Avila Editores, 1978. – 247 p. *Notes*: Includes bibliographical references. Venezuelan drama. 20th century. History and criticism.

Castillo, Susana D. **El 'desarraigo' en el teatro venezolano: marco histórico y manifestaciones modernas**. Caracas: Editorial Ateneo de Caracas, 1980. – 189 p. *Notes*: Originally presented as the author's thesis (doctoral)–UCLA, 1978. Bibliography: p. 185–9. *Subjects*: Drama. 20th century. History and criticism.

Chocrón, Isaac E. **Nueva crítica del teatro venezolano**. [A new analysis of Venezuelan theatre]. Colección Cuadernos de Difusión, no. 67. Caracas: FUNDARTE, 1981.

——. **El nuevo teatro venezolano**. [A new analysis of Venezuelan theatre]. Caracas: Oficina Central de Información. [n.d.].

——. **Sueño y tragedia en el teatro norteamericano**. Caracas: Alfadil Ediciones, 1984. – 163 p. American drama. History and criticism.

Feo Calcano, Guillermo. **Teatro municipal, 1881–1981**. [Municipal theatre, 1881–1981]. Caracas: FUNDARTE/CROMOTIP, 1981.

Guerrero Matheus, Fernando. **Teatro y gente de teatro en el Zulia**. Maracaibo: Universidad de Zulia, 1962.

Hernández, Gleider. **Tres dramaturgos venezolanos de hoy: Chalbaud, Cabrujas y Chocrón**. [Three contemporary Venezuelan playwrights: Chalbaud, Cabrujas and Chocrón]. Caracas: Ediciones El Nuevo Grupo, 1979.

Korn, Guillermo. **Unos pasos per el teatro**. [A few steps in the theatre]. Caracas: Ediciones Casuz/Italgráfica, 1979.

León, Enrique. **Fragmentos: una signatura de 'Dramática de Maracaibo'**. Maracaibo: Ediciones Pancho El Pájaro, Sociedad Dramática de Maracaibo, 1990. – 197 p. Venezuelan drama. 20th century. History and criticism/ Sociedad Dramática de Maracaibo.

Márquez, Carlos. **Juana Sujo: impulsora del teatro contemporáneo venezolano**. Caracas: FUNDARTE, 1996. – 142 p.: ill. *Notes*: Includes bibliographical references. Biography. Sujo, Juana, 1913–61.

Monasterios, Rubén. **Un enfoque crítico del teatro venezolano**. [A critical look at Venezuelan theatre]. Caracas: Monte Avila Editores, 1975.

——. **Un estudio crítico y longitudinal del teatro venezolano**. [A critical study of Venezuelan theatre]. Caracas: Universidad Central de Venezuela, 1974.

Moreno, Uribe and Edgard Antonio. **Bravo!: primera década de la Compañía Nacional de Teatro**. Caracas: La Compañía, 1995. – 99 p.: ill. *Notes*: 20th century/Compañía Nacional de Teatro (Caracas). History.

——, eds. **Carlos Giménez: tiempo y espacio**. Caracas: Vadell Hermanos Editores, 1993. – 151 p.: ill. *Notes*: Una selección de sus más valiosas declaraciones y una serie de artículos… que con su firma fueron publicados en el Periódico de Teatro y otros diarios de Caracas-Giménez, Carlos. Interviews/Fundación Rajatabla. History. The thoughts of a major director and theatrical shaker.

——. **Teatro 94: apuntes para su historia en Venezuela**. Caracas: Kairos, 1995. – 99 p. History. 20th century.

Ramón y Rivera, Luis Felipe. **Teatro popular venezolano**. [Venezuelan popular theatre]. Quito: Instituto de Artes Populares, 1981.

Rengifo, César and Jesús Mujica. **César Rengifo a viva voz**. [Caracas]: FUNDARTE, Alcaldía de Caracas, Dirección de Artes Escénicas, Cátedra Popular de Teatro Horacio Peterson, 1991. – 80 p.: ill. *Notes*: Rengifo, César. Interviews.

Rojas Uzcátegui, José de la Cruz and Lubio Cardozo. **Bibliografía del teatro venezolano**. Mérida: Universidad de Los Andes, Facultad de Humanidades y Educación, 1980. – 199 p. *Notes*: Includes index. Venezuelan drama. Bibliography.

Salas, Carlos. **Cien años de teatro municipal**. [100 years of municipal theatre]. Caracas: Consejo Municipal del Distrito Federal, 1980.

——. **Historia del teatro en Caracas**. [History

of theatre in Caracas]. Caracas: Secretaría General de la Gobernación del Distrito Federal, 1967.

Sánchez, Blanca and David Rojas. **Rajatabla: 20 años de vida para el teatro venezolano**. Caracas: Monte Ávila Latinoamericana, 1991. 420 p.: ill. *Notes*: Rajatabla, el grupo, 1971–91. History.

Suárez Radillo, Carlos. **Trece autores del nuevo teatro venezolano**. [Thirteen authors from the new Venzuelan theatre]. Caracas: Monte Avila Editores, 1971.

Various. **Imagen del teatro venezolano**. [Images of the Venezuelan theatre]. Caracas: Venezuelan Centre of the International Theatre Institute, 1978.

——. **Valores teatrales**. [Theatrical values]. Caracas: Círculo Musical, 1967.

A3a154. VIETNAM

Alter, Nora M. **The staged war: dramatization of the Vietnam War in German, French, British and American theatre**. 1992, 1991. 399 p. *Notes*: Includes bibliographical references (p. 383–99). Thesis (Ph. D.)–University of Pennsylvania, 1991. Photocopy. Ann Arbor, Mich.: UMI Dissertation Services, 1992. 399 p. Vietnamese War, 1961–1975. Protest movements/Political plays. 20th century. History and criticism.

Bích Lâm. **Luycen tcap ticeng nói cua dicen viên**. Ho Chí Minh City: Nhà xucat ban Thành phco Hco Chí Minh, 1978. – 154 p.: ill. *Notes*: Voice. Acting. Breathing exercises. Study and teaching.

Brandon, James R. **Theater in Southeast Asia**. Cambridge, Mass.: Harvard University Press, 1967. 370 p.

Durand, M. and Nguyen Tran Huan. **An introduction to Vietnamese theatre**. New York: Columbia University Press, 1985. 213 p.

Hà, Van Ccau, Châu Ký Hoàng and Nhu Mai Hoàng. **35 nam sân khcau ca kich cách mang**. Hanoi: Van hóa, 1980. 155 p. Vietnam (Democratic Republic). History. 20th century.

Hai muoi nam sân khcau Vicet Nam, 1975–1995. Hanoi: Sân khcau, 1995. 183 p., 3 p. of plates: ill. *Notes*: History. 20th century.

Ho Ngoc. **Nghce thuat vicet kich: mcay vcan dce co ban**. Hanoi: Van Hóa, 1973. – 199 p. *Notes*: Includes bibliographical references. Drama. Technique. History and criticism.

Ho, Trung An. **Sàn gco màn nhung: lich sân khcau cai luong Viet Nam**. Glendale, CA: Øai Nam, 1996. 348 p. *Notes*: Includes biblio-graphical references. Cai luong. Musical theatre. Vietnam drama. History and criticism.

Hoàng, Chuong. **Bác Ho vi nghe thucat sân khau**. Hanoi: Vicen sân khau, 1990. 253 p., 15 p. of plates: ill. *Notes*: Theatre and state. Ho Chí Minh, 1890–1969. Views on drama.

Jacquot, J., ed. 'Le Théâtre vietnamien'. [The Vietnamese theatre]. In **Les Théâtres d'Asie**, Paris, 1968.

Mackerras, Colin. 'Theatre in Vietnam'. **Asian Theatre Journal**, Spring 1987 Vol. 4, no. 1.

Nguycen, Ánh. **Sân khcau mcot doan trung**. Hanoi: Sân khcau, 1995. 317 p. *Notes*: History. 20th century.

Nguyen Ba Khoach, trans. **Vietnamese Water Puppets** [videorecording]. 1982.

Nguyen Huy Hong and Tran Trung Chinh. **Vietnamese Traditional Water Puppetry**. Hanoi: The Gioi, 1992. 79 p.

Tran, Bfang. **Sân khau Viet Nam, 1945–1985**. Hanoi: Sân khcau, 1987. 164 p. *Notes*: History. 20th century.

Tran, Van Thái. **Nghe-thucat sân-khau Viet-Nam: hát-boi, cai-luong, thoai-kich, thú xem dicen kich**. Saigon: Khai-Trí, 1970. 265 p., 8 p. of plates: ill. (some col.). *Notes*: History. 20th century. Study of forms such as hat boi and cai-luong.

'Vietnamese Water Puppets' in **Performing Arts Journal** (v. 9 No. 1), 1985.

A3a155. YEMEN

'Aulaqi, Sa'eed. **Sab'oun 'Aaman Min al-Masrah Fi l-Yaman**. [Seventy years of Yemeni theatre]. 1980.

Al-Haddad, Abdul-Rahman. **Cultural policy in the Yemen Arab Republic**. Paris: UNESCO, 1982. 74 p.

Luqmaan, Hamzah 'Ali. **Qisas min tarikh al-Yaman**. Sana'a: Dar al-Kalimah, 1985. 93 p.

Rahumah, Muhammad Mahmud. **Dirasat fi al-shi'r wa al-masrah al-Yamani**. Sana'a: Dar al'Kalimah, 1985. 184 p.

Zuwiyya, Jalal, compiler. 'Yemen'. In **The Near East (South-west Asia and North Africa): A bibliographic study**. Metuchen, NJ: Scarecrow Press, 1973: 306–409.

A3a156. YUGOSLAVIA

Batušić, Nikola. **Drama i pozornica: deset godina hrvatske drame na zagrebačkim pozornicama, 1964–1974**. [Drama and stage: ten years of Croatian drama on the stages of

Zagreb, 1964–74]. Novi Sad: Sterijino pozorje, 1975. 237 p.

Foretic, Dalibor. **Nova drama: svjedocenja o jugoslavenskim dramatikama i njihovim scenskim refleksima, 1972–1988**. Novi Sad: Sterijino pozorje, 1989. – 422 p. *Notes*: In Serbo-Croatian (Roman). Yugoslav drama. 20th century. History and criticism.

Hecimović, Branko. **Dramaturški tripthon**. [Dramaturgical triptych]. Zagreb: Hrvatsko društvo kazališnih kritičara i teatrologa, 1979. 188 p.

Histoire des spectacles: Encyclopédie de la Pléiade. Paris: 1965. S.v. 'Yugoslavia' by Marijan Matković.

Ivanovski, Ivan. **Plima i oseka**. Skopje: Makedonska kniga, 1981. – 240 p. *Notes*: Includes bibliographical references and index. History. 20th century.

Ivsic, Radovan. **U nepovrat: clanci, razgovori i dokumenti 1956–1989**. Zagreb: Graficki zavod Hrvatske, 1990. – 209 p. *Notes*: In Serbo-Croatian. Includes bibliographical references (p. 194–7) and index. Yugoslav literature. 20th century. History and criticism Surrealism. Intellectual life.

Jovanovic, Rasko V. **Pozoriste i drama**. Belgrade: Vuk Karadzic, 1984. – xi, 404 p.: ill. *Notes*: Includes index. Bibliography: p. 382–3. Dictionary of theatre. In Serbo-Croatian.

Jovanovic, Slobodan and Zoran Jovanovic. **Pozorisne studije i kritike**. Belgrade: Muzej pozorisne umetnosti Srbije, 1993. – 272 p. *Notes*: Includes bibliographical references (p. 255–8) and index. Dramatic criticism.

Jovanovic, Zoran. **Bibliografska grada za istoriju pozorista i dramske knjizevnosti u Vojvodini 1878–1983**. Novi Sad: Pozorisni muzej Vojvodine, 1984. – v. *Notes*: Yugoslavia. Voivodina (Serbia). Bibliography.

Karahasan, Dževad. **Kazalište i kritika**. [Theatre and criticism]. Sarajevo: Svjetlost, 1980. 241 p.

Marjanovic, Petar. **Jugoslovenski dramski pisci XX veka. 1**. Novi Sad: Akademija umetnosti u Novom Sadu, 1985. – 228 p. *Notes*: Yugoslav drama. 20th century. History and criticism.

Matković, Marijan, ed. **Le Théâtre yougoslave d'aujourd'hui/Yugoslav Theatre Today**. Zagreb-Belgrade-Dubrovnik: Yugoslavian Centre of the ITI, 1955.

Miletíc, Stjepan. **Hrvatsko Glumište: Dramaturški Zapisci**. [Croatian theatre: dramaturgical notes]. Zagreb: Centar za kulturnu djelatnost

Saveza socijalističke omladine Zagreba, 1978. 509 p.

Pervić, Muharem. **Premijera: naša drama u našem pozorištu**. [Première: our drama in our theatre]. Belgrade: Nolit, 1978. 337 p.

Petric, Vladimir. **Le Drame yougoslave d'aujourd'hui: notes et fragments**. Belgrade: Jugoslavija, 1962. – 137 p.: ill *Notes*: Includes bio-bibliographies of Yugoslav dramatists and brief excerpts from their works.

Popovic, Žorž: **Istorija arhitekture, pozorišta, kazališta gledališča i teatara Jugoslavije i Evrope**. [History of architecture and theatre of Yugoslavia and Europe]. Belgrade, 1986, 1977. 722 p.

Šovagović, Fabijan. **Glumčevi zapisi**. [Actor's notes]. Zagreb: Centar za kulturnu djelatnost Saveza socijalističke omladine, 1977. 214 p.

Stamenković, Vladimir. **Kraljevstvo eksperimenta**. [The kingdom of experimentation]. Belgrade: Prosveta pozorište u dramatizovanom društvu, 1987. 282 p.

——. **Pozoriste u dramatizovanom drustvu: kritike i eseji (1956–1986)**. Belgrade: Prosveta, 1987. – 295 p. *Notes*: In Serbo-Croatian (roman). Includes bibliographical references. Yugoslav drama. History and criticism.

Theatre in Yugoslavia. Belgrade: Museum of Theatre Art in Belgrade, 1955. 86 p.

A3a157. ZAÏRE

Biebuyck, Daniel P. **The arts of Zaïre**. Berkeley: University of California Press, 1986.

Bokonga Ekanga Botombele. **Cultural policy in the Republic of Zaïre: a study**. Paris: UNESCO, 1976. 119 p.

Cornevin, R. **Histoire du Congo, des origines préhistoriques à la République Démocratique du Congo**. [History of Congo, from Prehistoric Origins to a Democratic Republic]. 3rd edn. Paris: Berger Levrault, 1970.

De Rop. **Théâtre Nkundo**. Léopoldville: Édition de l'Université, 1959.

Duvingnaud, J. **Sociologie du théâtre, essai sur les ombres collectives**. [Sociology of theatre, an essay on Collective Shadows]. Paris: PUF, 1965.

Jadot, J.C. **Les Écrivains africains du Congo-Belge et du Rwanda-Urundi**. [African Writers of Belgian-Congo and Rwanda-Urundi.]. Vol. XVII. Brussels: Royal Academy of Colonial Sciences, 1959.

Kikufi, Mikanda, Kilesa Ndona and Tayaya Lumbombo. **Théâtre populaire de Bandundu**.

[The popular theatre of Bandundu]. Bandundu: CEEBA, 1980. 149 p.

Lapissade, G. **L'Arpenteur**. Paris: EPI, 1971.

Lebailly, Henry. **Catharsis, viol-violence**. [Catharsis, Rape-Violence]. Lubumbashi: PIC, 1979.

——. **La Fête révolutionnaire, le théâtre au Zaire avant 1960**. [The Revolutionary Festival Theatre in Zaïre before 1960]. Lubumbashi: Éditions Catharsis, 1983.

Le Théâtre zaïrois, dossier du premier festival. [Theatre of Zaïre: Record of the first festival]. Kisantu: 1977.

'Le Théâtre zaïrois'. [The Theatre of Zaïre]. **Poètes et Conteurs noire**.

Mukala, Kadima Nzuji. **Bibliographie littéraire de la République du Zaïre, 1931–1972**. Lubumbashi: Centre d'étude des littératures romanes d'inspiration africaine, Université nationale du Zaïre, 1973. 60 p.

Mwambayi, Kalengayi. **Initiation au théâtre Africain, technique du mouvement et de regroupement dans la création collective, guide pédagogique du maître**. [Introduction to African theatre, regrouping techniques of collective creations, pedalogical guide of the master]. Legon: Institute of African Studies, University of Ghana, 1981.

Schicho, Ndala M. **Le Groupe Mafwankolo**. [The Mafwankolo Group]. Vienna: 1981.

Yoka, L.M. **Le Rôle du théâtre au Zaïre, conférence au Goethe Institut, Kinshasa, 4 Juillet 1972**. [The Role of the Theatre in Zaïre, Conference at the Goethe Institute, Kinshasa, 4 July 1972]. Kinshasa: Goethe Institute, 1972.

A3a158. ZAMBIA

Balcomb, J. 'The beginning of a new beginning for Zambia'. **Le Théâtre dans le Monde**. (1965).

Chakulanda, P. 'Towards a Zambian national theatre'. **Chikwakwa Review** (1974–5).

Chifunyise, Stephen. 'Problems of transposing traditional narratives, myths and legends into contemporary performing arts'. **Bulletin of the Zambian Language Group** 3, no. 2 (1978): 37–42.

——, David Kerr and F. Dall. **Theatre for development: the Chalimbana Workshop, 1979**. Lusaka: Zambian Centre of the International Theatre Institute, 1980. 65 p.

Crehan, Stewart. 'Fathers and sons: politics and myth in recent Zambian drama'. **New Theatre Quarterly** 3, no. 9 (1987): 29–43.

Epskamp, Kees P. 'Historical outline of the development of Zambian national theatre'. **Canadian Journal of African Studies** 21, no. 2 (1987): 157–74.

Etherton, Michael. 'The development of a radio programme series in Zambia'. **University of Zambia Institute for Social Research Bulletin** (1968).

Idoye, Emeka Patrick. 'Ideology and the theatre: the case of Zambia'. **Journal of Black Studies** 19, no. 1 (September 1988): 70–8.

Kerr, David and Stephen Chifunyise. 'Popular theatre in Zambia: Chikwakwa reassessed'. **Theatre International** 11–12 (1984): 54–80.

Maxwell, Kevin B. **Bemba myth and ritual: the impact of literacy on an oral culture**. New York: P. Lang, 1983. 197 p.

Mwansa, Dickson. 'Theatre situation in Africa'. **Young Cinema and Theatre** 1, 3/5 (1985).

Mwondela, Willie R. **Mukanda and Makishi in northwestern Zambia**. Lusaka: National Educational Council of Zambia, 1972. 58 p.

Pownall, D. 'European and African influences in Zambian theatre'. **Theatre Quarterly** 10 (1973).

Richards, Audrey I. 'Theatrical situation in Zambia'. **World Theatre** 15, no. 1 (1966): 56–7.

——. **Chisungu: a girl's initiation ceremony among the Bemba**. London/New York: Tavistock, 1982. 224 p.

Turner, Edith. 'Phillip Kabwita, Ghost Doctor: the Ndembu in 1985'. **The Drama Review** 30, no. 4 (winter 1986), p. 12–35.

A3a159. ZIMBABWE

Anthrope, Raymond, and John Blacking. 'Field work co-operation in the study of Nsenga music and ritual'. **Africa** 32, no. 1 (1962).

Bourdillon, Michael. **Where are the Ancestors? Changing Culture in Zimbabwe**. Harare: University of Zimbabwe Publishers, 1993.

Chifunyise, Stephen. **Medicine for love and other plays**. Gweru: Mambo Press, 1984. 113 p.

Dube, Caleb. 'Amakhosi theatre Ako-Bulawayo'. **The Drama Review** 36, no. 2 (1992): 44–7.

Gelfand, Michael. 'A description of the ceremony of Kurova Guva'. **Zambezia** 2 (December 1971).

Globerman, Evie. 'Backstage on the frontline'. **Journal of Southern African Studies** 16, no. 2 (1990).

Kaarsholm, Preben. 'Mental Colonisation or

Catharsis? Theatre, Democracy and Cultural Struggle from Rhodesia to Zimbabwe'. **Journal of Southern African Studies** 16, no. 2 (1990).

Kavanagh, Robert. 'Theatre for development in Zimbabwe: an urban project'. **Journal of Southern African Studies** 16, no. 2 (1990).

Kidd, Ross. **From people's theatre for revolution to popular theatre for reconstruction: diary of a Zimbabwean workshop.** The Hague: Centre for the Study of Education in Developing Countries, 1984. 89 p.

McLaren, Robert. 'Theatre on the frontline: the political theatre of Zambuko/Izibuko'. **The Drama Review** 36, no. 1 (1992).

——, and Stephen J. Chifunyise. **Zimbabwe theatre report, University of Zimbabwe.** Harare: University of Zimbabwe Press, 1989.

Thompson, G. Caton. **The Zimbabwe culture: African pre-history.** London: Frank Press & Co. Ltd., 1971.

Wortham, C.J. 'The state of the theatre in Rhodesia'. **Zambezia** 1, no. 1 (January 1969): 47–53.

Zakes, M.D.A. 'Maratholi Travelling Theatre: Towards an Alternative Perspective of Development'. **Journal of Southern African Studies** 16, no. 2 (1990).

Zinyemba, Ranga M. **Zimbabwean drama: a study of Shona and English plays.** Gweru: Mambo Press, 1986. 112 p.

B. Genre, Style, Theory and Criticism

B1. Genre, Style, Theory

Banu, Georges. **Mémoires du théâtre: essai.** Arles: Actes Sud, 1987. – 141 p.: ill. *Notes:* Includes bibliographical references. Theatre. History. 20th century.

——. **Le théâtre, ou, L'instant habité: exercices et essais.** Paris: Editions de l'Herne, 1993. – 203 p. *Notes:* Includes bibliographical references. Theatre. History. 20th century.

——. **Le théâtre, sorties de secours: essais critiques.** Paris: Aubier, 1984. – 222 p. *Notes:* Bibliography: p. 207–19. Theatre. History. 20th century.

Beckerman, Bernard. **Dynamics of drama: theory and method of analysis.** New York: Drama Book Specialists, 1979 1970. – xii, 263, viii p. *Notes:* Originally published in 1970 by Knopf, New York. Includes bibliographical references and index.

Béhar, Henri. **Le théâtre Dada et surréaliste.** Nouv. éd. rev. et augm. [Paris]: Gallimard, 1979. – 444 p. *Notes:* Bibliography: p. 385–398. French drama. 20th century. History and criticism. Dadaism. Surrealism.

Bentley, Eric. **Theory, history and postmodernism.** Bloomington: Indiana: University Press, 1991. 240 p.

——. **The Theory of the modern stage: an introduction to modern theatre and drama.** New York: Applause, 1997. – 496 p. *Notes:* Includes index.

Birch, David Ian. **The language of drama: critical theory and practice.** New York: St. Martin's Press, 1991. – x, 175 p. *Notes:* Includes bibliographical references (p. 154–69) and index.

Birringer, Johannes H. **Theatre, theory, postmodernism.** Bloomington: Indiana University Press, 1993. – xiv, 235 p.: ill. *Notes:* Includes bibliographical references and index.

Bishop, Cynthia A. **The deconstructed actor: towards a postmodern acting theory.** 1988. – vi, 224 p. *Notes:* Includes abstract. Bibliography: p. 212–24. Thesis (Ph. D.)– University of Colorado, 1988. Photocopy. Ann Arbor, Mich.: University Microfilms, 1989. vi, 224 p.

Blau, Herbert. **The eye of prey: subversions of the postmodern.** Bloomington: Indiana University Press, 1987. – xxxvi, 213 p. *Notes:* Includes bibliographical references and index.

——. **To all appearances: ideology and performance.** New York: Routledge, 1992. – xv, 223 p. *Notes:* Includes bibliographical references (p. 200–13) and index.

Bradby, David and John McCormick. **People's theatre.** London: Totowa, N.J.: Croom Helm; Rowman & Littlefield, 1978. – 179 p., [8] p. of plates: ill. *Notes:* Includes indexes. Bibliography: p. 167–9. Theatre and society. 20th century.

Brockett, Oscar G. and Robert R. Findlay. **Century of innovation: a history of European and American theatre and drama since the late nineteenth century.** 2nd edn. Boston: Allyn and Bacon, 1991. – xii, 520 p.: ill. *Notes:* Includes bibliographical references (p. 482–98) and index. History and criticism.

Casas, Myrna, ed. **Teatro de la vanguardia** [Avant-garde theatre]. Lexington, KY: D.C. Heath, 1975.

Clark, Barrett H. **European theories of the drama, with a supplement on the American** drama; an anthology of dramatic theory and criticism from Aristotle to the present day, in a series of selected texts, with commentaries, biographies, and bibliographies. Rev. by Henry Popkin. New York: Crown Publishers, 1965. – xiv, 628 p. *Notes*: Bibliography: p. 543–613. A standard text.

Demastes, William W. **Theatre of chaos: beyond absurdism, into orderly disorder**. New York: Cambridge University Press, 1997. – p. *Notes*: Includes bibliographical references and index. History and criticism. Literature and science. Quantum chaos.

Dukore, Bernard Frank F. **Dramatic theory and criticism: Greeks to Grotowski**. New York: Holt, Rinehart & Winston, 1974. – xiv, 1003 p. *Notes*: Bibliography: p. 997–8. A standard text.

Eddleman, Floyd Eugene. **American drama criticism: supplement II to the second edition**. Hamden, Conn.: Shoe String Press, 1989. – 269 p. *Notes*: Includes indexes.

——. **American drama criticism: supplement III to the second edition**. Hamden, Conn.: Shoe String Press, 1992. – 436 p. *Notes*: Includes indexes.

——. **American drama criticism, supplement to the second edition**. Hamden, Conn.: Shoe String Press, Inc., 1984.

—— and Helen H. Palmer. **American drama criticism: interpretations, 1890–1977**. 2d edn. Hamden, Conn.: Shoe String Press, 1979. – viii, 488 p. *Notes*: First edn, by H.H. Palmer, published in 1967. Includes indexes. 'List of books indexed': p. 429–38. 'List of journals indexed': p. 439–47.

Esslin, Martin. **The theatre of the absurd**. 3rd edn. London; New York: Penguin Books, 1991 1980. – 480 p. *Notes*: Published 'in association with Eyre & Spottiswoode'. Includes index. Bibliography: p. 437–70. *Subjects*: The critic who coined the term explains the concept. This key book exists in French, German, Spanish and numerous other languages.

Fraga, Eudinyr. **Qorpo Santo: realismo ou absurdo?** [Qorpo Santo: Realism or Theatre of the Absurd?]. São Paulo: Perspectiva, 1990. 153 p.

Fiebach, Joachim. **Von Craig bis Brecht: Studien zu Künstlertheorien in der ersten Hälfte des 20. Jahrhunderts**. Berlin: Henschel, 1991. – 462 p. *Notes*: Includes bibliographical references (p. 391–458) and index. Study of the theories of Craig and Brecht.

Fortier, Mark. **Theory/theatre: an introduction**. London; New York: Routledge, 1997. – 195 p.

Notes: Includes bibliographical references (p. 170–86) and index.

Gaensbauer, Deborah B. **The French theatre of the absurd**. Boston: Twayne Publishers, 1991. – xix, 137 p.: ill. *Notes*: Includes bibliographical references (p. 117–29) and index. Jarry, the Dadaists, and the Surrealists – Antonin Artaud – Samuel Beckett – Eugène Ionesco – Arthur Adamov – Jean Genet – Fernando Arrabal – New directions.

Gilbert, Sandra M. and Susan Gubar. **Masterpiece theatre: an academic melodrama**. New Brunswick, N.J.: Rutgers University Press, 1995. – xxiv, 203 p.: ill. *Notes*: Includes bibliographical references (p. 189–202). Theory. Drama/Canon.

Godard, Colette and Natacha Decan. **Le Théâtre depuis 1968**. Paris: J.C. Lattès, 1980. – 246 p., [6] p. of plates: ill. *Notes*: Includes bibliographical references and index. Theatre. History. 20th century. Experimental theatre.

Graver, David. **The aesthetics of disturbance: anti-art in avant-garde drama**. Ann Arbor: University of Michigan Press, 1995. – 253 p.: ill. *Notes*: Includes index. Avant-garde aesthetics. History. 20th century/Modernism.

Gruber, William E. **Missing persons: character and characterization in modern drama**. Athens [Ga.]: University of Georgia Press, 1994. – xi, 222 p.: ill. *Notes*: Includes bibliographical references (p. 209–17) and index. Gordon Craig's depersonalized stage – Brecht and the social self – Character portraits/portraying character: Krapp's last tape, Rockaby, Catastrophe – Mental life in Thomas Bernhard's comic types – The characters of Maria Irene Fornes – Abstract art and the representation of character.

Hamon, Christine. **Le Constructivisme au théâtre**. Paris: Éditions du Centre national de la recherche scientifique, 1992, 1991. – 368 p.: ill. *Notes*: History. 20th century. Constructivism.

Herms, Dieter and Arno Paul. **Politisches Volkstheater der Gegenwart: Aufsätze**. Berlin: Argument-Verlag, 1981. – 109 p. *Notes*: Collection of previously published essays. Cover title. One summary in English. Includes bibliographical references. Kunst und Agitation/Dieter Herms – Mime Troupe, El Teatro, Bread and Puppet/Dieter Herms – Ein Theater mit Grips/Arno Paul – Agitation- und Strassentheater in den USA/Dieter Herms – Szene kritischen Vergnügens/Arno Paul – Engagement, commitment, and fresh air/Arno Paul – Zwischen Mythos, Anpassung und Rebellion/Dieter Herms – Anmerkungen zur Entwicklung der Bildersprache im europäisch-westlichen

Schauspiel/Arno Paul. Experimental theatre and street theatre. Critical studies in German.

Hewitt, Barnard. **Play production: theory and practice**. Ann Arbor: University Microfilms, 1973. – 488 p. illus.

Ho, Yong. **Kundae yon'guk**. [Modern theatre]. Seoul: Hansin Munhwasa, 1985. – 746 p.: ill. *Notes*: In Korean. Includes index. Bibliography 691–714. Drama. 20th century. History and criticism.

Jones, David E. **A history of drama theory**. Carbondale: Southern Illinois University Press, 1991. *Notes*: Includes bibliographical references and index.

Kern, Edith and Kenneth White. **Alogical modern drama: essays**. Amsterdam: Rodopi, 1982. – 74 p. *Notes*: Includes bibliographical references. Alogical drama/Edith Kern – The alogical in the plays of Brecht/John Fuegi – Frank Wedekind's Spring's awakening/Leroy R. Shaw – Transcending logic–Stoppard, Wittgenstein, and Aristophanes/Mary R. Davidson – The explosiveness of the planet–Ionesco and Einstein/Kenneth S. White.

Killinger, John. **World in collapse; the vision of an absurd drama**. New York: Dell Pub. Co., 1971. – 184 p. *Notes*: Bibliography: p. 172–7. Drama. 20th century. History and criticism.

Lebel, Jean Jacques, E.C. de Nimmo and Allan Kaprow. **New writers IV; plays and happenings**. London: Calder & Boyars, 1967. – 166 p. Antrobus, John S/Marowitz, Charles/Dewey, Ken/Obaldia, René. *Notes*: Theory and practice/ Jean-Jacques Lebel–Catastrophe in Paris/E.C. Nimmo–Happenings at Edinburgh/Charles Marowitz–Act of San Francisco at Edinburgh/ Ken Dewey–An Edinburgh impromptu/René de Obaldia–Five happenings/Allan Kaprow–You'll come to love your sperm test (play)/John Antrobus.

Lesić, Zdenko. **Teorija drama**. [The theory of drama]. 3 vols. 1977–91.

Levin, Harry. **Playboys and killjoys: an essay on the theory and practice of comedy**. New York: Oxford University Press, 1987. – viii, 214 p. *Notes*: Includes index. In European languages. Critical studies.

Lewis, Allan. **The contemporary theatre; the significant playwrights of our time**. New York: Crown Publishers, 1971. – ix, 374 p. *Notes*: Includes bibliographical references. Drama. 20th century. History and criticism.

Loney, Glenn Meredith. **20th century theatre**. New York, N.Y.: Facts on File, 1983. – 2 vols.

(xiii, 521 p.): ill. *Notes*: Includes index. Bibliography: p. 458–63.

Luzuriaga, Gerardo. **Introducción a las teorías latino-americanaa de teatro**. [Introduction to Latin American theatre theories]. Puebla: Universidad Autónoma de Puebla, 1990.

MacDonald, Erik. **Theater at the margins: text and the post-structured stage**. Ann Arbor: University of Michigan Press, 1993. – 202 p. *Notes*: Includes bibliographical references (p. 191–9) and index. Postmodernism (Literature)/Deconstruction. Philosophy/ Theatre and society.

Malekin, Peter and Ralph Yarrow. **Consciousness, literature, and theatre: theory and beyond**. Basingstoke: Macmillan, 1997. – ix, 197 p. *Notes*: Includes bibliographical references and index. Spirituality in literature. History and criticism.

Marranca, Bonnie. **Ecologies of theater: essays at the Century Turning**. Baltimore: Johns Hopkins University Press, 1996. – xix, 289 p.: ill. Series: PAJ books. *Notes*: History and criticism. Gertrude Stein. Heiner Müller. American avant-garde.

——. **Theatrewritings**. New York: Performing Arts Journal Publications, 1984. – 202 p., [1] p. of plates: ill. *Notes*: Includes bibliographical references. Performance art.

Melzer, Annabelle. **Dada and surrealist performance**. Baltimore: Johns Hopkins University Press, 1994. – xviii, 288 p.: ill. Series: PAJ books. *Notes*: Includes bibliographical references (p. 245–77) and index.

Mignon, Paul-Louis. **Le Théâtre au XXe siècle**. Paris: Gallimard, 1986. – 347 p. *Notes*: Includes index.

Nägele, Rainer. **Theater, theory, speculation: Walter Benjamin and the scenes of modernity**. Baltimore, Md.: Johns Hopkins University Press, 1991. – xviii, 232 p. *Notes*: Includes bibliographical references (p. 207–24) and index. History and criticism. Benjamin, Walter, 1892–1940. Aesthetics.

Nicoll, Allardyce. **The theatre and dramatic theory**. New York: Barnes & Noble, 1962. – 221 p. Drama. History and criticism. Theory.

——. **The theory of drama**. New York: Arno Press, 1980. – 261 p. *Notes*: Reprint of the 1931 edn which was a revised and enlarged edn of the work first published under title: **An introduction to dramatic theory**. Bibliography: p. 245–56. Drama/Tragedy/Comedy. A standard text.

Olson, Elder. **Tragedy and the theory of drama**. Detroit: Wayne State University Press, 1966

1961. – 269 p. *Notes*: Includes index. Drama. Tragedy. A standard text.

Orenstein, Gloria Feman. **The theatre of the marvelous: surrealism and the contemporary stage**. New York: New York University Press, 1975. – xv, 315 p.: ill. *Notes*: Includes index. Bibliography: p. 289–302.

Palmer, Helen H. **European drama criticism, 1900–1975**. 2nd edn. Hamden, Conn.: Shoe String Press, 1977. – 653 p. *Notes*: Includes index.

—— and Anne Jane Dyson. **American drama criticism; interpretations, 1890–1965 inclusive, of American drama since the first play produced in America**. Hamden, Conn.: Shoe String Press, 1974. – 239 p. *Notes*: Supplement I compiled by H.H. Palmer and A.J. Dyson, and Supplement II compiled by F.E. Eddleman.

——. **European drama criticism**. [Folcroft, Pa.]: Folcroft Library Editions, 1972. – 460 p. *Notes*: Companion volume to **American Drama Criticism**. Includes index. Kept up to date between editions by supplements.

——. **European drama criticism: supplement I**. Hamden, Conn.: Shoe String Press, 1970. – 243 p. *Notes*: Includes index.

——. **European drama criticism: supplement II**. Hamden: Conn.: Shoe String Press, 1974. – 209 p.

Pas, Elena and Gloria Waldman, eds. **Teatro contemporáneo**. [Contemporary theatre]. Boston, MA: Heinle & Heinle, 1983. 297 p.

Plesniarowicz, Krzysztof. **Mity teatru XX wieku: od Stanislawowskiego do Kantora**. [Twentieth century theatre: Stanislavsky to Kantor]. Kraków: Nakl. Uniwersytetu Jagiellonskiego, 1995. – 111 p. *Notes*: Includes bibliographical references.

Quackenbush, Howard L. **Teatro del absurdo hispanoamericano: antología anotada**. [Theatre of the absurd in Spanish America: annotated anthology]. México City: Editorial Patria, 1987. 270 p.

Rayner, Alice. **To act, to do, to perform: drama and the phemenology of action**. Ann Arbor: University of Michigan Press, 1994. – viii, 165 p. *Notes*: Includes bibliographical references (p. 157–61) and index. Philosophy in literature.

Reinelt, Janelle G. and Joseph R. Roach. **Critical theory and performance**. Ann Arbor: University of Michigan Press, 1992. – vii, 455: ill. *Notes*: Includes bibliographical references and index. Theatre. Philosophy.

Rose, Margaret. **The symbolist theatre tradition from Maeterlinck and Yeats to Beckett and Pinter**. Milan: Edizioni Unicopli, 1989. – 241 p.: ill. *Notes*: Includes bibliographical references (p. 219–41). Drama. History and criticism.

Sandford, Mariellen R. **Happenings and other acts**. London; New York: Routledge, 1995. – xxv, 397 p.: ill. *Notes*: Includes bibliographical references and index. Happenings: an introduction/Michael Kirby – The new theatre/Michael Kirby – Allan Kaprow's Eat/Michael Kirby – An interview with John Cage/Michael Kirby, Richard Schechner – Lecture 1960/La Monte Young – Fotodeath/Claes Oldenburg – The first and second wilderness/Michael Kirby – Fluxus/George Maciunas – The night time sky/Robert Whitman – Washes/Claes Oldenburg – Verdurous sanguinaria: Act 1/Jackson Mac Low – Graphis/Dick Higgins, Letty Eisenhauer – The tart, or Miss America/Dick Higgins – Yvonne Rainer interviews Ann Halprin – Some retrospective notes on a dance for 10 people and 12 mattresses called Parts of some sextets, performed at the Wadsworth Atheneum, Hartford, Connecticut, and Judson Memorial Church, New York, in March, 1965/Yvonne Rainer – Notes on Dance/Robert Morris – City scale/Ken Dewey, Anthony Martin, Ramon Sender – Three pieces: Evening, Kittyhawk, Combination wedding and funeral/The ONCE group – Calling/Allan Kaprow – The Great gaming house: A precis/Kelly Yeaton – X-ings/Ken Dewey – A monster model fun house/Paul Sills – Happenings/Richard Schechner – In response/A letter from Allan Kaprow – Extensions in time and space: an interview with Allan Kaprow/Richard Schechner – Self-service: a happening/Alan Kaprow – Excerpts from 'Assemblages, environments & happenings'/Allan Kaprow – From More than meat joy: from The notebooks, Meat joy, Snows/Carolee Schneemann – On the necessity of violation/Jean-Jacques Lebel – Reflections on happenings/Darko Suvin – Happenings in Europe: trends, events, and leading figures/Gunter Berghaus. European and American experimental theatre.

Sandier, Gilles. **Théâtre en crise: des années 70 à 82**. Grenoble: Editions La Pensée sauvage, 1982. – 487 p., [1] p. of plates: ill. (1 col.). *Notes*: Includes index. Bibliography: p. 472–80. Political theatre.

Schechner, Richard. **Essays on performance theory, 1970–1976**. New York: Drama Book Specialists, 1977. – 212 p. *Notes*: Bibliography: p. 202–12. Republished by Routledge in 1993 as **PerformanceTheory**, 304 p.

Shaland, Irene. **American theater and drama research: an annotated guide to information sources, 1945–1990**. Jefferson, N.C.:

McFarland, 1991. – xiv, 157 p. *Notes*: Includes index.

Szondi, Peter. **Theory of the modern drama: a critical edition**. Cambridge: Polity Press; in association with B. Blackwell, 1987. – xviii, 128 p. *Notes*: Translation of: **Theorie des modernen Dramas**. Includes index. Bibliography: p. 101–8. Drama. History and criticism.

Tharu, Susie J. **The sense of performance: post-Artaud theatre**. Atlantic Highlands, N.J.: Humanities Press, 1984. – 211 p. *Notes*: Includes index. Bibliography: p. 202–7. *Subjects*: Theatre. History. 20th century.

Tynan, Kenneth. **Curtains; selections from the drama criticism and related writings**. London: Longmans, 1961. – 495 p. One of the English-speaking world's foremost critics on American and European theatre.

——. **Tynan on theatre**. Harmondsworth. Penguin Books, 1964. – 363 p. Reviews and writings.

——. **Tynan right and left; plays, films, people, places and events**. London: Longmans, Green; New York: Atheneum, 1967. – ix, 479 p. Criticism. American and European.

Van Erven, Eugène. **Radical people's theatre**. Bloomington: Indiana University Press, 1988. – xiv, 238 p.: ill. *Notes*: Includes index. Bibliography: p. 207–33. Theatre and society. Populist approaches.

Zalacán, Daniel. **Teatro absurdista hispano-americano**. [Spanish-American theatre of the absurd]. Valencia, Spain: Albatros Hispanofilia, 1985.

B2. Criticism

Bennett, Benjamin. **Theater as problem: modern drama and its place in literature**. Ithaca: Cornell University Press, 1990. – x, 272 p. *Notes*: Includes bibliographical references and index.

Bentley, Eric. **The life of the drama**. New York, NY: Applause, 1991 1964. – ix, 371 p. *Notes*: Originally published: New York: Atheneum, 1964. Includes bibliographical references (p. 355–62) and index.

——. **In search of theater**. New York: Applause, 1992 1975. – xxii, 411, viii p., [24] p. of plates: ill. *Notes*: 'Travels in England, Ireland, France, Germany, Switzerland, Austria, Italy and the United states'. Originally published New York: Atheneum, 1975. Includes bibliographical references and index. 20th century/ Drama. 20th century. History and criticism.

——. **The modern theatre; a study of dramatists and the drama**. London: R. Hale, 1948. – xxv, 290 p. *Notes*: Errata slip inserted. American edn. (New York: Reynal & Hitchcock, 1946) has title: **The playwright as thinker**. Drama. History and criticism.

——. **The playwright as thinker: a study of drama in modern times**. San Diego: Harcourt Brace Jovanovich, 1987. – xxiii, 388 p. *Notes*: Reprint. Originally published: New York: Reynal & Hitchcock, 1946. Includes index. *Subjects*: Drama. 20th century. History and criticism.

——. **The theatre of commitment, and other essays on drama in our society**. New York: Atheneum; 1984; London: Methuen, 1968. – xi, 241 p. *Notes*: Drama. 20th century. History and criticism.

——. **Theatre of war: modern drama from Ibsen to Brecht**. New York: Viking Press, 1973. – xix, 236 p. *Notes*: Viking Compass edn. Includes bibliographical references and index. Drama. 20th century.

——. **Thinking about the playwright: comments from four decades**. Evanston, IL: Northwestern University Press, 1987. – x, 364 p. *Notes*: Includes index.

Berlogea, Ileana. **Teatrul si societatea contemporana: experiente dramatice si scenice ale anilor '60–'80**. Bucharest: Meridiane, 1985. – 339 p., 12 p. of plates: ill. *Notes*: Includes bibliographical references. Drama. 20th century. History and criticism.

Bermel, Albert. **Comic agony: mixed impressions in the modern theatre**. Evanston, Ill.: Northwestern University Press, 1993. – x, 223 p. *Notes*: Includes bibliographical references (p. 197–218) and index. Tragicomedy. Drama. 20th century. History and criticism.

——. **Contradictory characters: an interpretation of the modern theatre**. Evanston, IL: Northwestern University Press, 1996 1973. – xii, 298 p. *Notes*: Originally published: New York: Dutton, 1973. Includes bibliographical references and index. Drama. 20th century. History and criticism.

Brater, Enoch, ed. **The theatrical gamut: notes for a post-Beckettian stage**. Ann Arbor: University of Michigan Press, 1995. – xi, 304 p.: ill. *Notes*: Includes bibliographical references. Preface/Enoch Brater – Back to Bali/John Russell Brown – Training the French actor: From exercise to experiment/Bernard Dort – Molly's 'Happy Nights' and Winnie's 'Happy Days'/Antonia Rodriguez-Gago – Beckett's German context/Martin Esslin – Memory inscribed in the body: Krapp's last tape and the Noh Play Izutsu/Yasunari Takahashi – Delogocentering silence: Beckett's ultimate unwording/Carla Locatelli – Consorting with spirits: The arcane craft of Beckett's later drama/H. Porter Abbott – All my sons after the fall: Arthur Miller and rage for order/Hersh Zeifman – 'The garden is a mess': Maternal space in Bowles, Glaspell, Robins/Elin Diamond – Paranoia and celebrity in American dramatic writing: 1970–90/John Orr – The dramaturgy of the dream play: Monologues by Breuer, Chaikin, Shepard/Bill Coco – 'Codes form a mixed-up machine': The disintegrating actor in Beckett, Shepard and, surprisingly, Shakespeare/Gerry McCarthy – 'Aroun the Worl': The signifyin(g) theater of Suzan-Lori Parks/Linda Ben-Zvi – Is the English epic over?/Janelle Reinelt – Acting out the state agenda: Berlin, 1993/Sue-Ellen Case – Sitelines: A ground for theater/Jin Eigo – Afterthought from the vanishing point: Theater at the end of real/Herbert Blau – Afterword/Joseph Chaikin.

—— and Ruby Cohn, eds. **Around the absurd: essays on modern and postmodern drama**. Ann Arbor: University of Michigan Press, 1990. – viii, 316 p. *Notes*: Includes bibliographical references and index. Around the absurd/Ruby Cohn – Dagny and Lulu/Jan Kott – Maeterlinck in the light of the absurd/Katharine Worth – O'Neill and absurdity/Linda Ben-Zvi – Tradition and innovation in Ionesco's La Cantatrice chauve/James Knowlson – Late modernism; Samuel Beckett and the art of the oeuvre/H. Porter Abbott – Beckett, Shakespeare, and the making of theory/Charles R. Lyons – Harold Pinter/politics/Benedict Nightingale – Peter Barnes and the problem of goodness/Bernard F. Dukore – A trick of the light: Tom Stoppard's Hapgood and postabsurdist theater/Hersh Zeifman – Hen in a foxhouse: the absurdist plays of Maria Irene Fornes/Toby Silverman Zinman – The internationalization of the Paris stage/Rosette C. Lamont – Framing actuality: thirty years of experimental theater, 1959–89/Theodore Shank – The absurd, to and fro/Bernard Weiner – The oversight of ceaseless eyes/Herbert Blau – After the absurd: rethinking realism and a few other isms/Enoch Brater.

Brauneck, Manfred. **Theater im 20. Jahrhundert: Programmschriften, Stilperioden, Reformmodelle**. Hamburg: Rowohlt, 1989 1982. – 540 p.: ill. Series: Rowohlts Enzyklopädie. *Notes*: Bibliography: p. 495–516. Theatre. History. 20th century/Experimental theatre.

Brown, Hilda Meldrum. **Leitmotiv and drama: Wagner, Brecht, and the limits of 'Epic' theatre**. Oxford and New York: Clarendon Press; Oxford University Press, 1991. – 217 p. *Notes*: Includes bibliographical references (p. 206–11) and index. History and criticism. Criticism and interpretation.

Brownstein, Oscar Lee and Daphna Ben Chaim. **Analytical sourcebook of concepts in dramatic theory**. Westport, Conn.: Greenwood Press, 1981. – xxi, 560 p.

Brustein, Robert. **The theatre of revolt: an approach to the modern drama**. Boston: Little, Brown, 1964. *Notes*: 'Studies in modern drama from Ibsen to Genet'. Seminal critical study of modern drama.

Burkman, Katherine H. **The arrival of Godot: ritual patterns in modern drama**. Rutherford: London; Cranbury, NJ: Fairleigh Dickinson University Press; Associated University Presses, 1986. – 170 p. *Notes*: Includes index. Bibliography: p. 161–7.

Carpenter, Charles A. **Modern drama scholarship and criticism, 1966–1980: an international bibliography**. Toronto; Buffalo: University of Toronto Press, 1986. – xxxv, 587 p. *Notes*: Includes index.

——. **Modern drama scholarship and criticism 1981–1990: an international bibliography**. Toronto: University of Toronto Press, 1997. – xxxvii, 632 p. *Notes*: Includes indexes.

Chaudhuri, Una. **Staging place: the geography of modern drama**. Ann Arbor: University of Michigan Press, 1995. – xv, 310 p. *Notes*: Includes bibliographical references (p. 289–299) and index. Drama. 20th century. Setting (Literature) and Place (Philosophy) in literature.

Cirilov, Jovan. **Putovanje po pozoristu: teatralije**. Niksic: NIO 'Univerzitetska rijec', 1988. – 292 p. *Notes*: In Serbo-Croatian. Includes index. Theatre. History. 20th century.

Danan, Joseph. **Le Théâtre de la pensée**. Rouen: Editions Médianes, 1995. – 394 p. *Notes*: Includes bibliographical references (p. 361–87) and index. Drama. 20th century. History and criticism.

Driver, Tom. **Romantic quest and modern query: a history of the modern theatre**. Washington: University Press of America, 1980. – xvi, 496 p. *Notes*: Includes index. Bibliography: p. 471–9. Drama. 20th century. History and criticism.

Esslin, Martin. **Brief chronicles: essays on modern theatre**. London: Maurice Temple Smith, 1970. – 303 p. *Notes*: Drama. 20th century. History and criticism.

——. **Reflections: essays on modern theatre**. Anchor Books edn. Garden City, N.Y.:

Doubleday, 1971, 1969. – x, 226 p. *Notes*: Drama. 20th century/Theatre. History. 20th century.

Freedman, Morris. **The moral impulse; modern drama from Ibsen to the present**. Carbondale: Southern Illinois University Press, 1967. – vii, 136 p. *Notes*: Didactic drama. History and criticism. Ethics in literature.

Gassner, John. **The theatre in our times; a survey of the men, materials and movements in the modern theatre**. New York: Crown Publishers, 1963. – 609 p. illus. *Notes*: Drama. 20th century. History and criticism.

Gilbert, Helen and Joanne Tompkins. **Post-colonial drama: theory, practice, politics**. London; New York: Routledge, 1996. – ix, 344 p.: ill. *Notes*: Includes bibliographical references (p. 298–334) and index. Politics and literature. Commonwealth drama (English). History and criticism.

Gupta, Somnath. **Hindi natak sahitya ka itihas**. [A history of Hindi dramatic literature]. Allahabad: Hindi Bhawan, 1958.

Hayman, Ronald. **Theatre and anti-theatre: new movements since Beckett**. London: Secker & Warburg, 1979. – xiii, 272 p. *Notes*: Includes index. Bibliography: p. 263–5. Drama. 20th century. History and criticism.

Hodgson, Terry. **Modern drama: from Ibsen to Fugard**. London: Batsford, 1992. – ix, 244 p., [2] p. of plates: ill. *Notes*: Includes index. Includes bibliography: p. 228–32. History and criticism. Drama.

Holderness, Graham. **The Politics of theatre and drama**. London: Macmillan, 1992. – viii, 220 p. *Notes*: Theatre. Political aspects, history.

Houghton, Norris. **The exploding stage; an introduction to twentieth century drama**. New York: Weybright & Talley, 1971. – xii, 269 p. *Notes*: Drama. 20th century. History and criticism/Theatre.

Hye, Allen E. **The moral dilemma of the scientist in modern drama: the inmost force**. Lewiston, N.Y.: Edwin Mellen Press, 1996. – 218 p. *Notes*: Includes bibliographical references (p. 205–13) and index. Science. Moral and ethical aspects. Drama.

Innes, Christopher. **Avant garde theatre, 1892–1992**. London; New York: Routledge, 1993. – ix, 261 p.: ill. *Notes*: Rev. and updated edn. of: **Holy theatre**. 1981. Includes bibliographical references (p. 250–4) and index. History and criticism.

Kott, Jan. **The memory of the body: essays on theater and death**. Evanston, Ill.: Northwestern

University Press, 1992. – ix, 153 p.: ill. *Notes*: Translated from the Polish. Includes index.

Krutch, Joseph Wood. **'Modernism' in modern drama: a definition and an estimate**. Ithaca, N.Y.: Cornell University Press, 1966 1953. – ix, 138 p. *Notes*: Includes index. Drama. 20th century. History and criticism.

Lachaud, Jean-Marc. **Questions sur le réalisme: B. Brecht et G. Lukacs**. 2nd edn. Paris: Anthropos: diff. Economica, 1989. – xviii-176 p. *Notes*: Bibliography: p. 171–3.

Leiter, Samuel L. **From Stanislavski to Barrault**. Greenwood Press, 1991. – 250 p. Theatre: theory and criticism.

Lena Paz, Marta. 'La crítica teatral y América Latina'. [Theatre criticism in Latin America]. In **Hacia una crítica literaria latinoamericana** [Towards a Latin American literary criticism], ed. Graciela Maturo, 213–25. Buenos Aires: García Cambeiro, 1976.

Marowitz, Charles, Tom Milne and Owen Hale, eds. **The Encore reader; a chronicle of the new drama**. London: Methuen. 1970, 1956. – 308 p. illus. *Notes*: Articles originally published in **Encore** from 1956 through 1963. History and criticism.

Murphy, Patrick D. **Staging the impossible: the fantastic mode in modern drama**. Westport, Conn.: Greenwood Press, 1992. – viii, 245 p.: ill. *Notes*: Includes bibliographical references (p. 221–236) and index. When formula seizes form: Oscar Wilde's comedies/Susan Taylor Jacobs – A task most difficult: staging Yeats's mystical dramas at the Abbey/Frederick S. Lapisardi – The perilous edge: Strindberg, madness, and other worlds/Peter Malekin – Wassily Kandinsky's stage composition Yellow sound: the fantastic and the symbolic mode of communication/Kent W. Hooper – Ionesco and L'insolite/Elizabeth C. Hesson and Ian M. Hesson – Ambiguity and the supernatural in Cocteau's La machine infernale/Ralph Yarrow – Beckett and the horrific/Lance Olsen – Multiplicities of illusion in Tom Stoppard's plays/Peter N. Chetta – Leivick's The golem and the golem legend/Carl Schaffer – Dream on Monkey Mountain: fantasy as self-perception/Robert J. Willis – Spalding Gray's Swimming to Cambodia: a performance gesture/ Jessica Prinz – The shock of the actual: disrupting the theatrical illusion/Theodore Shank – Playing at the end of the world: postmodern theater/Veronica Hollinger – 'Infinity in a cigar box': the problem of science fiction on the stage/Joseph Krupnik. American drama. Fantasy drama. History and criticism.

Murray, Edward. **Varieties of dramatic struc-**

ture: a study of theory and practice. Lanham, Md.: University Press of America, 1990. – xiii, 143 p. *Notes*: Includes bibliographical references (p. 129–35).

Nair, Parmeshwar. **History of Malayalam literature**. New Delhi: Sahitya Academy, 1967.

Puzyna, Konstanty. **Szkola dramaturgów i inne szkice**. Wroclaw: Wiedza o Kulturze, 1993. – 185 p. *Notes*: Includes bibliographical references and index. *Subjects*: Drama. 20th century. History and criticism Realism.

Ratajczak, Dobrochna. **Przestrzen w dramacie i dramat w przestrzeni teatru**. Wyd. 1. Poznan: Wydawn. Nauk. Uniwersytetu im. Adama Mickiewicza, 1985. – 240 p., [11] p. of plates: ill. *Notes*: Summary in French. Includes bibliographical references and index. Theatre. Poland. Italy. Space and time in art.

Salmon, Eric. **Is the theatre still dying?** Westport, Conn.: Greenwood Press, 1985. – xiii, 294 p. *Notes*: Includes index. Bibliography: p. 275–281. English drama. American drama. Great Britain. History. 20th century. Stage history. 1950–80.

Schlueter, June. **Metafictional characters in modern drama**. New York: Columbia University Press, 1979. – x, 143 p. *Notes*: Includes index. Bibliography: p. 131–9. Characters and characteristics in dramatic literature.

Scolnicov, Hanna and Holland, Peter. **The Play out of context: transferring plays from culture to culture**. Cambridge [England]; New York: Cambridge University Press, 1989. *Notes*: 'Most of the essays are based on papers presented at the Jerusalem Theatre Conference in 1986'. Includes index. Introduction/Hannah Scolnicov – The play: gateway to cultural dialogue/ Gershon Shaked – Problems of translation for the stage: interculturalism and post-modern theatre/Patrice Pavis – Space: the final frontier/Peter Holland – 'If the salf have lost his savour': some 'useful' plays in and out of context on the London stage/James Redmond – Mimesis, mirror, double/Hanna Scolnicov – Greek drama in Rome: some aspects of cultural transposition/Dwora Gilula – Shakespeare and theatre politics in the Third Reich/Werner Habicht – The generation of Life is a dream from Oedipus the king/Eli Rozik – Claudel and Vitez direct Molière/Yehouda Moraly – The role of the target-system in theatrical adaptation: Jalal's Egyptian-Arabic adaptation of Tartuffe/Carol Bardenstein. Chekhov in limbo: British productions of the plays of Chekhov/ Vera Gottlieb – Intercultural aspects in postmodern theatre: a Japanese version of Chekhov's Three sisters/Erika Fischer-Lichte – Mr Godot will not come today/Shoshana Weitz

– The adaptation and reception in Germany of Edward Bond's Saved/Ruth von Ledebur – Whose life is it anyway? in London and on Broadway: a contrastive analysis of the British and American versions of Brian Clark's play/Albert-Reiner Glaap.

Stojanović, Velimir. **Šminka i znoj**. [Make-up and sweat]. Sarajevo, 1974. Theatre criticism.

Strem, George G. **Aspects of the 20th century Western theatre: synopses and analyses**. Los Angeles, 1990. – x, 200 p. *Notes*: Includes bibliographical references (p. 196–200). History and criticism.

Styan, J.L. **The dark comedy: the development of modern comic tragedy**. 2nd edn. New York: Cambridge Univ.Press, 1979. – vii, 311 p. History and criticism.

——. **Modern drama in theory and practice**. Cambridge and New York: Cambridge University Press, 1985 1981. – 3 vols: ill. *Notes*: Includes bibliographies and index. 1. Realism and naturalism. 2. Symbolism, surrealism, and the absurd. 3. Expressionism and epic theatre. Drama. History and criticism.

Sŭstav, Dimitŭr K. **Sŭvremenna teatralna teoriia i kritika: sbornik statii**. [Contemporary theatrical theory and criticism: a symposium]. Sofia: Nauka i Izkustvo, 1980. 355 p.

Il Teatro postmoderno. Turin: Tirrenia stampatori, 1983. – 300 p., 16 p. of plates: ill. *Notes*: Includes bibliographical references. Drama. 20th century. History and criticism. In Italian.

Ubersfeld, Anne. **Les Termes clés de l'analyse du théâtre**. Paris: Seuil, 1996. – 87, [6] p. *Notes*: Includes bibliographical references (p. 89–93). Literary and theatrical analytical terms explained in French.

Valency, Maurice. **The end of the world: an introduction to contemporary drama**. New York: Schocken Books, 1983 1980. – xii, 469 p. *Notes*: Reprint. Originally published: New York: Oxford University Press, 1980. Includes bibliographical references and index.

Vanden Heuvel, Michael. **Performing drama/dramatizing performance: alternative theater and the dramatic text**. 1st pbk. edn. Ann Arbor: University of Michigan Press, 1993 1991. – 262 p.: ill. *Notes*: Includes bibliographical references (p. 249–57) and index. The avant-garde urge and the margins of performance – 'The sad tale a last time told': closing performance and liberating the text in the plays of Samuel Beckett – The fractal dimensions of a fractious culture: the Wooster Group and the politics of performance – 'Of our origins: in ghostlier demarcations, keener sounds': Robert

Wilson's search for a new order of vision – The landlocked geography of a horse dreamer: performance and consciousness in the plays of Sam Shepard.

Wellwarth, George E. **Modern drama and the death of God**. Madison, Wis.: University of Wisconsin Press, 1986. – x, 177 p. *Notes*: Includes index. Bibliography: p. 165–72. Drama. 20th century. Religion and literature.

——. **The theater of protest and paradox; developments in the avant-garde drama**. [New York]: New York University Press, 1971. – xv, 315 p. *Notes*: Bibliography: p. 297–305. Drama. 20th century. History and criticism.

Wright, Elizabeth. **Postmodern Brecht: a representation**. London; New York: Routledge, 1989. – ix, 154 p. *Notes*: Includes index. Bibliography: p. 141–7. *Subjects*: Postmodernism. Brecht, Bertolt, 1898–1956. Criticism and interpretation.

C. Personal Visions, Statements, Manifestos and Related Studies

C1. Visions, Statements and Manifestos

Artaud, Antonin. **The theatre and its double**. New York: Grove Press, 1958. 159 p.

——. **Artaud on theatre**. London: Methuen, 1999. 320 p. Claude Schumacher and Brian Singleton, eds.

Barba, Eugenio and Ferdinando Taviani. **Beyond the floating islands**. New York: PAJ Publications, 1986. – 274 p.: ill. *Notes*: Theatre writings.

——. **The floating islands: reflections with Odin Teatret**. [Gråsten]: Drama, 1979. – 199 p., 40 p. of plates: ill. *Notes*: Odin teatret. Theatre writings.

Blau, Herbert. **Blooded thought: occasions of theatre**. New York: Performing Arts Journal Publications, 1982. 166 p.

——. **The impossible theatre**. New York: Collier-Macmillan, 1964. 309 p.

——. **Take up the bodies: theater at the vanishing point**. Urbana, Ill.: University of Illinois Press, 1982. – xxiv, 299 p.: ill. *Notes*: Includes index. An American director and theorist on contemporary theatre.

Boal, Augusto. **Categorías de teatro popular**. [Buenos Aires]: Ediciones Cepe, 1972. – 90p. *Notes*: Theatre and society.

——. **The rainbow of desire: the Boal method of theatre and therapy**. London; New York: Routledge, 1995. – xxvi, 188 p.: ill. Translated by Adrian Jackson. *Notes*: Acting. Psychological aspects.

——. **Stop: C'est magique!** Rio de Janeiro: Civilização Brasileira, 1980. – 163 p. *Notes*: Acting/Theatre. Political aspects.

——. **Teatro del oprimido y otras poéticas políticas**. [Buenos Aires]: Ediciones de la Flor, 1974. – 238 p. *Notes*: Political theatre: a theory.

——. **Técnicas latinoamericanas de teatro popular: una revolución copernicana al revés**. Buenos Aires: Corregidor, 1975. – 212 p. *Notes*: Latin America/Street theatre.

——. **Theater of the oppressed**. New York: Urizen Books, 1979. – xiv, 197 p. Translated from the Spanish by Charles A. and Maria-Odilia Leal McBride. *Notes*: Translation of Teatro del oprimido y otras poéticas políticas. Theatre. Political aspects. Boal's key text.

——. **Tres obras de teatro**. El gran acuerdo international del Tío Patilludo. Torquemada. Revolución en América del sur. Buenos Aires: Ediciones Noé, 1973, – 217 p.

Bond, Edward. **The hidden plot: notes on theatre and the state**. Methuen: London, 1999. 240 p.

Brook, Peter. **The empty space**. 1st Touchstone edn. New York: Simon & Schuster, 1996, 1968. – 141 p. *Notes*: The deadly theatre – The holy theatre – The rough theatre – The immediate theatre. An essential volume for an understanding of Brook and contemporary theatre practice.

——. **The shifting point: forty years of theatrical exploration, 1946–1987**. London: Methuen Drama, 1989 1987. – 254 p.: ill. *Notes*: Originally published: New York: Harper & Row, 1987. Includes index. Essays on theatre practice.

Croyden, Margaret. **Lunatics, lovers and poets: the contemporary experimental theatre**. New York: Delta, 1975. – xxvi, 320 p.: ill. *Notes*: Includes index. Bibliography: p. 307–14. Experimental theatre. 20th century. History and criticism. Includes Grotowski, Brook and others. An important study of the period.

Grotowski, Jerzy. **Towards a poor theatre**. Holstebro, Denmark: Odin Teatret, 1968. – 218 p., 44 p. of plates: ill. *Notes*: Later republished by New York: Simon and Schuster, 1968. – 262 p. 'Texts by Jerzy Grotowski, interviews with him and other supplementary material presenting his method and training'. A Methuen paperback. An essential text for studies of Grotowski and the contemporary theatre.

Ionesco, Eugène. **Notes et contre-notes**. [Paris]: Gallimard, 1975 1962. – xxxv, 256, 2 p., 24 p. of plates: ill. *Notes*: Bibliography: p. 257–8. A master of the absurd comments on his world and his art.

Kantor, Tadeusz and Michal Kobialka. **A journey through other spaces: essays and manifestos, 1944–1990**. Berkeley: University of California Press, 1993. – xxi, 430 p.: ill. *Notes*: Translated from Polish. Includes bibliographical references (p. 387–403) and index. Kantor, Tadeusz.

Kott, Jan. **Shakespeare our contemporary**. New York: Norton, 1974. – xxi, 372 p. *Notes*: Translation of **Szkice o Szekspirze** (Warsaw, 1962). Preface by Peter Brook. Bibliographical footnotes. Criticism and interpretation of Shakespeare for the contemporary theatre.

——. **The theatre of essence and other essays**. Evanston: Northwestern University Press, 1984. – vii, 218 p. *Notes*: Bibliography: p. 215–18. Introduction/by Martin Esslin – Shakespeare's riddle – The author of comedy, or The inspector general – Ibsen read anew – Witkiewicz, or The dialectic of anachronism – On Gombrowicz – Ionesco, or A pregnant death – Noh, or About signs – Bunraku and Kabuki, or About imitation – The icon of the absurd – Why should I take part in the sacred dance? – After Grotowski: the end of the impossible theater – The theater of essence: Kantor and Brook – Tadeusz Borowski: a European education – A cage in search of a bird – The serpent's sting – The seriousness of theatre.

——. **Theatre notebook, 1947–1967**. Garden City, N.Y.: Doubleday, 1968. – xiv, 268 p.

Ludlam, Charles and Steven Samuels. **Ridiculous theatre: scourge of human folly: the essays and opinions of Charles Ludlam**. New York: Theatre Communications Group, 1992. – xxi, 263 p. *Notes*: The founder of New York's Ridiculous Theatrical Company on theatre art.

Martin, Robert A. and Steve Centola, eds. **The theatre essays of Arthur Miller**. Rev. and expanded. New York: Da Capo Press, 1996 1978. – liv, 628 p. *Notes*: Includes bibliographical references (p. 587–612) and index. Miller, Arthur, 1915–. Aesthetics.

Piscator, Erwin. **The political theatre**. London: Eyre Methuen, 1980. – x, 373 p., 31 p. of plates. *Notes*: Translation of: **Das Politische Theater**. Berlin: Adalbert Schultz Verlag, 1929. 'List of contemporary plays produced by Piscator

between 1919 and 1930': p. 368–9. Includes bibliographical references and index. Also exists in innumerable translations. A major vision of theatre.

Schechner, Richard. **The end of humanism: writings on performance**. New York: Performing Arts Journal Publications, 1982. – 128 p.: ill. *Notes*: Includes bibliographical references. Includes Performance art.

——. **Environmental theatre**. Expanded edn. New York: Applause, 1994. – li, 339 p.: ill. *Notes*: Includes bibliographical references and index. Design and directing. Acting and audience.

——. **Public domain; essays on the theatre**. Indianapolis: Bobbs-Merrill, 1969. – 244 p. *Notes*: Comments on experimental theatre. Visions for the future.

Suzuki, Tadashi. **Enshutsuka no hasso**. [A director's vision]. Tokyo: Ota Shuppan, 1994. – 265 p. *Notes*: Thoughts of a major theatre thinker.

——. **Naikaku no wa: Suzuki Tadashi engeki ronshu**. [The sum of interior angles: essays]. Tokyo: Jiritsu Shobo, 1973. – 356 p., 4 p. of plates: ill.

—— and Betsuyaku, Minoru. **Suzuki Tadashi taidanshu**. [Interview with Suzuki]. Shohan. Tokyo: Riburo Poto, 1984. – 251 p., 1 p. of plates.

——. **The way of acting: the theatre writings of Tadashi Suzuki**. P. New York: Theatre Communications Group, 1986. – x, 158 p., 8 p. of plates: ill. *Notes*: Translation of: **Ekkyosuru chikara**. Includes 'A play: Clytemnestra'. Suzuki's key writings. In English.

Terayama, Shuji. **Meiro to shikai: waga engeki**. Shinsoban. Tokyo: Hakusuisha, 1993. – 227 p.: ill. *Notes*: In Japanese. Thoughts of a major experimental director.

Willett, John, ed. **Brecht on theatre**. London: Eyre Methuen, 1957. 283 p. *Notes*: Brecht's major critical writing on the theatre and aesthetics.

C2. Studies

'Artaud'. In **Revue Obliques**. Numéro 10–11. Paris: Obliques, 1976. – 360 p.

Artaud, Antonin. **Oeuvres complètes**. Nouv. édn. revue et augm. [Paris]: Gallimard, 1976. – vols 1–9. *Notes*: t. 1. Préambule. Adresse au Pape. Adresse au Dalaï-Lama. Correspondance avec Jacques Rivière. L'ombilic des limbes. Le pèse-nerfs. Fragments d'un journal d'enfer. L'art et la mort. Premiers poèmes (1913–1923).

Premières proses. Tric trac du ciel. Bibloquet. Poèmes (1924–35). Textes surréaliste. Lettres. 2 v.–t. 2. L'évolution du décor. Théâtre Alfred Jarry. Trois œuvres pour la scène. Notes sur Les tricheurs de Steve Passeur. Comptes rendus. A propos d'une pièce perdue. A propos de la litt´ erature et des arts plastiques.–t. 3. Scenari. A propos du cinéma. Lettres. Interviews.–t. 4. Le théâtre et son double. Le théâtre du Séraphin. Les Cenci.–t. 5. Autour du Théâtre et son double et des Cenci.–t. 6. Le moine de Lewis/ raconté par Antonin Artaud.–t. 7. Héliogabale, ou, L'anarchiste couronné. Les nouvelles révélations de l'être.–t. 8. De Quelques problèmes d'actualité aux Messages révolutionnaires.–t. 9. Les Tarahumaras. Lettres de Rodez. A shorter English edition was published in London: Calder and Boyars in 1968 under the title **Antonin Artaud: Collected Works**.

Banu, Georges. **Kantor, l'artiste à la fin du XXe siècle**. [Arles]: [Paris]: Actes sud; Diffusion, PUF, 1990. – 177 p.: ill. *Notes*: Kantor, Tadeusz. Criticism and interpretation.

——. **Peter Brook: de Timon d'Athènes à La tempête, ou, Le metteur en scène et le cercle**. [Paris]: Flammarion, 1991. – 263 p.: ill. *Notes*: Includes bibliographical references. Criticism and interpretation/Brook, Peter.

Barber, Stephen. **Antonin Artaud: blows and bombs**. London: Faber & Faber, 1994, 1993. – 182 p., 4 p. of plates: ill. *Notes*: Includes index. Bibliography: p. 173–5. History and criticism.

Borie, Monique. **Antonin Artaud: le théâtre et le retour aux sources: une approche anthropologique**. [Paris]: Gallimard, 1989. – 354 p. *Notes*: Includes bibliographical references. Anthropology/Artaud, Antonin, 1896–1948.

Bouthors-Paillart, Cathérine. **Antonin Artaud: l'énonciation ou l'épreuve de la cruauté**. Geneva: Droz, 1997. – xiii, 230 p. *Notes*: Includes bibliographical references (p. 219–24). Artaud, Antonin, 1896–1948. Criticism and interpretation.

Braun, Edward. **The theatre of Meyerhold: revolution on the modern stage**. New York: Drama Book Specialists, 1979. – 299 p.: ill. *Notes*: Bibliography: p. 287–91. Includes index.

Burzynski, Tadeusz and Zbigniew Osinski. **Grotowski's laboratory**. Warsaw: Interpress, 1979. – 147 p.: ill. *Notes*: Translation of: Grotowski i jego Laboratorium. Includes bibliographical references. Grotowski, Jerzy, 1933–/ Teatr Laboratorium (Wroclaw, Poland).

Carruthers, Ian and Patricia Mitchell. **Theatre east and west: problems of difference or problems of perception? (Suzuki Tadashi's Australian Macbeth, 1992)**. Bundoora, Vic.: School of Asian Studies, La Trobe University, 1995. – 43 p. *Notes*: Includes bibliographical references (p. 36). Suzuki, Tadashi, 1939–. Dramatic production.

Counsell, Colin. **Signs of performance: an introduction to twentieth-century theatre**. London and New York: Routledge, 1996. 256 p.

Dumoulié, Camille. **Nietzsche et Artaud: pour une éthique de la cruauté**. Paris: PUF, 1992. – 259 p. *Notes*: Includes bibliographical references and index. In French.

Esslin, Martin. **Antonin Artaud**. New York: Penguin Books, 1977, 1976. – 148 p. *Notes*: Includes index. Bibliography: p. 141–3. History and criticism.

Hagnell, Viveka. **On the borderline of theatre, art and life: interviews with P. Brook, R. Cieslak and E. Barba**. Lund: Institute for Research in the Dramatic Arts, University of Lund, 1977. – 1 vol. *Notes*: First two interviews in English, third in French.

Hirschman, Jack, ed. **Antonin Artaud anthology**. San Francisco: City Lights Books. – 253 p. *Notes*: Includes bibliography.

Horn, Barbara Lee. **Joseph Papp: a bio-bibliography**. New York: Greenwood Press, 1992. – xi, 409 p. *Notes*: Includes indexes.

Hossner, Ulrich. **Erschaffen und Sichtbarmachen: das theaterästhetische Wissen der historischen Avantgarde von Jarry bis Artaud**. Bern; New York: P. Lang, 1983. – 303 p. *Notes*: Includes index. Bibliography: p. 285–98. Drama. 20th century. History and criticism/ Experimental theatre.

Hozier, Anthony. **Augusto Boal: documents on the Theatre of the Oppressed**. London: Red Letters, 1985. – 52 p.: ill. *Notes*: Theatre and society.

Kiebuzinska, Christine Olga. **Revolutionaries in the theater: Meyerhold, Brecht, and Witkiewicz**. Ann Arbor: UMI Research Press, 1988. – 182 p. *Notes*: Includes bibliographical references (p. 147–76) and index. Photocopy. Ann Arbor: University Microfilms International, 1992. European drama. History and criticism. Semiotics and literature. Theatre and society.

Knapp, Bettina. **Antonin Artaud: man of vision**. Athens [Ohio]: Swallow Press: Ohio University Press, 1993. – xvi, 235 p.: 1 ill. *Notes*: Includes bibliographical references (p. 225–9) and index. Critical biography.

Kumiega, Jennifer. **The theatre of Grotowski**. London and New York: Methuen London Ltd;

Methuen Inc., 1987. – xiv, 290 p.: ill. *Notes*: Includes index. Bibliography: p. 272–87. A useful study.

Ley-Piscator, Maria and Jean Michel Palmier. **Piscator et le théâtre politique**. Paris: Payot, 1983. – 212 p., 8 p. of plates: ill. *Notes*: 'Liste des mises en scène réalisées par Erwin Piscator': p. 209–212. Includes bibliographical references. History. 20th century/Piscator, Erwin, 1893–1966. Politics.

Osinski, Zbigniew. **Grotowski and his laboratory**. New York, N.Y.: PAJ Publications, 1986. – 185 p.: ill. *Notes*: Translation of: **Grotowski i jego Laboratorium**. Includes bibliographical references. Grotowski, Jerzy, 1933–99. Teatr Laboratorium (Wroclaw).

Plunka, Gene A. **Antonin Artaud and the modern theater**. Rutherford: London; Cranbury, N.J.: Fairleigh Dickinson University Press; Associated University Presses, 1994. – ix, 285 p. *Notes*: Includes bibliographical references (p. 267–76) and index. Artaud, Antonin, 1896–1948. Criticism and interpretation.

Reinhardt, Max, Edda Fuhrich and Gisela Prossnitz. **Max Reinhardt: die Träume des Magiers**. Salzburg: Residenz, 1993. 215 p.: ill. (some col.). *Notes*: Chiefly a collection of letters, speeches, interviews, etc. by Max Reinhardt.

Rorrison, Hugh. **Erwin Piscator: politics on the stage in the Weimar Republic**. Cambridge: Chadwyck-Healey, 1987. – 58 p. *Notes*: Bibliography: p. 52. Biography. Piscator, Erwin.

Rudnitskii, Konstantin and Sydney Schultze. **Meyerhold, the director**. Ann Arbor: Ardis, 1981. – xv, 565 p.: ill. *Notes*: Translation of: **Rezhisser Meyerhold**. Includes bibliographical references and index. Soviet Union. Biography/Meyerhold, Vsevolod Emilevich, 1874–1940.

Schechner, Richard and Lisa Wolford. **The Grotowski Sourcebook**. London and New York: Routledge, 1997. 514 p.: ill. *Notes*: Includes bibliography (p. 503–7) and index. Definitive collection of essays and source materials on Grotowski.

Schumacher, Claude. **Artaud on theatre**. London: Methuen Drama, 1991. – 256 p. *Notes*: Theatre: theory and criticism.

Schutzman, Mady and Jan Cohen-Cruz, eds. **Playing Boal: theatre, therapy, activism**. London; New York: Routledge, 1994. – x, 245 p. *Notes*: Includes bibliographical references and index.

Stephanopoulou, Maria. **To theatro ton pegon kai he nostalgia tes katagoges: Jerzy Grotowski, Eugenio Barba: sto dromo tes outopias**. Athens:

Poreia, 1994. – 204 p.: ill. *Notes*: Includes bibliographical references. Criticism and interpretation.

Tatlow, Anthony. **The mask of evil: Brecht's response to the poetry, theatre and thought of China and Japan: a comparative and critical evaluation**. Bern/Las Vegas: P. Lang, 1977.

Temkine, Raymonde. **Grotowski**. New York: Avon, 1972. 160 p. illus. *Notes*: Biography and criticism by a French critic. Paperback edition in English.

Terayama, Shuji. **Theater contra Ideologie**. Frankfurt: Fischer, 1971. – 99 p. *Notes*: Theatrical provocations by one of Japan's most experimental directors. In German.

Unseld, Siegfried, ed. **Bertolt Brecht: Schriften zum Theater: über eine nicht-aristotelische Dramatik**. Berlin: Suhrkamp Verlag, 1971 1957. – 291 p. *Notes*: A collection of Brecht's significant writings.

Wanous, Sa'dallah. **Bayanat li masrah arabi jadid**. [Manifesto for a new Arab theatre]. Beirut: Dâr al-Farâbî, 1988.

Watson, Ian. **Towards a third theatre: Eugenio Barba and the Odin teatret**. London; New York: Routledge, 1993. – xx, 195 p., 8 p. of plates: ill. Foreword by Richard Schechner. *Notes*: Includes bibliographical references and index. History and criticism.

Weiler, Christel. **Kultureller Austausch im Theater: theatrale Praktiken Robert Wilsons und Eugenio Barbas**. Marburg: Tectum, 1994. – 149 p. *Notes*: Includes bibliographical references. Experimental theatre. History and criticism. Wilson, Robert and Barba, Eugenio.

Wiles, Timothy J. **The theatre event: modern theories of performance**. Chicago: University of Chicago Press, 1980. – vi, 209 p. *Notes*: Includes bibliographical references and index. Artaud, Antonin, 1896–1948/Brecht, Bertolt, 1898–1956/Grotowski, Jerzy, 1933–99/Stanislavsky, Konstantin, 1863–1938.

Willett, John. **The theatre of Erwin Piscator: half a century of politics in the theatre**. London: Methuen, 1986 1978. – 224 p.: ill. *Notes*: Originally published: London: Eyre Methuen, 1978. Includes index. Includes bibliographical references (p. 206–11). Theatrical producers and directors. Biography.

Williams, Dallas. **Edward Gordon Craig's theory of the theatre as seen through The Mask**. 1954. – ix, 256 p. *Notes*: Includes bibliographical references (p. 253–5). Thesis (Ph. D.)–Louisiana State University and Mechanical College, 1954. Microfilm. Ann Arbor, Mich.:

University Microfilms, 1962. 1 microfilm reel: positive; 35 mm. Craig, Edward Gordon, 1872–1966/The Mask, a journal of the art of the theatre.

Williams, David. **Peter Brook and the Mahabharata: critical perspectives**. London/New York: Routledge, 1991.

D. Gender Studies, Women's Theatre/Feminist Theatre and Drama/Gay and Lesbian Theatre

Andrade, Elba and Hilde Cramise, eds. **Dramaturgas latinamericanas contemporáneas (antología crítica)**. [Contemporary Latin American female dramatists (a critical anthology)]. Madrid: Editorial Verbum, 1991.

Aston, Elaine. **An introduction to feminism and theatre**. London; New York: Routledge, 1995. – ix, 166 p. *Notes*: Includes bibliographical references (p. 151–62) and index.

Austin, Gayle. **Feminist theories for dramatic criticism**. Ann Arbor: University of Michigan Press, 1990. – viii, 139 p. *Notes*: Includes bibliographical references (p. 117–35) and index. Drama. History and criticism.

Ben-Zvi, Linda. **Women in Beckett: performance and critical perspectives**. Illini books edn. Urbana: University of Illinois Press, 1992, 1990. – xviii, 260 p.: ill. *Notes*: Includes bibliographical references and index. Billie Whitelaw/interviewed by Linda Ben-Zvi – Dame Peggy Ashcroft/interviewed by Katharine Worth – Madeleine Renaud; Delphine Seyrig/interviewed by Pierre Chabert – Eva Katharina Schultz – Nancy Illig – Gudren Genest – Shivaun O'Casey; Aideen O'Kelly/interviewed by Rosette Lamont – Hanna Marron/interviewed by Linda Ben-Zvi – Irena Jun/interviewed by Antoni Libera – Brenda Bynum/interviewed by Lois Overbeck – Martha Fehsenfeld – Patterns of rejection: sex and love in Beckett's universe/Martin Esslin – Beckett and the heresy of love/James Acheson – 'Meet in paradize': Beckett's Shavian women/Kristin Morrison – Clods, whores, and bitches: misogyny in Beckett's early fiction/Susan Brienza – Stereoscopic or stereotypic: characterization in Beckett's fiction/Rubin Rabinovitz – Cartesian man and the woman reader: a feminist approach to Beckett's Molloy/Carol Helmstetter Cantrell – The Magna Mater myth in Beckett's fiction: subtext and subversion/Angela B. Moorjani – Homage to the dark lady/Lawrence Graver – Male or female voice: the significance of. (cont) the gender of the speaker in Beckett's late fiction and drama/Charles R. Lyons. The femme fatale on Beckett's stage/Ruby Cohn – The transformational grammar of gender in Beckett's dramas/Shari Benstock – Beckett and sexuality (terribly short version)/Peter Gidal – 'Her lips moving': the castrated voice of Not I/Ann Wilson – Portrait of a woman: the experience of marginality in Not I/Dina Sherzer – Speaking Parisian: Beckett and French feminism/Elin Diamond – Female subjectivity in Not I and Rockaby/Lois Oppenheim – Beckett's Eh Joe: lending an ear to the anima/Rosette Lamont – Women in Beckett's radio and television plays/Katharine Worth – Not I: through a tube starkly/Linda Ben-Zvi.

Berney, Kathryn Ann and N.G. Templeton. **Contemporary women dramatists**. London; Detroit: St. James Press, 1994. – xxi, 335 p.

Betsko, Kathleen and Rachel Koenig. **Interviews with contemporary women playwrights**. New York: Beech Tree-Morrow, 1987. 480 p.

Bornstein, Kate. **Gender outlaw: on men, women and the rest of us**. London: Routledge, 1994. 224 p.

Brater, Enoch. **Feminine focus: the new women playwrights**. New York: Oxford University Press, 1989. – xvi, 283 p. *Notes*: Includes bibliographical references. Images of women in modern English theatre/Katharine Worth – Stereotype and prototype: character in the plays of Caryl Churchill/Austin E. Quigley – Ariane Mnouchkine: playwright of a collective/Ruby Cohn – Benmussa's adaptations: unauthorized texts from elsewhere/Elin Diamond – The reverse side of a portrait: the Dora of Freud and Cixous/Rosette C. Lamont – In search of a feminist theater: Portrait of Dora/Jeannette Laillou Savona – Staging sexual difference: reading, recitation, and repetition in Duras' Malady of death/Sharon A. Willis – From split subject to split britches/Sue-Ellen Case – Susan Glaspell's contributions to contemporary women playwrights/Linda Ben-Zvi – Still playing games: ideology and performance in the theatre of Maria Irene Fornes/W.B. Worthen – The play of letters: possession and writing in Chucky's hunch/Timothy Murray – Distraught laughter: monologue in Ntozake Shange's theatre pieces/Deborah R. Geis – Rites and responsibilities: the drama of black American women/Helene Keyssar – The art of Tina Howe/Judith E. Barlow – The way out, the way in: paths to self in the plays of Marsha Norman/Leslie Kane.

Burke, Sally. **American feminist playwrights: a critical history**. New York: London: Twayne

Publishers; Prentice Hall International, 1996. – ix, 270 p.: ill. *Notes*: Includes bibliographical references (p. 242–58) and index. American drama. Women authors.

Canning, Charlotte. **Feminist theaters in the U.S.A.: staging women's experience**. London; New York: Routledge, 1996. – x, 271 p.: ill. *Series*: Gender in performance. *Notes*: Includes bibliographical references (p. 226–66) and index.

Case, Sue-Ellen. **Feminism and theatre**. New York: Routledge, 1988. – 149 p. *Notes*: Includes bibliographical references (p. 139–44) and index.

——. **Performing feminism: feminist critical theory and theatre**. Baltimore: Johns Hopkins University Press, 1990. – 327 p.: ill. *Notes*: Includes bibliographical references. Sexual indifference and lesbian representation/Teresa de Lauretis – 'Lesbian' subjectivity in realism: dragging at the margins of structure and ideology/Jill Dolan – Frame-up: feminism, psychoanalysis, theatre/Barbara Freedman – Hélène Cixous's Portrait de Dora: the unseen and the unscene/Sharon Willis – Refusing the romanticism of identity: narrative interventions in Churchill, Benmussa, Duras/Elin Diamond – The cult of true womanhood: toward a womanist attitude in African-American theatre/Glenda Dickerson – 'A raisin in the sun': anniversary of an American classic/Margaret Wilkerson – The female subject in Chicano theatre: sexuality, 'race,' and class/Yvonne Yarbro-Bejarano – Beyond Brecht: Britain's new feminist drama/Janelle Reinelt – Feminism and the Jewish subject in the plays of Sachs, Atlan, and Schenkar/Vivian Patraka. Unbodied figures of desire (on Troilus and Cressida)/Carol Cook – Playing the woman's part: feminist criticism and Shakespearean performance/Lorraine Helms – Anti-historians: women's roles in Shakespeare's histories/Phyllis Rackin – Painting women: images of femininity in Jacobean tragedy/Laurie A. Finke – Beatrice-Joanna and the rhetoric of love in The changeling/Sara Eaton – Women's performance art: feminism and postmodernism/Jeanie Forte – Performative acts and gender constitution: an essay in phenomenology and feminist theory/Judith Butler – Gender ideology and dramatic convention in progressive era plays, 1890–1920/Judith Stephens – Travesty and transgression: transvesticism in Shakespeare, Brecht and Churchill/Anne Herrmann – The female entertainment tradition in medieval Japan: the case of 'Asobi'/Ying-Hee Kim Kwon.

——. **Split britches: lesbian practice/feminist performance**. London; New York: Routledge, 1996. – viii, 276 p.: ill. *Notes*: Includes bibliographical references (p. 273–6).

Chesterman, Colleen and Virginia Baxter, eds. **Playing with fire: women writing for performance**. Darlinghurst: Playworks, 1995. 139 p.

Chinoy, Helen Krich and Linda Walsh Jenkins. **Women in American theatre**. Revised edn. New York: Theatre Communications Group, 1987. 442 p.

Cima, Gay Gibson. **Performing women: female characters, male playwrights, and the modern stage**. Ithaca, NY: Cornell University Press, 1996 1993. – xiii, 233 p.: ill. *Notes*: Includes bibliographical references and index. Role of women.

Clum, John. **Acting gay: male homosexuality in modern drama**. New York: Columbia University Press, 1992. 381 p.

Coaldrake, A. Kimi. **Women's gidayu and the Japanese theatre**. London: Routledge, 1997. *Notes*: First English book on traditional form of Japanese musical narrative.

Coven, Brenda. **American women dramatists of the twentieth century: a bibliography**. Metuchen, N.J.: Scarecrow Press, 1982. – v, 237 p. *Notes*: Includes index.

Curtin, Kaier. **We can always call them Bulgarians: the emergence of lesbians and gay men on the American stage**. Boston: Alyson Publications, 1987. – 342 p.: ill. *Notes*: Includes bibliographies and index.

Daniels, Rebecca. **Women stage directors speak: exploring the influence of gender on their work**. Jefferson, NC: McFarland & Co., 1996. – ix, 245 p.: ill. *Notes*: Includes bibliographical references (p. 231–9) and index. US directors.

De Jongh, Nicholas. **Not in front of the audience: homosexuality on stage**. London; New York: Routledge, 1992. – xiv, 214 p., 8 p. of plates: ill. *Notes*: Includes bibliographical references (p. 201–4) and index. Theatre. History/London and New York.

Diamond, Elin. **Unmaking mimesis: essays on feminism and theater**. London and New York: Routledge, 1997. – xvi, 226 p. *Notes*: Includes bibliographical references and index. Feminist drama. History and criticism.

Dolan, Jill. **The feminist spectator as critic**. Ann Arbor: University of Michigan Press, 1991 1988. – xii, 154 p.: ill. *Notes*: Reprint. Originally published: Ann Arbor, Mich.: UMI Research Press, c1988. Includes bibliographical references (p. 145–150) and index. Feminist criticism. Theatre audiences.

——. **Presence and desire: essays on gender, sexuality, performance**. Ann Arbor: University of Michigan Press, 1993. – xii, 217 p. *Series*: Critical perspectives on women and gender. *Notes*: Includes bibliographical references and index. Feminist criticism.

Donkin, Ellen. **Getting into the act: women playwrights in London 1776–1829**. London: Routledge, 1995. 256 p.: ill.

Eidelberg, Nora and María Mercedes Jaramillo. **Voces en escena: antología de dramaturgas latinoamericanas**. [Voices on stage: An anthology of Latin American women playwrights]. Medellín, Colombia: Universidad de Antioquía, 1991.

Feministische Theaterpädagogik: Grundlagen und Projekte. 1. [S.l.]: Küppelstein: Alexander T. Rolland; Akademie Remscheid, 1992. – 221 p.: ill. *Notes*: Women dramatists/Feminist theory. Germany.

Ferris, Leslie, ed. **Crossing the stage: controversies on cross dressing**. London: Routledge, 1993. 208 p.: ill.

Gale, Maggie Barbara. **West End women: women and the London stage, 1918–1962**. London; New York: Routledge, 1996. – x, 262 p. *Series*: Gender in performance. *Notes*: Includes bibliographical references (p. 245–55) and index. Women in the theatre. West End (London, England).

Goodman, Lizbeth. **Contemporary feminist theatres: to each her own**. London: Routledge, 1993. 328 p.

—— and Jane De Gay. **Feminist stages: interviews with women in contemporary British theatre**. Amsterdam, Netherlands: Harwood Academic Publishers, 1996. – xiv, 330 p.: ill. *Notes*: Includes index.

——. **The Routledge reader in gender and performance**. New York: Routledge, 1998. 360 p.

——. **Sexuality in performance: replaying of gender in theatre and culture**. London: Routledge, 1998. 256 p.: ill.

Griffiths, Trevor R. and Margaret Llewellyn-Jones. **British and Irish women dramatists since 1958: a critical handbook**. Buckingham [England]; Philadelphia: Open University Press, 1993. – viii, 193 p. *Series*: Gender in writing. *Notes*: Includes bibliographical references (p. 166–177) and indexes. Early stages: women dramatists 1958–68/Lib Taylor – Claiming a space: 1969–78/Margaret Llewellyn-Jones – Waving not drowning: the mainstream, 1979–88/Trevor R. Griffiths – Sister George is dead: the making of modern lesbian theatre/

Rose Collis – Black women playwrights in Britain/Susan Croft – On the margins: women dramatists in Wales/Margaret Llewellyn-Jones – Irish women playwrights since 1958/Anna McMulan – Transformations and transgressions: women's discourse on the Scottish stage/Susan C. Triesman – An alphabet of apocrypha: collaborations and explorations in women's theatre/Susan Croft, April de Angelis.

Hart, Lynda, ed. **Making a spectacle: feminist essays on contemporary women's theatre**. Ann Arbor, MI: University of Michigan Press, 1989. 347 p.

—— and Peggy Phelan. **Acting out: feminist performances**. Ann Arbor: University of Michigan Press, 1993. – vi, 406 p.: ill. *Notes*: Includes bibliographical references. Caught in the act of social definition: On the road with Anna Deavere Smith/Sandra L. Richards – From Lady Dick to ladylike: the work of Holly Hughes/Kate Davy – Cherrie Moraga's 'Shadow of a Man': touching the wound in order to heal/Yvonne Yarbro-Bejarano – Desire cloaked in a trenchcoat/Jill Dolan – Identity and seduction: lesbians in the mainstream/Lynda Hart – Unspeakable practices, unnatural acts: the taboo art of Karen Finley/C. Carr – 'Telling the Awfullest Truth': an interview with Karen Finley/C. Carr – Resisting Thatcherism: the monstrous regiment and the school of hard Knox/Janelle Reinelt – Siren theatre company: politics in performance/Joyce Devlin – The women's experimental theatre: transforming family stories into feminist questions/Julie Malnig, Judy C. Rosenthal – Split britches in Split Britches: performing history, vaudeville, and the everyday/Vivian M. Patraka – see the big show: spiderwoman theatre doubling back/Rebecca Schneider – Toward a lesbian theory of performance: refunctioning gender/Hilary Harris – Robbie McCauley: speaking history other-wise/Raewyn Whyte – Staging Hurston's life and work/Lynda M. Hill – 'Brought to you by fem-rage': stand-up comedy and the politics of gender/Philip Auslander – Is she or isn't she?: Madonna and the erotics of appropriation/Amy Robinson – Mimesis, mimicry, and the 'true-real'/Elin Diamond – White men and pregnancy: discovering the body to be rescued/Peggy Phelan.

Hodkinson, Yvonne. **Female parts: the art and politics of women playwrights**. Montreal and New York: Black Rose Books, 1991. – 163 p. *Notes*: Includes bibliographical references (p. 159–63). Restaging the past – Ever loving – Islands – The twisted leaf – A place on earth – La Sagouine – A woman from the sea. Canadian drama. Women authors. Maillet, Antonine, 1929–. A look at the author of La Sagouine.

Kent, Assunta Bartolomucci. **Maria Irene Fornes and her critics**. Westport, Conn.: Greenwood Press, 1996. – xi, 230 p.: ill. *Notes*: Includes bibliographical references (p. 215–23) and index. Feminism and theatre. United States. History. 20th century. Women in the theatre. Fornes, Maria Irene. Criticism and interpretation.

Keyssar, Helene. **Feminist theatre: an introduction to plays of contemporary British and American women**. New York: St. Martin's Press, 1985. – xvi, 223 p., 8 p. of plates: ill. *Notes*: Includes bibliographical references (p. 119–214) and index.

——. **Feminist theatre and theory**. Basingstoke: Macmillan, 1996. – ix, 288 p. *Notes*: Includes index. Bibliography: p. 275–280. History and criticism.

Kintz, Linda. **The subject's tragedy: political poetics, feminist theory and drama**. Ann Arbor, MI: University of Michigan Press, 1992. 329 p.

Krumholz, Linda and Estella Lauter. **Annotated bibliography of feminist aesthetics in the literary, performing, and visual arts, 1970–1990**. Madison, Wis.: University of Wisconsin System, Women's Studies Librarian, 1992. – 36 p. *Notes*: Includes a supplement of citations through 1991. Bibliography.

Laughlin, Karen Louise and Catherine Schuler. **Theatre and feminist aesthetics**. Madison: London; Cranbury, NJ: Fairleigh Dickinson University Press; Associated University Presses, 1995. – 331 p. *Notes*: Includes bibliographical references and index.

Leavitt, Dinah. **Feminist theatre groups**. Jefferson, SC: McFarland, 1980. 153 p.

Leite, Luiza Barreto. **A mulher no teatro brasileiro**. [Women in Brazilian theatre]. Rio de Janeiro: Espectáculo, 1965. 227 p.

Malpede, Karen. **Women in theatre: compassion and hope**. New York: Drama Book Publishers, 1983. 281 p.

Manful, Helen. **In other words: women directors speak**. Lyme, NH: Smith and Kraus, 1997. – xx, 185 p.: ill. *Notes*: Women theatrical directors. Great Britain.

——. **Taking stage: women directors on directing**. London: Methuen, 1999. 272 p. *Notes*: Follows the careers and approaches of thirteen top women directors of the British theatre.

Martin, Carol. **A sourcebook of feminist theatre and performance: on and beyond the stage**. London; New York: Routledge, 1996. – xix, 311 p.: ill. *Notes*: Includes bibliographical references and index.

Mlama Penina and A. Lihamba. 'Women in Communication: Popular Theatre as an Alternative Medium'. In **Women and the Mass Media in Africa/Femmes et média en Afrique**. Dakar: AAWORD/AFARD, 1992. 216 p.

Natalle, Elizabeth Jo. **Feminist theatre: a study in persuasion**. Metuchen, N.J.: Scarecrow Press, 1985. – vii, 155 p. *Notes*: Includes index. Bibliography: p. 137–46.

Partnow, Elaine and Lesley Hyatt. **The female dramatist: profiles of women playwrights from around the world from the Middle Ages to the present day**. New York: Facts On File, 1998. *Notes*: Includes bibliographical references and index.

Poole, Ralph J. **Performing bodies: Überschreitungen der Geschlechtergrenzen im Theater der Avantgarde**. Frankfurt am Main; New York: P. Lang, 1996. – 310 p. *Notes*: Includes bibliographical references (p. 281–310). Sex roles in literature.

Román, David. **Acts of intervention: performance, gay culture, and AIDS**. Bloomington: Indiana University Press, 1998. *Notes*: Includes bibliographical references and index. American drama. History and criticism/Gay actors.

Schlueter, June, ed. **Feminist rereadings of modern American drama**. Rutherford, N.J.: Fairleigh Dickinson University Press, 1989. – 249 p. *Notes*: Includes bibliographical references and index. Introduction/June Schlueter – 'A monster of perfection': O'Neill's 'Stella'/Anne Flèche – O'Neill's ghostly women/Suzanne Burr – Theatricality and otherness in All God's chillun got wings/Bette Mandl – The exchange of women and male homosocial desire in Arthur Miller's Death of a salesman and Lillian Hellman's Another part of the forest/Gayle Austin – Women and the American dream of Death of a salesman/Kay Stanton – Paper dolls: melodrama and sexual politics in Arthur Miller's early plays/Jeffrey D. Mason – Betrayal and blessedness: explorations of feminine power in The crucible, A view from the bridge, and After the fall/Iska Alter – Authorizing history: victimization in A streetcar named Desire/Anca Vlasopolos. 'Weak and divided people': Tennessee Williams and the written woman/John Timpane – What's new at the zoo?: rereading Edward Albee's American dream(s) and nightmares/Mickey Pearlman – Magnified and sanctified: Tiny Alice reconsidered/Naomi Conn Liebler – Sam Shepard's spectacle of impossible heterosexuality: Fool for love/Lynda Hart – Self as other: Sam Shepard's Fool for love and A lie of the mind/Rosemarie Bank.

——, ed. **Modern American drama: the female canon**. Rutherford: London: Fairleigh Dickinson University Press; Associated University Presses, 1990. – 308 p. *Notes*: Includes bibliographical references and index. Introduction/June Schlueter – The happy revolution: colonial women and the eighteenth-century theatre/Mary Anne Schofield – 'The new path': nineteenth-century American women playwrights/Doris Abramson – Rachel Crothers: Broadway feminist/Doris Abramson – Rebellion and rejection: the plays of Susan Glaspell/Barbara Ozieblo – 'Meeting the outside face to face': Susan Glaspell, Djuna Barnes, and O'Neill's The Emperor Jones/Ann E. Larabee – Zoe Akins and the age of excess: Broadway melodrama in the 1920s/Jennifer Bradley – Marriage, madness, and murder in Sophie Treadwell's Machinal/Barbara L. Bywaters – Gertrude Stein: exile, feminism, avant-garde in the American theatre/Dinnah Pladott – The fox's cubs: Lillian Hellman, Arthur Miller, and Tennessee Williams/Charlotte Goodman – Loneliness and longing in selected plays of Carson McCullers and Tennessee Williams/Mary McBride – Lorraine Hansberry and the great Black way/Leonard R.N. Ashley – Megan Terry's transformational drama: Keep tightly closed in a cool dry place and The possibilities of self/June Schlueter – No place but the funnyhouse: the struggle for identity in three Adrienne Kennedy plays/Susan E. Meigs – Whose name, whose protection: reading Alice Childress's Wedding band/Catherine Wiley – 'The poetry of a moment': politics and the open form in the drama of Ntozake Shange/John Tempane – Comic textures and female communities 1937 and 1977: Clare Boothe and Wendy Wasserstein/Susan L. Carlson – Gender perspective and violence in the plays of Maria Irene Fornes and Sam Shepard/Catherine A. Schuler. Ghosts of Chekhov's Three sisters haunt Beth Henley's Crimes of the heart/Joanne B. Karpinski – Disturbing women: Wendy Kesselman's My sister in this house/Bette Mandl – The Demeter myth and doubling in Marsha Norman's 'night, Mother/Katherine H. Burkman – The silver lining in the mushroom cloud: Meredith Monk's opera/music theater/Suzanne R. Westfall – Canonizing lesbians?/Lynda Hart.

Schneider, Rebecca. **The explicit body in performance**. London: Routledge, 1997. 256 p.: ill.

Schroeder, Patricia R. **The feminist possibilities of dramatic realism**. Madison, NJ: London: Fairleigh Dickinson University Press; Associated University Presses, 1996. – 185 p. *Notes*: Includes index. Bibliography: p. 167–79. History and criticism.

Schuler, Catherine. **Women in Russian theatre: the actress in the silver age**, 1996. 272 p.: ill.

Scolnicov, Hanna. **Woman's theatrical space**. Cambridge; New York: Cambridge University Press, 1994. – xiv, 177 p.: ill. *Notes*: Includes bibliographical references (p. 161–72) and index.

Senelick, Laurence. **Gender in performance: the presentation of difference in the performing arts**. Hanover [N.H.]: University Press of New England, 1992. – xxiv, 348 p.: ill. *Notes*: Includes bibliographical references and index. Gender impersonation onstage: destroying or maintaining the mirror of gender roles?/Jill Dolan – Mimesis and travesty in Iranian traditional theatre/William O. Beeman – Lady and the tramp: drag differentials in the progressive era/Laurence Senelick – The 'magic if': conflicting performances of gender in the Takarazuka Revue of Japan/Jennifer Robertson – Unveiling the word: science and narrative in transsexual striptease/Moe Meyer – Between difference and indifference: Marianne Hoppe in Robert Wilson's Lear/Erika Fischer-Lichte – Les Filles Errantes: emancipated women at the Comédie-Italienne, 1683–1691/Virginia Scott – Women in the Victorian theatre: images, illusions, realities/Joseph Donohue – Shotgun wedlock: Annie Oakley's power politics in the Wild West/Tracy C. Davis – Revolutionizing Galatea, iconic woman in early Soviet culture/Spencer Golub – The Orient, the feminine: the use of interculturalism by the Theatre du Soleil/Adrian Kiernander – Gender bending in Balinese performance/John Emigh and Jamer Hunt – Tradition, challenge, and the backlash: gender education through dance/Judith Lynne Hanna – Dance history and feminist theory: reconsidering Isadora Duncan and the male gaze/Ann Daly – Speech and sexual difference in Mary Wigman's dance aesthetic/Karl Toepfer – Freeing up: politics, gender, and theatrical form in the anglophone Caribbean/Elaine Savory Fido – Gender is attitude/Megan Terry, Jo Ann Schmidman, Sora Kimberlain – Kate Bornstein's gender and genre bending/Noreen C. Barnes – The theatre of sexual initiation/John Preston.

Soloman, Alisa. **Re-Dressing the canon: essays on theatre and gender**. London: Roultedge, 1997. 192 p. *Notes*: Theatre and Gender.

Steadman, Susan M. **Dramatic re-visions: an annotated bibliography of feminism and theatre, 1972–1988**. Chicago: American

Library Association, 1991. – xiv, 367 p. *Notes*: Includes indexes.

Tait, Peta. **Converging realities: feminism in Australian theatre**. Sydney: Melbourne: Currency Press; Artmoves, 1994. – 276 p., 8 p. of plates: ill. *Notes*: Includes bibliographical references (p. 255–66) and index.

—— and Elizabeth Schafer. **Australian women's drama: texts and feminisms**. Sydney: Currency Press, 1997. – xix, 286 p.: ill. *Notes*: Includes bibliographical references (p. 285–6).

Tompkins, Joanne and Julie Holledge. **Performing women, performing feminisms: interviews with international women playwrights**. [Brisbane?: Australasian Drama Studies Association], 1997. – 161 p. *Notes*: Includes bibliographic references.

Wandor, Michelene. **Carry on, understudies: theatre and sexual politics**. London; New York: Routledge & Kegan Paul, 1986. – xxi, 210 p. *Notes*: Rev. edn. of: **Understudies**. 1981. Includes index. Bibliography: p. 201–3.

Wilson, Ann and Rita Much. **Women on the Canadian stage: the legacy of Hrotsvit**. Winnipeg: Blizzard Pub., 1992. – xxiv, 133 p. *Notes*: Includes bibliographical references.

Witte, Ann. **Guiding the plot: politics and feminism in the work of women playwrights from Spain and Argentina, 1960–1990**. New York: P. Lang, 1996. – xii, 167 p. *Notes*: Includes bibliographical references (p. 149–63) and index.

Woods, Leigh. **Public selves, political stages: interviews with Icelandic women in government and theatre**. Amsterdam, Netherlands: Harwood Academic Publishers, 1997. – xiv, 285 p. *Notes*: Includes bibliographical references (p. 267–73) and index.

E. Theatre Anthropology and Intercultural Performance

Barba, Eugenio. **The paper canoe: a guide to theatre anthropology**. London; New York: Routledge, 1995. – x, 187 p. Translated by Richard Fowler. *Notes*: Includes bibliographical references and index.

—— and Nicola Savarese. **A dictionary of theatre anthropology: the secret art of the performer**. English-language edn. London and New York: Published for the Centre for Performance Research by Routledge, 1991. – 272 p.: ill. (some col.). Translated by Richard Fowler. *Notes*: Includes bibliographical references.

Bharucha, Rustom. **Theatre and the world: performance and the politics of culture**. London and New York: Routledge, 1993. 272 p.

Boon, Richard and Jane Plastow. **Theatre matters: performance and culture on the world stage**. Great Britain: Cambridge University Press, 1988. 152 p.

Burns, Elizabeth. **Theatricality: a study of convention in the theatre and in social life**. London: Longman, 1990 1972. – 246 p. *Notes*: Preservation photocopy. Includes bibliographical references and index. Photocopy. Atlanta, Ga.: Emory University Libraries, Preservation Office, 1990.

Hughes-Freeland, Felicia, ed. **Ritual, performance, media**. London: Routledge, 1997. 256 p. *Notes*: Cultural creativity and ritual.

Karampetsos, E.D. **The theatre of healing**. New York: P. Lang, 1995. – 137 p. *Notes*: Includes bibliographical references (p. 129–134) and index.

Núñez, Nicolás, Ronan J. Fitzsimons and Deborah Middleton. **Anthropocosmic theatre. Rite in the dynamics of theatre**. Amsterdam, Netherlands: Harwood Academic Publishers, 1996. – xx, 146 p.: ill. *Notes*: Includes index. Tibetan theatre – Nahuatlan theatre – Western theatre: Stanislavski, Brecht, The Old Vic, Strasberg, Grotowski – Anthropocosmic theatre: a guide.

Pavis, Patrice, ed. **The intercultural performance reader**. London and New York: Routledge, 1996. 280 p. *Notes*: Overview of intercultural performance. Key artists and scholars from around the world.

——. **Theatre at the crossroads of culture**. London and New York: Routledge, 1992. – vii, 219 p.: ill. *Notes*: Translation of: **Théâtre au croisement des cultures**. Includes bibliographical references and index. Theatre and society. Intercultural communication.

——, Guy Rosa, Michael Corvin and Erika Fischer-Lichte. **Confluences: Le Dialogue des cultures dans les spectacles contemporains: Essais en l'honneur d'Anne Ubersfeld**. Saint-Cyr L'Ecole: Prépublications du petit bricoleur de Bois-Robert, 1994. – 265 p.: couv. ill. Intercultural performance.

Pfaff, Walter, Erika Keil and Beat Schläpfer. **Der sprechende Körper: Texte zur Theater-anthropologie**. Zürich: Berlin: Museum für Gestaltung; Alexander Verlag, 1996. – 292 p.: ill. *Notes*: Issued on the occasion of the exhibition Tala, mudra, rasa held Dec. 4, 1996 to Jan. 26, 1997 at the Museum für Gestaltung, Zurich,

Switzerland. Includes bibliographical references. Der Körper als Werkzeug der Erinnerung/Jean Grädel – Grotowski, Kunst als Vehikel/Peter Brook – Der Performer/Jerzy Grotowski – Die Vielfalt der Performance/Richard Schechner – Was zuerst war/Dario Fo – Körpertechniken/ Marcel Mauss – Wiederkehrende Prinzipien/ Eugenio Barba – Theaterspielen im Alltagsleben und Alltagsleben im Theater/Victor Turner – Performer-Training Interkulturell/Richard Schechner – Die Lehre des Chackyar/Walter Pfaff – The Meeting/Manuel Bauer – Du bist jemandes Sohn/Jerzy Grotowski – Die Kollision der Kulturen/Rustom Bharucha – Die Kultur der Verknüpfungen/Peter Brook – Das eigene und das fremde Theater/Erika Fischer-Lichte – Kultur im Körper/Walter Pfaff im Gespräch mit Joanna Pfaff-Czarnecka.

Read, Alan. **Theatre and everyday life: an ethics of performance**. London and New York: Routledge, 1995. 304 p.

Schechner, Richard. **Between theatre and anthropology**. Philadelphia: University of Pennsylvania Press, 1985. – xiv, 342 p.: ill. Foreword by Victor Turner. *Notes*: Bibliography: p. 325–32. Includes index. Anthropology/Rites and ceremonies/Performing arts.

——. **The end of humanism: writings on performance**. New York: Performing Arts Journal Publications, 1982. – 128 p.: ill. *Notes*: Includes bibliographical references. Performance art.

——. **The future of ritual: writings on culture and performance**. London; New York: Routledge, 1993. – x, 283 p.: ill. *Notes*: Includes bibliographical references (p. 266–76) and index. Theatre and society/Performing arts. Rites and ceremonies/Play.

——. **Performance theory: writings on culture and performance**. London: Routledge, 1988. 320 p.

——. **Performative circumstances, from the avant garde to Ramlila**. Calcutta: Seagull Books, 1983. – xii, 337 p., 16 p. of plates: ill. *Notes*: Includes bibliographical references and index. Performing arts. India. Theatre and society.

—— and Mady Schuman, eds. **Ritual, play, and performance: readings in the social sciences/theatre**. New York: Seabury Press, 1976. – xviii, 230 p.: ill. *Notes*: Bibliography: p. 223–30. Introduction: the fan and the web.–Ethology: R. Schechner – The roots of art/A. Alland jr – Habit, ritual, and magic/ K. Lorenz–The chest-beating sequence of the mountain gorilla/G. Schaller–The rain dance– Play/J.V. Lawick-Goodall – Nature and significance of play as a cultural phenomenon/J.

Huizinga – A theory of play and fantasy/G.A. Bateson – The science of the concrete–Ritual and performance in everyday life/C. Lévi-Strauss – It depends on the point of view/ R.L. Birdwhistell – Performances/E. Goffman – Social dramas and ritual metaphors.– Shamanism, trance, meditation/V. Turner – The shaman's tent of the Evenks/A.F. Anisimov – The shamanistic origins of popular entertainments/E.T. Kirby – Trance experience in Bali–Rites, ceremonies, performances/J. Belo – Desert rituals and the sacred life/R.A. Gould – The theatre's new testament/J. Grotowski – From ritual to theatre and back./R. Schechner. Theater and society. Rites and ceremonies. Human behaviour.

—— and Willa Appel, eds. **By means of performance: intercultural studies of theatre and ritual**. Cambridge; New York: Cambridge University Press, 1990. – xv, 298 p.: ill. *Notes*: Includes bibliographical references (p. 275–83) and index. Rites and ceremonies.

Slawinska, Irena and Maria Barbara Stykowa. **Le Théâtre dans la pensée contemporaine: [anthropologie et théâtre]**. Louvain-la-Neuve: Cahiers théâtre Louvain, 1985. – 454 p., 2 p. of plates: ill. *Notes*: Translation of: **Wspólczesna refleksja o teatrze**. Includes bibliographies.

Taviani, Ferdinando. **Il Libro dell'Odin: il teatro-laboratorio di Eugenio Barba**. Milan: Feltrinelli, 1975. – xiv, 280 p., 8 p. of plates: ill. *Notes*: Bibliography: p. ix-xiii. One of Barba's closest colleagues on the Odin Teatret.

Turner, Victor. **The anthropology of performance**. New York, NY: PAJ Publications, 1986. – 185 p. Preface by Richard Schechner. *Notes*: Includes bibliographies and index. Rites and ceremonies.

Watson, Ian. **Towards a third theatre: Eugenio Barba and the Odin Teatret**. London: Routledge, 1995. 240 p.: ill. *Notes*: Introduction by Richard Schechner.

Zarrilli, Phillip, ed. **Acting (re)considered: theory and practice**. London and New York: Routledge, 1995. 320 p.: ill. *Notes*: Collection of essays about intercultural theories of acting and training.

F. Philosophy, Psychology and Drama Therapy

Evans, Richard Isadore. **Psychology and Arthur Miller**. [1st ed.]. New York: Dutton, 1969. –

xvii, 136 p. *Series*: His Dialogues with notable contributors to personality theory, vol 5. *Notes*: Bibliography: p. 129–30. Miller, Arthur, 1915–. Knowledge. Psychology.

Feldhendler, Daniel. **Psychodrama und Theater der Unterdrückten**. 2. erw. Aufl. Frankfurt am Main: W. Nold, 1992. – 145 p. *Notes*: Includes bibliographical references (p. 139–45). Psychodrama.

Ganz, Arthur F. **Realms of the self: variations on a theme in modern drama**. New York: New York University Press, 1980. – xvi, 240 p. *Notes*: Includes bibliographical references and index. Drama. Psychological aspects. Self in literature.

Garner, Stanton B. **Bodied spaces: phenomenology and performance in contemporary drama**. Ithaca, N.Y.: Cornell University Press, 1994. – x, 260 p. *Notes*: Includes bibliographical references (p. 231–49) and index. Phenomenology and performance – (Dis)figuring space: Visual field in Beckett's late plays – Object, objectivity, and the phenomenal body – The performing 'I': Language and the histrionics of place – Post-Brechtian anatomies: The politics of embodiment – Female landscapes: Phenomenology and gender.

Guerreschi, Jean. **Acting therapy et fin du théâtre: réflexions sur le trajet grotowskien**. Talence: Maison des sciences de l'homme d'Aquitaine, 1978. – 159 p. *Series*: Cahier/ CERT-CIRCE. (Centre d'études et de recherches théâtrales, University of Bordeaux III). Bibliography: p. 135–50. Grotowski and theatre as therapy.

Holmes, Paul, Marcia Karp and Michael Watson. **Psychodrama since Moreno: innovations in theory and practice**. London; New York: Routledge, 1994. – xii, 309 p.: ill. *Notes*: Includes bibliographical references and index. Moreno, Jacob Levy, 1889–1974. Drama therapy.

Jennings, Sue, ed. **Dramatherapy: theory and practice**. London and New York: Routledge, 1992–1997. Volume 1. 1992. 224 p. Volume 2. 1987. 256 p. Volume 3 1997. 368 p.: ill.

Jones, Philip. **Drama as therapy: theatre as living**. London and New York: Routledge, 1995. 352 p. *Notes*: Dramatherapy techniques.

Lutterbie, John Harry. **Hearing voices: modern drama and the problem of subjectivity**. Ann Arbor: University of Michigan Press, 1997. – 182 p. *Notes*: Includes bibliographical references (p. 173–6) and index. Identity in literature.

Moreno, Jacob Levy. **The theatre of spontaneity**.

3rd edn. Ambler, PA: Beacon House, 1983. 127 p., [1] p. of plates: ill. *Notes*: Translation of **Das Stegreiftheater**. Includes bibliographical references. *Subjects*: Psychodrama.

Ortega y Gasset, José. **Phenomenology and art**. [Selections. English. 1975]. 1st edn. New York: Norton, 1975. – 220 p. *Notes*: Includes bibliographical references. Autobiography and phenomenology: Preface for Germans (1934).– Phenomenology and theory of knowledge: Sensation, construction, and intuition (1913). On the concept of sensation (1913). Consciousness, the object, and its three distances (1916).–Phenomenology and esthetics: An essay in esthetics by way of a preface (1914). Esthetics on the streetcar (1916).–An esthetics of historical reason: The idea of theater: an abbreviated view (1946). Reviving the paintings (Velázquez, chapter I) (1946).

Rakoff, Vivian M. **Play and the theatre of fantasy**. [Stratford, Ont.]: Stratford Shakespearean Festival, 1983. – [19] p. *Series*: Celebrity lecture series. Theatre and psychology. A noted psychiatrist discusses play.

Shaffer, Elinor S., ed. **Knowledge and performance**. Cambridge; New York: Cambridge University Press, 1992. – xxvi, 281 p.: ill. *Notes*: Includes bibliographical references. pt. 1. Knowledge and performance. Acting women/ Michael Robinson – In the sign of Aquarius: Brecht and Eisenstein on the train to Moscow/ Lars Kleberg – The uses of Wittgenstein's philosophy in the study of literature/J.P. Stern – Performing theory: Wittgenstein and the trouble with Shakespeare/Peter Hughes – On open and closed doors, or, How dead is the sign: Kafka, Peirce and Derrida/Henriette Herwig – Theatre as communicative action: Augusto Boal's theatre of the oppressed/Drew Milne – pt. 2. Literature, translation and performance. Your blood: some sort of epic: interpretation/translation of a poem by Alain Bosquet, Ton sang, une epopée/Harry Guest – On puppet-shows/ Heinrich von Kleist – A double suicide/Charles Cros – Playback/Gabriel Josipovici. On the action of light in photography/August Strindberg – Trans-Atlantyk/Witold Gombrowicz – The burrow: an adaptation for the stage of Kafka's short story/Hannah Vincent – pt. 3. Essay reviews. Thinking postmodernisms: on Thomas Docherty, After theory and Fredric Jameson, Postmodernism/Nick Kaye – On Hoffmann's musical writings/Hanne Castein – Unbowdlerizing Bulgakov/Lesley Milne. Criticism. Philosophy.

States, Bert O. **Great reckonings in little rooms: on the phenomenology of theater**. Berkeley:

University of California Press, 1985. – 213 p. *Notes*: Includes index.

——. **The pleasure of the play**. Ithaca: Cornell University Press, 1994. – ix, 226 p.: ill. *Notes*: Includes bibliographical references (p. 215–20) and index. History and criticism.

Thoret, Yves. **La Théâtralité: étude freudienne**. [Paris]: Dunod, 1993. – viii, 207 p. *Notes*: Includes bibliographical references and index. Freudian theory. Drama. Psychoanalysis and audiences.

Witkiewicz, Stanislaw Ignacy. **Witkiewicz et la philosophie**. Lausanne: L'Age d'homme, 1984. – 108 p. *Other Authors*: Textes rassemblés par Bohdan Michalski. *Series*: Cahier Witkiewicz; no 5. *Notes*: Includes bibliographical references. Philosophy.

G. Theatre Semiotics, Performance Analysis, Reception

Alter, Jean. **A sociosemiotic theory of theatre**. Philadelphia: University of Pennsylvania Press, 1990. – xii, 281 p. *Notes*: Includes bibliographical references (p. 271–7) and index. Social aspects.

Aston, Elaine and George Savona. **Theatre as sign system: a semiotics of text and performance**. London and New York: Routledge, 1991. 224 p.

Balazard, Simone, Bernard Dort and Anne Ubersfeld. **Le Texte et la scène: études sur l'espace et l'acteur dans Woyzeck de Büchner, trois pièces de Maeterlinck, La Mouette de Tchékhov, Printemps 71 d'Adamov, L'Age d'or par le Théâtre du soleil**. Impr. F. Paillart, 1978. – 156 p.: ill. *Notes*: At head of title: Université de la Sorbonne nouvelle, Paris III, Groupes de recherche de l'Institut d'études théâtrales. Includes bibliographies. Studies of space and the actor.

Ben Chaim, Daphna. **Distance in the theatre: the aesthetics of audience response**. Epping: Bowker, 1984. – xi, 111 p. *Notes*: Includes index. Bibliography: p. 101–5. Drama. Participation of audiences. Theories, c1918–73.

Bennett, Susan. **Theatre audiences: a theory of production and reception**. 2nd edn. London; New York: Routledge, 1997. – xi, 248 p.: ill. *Notes*: Includes bibliographical references (p. 223–40) and index.

Castagnino, Raúl. **Semiótica, ideología y teatro hispano-americano contemporáneo**. [Semiotics and ideology in contemporary Spanish-American theatre]. Biblioteca Arte y Ciencia de la Expresión. Buenos Aires: Nova, 1974. 267 p.

de Toro, Fernando. **Semiótica y teatro latino-americano**. [Semiotics and Latin American theatre]. Buenos Aires: Editorial Galerna; Ottawa: IITCTL.

Donahue, Thomas. **Structures of meaning: a semiotic approach to the play text**. Rutherford, N.J.: London; Cranbury, NJ: Fairleigh Dickinson University Press; Associated University Presses, 1993. – 181 p.: ill. *Notes*: Includes bibliographical references (p. 171–8) and index.

Elam, Keir. **The semiotics of theatre and drama**. London: Methuen, 1980. 248 p. *Notes*: Includes index and bibliography (p. 221–39). Semiotics and literature.

Esslin, Martin. **The field of drama: how the signs of drama create meaning on stage and screen**. London: Methuen, 1987. 190 p. *Notes*: Includes index and bibliography (p. 179–85). Semiotics and literature.

Féral, Josette and Odette Aslan. **Théâtralité, écriture et mise en scène**. Ville de LaSalle, Québec: Hurtubise HMH, 1985. – 271 p.: ill. *Notes*: Bibliography: p. 267–8. Semiotics and literature.

Fischer-Lichte, Erika. **The semiotics of theatre**. Translated by Jeremy Gaines and Doris Jones. Bloomington: Indiana University Press, 1992. 336 p. *Notes*: Includes bibliographical references (p. 319–32) and indexes. Theatre, semiotics and literature.

Garzón Céspedes, Francisco, ed. **El teatro de participación popular y el teatro de comunidad: un teatro de sus protagonistas**. [Participatory and community theatre: a theatre that belongs to its protagonists]. Havana: Unión de Escritores y Artistas de Cuba, 1977. 146 p.

Horwood, Joanne E. **The semiotics of subtext in modern drama**. New York: P. Lang, 1996. *Notes*: Includes bibliographical references and index.

Martin, Jacqueline and Willmar Sauter. **Understanding theatre: performance analysis in theory and practice**. Stockholm: Almqvist & Wiksell, 1995. – 271 p.: ill. *Notes*: Includes bibliographical references (p. 264–71). Philosophy/Theatre audiences. Psychology/Dramatic criticism. Acting. History.

Martínez Arango, Gilberto. **Teatro, teoría y práctica**. Medellín, Colombia: Ediciones Autores Antioquenos, 1986. – 235 p.: ill. *Notes*: Includes bibliographies. Acting/Semiotics.

Matejka, Ladislava and I.R. Titunik, eds. **Semiotics of art: Prague School contributions**. 1st paperback printing. Cambridge, Mass.: MIT Press, 1984. – xxi, 298 p. *Notes*: Includes bibliographical references and index. Mukarovský, J. Art as semiotic fact.–Bogatyrev, P. Costume as a sign.–Bogatyrev, P. Folk song from a functional point of view.–Bogatyrev, P. Semiotics in the folk theater.–Bogatyrev, P. Forms and functions of folk theater.–Brusák, K. Signs in the Chinese theater.–Honzl, J. Dynamics of the sign in the theater.–Veltruský, J. Dramatic text as a component of theater.–Honzl, J. The hierarchy of dramatic devices.–Veltruský, J. Basic features of dramatic dialogue.–Veltruský, J. Construction of semantic contexts,–Jakobson, R. Is the cinema in decline?–Mukarovský, J. Poetic reference.–Jakobson, R. What is poetry?–Jakobson, R. Signum et signatum.–Jakobson, R. The contours of The safe conduct.–Vodicka, F. Response to verbal art.–Dolezel, L. A scheme of narrative time.–Levý, J. The translation of verbal art.–Mukarovský, J. The essence of the visual arts.–Veltruský, J. Some aspects of the pictorial sign.–Matejka, L. Postscript: Prague School semiotics.

Melrose, Susan. **A semiotics of the dramatic text**. Basingstoke: Macmillan, 1994. – ix, 338 p. *Notes*: Includes index. Bibliography: p. 315–21.

Pavis, Patrice. **L'analyse des spectacles: théâtre, mime, danse, danse-théâtre, cinéma**. Paris: Nathan, 1996. – 319 p.: ill. *Notes*: Includes bibliographical references (p. 300–10) and index. Performing arts. Audiences.

——. **Dictionnaire du théâtre: termes et concepts de l'analyse théâtrale**. Paris: Éditions sociales, 1980. – 482 p. *Notes*: Bibliography: p. 443–70. A semiotic emphasis on theatre concepts.

——. **Languages of the stage: essays in the semiology of the theatre**. New York: Performing Arts Journal Publications, 1982. – 206 p.

——. **Problèmes de sémiologie théâtrale**. Montréal: Presses de l'Université du Québec, 1976. – 167 p.: ill., diagrs. *Notes*: Includes index. Bibliography: p. 151–9.

——. **Voix et images de la scène: essais de sémiologie théâtrale**. [Lille]: Presses universitaires de Lille, 1982. – 225 p., 16 p. of plates: ill. *Notes*: Includes bibliographical references.

——. **Voix et images de la scène: vers une sémiologie de la réception**. Nouv. édn. rev. et augm. [Lille]: Presses universitaires de Lille, 1985. – 340 p., 36 p. of plates: ill. *Notes*: Bibliography: p. 325–40.

Quinn, Michael L. **The semiotic stage: Prague school theatre theory**. New York: P. Lang, 1995. – 166 p.: ill. *Notes*: Includes bibliographical references (p. 145–60).

Rask, Elin. **Teatersemiologi**. [Semiology of theatre]. Copenhagen: Berlingske leksikon Bibliotek, 1976.

——. **Teaterforestillingen**. [Theatre performance]. Gråsten: Forlaget Drama, 1980.

Raz, Jacob. **Audience and actors: a study of their interaction in the Japanese traditional theatre**. Leiden: E.J. Brill, 1983. – xii, 307 p. *Notes*: Includes index. Bibliography: p. 293–302.

Roach, Joseph R. **The player's passion: studies in the science of acting**. Ann Arbor: University of Michigan Press, 1993 1985. – 255 p.: ill. *Notes*: Originally published: Newark: University of Delaware Press; London: Associated University Presses, c1985. Includes bibliographical references and index. Semiotics.

Sauter, Willmar. **Acting and dancing**. [Copenhagen]: Munksgaard, 1992. – 159 p.: ill. *Notes*: Cover title: In homage to Kirsten Gram Holmström. Includes several articles by Kirsten Gram Holmström, published on the occasion of her retirement. Includes bibliographical references. Scandinavia. History/Dance.

Schmid, Herta and Aloysius van Kesteren. **Semiotics of drama and theatre: new perspectives in the theory of drama and theatre**. Amsterdam; Philadelphia: J. Benjamins, 1984. – 548 p.: ill. *Notes*: English, French, and German. Bibliography: p. 511–48.

Schmid, Herta and Jurij Striedter. **Dramatische und theatralische Kommunikation: Beiträge zur Geschichte und Theorie des Dramas und Theaters im 20. Jahrhundert**. Tübingen: Narr, 1992. – 272 p. *Notes*: Three contributions in English. Includes bibliographical references.

Ubersfeld, Anne. **L'École du spectateur: lire le théâtre 2**. Paris: Editions sociales, 1981. – 352 p.: ill. *Notes*: Bibliography: p. 345–50. Includes index. Audience reception.

——. **Lire le théâtre**. Paris: Éditions Sociales, 1978. – 309 p.; 18 cm. *Notes*: Bibliography: p.305–309. Dramatic criticism. Audience reception.

Vallauri, Carlos. **Il pubblico in palcoscenico. Ricerca sugli spettatori di teatro**. [The audience on the stage: research on theatre audiences]. Rome: Regione Lazio, 1980.

Whitmore, Jon. **Directing postmodern theatre: shaping signification in performance**. Ann Arbor: University of Michigan Press, 1994. – viii, 242 p.: ill. *Notes*: Includes bibliographical references (p. 229–34) and index.

H. Acting and Directing

H1. Acting

H1a. GENERAL STUDIES

The actor. Bruxelles. Elsevier, 1955. – 78, [2] p. illus. *Series*: World Theatre, vol. 4, no. 1. *Notes*: Editorial, by René Hainaux.–The Stanislavski method, by Nina Gourfinkel.–A new technique of the art of acting, by Bertolt Brecht.–Actors' comments: A French reaction, by Jean-Louis Barrault; A British reaction, by Michael Redgrave.–A school of dramatic art, by Michel Saint-Denis.

Ahn, Mim-Soo, Suk-Kee Yoh and Taw-Ju Lee. **Yeun-ki**. [Acting]. Seoul, 1988. 267 p.

Aleksidze, Dimitri. **Msakhiobis aghsrdis sakitkhisatvis**. [Training an actor]. Tbilisi: Literatura da Khelovneba, 1956. 204 p.

Barba, Eugenio and Nicola Savrese. **A dictionary of theatre anthropology: the secret art of the performer**. London: Published for the Centre for Performance Research by Routledge, 1991. 272 pp.: ill. *Notes*: Includes index.

Barker, Clive. **Theatre games: a new approach to drama training**. London: Methuen Drama, 1989. – xi, 226 p.: ill. *Notes*: Includes bibliographical references (p. 225–6).

Belich, Margaret, ed. **Performance**. Wellington: Association of Community Theatres, 1985. 62 p.

Boal, Augusto. **Games for actors and non-actors**. London: Routledge, 1992. 288 p.: ill. *Notes*: Translated into English by Adrian Jackson. Analysis of the actor's art. Games, methods and techniques.

——. **The rainbow of desire: the Boal method of theatre and therapy**. London: Routledge, 1994. 219 p. *Notes*: Translated into English by Adrian Jackson. Theatre as therapeutic and liberating.

Brook, Peter. **The open door: thoughts on acting and theatre**. New York: Theatre Communications Group, 1995. – 147 p. *Notes*: Includes bibliographical references (p. 147). American edition of **There are no secrets**.

——. **There are no secrets: thoughts on acting and theatre**. London: Methuen Drama, 1995 1993. – 118 p.

Cohen-Cruz, Jan and Mady Schutzman, eds. **Playing Boal**. London and New York: Routledge, 1993. 256 p. *Notes*: Examination of Augusto Boal's techniques.

Drama and the actor. Cambridge and New York: Cambridge University Press, 1984. – xiii, 290 p.: ill. *Notes*: Includes bibliographies and index.

Efros, Anatolii. **Professiia, rezhisser**. Moscow: Iskusstvo, 1979. – 367 p. *Notes*: Efros on directing as a career.

——. **Repetitsiia-liubov' moia**. Moscow: Iskusstvo, 1975. – 319 p.: ill. *Notes*: Efros on the rehearsal process.

Fitzpatrick, Tim. **Performance, from product to process**. Sydney: University of Sydney, 1989. 253 p.

Gourdon, Anne-Marie. 'La Formation du comédien'. [The actor's training]. In **Les Voies de la création théâtrales** vol. IX. Paris: CNRS. 280 p.

Harrop, John. **Acting**. London and New York: Routledge, 1992. – vii, 135 p. *Notes*: Includes bibliographical references (p. 130–1) and index. Acting. Study and teaching.

Hobgood, Burnet M., ed. **Master teachers of theatre: observations on teaching theatre by nine American masters**. Carbondale: Southern Illinois University Press, 1988. – ix, 212 p. *Notes*: The play's the thing– but what's a play?/Bernard Beckerman – Historical study in the theatre curriculum/Oscar Brockett – In the beginning was the word/Claribel Baird – Zen in the art of actor training/Robert Benedetti – Movement for actors/Jewel Walker – The craft of the eclectic/Carl Weber – Teaching design for theatre/Howard Bay – Essential theatre for the high school/Wallace Smith – The drama of childhood/the childhood of theatre/Agnes Haaga.

Mitchell, John Dietrich. **The director–actor relationship: essays and articles**. New York: Institute for Advanced Studies in the Theatre Arts Press, 1992. – vi, 170 p.: ill. *Notes*: Applied psychoanalysis in the drama – Applied psycho-analysis in the director-actor relationship – Contemporary American theatre... a psycho-logic sounding board – Psychoanalytic approach to Kabuki: a study in personality and culture – The actor's 'method', backstage at the Kabuki-za, Tokyo – A psychosocial approach to the Peking Opera – How the Chinese actor trains; interviews with two Peking Opera performers – Two faces of China – East-West understanding through the arts – Discussion – The theatre in India – A Sanskrit classic: Shakuntala – The Sanskrit drama Shakuntala – The theatre of India and Southeast Asia – Theatre of Western Europe – The theatre in Russia – The Moscow Art Theatre in rehearsal – The theatre of Western Europe: some highlights – Brecht's theatre, the Berliner Ensemble – In search of Commedia Dell'Arte – André Gide, rebel and conformist – The challenge of directing a neo-classical verse tragedy – Theatre in Mexico moves ahead – Riches from abroad – IASTA, an American innovation in workshop production – The International Amateur Theatre Association – Is the play the thing? Acting/Theatre. Production and direction. China. USA. Japan. India. Russia. Germany. Mexico.

Trobisch, Stephen. **Theaterwissenschaftliche Studien zu Sinn und Anwendbarkeit von Verfahren zur Schauspieler-Ausbildung: mit besonderer Berücksichtigung der Lehr-Methoden von Richard Boleslavsky, Lee Strasberg, Uta Hagen, und Michael Tschechow**. Frankfurt am Main; New York: Lang, 1993. – 220 p. *Notes*: Includes bibliographical references (p. 215–20). Acting. Study and teaching.

Urushadze, Natela. **Msakhiobis Khelovneba**. [The actor's art]. Tbilisi: Literatura da Khelovneba, 1957. 248 p.

Worthen, William B. **The idea of the actor: drama and the ethics of performance**. Princeton, N.J.: Princeton University Press, 1984. – 269 p. *Notes*: Includes index. Bibliography: p. 233–59.

Zarrilli, Phillip, ed. **Acting (re)considered: theory and practice**. London and New York: Routledge, 1995. 320 p.: ill. *Notes*: Collection of essays about intercultural theories of acting and training.

H1b. METHODOLOGY, TECHNIQUES AND STUDIES OF SPECIFIC ACTORS

Beck, Alan. **Radio acting**. London: A & C Black, 1997. – vi, 170 p.: ill. *Notes*: Includes bibliographical references (p. 164) and index.

Benedetti, Robert L. **The actor at work**. 3rd edn. Englewood Cliffs, N.J.: Prentice-Hall, 1981. – xvii, 286 p.: ill. *Notes*: Includes index.

Bibliography: p. 279–281. Standard acting text.

Brook, Peter and Jim MacAndrew. **The magic of Peter Brook, pt. 1**. New York: Columbia Broadcasting System, 1971. – 1 videocassette (ca. 25 min.): sd., col.; $\frac{1}{2}$ in. VHS. *Series*: Camera three. *Notes*: Prog. #11-71. English theatre director Peter Brook explains and shows how he staged his version of The Tempest.

Brovelli, Claude. **Ils ont réussi**. Paris: Éditions France-Empire, 1984. – 221 p. *Notes*: Includes index. Jean-Louis Barrault – Maurice Béjart – Paul Bocuse – Bernard Buffet – César – Guy Des Cars – Edouard Leclerc – Michel Legrand – Paul Ricard – Yves Saint-Martin – Léon Schwarzenberg – Madame Soleil – Marguerite Yourcenar. Interviews. In French.

Bruehl, Bill. **The technique of inner action: the soul of a performer's work**. Portsmouth, NH: Heinemann, 1996. – xiii, 97 p. *Notes*: Includes bibliographical references (p. 93–7).

Chekhov, Michael. **To the actor: on the technique of acting**. New York; London: Barnes & Noble, 1985 1953. – xiii, 201 p.: ill. *Notes*: Originally published: New York: Harper & Row, 1953.

Cole, Toby. **Acting, a handbook of the Stanislavski method; introd. by Lee Strasberg**. New York: Lear, 1947. – 223 p. illus., ports.

—— and Helen K. Chinoy. **Actors on acting: the theories, techniques and practices of the great actors of all times as told in their own words**. New York: Crown, 1970. 715 p.

Davis, Debora Fay. **Mime as an actor training technique: a professional problem**. 1991. – vi, 305 p. *Notes*: Discography: p. 211–13. Includes abstract. Includes bibliographical references (p. 209–11). Thesis (Ph. D.)–Texas Tech University, 1991. Photocopy. Ann Arbor, Mich.: University Microfilms, 1991. *Subjects*: Acting. Study and teaching/Mime. Study and teaching/Movement (Acting). Study and teaching.

Fo, Dario and Stuart Hood. **The tricks of the trade**. London: Methuen Drama, 1992, 1991. – 217 p., 4 p. of plates: ill. *Notes*: Translation of **Manuale minimo dell'attore**. Includes index.

Gordon, Hayes. **A complete compendium of acting and performing, in two parts**. Milsons Point, N.S.W.: Ensemble Press, 1992, 1987. – ii, 299 p.: ill. *Notes*: Includes index.

Gordon, Mel. **The Stanislavsky technique: Russia: a workbook for actors**. New York: Applause, 1988 1987. – xv, 252 p. *Notes*: Bibliography: p. 251–2. Method (acting).

Green, Michael Frederick. **The art of coarse acting**. New rev. edn., 4th Limelight edn. New York: Limelight Editions, 1996, 1964. – 127 p., 8 p. of plates: ill. *Notes*: Humour. How to act badly.

Grotowski, Jerzy and Eugenio Barba. **Towards a poor theatre**. London: Methuen, 1991 1968. – 218 p.: ill. *Notes*: 'Texts by Jerzy Grotowski, interviews with him and other supplementary material presenting his method and training'. 'A Methuen drama book'. *Subjects*: Acting. An essential text covering Grotowski's 'Poor Theatre' phase.

—— and Ludwik Flaszen. **Institut de Recherches sur le Jeu de l'Acteur: théâtre laboratoire**. Wroclaw: 1960, 1969, – 36 p., 14 p. of plates: ill. *Notes*: Acting. Research. Poland/Instytut Badan Metody Aktorskiej. In Polish.

Hilton, Julian. **Performance**. Basingstoke: Macmillan, 1987. – 173 p. *Notes*: Includes index. Bibliography: p. 164–6. Acting techniques.

Jilinsky, Andrius and Helen C. Bragdon. **The joy of acting: a primer for actors**. New York: P. Lang, 1990. – xix, 186 p.: ill.

Kuchtówna, Lidia. **Sztuka aktorska a dramat**. Warsaw: Instytut Sztuki Polskiej Akademii Nauk, 1993. – 290 p.: ill. *Notes*: Includes bibliographical references and index. Acting. Theatre Poland.

Laurie, Rona. **The actor's art and craft**. Colwall: J. Garnet Miller, 1994. – 164 p.: ill. *Notes*: Includes index.

McMenamin, Milton J. and Ann Marie McMenamin. **Designs in drama**. Malabar, Fla.: Krieger Pub. Co., 1991. – xvii, 169 p.: ill. *Notes*: Includes bibliographical references (p. 161), indexes. Acting. Direction/Image processing.

McTeague, James H. **Playwrights and acting: acting methodologies for Brecht, Ionesco, Pinter, and Shepard**. Westport, Conn.: Greenwood Press, 1994. – xviii, 176 p.: ill. *Notes*: Includes bibliographical references (p. 155–9) and index.

Moore, Sonia. **The Stanislavski system: the professional training of an actor: digested from the teachings of Konstantin S. Stanislavski**. 2nd rev. edn. New York, NY: Penguin Books, 1984. – xvi, 96 p. *Notes*: Originally published as **The Stanislavski method**. Bibliography: p. 91–2. Includes index.

——. **Training an actor; the Stanislavski system in class**. New York: Viking Press, 1968. – 260p. *Subjects*: Acting. Study and teaching.

——, ed. **Stanislavski today; commentaries on K.S. Stanislavski**. New York: American Center for Stanislavski Theatre Art, 1973. – 112 p. *Notes*: Includes bibliographical references. The mastery of the actor and the director/B.E. Zakhava–The training of an actor in the Stanislavski school of acting/G.V. Kristi–The method of K.S. Stanislavski and the physiology of emotions/P.V. Simonov–Superior simplicity/M.O. Knebel–The Nemirovitch-Dantchenko school of directing/M.O. Knebel–The profession of a director/G.A. Tovstonogov–William Shakespeare, our contemporary/G. Kozintsev–Reminiscences and reflections about theatre/A.D. Popov–About the art of the theatre/Yu. Zavadsky–Meyerhold: innovator and example/S. Moore.

Moossen, Inge. **Theater als Kunst: Sinn und Unsinn des Stanislawski-Systems**. Frankfurt am Main: Haag und Herchen, 1993. – 372 p. *Notes*: Includes bibliographical references. *Subjects*: Method (Acting). Stanislavsky, Konstantin, 1863–1938.

Morrison, Hugh. **Acting skills**. London and New York: Theatre Arts/Routledge, 1992. – vi, 175 p.: ill. *Notes*: Includes bibliographical references (p. 171–2) and index.

Morrison, Malcolm. **Classical acting**. London: A & C Black, 1995. – vii, 128 p. *Notes*: Includes bibliographical references (p. 124–5) and index.

Munk, Erika, ed. **Stanislavski and America; an anthology from the Tulane Drama Review**. Introd. by Richard Schechner. Tulane drama review. New York: Hill and Wang, 1966. – 279 p.

Olivier, Laurence. **On acting**. New York: Simon & Schuster, 1987, 1986. – 397 p., 2 p. of plates: ill. *Notes*: Includes index. 'Performances': p. 379–88.

Paxton, Steve. **Contact improvisation**. Devon: Dept. of Theatre, Dartington College of Arts, 1982. – 27 p. *Subjects*: Acting. Study and teaching.

Powers, Mala and Michael Chekhov. **Michael Chekhov: on theatre and the art of acting: the six-hour master class: a guide to discovery with exercises**. New York, NY: Applause, 1992. – 53 p.; 22 cm. + 4 sound cassettes. *Notes*: Accompanied by lectures recorded by Michael Chekhov in 1955. Includes bibliographical references.

Richards, Thomas. **At work with Grotowski on physical actions**. London and New York: Routledge, 1995. 160 p. *Notes*: With preface and essay by Jerzy Grotowski.

Rumbelow, Steven and Frances Clarke. **The training of Triple Action Theatre**. Devon: Dept. of Theatre, Dartington College of Arts, 1982. –

44 p. *Subjects*: Acting. Study and teaching. England/Triple Action Theatre.

Stanislavsky, Konstantin. **An actor prepares**. New York: Routledge/Theatre Arts Books, 1989 1936. – 313 p. Translated by Elizabeth Reynolds Hapgood. *Notes*: An essential text on actor training. Translation of: **Rabota aktera nad soboi**.

——. **An actor's handbook: an alphabetical arrangement of concise statements on aspects of acting**. London: Methuen Drama, 1990, 1963. 160 p. Edited and translated by Elizabeth Reynolds Hapgood. *Notes*: Originally published: New York: Theatre Arts Books, 1963.

——. **Building a character**. New York: Routledge/Theater Arts Books, 1989 1977. – 299 p. Translated by Elizabeth Reynolds Hapgood. *Notes*: Translation of: **Rabota aktera nad soboi**. (Additional selections.)

——. **Creating a role**. New York: Routledge, 1989. – xiv, 271 p. Translated by Elizabeth Reynolds Hapgood; edited by Hermine I. Popper; foreword by Robert Lewis. *Notes*: Acting.

——. **My life in art**. New York: Theatre Arts Books, 1952. – ix, 582 p.; 21 cm. Translated by J.J. Robbins. *Series*: TAB paperbook; no. 50. *Notes*: Translation of: **Moia zhizn' v iskusstve**. Includes index. Autobiography.

—— and Hapgood, Elizabeth Reynolds. **Stanislavski's legacy**. A collection of comments on a variety of aspects of an actor's art and life. Rev. and expanded edn. New York: Theatre Arts Books, 1989, 1968. – x, 209 p.

Strasberg, Lee and Evangeline Morphos. **A dream of passion: the development of the method**. London: Methuen Drama, 1989 1987. – 201 p., [16] p. of plates: ill., ports., facsims. *Notes*: Originally published: Boston, Mass: Little Brown, 1987; London: Bloomsbury, 1988. Acting techniques.

Tremblay, Larry. **Le Crâne des théâtres: essai sur le corps de l'acteur**. Montréal: Leméac, 1993. – 135 p. *Notes*: Includes bibliographical references (p. 131–3). Body image/Gesture.

Veinstein, André. **Théâtre: étude, enseignement, éléments de méthodologie**. Louvain-la-Neuve: Cahiers théâtre Louvain, 1983. – 174 p. *Notes*: Includes bibliographical references. History. 20th century. Towards a methodology of training.

Woods, Leigh. **On playing Shakespeare: Advice and commentary from actors and actresses of the past**. Greenwood Press, 1991. – 1 v. *Notes*: Acting techniques/Shakespeare: studies and criticism.

H1c. IMPROVISATION

Bernardi, Philip. **Improvisation starters: a collection of 900 improvisation situations for the theater**. White Hall, Va.: Betterway Publications, 1992. – 159 p. *Subjects*: Improvisation (Acting).

Clark, Brian. **Group theatre**. New York: Theatre Arts Books, 1972 1971. – vi, 119 p. *Notes*: Bibliography: p. 118–19.

Fox, Jonathan. **Acts of service: spontaneity, commitment, tradition in the nonscripted theatre**. New Paltz, NY: Tusitala Pub., 1994. – 276 p. *Notes*: Includes bibliographical references (p. 262–70) and index.

Frost, Anthony and Ralph Yarrow. **Improvisation in drama**. New York: St. Martin's Press, 1990. – ix, 214 p., 4 p. of plates: ill. *Series*: Theatre studies. *Notes*: Includes bibliographical references (p. 199–205) and index.

Gravel, Robert and Jan-Marc Lavergne. **Impro: réflexions et analyses**. [Montréal]: Leméac, 1987. – 159 p.: ill.

Johnstone, Keith. **Impro: improvisation and the theatre**. London: Methuen Drama, 1994 1979. – 208 p. *Notes*: First published in the USA 1979 by Theatre Arts Books. A core text in the field.

Kirby, Michael. **Happenings**. New York: Dutton, 1965. 288 p.

Oddey, Alison. **Devising theatre: a practical and theoretical handbook**. London; New York: Routledge, 1994. – xiv, 254 p.: ill. *Notes*: Includes bibliographical references (p. 242–5) and index. A British perspective.

Spolin, Viola. **Improvisation for the theatre: a handbook of teaching and directing techniques**. Evanston, Ill.: Northwestern University Press, 1985. – xxxi, 397 p.: ill. Essential text in the field.

Zaporah, Ruth. **Action theater: the improvisation of presence**. Berkeley, Calif.: North Atlantic Books, 1995. – xxiii, 275 p.: ill. *Notes*: Includes bibliographical references and index.

H1d. MOVEMENT FOR ACTORS

Bernd, Christine. **Bewegung und Theater: Lernen durch Verkörpern**. Frankfurt am Main: AFRA Verlag, 1988. – 235 p. *Notes*: Includes bibliographical references (p. 214–35).

Caune, Jean. **La Dramatisation: une méthode et des techniques d'expression et de communiction par le corps**. Louvain-la-Neuve: Cahiers théâtre Louvain, 1981. – 368 p. *Notes*: Includes bibliographical references.

Fleshman, Bob. **Theatrical movement: a bibliographical anthology**. Metuchen, N.J.: Scarecrow Press, 1986. – xiv, 742 p. *Notes*: Movement (Acting). Bibliography.

Hulton, Peter. **From action to theatre image**. Dartington, England: Dept. of Theatre, Dartington College of Arts, 1978. *Series*: Theatre papers; 2nd ser. (1978), no. 10. *Subjects*: Movement (Acting).

King, Nancy. **Theatre movement: the actor and his space**. New York: Drama Book Specialists/ Publishers, 1971. – viii, 175 p. illus.

Kline, Peter, Nancy Meadors Kline and Harold Isen. **Physical movement for the theatre**. New York: Richards Rosen Press, 1971. – 156 p. illus. *Notes*: Bibliography: p. 149–56. Suggests exercises to help develop controlled body movements that can facilitate the student actor's communication of ideas, words, and emotions.

Koner, Pauline. **Elements of performance: a guide for performers in dance, theatre, and opera**. Chur, Switzerland; Langhorne, Pa.: Harwood Academic Publishers, 1993. – xiii, 107 p.: ill. *Notes*: Based on the course of the same title the author taught at the Juilliard School. Includes index. Dance. Study and teaching.

Law, Alma H. and Mel Gordon. **Meyerhold, Eisenstein, and biomechanics: actor training in revolutionary Russia**. Jefferson, N.C.: McFarland, 1996. – xi, 282 p.: ill. *Notes*: Includes bibliographical references (p. 273–4) and index.

Rose, Mark V. **The actor and his double: mime and movement for the theatre of cruelty**. Chicago: Actor Training & Research Inst. Press, 1986. – xii, 56 p., 11 p. of plates: ill. *Notes*: Bibliography: p. 52–6.

Sullivan, Claudia N. **The actor moves**. Jefferson, N.C.: McFarland, 1990. – xiv, 151 p. *Notes*: Includes bibliographical references (p. 141–6) and index.

H1e. SPEECH

Berry, Cicely. **The actor and the text**. Rev. edn. London: Virgin, 1993 1992. – 303 p. *Notes*: Includes indexes. Acting/voice exercises. Vocal communication. An essential text in the field.

Colaianni, Louis and Gale Nelson. **The joy of phonetics and accents**. New York: Drama Book Publishers, 1994. – ix, 172 p.: ill. *Notes*: Includes bibliographical references. English language. Pronunciation by foreign speakers.

Hampton, Marian E. and Barbara Acker. **The vocal vision: views on voice**. New York: Applause, 1997. – viii, 276 p. *Notes*: 'By 24 leading teachers, coaches & directors'. Includes bibliographical references and index.

Herman, Lewis and Marguerite Shalett. **Foreign dialects: a manual for actors, directors and writers**. New York, N.Y.: Routledge, 1997. – 376 p.: ill. English language. Pronunciation by foreign speakers.

Hill, Harry and Robert Barton. **A voice for the theatre**. New York: Holt, Rinehart & Winston, 1985. – ix, 270 p. *Notes*: Includes index. Bibliography: p. 259–61. Voice production.

Jones, Chuck. **Make your voice heard: an actor's guide to increased dramatic range through vocal training**. New York: Back Stage Books, 1996. – 144 p. *Notes*: Includes index.

Linklater, Kristin. **Freeing Shakespeare's voice: the actor's guide to talking the text**. New York: Theatre Communications Group, 1992. – vii, 214 p. *Subjects*: Voice. Acting/Shakespeare, William, 1564–1616. Words from a master teacher.

Macdonald, Robert. **The use of the voice: sensory appreciation, posture, vocal functioning and Shakespearean text performance**. London: Macdonald Media, 1997. – 171 p. *Notes*: Includes bibliographical references. Exercises/Voice. Physiological aspects/ Alexander technique.

Machlin, Evangeline. **Speech for the stage**. New York: Routledge, 1992 1980. – viii, 254 p.: ill. *Notes*: 'A Theatre Arts Book'. Includes bibliographical references (p. 221) and index. A standard in the field.

Martin, Jacqueline. **Voice in modern theatre**. London and New York: Routledge, 1991. – xviii, 229 p.: ill. *Notes*: Includes bibliographical references (p. 193–218) and index.

McCallion, Michael. **The voice book: for actors, public speakers and everyone else who wants to make the most of their voice**. London: Faber, 1988. – 300 p.: ill. *Notes*: Includes bibliography and index.

Mrevlishvili, Maliko. **Kartuli sastseno metkvelebis phonetikuri gapudzvlebi**. [Basic phonetic speech principles of Georgian stage speech]. Tbilisi: Ganatleba, 1966. 153 p.

Nikolaishvili, Barbale. **Kartuli sastseno metkveleba**. [Georgian artistic speech]. Tbilisi: Ganatleba, 1979. 378 p.

——. **Mkhatvruli kithvis khelovneba**. [The basic principles of artistic speech]. Tbilisi: Literatura da Khelovneba, 1971. 194 p.

Rodenburg, Patsy. **The actor speaks: voice and the performer**. London: Methuen Drama, 1997. – xii, 388 p.

H1f. PSYCHOLOGY OF THE ACTOR

Beckerman, Bernard, Gloria Brim Beckerman and William Coco. **Theatrical presentation: performer, audience, and act**. New York: Routledge, 1990. – xi, 212 p. *Notes*: Includes bibliographical references (p. 198–202) and index. Philosophy. Acting.

Caune, Jean. **Acteur-spectateur: une relation dans le blanc des mots**. [Paris]: Libr. Nizet, 1996. – 222 p. *Notes*: Includes bibliographical references and index. Acting. Psychological aspects. Semiotics/Theatre audiences. Psychology.

Gillibert, Jean. **Les illusiades: essai sur le théâtre de l'acteur**. Paris: Editions Clancier-Guénaud, 1983. – 333 p. Acting. Psychological aspects.

Huston, Hollis. **The actor's instrument: body, theory, stage**. Ann Arbor: University of Michigan Press, 1992. – vi, 218 p. *Notes*: Includes bibliographical references (p. 201–11) and index.

Meyer-Dinkgräfe, Daniel. **Consciousness and the actor: a reassessment of Western and Indian approaches to the actor's emotional involvement from the perspective of Vedic psychology**. Frankfurt am Main; New York: Peter Lang, 1996. – 203 p. *Notes*: Includes bibliographical references (p. 169–203). *Subjects*: Acting. Psychological aspects/Acting. Philosophy/Transcendental meditation.

Pidoux, Jean-Yves. **Acteurs et personnages: l'interprétation dans les esthétiques théâtrales du XXe siècle**. [Lausanne]: Éditions de l'Aire, 1986. – 372 p. *Notes*: Bibliography: p. 345–70. Drama. 20th century. History and criticism/Brecht, Bertolt, 1898–1956. Stanislavsky, Konstantin, 1863–1938.

H2. Directing

Alberts, David. **Rehearsal management for directors**. Portsmouth, NH: Heinemann, 1995. – x, 160 p.: ill. *Notes*: Includes bibliographical references (p. 159–60).

Aleksidze, Dimitri. **Rejisoris mushaoba spektakles**. [The director's work on performance]. Tbilisi: Literatura da Khelovneba, 1961. 261 p.

Aslan, Odette. **Roger Blin**. Paris: La Manufacture, 1990. – 358, 15 p.: ill. *Notes*: Includes bibliographical references (p. 355–9). Theatrical producers and directors. France. Biography/Blin, Roger.

—— and Jean Jacquot, eds. **Les Voies de la création théâtrale. 1**. Paris: Éd. du CNRS, 1985. – 345 p.: ill. *Notes*: Index. Réunit: 'Le Prince Constant/Jerzy Grotowski; Kaspariana/Eugenio Barba; The Brig, Frankenstein, Antigone, Paradise now/Julian Beck et Judith Malina; The serpent/Joseph Chaikin, J.C. Van Itallie; Le cimetière des voitures/Arrabal. Victor Garcia'. Major directors speak of their work. In French.

Ball, William. **A sense of direction: some observations on the art of directing**. New York: Drama Book Publishers, 1984. – xiv, 182 p. *Notes*: An American director speaks of his approach.

Bannour, Wanda. **Meyerhold: un saltimbanque de génie**. Paris: La Différence, 1996. – 309 p., 24 p. of plates: ill. *Notes*: 'Index des mises en scène de V. Meyerhold': p. 295–8. Includes bibliographical references (p. 293–4) and index. Meyerhold, Vsevolod Emilievich (1874–1940).

Banu, Georges. **Peter Brook**. Paris: Flammarion, 1991. 264 p.

Barowski, Wieslaw. **Tadeusz Kantor**. Warsaw: Wydawn. Artystyczne i Filmowe, 1982. – 176 p.

Bartow, Arthur. **The director's voice: twenty-one interviews**. New York: Theatre Communications Group, 1988. – xv, 382 p. *Notes*: American directors on directing.

Batchelder, Vernita Mallard. **The theatre theory and theatre practice of Jurij Ljubimov, 1964–1971**. 1988 1978. – v, 335 p. *Notes*: Bibliography: p. 313–35. Thesis (Ph. D.)–University of Georgia, 1978. Photocopy. Ann Arbor, Mich.: University Microfilms International, (1988). Russia (Federation). Moscow. Taganka theatre.

Battistini, Fabio. **Giorgio Strehler**. Rome: Gremese Editore, 1980. – 291 p.: ill. *Notes*: Includes index. Bibliography: p. 276–84. Italy. Directors. Strehler, Giorgio.

Bene, Carmelo and Dario Ventimiglia. **La ricerca impossibile: Biennale teatro '89**. Venice: Marsilio editori, 1990. – 160 p. *Notes*: 'Questo libro è stato realizzato durante il periodo di permanenza di Carmelo Bene alla direzione del Settore Teatro della Biennale ed è stato curio da Dario Ventimiglia'–P. [6]. Essays in Italian and French, with Italian translations of the French in Appendix. 'Biennale teatro '89, Giardini di Castello, 1–30 settembre, Padiglioni Italia, Belgio, Svizzera'–T.p. verso. Criticism and interpretation. Carmelo Bene.

Benedetti, Jean. **Stanislavski: his life and art**. London: Methuen, 1999. 320 p. *Notes*: Fully revised and expanded biography.

Benedetti, Robert L. **The director at work**. Englewood Cliffs, N.J.: Prentice-Hall, 1985. –

xiv, 240 p.: ill. *Notes*: Includes index. Bibliography: p. 237. Important study by a major American teacher.

Benhamou, Anne-Françoise, Claudine Amiard-Chevrel and François Regnault. **Antoine Vitez: toutes les mises en scène**. [Bourges]: J.-C. Godefroy, 1981. – 282 p.: ill. *Notes*: Includes bibliographical references.

Bergman, Ingmar. **Laterna magica**. Stockholm: Mânpocket, 1989, 1987. – 336 p. *Notes*: Biography of the Swedish director.

Berry, Ralph. **On directing Shakespeare: interviews with contemporary directors**. London and New York: H. Hamilton; Viking Penguin, 1989. – viii, 227 p., 24 p. of plates: ill. *Notes*: Includes index. Jonathan Miller – Konrad Swinarski – Trevor Nunn – Michael Kahn – Robin Phillips (I) – Giorgio Strehler – Peter Brook – Robin Phillips (II) – Adrian Noble – Bill Alexander – Declan Donnellan – Sir Peter Hall – Michael Bogdanov.

Blin, Roger and Lynda Bellity Peskine. **Roger Blin, souvenirs et propos**. [Paris]: Gallimard, 1986. – 330 p., 1 p. of plates. *Notes*: Includes index. 'Distributions des pièces de théâtre créées par Roger Blin': p. 303–21. Theatrical producers and directors. France.

Blumenthal, Eileen. **Joseph Chaikin: exploring at the boundaries of theater**. Cambridge and New York: Cambridge University Press, 1984. – xvi, 261 p. *Series*: Directors in perspective. *Notes*: Includes index. Bibliography: p. 250–5. A study of the director of the Open Theatre.

Bondy, Luc and Georges Banu. **La fête de l'instant: dialogues avec Georges Banu**. Arles: Actes sud; Académie expérimentale des théâtres, 1996. – 251 p.: ill. *Notes*: Contains contributions from the cycle Une œuvre à questionner à Luc Bondy held at the Académie expérimentale des théâtres, Oct. 28–9 and Nov. 5–6, 1994.

Bradby, David. **The theatre of Roger Planchon**. Teaneck, N.J.: Chadwyck-Healey in association with the Consortium for Drama and Media in Higher Education, 1984. – 56 p.: ill.; 21 cm. + 50 slides. *Notes*: Bibliography: p. 43–5. France/Planchon, Roger.

—— and David Williams. **Directors' theatre**. London: Macmillan, 1988. – xii, 275 p.: ill. *Notes*: Includes index. Bibliography: p. 262–7.

Braun, Edward. **The director and the stage: from naturalism to Grotowski**. London: Methuen, 1982. – 218 p., 8 p. of plates: ill. *Notes*: Includes bibliographical references and index. The Meiningen theatre – Antoine and the théâtre libre – The symbolist theatre – Alfred Jarry – Stanislavsky and Chekhov – Edward Gordon Craig – Max Reinhardt in Germany and Austria – Meyerhold: the first five years – Meyerhold: theatre as propaganda – Piscator in Berlin – Brecht's formative years – Artaud's theatre of cruelty – Grotowski's laboratory theatre/[by Jennifer Kumiega].

——. **Meyerhold: a revolution in theatre**. Iowa City: University of Iowa Press, 1995. – 347 p.: ill. *Notes*: Rev. edn. of: **Theatre of Meyerhold**. London: Methuen, 1979. Includes bibliographical references (p. 334–8) and index. Biography. History. 20th century. Meyerhold, Vsevelod Emilovich.

——, ed. **Meyerhold on theatre**. Rev. edn. London: Methuen Drama, 1991. – 336 p.: ill. *Notes*: Includes bibliographical references (p. 325–7) and index. A valuable collection of Meyerhold's own writings with useful introductions.

Brauneck, Manfred. **Klassiker der Schauspielregie: Positionen und Kommentare zum Theater im 20. Jahrhundert**. Reinbek bei Hamburg: Rowohlt, 1988. – 445 p.: ill. *Notes*: Comprises biographical sketches of directors and bibliographies by M. Brauneck and selected works by personalities of the 20th century theatre. Includes bibliographical references.

Brook, Peter. **Threads of time: recollections**. Washington, DC: Counterpoint, 1998. – p. cm. *Notes*: Includes index. Biography/Brook, Peter.

——, Richard Eyre, Genista McIntosh, Jean-Guy Lecat and Alan Read. **Peter Brook**. [London]: Royal National Theatre, 1994. – 43 p. *Series*: Platform papers; 6. *Notes*: Includes bibliographical references (p. 43). Introduction/by Richard Eyre – Peter Brook: 5 November 1993, Olivier Theatre/introduced by Genista McIntosh – The empty space and after/Jean-Guy Lecat in conversation with Alan Read – Peter Brook addresses an invited audience of theatre practitioners, 16 May 1994, Cottesloe Theatre.

Catron, Louis E. **The director's vision: play direction from analysis to production**. Mountain View, Calif.: Mayfield Pub. Co., 1989. – xix, 358 p.: ill. *Notes*: Includes index. Bibliography: p. 336–40.

Chaikin, Joseph and Sam Shepard. **Joseph Chaikin and Sam Shepard: letters and texts, 1972–1984**. New York: Theater Communications Group, 1994. – xii, 255 p. Daniels, Barry V., ed. *Notes*: Originally published: New American Library, a division of Penguin Books. Includes bibliographical references (p. 251–2). Correspondence between a major American writer and director.

Chothia, Jean. **André Antoine**. Cambridge: Cambridge University Press, 1991. – 230 p.: ill. *Series*: Directors in perspective. *Notes*: Includes bibliography and index. France.

Cole, Susan Letzler. **Directors in rehearsal: a hidden world**. New York: Routledge, 1992. – xiii, 282 p.: ill. *Notes*: 'A Theatre Arts book'. Includes bibliographical references (p. 275–8) and index. A hidden world – Elinor Renfield directs The cherry orchard – Maria Irene Fornes directs Uncle Vanya and Abingdon Square – Emily Mann directs Execution of justice – JoAnne Akalaitis directs The voyage of the Beagle – Elizabeth LeCompte directs Frank Dell's The temptation of Saint Antony – Richard Foreman directs The birth of the poet – Robert Wilson directs The golden windows and Hamletmachine – Liviu Ciulei directs Hamlet – Peter Sellars directs Two figures in dense violet light – Lee Breuer directs The warrior ant.

Cole, Toby and Helen Krich Chinoy. **Directors on directing: a source book of the modern theatre**. 2nd (rev.) edn. New York: London: Macmillan; Collier Macmillan, 1986, 1985. – xv, 464 p.: ill. *Notes*: First edn. published in 1953 under title: **Directing the play**. Includes index. Bibliography: p. 441–56. Standard text in the field.

Colombo, Laura and Federica Mazzocchi. **Luigi Squarzina e il suo teatro**. Rome: Bulzoni, 1996. – 438 p. *Notes*: 'Scelta di recensioni degli spettacoli di Luigi Squarzina': p. 385–428. 'Bibliografia essenziale degli scritti di Luigi Squarzina': p. 371–384. Includes bibliographical references and index. Italy. Production and direction.

Copfermann, Emile. **Roger Planchon**. [Lausanne]: La Cité-Éditeur (Éditions l'Age d'homme), 1969. – 317 p. illus., 12 plates. *Notes*: Bibliography: p. 301–7. Planchon, Roger.

——. **Théâtres de Roger Planchon**. Paris: Union générale d'éditions, 1977. – 445 p. *Notes*: Bibliography: p. 440–6.

Creamer, Richard. **Athol Fugard: the playwright as director of his own works**. 1990. – 392 p. *Notes*: Includes abstract. Bibliography: 387–92. Thesis (Ph. D.)–City University of New York, 1990. Photocopy. Ann Arbor, Mich.: University Microfilms, 1992. Includes interviews.

Daoust, Yvette. **Roger Planchon, director and playwright**. Cambridge and New York: Cambridge University Press, 1981. – x, 252 p.: ill. *Notes*: Includes index. Bibliography: p. 240–3. Theatrical producers and directors. France. Biography.

Delgado, Maria M. and Paul Heritage. **In contact with the gods?: directors talk theatre**. Manchester and New York: Manchester University Press, 1996. – x, 342 p. *Notes*: Includes bibliographical references and index. Augusto Boal – Peter Brook – Ion Caramitru – Lev Dodin – Declan Donnellan and Nick Ormerod – Maria Irene Fornes – Jorge Lavelli – Robert Lepage – Jonathan Miller – Ariane Mnouchkine – Yukio Ninagawa – Lluís Pasqual – Peter Sellars – Peter Stein – Giorgio Strehler – Jatinder Verma – Robert Wilson – Epilogue: 'Six hemispheres in search of'. Peter Brook, Jonathan Miller and Oliver Sacks in conversation. Interviews.

Déprats, Jean-Michel. **Antoine Vitez: le devoir de traduire: études**. [Castelnau-le-Lez]: [Montpellier]: Editions Climats; Maison A. Vitez, 1996. – 99 p. *Notes*: Includes bibliographical references. Study of the work of a major French director.

Dexter, John. **The honourable beast: a posthumous autobiography**. New York: Theatre Arts Books/Routledge, 1993. – xi, 340 p.: ill. *Notes*: Includes index. Great Britain. Biography/Opera producers and directors. Dexter, John, 1925–90.

Djafarov, Djafar. **Redjisser sanati: M. Mammadovun jaradygylygy**. [The art of the director: the creative journey of M. Mamedov]. Baku: Azerneshr, 1968. 380 p.

Douël Dell'Agnola, Catherine. **Gli spettacoli goldoniani di Giorgio Strehler: 1947–1991**. Rome: Bulzoni, 1992. – 194 p., 36 p. of plates: ill. *Notes*: Italian and French. Includes bibliographical references and index. Study of Strehler's work on Goldoni.

——. **Strehler e Brecht: L'anima buona di Sezuan, 1981: studio di regia**. Rome: Bulzoni, 1994. – 133 p., [60] p. of plates: ill. *Notes*: Includes bibliographical references. Study of Strehler's work on Brecht.

Dvorák, Cordelia. **Passione teatrale: Giorgio Strehler und das Theater**. Berlin: Henschel, 1994. – 224 p.: ill. *Notes*: Includes bibliographical references (p. 217–21) and index. Study of Giorgio Strehler as director.

Efros, Anatoli. **Prodolzhenie teatral'nogo rasskaza**. Moscow: Iskusstvo, 1983. – 397 p. *Notes*: Study of Anatoli Efros, one of Russia's major directors.

Everding, August and Klaus Jürgen Seidel. **Die ganze Welt ist Bühne: August Everding**. München: Piper, 1988. – 211 p.: 154 ill. (some col.). Biography/Everding, August.

Eynat-Confino, Irène. **Beyond the mask: Gordon Craig, movement, and the actor**. Carbondale: Southern Illinois University Press,

1987. – xiii, 239 p.: ill. *Notes*: Includes index. Bibliography: p. 221–9.

Eyre, Richard, ed. **Directors**. [London]: Royal National Theatre, 1994, 1993. – 42 p. *Series*: Platform papers. *Notes*: Stephen Daldrey. Interviewed by Giles Croft – Nicholas Hytner interviewed by Michael Ratcliffe – Robert Lepage interviewed by Richard Eyre.

——. **Utopia and other places**. London: Bloomsbury, 1995, 1993. – 256 p. *Notes*: Theatrical producers and directors. England. Biography/Eyre, Richard.

Fay, Stephen. **Power play: the life and times of Peter Hall**. London: Hodder & Stoughton, 1995. – xii, 402 p., 16 p. of plates. *Notes*: Includes bibliographical references (p. 379–82) and index. Study of Peter Hall.

Ferla, Patrick. **Conversation avec Marcel Maréchal**. Lausanne: Editions P.-M. Favre, 1983. – 241 p., 64 p. of plates: ill. *Notes*: A major French director on his life and art.

Forsyth, James. **Tyrone Guthrie: a biography**. London: Hamilton, 1976. – xi, 372 p., 12 p. of plates: ill. *Notes*: Includes index. Bibliography: p. 355. Study of one of the figures who created the 'director's theatre'.

Fuegi, John. **Bertolt Brecht: chaos, according to plan**. Cambridge and New York: Cambridge University Press, 1987. – xiv, 223 p.: ill. *Series*: Directors in perspective. *Notes*: Includes index. Bibliography: p. 200–17. Study of Brecht as director.

Gaskill, William. **A sense of direction**. 1st Limelight edn. New York: Limelight Editions, 1990 1988. – x, 166 p., 8 p. of plates: ill. *Notes*: Includes index. Originally published in London and Boston: Faber & Faber, 1988. *Subjects*: Theatrical producers and directors. Great Britain. Biography/Gaskill, William.

Gershkovich, Aleksandr Abramovich. **The theater of Yuri Lyubimov: art and politics at the Taganka Theater in Moscow**. 1964–1984. New York: Paragon House, 1989. – xvi, 228 p., [12] p. of plates: ill. *Notes*: Translation of: **Teatr na Taganke, 1964–1984**. Includes index. Bibliography: p. 201.

Gielgud, John and Clive Unger-Hamilton. **The entertainers**. London: Pitman House, 1980. – 320 p.: ill. (some col.). *Notes*: On cover of dust jacket: A biographical history of the stage, its players, writers, directors, showmen and clowns. 'General editor, Clive Unger-Hamilton'. Includes indexes. *Subjects*: Theatre. Dictionaries/Theatre, to 1980 – Biographies.

Godard, Colette. **Jérôme Savary, l'enfant de la fête**. Monaco: Editions du Rocher, 1996. –

165 p. *Notes*: Theatrical producers and directors. France. Biography.

Goncharov, Andrei. **Rezhisserskiye tetradi**. [Director's notebooks]. Moscow: All-Union Theatre Society, 1980.

Gorfunkel, Elena. **Premery Tovstonogova**. Moscow: Izd-vo 'Artist, rezhisser, teatr': Professional'nyi fond 'Russkii teatr', 1994. – 366 p. *Notes*: Includes bibliographical references. Theatrical producers and directors. Soviet Union. Biography. Tovstonogov, Georgii Aleksandrovich.

Goto, Yukihiro. **Suzuki Tadashi: innovator of contemporary Japanese theatre**. 1988. – x, 341 p.: ill., music. *Notes*: Includes abstract. Bibliography: p. 325–41. Thesis (Ph. D.)–University of Hawaii, 1988. Photocopy. Ann Arbor, Mich.: University Microfilms, 1989. Suzuki, Tadashi, 1939–. A study of the Japanese director.

Guthrie, Tyrone. **A life in the theatre**. New York: Limelight Editions, 1985 1959. – vi, 357 p. *Notes*: Originally published: New York: McGraw-Hill, 1959. Includes index. Autobiography.

Hall, Peter. **Making an exhibition of myself**. London: Sinclair-Stevenson, 1993. – 419 p., 32 p.: ill. *Notes*: 'List of productions': p. 401–5. Includes index. Autobiography.

——. **Peter Hall's Diaries: the story of a dramatic battle**. New York: Limelight Editions, 1985, 1984. – xiii, 507 p., 32 p. of plates. Edited by John Goodwin. *Notes*: Originally published: New York: Harper & Row, 1984.

Heed, Sven Åke. **Roger Blin: metteur en scène de l'avant-garde (1949–1959)**. [Paris]: Circé, 1996. – 153 p. *Notes*: Abstract in English. Study of an experimental master.

Heilpern, John. **Conference of the birds: the story of Peter Brook in Africa**. London: Methuen Drama, 1989. – 327 p.: 1 map. *Notes*: Previous edn.: London: Faber, 1977. Brook's International Centre of Theatre Research and its tour of Africa.

Henrichs, Benjamin and Ivan Nagel. **Liebe! Liebe! Liebe! Ist die Seele des Genies: Vier Regisseure des Welttheaters**. Munich: Hanser Verlag, 1996. – 214 p.: ill. *Notes*: Includes bibliographical references. Studies/discussions with Luc Bondy, Frank Castorf, Peter Sellars and Robert Wilson.

Hirst, David L. **Giorgio Strehler**. New York: Cambridge University Press, 1993. – xi, 140 p.: ill. *Series*: Directors in perspective. *Notes*: Includes bibliographical references (p. 135) and index. Study of Strehler as director.

Holmberg, Arthur. **An eye with a mind of its own: the theatre of Robert Wilson**. Cambridge: Cambridge University Press, 1995.

——. **The theatre of Robert Wilson**. Cambridge and New York: Cambridge University Press, 1996. – xix, 229 p.: ill. *Series*: Directors in perspective. *Notes*: Includes bibliographical references (p. 218–25) and index. Criticism and interpretation.

Hunt, Albert and Geoffrey Reeves. **Peter Brook**. Cambridge and New York: Cambridge University Press, 1995. – xvii, 288 p.: ill. *Series*: Directors in perspective. *Notes*: Includes bibliographical references (p. 279–83) and index. Study of Brook as director.

Hunt, Hugh. **The director in the theatre**. London: Routledge & Kegan Paul, 1976 1954. – ix, 111 p. *Notes*: Photocopy. Ann Arbor, Mich.: University Microfilms, 1976. Great Britain. History.

Ichikawa, Hiroshi. **Terayama Shuji no uchu**. Shohan. Tokyo: Shinshokan, 1992. – 262 p.: ill. *Other Authors*: Kotake, Nobutaka. Miura, Masashi. Terayama, Shuji. Criticism and interpretation.

Jomaron, Jacqueline. **Georges Pitoëff, metteur en scène**. Lausanne: Éditions L'Age d'homme, 1979. – 369 p., 40 p. of plates. *Notes*: 'Écrits et interviews de Georges Pitoëff': p. 348–351. Includes indexes. Bibliography: p. 352–3. Pitoëff, Georges, 1886–1939.

Jones, David Richard. **Great directors at work: Stanislavsky, Brecht, Kazan, Brook**. Berkeley: University of California Press, 1986. – x, 289 p. *Notes*: Includes index. Bibliography: p. 265–280. Case studies.

Jones, Edward. **Following directions: a study of Peter Brook**. New York: P. Lang, 1985. – 220 p. *Notes*: Includes index. Bibliography: p. 211–13. History and criticism.

Kantor, Tadeusz. **Ma création, mon voyage: commentaires intimes**. Paris: Ed. Plume, 1991. – 240 p.: ill. *Other Authors*: Scarpetta, Guy, préf. Vido-Rzewuska, Marie-Thérèse. *Notes*: Kantor on his life and art.

——. **Métamorphoses**. Paris: Chêne, 1982. – 141 p.: ill. *Notes*: Kantor on his move from art to theatre.

——. **T. Kantor: le Théâtre Cricot 2, La classe morte, Wielopole-Wielopole**. Paris: Centre national de la recherche scientifique, 1983. – 287 p.: ill. *Other Authors*: Eruli, Brunella. Bablet, Denis. *Notes*: Bibliography: p. 276–7. Filmography: p. 278. Study of Kantor's work.

——. **T. Kantor: Retour à la baraque de foire, Qu'ils crèvent les artistes, Je ne reviendrai jamais...** Paris: Centre national de la recherche scientifique, 1993. – 285 p.: ill. *Other Authors*: Bablet, Denis, éd. *Notes*: Bibliographie: p. 275–8. Filmographie: p. 279.

——. **Tadeusz Kantor (1915–1990): Leben im Werk**. Nuremberg: Verlag für Moderne Kunst, 1996. – 144 p.: ill. (some col.). *Other Authors*: Jedlinski, Jaromir. Ladnowska, Janina. *Notes*: Includes bibliographical references (p. 142–3). Exhibitions.

—— and Wlodzimierz Nowaczyk. **Dziela Tadeusza Kantora w kolekcji Muzeum Narodowego w Poznaniu: katalog obrazów i prac na papierze**. Poznan: Muzeum Narodowe, 1993. – 114 p.: ill. (some col.). *Notes*: Polish and English. Includes bibliographical references. Muzeum Narodowe w Poznaniu. Catalogues. Kantor's artwork.

Karpinski, Maciej. **The theatre of Andrzej Wajda**. Cambridge and New York: Cambridge University Press, 1989. – xviii, 135 p.: ill. *Series*: Directors in perspective. *Notes*: Translation of: **Andrzej Wajda–teatr**. Includes bibliographical references and index. Criticism and interpretation of this major Polish director.

Kazan, Elia. **Elia Kazan: a life**. New York: Da Capo Press, 1997 1988. *Notes*: Originally published: New York: Knopf, 1988. Includes index. United States. Biography. Directors.

Kennedy, Dennis, ed. **Foreign Shakespeare: contemporary performance**. Cambridge and New York: Cambridge University Press, 1993. – xviii, 311 p.: ill. *Notes*: Includes bibliographical references and index. John Russell Brown – Titus resartus: Warner, Stein, and Mesguich have a cut at Titus Andronicus/Dominique Goy-Blanquet – Transformations of authenticity: The merchant of Venice in Israel/Avraham Oz – Translation and mise en scène: the example of contemporary French Shakespeare/Leanore Lieblein – Audience, style, and language in the Shakespeare of Peter Zadek/Ron Engle – Brecht and beyond: Shakespeare on the East German stage/Lawrence Guntner – Theatrical continuities in Giorgio Strehler's The tempest/Pia Kleber – Between the curtain and the grave: the Taganka in the Hamlet gulag/Spencer Golub – Woman scorned: Antony and Cleopatra at Moscow's Vakhtangov Theatre/Irena R. Makaryk – Hamlet in postwar Czech theatre/Jarka Burian. Daniel Mesguich and intertextual Shakespeare/Marvin Carlson – Word into image: notes on the scenography of recent German productions/Wilhelm Hortmann – Shakespeare and the Japanese stage/Andrea J. Nouryeh – Wilson, Brook, Zadek: an intercultural encounter?/Patrice Pavis – Afterword: Shakespearean orientalism/Dennis Kennedy.

Kiernander, Adrian. **Ariane Mnouchkine and the Théâtre du Soleil**. Cambridge; New York: Cambridge University Press, 1993. – xiv, 172 p.: ill. *Series*: Directors in perspective. *Notes*: Includes bibliographical references (p. 161–7) and index. Mnouchkine, Ariane, 1938–. Criticism and interpretation. France.

Kitagawa, Takanobu. **Shokugyo Terayama Shuji: kyoko ni ikita tensai no densetsu**. Tokyo: Nihon Bungeisha, 1993. – 243 p.: ill. *Notes*: Biography/Teryama, Shuji, 1936–.

Kleber, Pia. **Exceptions and rules: Brecht, Planchon, and 'The good person of Szechwan'**. Frankfurt am Main; New York: P. Lang, 1987. – 334 p., 68 p. of plates: ill. *Notes*: Bibliography: p. 307–19.

Kłossowicz, Jan. **Tadeusz Kantor: teatr**. Warszawa: PIW, 1991. – 203 p., 20 p. of plates: ill. *Notes*: Includes bibliographical references (p. 190–3). History and criticism.

Köller, Thomas. **Die Schauspielpädagogik Jacques Lecoqs**. Frankfurt am Main; New York: Lang, 1993. – ix, 225 p.: ill. *Notes*: Includes bibliographical references (p. 217–25). Lecoq, Jacques. Technique and pedagogy.

Kranz, Dieter. **Positionen: Strehler, Planchon, Koun, Dario Fo, Långbacka, Stein: Gespräche mit Regisseuren des europäischen Theaters**. Berlin: Henschelverlag, 1981. – 208 p.: ill. *Notes*: European directors interviewed.

Kumiega, Jennifer. **Theatre of Grotowski**. London: Methuen, 1985.

Kuritsubo, Yoshiki. **Terayama Shuji**. [Selections. 1995]. Shohan. Tokyo: Nihon Tosho Senta, 1995. – 233 p.: ill. *Notes*: Includes chronological list of his works. Biography.

Lavelli, Jorge and José Tcherkaski. **El teatro de Jorge Lavelli: el discurso del gesto**. Buenos Aires: Editorial de Belgrano, 1983. – 196 p., 32 p. of plates. *Notes*: 'Cronología general de la obra realizada por Jorge Lavelli (teatro dramático y lírico desde 1961 hasta 1982)': p. 189–194. Correspondencia de Witold Gombrowicz a Jorge Lavelli (1963 a 1969). Theatrical directors. Argentina. Interviews.

Leach, Robert. **Vsevolod Meyerhold**. Cambridge: Cambridge University Press, 1989. – 1 v.: ill. *Series*: Directors in perspective. *Notes*: Includes bibliography and index.

Leiter, Samuel L. **From Belasco to Brook: Representative directors of the English-speaking stage**. Greenwood Press, 1991. – 320 p.

——. **From Stanislavsky to Barrault: representative directors of the European stage**. New York: Greenwood Press, 1991. – xvi, 241 p. *Notes*: Includes bibliographical references (p. 215–25) and index. Konstantin Stanislavsky – Vsevolod Meyerhold – Max Reinhardt – Jacques Copeau – Bertolt Brecht – Jean-Louis Barrault.

——. **The great stage directors: 100 distinguished careers of the theater**. New York, NY: Facts on File, 1994. – xi, 340 p.: ill.v *Notes*: Includes bibliographical references (p. 324–6) and index.

Léonardini, Jean Pierre. **Profils perdus d'Antoine Vitez**. Paris: Messidor, 1990. – 93 p.

Lepage, Robert and Rémy Charest. **Robert Lepage: quelques zones de liberté**. Québec: L'Instant même, 1995. – 221 p.: ill. *Notes*: Interviews/Lepage, Robert, 1957–.

Ley-Piscator, Maria. **Der Tanz im Spiegel: mein Leben mit Erwin Piscator**. Reinbek bei Hamburg: Wunderlich, 1989. – 381 p., 8 p. of plates: ill. *Notes*: Translation of: **Mirror people**. Theatrical directors. Germany. Piscator, Erwin and Ley-Piscator, Maria.

Littlewood, Joan. **Joan's book: Joan Littlewood's peculiar history as she tells it**. London: Minerva, 1995, 1994. – xvii, 796 p., 24 p. of plates: ill. *Notes*: Originally published: London: Methuen, 1994. Includes index. Theatrical directors. England. Autobiography.

Liubimov, Yuri and Marc Dondey. **Le Feu sacré: souvenirs d'une vie de théâtre**. Paris: Fayard, 1985. – 246 p., 32 p. of plates: ill. *Notes*: Bibliography: p. 237–40. Soviet Union. Biography. Liubimov, Yuri.

Loubier, Jean-Marc. **Louis Jouvet: biographie**. Paris: Editions Ramsay, 1986. – 473 p., 8 p. of plates. *Notes*: Includes index. Bibliography: p. 455–9. Theatrical directors. France. Biography/Jouvet, Louis.

Loyer, Emmanuelle. **Le Théâtre citoyen de Jean Vilar: une utopie d'après-guerre**. Paris: Presses universitaires de France, 1997. – ix, 253 p., 12 p. of plates: ill. *Notes*: Includes bibliographical references (p. 245–7) and index. *Subjects*: Vilar, Jean, 1912–71. Criticism and interpretation.

Magaldi, Sábato. **Nelson Rodrigues: dramaturgia e encenação**. [Nelson Rodrigues: his plays and his productions]. São Paulo: Perspectiva, 1987. 200 p.

Magarshack, David. **Stanislavsky: a life**. Boston: Faber & Faber, 1986 1950. – xi, 416 p. *Notes*: Reprint. Originally published: London: Macgibbon & Kee, 1950. Includes index. *Subjects*: Theatrical producers and directors. Soviet Union. Biography.

Mainusch, Herbert. **Regie und Interpretation: Gespräche mit Achim Benning, Peter Brook, Dieter Dorn, Adolf Dresen, Boy Gobert, Hans Hollmann, Takis Mouzenidis, Hans-Reinhard Müller, Claus Peymann, Peter Stein, Giorgio Strehler und Georgij Towstonogov.** Munich: W. Fink, 1985. – 139 p.: ill. *Notes*: Interviews with major European directors from the UK to Russia, from Germany to Greece.

Malina, Judith. **The diaries of Judith Malina, 1947–1957.** New York: Grove Press, 1984. – 485, 10 p. of plates: ill. *Notes*: Theatrical directors. United States. Biography. Malina, Judith, a co-founder of the living theatre.

Maltseva, Olga. **Akter teatra Liubimova.** St. Petersburg: LenNar, 1994. – 60 p. *Notes*: Includes bibliographical references (p. 58–60). Theatrical directors. Russia. Biography/Liubimov, Yuri.

Mantzopoulou, Liza and Paulos Matesis. **Architektones tou synchronou theatrou: Artaud, Pirandello, Brecht, Piscator, Bergman, Gets,** Athens: Vivliopoleio 'Dodone', 1980, 1990, – 202 p.

Marker, Lise-Lone and Frederick J. Marker. **Ingmar Bergman: a life in the theater.** Cambridge and New York: Cambridge University Press, 1992. – xx, 323 p.: ill. *Series*: Directors in perspective. *Notes*: Rev. edn. of: **Ingmar Bergman, four decades in the theatre.** 1982. Includes bibliographical references (p. 308–18) and index.

Marowitz, Charles. **Directing the action: acting and directing in the contemporary theatre.** New York: Applause, 1986. – xix, 194 p.: ill. *Notes*: Previously published as: **Prospero's staff.**

——. **The other way: an alternative approach to acting and directing.** New York: Applause, 1998.

——. **Prospero's staff: acting and directing in the contemporary theatre.** Bloomington: Indiana University Press, 1986. – xix, 194 p.

Mennicken, Rainer. **Peter Palitzsch.** Frankfurt am Main: Fischer Taschenbuch Verlag, 1993. – 144 p.: ill. *Notes*: Includes bibliographical references (p. 143). Theatrical directors. Germany. Biography. Palitzsch, Peter.

Mitchell, John Dietrich. **Theatre, the search for style: master directors on style, Chekhov to kabuki to musical comedy.** 2nd edn. Midland, Mich.: Northwood Institute Press, 1997 1982. – xxvii, 332 p.: ill. *Notes*: Interviews with Lehman Engel and others. Includes bibliographies.

Mitter, Shomit. **Systems of rehearsal: Stanislavsky, Brecht, Grotowski, and Brook.** London; New York: Routledge, 1992. – ix, 179 p. *Notes*: Includes bibliographical references (p. 159–73) and index.

Miura, Masashi. **Terayama Shuji kagami no naka no kotoba.** Tokyo: Shinshokan, 1987. – 315 p. *Notes*: List of works by S. Terayama: p. 310–13. Criticism and interpretation.

Mnouchkine, Ariane and Josette Féral. **Dresser un monument à l'éphémère: rencontres avec Ariane Mnouchkine.** Paris: Éditions théâtrales, 1995. – 86 p. of 8 p. de pl.: ill. *Notes*: Production and direction/Mnouchkine, Ariane. Interviews.

Morawiec, Elzbieta, Józef Szajna and Jerzy Madeyski. **Józef Szajna: plastyka, teatr.** Kraków: Wydawn. Literackie, 1974. – 152 p., 6 p. of plates: ill. (some col.). *Notes*: Study of the Polish director/designer.

Moscati, Italo. **Strehler: vita e opere di un regista europeo.** Brescia: Camunia, 1985. – 231, 5 p. *Notes*: Bibliography: p. 233. Theatrical producers and directors. Italy. Biography/Strehler, Giorgio, 1921–97.

Murphy, Brenda. **Miller: death of a salesman.** Cambridge and New York: Cambridge University Press, 1995. – xix, 246 p.: ill. *Notes*: Discography: p. 206. Filmography: p. 207. Includes bibliographical references (p. 208–39) and index.

Nojima, Naoko. **Koji e no ishi: Terayama Shuji ron.** Kyoto-shi: Hozokan, 1995. – 237 p. *Notes*: Terayama, Shuji. Criticism and interpretation.

O'Connor, Garry and Gilles Abegg. **The Mahabharata: Peter Brook's epic in the making.** San Francisco and St. Paul: Mercury House, 1990, 1989. – 159 p.: ill. (some col.). *Notes*: Includes index. History and criticism.

Ogawa, Taro. **Terayama Shuji sono shirarezaru seishun: uta no genryu o sagutte.** Tokyo: San'ichi Shobo, 1997. – 243 p.: ill. Terayama, Shuji. Biography.

Ortolani, Olivier. **Peter Brook.** Frankfurt: Fischer Taschenbuch Verlag, 1988. – 140 p.: ill. *Notes*: Includes bibliographical references (p. 135–9). Criticism and interpretation.

Osiński, Zbigniew. **Grotowski i jergo Laboratorium.** Warsaw: Państwowy Instytut Wydawniczy, 1980. Published in English as **Grotowski and his laboratory.** New York: PAJ, 1986.

Osten, Suzanne and Helena von Zweigbergk. **Barndom, feminism och galenskap: Osten om Osten.** [Stockholm]: Alfabeta Bokforlag, 1990. – 280 p., [8] p. of plates: ill. *Notes*: Includes index. Women theatrical producers and directors. Sweden. Interviews with one of Sweden's most innovative directors – Suzanne Osten.

Pandolfi, Vito. **Regia e registi nel teatro moderno**. [Directing and directors in the modern theatre]. Bologna: Cappelli, 1973.

Patterson, Michael. **Peter Stein: Germany's leading theatre director**. Cambridge: Cambridge University Press, 1982. – xv, 186 p.: ill. *Series*: Directors in perspective. *Notes*: Includes index. Bibliography: p. 178–80. Critical studies.

Plesniarowicz, Krzysztof. **Teatr smierci Tadeusza Kantora**. Chotomów: Verba, 1990. – 177 p., 16 p. of plates: ill. *Notes*: Summary in English, French, and German. Includes bibliographical references and index. Criticism and interpretation.

Poliakova, Elena. **Stanislavski**. Translated by Liv Tudge. Moscow: Progress, 1986.

Quadri, Franco. **Il teatro degli anni Settanta**. Turin: G. Einaudi, 1982. – v. <1>: ill. *Notes*: Includes bibliographies. Chéreau, Ronconi, Mnouchkine, Grüber, Bene. European directors of the 70s.

——. **Luca Ronconi, ou, Le rite perdu**. Paris: Union Générale d'Éditions, 1974. – 443 p. *Notes*: Biography/Ronconi, Luca.

——. **Peter Brook: o, Il teatro necessario**. [Venezia]: Edizioni de La biennale di Venezia, 1976. – 75 p.: ill. Theatrical producers and directors. Great Britain. Interviews/Brook, Peter.

——. **Tradizione e ricerca: il teatro degli anni settanta: Stein, Chéreau, Ronconi, Mnouchkine, Grüber, Bene**. Turin: Giulio Einaudi, 1982. – 371 p., 24 p. of plates: ill. *Notes*: Includes bibliographical references. European directors – a view of the 70s.

Quintero, José. **If you don't dance they beat you**. New York: St. Martin's Press, 1988 1974. – viii, 306 p. *Notes*: Reprint. Originally published: Boston: Little, Brown, 1974. Autobiography of one of America's foremost directors of O'Neill.

Reinhardt, Gottfried. **The genius: a memoir of Max Reinhardt**. New York: Knopf, 1979. – xv, 420 p., 16 p. of plates: ill. *Notes*: Translation of **Der Liebhaber**. Includes index. Biography/Reinhardt, Max, 1873–1943.

Richards, Thomas. **At work with Grotowski on physical actions**. London and New York: Routledge, 1995. – 135 p. *Notes*: Includes bibliographical references.

Richardson, Helen Elizabeth. **The Théâtre du Soleil and the quest for popular theatre in the twentieth century**. 1990. – v, 438 p. *Notes*:

Includes bibliographical references. Thesis (Ph. D.)–University of California, Berkeley, 1990. Microfilm. Ann Arbor, Mich.: University Microfilms International, 1991. 1 microfilm reel; 35 mm.

Roose-Evans, James. **Experimental theatre: from Stanislavsky to Peter Brook**. New, enlarged edn. London; New York: Routledge, 1996 1989. – ix, 225 p., 22 p. of plates: ill. *Notes*: Includes bibliographical references (p. 203–14) and index.

Rousseau, Nita. **Marcel Maréchal, 'un colossal enfant': entretiens avec Nita Rousseau**. Arles: Actes Sud; Théâtre national de Marseille/La Criée, 1992. – 105 p.: ill. *Note*: Interviews.

Rudlin, John. **Jacques Copeau**. Cambridge and New York: Cambridge University Press, 1986. – xvii, 141 p.: ill. *Series*: Directors in perspective. *Notes*: Includes index. Bibliography: p. 137. Biography/Copeau, Jacques, 1879–1949. France. Theatre. Directing.

Sanders, James. **André Antoine, directeur à l'Odéon: dernière étape d'une odyssée**. Paris: Minard, 1978. – 305 p., 15 p. of plates: ill. *Notes*: Includes index. Bibliography: p. 291–5. France. Biography/Antoine, André, 1858–1943.

Savary, Jérôme. **Ma vie commence à 20 h 30**. [Life begins at 8:30]. Paris: Stock/Laurence Pernoud, 1991. – 297 p.: ill. *Notes*: Theatrical producers and directors. France. Biography/Savary, Jérôme.

——. **La Vie privée d'un magicien ordinaire**. [The private life of an ordinary magician]. Paris: Ramsay, 1985. – 323, [1] p., xvi p. of plates: ill. *Notes*: 'Théâtrographie': p. 320–3. Filmography: p. 323–4. Biography/Savary, Jérôme.

—— and André Bercoff. **Album du Grand Magic Circus**. Paris: P. Belfond, 1974. – 127 p.: ill. (some col.). *Notes*: Autobiographical. The director of France's Grand Magic Circus looks at his work.

Sayonara terayama shuji. Tokyo: Shinshokan, 1983. – 144 p. *Notes*: Reflections on the death of Japan's leading experimental director.

Schmidt, Dietmar N. **Regie–Luc Bondy**. Berlin: Alexander, 1991. – 232 p.: ill. *Notes*: Includes index. Germany. Biography of director Bondy, Luc.

Schmidt, Paul. **Meyerhold at work**. Manchester: Carcanet New Press, 1981. – xxii, 241 p. *Notes*: Theatrical producers and directors. Soviet Union. Biography/Meyerhold, V.E.

——, Ilya Levin and Vern McGee. **Meyerhold at work**. New York: Applause, 1996. – xxii, 241 p.

Notes: Includes 'Glossary of names' (p. 233–41). Includes bibliographical references. Updated.

Schneider, Alan. **Entrances: an American director's journey**. 1st Limelight edn. New York: Harper & Row, 1987. – xv, 416 p., 24 p. of plates: ill. *Notes*: Includes index. 'Productions by Alan Schneider': p. 389–401. Autobiography of avant-garde American director who staged the first US productions of such dramatists as Beckett and Albee.

Schütt, Hans-Dieter. **Die Erotik des Verrats: Gespräche mit Frank Castorf**. Berlin: Dietz, 1996. – 157 p. *Notes*: Theatrical producers and directors. Germany. Interviews/Castorf, Frank.

Selbourne, David. **The making of A Midsummer Night's Dream: an eye-witness account of Peter Brook's production from first rehearsal to first night**. London: Methuen, 1983 1982. – xxxvii, 327 p.: ill. *Notes*: Stage history. Production by Brook, Peter.

Seym, Simone. **Das Théâtre du Soleil: Ariane Mnouchkines Ästhetik des Theaters**. Stuttgart: J.B. Metzler, 1992. – 264 p.: ill. *Notes*: Includes bibliographical references (p. 237–263) and indexes. Mnouchkine, Ariane. Criticism and interpretation.

Smith, Anthony. **Orghast at Persepolis: an international experiment in theatre directed by Peter Brook and written by Ted Hughes**. New York: Viking Press, 1973. – 264 p.: ill. *Notes*: Includes bibliographical references. Brook, Peter/International Centre for Theatre Research. An experiment in language.

Sokorski, Wlodzimierz. **Leon Schiller**. Warsaw: Iskry, 1978. – 83, 1 p., 4 p. leaves of plates: ill., ports. *Notes*: Biography of Leon Schiller (1887–1954), a Polish master director.

Sorgenfrei, Carol Jay. **Shuji Terayama: avant garde dramatist of Japan**. 1980, 1978. – ix, 318 p. *Notes*: Mich.: University Microfilms, 1980. Bibliography: p. 312–18. Thesis (Ph. D.)– University of California, Santa Barbara. Criticism and interpretation.

Squarzina, Luigi. **Luigi Squarzina**. [Plays. Selections]. Roma: Editori & Associati, 1991. – 275 p. *Series*: Teatro italiano contemporaneo 20. *Notes*: A major Italian director talks about theatre.

—— and Claudio Meldolesi, Arnaldo Picchi and Paolo Puppa. **Passione e dialettica della scena: studi in onore di Luigi Squarzina**. Rome: Bulzoni, 1994. – 349 p.: ill. *Notes*: Includes bibliographical references. Drama. History and criticism/Squarzina, Luigi, 1922–.

Swinarski, Konrad, Marta Fik and Jacek Sieradzki. **Wiernosc wobec zmiennosci**. Warsaw: Wydawnictwa Artystyczne i Filmowe, 1988. – 282 p. *Notes*: Includes index. Bibliography: p. 276–7. Polish director Konard Swinarski. Interviews. In Polish.

Tairov, Aleksandr. **Notes of a director**. Coral Gables: Fla.: University of Miami Press, 1969. – 153 p. illus. *Notes*: Translation of **Zapiski rezhissera**.

Takatori, Ei and Shuji Terayama. **Terayama Shuji ron: sozo no mashin**. Tokyo: Shichosha, 1992. – 294 p.: ill. *Notes*: Includes chronological list of works by S. Terayama: p. 276–90. Biography/Japanese director, Terayama, Shuji.

Tazawa, Takuya. **Kyojin Terayama Shuji den**. Tokyo: Bungei Shunju, 1996. – 270 p. *Notes*: Includes bibliographical references (p. 267–9). Biography. Terayama, Shuji.

Temkine, Raymonde. **Mettre en scène au présent**. Lausanne: Éditions La Cité-L'Age d'homme, 1977. – v.: ill. *Notes*: Includes bibliographical references. Victor Garcia, Gérard Gélas, Daniel Mesguich, Ariane Mnouchkine, Henri Ronse, Antoine Vitez. Theatrical directors. France. Biography.

Terayama Shuji memoriaru. Tokyo: Yomiuri Shinbunsha, 1993. – 176 p.: ill. (some col.). *Notes*: In Japanese. Essays about Terayama.

Terayama, Shuji. **Terayama Shuji korekushon**. [Shuji Terayama Selections]. Tokyo: Shichosha, 1992. 3 vols. *Notes*: Vol. 1: 1993 printing. vol. 1. Zenkashu, zenkushu – vol. 2. Dokuyaku monogatari: zen shishu I – vol. 3. Enpitsu no dorakyura: sakka ronshu.

——. **Terayama Shuji no tokushu**. [Selections. 1996]. Tokyo: Jiyu Kokuminsha, 1996. – 277 p., 7 p. of plates: ill. *Notes*: Terayama, Shuji. Interviews.

——. **Terayama Shuji wandarando**. Tokyo: Chusekisha, 1993. – 127 p.: ill. *Notes*: List of works by S. Terayama: p. 109–19. Terayama, Shuji. Criticism and interpretation..

Toporkov, Vasilii. **Stanislavski in rehearsal: the final years**. Translated by Christine Edwards. New York: Theatre Arts Books (c1979), – 224 p. *Notes*: Translation of **K.S. Stanislavskii na repetitsii**.

Touzoul, Melly and Jacques Téphany, eds. **Jean Vilar mot pour mot**. [Paris]. Stock, 1972. – 283 p. *Notes*: Bibliography: p. 269–74. Comments on the theatre by a French master.

Tovstonogov, Giorgi. **O professii rezhissera**.

[On the director's profession]. Moscow: All-Union Theatre Society, 1965.

——. **Stat'l; Zapisi repetitsii**. [Selections. 1984]. Leningrad: Iskusstvo, Leningradskoe otd-nie, 1984. – 367 p., 9 p. of plates: ill. *Notes*: 'Literaturnye raboty G.A. Tovstonogova': p. 353–67. Production and direction. History. 20th century.

Ubersfeld, Anne. **Antoine Vitez: metteur en scène et poète**. Paris: Editions des Quatre-Vents, 1994. – 175 p.: ill. (some col.). *Notes*: Criticism and interpretation.

Vilar, Jean. **Jean Vilar par lui-même**. Avignon: [Arles]: Maison Jean Vilar; Diffusion, Actes Sud, 1991. – 340 p.: ill. (some col.). *Notes*: 'Filmographie, bibliographie, discographie, phonographie, vidéothèque': p. 316–34. *Subjects*: Vilar, Jean, 1912–71.

——. **Le Théâtre, service public et autres textes**. [Paris]: Gallimard, 1975. – 562 p., 8 p. of plates: ill. *Notes*: Includes bibliographical references and indexes. Collected works.

Vinogradskaia, I.N. **Stanislavskii repetiruet: zapisi i stenogrammy repetitsii**. Moscow: Soiuz teatral'nykh deiatelei RSFSR, 1987. – 590 p., 1 p. of plates: ill. *Notes*: Includes bibliographical references. Stanislavsky as director.

Vitez, Antoine. **L'Ecole**. Paris: P.O.L., 1994. – 277 p. *Notes*: Includes bibliographical references. France. Production and direction/Vitez, Antoine. Diaries.

Volkova, Marianna and Solomon Volkov. **Yuri Liubimov v Amerike: odisseia rezhissera v fotografiiakh, tekstakh i besedakh**. [Yuri Lyubimov in America]. New York: Slovo, 1993. – 160 p.: ill. *Subjects*: Theatrical producers and directors. Criticism and interpretation. The Russian director's work in America.

Williams, David. **Peter Brook and the Mahabharata: critical perspectives**. London; New York: Routledge, 1991. – xiii, 337 p.: ill. *Notes*: Includes bibliographical references (p. 312–22) and index. History and criticism.

——. **Peter Brook: Theatrical Casebook**. Methuen, 1992. – 448 p.: ill.

Wolford, Lisa. **Action: the unrepresentable origin**. 1996. *Notes*: Describes the performance piece, Action, directed by Jerzy Grotowski, staged at the Workcenter under the sponsorship of the Centro per la Sperimentazione e la Ricerca Teatrale, in Pontedera, Italy. Action is also the name of a performance structure under development at the Workcenter, which blends ritual, movement and theatrical performance.

——. **Grotowski's objective drama research**. Jackson: University Press of Mississippi, 1996. – xxiv, 212 p.: ill. *Series*: Performance studies. Performance studies (Jackson, Miss.). *Notes*: Includes bibliographical references (p. 203–8) and index. *Subjects*: Experimental theatre/Grotowski, Jerzy, 1933–. Criticism and interpretation.

Zaki, Ahmed. **On directing**. Cairo: Egyptian Book Organization, 1978. In Arabic.

I. Playwriting and Dramaturgy

I1. General Studies

Autant-Mathieu, Marie-Christine. **Ecrire pour le théâtre: les enjeux de l'écriture dramatique**. Paris: CNRS, 1995. – 199 p. *Notes*: Includes bibliographical references and index. Playwriting technique.

Cardullo, Bert. **What is dramaturgy?** New York: P. Lang, 1995. – viii, 258 p. *Notes*: Includes bibliographical references (p. 249–258). Enter dramaturgs/Bert Cardullo – The compleat dramaturg/Leon Katz – Ten dramaturgical myths/David Copelin – Lessing, jugglers, and dramaturgs/Joel Schechter – The role of the dramaturg in European theater/Martin Esslin – Dramaturgy in Stuttgart: an interview with Hermann Beil/Reinhardt Stumm – Bertolt Brecht as dramaturg/Russell E. Brown – American dramaturgy: a critical re-appraisal/Peter Hay – The American view: the future for dramaturgs on U.S. campuses/C.J. Gianakaris – Dramaturgs in America: two interviews and six statements: Dramaturgy at the Guthrie: an interview with Mark Bly/David Moore, Jr – The literary manager as 'resident highbrow': an interview with Russell Vandenbroucke at the Mark Taper Forum/Carol Rosen – Dramaturgs in America/Jonathan Alper; André Bishop; Oscar Brownstein; John Lahr; Jonathan Marks; Richard Pettengill – Dramaturgy in two senses: towards a theory and some working principles of new-play dramaturgy/Art Borreca – The ghost lights of our theaters: the fate of contemporary American dramaturgs/Carol Rosen – The critic comes full circle: an interview with Kenneth Tynan/by the Editors of Theatre Quarterly – Literary management at the National Theatre, London: an interview with John Russell Brown/Richard Beacham – Directors, dramaturgs, and war in Poland: an interview with Jan Kott/Rustom Bharucha, Janice Paran, and Laurence Shyer – The dramaturg in Yugoslavia/Sanja Ivic – The program as performance text/Nicholas Rzhevsky.

Culpeper, Jonathan, Michael H. Short and Peter Verdonk. **Exploring the language of drama: from text to context**. London and New York: Routledge, 1998. *Notes*: Includes bibliographical references and index. English drama. English language. Style/Drama. Technique.

Czerwinski, Edward Joseph and Nicholas Rzhevsky. **Dramaturgs and Dramaturgy**. Stony Brook, N.Y.: Slavic Cultural Center Press, 1986. – 145 p.: ill. *Subjects*: Drama. Technique.

Féral, Josette, Jeannette Laillou Savona and Edward A. Walker. **Théâtricalité, écriture et mise en scène**. Québec: Hurtuise HMH, 1985. – 271 p.: ill. *Notes*: Communications d'un colloque… qui eut lieu à Trinity College les 13, 14 et 15 novembre 1980 sous les auspices du département de français de l'Université de Toronto. Includes bibliographies. Philosophy. Drama. History and criticism.

Friedman, Robert. **Playwright power: a concise how-to book for the dramatist**. Lanham, MD: University Press of America, 1996. – xiii, 150 p. *Notes*: Includes index.

Frome, Shelly. **Playwriting – a complete guide to creating theatre**. Jefferson, N.C.: McFarland, 1990. – xii, 179 p. *Notes*: Includes bibliographical references (p. 165–6). Playwriting/Drama. Technique/Drama. Composition.

Grebanier, Bernard D.N. **Playwriting**. New York: Barnes & Noble, 1979 1961. – xiii, 386 p.: ill. *Notes*: Includes bibliographical references and index. Drama. Technique.

Griffiths, Stuart. **How plays are made: the fundamental elements of play construction**. Rev. American edn. Englewood Cliffs, N.J.: Prentice-Hall, 1984. – x, 158 p. *Notes*: Includes index. Bibliography: p. 152–4.

Hornby, Richard. **Script into performance: a structuralist approach**. New York and London: Applause, 1995. – xvii, 229 p. *Notes*: Previously published under title: **Script into performance, a structuralist view of play production**. Includes bibliographical references (p. 215–19) and index.

Kindelan, Nancy Anne. **Shadows of realism: dramaturgy and the theories and practices of modernism**. Westport, Conn.: Praeger, 1996. – 171 p.: ill. *Notes*: Includes bibliographical references (p. 159–63) and index.

Levitt, Paul M. **A structural approach to the analysis of drama**. The Hague: Mouton, 1971. – 119 p. *Notes*: Bibliographical footnotes. Drama. History and criticism/Drama. Technique.

Macgowan, Kenneth. **A primer of playwriting**. Westport, Conn.: Greenwood Press, 1981 1962.

– 199 p. *Notes*: Reprint of the 1962 edn. published by Doubleday, New York. Includes index. Bibliography: p. 187–9. Drama. Technique.

Mayer, David, ed. **Schirmer Books theatre manuals**. 1st American edn. New York: Schirmer Books, 1989 1988. – 5 vols.: ill. (some col.). *Notes*: Includes bibliographies and indexes. vol. 1. Directing a play/Michael McCaffery. – vol. 2. Stage design and properties/Michael Holt. – vol. 3. Stage management and theatre administration/Pauline Menear and Terry Hawkins. – vol. 4. Lighting and sound/Neil Fraser. – vol. 5. Costume and make-up/Michael Holt.

Packard, William. **The art of the playwright: creating the magic of theatre**. New York and San Francisco: Thunder's Mouth Press, 1997, 1987. – xxv, 214 p.: ill. *Notes*: Originally published: Paragon House Publishers, c1987. Includes bibliographical references (p. 181–2) and index. Playwriting technique.

Pereira, Teresinha. **La actual dramaturgia latinoamericana**. [Playwriting in Latin America today]. Bogotá: Tercer Mundo, 1979. 87 p.

Schumacher, Claude. **Forty years of mise en scène**. Dundee: Lochee, 1986.

Sweet, Jeffrey. **The dramatist's toolkit: the craft of the working playwright**. Portsmouth, N.H.: Heinemann, 1993. – xiv, 162 p.

I2. Methodology, Techniques and Studies of Specific Internationally-produced Writers

Abastado, Claude. **Eugène Ionesco**. [Paris]. Bordas, 1977, 1971. – 286 p. illus. *Notes*: Bibliography: p. 268–73.

Abbott, H. Porter. **Beckett writing Beckett: the author in the autograph**. Ithaca, N.Y.: Cornell University Press, 1996. – xii, 196 p. *Notes*: Includes bibliographical references and index. Authorship. Psychological aspects. Self in literature/Beckett, Samuel.

Acheson, James. **Samuel Beckett's artistic theory and practice: criticism, drama, and early fiction**. Houndsmills, Basingstoke and New York: Macmillan Press and St. Martin's Press, 1997. – xii, 254 p. *Notes*: Includes bibliographical references (p. 242–250) index. Towards a theory of art – Belacqua – Murphy's metaphysics – Watt and the gentle skimmer – The transition to French – The art of failure: Molloy, Malone dies, The unnamable – First plays for the stage – Stage, screen and radio: Not I, Film and All that fall – The shape of ideas: That time – Last plays for the stage. Criticism and interpretation.

Adewale, Maja-Pearce, ed. **Wole Soyinka: an appraisal**. Portsmouth, NH, USA: Heinemann, 1994. – ix, 166 p. *Notes*: Includes bibliographical references and index. Nobel Lecture 1986: This past must address its present/Wole Soyinka – The complexity of freedom/Wilson Harris – Soyinka the tiger/Nadine Gordimer – Wole Soyinka and a living dramatist: a playwright's encounter with Soyinka's drama/Femi Osofian – The fiction of Wole Soyinka/Abdulrazak Gurnah – Wole Soyinka and the Àtundá ideal: a reading of Soyinka's poetry/Niyi Osundare – Myth, literature and the African world/Kwame Anthony Appiah – Madmen and specialists: new nation states and the importance of a tragic art/Gabriel Gbadamosi – On being squelched in the spittle of an alien race/Martin Banham – Against ideology: Soyinka vs. Hunt/Adewale Maja-Pearce – Wole Soinka interviewed, 3 July 1993, Notting Hill Gate, London/'Biyi Bandele-Thomas. Criticism and interpretation.

Adolphs, Ulrich. **Die Tyrannei der Bilder: Sam Shepards Dramen**. Frankfurt am Main; New York: P. Lang, 1990. – xi, 246 p. *Notes*: Originally presented as the author's thesis (doctoral)–Universität Freiburg (Breisgau), 1989. Summary in English. Includes bibliographical references (p. 228–43). Criticism and interpretation.

Ahuja, Chaman. **All life long the same questions, the same answers: reinterpreting Samuel Beckett**. New Delhi: Manohar, 1996. – viii, 225 p. *Notes*: Includes bibliographical references (p. 203–17) and index. Criticism and interpretation.

Akerholt, May-Brit. **Patrick White**. Australian Playwrights Monograph Series. Amsterdam: Rodopi, 1988.

Albee, Edward and Philip C. Kolin. **Conversations with Edward Albee**. Jackson: University Press of Mississippi, 1988. – xxix, 223 p. *Notes*: Includes index. 'Books by Edward Albee': p. [iv]. Albee/Lillian Ross – Social critics, like prophets, are often honored from afar/Edward Kosner – Interview with Edward Albee/Paul Zindel and Loree Yerby – Edward Albee interviewed/Digby Diehl – Playwright at work: Edward Albee/Walter Wager – Albee asks and Albee answers/R.H. Gardner – The art of the theatre IV: Edward Albee: an interview/William Flanagan – Is the American theatre in a vacuum, part II/Dorothy Gordon – The private world of Edward Albee/Adrienne Clarkson – Edward Albee returns to view Zoo story/The Choate News – Albee looks at himself and at his plays/Irving Wardle – Edward Albee fights back/Guy Flatley – Albee on the real thing (theatre) versus a film/Tom Donnelly – Jeanne

Wolf in conversation with Edward Albee/Jeanne Wolf – Edward Albee takes to the air/Alan Rich – Edward Albee speaks/Brooks von Ranson – Edward Albee 'if the play can be described in one sentence, that should be its length'/Allan Wallach – Edward Albee: a playwright versus the theatre/Peter Adam – Edward Albee: an interview/Patricia De La Fuente – The writing life: avant-garde Albee/Bob Woggon – Living on the precipice: a conversation with Edward Albee/Mark Anderson and Earl Ingersoll – The playwright as curator/ARTnews – Albee after the plunge/David Richards – Albee at Notre Dame/Kathy Sullivan – Well-known playwright directs University of Houston students/Jane Holt – Edward Albee in conversation with Terrence McNally/Terrence McNally – Outrageous Edward Albee/Joe Pollack.

Almansi, Guido and Simon Henderson. **Harold Pinter**. London and New York: Methuen, 1983. – 111 p. *Notes*: Bibliography: p. 108–11. Criticism and interpretation.

Alphenaar, Carel. **De goden van het theater. 22 Nederlandse en Vlaamse toneelschrijvers aan het woord**. [The Gods of theatre: twenty-two Dutch and Flemish playwrights talk about their craft]. Harlekijn: Westbroek, 1983.

Amacher, Richard E. **Edward Albee**. Boston: Twayne Publishers, 1982. – 219 p. *Notes*: Includes index. Bibliography: p. 208–12. Criticism and interpretation.

Ames, Sanford Scribner. **Remains to be seen: essays on Marguerite Duras**. New York: P. Lang, 1988. – vii, 298 p. *Notes*: Bibliography: p. 291–5. Criticism and interpretation.

Amosu, Tundonu. **The Nigerian dramatist and his audience: the questions of language and culture**. 1985. *Subjects*: Playwrights. Nigeria/Theatre audiences. Nigeria.

Andonian, Cathleen Culotta. **The critical response to Samuel Beckett**. Westport, Conn.: Greenwood Press, 1998. – p. *Notes*: Includes bibliographical references and index. Criticism and interpretation.

——. **Samuel Beckett: a reference guide**. Boston, Mass.: G.K. Hall, 1989. – xxviii, 754 p. *Notes*: Includes indexes. Bibliography.

Andretta, Richard A. **Tom Stoppard, an analytical study of his plays**. New Delhi: Har-Anand Publications in association with Vikas Pub. House, 1992. – x, 388 p. *Notes*: Includes bibliographical references (p. 384–8). Criticism and interpretation.

Angermeyer, Hans Christoph. **Zuschauer im Drama; Brecht, Dürrenmatt, Handke**. [Frankfurt am Main]. Athenäum Verlag, 1971.

– 144 p. *Notes*: Bibliography: p. 141–4. Study of three major German-language dramatists.

Astro, Alan. **Understanding Samuel Beckett**. Columbia, S.C.: University of South Carolina Press, 1990. – xviii, 222 p. *Notes*: Includes bibliographical references (p. 209) and index. Criticism and interpretation.

Auerbach, Doris. **Sam Shepard, Arthur Kopit, and the Off Broadway theatre**. Boston: Twayne Publishers, 1982. – 145 p. *Notes*: Includes index. Bibliography: p. 138–42. American drama. History and criticism. Shepard, Sam. Kopit, Arthur.

Bair, Deirdre. **Samuel Beckett: a biography**. 1st Touchstone edn. New York: Simon & Schuster, 1993 1990. – xxiii, 736 p., 24 p. of plates: ill. *Notes*: Includes bibliographical references (p. 641–723) and index. Among the standard biographies of Beckett.

Banu, Georges. **Bertolt Brecht, ou, Le petit contre le grand**. Paris: A. Montaigne, 1981. – 192 p. *Notes*: Includes bibliographical references. Criticism and interpretation.

Bänziger, Hans. **Frisch und Dürrenmatt. Bern and Munich**: Francke, 1976 1960. – 312 p. *Notes*: Includes bibliographical references and index. Frisch, Max, 1911. Dürrenmatt, Friedrich.

Barbera, Jack. **Athol Fugard**. Hempstead, NY: Hofstra University Press, 1993. – xix, 540 p.: ill. *Notes*: Cover title. Includes bibliographical references. Introduction: Fugard, women, and politics/Jack Barbera – Some problems of a playwright from South Africa/Athol Fugard – The apprenticeship years/Sheila Fugard – Crossing boundaries: The genesis of the township plays/Dennis Walder – Power, self, and other: the absurd in Boesman and Lena/Craig W. McLuckie – Fugard as director: An interview with the cast of Boesman and Lena, 1992/Jack Barbera – 'No way out': Sizwe Bansi is dead and the dilemma of political drama in South Africa/Andre Brink – Encounters with Fugard: Native of the Karoo/Mary Benson – Life in the theatre: Autobiography, politics, and romance in 'Master Harold … and the boys'/John O. Jordan – The artist as an outcast and a mother in The Road to Mecca/Janet Ruth Heller – Realizing Fugard/Susan Hilferty – Drama and politics in a state of emergency: My children! My Africa!/Nicholas Visser – Fugard masters the code/Gerald Weales – A tribute for Athol Fugard at sixty/Don Maclennan – Recent notebook entries/Athol Fugard.

Bareham, Tony. **Tom Stoppard: Rosencrantz and Guildenstern are dead, Jumpers, Travesties: a casebook**. Basingstoke: Macmillan,

1990. – 220 p. *Notes*: Includes index. Bibliography: p. 211.

Bartram, Graham and Anthony Waine. **Brecht in perspective**. London and New York: Longman, 1982. – xv, 231 p. *Notes*: Includes bibliographies and index. Criticism and interpretation.

Basal, Muhammad Isma'il. **Nahwa nazariyat lisaniyah masrahiyah: masrah Sa'd Allah Wannus namudhajan tatbiqiyan**. Damascus: Dar al-Yanabi', 1996. – 225 p. *Notes*: Includes bibliographical references. Study of Syrian dramatist Wannus, Sa'd Allah.

Bassnett, Susan. **File on Pirandello**. London: Methuen Drama, 1989. – 94 p. *Notes*: Bibliography: p. 92–4. *Subjects*: Pirandello, Luigi, 1867–1936. Criticism and interpretation. Stage history. Bibliography.

—— and Jennifer. **Luigi Pirandello in the theatre: a documentary record**. Chur, Switzerland; Philadelphia, Pa.: Harwood Academic Publishers, 1993. – xxi, 203 p.: ill. *Notes*: Includes bibliographical references (p. 192–4) and index.

Beach, Cecilia. **French women playwrights of the twentieth century: a checklist**. Westport, Conn.: Greenwood Press, 1996. – xi, 515 p. *Notes*: Includes bibliographical references (p. 451–6) and index. French drama. 20th century. Women and literature.

Bechert, Frank. **Keine Versöhnung mit dem Nichts: zur Rezeption von Samuel Beckett in der DDR**. Frankfurt am Main; New York: P. Lang, 1997. – 428 p. *Notes*: Originally presented as the author's thesis (doctoral)– Universität Leipzig, 1996. Includes bibliographical references (p. 368–411) and index. Beckett in Germany.

Beckers, Anne-Marie. **Michel de Ghelderode: Barabbas, Escurial**. Brussels: Labor, 1987. – 109 p. *Notes*: Bibliography: p. 101–4. Criticism and interpretation/Ghelderode, Michel de.

Begam, Richard. **Samuel Beckett and the end of modernity**. Stanford, Calif.: Stanford University Press, 1996. – x, 237 p. *Notes*: Includes index. Bibliography: p. 221–8. Postmodernism (Literature). Criticism and interpretation.

Bentley, Eric. **The Brecht memoir**. Manchester: Carcanet, 1989 1985. – 135 p.: ill. *Notes*: Originally published: New York: P.A.J., 1985. Includes index. Bentley on Brecht.

——. **The Pirandello commentaries**. Evanston, Illinois: Northwestern University Press, 1986. – xii, 119 p. *Notes*: Includes index. 'An earlier version of this collection appeared in Pirandellian studies 1 (Winter 1985)'–T.p. verso. Bibliography: p. 111–13. *Subjects*: Pirandello, Luigi. Criticism and interpretation.

Ben-Zvi, Linda. **Samuel Beckett**. Boston: Twayne Publishers, 1986. – 230 p., 1 p. of plates. *Notes*: Includes index. Bibliography: p. 219–24. Criticism and interpretation.

Bernard, Michel. **Samuel Beckett et son sujet: une apparition évanouissante**. Paris: L'Harmattan, 1996. – 303 p. *Notes*: Includes bibliographical references (p. 289–96) and index. Psychoanalysis and drama. Criticism and interpretation.

Bernold, André. **L'Amitié de Beckett: 1979–1989**. Paris: Hermann, 1992. – 109 p.: ill. *Notes*: Includes bibliographical references. Beckett, Samuel. Friends and associates.

Beyen, Roland. **Michel de Ghelderode, ou, La hantise du masque: essai de biographie critique**. 3rd edn. Brussels: Académie royale de langue et de littérature françaises: Palais des Académies, 1980. – 554 p. *Notes*: Includes index. 'Mémoire couronné par l'Académie royale de langue et de littérature françaises'. Bibliography: p. 509–36. Ghelderode, Michel de, 1898–1962. Biography.

Bigsby, C.W.E. **Arthur Miller and company: Arthur Miller talks about his work in the company of actors, designers, directors, reviewers, and writers**. London: [East Anglia]: Methuen; Arthur Miller Centre for American Studies, 1990. – xv, 240 p.: ill. *Notes*: Includes index. Interviews/Playwriting/Miller, Arthur.

——. **The Cambridge companion to Arthur Miller**. Cambridge, U.K.; New York: Cambridge University Press, 1997. – xix, 277 p.: ill. *Notes*: Includes bibliographical references and index. 'Arthur Miller: a bibliographic essay': p. 245–66. Criticism and interpretation.

——. **A critical introduction to twentieth-century American drama: Tennessee Williams, Arthur Miller, Edward Albee**. Cambridge: Cambridge Univ., 1986 1984. – vii, 355 p.: ill. *Notes*: Includes bibliography and index.

——. **Edward Albee: a collection of critical essays**. Englewood Cliffs, N.J.: Prentice-Hall, 1975. – xii, 180 p. *Notes*: Bibliography: p. 179–180. Weales, G. Edward Albee: don't make waves.–Esslin, M. The Theatre of the Absurd: Edward Albee.–Way, B. Albee and the Absurd: The American dream and The zoo story.– Zimbardo, R. A. Symbolism and naturalism in Edward Albee's The zoo story.–Debusscher, G. The death of Bessie Smith.–Schechner, R. Who's afraid of Edward Albee?–Schneider, A. Why so

afraid?–Schechner, R. Reality is not enough: an interview with Alan Schneider.–Clurman, H. Who's afraid of Virginia Woolf?–Trilling, D. The riddle of Albee's Who's afraid of Virginia Woolf?–Rutenberg, M. E. The ballad of the sad café.–Hewes, H. The Tiny Alice caper.–Roth, P. The play that dare not speak its name.– Franzblau, A. N. A psychiatrist looks at Tiny Alice.–Stewart, R. S. John Gielgud and Edward Albee talk about the theater.–Bigsby, C. W. E. Tiny Alice.–Brustein, R. Albee decorates an old house: A delicate balance.–Paolucci, A. A vision of Baal: A delicate balance.–Bigsby, C. W. E. Box and Quotations from Chairman Mao Tse-tung: Albee's diptych.–Hewes, H. Death prattle.–Bigsby, C. W. E. To the brink of the grave: Edward Albee's All over.

Billington, Michael. **The life and work of Harold Pinter**. London: Faber & Faber, 1996. – x, 414 p.: ill. *Notes*: Includes bibliographic references (p. 391–4) and index. Criticism and interpretation.

——. **Stoppard, the playwright**. London; New York: Methuen, 1987. – 188 p., 8 p. of plates: ill. *Notes*: Includes index. Bibliography: p. 181–2. Criticism and interpretation.

Binot, Lucien. **Conversations autour de Michel de Ghelderode**. Bruxelles: Editions la Rose de Chêne, 1993. – 540 p. *Notes*: Includes bibliographical references and index. Criticism and interpretation.

Blonski, Jan. **Wszystkie sztuki Slawomira Mrozka**. Craków: Wydawn. Literackie, 1995. – 285 p. *Notes*: Includes bibliographical references and index. Mrozek, Slawomir. Criticism and interpretation.

Bloom, Harold, ed. **Arthur Miller**. New York: Chelsea House Publishers, 1987. – viii, 164 p. *Notes*: Includes index. Bibliography: p. 151–3. Arthur Miller/Raymond Williams – Strength and weakness in Arthur Miller/Tom F. Driver – Death of a salesman/Esther Merle Jackson – Clinton W. Trowbridge – The action and its significance/Orm Overland – The drama of forgiveness/Dennis Welland – The perspective of a playwright/Leonard Moss – A view from the bridge and the expansion of vision/Neil Carson– Drama from a living center/C.W.E. Bigsby – History and other spectres in Arthur Miller's The crucible/E. Miller Budick.

——, ed. **Edward Albee**. New York: Chelsea House Publishers, 1987. – vii, 181 p. *Notes*: Includes index. Bibliography: p. 169–72. Albee and the absurd/Brian Way – Edward Albee/Gerald Weales – Albee's Gothic/Paul Witherington – All over/Ronald Hayman – Conventional Albee/Anthony Hopkins –

Staging the unconscious/Mary Castiglie Anderson – The idea of language in the plays of Edward Albee/Julian Wasserman – The limits of reason/ Liam O. Purdon – The Pirandello in Albee/ Thomas P. Adler – Who's afraid of Virginia Woolf?/C.W.E. Bigsby – The man who had three arms/Matthew C. Roudané.

——, ed. **Harold Pinter**. New York: Chelsea House Publishers, 1987. – vii, 183 p. *Notes*: Includes index. Bibliography: p. 171–3. Home-coming/Bert O. States – The birthday party/ Raymond Williams – Words and silence/ John Russell Brown – Landscape/James Eigo – The room/Austin E. Quigley – Time and possible realities/Barbara Kreps – Idiom of lies/Guido Almansi – Cinematic fidelity and the forms of Betrayal/Enoch Brater – The dumb waiter/Thomas F. Van Laan – Parody play/Elin Diamond – Language and silence/Martin Esslin.

——, ed. **Samuel Beckett's Waiting for Godot**. New York: Chelsea House Publishers, 1987. – vii, 131 p. *Notes*: Includes index. Bibliography: p. 123–4. Bailing out the silence/John Fletcher – The search for the self/Martin Esslin – Waiting/Ruby Cohn – Waiting for Godot/Hugh Kenner – The waiting since/Richard Gilman – The language of myth/Bert O. States – Beckett and the problem of modern culture/Eric Gans – Beckett's modernity and medieval affinities/ Edith Kern.

——, ed. **Tennessee Williams**. New York: Chelsea House, 1987. – viii, 168 p. *Notes*: Includes index. Bibliography: p. 157–9. Truth and dramatic mode in A streetcar named Desire/Alvin B. Kernan – A streetcar named Desire: Nietzsche descending/Joseph N. Riddel – The synthetic myth/Esther Merle Jackson – Tennessee Williams's persistent Battle of angels/Leonard Quirino – The garrulous gro-tesques of Tennessee Williams/Ruby Cohn – The middle years/Robert Bechtold Heilman – Irony and distance in The glass menagerie/ Thomas L. King – Time and tide on the Camino real/James Coakley – A desperate morality/ Arthur Ganz – 'Minting their separate wills': Tennessee Williams and Hart Crane/Gilbert Debusscher – Valedictory/C.W.E. Bigsby. A collection of critical essays on Williams and his works arranged in chronological order of publication.

——. **Willy Loman**. New York: Chelsea House, 1991. – xv, 168 p. *Notes*: Includes biblio-graphical references (p. 159–61) and index. A study of Miller's hero.

Blot-Labarrère, Christiane. **Marguerite Duras**. Buenos Aires: Ediciones de la Flor, 1994. – 303 p. *Notes*: Includes bibliographical references (p. 272–303). Criticism and interpretation.

Bohler, Liette. **Der Mythos der Weiblichkeit im Werke Max Frischs**. New York: Peter Lang, 1998. *Notes*: Originally presented as the author's thesis (doctoral)–University of California, Los Angeles, 1995. Includes biblio-graphical references and index. Femininity in literature/Women in literature/Frisch, Max. Criticism and interpretation.

Bold, Alan Norman. **Harold Pinter, you never heard such silence**. London: Totowa, NJ: Vision Press; Barnes & Noble, 1985 1984. – 184 p. *Notes*: Includes bibligraphies and index. Pinter, Harold – Critical studies.

Bolliger, Luis and Ernst Buchmüller. **Play Dürrenmatt: ein Lese- und Bilderbuch**. Zürich: Diogenes: Schweizer Fernsehen DRS, 1996. – 325 p.: ill. *Notes*: 'Dieses Buch erscheint zur grossen Dürrenmatt-Retrospektive im Satelliten-Fernsehprogramm sat, im Herbst 1996–t.p. verso. Dürrenmatt, Friedrich. Criticism and interpretation.

Bonnefoy, Claude, ed. **Conversations with Eugène Ionesco**. New York: Holt, Rinehart and Winston, 1971 1970. – 187 p. *Notes*: Trans-lation of **Entretiens avec Eugène Ionesco.**

Boon, Richard. **Brenton, the playwright**. London: Methuen Drama, 1991. – xviii, 355 p., 8 p. of plates: ill. *Notes*: Includes bibliographical references (p. 337–49) and index. Brenton, Howard. Criticism and interpretation.

Böttcher-Wöbcke, Rita. **Komik, Ironie und Satire im dramatischen Werk von Wole Soyinka**. Hamburg: Buske, 1976. – vi, 290 p. *Notes*: Bibliography: p. 275–90. Originally pre-sented as the author's thesis, Hamburg, 1975. Soyinka, Wole. Criticism.

Bottoms, Stephen James. **The theatre of Sam Shepard: states of crisis**. Cambridge, and New York: Cambridge University Press, 1998. – xii, 301 p.: ill. *Notes*: Includes bibliographical refer-ences (p. 293–6) and index. Criticism and inter-pretation.

Bradby, David. **The theatre of Michel Vinaver**. Ann Arbor: University of Michigan Press, 1993. – 170 p.: ill. *Notes*: Includes bibliographical ref-erences (p. 161–6) and index. Vinaver, Michel. Criticism and interpretation.

Bratt, David. **Tom Stoppard: a reference guide**. Boston, MA: G.K. Hall, 1982. – xxxiv, 264 p. *Notes*: Includes index. Bibliography.

Breuer, Rolf and Werner Huber. **A checklist of Beckett criticism in German**. Paderborn, Germany: F. Schöningh, 1996. – x, 90 p. *Notes*: Text in English and German. 2nd rev. edn. of: **Beckett criticism in German**, 1986. Includes indexes. Bibliography.

Brito, Ferreira de. **Le Réel et l'iréel dans la dramaturgie de Beckett, Ionesco et Tardieu**. Porto [Portugal]: Associação de Jornalistas e Homens de Letras do Porto, 1983. – 481 p. *Notes*: Includes bibliographical references (p. 455–81). Reality in literature/Illusion in literature/Beckett, Samuel. Ionesco and Tardieu. Criticism and interpretation. French drama.

Brown, John Russell. **Theatre language: a study of Arden, Osborne, Pinter and Wesker**. [London]: The Penguin Press, 1972. – 255 p. *Notes*: Bibliography: p. 252–3. English drama.

Bryer, Jackson R. **The playwright's art: conversations with contemporary American dramatists**. New Brunswick, N.J.: Rutgers University Press, 1995. – xx, 316 p.: ill. *Notes*: Includes index. Edward Albee – Robert Anderson – Alice Childress – John Guare – A.R. Gurney – Beth Henley – David Henry Hwang – Larry L. King – Jerome Lawrence – Terrence McNally – Ntozake Shange – Neil Simon – Jean-Claude van Itallie – Wendy Wasserstein – Lanford Wilson.

Bu Shu'ayr, al-Rashid. **Athar Bertolt Brecht fi masrah al-mashriq al-'Arabi**. Damascus: al-Ahali lil-Tiba'ah wa-al-Nashr wa-al-Tawzi', 1996. – 384 p. *Notes*: Includes bibliographical references (p. 363–80). Brecht, Bertolt, 1898–1956 influence in the Arab world. In Arabic.

Burkman, Katherine H., ed. **Simon Gray: a casebook**. New York: Garland Pub. Inc., 1992. – xx, 205 p.: ill. *Notes*: Includes bibliographical references (p. 185–94) and index. Experimental drama and the well-made play: Simon Gray and Harold Pinter as collaborators/Robert Gordon – Simon Gray and the pedagogical erotics of theatre/Judith Roof – Homosexual from necessity: the oedipal, the homoerotic, and the rhetorical woman in three plays by Simon Gray/Paula Jayne White – 'Being took queer': homosexuality in Simon Gray's plays/John M. Clum – Simon Gray's Butley: from stage to screen/ Steven H. Gale – Snatching at a monopoly: Simon Gray's rendering of Dostoyevsky's The idiot/Anne Marie Drew – Deceit, desire, and Simon Gray's Otherwise engaged/Ann C. Hall – The powers of detachment: inside and out of The rear column/Jeanne Colleran – Some particular pursuits: the double fiction of Simon Gray/ Marya Bednerik – The unravelling of Melon/ Kimball King – Hedda's children: Simon Gray's anti-heroes/Katherine H. Burkman – Hidden laughter and middle-aged complacency/John M. Clum – Hidden laughter: a review/ Kimball King – Theatre review of Simon Gray's Hidden laughter/Ann C. Hall.

—— and John Kundert-Gibbs, eds. **Pinter at sixty**. Bloomington: Indiana University Press, 1993. – xvii, 219 p.: ill. *Notes*: Papers presented at the Pinter Festival which was held Apr. 19–21, 1991, Ohio State University in honour of Pinter's 60th birthday. Includes bibliographical references (p. 201–8) and index. Pinter in rehearsal: from The Birthday Party to Mountain Language/Carey Perloff – Producing Pinter/Louis Marks – Harold Pinter's Theatre of Cruelty/Martin Esslin – Harold Pinter's The Hothouse: a parable of the holocaust/Rosette C. Lamont – Disjuncture as theatrical and postmodern practice in Griselda Gambaro's The Camp and Harold Pinter's Mountain Language/ Jeanne Colleran – The outsider in Pinter and Havel/Susan Hollis Merritt – The betrayal of facts: Pinter and Duras beyond adaptation/ Judith Roof – Image and attention in Harold Pinter/Alice Rayner – Pinter and the ethos of minimalism/Jon Erickson – Chekhov, Beckett, Pinter: the st(r)ain upon the silence/Alice N. Benston – 'That first last look ...'/Martha Fehsenfeld – A rose by any other name: Pinter and Shakespeare/Hersh Zeifman – From novel to film: Harold Pinter's adaptation of The Trial/Francis Gillen – 'I am powerful ... and I am only the lowest doorkeeper': power play in Kafka's The Trial and Pinter's Victoria Station/John L. Kundert-Gibbs – Art objects as metaphors in the filmscripts of Harold Pinter/ Steven H. Gale – Pinter and Bowen: The Heat of the Day/Phyllis R. Randall – Portrait of Deborah: A Kind of Alaska/Moonyoung C. Ham – Deborah's homecoming in A Kind of Alaska: an afterword/Katherine H. Burkman. Pinter, Harold, 1930–. Criticism and interpretation.

Butler, Lance St. John and Robin Davis, eds. **Rethinking Beckett: a collection of critical essays**. New York: St. Martin's Press, 1990. – xi, 207 p. *Notes*: Includes bibliographical references and index. 'What? where?': presence and repetition in Beckett's theatre/Steven Connor – Beckett's devious deictics/Angela Moorjani – Repetition and underlying meanings in Samuel Beckett's trilogy/Rubin Rabinovitz – The figure in Beckett's carpet: Molloy and the assault on metaphor/Kevin J.H. Dettmar – 'Babel of silence': Beckett's post-trilogy prose articulated/ Barbara Trieloff – Fizzles by Samuel Beckett: the failure of the dream of a never-ending verticality/Paola Zaccaria – Worstward ho and on-words: writing to(wards) the point/Charles Krance – Beckett's Company, post-structuralism, and mimetalogique/Ed Jewinski – Watt: Samuel Beckett's sceptical fiction/Michael E. Mooney – A new approach to Watt/Gottfried Büttner – Conspicuous absence: tracé and power in Beckett's drama/ Stephen Barker.

Butler, Michael. **The plays of Max Frisch**. London: Macmillan in association with Humanities Research Centre of the Australian National University, Canberra, 1985. – ix, 182 p. *Notes*: Includes index. Criticism and interpretation/Drama in German.

Cahn, Victor L. **Beyond absurdity: the plays of Tom Stoppard**. Rutherford [N.J.]: Fairleigh Dickinson University Press, 1979. – 169 p. *Notes*: Includes index. Bibliography: p. 163–6. Criticism and interpretation.

Canziani, Roberto and Gianfranco Capitta. **Harold Pinter: un ritratto**. Milan: Anabasi, 1995. – 219 p.

Capone, Giovanna. **Drammi per voci. Dylan Thomas, Samuel Beckett, Harold Pinter**. Bologna: R. Parron, 1967. – 232 p. *Notes*: Bibliography: p. 217–26.

Carson, Neil. **Arthur Miller**. New York: St. Martin's Press, 1988 1982. – 167 p., 8 p. of plates: ill. *Notes*: Includes bibliographical references. Criticism and interpretation.

Carter, Alan. **John Osborne**. New York: Harper & Row, 1973. – 213 p. *Notes*: Includes bibliography and index.

Centola, Steve. **The achievement of Arthur Miller: new essays**. Dallas, Tex.: Contemporary Research Press, 1995. – 158 p. *Notes*: Includes bibliographical references and index. Criticism and interpretation.

——. **Arthur Miller in conversation**. Dallas: Northouse & Northouse, 1993. – 84 p. *Notes*: Includes bibliographical references (p. 65–80) and index. Interviews.

Chabert, Pierre. **Samuel Beckett**. Toulouse: Privat, 1986. – 475 p.: ill. *Series*: Revue d'esthétique; numéro spécial hors série, 1986. *Notes*: 'Ce numéro a été préparé par Pierre Chabert'–T.p. verso. 'Liste chronologique des oeuvres de Samuel Beckett': p. 416–22. Bibliography: p. 423–33. Criticism and interpretation.

Chick, Edson M. **Dances of death: Wedekind, Brecht, Dürrenmatt, and the satiric tradition**. Columbia, S.C.: Camden House, 1984. – 181 p.: ill. *Notes*: Includes index. Bibliography: p. 167–173. German drama. 20th century. History and criticism.

Clément, Bruno. **L'Oeuvre sans qualités: rhétorique de Samuel Beckett**. Paris: Seuil, 1994. – 441 p. *Notes*: Includes bibliographical references (p. 427–40) and index.

Coe, Richard N. **Ionesco; a study of his plays**. London: Methuen, 1971. – 206 p. illus., plates.

Notes: Originally published in 1961. Bibliography: p. 177–98.

Cohn, Ruby. **Just play: Beckett's theater**. Princeton, N.J.: Princeton University Press, 1980. – 313 p., 2 p. of plates: ill. *Notes*: Includes bibliographical references (p. 289–92) and index. Criticism and interpretation. Stage history.

Cole, Toby. **Playwrights on playwriting: the meaning and making of modern drama from Ibsen to Ionesco**. New York: Hill & Wang, 1969, 1960. – 299 p. *Notes*: Includes index. Bibliography: p. 289–94.

Connor, Steven. **Waiting for Godot and Endgame**. Basingstoke: Macmillan, 1992. – ix, 172 p. *Notes*: Bibiliography: p. 165–7. Includes index. Casebook.

Cook, Bruce. **Brecht in exile**. 1st edn. New York: Holt, Rinehart and Winston, 1983, 1982. – xiii, 237 p. *Notes*: Includes bibliographical references and index. Biography/Brecht, Bertolt.

Coupry, François. **Eugène Ionesco**. Paris: Editions Julliard, 1994. – 172, 12 p.: ill. *Notes*: Includes bibliographical references (p. 171–173).

Cousin, Geraldine. **Churchill, the playwright**. London and Portsmouth, N.H.: Methuen Drama. 1989. – 135 p., 8 p. of plates: ill. *Notes*: Includes bibliographical references (p. 129–35) and index. Churchill, Caryl. Criticism and interpretation.

Cowan, Suzanne. **Dario Fo: bibliography, biography, playography**. London: TQ Publications, 1978. – 24 p.: ill. *Series*: Theatre checklist; no. 17. *Notes*: Bibliography: p. 21–4.

Crandell, George W. **Tennessee Williams: a descriptive bibliography**. Pittsburgh: University of Pittsburgh Press, 1995. – xxiii, 673 p.: ill. *Notes*: Includes index. Williams, Tennessee, 1911–83. Bibliography.

——. **The critical response to Tennessee Williams**. Westport, Conn.: Greenwood Press, 1996. – xxxix, 307 p. *Notes*: Includes bibliographical references (p. 285–94) and index. Criticism and interpretation.

Crockett, Roger Alan. **Understanding Friedrich Dürrenmatt**. Columbia: University of South Carolina Press, 1997. *Notes*: Biography – Earliest prose and dramatic works – The turn to comedy – Three detective stories – Two plays about ideologies and God's remoteness – The radio plays – Consolation from Dürrenmatt – The corruption of justice – Of heroism, failure, and resignation – Improbable grace – The adaptations – Four that failed: the late plays –

The prose of the 1970s and 1980s – Conclusion.

Cronin, Anthony. **Samuel Beckett: the last modernist**. London: Flamingo, 1997 1996. – ix, 645 p., 12 p. of plates. *Notes*: First published 1996 by HarperCollins. Includes bibliographical references and index. Biography.

Crugten, Alain van. **S. I. Witkiewicz aux sources d'un théâtre nouveau**. [Lausanne]. Éditions L'Age d'homme, 1971. – 385 p. *Notes*: Bibliography: p. 377–81. Originally presented as the author's thesis, Brussels. Witkiewicz, Stanislaw Ignacy, 1885–1939. In French.

——. **S.I. Witkiewicz: génie multiple de Pologne**. Lausanne: L'Age d'Homme, 1981. – 109 p.: ill. (some col.). *Notes*: 'Mélange d'études de dessins, de peintures et de photographies assemblé et édité par Alain Van Crugten à l'occasion du Festival Witkiewicz, Bruxelles, novembre 1981'. Includes bibliography. Poland. Biography/Witkiewicz, Stanislaw Ignacy.

Dashwood, Julie R. **Luigi Pirandello: the theatre of paradox**. Lewiston, N.Y.: Edwin Mellen Press, 1996. – 292 p. *Notes*: Includes bibliographical references (p. 285–7) and index. *Subjects*: Drama. 20th century. History and criticism/Pirandello, Luigi, 1867–1936. Criticism and interpretation/Pirandello, Luigi, 1867–1936. Influence.

Davies, Robertson. **Robertson Davies, dramatist**. Waterloo: Ont., 1981. – iv, 198 p. *Notes*: Special issue: **Canadian drama** 7, no. 2, 1981. 'Leaven of malice, a theatrical extravaganza adapted from the novel by Robertson Davies': p. 117–90. Includes bibliographical references.

Davis, Katie Brittain Adams. **Federico García Lorca and Sean O'Casey: powerful voices in the wilderness**. Salzburg: Inst. f. Engl. Sprache u. Literatur, Univ. Salzburg, 1978. – v, 147 p. *Notes*: Bibliography: p. 144–7.

Delaney, Paul. **Tom Stoppard: the moral vision of the major plays**. Houndmills, Basingstoke, Hampshire: Macmillan, 1990. – xii, 202 p. *Notes*: Includes bibliographical references (p. 179–97) and index. Art as a moral matrix – Through a glass darkly: mortality and the outer mystery in Rosencrantz and Guildenstern are dead – Flesh and the word in Jumpers – Mortal flesh in a moral matrix of words: the temporal and the timeless in Travesties – Word made flesh: moral action in the body politic (Professional foul, Every good boy deserves favour, Night and day, Dogg's Hamlet, Cahoot's Macbeth) – 'Not of the flesh but through the flesh': knowing and being known in The real thing – Particle physics and particular persons: the join between happenstance and goodness in Hapgood – Moral absolutes and mortal contexts.

Demastes, William W. **Clifford Odets: a research and production sourcebook**. New York: Greenwood Press, 1991. – viii, 209 p. *Notes*: Includes bibliographical references and indexes. Odets, Clifford, 1906–63.

Denison, Patricia D. **John Osborne: a casebook**. New York: Garland Pub., 1997. – xxxiv, 231 p.: ill. *Notes*: Includes bibliographical references (p. 197–221) and index. Criticism and interpretation.

DeRose, David J. **Sam Shepard**. New York and Toronto: Twayne, 1992. – xv, 171 p.: ill. *Notes*: Includes bibliographical references (p. 151–64) and index. Criticism and interpretation.

DiGaetani, John Louis. **A search for a postmodern theater: interviews with contemporary playwrights**. New York: Greenwood Press, 1991. – xv, 313 p. *Notes*: Includes bibliographical references (p. 305–8) and index. Robert Anderson – Alan Ayckbourn – Eric Bentley – Ed Bullins – Mart Crowley – Jules Feiffer – Horton Foote – Michael Frayn – Larry Gelbart – Amlin Gray – Simon Gray – John Guare – A.R. Gurney – Christopher Hampton – William M. Hoffman – Israel Horovitz – Tina Howe – David Henry Hwang – Albert Innaurato – David Ives – Barrie Keeffe – Romulus Linney – Craig Lucas – Terrence McNally – Adrian Mitchell – Richard Nelson – Marsha Norman – Eric Overmyer – David Storey – Timberlake Wertenbaker – August Wilson – Lanford Wilson – Paul Zindel.

Donati, Corrado. **Bibliografia della critica pirandelliana, 1962–1981**. Florence: La Ginestra, 1986. – 197 p. *Notes*: Includes index. Pirandello, Luigi, 1867–1936. Bibliography.

Dort, Bernard. **En attendant Godot, pièce de Samuel Beckett**. 1953. *Notes*: A major critical essay by a major French critic.

Dubois, Félicie. **Tennessee Williams: l'oiseau sans pattes**. Paris: Editions Balland, 1992. – 259 p. – 8 p. of plates. *Notes*: Chronology and filmography. Bibliography.

Dukore, Bernard F. **Harold Pinter**. 2nd edn. London: Macmillan, 1988. – xi, 162 p., 8 p. of plates. *Notes*: Previous edn.: 1982. Includes index. Bibliography: p. 151–158. Criticism and interpretation.

Duras, Marguerite and Jérôme Beaujour. **La Vie matérielle: Marguerite Duras parle à Jérôme Beaujour**. [Paris]: Gallimard, 1994. – 179 p. *Notes*: Duras, Marguerite. Interviews.

Duras, Marguerite and Xavière Gauthier. **Les Parleuses**. Paris: Éditions de Minuit, 1993, 1974. – 243 p. *Notes*: Duras, Marguerite. Interviews.

Dürrenmatt, Friedrich. **Gespräche [1961– 1990]**. Zürich: Diogenes, 1996. – 4 vols. Edited by H. Arnold, A. von Planta and Jan Strümpel. *Notes*: Includes bibliographical references and index. Vol. 1. Der Klassiker auf der Bühne – Vol. 2. Die Entdeckung des Erzählers – Vol. 3. Im Bann der 'Stoffe' – Vol. 4. Dramaturgie des Denkens. Dürrenmatt, Friedrich.

—— and Michael Haller. **Über die Grenzen: Friedrich Dürrenmatt**. Munich: Piper, 1993. – 159 p. *Notes*: Dürrenmatt, Friedrich. Interviews.

Esslin, Martin. **Brecht, a choice of evils: a critical study of the man, his work, and his opinions**. London: Methuen Drama, 1990, 1984. – xix, 315 p. *Notes*: Includes index. Published in paperback in 1984 by Methuen London 'A descriptive list of Brecht's works'– p. 251–89. Bibliography: p. 290–302. Critical studies.

——. **Mediations: essays on Brecht, Beckett, and the media**. New York: Grove Press, 1982, 1980. – 248 p. *Notes*: Originally published: Baton Rouge: Louisiana State University Press, c1980. Includes index. Bibliography: p. 243–4. Criticism and interpretation.

——. **Pinter: the playwright**. 5th edn. London: Methuen Drama, 1992, 1982 – vii, 279 p. *Notes*: Includes index. Bibliography: p. 265–72. Criticism and interpretation.

——. **Samuel Beckett: a collection of critical essays**. Englewood Cliffs, N.J.: Prentice-Hall International, 1987. – vi, 182 p. *Notes*: Includes bibliographical references (p. 181–2). Criticism and interpretation.

Fassmann, Kurt. **Brecht, eine Bildbiographie**. Berlin: Deutsche Buch-Gemeinschaft, 1967. – 144 p. illus. *Notes*: First published in 1958 by Kindler Verlag. *Subjects*: Brecht, Bertolt, 1898–1956.

Fischer, Matthias-Johannes. **Brechts Theatertheorie: Forschungsgeschichte, Forschungsstand, Perspektiven**. Frankfurt am Main; New York: P. Lang, 1989. – 351 p. *Notes*: Includes bibliographical references (p. 328–351). Brecht, Bertolt, 1898–1956. Aesthetics. In German.

Fo, Dario. **Il teatro politico di Dario Fo**. Milan: G. Mazzotta, 1977. – 152 p., 8 p. of plates: ill. *Notes*: Bibliography: p. 51–3.

—— and Luigi Allegri. **Dario Fo, dialogo provocatorio sul comico, il tragico, la follia e la ragione con Luigi Allegri**. Rome: Laterza, 1990. – 163 p. *Notes*: Fo, Dario. Interviews.

Frick, John W. and Stephen M., Vallillo. **Theatrical directors: a biographical dictionary**. Westport, Conn.: Greenwood Press, 1994. – xi, 567 p. *Notes*: Includes bibliographical references (p. 465–6) and index.

Fritsch, Rudolf. **Absurd oder grotesk?: über literarische Darstellung von Entfremdung bei Beckett und Heller**. Frankfurt am Main; New York: P. Lang, 1990. – 445 p. *Notes*: Originally presented as the author's thesis (doctoral)– Universität Bremen, 1987. Includes bibliographical references (p. 426–45). Criticism and interpretation/Joseph Heller and Samuel Beckett.

Fuegi, John. **Brecht in Asia and Africa**. Univ. of Hong Kong, 1989. – iii, 209 p.: ill. *Series*: The Brecht yearbook. *Notes*: Abstracts in English, German, French, and Spanish. Includes bibliographical references.

Gale, Steven H. **Critical essays on Harold Pinter**. Boston: G.K. Hall, 1990. – x, 356 p. *Notes*: Includes bibliographical references and index.

Galle, Etienne. **L'Homme vivant de Wole Soyinka**. Paris: Silex, 1987. – 270 p. *Notes*: Bibliography: p. 263–5. Includes index.

Gauthier, Brigitte. **Harold Pinter, 'the Caretaker' of the Fragments of Modernity: étude de l'oeuvre de Pinter**. Paris: Ellipses-Marketing, 1996. – 127 p. *Notes*: Bibliography. Index.

Geissler, Rolf, Therese Poser and Wihelm Ziskoven. **Zur Interpretation des modernen Dramas: Brecht, Dürrenmatt, Frisch**. Frankfurt am Main: Diesterweg, 1981. – 144 p. *Notes*: Includes bibliographies. Criticism and interpretation.

Giantvalley, Scott. **Edward Albee: a reference guide**. Boston, Mass.: G.K. Hall, 1987. – xxiv, 459 p. *Notes*: Includes index. Albee, Edward, 1928–. Bibliography.

Gontarski, S.E. **A choice of the best writings on Beckett: essays and criticism**. New York: Grove Press, 1986. – 427 p. *Notes*: 'Getting known' – Beckett and Merlin – Samuel Beckett and the visual arts – When is the end not the end? the idea of fiction in Beckett – Murphy and the uses of repetition – Watt – Mercier and Camier – Molloy's silence – Where now? who now? – Voice and its words – Shards of ends and odds in prose: from Fizzles to the Lost ones – Between verse and prose – Worstward Ho – MacGowran on Beckett – Blin on Beckett – Working with Beckett – Notes from the underground: waiting for Godot and Endgame – Beckett directs Godot – Beckett directs: Endgame and Krapp's last tape

– Literary allusions in Happy days – Counterpoint, absence, and the medium in Beckett's Not I – Rehearsal notes for the German premiere of Beckett's That time and Footfalls – Footfalls – Samuel Beckett and the art of radio – Light, sound, movement, and action in Beckett's Rockaby – Beckett's Ohio impromptu – Quad and catastrophe – Burroughs with Beckett in Berlin.

Gordon, Lois G. ed. **Harold Pinter: a casebook**. New York: Garland Pub., 1990. – xlv, 277 p.: ill. *Notes*: Includes bibliographical references (p. 243–67) and index. Creative process and meaning–some remarks of Pinter's 'Letter to Peter Wood'/Martin Esslin – Economy of Betrayal/ Ruby Cohn – Time for change in No Man's Land/Austin E. Quigley – Last to go: a structuralist reading/David Lodge – Monologue:the play of words/Linda Ben-Zvi – The Dumb Waiter, The Collection, The Lover and The Homecoming: a revisionist approach/George E. Wellwarth – Displacement in time and space:Harold Pinter's Other Places/Katherine Burkman – Film and drama:the opening sequence of the filmed version of Harold Pinter's The Caretaker (The Guest)/Steven H. Gale – Pinter and politics/Susan Hollis Merritt – 'Yes! in the Sea of Life Enisled': Harold Pinter's Other Places/Ewald Mengel – 'To Lay Bare': Pinter, Shakespeare, and The Dwarfs/Francis Gillen – Mind-less men: Pinter's dumb waiters/Robert Gordon – Harold Pinter in New York/Lois Gordon.

Graver, Lawrence and Federman, Raymond. **Samuel Beckett: the critical heritage**. London and New York: Routledge, 1997, 1979. – xx, 372 p. *Notes*: Reprint. Originally published: London and Boston: Routledge & Kegan Paul, 1979. Includes bibliographical references (p. 359) and index. Criticism and interpretation.

Gray, Ronald D. **Brecht the dramatist**. Cambridge and New York: Cambridge University Press, 1977, 1976. – 232 p. *Notes*: 'Reprinted with corrections 1977'. Includes index. 'A chronological list of Brecht's plays and translations': p. 217–20. Bibliography: p. 221–4. Criticism and interpretation.

Gray, Stephen. ed. **Athol Fugard**. Cape Town: Maskew Miller, 1980.

Griffin, Alice. **Understanding Arthur Miller**. Columbia, S.C.: University of South Carolina Press, 1996. – xii, 208 p. *Notes*: Includes bibliographical references (p. 191–8) and index. Understanding Arthur Miller – All my sons – Death of a salesman – The crucible – A view from the bridge – Two plays of the Depression: A memory of two mondays and The American clock – After the fall and Incident at Vichy – The price – Plays of the 1980s: Some kind of love story, Elegy for a lady, I can't remember anything, Clara, and The Archbishop's ceiling – Plays of the 1990s: The ride down Mount Morgan, The last Yankee, and Broken glass. Criticism and interpretation.

——. **Understanding Tennessee Williams**. Columbia, S.C.: University of South Carolina Press, 1995. – xv, 266 p.; 21 x. *Notes*: Includes bibliographical references (p. 242–52) and index. Understanding Tennessee Williams – The glass menagerie – A streetcar named Desire – Summer and smoke – The rose tattoo – Camino Real – Cat on a hot tin roof – Orpheus descending – Sweet bird of youth – The night of the iguana. Criticism and interpretation.

Griffiths, Gareth. **John Romeril**. Australian Playwrights Monograph Series. Amsterdam: Rodopi, 1993.

Grossvogel, David I. **The blasphemers: the theater of Brecht, Ionesco, Beckett, Genet**. Ithaca, N.Y.: Cornell University Press, 1965. – xviii, 209 p. *Notes*: Previously published as: **Four playwrights and a postscript**. Includes bibliographical references and index.

Gunn, Drewey Wayne. **Tennessee Williams, a bibliography**. 2nd edn. Metuchen, N.J.: Scarecrow Press, 1991. – xxxi, 434 p. *Notes*: Includes indexes. Williams, Tennessee, 1911–83. Bibliography.

Guralnick, Elissa S. **Sight unseen: Beckett, Pinter, Stoppard, and other contemporary dramatists on radio**. Athens: Ohio University Press, 1996. – xviii, 238 p.: ill. *Notes*: Includes bibliographical references (p. 225–32) and index. Howard Barker's Scenes from an execution – Tom Stoppard's Artist decending a staircase – Robert Gerguson's Transfigured night from three perspectives: in itself, in the orbit of Schoenberg, and in the shadow of Beckett's radio drama … with a coda on Cage's Roaratorio – Arthur Kopit's Wings and Harold Pinter's A slight ache – David Rudkin's Cries from Casement as his bones are brought to Dublin – John Arden's Pearl, and The bagman, too. English drama. 20th century. History and criticism.

Gussow, Mel. **Conversations with and about Beckett**. London: Nick Hern Books, 1996. – 192 p. *Notes*: Includes index. Beckett, Samuel. Interviews. Criticism and interpretation.

——. **Conversations with Pinter**. London: Nick Hern Books, 1994. – 158 p. *Notes*: Includes index. Pinter, Harold. Interviews.

——. **Conversations with Stoppard**. London: Nick Hern, 1995. – xii, 146 p. *Notes*: Stoppard, Tom. Interviews.

Hagiwara, Sakumi. **Omoide no naka no Terayama Shuji**. Tokyo: Chikuma Shobo, 1992. – 205 p.: ill. *Notes*: Biography of the noted director Terayama Shuji.

Hamdan, Alexandra. **Ionescu avant Ionesco: portrait de l'artiste en jeune homme**. Berne; New York: P. Lang, 1993. – 285, 65 p.: ill. *Notes*: Text in French, annexes in French translation, followed by the original in Romanian. Includes bibliographical references (p. 239–245). Ionesco, Eugène. Criticism and interpretation.

Hansel, Johannes. **Friedrich Dürrenmatt Bibliographie**. Bad Homburg v.d.H., Berlin, Zürich: (Dr.) Gehlen, 1968. – 87 p. Dürrenmatt, Friedrich. Bibliography.

Hart, Lynda. **Sam Shepard's metaphorical stages**. Westport, Conn.: Greenwood Press, 1987. – viii, 157 p., 4 p. of plates: ill. *Notes*: Includes index. Bibliography: p. 149–52. Criticism and interpretation.

Harvey, Robert; Volat-Shapiro, Hélène. **Marguerite Duras: a bio-bibliography**. Westport, Conn.; London: Greenwood Press, 1997. – xiv, 273 p. *Notes*: Includes index.

Hauptfleisch, Temple, Wilma Viljoen and Câeleste Van Greunen. **Athol Fugard: a source guide**. Johannesburg: Ad Donker, 1980. 126 p.

Hayashi, Tetsumaro. **An index to Arthur Miller criticism**. 2d edn. Metuchen, N.J.: Scarecrow Press, 1976. – xiv, 151 p. *Notes*: First edn. published under title: **Arthur Miller criticism, 1930–1967**. Includes index. Miller, Arthur, 1915–. Bibliography.

Hayman, Ronald. **Tennessee Williams: everyone else is an audience**. New Haven, Conn.: Yale University Press, 1993. – xx, 268 p.: ill. *Notes*: Includes bibliographical references (p. 262–4) and index. Criticism and interpretation.

Herdeck, Donald E., ed. **Three dynamite authors: Derek Walcott (Nobel 1992), Naguib Mahfouz (Nobel 1988), Wole Soyinka (Nobel 1986): ten bio-critical essays from their works as published by Three Continents Press**. Colorado Springs, Colo.: Three Continents Press, 1995. – xi, 132 p. *Notes*: Includes bibliographical references. West Indies. Egypt. Nigeria.

Hinderer, Walter. **Brechts Dramen**. Stuttgart: Reclam, 1995. – 188 p. *Notes*: Includes bibliographical references (p. 179–82). Criticism and interpretation.

Hoare, Philip. **Noël Coward: a biography**. London: Sinclair-Stevenson, 1996, 1995. – xii, 605 p., 24 p. of plates: ill. *Notes*: Includes bibliographic references and index. Biography/ Coward, Noël, 1899–1973.

Hochman, Stanley. **McGraw-Hill encyclopedia of world drama: an international reference work in 5 volumes**. 2nd edn. New York, N.Y.: McGraw-Hill, 1984. – 5 vols: ill. *Notes*: Includes biographies, bibliographies and index.

Hubert, Marie-Claude. **Eugène Ionesco**. [Paris]: Seuil, 1990. – 284 p.: ill. *Notes*: Includes bibliographical references (p. 279–82). Biography/ Ionesco, Eugène.

——. **Langage et corps fantasmé dans le théâtre des années cinquante: Ionesco, Beckett, Adamov**. [Paris]: Libr. J. Corti, 1987. 296 p. *Notes*: Bibliography: p. 291–3. French drama. 20th century. History and criticism.

Iglésis, Roger and Alain Trutat, eds. **Les Entretiens d'Ostende: Michel Ghelderode**. Toulouse: L'Ether vague/P. Thierry, 1992. – 196 p.: ill. *Notes*: Interview. Ghelderode, Michel de.

Iji, Edde. **Understanding Brecht and Soyinka: a study in anti-heroism**. Yaba, Lagos: Kraft Books, 1991. – ix, 216 p. *Notes*: Includes bibliographical references (p. 204–10) and index. Criticism and interpretation.

——. **Three radical dramatists: Brecht, Artaud, Soyinka a study**. Lagos: Kraft Books, 1991. – 120 p. *Notes*: Includes bibliographical references (p. 113–16) and index.

Ionesco – Beckett – Pinget. Paris: Gallimard, 1966. – 128 p. illus. *Series*: Cahiers Renaud Barrault, 53. *Notes*: Criticism and interpretation.

Ionesco, Eugène. **La Quête intermittente**. [Paris]: Gallimard, 1987. – 168 p. *Notes*: Ionesco, Eugène. Diaries.

——. **Notes et contrenotes**. [Notes and counternotes]. Paris: Gallimard, 1962. Published in English: New York: Grove Press, 1964. 271 p.

——. **Present past, past present: a personal memoir**. [Présent passé, passé présent]. New York: Da Capo Press, 1997. *Notes*: Ionesco, Eugène. Biography.

Ionesco, Eugène and Claude Bonnefoy. **Entre la vie et le rêve: entretiens avec Claude Bonnefoy**. Paris: Gallimard, 1996. – 227 p. *Notes*: Entretiens parue en 1977 aux éditions Belfond. Les annexes et la biographie de l'auteur ont fait l'objet d'une mise à jour. Ionesco, Eugène. Interviews.

Ionesco, Eugène and André Coutin. **Ruptures de silence: rencontres avec André Coutin**. Paris: Mercure de France, 1995. – 92 p. *Notes*: Ionesco, Eugène. Interviews.

Jacobsen, Josephine and William Randolph Mueller. **Ionesco and Genêt; playwrights of silence**. New York: Hill & Wang, 1968. – xii, 242 p. *Notes*: Bibliography: p. 236–8. French drama. 20th century. History and criticism.

Jacquart, Emmanuel C. **Le Théâtre de dérision: Beckett, Ionesco, Adamov**. [Paris]: Gallimard, 1974. – 313 p. *Notes*: Includes index. Bibliography: p. 285–306. French drama. 20th century. History and criticism.

Jeffers, Jennifer M. **Samuel Beckett: a casebook**. New York: Garland Pub., 1998. *Notes*: Includes index. Criticism and interpretation.

Jenkins, Anthony, ed. **Critical essays on Tom Stoppard**. Boston, Mass.: G.K. Hall, 1990. – x, 230 p. *Notes*: Includes bibliographical references (p. 219–20) and index. An interview with Tom Stoppard/Joost Kuurmann, with Wim van Klaveren and Simon Popma – Count Zero splits the infinite/Clive James – [Lord Malquist and Mr Moon]/Michael Billington – [Death in Rosencrantz and Guildenstern: I]/Normand Berlin – [Death in Rosencrantz and Guildenstern: II]/Anthony Jenkins – [An art of literary travesty: Rosencrantz and Guildenstern, Jumpers]/Richard Allen Cave – Philosophy and Mr Stoppard/Jonathan Bennett – Philosophy as farce, or farce as philosophy/Roy W. Perrett – Ethics on the wane/Tim Brassell – Logics of the absurd/Thomas R. Whitaker – [Travesties]/Michael Billington – [Moral dilemmas]/C.W.E. Bigsby – A politics of disengagement/Neil Sammells – Cricket bats and commitment:the real thing in art and life/Paul Delaney – Moles and molecules: Tom Stoppard's Hapgood/Anthony Jenkins – Tomfoolery: Stoppard's theatrical puns/Hersh Zeifman – Stoppard's idea of woman: 'Good, bad or indifferent?'/Doreen Thompson – Talking/Jim Hunter.

Jones, Eldred Durisimi. **The Writings of Wole Soyinka**. London: Heinemann Educational Books, 1976.

Kacou-Koné, Denise. **Shakespeare et Soyinka: le théâtre du monde**. Abidjan: Nouvelles éditions africaines, 1989. – 207 p. *Notes*: Bibliography: p. 201–7.

Kalb, Jonathan. **The theatre of Heiner Müller**. Great Britain: Cambridge University Press, 1998. 275 p. *Notes*: First comprehensive English study of an important German theatre figure.

Kamyabi Mask, Ahmad. **Qu'attendent Eugène Ionesco et Samuel Beckett? et qu'en pensent: Jean Louis Barrault, Jacques Mauclair, Marcel Maréchal, Paul Vernois, Terence Brown, August Grodzicki, Roger Benski, Alvin Epstein, Rosette Lamont, Richard Schechner?** (Interviews). Paris: A. Kamyabi Mask, 1991. – 208 p.: ill.

Kane, Leslie. **Israel Horovitz: a collection of critical essays**. Westport, Conn.: Greenwood Press, 1994. – xxi, 221 p. *Notes*: Includes bibliographical references (p. 211–18). Criticism and interpretation.

Katrak, Ketu H. **Wole Soyinka and modern tragedy: a study of dramatic theory and practice**. New York: Greenwood Press, 1986. – xii, 192 p.: ill. *Notes*: Bibliography: p. 175–88. Includes index. Tragedy.

Kelly, Katherine E. **Tom Stoppard and the craft of comedy: medium and genre at play**. Ann Arbor: University of Michigan Press, 1991. – 179 p. *Notes*: Includes bibliographical references p. (161–73) and index. Criticism and interpretation.

Kelly, Veronica. **Louis Nowra**. Australian Playwrights Monograph Series. Amsterdam: Rodopi, 1987.

Kleber, Pia and Visser, Colin, eds. **Re-interpreting Brecht: his influence on contemporary drama and film**. Cambridge and New York: Cambridge University Press, 1990. – xiii, 220 p. *Notes*: Includes index. Introduction/Pia Kleber – Questions concerning Brecht/Manfred Wekwerth – The origins, aims, and objectives of the Berliner Ensemble/Joachim Tenschert – Two generations of post-Brechtian playwrights in the German Democratic Republic/Rolf Rohmer – Productions of Brecht's plays on the West German stage, 1945–86/Klaus Völker – Ups and downs of British Brecht/John Willett – Crossing the desert: Brecht in France in the eighties/Bernard Dort – 'His liberty is full of threats to all': Benno Besson's Helsinki Hamlet and Brecht's dialectical appropriation of classic texts/Paul Walsh – Blocking Brecht/Maarten Van Dijk – Some reflections on Brecht and acting/Martin Esslin – Brechtian theory and American feminist theatre/Karen Laughlin. The influence of Brecht on women's cinema in West Germany/Renate Möhrmann – From anti-illusionism to hyper-realism: Bertolt Brecht and contemporary film/Thomas Elsaesser – The influence of Brecht/Eric Bentley.

Kluback, William and Michael Finkenthal. **The clown of the agora: conversations about Eugène Ionesco**. New York: P. Lang, 1998. *Notes*: Criticism.

Knowles, Ronald. **Understanding Harold Pinter**. Columbia, S.C.: University of South Carolina Press, 1995. – xii, 232 p. *Notes*: Includes bibliographical references (p. 212–20) and index. Criticism and interpretation.

Knowlson, James. **Damned to fame: the life of Samuel Beckett**. New York: Touchstone, 1997, 1996. – 800 p., 32 p. of plates: ill. *Notes*:

Includes bibliographical references (p. 747–62) and index. Biography.

Kolin, Philip C. and J. Madison Davis. **Critical essays on Edward Albee**. Boston, Mass.: G.K. Hall, 1986. – ix, 222 p. *Notes*: An annotated bibliography of Albee interviews, with an index to names, concepts, and places: p. 200–18. Includes bibliographies and index. Criticism and interpretation.

Krüger, Axel E. **Beckett; Schwarze Serie: Photo-graphien**. Berlin: [s.n.] Druckerei Gebrüder Höltje, 1990. – 1 v. (unpaged): chiefly ill. *Notes*: 'Privatdruck, Auflage. Exemplare'–Colophon. 'Beckett' consists of photographs of the San Quentin Drama Workshop's production of Waiting for Godot, Endgame, and Krapp's Last Tape given in Hannover and Hamburg in May 1986. 'Schwarze Serie' consists of photographs selected from a series of self-portraits taken by Krüger in 1985 and 1986 prior to his death. Krüger, Axel E., 1951–87. Pictorial works.

Krysinski, Wladimir. **El paradigma inquieto: Pirandello y el campo de la modernidad**. Frankfurt am Main; Madrid: Iberoamericana, Vervuert, 1995. – 357 p. *Notes*: Includes bibliographical references (p. 341–57). *Subjects*: Pirandello, Luigi, 1867–1936. Criticism and interpretation. In Spanish.

Kuntze, Gisela. **Bibliographie Bertolt Brecht**. Berlin and Weimar: Aufbau-Verlag, 1975.

Lamont, Rosette C. **Ionesco's imperatives: the politics of culture**. Ann Arbor: University of Michigan Press, 1993. – 328 p. *Notes*: Includes bibliographical references (p. 307–13) and index. *Subjects*: Ionesco, Eugène. Political and social views.

—— and Melvin J. Friedman, eds. **The Two faces of Ionesco**. Troy, N.Y.: Whitston Pub. Co., 1978. – xxiii, 283 p., 2 p. of plates. *Notes*: Bibliography: p. 269–83. Peyre, H. Foreword.–Lamont, R.C. Introductory remarks to Eugene Ionesco's 'Why do I write?'.–Ionesco, E. Why do I write? a summing up; translated by R.C. Lamont.–Eliade, M. Eugene Ionesco and 'La nostalgie du paradis'.–Lamont, R.C. Father of the man.–Morrissette, B. A 'lost' play by Ionesco: La nièce-épouse.–Rainof, A. Ionesco and the film of the twenties and thirties: from Groucho to Harpo.–Benamou, M. Philology can lead to the worst.–Malin, I. The fragments of Eugene Ionesco.–Brée, G. Ionesco's later plays: experiments in dramatic form.–Swanson, R.A. Ionesco's classical absurdity.–Champigny. R. Designation and gesture in The chairs.–Fletcher, J. 'A psychology based on antagonism:' Ionesco, Pinter, Albee, and others.–Hunger and thirst: a conversation with Simone Benmussa and an analysis.–Kern, E. Macbett in the light of Verfremdung.–Ionesco, E. Towards a dream theatre; translated by R.C. Lamont.–Lamont, R.C. L'homme aux valises; Ionesco's absolute stranger.

Lamy, Suzanne and André Roy. **Marguerite Duras à Montréal**. Malakoff: Spirale: Solin, 1984, 1981. – 175 p.: ill., facsims. Criticism and interpretation. Interviews.

Larsen, Linda Lee. **Bertolt Brecht: a comprehensive bibliography in English, 1924–1982**. 1986. – xvii, 309 p. *Notes*: Includes abstract. Bibliography: leaves xi–xvii. Thesis (M.A.)–Baylor University, 1986. *Subjects*: Brecht, Bertolt, 1898–1956.

Laurence, Dan H. **Bernard Shaw, a bibliography**. Oxford: New York: Clarendon Press; Oxford University Press, 1983. – 2 v. (xxiii, 1058 p.): ill. *Notes*: Includes index. Shaw, Bernard, 1856–1950. Bibliography.

Lebelley, Frédérique. **Duras, ou, Le poids d'une plume**. Paris: Grasset, 1996. – 379, 1 p. *Notes*: Includes bibliographical references (p. 377–80). Duras, Marguerite. Biography.

Leiner, Wolfgang. **Bibliographie et index thématique des études sur Eugène Ionesco**. Fribourg: Éditions universitaires, 1980. – 192 p. *Notes*: Includes indexes. Ionesco, Eugène. Criticism and interpretation. Bibliography.

Liebman, Herbert. **The dramatic art of David Storey: the journey of a playwright**. Westport, Conn.: Greenwood Press, 1996. – 183 p. *Notes*: Includes bibliographical references (p. 169–79) and index. Storey, David. Criticism and interpretation.

Lifton, Paul. **Vast encyclopedia: the theatre of Thornton Wilder**. Westport, Conn.: Greenwood Press, 1995. – xii, 225 p. *Notes*: Includes bibliographical references (p. 211–17) and index on U.S. Wilder (1897–1975). Criticism and interpretation.

Lurdos, Michèle. **Côté cour, côté savane: le théâtre de Wole Soyinka**. Nancy: Presses universitaires de Nancy, 1990. –133 p. *Notes*: Includes bibliographical references.

Lyon, James K. **Bertolt Brecht in America**. Princeton, N.J.: Princeton University Press, 1980. –xiv, 408 p., 8 p. of plates: ill. *Notes*: Includes bibliographies and index.

Malick, Javed. **Toward a theatre of the oppressed: the dramaturgy of John Arden**. Ann Arbor: University of Michigan Press, 1995. – 208 p. *Notes*: Includes bibliographical references and index. Political and social views/Arden, John.

Mamet, David. **Three uses of the knife: on the nature and purpose of drama**. New York: Columbia University Press, 1998. *Notes*: Includes index.

Manceaux, Michèle. **L'Amie**. Paris: Albin Michel, 1997. – 214 p. *Notes*: Duras, Marguerite. Biography.

Marranca, Bonnie. **American dreams: the imagination of Sam Shepard**. New York: Performing Arts Journal Publications, 1981. – 223 p. Criticism and interpretation.

—— and Gautum Dasgupta. **American playwrights: a critical survey**. New York: Drama Book Specialists, 1981.

Martin, Robert A. **Critical essays on Tennessee Williams**. New York and London: G.K. Hall and Prentice Hall International, 1997. – xviii, 312 p.: ill. *Notes*: Includes bibliographical references and index. Criticism and interpretation.

Mayberry, Bob. **Theatre of discord: dissonance in Beckett, Albee, and Pinter**. Rutherford [N.J.]: Fairleigh Dickinson University Press, 1989. – 90 p. *Notes*: Includes index. Bibliography: p. 82–5.

McGhee, Jim. **True lies: the architecture of the fantastic in the plays of Sam Shepard**. New York: P. Lang, 1993. – 224 p. *Notes*: Includes bibliographical references (p. 221–4). Criticism and interpretation.

McGillick, Paul. **Jack Hibberd**. Australian Playwrights Monograph Series. Amsterdam: Rodopi, 1988.

McMillan, Dougald and Martha, Fehsenfeld. **Beckett in the theatre: the author as practical playwright and director**. London: John Calder, 1988. – 333 p.: ill. *Notes*: Vol. 1. From Waiting for Godot to Krapp's last tape. 1988. Productions.

McMullan, Anna. **Theatre on trial: Samuel Beckett's later drama**. New York: Routledge, 1993. – vi, 155 p. *Notes*: Includes bibliographical references (p. 137–50) and index.

Meister, Charles W. **Chekhov bibliography: works in English by and about Anton Chekov; American, British, and Canadian performances**. Jefferson, N.C.: McFarland, 1985. – vi, 184 p. *Notes*: Includes index. Chekhov, Anton Pavlovich, 1860–1904.

Micinska, Anna. **Witkacy: Stanislaw Ignacy Witkiewicz, life and work**. Warsaw: Interpress, 1990. – 300 p.: ill. *Notes*: Includes bibliographical references (p. 336–355). Witkiewicz, Stanislaw Ignacy, 1885–1939.

Mikotowicz, Thomas J. **Oliver Smith: a bio-bibliography**. Westport, Conn.: Greenwood Press, 1993. – xii, 250 p.: ill. *Notes*: Includes index. Set designers. United States. Biography/Smith, Oliver Lemuel, 1918–.

Miller, Arthur. **'Salesman' in Beijing**. London: Methuen Drama, 1991 1984. – xii, 254 p.: ill. *Notes*: Arthur Miller's impressions and strategies on directing his **Death of a Salesman** in China.

——. **Timebends: a life**. New York: Penguin Books, 1995. – 614 p., 32 p. of plates. *Notes*: Includes index. Autobiography.

—— and Matthew Charles Roudané. **Conversations with Arthur Miller**. Jackson: University Press of Mississippi, 1987. – xvii, 394 p. *Notes*: Includes index. Dramatists, American. 20th century. Interviews. Miller, Arthur.

Mitchell, Tony. **Dario Fo: people's court jester**. London and New York: Methuen, 1999. – 135 p., 10 p. of plates: ill. *Notes*: Bibliography: p. 128–35. Updated and expanded. Fo, Dario. Stage history. Political and social views.

Moore, Gerald. **Wole Soyinka**. London: Evans Bros, 1978. – x, 177 p. *Notes*: Bibliography: p. 166–171. Includes index.

Mrozek, Slawomir. **Oeuvres complètes. IV, dessins humoristiques et satiriques, 1: La Pologne en images; Vu par Slawomir Mrozek; Dessins**. Montricher: Noir sur blanc, 1993. – 362 p.: ill. Mrozek as visual artist and satirist.

Murphy, Brenda. **Tennessee Williams and Elia Kazan: a collaboration in the theatre**. Cambridge [England]; New York: Cambridge University Press, 1992. – xv, 201 p., [16] p. of plates, ill. *Notes*: Includes bibliographical references (p. 178–194) and index. Tennessee Williams and Elia Kazan: the aesthetic matrix – Subject and object: A streetcar named Desire – Realism and fantasy: Camino Real – Presentation and representation: Cat on a hot tin roof – Realism and metatheatre: Sweet bird of youth.

Murphy, Peter John. **Critique of Beckett criticism: a guide to research in English, French, and German**. 1st edn. Columbia, SC: Camden House, 1994. – xii, 173 p. *Notes*: 'Beckett's work in chronological order'– 119–21. Includes bibliographical references (p. 122–62) and indexes.

Northouse, Cameron and Thomas P. Walsh. **John Osborne: a reference guide**. Boston: G. K. Hall, 1974. – ix, 158 p. *Notes*: Osborne, John, 1929– Bibliography.

Oba, Masaharu. **Bertolt Brecht und das Nô-Theater: das Nô-Theater im Kontext der**

Lehrstücke Brechts. Frankfurt am Main and New York: P. Lang, 1984. – v, 350 p. *Notes*: Bibliography: p. 314–37. Noh plays/Brecht, Bertolt. Criticism and interpretation.

Okpu, B.M. **Wole Soyinka: a bibliography**. Lagos, Nigeria: Libriservice, 1984. – vi, 54 p. *Notes*: Includes index. Introduction by F. Odun Balogun.

Orr, John. **Tragicomedy and contemporary culture: play and performance from Beckett to Shepard**. Ann Arbor: University of Michigan Press, 1991. – 170 p. *Notes*: Includes bibliographical references (p. 162–5) and index. Tragicomedy. History and criticism.

Ortolani, Olivier. **Dario Fo, Theater und Politik: eine Monographie**. Berlin: Basis Verlag, 1985. – 62 p. *Notes*: Bibliography: p. 57–62. Fo, Dario. Political and social views.

Osborne, John. **Almost a gentleman: an autobiography: volume II, 1955–1966**. London: Faber & Faber, 1992 1991. – 283 p., 32 p.: ill. *Notes*: Includes index.

——. **A better class of person: an autobiography 1929–1956**. London: Faber, 1991, 1981. – 285 p., 8 p. of ill. *Notes*: Includes index.

Page, Malcolm. **File on Stoppard**. London; New York: Methuen, 1986. – 96 p. *Notes*: Bibliography: p. 91–6.

——. **Peter Shaffer: bibliography, biography, playography**. London: TQ publications, 1978. – 16 p.: ill. *Series*: Theatre checklist; no. 16. Shaffer, Peter, 1926–. Bibliography.

——. **Wole Soyinka: bibliography, biography, playography**. London: TQ Publications, 1979. *Series*: Theatre checklist, no. 19.

Parsell, David B. **Michel de Ghelderode**. New York and Toronto: Twayne Publishers and Maxwell Macmillan Canada, 1993. – xv, 109 p.: ill. *Notes*: Includes bibliographical references (p. 103–6) and index. Ghelderode, Michel de. Criticism and interpretation.

Pennington-Jones, Paulette. **Amiri Baraka. bibliography, biography, playography**. London: TQ Publications, 1978. – 21 p.: ill., port. *Notes*: Microfilm. New York: New York Public Library, 1982. 1 microfilm reel; 35 mm. (MN *ZZ-19947). Baraka, Imamu Amiri, 1934–. Bibliography.

Perkins, Elizabeth. **The Plays of Alma De Groen**. Australian Playwrights Monograph Series. Amsterdam: Rodopi, 1994.

Pike, David. **Lukács and Brecht**. Chapel Hill: University of North Carolina Press, 1985. – xvi, 337 p. *Notes*: Includes index. Bibliography: p. 323–32. Biography/Lukács, György, 1885–1971/Brecht, Bertolt, 1898–1956. Political and social views.

Piotrowski, Piotr. **Stanislaw Ignacy Witkiewicz**. Warsaw: Krajowa Agencja Wydawnicza, 1989. – 164 p.: ill. (some col.). *Notes*: Includes bibliographical references (p. 158–60). Poland. Biography/Witkiewicz, Stanislaw Ignacy, 1885–1939.

Pirandello, Luigi. **Non parlo di me**. Como: Ibis, 1994. – 86 p. *Notes*: Biography/Pirandello, Luigi.

Plazy, Gilles. **Eugène Ionesco: le rire et l'espérance: une biographie**. Paris: Julliard, 1994. – 299 p., 12 p.: ill. *Notes*: Includes bibliographical references (p. 285).

Plimpton, George. **Writers at work: the Paris review interviews, ninth series**. New York: Viking, 1992. – xx, 299 p.: ill. *Notes*: Includes Samuel Beckett, Harold Bloom, Mario Vargas Llosa, Tom Stoppard.

Prentice, Penelope. **The Pinter ethic: the erotic aesthetic**. New York: Garland, 1994. – lxxix, 396 p.: ill. *Notes*: Includes bibliographical references (p. 373–86) and indexes. Criticism and interpretation.

Quigley, Austin E. **The Pinter problem**. Princeton, N.J.: Princeton University, 1992. – xix, 294 p. *Notes*: Includes index. Bibliography: p. 279–91. Criticism and interpretation.

Ramer, Rudolf Ulrich. **Max Frisch Gesamtbibliografie**. Frankfurt: R.G. Fischer, 1993. – 155 p. *Notes*: Frisch, Max, 1911–. Bibliography.

Ranald, Margaret Loftus. **The Eugene O'Neill companion**. Westport, Conn.: Greenwood Press, 1984. – xi, 827 p.: port. *Notes*: Includes index. Bibliography: p. 765–89.

Read, John. **Athol Fugard: a bibliography**. Grahamstown: NELM, 1991.

Regal, Martin S. **Harold Pinter: a question of timing**. Basingstoke: Macmillan, 1995. – ix, 169 p. *Notes*: Includes bibliographical references (p. 161–4) and index. Criticism and interpretation.

Reinelt, Janelle G. **After Brecht: British epic theater**. 1st paperback edn. Ann Arbor: University of Michigan Press, 1996, 1994. – vi, 237 p.: ill. *Notes*: Includes bibliographical references (p. 211–31) and index. Socialism and theater. Political plays. History and criticism. Brecht, Bertolt, 1898–1956. Influence.

Ricard, Alain. **Theatre and nationalism: Wole Soyinka and LeRoi Jones/Alain Ricard;**

translated by Femi Osofisan. Ile-Ife, Nigeria: University of Ife Press, 1983. – 205 p. *Notes*: Bibliograhy: p. 188–98. Index. Translation of: Théâtre et nationalisme: Wole Soyinka et LeRoi Jones. History and criticism.

Riordan, Mary Marguerite. **Lillian Hellman, a bibliography, 1926–1978**. Metuchen, N.J.: Scarecrow Press, 1980. – xxiv, 210 p.: port. *Notes*: Includes index. Hellman, Lillian.

Rivera-Rodas, Oscar. **El metateatro y la dramática de Vargas Llosa: hacia una poética del espectador**. Amsterdam; Philadelphia: J. Benjamins Pub. Co., 1992. – vii, 213 p.: ill. *Series*: Purdue University monographs in Romance languages, 0165–8743; vol. 41. *Notes*: Includes bibliographical references (p. 209–13). Vargas Llosa, Mario, 1936–. Criticism and interpretation.

Roelcke, Thorsten. **Dramatische Kommunikation: Modell und Reflexion bei Dürrenmatt, Handke, Weiss**. Berlin; New York: W. de Gruyter, 1994. – xii, 312 p.: ill.

Roudané, Matthew Charles. **The Cambridge companion to Tennessee Williams**. New York: Cambridge University Press, 1997. *Notes*: Includes bibliographical references and index.

Roy, Ranendra Narayan. **Rabindranath Tagore the dramatist**. Calcutta: A. Mukherjee & Co., 1992. – xvi, 333 p. *Notes*: Bengali drama. History and criticism. Tagore, Rabindranath, 1861–1941. Criticism and interpretation.

Rykner, Arnaud. **Théâtres du nouveau roman: Sarraute, Pinget, Duras**. [Paris]: J. Corti, 1988. – 241 p. *Notes*: Includes bibliographical references. History and criticism. Sarraute, Nathalie. Pinget, Robert. Duras, Marguerite.

Salmon, Eric. **The dark journey: John Whiting as dramatist**. London: Barrie & Jenkins, 1979. – 326 p., 4 p. of plates: ill. *Notes*: Includes index. Bibliography: p. 318–20. Whiting, John, 1917–1963. Criticism and interpretation.

Sánchez, José A. **Brecht y el expresionismo: reconstrucción de un diálogo revolucionario**. [Cuenca, Spain?]: Servicio de Publicaciones de la Universidad de Castilla-La Mancha, 1992. – 205 p. *Notes*: Includes bibliographical references (p. 183–205). Expressionism. Brecht, Bertolt, 1898–1956. Political and social views. Aesthetics.

Savran, David. **Communists, cowboys, and queers: the politics of masculinity in the work of Arthur Miller and Tennessee Williams**. Minneapolis: University of Minnesota Press, 1992. – xi, 204 p.

Schings, Dietmar. **Über die Bedeutung der Rolle als Medium der Entpersonalisierung im**

Theater des XX. Jahrhunderts: Strindberg, Pirandello, Brecht, Ionesco. Munich: Schön, 1969. – 125 p. *Notes*: History and criticism.

Schrank, Bernice. **Sean O'Casey: a research and production sourcebook**. Westport, Conn: Greenwood Press, 1996. – viii, 298 p. *Notes*: Includes bibliographical references and indexes.

Schwarz, Alfred. **From Büchner to Beckett: dramatic theory and the modes of tragic drama**. Athens: Ohio University Press, 1978. – xxiv, 360 p. *Notes*: Includes bibliographical references and index. History and criticism.

Sciascia, Leonardo. **Pirandello dall' A alla Z**. Rome: Editoriale L'Espresso, 1986. – 50 p.: ill., ports. *Notes*: Pirandello, Luigi, 1867–1936.

Senda, Koreya. **Nijissseiki no engeki: Brecht to watakushi**. Tokyo: Yomiuri Shinbunsha, 1976. – 286 p., 4 p. of plates: ill. *Notes*: Brecht, Bertolt, 1898–1956. Stage history. Japan.

Shewey, Don. **Sam Shepard**. Updated edn., New York: Da Capo Press, 1997. – 269 p., 12 p. of plates: ill. *Notes*: Includes bibliographical references and index. Shepard, Sam, 1943–. Biography and criticism.

Sidoruk, Elzbieta. **Antropologia i groteska w dzielach Slawomir Mrozek**. Bialystok: Tow. Literackie im. Adama Mickiewicza, Oddz, 1995. – 116 p. *Notes*: Includes bibliographical references. Grotesque in literature/Mrozek, Slawomir. Criticism and interpretation.

Siebold, Thomas. **Readings on Arthur Miller**. San Diego, CA: Greenhaven Press, 1997. – 190 p. *Notes*: Includes bibliographical references (p. 182–3) and index. General introduction to the playwright – Major themes in Miller's plays – Death of a Salesman – The Crucible – Other works – All My Sons. Criticism and interpretation.

Simpson, Alan. **Beckett and Behan, and a theatre in Dublin**. London: Routledge & Kegan Paul, 1962. – xiv, 193 p. ills. *Notes*: Ireland/Behan, Brendan/Beckett, Samuel/Dublin. Pike Theatre.

Smith, Joseph H., ed. **The World of Samuel Beckett**. Baltimore: Johns Hopkins University Press, 1991. – xxiv, 226 p., 9 p. of plates: ill. *Series*: Psychiatry and the humanities; vol. 12. *Notes*: Includes bibliographical references and index. Quaquaquaqua: the babel of Beckett/Herbert Blau – Enough or too little?: voicings of desire and discontent in Beckett's 'Enough'/Mary F. Catanzaro – Seven types of postmodernity: several types of Samuel Beckett/Nicholas Zurbrugg – A cryptanalysis of Beckett's Molloy/Angela Moorjani – The whole story/Robert Winer – 'Tender mercies': subjectivity and subjection in Samuel Beckett's Not I/John H. Lutterbie – Post apocalypse without figures: the trauma of theatre in Samuel Beckett/Anthony Kubiak – Recovering the Néant: language and the unconscious in Beckett/Stephen Barker – The fragmented self, the reproduction of the self, and reproduction in Beckett and in the Theatre of the Absurd/Bennett Simon – Self-objectification and preservation in Beckett's Krapp's last tape/Jon Erickson – Notes on Krapp, Endgame, and 'applied' psychoanalysis/Joseph H. Smith – Telling it how it is: Beckett and the mass media/Martin Esslin. Psycho-analysis and literature.

Smith, Madeline and Richard Eaton. **Eugene O'Neill: an annotated bibliography**. New York: Garland, 1988. – 320 p. *Notes*: Includes indexes. O'Neill, Eugene, 1888–1953. Bibliography.

Song, Tong-jun. **Brecht ui sosaguk: yuhyong-hakchok koch'al**. Seoul: Taehakkyo Ch'ulp'anbu, 1993. – x, 321 p. *Notes*: Table of contents also in German with caption title. Includes bibliographical references. *Subjects*: Brecht, Bertolt, 1898–1956. Criticism and interpretation. Brecht in Korea (South).

Song, Yun-Yeop. **Bertolt Brecht und die chinesische Philosophie**. Bonn: Bouvier, 1978. – viii, 304 p. *Notes*: Originally presented as the author's thesis, Göttingen, 1977. Bibliography: p. 294–304. Philosophy, Chinese/ Brecht, Bertolt, 1898–1956.

Spencer, Jenny S. **Dramatic strategies in the plays of Edward Bond**. Cambridge and New York: Cambridge University Press, 1992. – xv, 270 p.: ill. *Notes*: Includes bibliographical references (p. 247–67) and index. Bond, Edward, 1934–. Criticism.

Spoto, Donald. **The kindness of strangers: the life of Tennessee Williams**. New York: Da Capo Press, 1997 1985. – xix, 409 p., 16 p. of plates: ill. *Notes*: Originally published: Boston: Little, Brown, 1985. Includes bibliographical references (p. 385–8) and index. Biography.

Steele, Thomas, David Stryker and Vernon Ruland. **Studies in drama**. New York: Random House, 1967. – 289 p. *Notes*: Drama. History and criticism.

Stephan, Halina. **Transcending the absurd: drama and prose of Slawomir Mrozek**. Amsterdam and Atlanta, GA: Rodopi, 1997. – 276 p. *Notes*: Includes bibliographical references and index. Mrozek, Slawomir. Criticism and interpretation.

Stoppard, Tom and Paul Delaney. **Tom Stoppard in conversation**. Ann Arbor: University of Michigan Press, 1994. – xix, 304 p.

Notes: Includes bibliographical references and index. Stoppard, Tom. Interviews.

Strelka, Joseph. **Brecht, Horváth, Dürren-matt; Wege und Abwege des modernen Dramas**. [Vienna]. Forum, 1962. – 175, 1 p. *Notes*: Bibliographical references included in 'Anmerkungen' (p. 167–76). German drama. 20th century. History and criticism.

Studeny, Doris. **Epische Verfahren bei Fernando Arrabal: Le jardin des délices und Et ils passèrent des menottes aux fleurs**. Frankfurt am Main; New York: P. Lang, 1990. – 226 p.: ill. *Notes*: Originally presented as the author's thesis (doctoral) – Ludwig-Maximillians-Universität München, 1989. Includes bibliographical references (p. 221–6). Arrabal, Fernando.

Sugiera, Malgorzata. **Dramaturgia Slawomira Mrozka**. [Dramaturgy of Slawomir Mrozek]. Craków: Universitas, 1997. – 294 p. *Notes*: Includes bibliographical references (p. 283) and index. Mrozek, Slawomir. Criticism and inter-pretation.

Suvin, Darko. **To Brecht and beyond: sound-ings in modern dramaturgy**. Brighton, Sussex: Totowa, N.J.: Harvester Press; Barnes & Noble, 1984. – xii, 283 p. *Notes*: Includes bibli-ographies and index. History and criticism.

Szydlowski, Roman. **Dramaturgia Bertolt Brecht**. Warsaw: Wydawnictwo Artyczne i Filmowe, 1965. – 338 p. *Notes*: Includes index. Bibliography: p. 320–6. Brecht, Bertolt, 1898–1956. Criticism and interpretation. Study by a leading Polish reviewer.

——. **Brecht w oczach krytyki swiatowej**. Warsaw: Panst. Instytut Wydawniczy. WZG, 1977. – 569, 3 p. *Series*: Wielcy pisarze w oczach krytyki swiatowej. *Notes*: Includes indexes. Bibliography: p. 546–7. *Subjects*: Brecht, Bertolt, 1898–1956. Criticism and interpreta-tion. Study by a leading Polish reviewer.

Tanner, James T. F. and Jerry Don Vann. **Samuel Beckett: a checklist of criticism**. Ohio: Kent State University Press, 1997, 1969. – vi, 85 p. *Notes*: Photocopy. Ann Arbor, MI: UMI, 1997. Beckett, Samuel. Bibliography.

Tantow, Lutz. **Friedrich Dürrenmatt: Moralist und Komödiant**. Munich: W. Heyne, 1992. – 272 p.: ill. *Notes*: Includes bibliographical refer-ences (p. 265–6) and index. Swiss dramatist. Dürrenmatt, Friedrich. Biography.

Tatlow, Antony. **The mask of evil: Brecht's response to the poetry, theatre and thought of China and Japan: a comparative and critical evaluation**. Bern; Las Vegas: P. Lang, 1977. – 629 p.: ill. *Notes*: Includes index. Bibliography: p. 561–575. Brecht, Bertolt. Japan and China.

Taylor, John Russell, comp. **John Osborne: Look back in anger: a casebook**. London: Macmillan, 1982, 1968. – 206 p. *Notes*: Reprint of the 1968 edn. Includes index. Bibliography: p. 197–200.

Thomas, Eberle. **Peter Shaffer: an annotated bibliography**. New York: Garland, 1991. – xxviii, 270 p. *Notes*: Includes index. Shaffer, Peter, 1926–. Bibliography.

Thompson, Edward John. **Rabindranath Tagore, Poet and Dramatist**. New edn. OUP (India), 1992. – 380 p. *Notes*: Biography.

Thomson, Peter and Glendyr Sacks. **The Cambridge companion to Brecht**. Cambridge [England]; New York, NY: Cambridge University Press, 1994. – xxxii, 302 p.: ill. *Notes*: Includes bibliographical references (p. 288–92) and index. Brecht, Bertolt, 1898–1956. Criticism and interpretation.

Tiusanen, Timo. **Dürrenmatt: a study in plays, prose, theory**. Princeton, N.J.: Princeton University Press, 1977. – xiii, 486 p., 4 p. of plates: ill. *Notes*: Includes index. Bibliography: p. 443–67. Dürrenmatt, Friedrich. Criticism and interpretation.

Topsfield, Valerie. **The humour of Samuel Beckett**. Basingstoke: Macmillan, 1988. – v, 160 p. *Notes*: Includes bibliography and index. Critical studies.

Tyce, Richard. **Edward Albee, a bibliography**. Metuchen, N.J.: Scarecrow Press, 1986. – viii, 212 p. *Notes*: Includes index. Albee, Edward, 1928–. Bibliography.

Valentini, Chiara. **La storia di Dario Fo**. Milan: Feltrinelli, 1997. – 205 p., 8 p. of plates: ill. *Notes*: First edn. 1977, now revised and enlarged. Contains bibliography and chronology. Dario Fo (1926–).

Vandenbroucke, Russell. **Truths the hand can touch: the theatre of Athol Fugard**. Johannesburg: Ad Donker, 1986.

Vasilinina, Irina. **Teatr Arbuzova**. Moscow: Iskusstvo, 1984. – 263 p. *Notes*: Includes bibliographical references. Arbuzov, Aleksei Nikolaevich. Criticism and interpretation.

Vinson, James and Daniel Lane Kirkpatrick. **Contemporary dramatists**. 2nd edn. with a preface by Ruby Cohn. London: St James Press, 1977. – xiv, 1088 p. *Notes*: Previous edn.: 1973. Includes bibliographies and index.

Volodin, Aleksandr. **Tak nespokoino na dushe: zapiski s otstupleniiami**. St Petersburg: Sankt-Peterburgskoe otd-nie, 1993. – 125 p. *Notes*: Dramatists, Russian. 20th century. Biography/ Volodin, Aleksandr.

—— and Ariadne Nicolaeff. **Five evenings**. Minneapolis: University of Minnesota Press in association with the Minnesota Theater Co, 1966. – 101 p., 21 cm. *Series*: Minnesota drama editions; no. 3.

Wade, Leslie A. **Sam Shepard and the American theater**. Westport, Conn.: Greenwood Press, 1997. – xii, 188 p. *Notes*: Includes bibliographical references (p. 173–9) and index. Criticism and interpretation.

Walder, Dennis. **Athol Fugard**. London: Macmillan, 1984. 142 p.

Watson, Ian. **Alan Ayckbourn: bibliography, biography, playography**. London: TQ Publications, 1980. – [24] p.: ill. *Subjects*: Ayckbourn, Alan, 1939–. Bibliography.

White, Alfred D. **Max Frisch, the reluctant modernist**. Lewiston: E. Mellen Press, 1995. – xviii, 428 p. *Notes*: Includes bibliographical references (p. 409–22) and index. Biography.

Wilcox, Leonard. **Rereading Shepard: contemporary critical essays on the plays of Sam Shepard**. Basingstoke: Macmillan, 1993. – xii, 229 p. *Notes*: Includes index. Shepard, Sam. United States.

Willett, John. **Brecht in context: comparative approaches**. London: Methuen, 1986 1984. – 272 p. *Notes*: Criticism and interpretation.

——. **The theatre of Bertolt Brecht: a study from eight aspects**. London: Methuen Drama, 1991 1977. – 240 p.: ill. *Notes*: Originally published: Eyre Methuen, 1977. Includes bibliographical references (p. 226–32) and index. Criticism and interpretation.

Williams, Tennessee. **Memoirs**. Garden City, N.Y.: Anchor Press/Doubleday, 1983, 1975. – xix, 264 p., 64 p. of plates: ill. *Notes*: Includes index.

——. **Where I live: selected essays**. New York: New Directions, 1978. – xv, 171 p. *Other Authors*: Day, Christine R., Woods, Bob. *Notes*: Introduction: personal lyricism/by Christine R. Day – Preface to my poems – 'Something wild' – On a streetcar named success – Questions without answers – A writer's quest for a Parnassus – The human psyche, alone – Introduction to Carson McCullers's Reflections in a golden eye – The timeless world of a play – The meaning of The rose tattoo – Facts about me – Foreword to Camino real – Afterword to Camino real – Critic says 'evasion,' writer says 'mystery' – Person-to-person – The past, present, and the perhaps – The world I live in – Author and director: a delicate situation – If the writing is honest – Foreword to Sweet bird of youth – Reflections on a revival of a controversial fantasy – Tennessee Williams presents his POV. (Cont'd) Prelude to a comedy – Five fiery ladies – Biography of Carson McCullers – A summer of discovery – T. Williams's view of T. Bankhead – Too personal? – Homage to Key West – The pleasures of the table – The misunderstandings and fears of an artist's revolt.

—— and Albert J. Devlin. **Conversations with Tennessee Williams**. Jackson: University Press of Mississippi, 1986. – xx, 369 p. *Notes*: Includes index. Interviews.

Winter, Scarlett Christiane. **Spielformen der Lebenswelt: zur Spiel- und Rollenmotivik im Theater von Sartre, Frisch, Dürrenmatt und Genet**. Munich: W. Fink, 1995. – 183 p.: 3 ill. *Notes*: Includes bibliographical references (p. 175–183). European drama. Criticism and interpretation.

Witkiewicz, Stanislaw Ignacy. **Introduzione alla teoria della forma pura nel teatro: e altri saggi di teoria e critica**. Rome: Bulzoni, 1988. – 172 p. *Other Authors*: Bigazzi, Francesco. Kozarzewska, Anna Maria. De Marco, Pietro. *Notes*: Originally published: Warsaw: Wydawnictwa Artystyczne i Filmowe, 1977. Includes bibliographical references. Translation of: **Czysta forma w teatrze**. History and criticism.

Wren, Robert M. **J.P. Clark**. Boston: Twayne, 1984. 181 p.

Wright, Derek. **Wole Soyinka: life, work, and criticism**. Fredericton: York Press, 1996. – 42 p. *Notes*: Includes bibliographical references (p. 31–9) and index. Chronological list of Soyinka's works: p. 10–13.

Yang, Peter. **Theater ist Theater: ein Vergleich der Kreidekreisstücke Bertolt Brechts und Li Xingdaos**. New York: P. Lang, 1998. *Series*: Studies in modern German literature; vol. 91. *Notes*: Includes bibliographical references and index. China. In literature/Brecht, Bertolt, 1898–1956. Li, Hsing-tao.

Zaiser, Rainer. **Themen und Techniken des Dramatikers Luigi Pirandello im französischen Theater der fünfziger und sechziger Jahre: ein Vergleich mit ausgewählten Stücken von Jean Anouilh, Eugène Ionesco, Jean Genet und Samuel Beckett**. Frankfurt am Main; New York: P. Lang, 1988. – 473 p. *Notes*: Bibliography: p. 450–73. 20th century. History and criticism.

Zakowski, Jacek. **Co dalej panie Mrozek?** Warsaw: Iskry, 1996. – 114 p.: ill. *Notes*: Mrozek, Slawomir. Biography.

Zeineddine, Nada. **Because it is my name: problems of identity experienced by women,** artists, and breadwinners in the plays of Henrik Ibsen, Tennessee Williams, and Arthur Miller. Braunton, Devon: Merlin Books, 1991. – 231 p. *Notes*: Includes bibliographical references (p. 222–31). *Subjects*: American drama. 20th century. History and criticism/Characters and characteristics in literature/Identity (Psychology) in literature/Williams, Ibsen and Miller.

Zuber-Skerritt, Otrun. **David Williamson**. Australian Playwrights Monograph Series. Amsterdam: Rodopi, 1988.

J. Costume, Set/Scenography and Lighting Design

J1. General Studies

Adix, Vern. **Theatre scenecraft: for the backstage technician and artist**. Rev. edn. New Orleans, La.: Anchorage Press, 1981. – xx, 309 p.: ill. *Notes*: Includes index. Bibliography: p. 287–90.

Bataille, André. **Lexique de la machinerie théâtrale: à l'intention des praticiens et amateurs**. Paris: Libr. Théâtrale, 1989. – 115 p.: ill. *Notes*: Stage setting and scenery. Terminology.

Carnaby, Ann J. **A guidebook for creating three-dimensional theatre art**. Portsmouth, NH: Heinemann, 1997. – ix, 190 p.: ill. *Notes*: Includes bibliographical references (p. 185) and index. Stage props. Design and construction. Costume.

Cook, Judith. **Backstage: who does what in the theatre**. London: Harrap, 1987. – 141 p.: ill. *Notes*: Backstage. Technical aspects.

Corey, Irene. **The mask of reality; an approach to design for theatre**. Anchorage: Ky.: Anchorage Press, 1968. – 124 p. illus. (part col.). *Notes*: Bibliography: p. 113. Stage-setting and scenery/Theatrical makeup/Costume.

Dorn, Dennis and Mark Shanda. **Drafting for the theatre**. Carbondale: Southern Illinois University Press, 1992. – xiii, 262 p.: ill. *Notes*: Includes index. Mechanical drawing.

Frenkel, Mykhailo. **Suchasna stsenohrafiia**. [Contemporary scenography]. Kiev: Mystetstvo, 1980. 132 p.

Gassner, John and Philip Willson Barber. **Producing the play**. Rev. edn. New York: Holt, 1967. – 915 p. illus. *Notes*: Production and direction. Stage-setting and scenery. A standard in 'how-to' books.

Govier, Jacquie. **Create your own stage props**. London: Black, 1988 1984. – 192 p.: ill. *Notes*: Includes index. Bibliography: p. 189. Making stage properties.

Hainaux, René *et al*. **Le Lieu théâtral, sa construction et son équipement, le décor et le costume; guide bibliographique**. [The physical theatre, buildings and equipment, stage design and costume; bibliographical guide.] Liège: Bruxelles: Information-arts de diffusion, Université de Liège; INSAS, 1976. – xii, 177 p. *Notes*: Performing arts international bibliography. 'Sponsored by the International Theatre Institute and the International Society for Performing Arts Libraries and Museums'. Includes index. A selection of books in German, English, French, Italian and Russian. Construction. Stage-setting and scenery. Costume. Bibliography.

Herbert, Jocelyn and Cathy Courtney. **Jocelyn Herbert: a theatre workbook**. London: Art Books International, 1993. – 240 p.: ill. (some col.). *Notes*: 'This book is a record of the work of Jocelyn Herbert ... This Workbook tries to re-create a little of the chemistry that ... flows between director, designer and writer throughout the process of bringing a play to the stage ... .' – Preface. Includes index. Introduction/by Jocelyn Herbert–The Royal Court and The English Stage Company – The Royal National Theatre – Other Theatres – Opera – Contributions from colleagues – Cast lists.

Holt, Michael. **Stage design and properties**. Rev. edn. London: Phaidon, 1993. – 128 p.: ill. *Notes*: Includes bibliographical references (p. 125) and index. Stage-setting and scenery/Stage props/Set designers.

Izenour, George C. **Theater Design**. New York: McGraw-Hill, 1977. 631 p.

James, Thurston. **The theater props handbook: a comprehensive guide to theater properties, materials, and construction**. White Hall, Va.: Betterway Publications, 1987. – xvi, 272 p.: ill. *Notes*: Includes index. Design and construction.

Javier, Francisco. **Notas para la historia científica de la puesta en escena**. [Notes on the scientific history of theatre production]. Buenos Aires: Editorial Leviatán, 1985. 121 p.

Karvăs, Peter and Ladislav Laicha. **Súčasná slovenská scénografia**. [Contemporary Slovak stage design]. Bratislava: Pallas, 1977. 244 p.

Kenton, Warren. **Stage properties and how to make them**. 2nd edn. London: Pitman; New York: Drama Book Specialists, 1978. – viii, 151 p.: ill. *Notes*: Stage properties. Manuals.

Lee, Briant Hamor, Daryl M. Wedwick and

William-Alan Landes. **Corrugated cardboard scenery: environmentally acceptable, biodegradable, recyclable, economical: a cost effective solution for the theatre of the 1990's and beyond–**. 2nd edn., rev. Studio City, CA: Players Press Inc., 1993. – xiii, 159 p.: ill. *Notes*: Includes bibliographical references (p. 157–8) and index.

Lee James, Thurston. **The theater props handbook: a comprehensive guide to theater properties, materials, and construction**. White Hall, Va.: Betterway Publications, 1987. – xvi, 272 p.: ill. *Notes*: Includes index. Design and construction.

Lounsbury, Warren C. **Theatre backstage from A to Z; a glossary of technical stage terms**. Rev. edn., Illustrated by Alanson Davis. Seattle: Distributed by University of Washington Press, 1968. – 131 p. ills. *Notes*: Dictionary.

Mikotowicz, Thomas J., ed. **Theatrical designers: an international biographical dictionary**. Westport, CT: Greenwood Press, 1992. 365 p.

Milanović, Olga. **Beogradska scenografija i kostimografija 1868–1941**. [Belgrade stage and costume design 1868–1941]. Belgrade: Muzej pozorišne umetnosti SR Srbije and Univerzitet umetnosti, 1983. 396 p.

Ptáčková, Věra. **Česká scénografie 20. stoletî**. [Czech theatre design in the twentieth century]. Prague: Odeon, 1982. 365 p.

Reinking, Wilhelm. **Spiel und Form: Werkstattberichte. Bühnenbildner zum Gestaltwandel d. Szene in d. zwanziger u. dreissiger Jahren**. [Play and form: designers and the transformation of stage design in the 1920s and 1930s]. Hamburg: Christians, 1979. 326 p.

Rosenfeld, Sybil. **A short history of scene design in Great Britain**. London: Basil Blackwell, 1973.

Scenografia in Italia oggi. [Italian stage design today]. Foreword by Roberto Rebora. Milan: Gorlich, 1974.

J2. Costume

Anderson, Barbara Benz and Cletus Anderson. **Costume design**. New York: Holt, Rinehart & Winston, 1984. – viii, 401 p.: ill. (some col.). *Notes*: Includes index. Bibliography: p. 374–90.

Barton, Lucy. **Historic costume for the stage**. Boston, MA: W.H. Baker, 1961.

Blaho, Jaroslav, Ivan Lacika and Vlasta Vaculová. **Mladá slovenská scénografia, kostýmová a bábkárska tvorba**. Bratislava:

Národné divadelné centrum, 1991. – 47 p.: ill. *Notes*: Preface in Slovak and English. Puppet costumes. Slovakia.

Boari, Annie and Bonizza Giordani-Aragno. **1950/60: palcoscenico e moda**. Rome: Il Ventaglio, 1987 1985. – 141 p.: ill. (some col.). *Notes*: Includes index. Costume. History. In Italian.

Bogel, József and Lajos Jánosa, eds. **Scenographia Hungarica: Mai magyar díszlet és jelmez**. [Contemporary stage and costume design in Hungary]. Budapest: Corvina Kiadó, 1973. – 43 p., 48 p. of plates: ill. (some col.). *Notes*: Hungarian, English, and French. Stage-setting and costume. Hungary.

Brandt, Klaus J. **No: Gewänder und Masken des japanischen Theaters**. Tokyo: Stuttgart: Japan Foundation; Linden-Museum, 1993. – 165 p.: ill. *Notes*: Catalogue d'exposition. Bibliography. p. 165. Costume. Mask.

Brayer, Yves. **Yves Brayer: décorateur de théâtre**. Luisant, France: Éditions Archimbaud, 1986. – 62 p.: ill. (some col.). *Notes*: Parallel text in French and English. Includes bibliographical references (p. 62). Set and costume design. France. Brayer, Yves, 1907–.

Brooke, Iris. **Medieval theatre costume: a practical guide to the construction of garments**. London: Adam & Charles Black, 1969, 1967. – 112 p.: ill. *Notes*: Reprint. Originally published: London: Adam & Charles Black, 1967. Includes index. Costume.

Castle, Charles. **Oliver Messel: a biography**. New York, N.Y.: Thames & Hudson, 1986. – 264 p.: ill. (some col.). *Notes*: Includes index. Set designers. Great Britain. Biography/Messel, Oliver, 1904–78.

Costume Society. **Costume for the theatre, ballet, opera, film, television**. [S.l.]: The Costume Society, 1991. – [5] p. *Notes*: Costume bibliography.

Cunningham, Rebecca. **The magic garment: principles of costume design**. Prospect Heights, Ill.: Waveland Press, 1994, 1989. – xiv, 395 p., [8] p. of plates: ill. (some col.). *Notes*: Bibliography: p. 369–77.

Dryden, Deborah M. **Fabric painting and dyeing for the theatre**. Portsmouth, NH: Heinemann, 1993. – xiv, 256 p., 8 p. of plates: ill. (some col.). *Notes*: Includes bibliographical references (p. 239–40) and index.

Erté. **Erte's theatrical costumes: in full color**. New York; London: Dover; Constable, 1979. – 49 p.: of col. ill.

Esrig, David, Evelin Kohl, Hans-Jürgen Frintrop and Olympia Esrig. **Commedia dell'arte: eine Bildgeschichte der Kunst des Spektakels**. Nördlingen: Delphi, 1985. – 255 p.: ill. (some col.). *Notes*: Bibliography: p. 254–5. Commedia dell'arte.

Exter, Alexandra. **Artist of the theatre–Alexandra Exter: four essays, with an illustrated check list of scenic and costume designs exhibited at the Vincent Astor Gallery, the New York Public Library at Lincoln Center (spring-summer 1974)**. New York: New York Public Library, 1974. – 40 p.: ill. *Notes*: Bibliography: p. 40. Exter, Alexandra.

Fotopoulos, Dionysis. **Costume design in the Greek theatre**. Athens: Commercial Bank, 1986.

Gontard, Denis. **Nô-kyôgen: le masque et le rire [mask and laughter]**. Marburg: Hitzeroth, 1987. – 88 p.: ill. (some col.). *Notes*: French, English, German. Cover title also in Japanese. Noh. Kyogen. Japan. Costume. Masks.

Govier, Jacquie and Gillian Davies. **Create your own stage costumes**. London: A & C Black, 1996. – 160 p.: ill. *Notes*: Includes index. Costume. Design.

Green, Ruth M. **The wearing of costume: the changing techniques of wearing clothes and how to move in them, from Roman Britain to the Second World War**. London: Pitman, 1969, 1966. – ix, 171 p.: ill. *Notes*: Costume. History.

Hardy, Dot. **Costumes and masks**. Leeds: E.J. Arnold, 1988. – 127 p.: ill. *Notes*: Children's theatre costumes. Design and making.

Holkeboer, Katherine Strand. **Patterns for theatrical costumes: garments, trims, and accessories from ancient Egypt to 1915**. Englewood Cliffs, N.J.: Prentice-Hall, 1984. – viii, 342 p.: ill. *Notes*: Includes index. Bibliography: p. 339–40. Costumes. Design and making.

Holt, Michael. **Costume and make-up**. Rev. edn. London: Phaidon, 1993. – 136 p.: ill. (some col.). *Notes*: Includes bibliographical references (p. 133) and index.

Hunnisett, Jean. **Period costume for stage and screen. Patterns for women's dress, 1500–1800**. London: Bell & Hyman, 1986. – 176 p.: ill. *Notes*: Bibliography: p. 175. Dressmaking. Patterns, 1500–1800.

Ingham, Rosemary and Liz Covey. **The costume designer's handbook: a complete guide for amateur and professional costume designers**. Englewood Cliffs, N.J.: Prentice-Hall, 1983. – 264 p.: ill. *Notes*: Includes index. Bibliography: p. 213–25.

Jackson, Sheila. **Costumes for the stage: a complete handbook for every kind of play**. London: Herbert, 1988 1978. – 144 p.: ill. *Notes*: Includes bibliography and index.

——. **More costumes for the stage**. London: Herbert Press, 1993. – 144 p.: ill. *Notes*: Includes index. Bibliography: p. 141–2. Design.

Kirihata, Ken, Masafumi Sugai, Iwao Nagasaki and Sadao Hibi. **Kabuki isho**. [Kabuki costumes]. Tokyo: Kodansha, 1993. – 299, [1] p.: ill. *Notes*: Includes bibliographical references. Costume. Japan.

Kondo, Dorinne K. **About face: performing race in fashion and theatre**. New York: Routledge, 1997. – xiii, 277 p.: ill. *Notes*: Includes bibliographical references (p. 261–70) and index. Asian-Americans. Ethnic identity and fashion.

Król-Kaczorowska, Barbara. **Teatr dawnej polski: budynki, dekoracje, kostiumy**. Warsaw: Panstwowy Instytut Wydawniczy, 1971. – 270 p.: illus. Costume. Poland.

Kundu, Ananga Mohana. **Natakera besabhusha**. Calcutta: Ka. Ra, 1992. – 6, 109, ii p.: ill. *Notes*: In Bengali. Includes bibliographical references (p. i-ii). Stage costume and accessories for the Indian theatre.

Laver, James. **Costume in the theatre**. New York: Hill & Wang, 1967, 1964. – xi, 212 p.: ill. *Notes*: Includes index. Bibliography: p. 200–4. Costume history.

Lukes, Milan. **Costumes de théâtre**. Prague: Artis, 1962. – viii, 183 p. 326 fig.

Marshall-Martin, David. **Ecclesiastical dress and vestments of the Roman Catholic Church from the eleventh century to the present: a handbook of patterns, construction and vesting procedures for use in the theatre**. 1983, 1980. – ix, 247 p., 48 p. of plates: ill. *Notes*: Bibliography: p. 237–42. Thesis (Ph. D.)– Florida State University, 1980. Photocopy. Ann Arbor, Mich.: University Microfilms International, 1983. Costume design. Catholic church.

Milanovic, Olga. **Beogradska scenografija i kostimografija 1868–1941**. Belgrade: Muzej pozorisne umetnosti SR Srbije: Univerzitet umetnosti u Beogradu, 1983. – 396 p., [48] p. of plates: ill. *Notes*: In Serbo-Croatian (Roman). Bibliography: p. 386–93. Costume and scenography. Yugoslavia. Belgrade (Serbia).

Mullin, Michael. **Designing and making stage costumes**. Rev. edn, edited and introduced by Michael Mullin. London: Herbert Press, 1992. – 140 p.: ill. *Notes*: Previous edn.: London: Studio Vista, 1964.

Owen, Bobbi. **Costume design on Broadway: designers and their credits, 1915–1985**. New York: London: Greenwood, 1987. – 368 p.: ill. *Notes*: Includes index. Broadway. Theatre. Costumes. 1915–85. Biographies.

Photopoulos, Dionyses. **Costume design in the Greek theatre**. Athens: Published by the Commercial Bank of Greece, 1986. – 324 p.: chiefly ill. *Notes*: Translation of: **Endymatologia sto Helleniko theatro**. Costume design. Greece.

Prisk, Berneice and Jack A. Byers. **Costuming**. Rev. edn. New York: Richards Rosen Press, 1970. – 108 p.: ill. *Notes*: Bibliography: p. 107–8. Explains the primary steps in costume design, planning, and construction.

Rickards, Jocelyn. **The painted banquet: my life and loves**. London: Weidenfeld & Nicolson, 1987. – viii, 172 p.: ill. *Notes*: Includes index. Costume designers. England. Biography. Rickards, Jocelyn.

Saint Laurent, Yves. **Yves Saint Laurent et le théâtre**. [Paris]: Herscher: Musée des arts décoratifs, 1986. – 130 p.: ill. (some col.). *Notes*: 'Publié à l'occasion de l'exposition … qui se tiendra au Musée des Arts Décoratifs du 25 juin au 7 septembre 1986'. Costume design. Exhibitions.

Shaver, Ruth M. **Kabuki costume**. London: Simon & Schuster, 1991. – 396 p.: ill. *Notes*: Includes bibliography and index. Japan.

Simpson, Jeannette. **Theatrical costume**. Wayland, 1988. – 32 p.

Smith, C. Ray, comp. **The theatre crafts book of costumes**. Emmaus: Pa.: Rodale Press, 1973. – 224 p. illus. *Notes*: 'Theatre crafts books'. Aldredge, T.V. Costumes and the budget.–Potts, N. Costumes for a repertory theatre.–Brady, J.E. Designing for regional theatre.–Slaiman, M. Managing a regional theatre costume shop.– Van Witsen, L. Feathers for bird costumes are for the birds.–Weldy, M. Costumes for the circus.–MacKay, P.J. Dressing up for children's plays.–MacKay, P.J. Man in space: from Bauhaus to moonwalk.–Nikolais, A. Environments for the human figure.–MacKay, P.J. Plastics in costumes.–Matheson, B.B. Polyurethane trolls for 'Peer Gynt.'–Roberts, W.D. The contemporaneity of 'Love for love.'– Wilhelm, K. Stocky bourgeoisie in 'The miser.'–Campbell, P. The true vintage of 'La Traviata.'–Greenwood, J. American primitives for 'More stately mansions.'–Harvey, P. Busby Berkeley on a budget.–Somner, P. Modern dress is no accident.–MacKay, P.J. Covering (and uncovering) in environmental theatre.– Campbell, P. Stylized rustics in 'Man of La

Mancha.'–Voelpel, F. Antediluvian handcrafts for 'Two by two.'–Russell, D.A. Primeval crystals for 'Prometheus bound.'–Loney, G.M. Florence Klotz's recollections for 'Follies.'

Tompkins, Julia. **Stage costumes and how to make them**. London: Pitman, 1978, 1969. – xvi, 160 p.: ill. *Notes*: Originally published: 1969. Includes index. Bibliography: p. 158.

Walkup, Fairfax Proudfit. **Dressing the part: a history of costume for the theatre**. Rev. edn. New York: Appleton-Century Crofts, 1966. – x, 423 p. illus. *Notes*: Bibliography: p. 399–409. Costume. History.

Weir, Shelagh. **Palestinian costume**. London: British Museum, 1989.

Wilcox, R. Turner. The dictionary of costume. New York: Scribner, 1969.

J3. Set Design, Scenography, Studies of Specific Designers

Appia, Adolphe. **Attore, musica e scena**. Milan: Feltrinelli, 1975. – 252 p., 16 p. of plates: ill. *Notes*: Translation of: **La mise en scène du drame wagnérien**/translated by Delia Gambelli; **La musique et la mise en scène**/translated by Delia Gambelli; **L'oeuvre d'art vivant**/translated by Marco De Marinis. Bibliography: p. 237–50. Stage-setting and scenery. Dramaturgy/Wagner, Richard, 1813–83.

Aronson, Arnold. **American set design**. New York: Theatre Communications Group, 1985. 182 p.

——. **The history and theory of environmental scenography**. Ann Arbor, Mich.: U-M-I Out-of-Print Books on Demand, 1992, 1981. – xiv, 282 p.: ill. *Notes*: Originally published: Ann Arbor, Mich.: UMI Research Press, c.1981. Includes index. Bibliography: p. 267–76. Revision of thesis (Ph. D.)–New York University, 1977.

Artists of the theatre. Moscow: Soviet Khudozh, 1970. – 272 p.: ill. *Notes*: Soviet design. USSR.

Atkinson, Patrick. **Theatrical design in the twentieth century: an index to photographic reproductions of scenic designs**. Westport, Conn.: Greenwood Press, 1996. – x, 475 p. *Notes*: Includes bibliographical references. Indexes. Stage design.

Bablet, Denis. **The theatre of Edward Gordon Craig**. London: Eyre Methuen, 1981, 1966. – 207 p., 24 p. of plates: ill. *Notes*: Originally published: London: Heinemann, 1966. Includes index. Translation of Bablet's original in French. Design.

——, Erika Billeter and Christiane Bauermeister. **Die Maler und das Theater im 20. Jahrhundert: Schirn Kunsthalle Frankfurt, Ausstellung vom 1. März bis 19. Mai 1986**. [Frankfurt]: Die Kunsthalle, 1986. – 577 p.: ill. (some col.). *Notes*: Bibliography: p. 575–7. Scene painting. Stage-setting and scenery. Costume. History. 20th century. Exhibitions.

Bablet-Hahn, Marie-Louise, ed. **Adolphe Appia: Oeuvres complètes**. [Works. 1983]. [Lausanne?]: L'Age d'homme, 1983. – v.: ill. *Notes*: Includes bibliographies. 1. 1880–94.–2. 1895–1905. Stage design.

Baer, Nancy Van Norman and John E. Bowlt. **Theatre in revolution: Russian avant-garde stage design, 1913–1935**. New York: San Francisco: Thames & Hudson; Fine Arts Museums of San Francisco, 1991. – 207 p.: ill. (some col.). *Notes*: Constructivism. Soviet Union.

Ballagh, Robert. **Robert Ballagh on stage: theatre set design by Robert Ballagh**. Dublin: Project Arts Centre, 1990. – 65 p., 1 fold. plate: ill. (some col.). *Notes*: Set designers. Ireland/ Ballagh, Robert, 1943–.

Banu, Georges. **Yannis Kokkos: le scénographe et le héron**. Arles: Actes Sud; Diffusion PUF, 1989. – 211 p.: ill. *Notes*: Stage-setting and scenery/Kokkos, Yannis.

—— and Mark Blezinger. **Klaus Michael Grüber: – il faut que le théâtre passe à travers les larmes–**. Paris: Ed. du Regard, Académie expérimentale de théâtre, Festival d'automne, 1993. – 238 p.: ill. *Notes*: Includes bibliographical references. Stage-setting and scenery. Biography. Grüber, Klaus Michael.

Bassekhes, Alfred and Militsa Nikolaevna, Pozharskaia. **Khudozhniki na stsene MKHAT**. Moscow: Vserossiiskoe teatral'noe obshchestvo, 1960. – 138 p.: ill. *Notes*: Includes bibliographical references. Stage-setting and scenery. Moscow Art Theatre.

Battistini, Fabio and Caterina, Pirina. **Gli Spazi dell'incanto: bozzetti e figurini del Piccolo teatro, 1947–1987**. [Italy]: Silvana, 1987. – 221 p.: col. ill. *Notes*: Includes bibliographical references. History. Stage-setting and scenery. Piccolo Teatro of Milan (Italy).

Bay, Howard. **Stage design**. London: Pitman, 1975 1974. – 219 p.: ill., plans. *Notes*: Originally published: New York: Drama Book Specialists, 1974. Design.

Bazaine, Jean. **Bazaine et le théâtre: maquettes de décors et de costumes, 1936–1981**. Bourges: Maison de la culture: Scène nationale, 1992. – 120 p.: ill. (some col.). *Notes*: Catalogue of an exhibition held at the Maison de la culture de Bourges, Dec. 18, 1992–Jan. 18, 1993. Includes bibliographical references. Stage-setting, scenery, costume. Bazaine, France. Jean.

Beacham, Richard C. **Adolphe Appia, theatre artist**. Cambridge and New York: Cambridge University Press, 1987. – xiii, 190 p.: ill. *Series*: Directors in perspective. *Notes*: Includes index. Bibliography: p. 185–6. Criticism and interpretation.

——. **Adolphe Appia: artist and visionary of the modern theatre**. Chur, Switzerland; Philadelphia, Pa.: Harwood Academic Publishers, 1994. – xv, 307 p.: ill. *Notes*: Rev. edn. of: **Adolphe Appia, theatre artist**. 1987. Theatrical chronology: p. 299–301. Includes bibliographical references (p. 297–8) and index. Criticism and interpretation.

Behl, Dennis L. **Tanya Moiseiwitsch: her contribution to theatre arts from 1935–1980**. 1984, 1981. – x, 391 p.: ill. *Notes*: Bibliography: p. 379–91. Thesis (Ph. D.)–Kent State University, 1981. Photocopy. Ann Arbor, Mich.: University Microfilms International, 1984. Stage-setting and scenery. Costume. History/Moiseiwitsch, Tanya.

Bellman, Willard F. **Scenography and stage technology: an introduction**. New York: Crowell, 1977. – xiv, 625 p.: ill. *Notes*: Rev. edn. published as: **Scene design, stage lighting, sound, costume and makeup**. c1983. Includes index. Bibliography: p. 610–612.

Berezkin, Viktor Iosifovich. **Sovetskaia literatura po stsenografii (1917–1983)**. [Soviet literature on scenography (1917–1983]. Moscow; Prague: Ministerstvo Kul'tury SSSR, 1983. – 96 p. *Notes*: Text in Russian, 'Compiler's Notes', marginal notes and contents also in English. At head of title: Ministry of Culture of the USSR. Soviet centre of the international organization of scenographers and theatre technicians (OISTT). Includes bibliographical references (p. 80–94). Soviet Union. Stage setting and scenery.

Berger, Genia. **Genia Berger, 'avodot late'atron**. Tel-Aviv: Shapir 'al shem A.D. Shapir, 1994. – 1 v. (unpaged): ill. (some col). *Notes*: Works for the theatre. Text in Hebrew and English. Set designers. Costume designers. Israel.

Bibliothèque nationale (France). **André Barsacq: cinquante ans de théâtre**. Paris: Bibliothèque Nationale, 1978. – xxviii, 179 p.,: 4 p. of plates: ill. (some col.). *Notes*: Includes bibliographical references. Stage-setting and scenery/Barsacq, André. France.

Bílková, Marie and Jan Sramek. **Prague quadrennial of theatre design and architecture, 1995: Industry Palace, Výstaviste Praha 26.6–16.7.1995**. 1st edn. Prague: Czech Theatre Institute, 1995. – 229 p.: ill.; 20 x. *Notes*: Commissioned by the Ministry of Culture of the Czech Republic. Stage-setting and scenery including International designers biography. Also costume design.

Bogel, József and Lajos Jánosa. **Scenographia Hungarica: Mai magyar díszlet és jelmez**. [Contemporary stage and costume design in Hungary]. Budapest: Corvina, 1973. – 43 p. 131 plates. *Notes*: Hungary.

Bogomolova, Marina Timofeevna. **Dekoratsionnye materialy – khudozhnikam teatra: o predmetnoi osnove, sluzhashchei khudozhniku dlia raskrytiia idei dramaturgicheskogo i muzykal'nogo proizvedeniia**. Moscow: Soiuz teatral'nykh deiatelei RSFSR, 1988. – 117 p., 48 p. of plates: ill. *Notes*: Bibliography: p. 116–17. Stage-setting and scenery. USSR.

Burian, Jarka. **The scenography of Josef Svoboda**. Middletown, Conn.,: Wesleyan University Press, 1983, 1971. – xxii, 198 [4] p.: ill. *Notes*: 'First paperback edition, 1974; third printing, 1983'. 'A register of Svoboda productions': p. 172–98. Bibliography: p. 201–2. Svoboda, Josef, 1920–. Czech.

Carrick, Edward. **Gordon Craig: the story of his life**. 1st Limelight edn. New York: Limelight Editions, 1985, 1968. – 398 p.: ill. *Notes*: Originally published: 1st American edn. New York: Knopf, 1968. Includes index. Bibliography: p. 385–6. Biography/Craig, Edward Gordon, 1872–1966.

Cave, Richard Allen. **Charles Ricketts' stage designs**. Cambridge: Chadwyck-Healey in association with the Consortium for Drama and Media in Higher Education, 1987. – 102 p. *Notes*: Bibliography: p. 101–2. Stage-setting and scenery. Ricketts, Charles S., 1866–1931.

Chmura, Lubomír. **Prazské quadriennale jevistního výtvarnictví a divadelní architektury, 1991: Palác kultury, Praha**. [Prague Quadrennial of Theatre Design and Architecture, 1991]. Prague: s.n., 1992. – 242 p. *Notes*: Czech, English, and French. Includes biographical sketches of artists. Stage-setting and scenery. Costume.

Cogniat, Raymond. **Cinquante ans de spectacles en France. Les décorateurs de théâtre**. Paris: Librairie théâtrale, 1955. – 222 p., plates. *Notes*: Stage-setting and scenery. France.

Cooper, Douglas. **Picasso theatre**. New York: H.N. Abrams, 1968. – 360 p. ill. (part col.).

Notes: Includes facsims. of MS. letters, etc. of Picasso, É. Satie, and J. Cocteau. Bibliography: p. 359–60. Stage-setting and scenery. Picasso, Pablo, 1881–1973.

Craig, Edward Gordon. **Craig on theatre**. London: Methuen Drama, 1991, 1983. – 192 p.: ill. *Notes*: Ed. by J. Michael Walton. Reprint. Originally published: London: Methuen, 1983. Includes bibliographical references (p. 188–90). Craig, Edward Gordon, 1872–1966. Views on theatre.

Cruciani, Fabrizio and Luca, Ruzza. **Lo spazio del teatro**. Bari: Laterza, 1992. – 219 p.: ill. *Notes*: Includes bibliographical references. Stage-setting and scenery.

Czechoslovak scenography. Prague: Divadelní ústav Praha, 1969. – 17, 10 p.: ill. *Notes*: 'Edited by Theatre Institute Prague for the exhibition of Czechoslovak Scenography'. Czechoslovakia.

DeShong, Andrew. **The theatrical designs of George Grosz**. Ann Arbor, Mich.: UMI Research Press, 1982. – xiv, 182 p.: ill. *Notes*: Revision of thesis (Ph. D.)–Yale University, 1970. *Notes*: Includes index. Bibliography: p. [173]–7. Germany.

Dieckmann, Friedrich, ed. **Bühnenbildner der Deutschen Demokratischen Republik. Arbeiten aus den Jahren 1971 bis 1977**. [Stage designers of the German Democratic Republic: designs from 1971 to 1977]. Berlin: Sektion DDR der OISTAT, 1978. 120 p.

Dinova-Russeva, Vera. **Bulgarian Set Design**. Bulgarian Artistic Publishing House, 1975.

Fletcher, Ifan Kyrle and Arnold Rood. **Edward Gordon Craig: a bibliography**. London: Society for Theatre Research, 1967. – 117 p. plate.

Fotopoulos, Dionysis. **Stage design in the Greek theatre**. Athens: Commercial Bank, 1987.

Frette, Guido. **Stage design**. Milan: G.G. Görlich, 1955. – xl p., 182 p. of illus. *Notes*: Microfilm (positive). Original in Library of Congress. Stage-setting and scenery. Italy.

Den Freunden zur Erhaltung des künstlerischen Nachlasses von Fritz Wotruba, eds. **Fritz Wotruba: der Bildhauer als Bühnenbildner**. [Fritz Wotruba: the sculptor as stage designer]. Bremen: Gerhard-Marcks-Stiftung, 1992.

Friedman, Martin L. **Hockney paints the stage**. London: Thames & Hudson, 1983. – 227 p.: ill. (some col.). *Notes*: Includes index. Ill. on lining papers. Bibliography: p. 212–14. Stage-setting and scenery/Hockney, David/Theatre. Sets.

Frycz, Karol. **O teatrze i sztuce**. Warsaw: Wydawn, Artystyczne i Filmowe, 1967. – 298 p.

Woycicki, Alfred, ed. *Notes*: Includes bibliography. Stage-setting and scenery. Poland.

Gall, Iwo. **Mój teatr**. Kraków: Wydawn. Literackie, 1963. – 246 p.: ill. *Notes*: Stage-setting and scenery/Osterwa, Juliusz, 1885–1947. Poland.

Gillette, Arnold S. and J. Michael Gillette. **Stage scenery, its construction and rigging**. New York: Harper & Row, 1981. – xv, 448 p.: ill. *Notes*: Includes index. Bibliography: p. 440–1. Scenery. Construction.

Gillette, J. Michael. **Theatrical design and production: an introduction to scene design and construction, lighting, sound, costume, and makeup**. 3rd edn. Mountain View, Calif.: Mayfield Pub. Co., 1997. – xv, 573 p.: ill. (some col.). *Notes*: Includes bibliographical references (p. 565–6) and index.

Goodwin, John, ed. **British theatre design: the modern age**. London: Weidenfeld & Nicolson, 1995, 1989. – 208 p.: ill. (some col.). *Notes*: Foreword/Peter Hall – The years before/Roy Strong – Plays/Michael Ratcliffe – Opera/John Higgins – 'The great British musical'/Trevor Nunn – Dance/Mary Clarke and Clement Crisp – The painter as designer/Bryan Robertson – Using the space/Pamela Howard – Time future/Timothy O'Brien. Stage-setting and scenery. History. Great Britain.

Gorelik, Mordecai. **New theatres for old**. New York: Dutton, 1962. – 553 p. illus. *Notes*: Includes bibliography. Stage-setting and scenery.

Greisenegger, Wolfgang. **Österreich. Bühnenbildner der Gegenwart: Ausstellung im Tiroler Kunstpavillon in Innsbruck**. [Contemporary Austrian stage designers: exhibition at the Tiroler Kuntspavillon in Innsbruck]. Exhibition catalogue. Innsbruck: 1968.

Grodzicki, August. **Teatr narodów**. Warsaw: [Agencja Autorska-Biuro Teatru narodów], 1975. – 143 p.: ill. *Notes*: Stage-setting and scenery. Theatre. History. 20th century.

Gronius, Jörg Werner and Franz Wille. **Willi Schmidt: das Bühnenwerk**. Berlin: Hentrich, 1990. – 193 p.: ill. (some col.). Stage-setting and scenery. Germany (East). Schmidt, Willi.

Hainaux, René, ed. **Stage design throughout the world since 1935**. London: Harrap, 1956. – 219 p. (chiefly plates (part col.)). *Notes*: International Theatre Institute publication.

——. **Stage design throughout the world since 1950**. London: Harrap, 1964. – 276 p.: ill. *Notes*: Includes indexes.

——. **Stage design throughout the world, 1970–75**. London: Harrap, 1976. – 159 p. (2 fold.): chiefly ill. (some col.), plans. *Notes*: Captions in English and French. Includes indexes. Bibliography: p. 158.

——— and Yves Bonnat. **Stage design throughout the world since 1960**. London: Harrap, 1973. – 239 p. (chiefly illus. (part col.)). *Notes*: Bibliography: p. 227–30.

Hanguk Mudae Design ui Pyoenhwa as Kwanhan Yeongu. [History of Korean stage setting: From 1945 to present]. Seoul: Kim Im-Ode, 1986. 281 p.

Henderson, Mary C. **Jo Mielziner and the theatre of his time**. New York: Alfred A. Knopf, 1997. *Notes*: Includes bibliographical references and index. Set designers. United States. Biography. Mielziner, Jo.

Hewitt, Barnard, ed. **Appia, Adolphe: The work of living art; a theory of the theatre**. Coral Gables, Fla.: University of Miami Press, 1981. – xix, 131 p.: ill. *Notes*: Stage design.

Ingham, Rosemary. **From page to stage: how theatre designers make connections between scripts and images**. Portsmouth, NH: Heinemann, 1997. *Notes*: Stage setting and scenery. Explication.

Ingram, Raymond. **The stage designs of Leslie Hurry**. Cambridge: Chadwyck-Healey in association with the Consortium for Drama and Media in Higher Education, 1990. – 168 p. *Notes*: Set designers. Great Britain/Hurry, Leslie, 1909–1978.

Innes, Christopher. **Edward Gordon Craig**. Cambridge and New York: Cambridge University Press, 1983. – xiv, 240 p.: ill. *Series*: Directors in perspective. *Notes*: Includes index. Bibliography: p. 236. Critical studies.

Isgrò, Giovanni. **Antonio Valente, architetto scenografo e la cultura materiale del teatro in Italia fra le due guerre**. Palermo: S.F. Flaccovio, 1988. – 214 p.: ill. (some col.). *Notes*: Includes bibliographical references (p. 211–14). Set designers. Architects. Italy. Biography/Valente, Antonio, d. 1975.

Jahnke, Manfred and Manfred Linke. **Theater 1967–1982**. Berlin: Felgentreff & Goebel, 1983. – 352 p.: ill. *Notes*: German and English. Includes index. Stage-setting and scenery. Germany (West).

Keresztury, Dezso, Geza Staud and Zoltan Fulop. **A magyar opera es balettszcenika**. [Hungarian opera and ballet scenography]. Budapest: Magveto, 1976.

Kesler, Jackson. **Theatrical costume: a guide to information sources**. Detroit: Gale Research Co., 1979. – x, 308 p.

Kirchmann, Kay. **Bühnenkonzept der Moderne: Aspekte der Theater- und Tanzformen zur Zeit Oskar Schlemmers**. 1994. *Notes*: Shortened version of a talk given in conjunction with the exhibition, 'Oskar Schlemmer – Tanz Theater Bühne', in Düsseldorf, September 1994. Includes bibliographical references (p. 16). History. 20th century/Schlemmer, Oskar, 1888–1943/Bauhaus.

Kokkos, Yannis. **Le Scénographe et le héron**. [The scenographer and the heron]. Arles: Actes-Sud, 1989. 215 p.

Konechna, G.P. and Sergei Lifatov. **50 let sovetskogo iskusstva: khudozhniki teatra**. Moscow: Sovetskii Khudozhnik, 1969. – 271 p.: chiefly ill. (some col.), plates. *Notes*: Text in Russian; summary in English, French, and German; lists of illus. also in the same languages. Stage-setting and scenery. USSR.

Kosinski, Jan. **Ksztalt teatru**. Warsaw: Panstwowy Instytut Wydawniczy, 1984. – 267 p., 10 p. of plates: ill. *Notes*: Bibliography: p. 264–5. Stage-setting and scenery. Poland.

Die Künstler und das Theater. Zurich: Conzett & Huber, 1964. – 116 p.: ill. *Notes*: Stage-setting and scenery. Switzerland.

Lajcha, Ladislav. **Súcasná slovenská scénografia**. Bratislava: Pallas, 1977. – 244, 2 p.: ill. (some col.). *Notes*: Summary in English, German, Spanish and Russian. Stage-setting and scenery. Slovakia.

Larson, Orville Kurth. **Scene design in the American theatre from 1915 to 1960**. Fayetteville: University of Arkansas Press, 1989. – xx, 385 p.: ill. (some col). *Notes*: A chronicle of the activities of the new stagecraft designers and their followers with an appraisal of the state of the art and the European influences previous to their appearance. Includes index. Bibliography: p. 369–75. United States.

Leeper, Janet. **Edward Gordon Craig: designs for the theatre**. [Harmondsworth, Middlesex]: Penguin Books, 1973, 1948. – 47 p., ill. (part col.). *Notes*: Photocopy. Ann Arbor, Mich.: University Microfilms, 1973.

Macgowan, Kenneth and Robert Edmond Jones. **Continental stagecraft**. New York: B. Blom, 1964 (reproduction). – xvi, 233 p. plates. *Notes*: Stage-setting and scenery. Europe.

Mancini, Franco. **L'illusione alternativa: lo spazio scenico dal dopoguerra ad oggi**. Turin: Einaudi, 1980. – xxiv, 389 p., [56] p. of plates: ill. *Notes*: Includes bibliographical references and indexes. Stage-setting and scenery.

Mango, Achille. **La Macchina del tempo, dal**

teatro al teatro. Perugia: Editrice umbra co-operativa, 1981. – 154 p.: ill. *Notes*: Includes bibliographical references. Experimental theatre. Stage-setting and scenery.

Manherz, Karoly, ed. **Hungarian State Ballet Institute**. Budapest: State Ballet Institute, 1981.

Marcheschi, Jean-Paul. **L'Art en scènes**. Bois-le-Roi (France): Editeurs Evidant, 1992. – 204 p.: ill. *Notes*: 'Cet ouvrage prolonge le colloque "Arts de la scène/scène de l'art" organisé par l'Ecole d'art d'Avignon les 25, 26 et 27 juillet 1991 au centre des congrès du Palais des papes'–P. opposite t.p. Includes bibliographical references. L'artiste en répresentation – L'art mis en scène – Transversalités. Stage-setting and scenery/Performance art. Experimental theatre.

Matt, Frits. **Eesti teatri lavapilt**. Tallinn: Kunst, 1969. – 179, 68 p. illus. (part col.). *Notes*: Includes bibliographical references. Stage-setting and scenery. Estonia.

Mayer, David, ed. **Schirmer Books theatre manuals**. 1st American edn. New York: Schirmer Books, 1989 1988. – 5 vols.: ill. (some col.). *Notes*: Includes bibliographies and indexes. vol. 1. Directing a play/Michael McCaffery. – vol. 2. Stage design and proper-ties/Michael Holt. – vol. 3. Stage management and theatre administration/Pauline Menear and Terry Hawkins. – vol. 4. Lighting and sound/Neil Fraser. – vol. 5. Costume and make-up/Michael Holt.

McNamara, Brooks, Jerry Rojo and Richard Schechner. **Theatres, spaces, environments: 18 projects**. New York: Drama Book Specialists, 1975. [viii], 181 p.: ill., plans. *Notes*: Theatres. United States. Design and scenography. Environmental theatres.

Mello, Bruno. **A treatise on scene design**. Novara: G.G. Gorlich, Instituto Geografico de Agostini, 1979.

Mielziner, Jo. **Designing for the theatre; a memoir and a portfolio**. New York: Atheneum, 1965. – x, 242 p. illus. (part col.). *Notes*: 'Productions designed by Jo Mielziner': p. 225–36. Stage-setting and scenery.

——. **The shapes of our theatre**. New York: Clarkson Potter, 1970. 160 p.

Mikhail, Edward Halim. **Sean O'Casey and his critics: annotated bibliography, 1916–1982**. Metuchen, N.J.; London: Scarecrow, 1985. – x, 348 p. *Notes*: Includes index. O'Casey, Sean, 1880–1964. Bibliography.

Mikotowicz, Thomas J. and Arnold Aronson. **Theatrical designers: an international biographical dictionary**. New York: Greenwood

Press, 1992. – xli, 365 p. *Notes*: Includes bibliographical references (p. 289–95) and index.

Morgan, Harry. **Perspective drawing for the theatre**. New York: Drama Book Specialists, 1979. – 254 p.: ill. *Notes*: Bibliography: p. 253–4. Drawing, technique.

Nelms, Henning. **Scene design: a guide to the stage**. New York: Dover and London: Constable, 1975, 1970. – 3 –96 p.: ill., plans. *Notes*: Originally published: New York: Sterling, 1970. Includes index. Manual.

Nematomi menininkai. Vilnius: 'Periodika', 1969. – 72 p. with illus. *Notes*: Stage-setting and scenery. Lithuania.

Obraztsova, Anna and IUrii Fridshtein. **Eduard Gordon Craig: vospominaniia, stat'i, pis'ma**. Moscow: Iskusstvo, 1988. – 397 p.: ill. *Notes*: Includes bibliographical references and index. Critical biography.

Ocana, Maria-Teresa. **Picasso y el teatro: Parade, Pulcinella, Cuadro Flamenco, Mercure**. Barcelona: Museo Picasso: Adjuntament de Barcelona, Institut de Cultura: Ambit Serveis Editorials, 1996. – 166 p.: ill. (some col.). *Notes*: Catalogue of an exhibition held at the Museu Picasso de Barcelona, Nov. 19, 1996 – Feb. 23, 1997. Includes bibliographical references (p. 164–5).

Oenslager, Donald. **Scenery then and now**. New York: W.W. Norton, 1973 1936. – xiv, 265 p.: ill., plates, col. mounted front. *Notes*: Stage-setting and scenery/Theatre. History.

——. **The theatre of Donald Oenslager**. Middletown, Conn.: Wesleyan University Press, 1990, 1978. – xv, 176 p., 8 p. of plates: ill. *Notes*: 'Productions designed by Donald Oenslager': p. 147–67. Includes index. Set designers. United States.

Owen, Bobbi. **Scenic design on Broadway: designers and their credits, 1915–1990**. New York: Greenwood Press, 1991. – xvi, 286 p.: ill. *Notes*: Includes bibliographical references (p. 211–12) and index.

Parmelin, Hélène. **Cinq peintres et le théâtre: décors et costumes de Léger, Coutaud, Gischia, Labisse, Pignon**. Paris: Éditions Cercle d'art, 1956. – 152, 2 p. illus. (part. col.). *Notes*: Bibli-ography: p. 153. Stage-setting and scenery/Costume/Scene painting.

Pecktal, Lynn. **Designing and drawing for the theatre**. New York: McGraw-Hill, 1995. – vii, 601 p., 16 p. of plates: ill. (some col.). *Notes*: Includes index. Stage design.

Pendleton, Ralph, ed. **The theatre of Robert Edmond Jones**. Middletown, Conn.: Wesleyan

University Press, 1977. – xiii, 198 p.: ill., port.; 23 x. *Notes*: First published in 1958. Stage-setting and scenery. Jones, Robert Edmond, 1887–1954.

Pépin, Lucien. **Robert Prévost: scénographe et favori des dieux**. Sillery, Québec: Pélican, 1994. – 124 p.: ill. *Notes*: Stage-setting and scenery/ Set designers. Quebec (Province). Biography. Prévost, Robert.

Photopoulos, Dionyses. **Stage design in the Greek theatre**. Athens: Published by the Commercial Bank of Greece, 1987. – 414 p.: chiefly ill. *Notes*: Translation of: **Skenographia sto Helleniko theatro**. Set designers. Greece.

Pietzsch, Ingeborg, Gunter Kaiser, and Detlef Schneider, eds. **Bild und Szene. Bühnenbildner der DDR 1978 bis 1986**. [Stage design in the GDR from 1978 to 1986]. Berlin: Henschel, 1988. 119 p.

Pinnell, William H. **Perspective rendering for the theatre**. Carbondale: Southern Illinois University Press, 1996. – viii, 179 p.: ill. *Notes*: Includes bibliographical references (p. 173–4) and index. Computer-aided design.

Pleskacová, Jana. **PQ–Prazské quadriennale jevistního výtvarnictví a divadelní architektury, 1987**. [Prague Quadrennial of Theatre Design and Architecture, 1987] Prague: Divadelní ústav, 1987. – 530 p.: ill.; 20 x.

Polieri, Jacques. **Scénographie: théâtre, cinéma, télévision**. Paris: J.M. Place, 1990. – xxiii, 191 p.: ill. (some col.). *Notes*: Stage-setting and scenery.

——, Pierre Lacombe and Ned Alan Bowman. **Contemporary scenography**. Pittsburgh, 1965. – 303 p. *Notes*: Translation of **Scénographie nouvelle**, originally published as a special issue of **Aujourd'hui, Art et Architecture**, 42–3 (Oct. 1963). Stage setting and scenery.

Prampolini, Enrico. **Lineamenti di scenografia italiana, dal Rinascimento ad oggi**. Rome: C. Bestetti, 1950. – 16, 23 p. plates. Stage-setting and scenery. Italy.

Ptácková, Vera and Vladimír Adamczyk. **A mirror of world theatre: the Prague Quadrennial, 1967–1991**. Prague: Theatre Institute, 1995. – 382 p.: ill. (chiefly col.). *Notes*: Stage-setting and scenery. Exhibitions.

Raftis, Alkis. **40 Greek costumes from the Dora Stratou Theatre collection**. Athena: Dora Stratou Theatre, 1994. – 90 p.: col. ill. *Notes*: Costume. Greece. Catalogues.

Rassegna stampa: palcoscenico e spazio scenico: percorsi attraverso la scenografia teatrale italiana. Rome: Circuito Teatro Musica Coop., 1985. – 18 p.: ill. *Notes*: Stage-setting and scenery. Italy.

Reid, Francis. **Designing for the theatre**. 2nd edn. London and New York: A & C Black; Theatre Arts Books/Routledge, 1996. – 106 p.: ill. *Notes*: Includes bibliographical references (p. 93–4) and index.

Reinking, Wilhelm. **Spiel und Form: Werkstattberichte. Bühnenbildner zum Gestaltwandel d. Szene in d. Zwanziger u. Dreissiger Jahren**. [Play and form: designers and the transformation of stage design in the 1920s and 1930s]. Hamburg: Christians, 1979. 326 p.

Rich, Frank and Lisa Aronson. **The theatre art of Boris Aronson**. New York: Knopf, 1987. – xi, 322 p.: ill. (some col.). *Notes*: Includes index. Bibliography: p. 311–12. Stage-setting and scenery/Set designers. United States. Biography/Aronson, Boris.

Rischbieter, Henning and Wolfgang Storch. **Art and the stage in the 20th century; painters and sculptors work for the theatre**. Greenwich: Conn.: New York Graphic Society, 1970 1968. – 306 p. illus. (part col.). *Notes*: Translation of **Bühne und bildende Kunst im XX. Jahrhundert**. Bibliography: p. 300–1. Stage-setting and scenery.

Rose, Enid. **Gordon Craig and the theatre; a record and an interpretation**. London: S.Low: Marston, 1973. – ix, 250 p. illus. *Notes*: Bibliography: p. 223–9.

Rose, Rich. **Autocad onstage: a computer-aided design handbook for theater, film, and television**. White Hall, Va.: Betterway Publications, 1990. – 280 p.: ill. *Notes*: Includes index. Stage-setting and scenery.

Russell, Douglas A. **Period style for the theatre**. 2nd edn. Boston: Allyn & Bacon, 1987. – xix, 375 p.: ill. *Notes*: Includes index. Bibliography: p. 365–66. Costume. History. Stage-setting and scenery.

Scenography in Latvia. Riga, Latvia: The Union, 1995. – 1 v.: chiefly ill. (some col.). *Notes*: Stage-setting and scenery. Latvia.

Schechner, Richard. **Environmental theater**. Expanded edn. New York: Applause, 1994. – li, 339 p.: ill. *Notes*: Includes bibliographical references and index. Design and directing. Acting and audience.

Schlemmer, Oskar, C. Raman Schlemmer and Maria Müller. **Oskar Schlemmer: Tanz, Theater, Bühne**. Ostfildern-Ruit: G. Hatje, 1994. – 311 p.: ill. (some col.). *Notes*: Published in conjunction with the exhibition held at the Kunstsammlung Nordrhein-Westfalen, Düsseldorf, July 30–October 16, 1994; Kunsthalle Wien, November 11, 1994–January 29, 1995; Sprengel Museum Hannover, February 19–May 21, 1995. Includes bibliographical references (p. 307–9). Germany. Stage-setting and scenery. Exhibitions/Schlemmer, Oskar, 1888–1943. Bauhaus influence.

Schlemmer, Oskar, László Moholy-Nagy, Farkas Molnár, Walter Gropius and Arthur S. Wensinger. **The theatre of the Bauhaus**. [Bühne im Bauhaus]. Baltimore: Johns Hopkins University Press, 1996, 1961. – 109 p.: ill. *Series*: PAJ books. *Notes*: Originally published (in English): Middletown, Conn.: Wesleyan University Press, 1961. Includes bibliographical references. Design. Bauhaus.

Schouvaloff, Alexander and Simon De Pury. **Set and costume designs for ballet and theater**. New York City: Vendome Press, 1987. – 268 p.: ill. (some col.). *Notes*: 'The Thyssen-Bornemisza Collection'. Includes index. Bibliography: p. 260–1. Ballet. Stage-setting and scenery. Catalogues.

Senelick, Laurence. **Gordon Craig's Moscow Hamlet: a reconstruction**. Westport, Conn.: Greenwood Press, 1982. – xviii, 234 p.: ill. *Notes*: Includes index. Bibliography: p. 223–6.

Simhandl, Peter. **Bildertheater: bildende Künstler des 20. Jahrhunderts als Theaterreformer**. Berlin: Gadegast, 1993. – 160 p.: ill. *Notes*: Includes bibliographical references and index. Stage-setting and scenery.

Simonson, Lee. **The stage is set**. New York: Theatre Arts Books, 1964, 1963. – xxv, 581 p. illus., plans. *Notes*: 'A critical bibliography': p. 531–45. Stage-setting and scenery.

Sinisi, Silvana. **Cambi di scena: teatro e arti visive nelle poetiche del Novecento**. Rome: Bulzoni, 1995. – 242 p., 13 p. of plates: ill. *Notes*: Includes bibliographical references. Set designers/Costume design. History. 20th century.

Smith, Ronn. **American set design 2**. New York: Theatre Communications Group, 1991. 210 p.

Society of British Theatre Designers. **British theatre design 1983–1987**. Faringdon, Oxfordshire: Twynam, 1987. – 80 p.: ill. (some col.). *Notes*: Great Britain.

Sovetskaya literatura po stzenographii (1917–1983). [Soviet literature on scenography (1917–1983)]. Moscow/Prague: 1983.

Sporre, Dennis J. and Robert C. Burroughs. **Scene design in the theatre**. Englewood Cliffs,

N.J.: Prentice Hall, 1990. – viii, 312 p., 4 p. of plates: ill. (some col.). *Notes*: Includes index. Bibliography: p. 305–7.

Stadler, Edmund. **Le Décor du théâtre suisse depuis Adolphe Appia**. [Swiss scene designs since Adolphe Appia]. Thalwil: Theaterkultur-Verlag, 1954. – 85 p.: ill. *Notes*: Exposition organisée par la Société Suisse du Théâtre en collaboration avec la Fondation Pro Helvetia. Text in French, German, and English. Stage-setting and scenery. Switzerland.

Strzelecki, Zenobiusz. **Wspólczesna scenografia polska**. Warsaw: Arkady, 1983, 1984. – 2 vols: chiefly ill. (some col.). *Notes*: Text in English and Polish. vols 1–2: Contemporary Polish stage design. Poland.

Svoboda, Josef and Jarka Burian. **The secret of theatrical space: the memoirs of Josef Svoboda**. New York: Applause, 1993. – 144 p.: ill. *Notes*: Includes index. Translation of: **Tajemství divadelního prostoru**. Stage-setting and scenery/Set designers. Czechoslovakia/Svoboda, Josef.

Syskind, Povl and Paul Brandt. **Alfred Jacobsens Danske Teaterdekorationer & Danske billeder**. [Copenhagen]. Dansk Dukketeaterforening, 1967. – 132 p. illus. *Notes*: Stage-setting and scenery. Denmark.

Tanaka, Ryo. **Kabuki joshiki butai zushu**. Tokyo: Kodansha, 1979, 1958. – 227 p.: chiefly col. ill.; 22 x. *Notes*: Reprint, with new introd. Originally published: 1958. Kabuki. Stage-setting and scenery. Pictorial works. Japan.

Tritten, Hélène and Rosa-Th. Creton. **Les Potiers d'étain à Morges**. [Rolle?]: Société d'histoire de la Côte, 1993. – 44 p.: ill. *Notes*: Includes bibliographical references. Biography. Set designers. Costume designers. Switzerland.

Vakalo, Yorgos. **Short history of scenography**. Athens: Kedros, 1979.

The Vandamm collection. [7, Landmarks in American stage design]. Theater photographs from the studios of Florence Vandamm and Francis Joseph Bruguière from 1915 to 1960 in the New York Public Library, Library and Museum of the Performing Arts. Teaneck, NJ: Somerset House, 1980. – 94 microfiches: chiefly ill.; 11 x. *Notes*: Subset of the complete microfiche edition of photographs of theatre productions from the Vandamm collection. Title of subset supplied by publisher. Stage-setting and scenery. Pictorial works. USA.

Verykivs'ka, Iryna M. **Stanovlennia ukraïns'koï radianskoï stsenohrafiï**. [Development of

Ukrainian Soviet scenography]. Kiev: Nauk dumka, 1981. 205 p.

Vogelsang, Bernd and Rudi, Strauch. **Universität zu Köln, Institut für Theater-, Film- und Fernsehwissenschaft, Theatersammlung: Findbuch der Szenischen Graphik.** [University of Cologne Institute of Theatre-, Film- and Television Studies, Theatre Collection: Index of Scenographic Design]. Munich; New York: Saur, 1993. – 4 vols. *Notes:* Includes bibliographical references vol. 1. Künstler-Index – vol. 2. Titel-Index – vol. 3. Verfasser-Index – vol. 4. Orts- und Jahres-Index. Stage-setting and scenery. Theatersammlung. Indexes.

Volbach, Walther and Richard Beacham. **Adolphe Appia – essays, scenarios, and designs.** Ann Arbor, Mich.: UMI Research Press, 1989. – xvii, 480 p.: ill. *Notes:* Translations from the French. Includes index. Bibliography: p. 473–5.

Willett, John. **Caspar Neher, Brecht's designer.** London and New York: Methuen, in association with the Arts Council of Great Britain, 1986. – 141 p.: ill. *Notes:* Bibliography: p. 135–8.

J4. Stage Lighting and Sound

Baumann, Carl-Friedrich. **Licht im Theater: von der Argand-Lampe bis zum Glühlampen-Scheinwerfer.** Stuttgart: F. Steiner Verlag Wiesbaden, 1988. – xii, 397 p., 66 p. of plates: ill. *Notes:* Includes bibliographical references. Stage lighting. History.

Bentham, Frederick. **The art of stage lighting.** 3rd edn. London: Pitman House, 1980. – 361 p.: ill. *Notes:* Includes bibliographical references and index. Manuals.

——. **Sixty years of light work.** Isleworth: Strand Lighting, 1992. – vi, 266 p.: ill., ports. *Notes:* Includes index. Lighting/Great Britain.

Bonnat, Yves. **L'Éclairage des spectacles.** Paris: Librairie théâtrale, 1982. – 86 p.: ill. *Notes:* Bibliography: p. 81.

Boulanger, Norman and Warren C. Lounsbury. **Theatre lighting from A to Z.** Seattle: University of Washington Press, 1992. – 197 p.: ill. *Notes:* Includes bibliographical references (p. 196–7) and index.

Bracewell, John L. **Sound design in the theatre.** Englewood Cliffs, N.J.: Prentice Hall, 1993. – xi, 274 p.: ill. *Notes:* Includes index. Basic characteristics of sound – The electrical basis of audio – Audio measurements – Overview of audio systems – Loudspeakers – Microphones – Amplifiers – Basic signal processing – Mixers and control consoles – Audio signal storage – Time domain processors – Synthesizers and samplers – Survey of audio systems – Assembling audio components into audio systems – Basic characteristics of human hearing – Binaural perception and psychoacoustics – The psychological basis of auditory aesthetics – Creativity, craftsmanship, and design – Sound and dramatic art – Reading the playscript for sound design – Developing the design: deriving a concept – Developing the design: organizing ideas – Constructing the design: organizing resources – Constructing the design: recording and editing – Rehearsing sound – Postscript on the design process – Notes on The Rose Tattoo in the computer age. Electronic sound control. Acoustic engineering.

Brown, Bill. **Light the way.** 1996. *Notes:* Production and direction.

Bunn, Rex. **Practical stage lighting.** Sydney: Currency Press, 1993. – 108 p., 4 p. of plates: ill. (some col.). *Notes:* Includes bibliographical references (p. 106) and index.

Carpenter, Mark. **Basic stage lighting.** Kensington, Aus.: New South Wales University Press, 1982. – vii, 107 p.: ill.; 16 X. *Notes:* Includes index. Bibliography: p. 104.

Cunningham, Glen. **Stage lighting revealed: a design and execution handbook.** Cincinnati, Ohio: Betterway Books, 1993. – 176 p.: ill. *Notes:* Includes index. Stage lighting. Handbooks, manuals, etc.

Essig, Linda. **Lighting and the design idea.** Fort Worth: Harcourt Brace College Publishers, 1997. – xi, 238 p.: ill. (some col.). *Notes:* Includes index.

Fitt, Brian and Joe Thornley. **Lighting by design: a technical guide.** Oxford and Boston: Focal Press, 1992. – viii, 321 p.: ill. (some col.). *Notes:* Includes bibliographical references (p. 314) and index. Cinematography. Television. Theatre.

Fraser, Neil. **Lighting and sound.** Rev. edn. London: Phaidon, 1993. – 130 p.: ill. (some col.). *Notes:* Includes bibliographical references (p. 129) and index. Stage lighting. Sound effects. Manual.

Freeman, Tim. **Easy stage lighting.** Kansas City, Mo.: Lillenas, 1995. – 47 p.: ill. *Notes:* Includes reproducible forms.

Gillette, J. Michael. **Designing with light: an introduction to stage lighting.** 2nd edn. Mountain View, Calif.: Mayfield Pub. Co., 1989. – xi, 244 p., [8] p. of plates: ill. (some col.). *Notes:* Includes index.

Hays, David. **Light on the subject: stage lighting for directors and actors – and the rest of us**. 4th Limelight edn. New York: Limelight Editions, 1995. – 173 p.: ill. *Notes*: Originally published: Calcutta: Seagull Books, 1988. First Limelight edn. published 1989. Includes bibliographical references (p. 171–3).

Huntington, John. **Control systems for live entertainment**. Boston: Focal Press, 1994. – xx, 292 p.: ill. *Notes*: Includes bibliographical references (p. 279–82) and index. Electronic sound control.

Izenour, George C. **Theatre technology**. 2nd edn. New Haven; London: Yale University Press, 1996. – xxix, 558 p.: ill., plans. *Notes*: Previous edn.: New York: McGraw-Hill, 1988. Includes index. Bibliography: p. 535–40. Stage machinery/Stage lighting.

McCandless, Stanley. **A method of lighting the stage**. 4th edn. amended and rev. New York: Theatre Arts Books, 1984 1958. – 143 p.: ill. *Notes*: Reprint of the 1963 edn.

McGrath, Ian. **A process for lighting the stage**. Boston: Allyn & Bacon, 1990. – xviii, 331 p., [2] p. of plates: ill. (some col.). *Notes*: Includes index. Bibliography: p. 325–6.

Morgan, Nigel H. **Stage lighting for theatre designers**. London: Herbert Press, 1995. – 128 p.: ill. (some col.). *Notes*: Bibliography: p. 125–6. Includes index.

Mumm, Robert C. **Photometrics handbook**. 2nd print. with corr. Shelter Island, NY: Broadway Press, 1994 1992. – xviii, 492 p.: ill. *Notes*: Includes index. Photometry. Handbooks, manuals, etc.

Nihon butai terebi shomei kindaishi: Showa yori Heisei ni itaru shomeika no ayumi to Kyokai 20-nen no sokuseki. Tokyo: Nihon Shomeika Kyokai, 1993. – 336 p.: ill. *Notes*: Stage lighting. Japan. History.

Palmer, Richard H. **The lighting art: the aesthetics of stage lighting design**. Englewood Cliffs, N.J.: Prentice-Hall, 1985. – xvii, 237 p., 4 p. of plates: ill. (some col.). *Notes*: Includes index. Bibliography: p. 217–20.

Parker, Wilford Oren and R. Craig Wolf. **Scene design and stage lighting**. 7th edn. Fort Worth: Harcourt Brace College Publishers, 1996. – xvi, 670 p., 24 p. of plates: ill. (some col.). *Notes*: Includes bibliographical references (p. 657–60) and index.

Pilbrow, Richard. **Stage lighting design: the art, the craft, the life**. New York: By Design Press, 1997. – xxvi, 481 p.: ill. (some col.). *Notes*:

Includes bibliographical references (p. 471–2) and index.

Practical projects for teaching lighting design: a compendium. 2nd edn. New York: United States Institute for Theatre Technology, 1992. – vii, 82 p.: ill. *Notes*: 'June 1992'. 'A project of the USITT Lighting Design Commission'. Study and teaching.

Reid, Francis. **The ABC of stage lighting**. London; New York: A & C Black Drama Book Publishers, 1992. – 129 p.: ill. Dictionaries.

——. **Discovering stage lighting**. Oxford and Boston: Focal Press, 1993. – viii, 118 p.: ill. *Notes*: Includes bibliographical references (p. 113) and index.

——. **Lighting the stage: a lighting designer's experiences**. Oxford; Boston: Focal Press, 1995. – x, 113 p.: ill. *Notes*: Biography.

——. **The stage lighting handbook**. 5th edn. London; New York: A & C Black Theatre Art Books/Routledge, 1996. – 224 p.: ill. *Notes*: Includes index.

Rosenthal, Jean and Lael Tucker Wertenbaker. **The magic of light: the craft and career of Jean Rosenthal, pioneer in lighting for the modern stage**. Boston: Little, Brown, 1972. – ix, 256 p. illus. *Notes*: Bibliography: p. 249–50.

Rubin, Joel E. and Lee Watson. **Theatrical lighting practice**. New York: Theatre Arts Books, 1968 1954. – xiv, 142 p.: ill. *Notes*: Includes bibliographical references (p. 127–34).

Sammler, Ben and Don Harvey. **The Technical Brief collection: ten years of solutions to recurring problems in technical theatre**. New Haven, CT: Department of Technical Design and Production, the Yale School of Drama, 1992. – xiv, 265 p. *Notes*: Reprint of articles from **Technical Brief**, vols. 1–10. Includes index. Lighting. Safety measures. Sound effects.

Sandström, Ulf. **A guide to modern stage lighting controls**. Oxford; Boston: Focal Press, 1997. *Notes*: Includes bibliographical references and index.

Streader, Tim and John Arthur Williams. **Create your own stage lighting**. London: Bell & Hyman, 1985. – 192 p.: ill. (some col.), plans. *Notes*: Includes index. Bibliography: p. 192. Manuals.

Valentin, François-Eric. **Lumière pour le spectacle**. Paris: P. Olivier, 1982. – 190 p.: ill. *Notes*: Bibliography: p. 186–188.

Vasey, John. **Concert sound and lighting systems**. Boston: Focal Press, 1989. – xiii, 178 p.: ill. *Notes*: Includes index. Electronic sound control/Stage lighting/Concerts. Acoustic engineering.

Walne, Graham. **Projection for the performing arts**. Oxford and Boston: Focal Press, 1995. – xii, 139 p., 8 p. of plates: ill. (some col.). *Notes*: Includes bibliographical references (p. 115–16) and index. Projections.

Walters, Graham. **Stage lighting step-by-step: basic techniques to achieve professional results**. London: A & C Black, 1997. – 144 p.: ill. (some col.). *Notes*: Includes index.

Warfel, William B. **The new handbook of stage lighting graphics**. New York: Drama Book Publishers, 1990. – 112 p.: ill. *Notes*: Stage lighting. Planning. Drawings.

—— and Walter R. Klappert. **Color science for lighting the stage**. New Haven: Yale University Press, 1981. – xiv, 158 p.: ill. (2 fold. in pocket). *Notes*: Includes bibliographical references. Stage lighting/Colorimetry. Charts, diagrams, etc.

Watson, Lee. **Lighting design handbook**. New York: McGraw-Hill, 1990. – xxii, 458 p., 16 p. of plates: ill. (some col.). *Notes*: Includes bibliographical references (p. 447–50) and index. On being a creative artist: designing – Keys to mastery – On being a master technician: the building blocks – Non musical performance theatre – Musical theatre – Other theatrical forms – Photographic lighting design – Nightclubs, discos and concert lighting – Spectacle – Architectural/commercial/industrial lighting – Employment and career prospects – Unions – Professional organizations – Lighting design training and education – Agents and taxes – World of tomorrow.

Wehlburg, Albert F.C. **Theatre lighting: an illustrated glossary**. 1st edn. New York: Drama Book Specialists, 1975. – 62 p.: ill.

West, Martha Ullman. **Fuller, Rosenthal and Tipton: the light fantastic**. 1996. *Notes*: Discussion of the use of light by choreographer, dancer Loïe Fuller and lighting designers Jean Rosenthal and Jennifer Tipton.

K. Theatre Space, Architecture, Technology and Management

American Federation of Arts. **The ideal theatre: eight concepts: an exhibition of designs and models resulting from the Ford Foundation Program for Theatre Design; prepared and circulated by the American Federation of Arts**. American Federation of Arts; Owen, 1965. – 144 p.: ill. *Notes*: Originally published, American Federation of Arts, 1962. Ideal theatre designs.

Architecture of the theatre. a bibliographical overview. Monticello, Ill.: Vance Bibliographies, 1984. – 11 p. *Notes*: Cover title. 'October 1984'. Microfiche. New York: New York Public Library, 1987. 1 microfiche: negative. (FSN 41, 751). Bibliography.

Armstrong, Leslie, Roger Morgan and Mike Lipske. **Space for dance: an architectural design guide**. New York: Pub. Center for Cultural Resources, 1984. – 191 p.: ill. *Notes*: 'Commissioned by the Design Arts Program and the Dance Program of the National Endowment for the Arts'–T.p. verso. Includes index. Bibliography: p. 182–5. Theatre architecture. Dance.

Arnold, Richard L. **Scene technology**. Englewood Cliffs, N.J.: Prentice-Hall, 1985. – viii, 343 p.: ill. *Notes*: Includes bibliographies and index. Scenery. Construction.

Athanasopoulos, Chrestos Georgiou. **Contemporary theater: evolution and design**. New York: Wiley, 1983. – xvi, 341 p.: ill. *Notes*: Translation of: **Provlemata stis exelixeis tou synchronou theatrou**. Includes index. Bibliography: p. 330–2.Theatre architecture design, to 1982.

Atkinson, Patrick. **Theatre design and technology: index 1965–1984**. [New York]: United States Institute for Theatre Technology, 1984. – 47 p. *Notes*: Theatre architecture. Indexes.

Baker, Hendrik. **Stage management and theatrecraft: a stage manager's handbook**. 4th ed. New York: Theatre Arts Books/Routledge, 1988. – xv, 392 p.: ill. *Notes*: Includes bibliographical references (p. 389–92) and index.

Baker, James W. **Elements of stagecraft**. Sherman Oaks, CA: Alfred Pub. Co., 1978. – xii, 241 p.: ill. *Notes*: Includes index. Stage management. Terminology.

Bayón, Mariano. **Arquitecturas de papel: una iconografia popular de la arquitectura**. Madrid: Colegio Oficial de Arquitectos de Madrid, Comisión de Cultura, 1980. – 133 p.: ill. (some col.). *Notes*: Publicación-catalogo de la exposición 'Arquitecturas de papel. Una iconografia popular de la arquitectura', Sala 'Barquillo' de la Caja de Ahorros y Monte de Piedad de Madrid, Obra Cultural, Mayo–junio de 1980.

Bellman, Willard F. **Scene design, stage lighting, sound, costume and makeup: a scenographic approach**. Ann Arbor, Mich.: UMI Books on Demand, 1996 1983. – xiv, 474 p., 16 p. of plates: ill. (some col.). *Notes*: Rev. edn. of: **Scenography and stage technology**. c1977. Reprint. Originally published: New York:

Harper & Row. Includes bibliography (p. 466–7) and index.

Bond, Daniel. **Stage management: a gentle art**. 2nd edn. London: A & C Black, 1997. – 151 p.: ill. *Notes*: Includes index. Stage management.

Bowman, Ned Allan, William L. Coleman and Glorianne Engel. **Planning for the theatre: a detailed checklist and bibliography of theatre building design for users, architects, and consultants**. Pittsburgh: Arts Information International: University of Pittsburgh, 1965. – 75 p. Theatre architecture/Theatres.

Brenner, Klaus Theo. **Stadttheater: Manifeste für eine stillose Architektur**. [Urban theatre: manifesto for a style-free architecture]. Berlin: Ernst & Sohn, 1994. – 118 p.: ill. (some col.). *Notes*: German and English in parallel columns. Includes the author's 'Projektliste/Project list' (p. 110–12) and 'Publikationen/Publications' (p. 116–17). Includes bibliographical references (p. 118). City planning/Urban renewal.

Bühnentechnik. Stuttgart: IRB Verlag, 1987. – 58 p. *Notes*: Theater architecture. Germany. Bibliography.

Building theatres for communities: a symposium on theatre design. Adelaide: Adelaide Festival Centre, 1974. – 197 p. Theatre architecture. Australia.

Burnett, Kate and Peter Ruthven Hall. **Make space!: design for theatre and alternative spaces**. London: Society of British Theatre Designers, 1996 1994. – 131 p.: ill. (some col.), plans. *Notes*: Designs and plans.

Busti, Kathryn Michèle. **Stage production handbook: job responsibilities for all technical backstage crews**. Littleton, CO: Theatre Things, 1992. *Notes*: Director – Technical director – Stage manager – Set designer – Lighting designer – Costume designer – Props master – Master carpenter – Scenic artist – Sound designer – Video master – Make-up artist – Publicist – Program editor – House manager. *Subjects*: Stage management. Handbooks, manuals, etc.

Dahle, Terje Nils. **Theater in Mehrzweckbauten**. Stuttgart: IRB Verlag, 1985. – 92 p. *Notes*: 'Die nachgewiesenen Informationen wurden den Datenbanken des Informationszentrums Raum und Bau der Fraunhofer-Gesellschaft entnommen'. Includes indexes. Theatre architecture. Joint occupancy of buildings. Bibliography.

——. **Theaterbau im Ausland**. Stuttgart: IRB Verlag, 1985. – 167 p. *Notes*: 'Die nachgewiesenen Informationen wurden den Datenbanken des Informationszentrums Raum und Bau der Fraunhofer-Gesellschaft entnommen'. Includes indexes. Theatre architecture. Bibliography.

——. **Theaterbau in der Bundesrepublik Deutschland**. 1. Aufl. Stuttgart: IRB-Verlag, 1985. – 129 p. *Notes*: 'Die nachgewiesenen Informationen wurden den Datenbanken des Informationszentrums Raum und Bau der Fraunhofer-Gesellschaft entnommen'. Includes indexes. Theatre architecture. Germany (West). Stage-setting and scenery.

Deutsche Theatertechnische Gesellschaft. **Theaterszene, Theaterbau 1971–1975: eine Dokumentation des Theaters in der Bundesrepublik Deutschland**. Hamburg: Die Gesellschaft, ? 1976, – ca. 150 p.: chiefly ill., plans. *Notes*: Includes bibliographical references. Stage-setting and scenery/Theatre architecture. Germany.

Dunning, Glenna. **Theater architecture in California: an annotated bibliography**. Monticello, Ill.: Vance Bibliographies, 1981. – 29 p. *Notes*: Includes index. Microfilm. New York: New York Public Library. 1983. l microfilm reel; 35 mm. (MN*ZZ-22580). California. Construction. Theatres. Decoration. Bibliography.

Fiorillo, Clara. **Scenographia: note di estetica sull'architettura della scena**. Naples: Liguori, 1996. – 239 p.: ill. *Notes*: Includes bibliographical references and index. Theatre architecture.

Frenkel, Mykhailo. **Plastyka stsenichnoho prostoru**. [The plasticity of stage space]. Kiev: Mystetstvo, 1987. 183 p.

Gaulme, Jacques. **Architectures, scénographiques et décors de théâtre**. Paris: Magnard, 1985. – 142 p.: ill. *Notes*: Theatre architecture/Theaters. Decoration.

Greisenegger, Wolfgang. 'Theater'. In **Clemens Holzmeister. Architekt in der Zeitwende. Sakralbau, Profanbau, Theater**. [Clemens Holzmeister. Architect at a time of change. Religious and profane buildings, theatre]. Salzburg/Stuttgart/Zürich: Verlag Das Bergand-Buch, 1978.

Griffiths, Trevor R. **Stagecraft: the complete guide to theatrical practice**. Oxford: Phaidon, 1990, 1982. – 192 p.: ill. *Notes*: Includes index. Stage management.

Ham, Roderick. **Theatres: planning guidance for design and adaptation**. London; Boston: Butterworth Architecture, 1988, 1987. – x, 246 p.: ill., plans. *Notes*: First edn published with title: **Theatre planning**. London: Architectural Press, 1972. 'This edition published 1987. Reprinted by Butterworth Architecture, 1988.'– T.p. verso. Includes bibliographical references and index. Theatre architecture.

Hodge, Francis, ed. **Innovations in stage and theatre design**. [New York]: American Society for Theatre Research, 1972. – 165 p. illus. *Notes*: Papers presented at the sixth congress of the International Federation for Theatre Research, held Oct. 6–10, 1969, at Lincoln Center, New York. Sponsored by the American Society for Theatre Research and the Theatre Library Association. Includes bibliographical references. Theatre architecture.

Howard, John T. **A bibliography of theatre technology: acoustics and sound, lighting, properties, and scenery**. Westport, Conn.: Greenwood Press, 1982. – xii, 345 p. *Notes*: Includes indexes. Stage-setting and scenery. Stage lighting. Architectural acoustics. Theatre architecture.

Ionazzi, Daniel A. **The stage management handbook**. White Hall, Va.: Betterway Publications, 1992. – 190 p.: ill. *Notes*: Includes bibliographical references (p. 167–70) and index.

Izenour, George. **Theatre design and modern architecture**. Pittsburgh, PA: Carnegie Mellon University Press, 1978. 105 p.

——, Vern Oliver Knudsen and Robert Newman. **Theatre design**. 2nd edn. New Haven: Yale University Press, 1996. – xxxv, 639 p.: ill.; 30 x. *Notes*: Includes bibliographical references (p. 620–3) and indexes. Theatre architecture.

Javier, Francisco. **Notas para la historia científica de la puesta en escena**. Buenos Aires: Editorial Leviatán, 1984. – 121, 17 p.: ill. *Notes*: Includes bibliographical references. Designs and plans. Argentina.

——. **La renovación del espacio escénico**. [Buenos Aires: Fundación Banco de la Provincia de Buenos Aires], 1981. – 111 p.: ill. *Notes*: Bibliography: p. 61–2. Theatre architecture.

Kelly, Kevin A. and James B. Gatton. **Large multi-purpose halls for the performing arts: issues and concepts to consider before design**. Houston, Tex.: CRS Sirrine, 1985. – 43, v p.: ill. *Notes*: Includes bibliographical references. Centers for the performing arts. Design/Theater architecture/Arts facilities. Design.

Koho, Timo. **Teatteriarkkitehtuurin merkitysarvot: teatterirakentamisen suhde yhteiskunnan arvomaailmaan kaupungistuvassa Suomessa**. Helsinki: Suomen Muinaismuistoyhdistys, 1991. – 147 p.: ill. (one col.), plans. *Notes*: Summary in English. Includes bibliographical references (p. 141–6). Theatre architecture. Finland. Designs and plans.

Leacroft, Richard. **The development of the English playhouse: an illustrated survey of theatre building in England from medieval to modern times**. London; New York: Methuen, 1988. – xiii, 354 p.: ill. *Notes*: Includes index. Bibliography: p. 338–45. Theatres. Architectural design, to 1985.

—— and Helen Leacroft. **Theatre and playhouse: an illustrated survey of theatre building from ancient Greece to the present day**. London; New York: Methuen, 1984. – x, 246 p.: ill. *Notes*: Includes index. Bibliography: p. 236–42. Theatres. Architectural design, to 1982.

Lord, Peter and Duncan Templeton. **The architecture of sound: designing places of assembly**. New York: Van Nostrand Reinhold, 1986. – xii, 300 p.: ill. *Notes*: Includes bibliography and index. Architectural acoustics/Acoustical engineering/Soundproofing/Theatre architecture.

Lounsbury, Warren C. and Alanson Davis. **Theatre backstage from A to Z**. Revised edn. Seattle: University of Washington Press, 1973 1968. – xxviii, 191 p.: ill. *Notes*: Bibliography: p. 189–91. Stage equipment.

Luere, Jeane and Sidney Berger. **The theatre team: playwright, producer, director, designers, and actors**. Westport, CT: Greenwood Press, 1998. *Notes*: Includes bibliographical references and index.

Market the arts! Rev. edn., 1995/edited by Patricia Lavender. New York, NY: Publication of ARTS Action Issues, 1995. – 194 p.: ill. *Notes*: Originally published by Foundation for the Extension and Development of the American Professional Theatre, 1983. Bibliography: p. 192–3. Marketing the performing arts: a personal view/Patricia Cox – Relationship building in your community/Ruby Lerner – Audiences/Robert Schlosser – The marketing plan and a plan for planning/Douglas Eichten – The marketing mix/Michael W. House – Making the marketing plan and mix work/Michalann Hobson – Financial needs in marketing/Cora Cahan and Elizabeth Cashour – Computers and test marketing/Charles Ziff – Essentials of effective public relations/Bill Rudman – Design promotional materials that work/David J. Skal. (cont.) Production: working with an agency/Michael Prewitt – Media: print and electronic/Harry Clark – Telephone campaigns/Mark Arnold – Theatre: a case history (McCarter Theater Company)/Linda Kinsey – Opera: the people's theater (Minnesota Opera)/Edward Corn – Music: product, market, media, message (The Cleveland Orchestra)/David Levenson – Dance: management, marketing, and schizophrenia (Paul Taylor Dance Company)/Robert Yesselam – Ballet and the art of marketing (The Hartford Ballet)/John Simone – Touring/Rena Shagan. – Performing arts centers (Arvada Center for the Arts)/Frank Jacobson – Sponsors and presenters: community groups (Cultural Resources Council of Syracuse and Onondaga County)/Joseph Golden.

Mayer, David, ed. **Schirmer Books theatre manuals**. 1st American edn. New York: Schirmer Books, 1989 1988. – 5 vols.: ill. (some col.). *Notes*: Includes bibliographies and indexes. vol. 1. Directing a play/Michael McCaffery. – vol. 2. Stage design and properties/Michael Holt. – vol. 3. Stage management and theatre administration/Pauline Menear and Terry Hawkins. – vol. 4. Lighting and sound/ Neil Fraser. – vol. 5. Costume and make-up/ Michael Holt.

McNamara, Brooks, Jerry Rojo and Richard Schechner. **Theatres, spaces, environments: eighteen projects**. New York: Drama Book Specialists, 1975. – 181 p.: ill.; 21 x. *Notes*: The creators of environmental theatre speak about their work.

Miller, James Hull. **Designing small theatres: thirty years of highlights in designing small arena, flexible, open, proscenium and thrust theatres**. Colorado Springs, Colo.: Meriwether Pub., 1974. – 24 p.: ill. *Notes*: Theatre architecture.

Pagan, Hugh. **Theatres, festivals and great occasions: an architectural catalogue**. London: Weinreb Architectural Books, 1987. – 56 p.: ill. *Notes*: Theatre architecture. Bibliography.

Perković, Zdeslav. **Arhitektura dalmatinskih kazališta**. [Dalmatian theatre architecture]. Split: Logos, 1989. 74 p.

Reid, Francis. **The ABC of stage technology**. London: A & C Black, 1995. – 108 p.: ill., plans.

Schneider, Doris. **The art and craft of stage management**. Fort Worth: Harcourt Brace College Publishers, 1997. – xvii, 264 p.: ill. *Notes*: Includes index.

Schreck-Offermann, Ursula. **Freilichttheater**. [Open air theatre]. 2. erw. Aufl. Stuttgart: IRB, 1994. – 111 p. *Notes*: Includes index. Bibliography.

Sekai gekijo kaigi happyo ronbunshu = International Theatre Conference proceedings. Nagoya, Japan: Sekai Gekijo Kaigi Jikko Iinkai Jimukyoku, 1993. – 1 vol. (various pagings): ill. *Notes*: In Japanese and English, with some in Italian, Russian, and German. 1. Culture and economics session – 2. Stage arts and management session: A – 3. Stage arts and management session: B – 4. Stage arts and management forum – 5. Stage arts and cultural administration session – 6. Stage arts and technology session: A – 7. Stage arts and technology session: B – 8. Stage arts and technology forum – 9. Theatre architecture session – 10. Theatre architecutre forum.

Silfen, Martin E. **Counseling clients in the entertainment industry, 1992**. New York: Practising Law Institute, 1992. – 2 vols.: forms. *Notes*: Contents include: Sound recordings and music videos – Music publishing and songwriting – Ethical aspects of entertainment law practice – Entertainment law practice development – Personal management – Counseling clients in the theatre – Television production, distribution and financing – Motion picture production, distribution and financing.

Sonrel, Pierre. **Traité de scénographie: évolution du matériel scénique, inventaire et mise en oeuvre du matériel scénique actuel, technique de l'établissement des décors, perspective théâtrale, autres scènes en usage**. Paris: Librairie Théâtrale, 1984. – 301 p., 28 p. of plates: ill., facsims., plans (some folded). *Notes*: Bibliography: p. 289–92. Theatre architecture.

Southern, Richard. **The open stage and the modern theatre in research and practice**. New York: Theatre Arts Books, 1959. – 125 p. illus. *Notes*: Theatre architecture.

——. **Proscenium and sight-lines; a complete system of scenery planning and a guide to the laying out of stages for scene designers, stage managers, theatre architects and engineers, theatrical history and research workers and those concerned with the planning of stages for small halls**. London: Faber & Faber, 1983 1964. – 235 p. illus. *Notes*: Theatre architecture.

Spinks, Kim. **Australian theatre design**. Paddington, N.S.W.: Australian Production Designers Association NSW, 1992. *Notes*: Available from Centre for Performance Studies, Sydney University NSW 2006. Designs and plans/Theatres. Australia.

Starck, Philippe. **Nouveau Théâtre National de Tokyo**. [New National Theater, Tokyo, Japan]. Seyssel, France: Champ Vallon, 1987. – 24 p.: ill. *Notes*: Parallel text in French and English. *Subjects*: Designs and plans.

Stark, Ulrike. **Competitions: operas, theatres and concert buildings**. Stuttgart: IRB Verlag, 1990. – 48 p. *Notes*: Includes indexes. Theatres. Designs and plans. Music-halls. Centres for the performing arts. Architecture plans. Bibliography.

Stern, Lawrence. **Stage management**. 6th edn. Boston: Allyn & Bacon, 1998. – xv, 362 p.: ill. *Notes*: Includes index.

Stoddard, Richard. **Theatre and cinema architecture: a guide to information sources**. Detroit: Gale Research Co., 1978. – xi, 368 p. *Notes*: Includes indexes. Theatre architecture.

Stürzebecher, Peter. **Szenische Architektur heute: 28 Entwürfe für Raum und Bühne: Deutsches Architekturmuseum, Frankfurt am Main, 16. November 1988 bis 8. Januar 1989**. Munich: Das Architekturmuseum, 1988. – 72 p.: ill. *Notes*: Theatre stage design.

Theatre spaces: issues in design. Canberra: ACT Administration, 1989. – 3, 84 p.: 1 map. *Notes*: 'A public seminar held at the Arts Centre, Australian National University, Canberra, on Friday 16 June 1989'. Includes bibliographical references and index. Theatres. Construction. Arts centres. Australia.

Tidworth, Simon. **Theatres: an architectural and cultural history**. New York: Praeger, 1973. 224 p.

Vance, Mary A. **Theater architecture: a basic bibliography**. Monticello, Ill.: Vance Bibliographies, 1981. – 6 p. *Notes*: Microfiche. New York: New York Public Library, 1982. 1 microfiche: negative. (FSN 37,458).

Walker, Bradford C. **Boston performing arts center: order, significance and an architectural process**. 1985. – 106 p.: ill. *Notes*: Includes bibliographies. Thesis (M. Arch.)–Harvard University, 1985. Theatre architecture. Designs and plans. Buildings, structures, etc.

Welker, David. **Stagecraft: a handbook for organization, construction, and management**. 2nd edn. Boston: Allyn & Bacon, 1987. – xvi, 492 p.: ill. *Notes*: Includes bibliographical references and index.

Woll, Stefan. **Das Totaltheater: ein Projekt von Walter Gropius und Erwin Piscator**. Berlin: Gesellschaft für Theatergeschichte, 1984. – 213 p.: ill. *Notes*: Includes index. Bibliography: p. 192–209. Theatre architecture. Germany. History. 20th century/Gropius, Walter, 1883–1969/Piscator, Erwin, 1893–1966.

Young, Edgar. **Lincoln Center: the building of an institution**. New York: New York University Press, 1980. 334 p.

Young, William, ed. **Famous American playhouses, 1716–1971**. 2 vols. Chicago: American Library Association, 1973.

Zodiac 2: theatre history and design. Milan and New York: B. Alfieri, R. Minetto, 1989. – 222 p.: ill. (some col.). *Notes*: Julius Posener – Daniel Rabreau – Guido Canella – Theo Crosby – Gottfried Böhm and Stefan Böhm – Aldo Rossi and Morris Adjmi – Carol McMichael Reese and Thomas Ford Reese – Gottfried Böhm – Frank O. Gehry – Hans Hollein – James Stirling – Kurt W. Forster. Architecture.

L. Puppetry and Masks

L1. Puppetry

Adachi, Barbara C. and Joel Sackett. **Backstage at Bunraku: a behind-the-scenes look at Japan's traditional puppet theatre**. New York: Weatherhill, 1985. – xiv, 192 p.: ill. *Notes*: Based on: **The voices and hands of Bunraku**, c.1978. Includes index. *Subjects*: Bunraku.

'Adel Abu-Shanab. **Karaküz**. Damascus: Ministry for the Preservation and Promulgation of Antiquities, n.d.

Amaral, Ana Maria. **Teatro de bonecos no Brasil e em São Paulo de 1940 a 1980**. São Paulo: Com-Arte, 1994. – 74 p.: ill. *Notes*: Puppet theatre. Brazil.

And, Metin. **Karagöz: Turkish shadow theatre with an appendix on the history of Turkish puppet theatre**. Rev. new edn. Istanbul: Dost Yayinlari, 1979. – 116, 2 p.: ill. (some col.). *Notes*: Bibliography: p. 117. History/Karagöz.

Ando, Tsuruo. **Bunraku: the puppet theater**. 1st edn. New York: Walker/ Weatherhill, 1970. 222 p. illus. (part col.). *Notes*: Translation of **Bunraku** originally published as vol. 3 of **Nihon no dento**.

Baird, Bill. **The art of the puppet**. New York: Macmillan, 1965. 251 p.

Belitska-Scholtz, Hedvig. **Théâtre forain de marionnettes et de guignols en Hongrie**. [Itinerant puppet and marionette theatres in Hungary]. Charlesville-Mézières, France: IMPR Moderne, 1976.

Beloff, Angelina. **Historia técnica y función educativa del teatro de muñecos en México y en el mundo**. [The technical history and educational function of puppet theatre in México and in the world]. México City: Secretaría de Educación Pública, 1945.

Benegal, Som. **Puppet theatre around the world**. New Delhi: Bharariya Natya Sangh, 1960. – 180 p.: ill. *Notes*: 'The contents of this volume originally appeared in Natya, Theatre Arts Journal'. Puppets and puppet-plays.

Bezděk, Zdeněk. **Československá loutková divadla, 1949–1969**. [Czechoslovak puppet theatre, 1949–69]. Prague: Divadelní ústav, 1973. 160 p.

Bissegger, Ursula. **Puppentheater in der Schweiz**. [Puppet theatre in Switzerland]. Zürich: Theater Kultur-Verlag, 1978.

Brecht, Stefan. **Peter Schumann's Bread and Puppet Theatre**. London: Methuen, 1988. – 813 p., 48 p. of plates: ill. *Notes*: Vol. 2. Of a series on theatre. Criticism and interpretation/ Puppet theatre. Critical studies.

Burger, Gerd. **Agitation und Argumentation im politischen Theater: die San Francisco Mime Troupe und Peter Schumanns Bread and Puppet Theater als komplementäre Modelle aufklärerischen Theaters**. Berlin: Verlag für Wissenschaft und Bildung, 1993. – 212 p. *Notes*: Includes bibliographical references (p. 203–12). San Francisco Mime Troupe/Bread and Puppet Theatre.

Buurman, P. **Wayang golek: the entrancing world of classical West Javanese puppet theatre**. Singapore and Oxford: Oxford University Press, 1991 1988. – x, 152 p.: ill. (some col.), 1 col. map. *Notes*: Translation of: Wayang golek. Bibliography: p. 150–1. Puppets/Java (Indonesia).

Byrom, Michael. **Punch in the Italian puppet theatre**. Fontwell, Sussex: Centaur Press, 1983. – 229 p., 30 p. of plates: ill. *Notes*: Includes index. Bibliography: p. 219–24. Puppets and puppet-plays. Italy/Punch and Judy.

Callahan, Pegg. **Puppets, stop the flap!: the Arpeggio method of mouth puppet manipulation**. Atlanta, GA: Arpeggio, 1994. – 86 p.: ill.

Cecchi, Doretta. **Attori di legno: la marionetta italiana tra '600 e '900**. Rome: Fratelli Palombi Editori, 1988. – 115 p.: ill. *Notes*: Includes bibliographical references and indexes. Marionettes. Italy. History.

Cho, Yong-su. **Inhyongguk kaeron: iron kwa silche**. [Seoul]: Chongdong Ch'ulp'ansa, 1987. – 252 p.: ill. Korea.

Contractor, M.R. **Creative drama and puppetry in education**. New Delhi: National Book Trust, 1984. 100 p.

–––– and Jordi Coca. **Les Grans tradicions populars, ombres i titelles**. Barcelona: Institut del Teatre: Edicions 62, 1977. – 173 p., 24 p. of plates: ill. *Notes*: Includes bibliographies. Puppet theatre. Spain.

Currell, David. **The complete book of puppet theatre**. Totowa, N.J.: Barnes & Noble Books, 1987 1985. – 342 p.: ill. *Notes*: Rev., updated edn of: The complete book of puppetry, 1974. Includes index. Bibliography: p. 323–31. Introduces the history of puppetry and gives instruc-

tions for making various types of puppets, creating stage sets, and producing plays.

Dagan, Esther A. **Emotions in motion: theatrical puppets and masks from Black Africa**. Montréal: Galerie Amrad African Arts, 1990. – 167 p.: ill. Col. ill. on folded covers. *Notes*: Includes bibliographical references. Puppets and puppet-plays. Masks. Africa, Sub-Saharan.

Darkowska-Nidzgorski, Olenka. **L'Afrique noire en marionettes**. Charleville-Mézières: Unione internationale de la marionette, 1988. – 80 p.: ill. *Notes*: Special issue of: **Unima informations**. Puppets and puppet-plays. Africa, Sub-Saharan.

––––. **Théâtre populaire de marionnettes en Afrique sud-Saharienne**. [Popular puppet theatre in sub-Saharan Africa]. Bandundu, Zaïre: Centre d'études ethnologiques, 1980. 259 p.

Dasa, Gauranga Carana. **Lokanatya parampara o kandheinata**. Kataka: Phrends Pablisarsa, 1993. – 5, 294 p.: ill. *Notes*: In Oriya. Includes bibliographical references (p. 287–94). History and development of folk and puppet theatre; with special reference to Orissa. History/ Puppets and puppet plays. India. Orissa.

Devens, Tuur and Koen Kwanten. **Tussen pop en theater: een cultuursociologische zoektocht naar het fenomeen poppentheater in Vlaanderen**. Neerpelt [Belgium]: Culturele Aangelegenheden, PICS Dommelhof, 1991. – 110 p.: ill. *Notes*: Includes bibliographical references (p. 99–105). Puppet theatre. Belgium. Flanders.

Di Rosa, Gino. **A scuola con i burattini: didattica dei burattini**. Brescia: La scuola, 1986, 1981. – 186 p.: ill. (some col.). *Notes*: Includes bibliographical references (p. 185–6). Puppet theatre. Italy.

Drewal, Margaret Thompson, ed. **Africa: prophecy and puppetry, weddings and worship, ritual, rivalry and opera**. Cambridge, MA; London: MIT Press, 1988. – 207 p.: ill., maps. *Series*: TDR; v. 32, no. 2 (T118). *Notes*: Includes bibliographies. Rites and ceremonies. Africa.

Dupavillon, Christian. **Bread and Puppet Theatre: black and white shows, spectacles en noir et blanc**. Paris: Les Loges, 1978. – 93 p.: ill. *Notes*: Bibliography: p. 91. French language. Texts/Puppets and puppet-plays. France/Street theatre.

Felix, Geoff. **Conversations with Punch: Punch and Judy men talk about their lives**. Wembley Park, Middlesex: G. Felix, 1994. – xii, 79 p., [4] p. of plates: ill. *Notes*: Puppeteers. Punch and Judy. UK.

Feustel, Gotthard. **Prinzessin und Spass-macher: eine Kulturgeschichte des Puppen-theaters der Welt**. Leipzig: Edition Leipzig, 1991. – 228 p.: ill. (some col.). *Notes*: Includes bibliographical references (p. 212–16) and indexes. Puppet theatre. History.

Fijan, Carol, Frank Ballard and Christina Starobin. **Directing puppet theatre step by step**. San Jose, Calif.: Resource Publications, 1989. – x, 96 p.: ill. *Notes*: Bibliography: p. 94–6.

Fisher, James, ed. **The puppetry yearbook. Volume one**. Lewiston, N.Y.: Edwin Mellen Press, 1995. – vii, 203 p.: ill. *Notes*: Includes bibliographical references. Introduction/James Fisher – The voice of the people/George Speaight – Puppets and the Commedia dell'Arte in the sixteenth, seventeenth, and eighteenth centuries/Ryan Howard – Chapbooks and English puppet plays/John Phillips – Bunraku: the traditional puppet theater of Japan/Kinko Ito – The development and characterization: puppet figures of Kasperltheater/Martha Freehan – The Argentine creole puppet theatre (el teatro criollo argentino de títeres): an exploratory essay/Donald S. Castro – A chronology of European theater events involving masks, puppets, and other performing objects, 1887–1939/John Bell – An interview with Lou Bunin: 'being a puppet'/Kathryn Grow-McCromick – Po(p)litieke satire Vlaamse realiteit?/Freek Neirynck – Theatre of the twentieth century as theatre of the performing object/John Bell – Domestic resurrection: The Bread and Puppet Theatre/James Fisher – Book reviews.

Foulquié, Philippe and Gérard Lo Monaco. **Les Théâtres de marionnettes en France: les compagnies membres de Centre national des marionnettes**. Lyon: La Manufacture, 1985. – 214 p.: ill.; 19 x. *Notes*: Includes index. Bibliography: p. 209–14. France.

Fournel, Paul. **L'Histoire véritable de Guignol**. Lyon: Fédérop, 1975. – 298 p.: ill. *Notes*: Bibliography: p. 285–98. History/Popular culture. France. Guignol.

Fraser, Peter. **Punch and Judy**. London and New York: Batsford Van Nostrand Reinhold Co., 1970. – 120 p. illus. *Notes*: Bibliography: p. 120. History/Punch and Judy.

Froschan, Frank. **The puppetry tradition of Sub-Saharan Africa: Descriptions and defin-itions**. Austin: University of Texas, 1980.

Gitza, Letitia, Iordan Chimet and Valentin Silvestru. **Teatrul de püapuşi in România**. [Puppet theatre in Romania]. Bucharest, 1969.

Gontard, Denis. **Nô-kyôgen: le masque et le rire [mask and laughter]**. Marburg: Hitzeroth, 1987. – 88 p.: ill. (some col.). *Notes*: French, English, German. Cover title also in Japanese. Noh. Kyogen. Japan. Costume. Masks.

Gradev, Dimiter, ed. **Bulgarian puppet theatre**. Sofia: Information Centre, 1979. 144 p.

Grano, Enzo and Alberto Carpino. **Il teatro di figura: guaratelle e pupi**. Naples: Società editrice napoletana, 1988. – 157, 19 p., 32 p. of plates: ill. *Notes*: Bibliography: p. 168–70. Puppet plays, Italian. History.

Groenendael, Victoria M. Clara van. **Wayang theatre in Indonesia: an annotated bibli-ography**. Dordrecht-Holland; Providence, R.I.: Foris, 1987. – 221 p. *Notes*: Includes indexes. Puppet theatres. Indonesia. Bibliography.

Hagher, Iyorwuese Harry. **The Tiv Kwagh-Hir: a popular Nigerian puppet theatre**. Lagos: Centre for Black and African Arts and Civilization, 1990. – vii, 224 p., 8 p. of plates: ill. (some col.). *Notes*: Includes bibliographical references and index.

Halász, László and Dezso Szilágyi. **Contem-porary Hungarian puppet theatre**. Budapest: Corvina, 1978. – 78 p., 48 p. of plates: ill. (some col.) *Notes*: Translation of **A Mai magyar bábsz´ ınház**. Állami Bábszínház (Company).

Hamilton, Robert Craig. **The Bread and Puppet Theatre of Peter Schumann: history and ana-lysis**. 1990 1978. – xi, 385 p.: ill. *Notes*: Includes bibliographical references (p. 380–5). Thesis (Ph. D.)–Indiana University, 1978. Photocopy. Ann Arbor, Mich.: University Microfilms International, 1990. Bread and Puppet Theatre. History.

Harmignies, Magda. **Guide de ressources pour les intervenants dans le domaine de la marionnette au Québec**. Montréal: Association québécoise des marionnettistes, 1990. – 1 vol. (pag. multiple). *Notes*: Directories/Puppet theater. Quebec (Province). Puppet making. Study and teaching.

Iglesias, Sonia and Guillermo Murray Prisant. **Piel de papel, manos de palo: historia de los títeres en México**. México City: Consejo Nacional para la Cultura y las Artes: FONCA: Espasa-Calpe Mexicana, 1995. – 223 p.: ill. (some col.). *Notes*: Includes bibliographical references (p. 222–3). Puppet theatre. Mexico. History.

Jurkowski, Henryk. **Dzieje teatru lalek. Od wielkiej reformy do wspólczesnóśi**. [History of the puppet theatre. From theatre's reform to today]. Warsaw: 1984.

——. **Ecrivains et marionettes. Quatre siècles de littérature dramatique**. [Writers and puppets: four centuries of dramatic literature]. Charleville-Mezieres: Institut National de la Marionnette, 1991.

——. **A history of European puppetry from its origins to the end of the 19th century**. Lewiston: Edwin Mellen Press, 1996. – 426 p. *Notes*: Includes bibliographical references (p. 402–13) and index.

—— and Penny Francis. **Aspects of puppet theatre: a collection of essays**. London: Puppet Centre Trust, 1988. – viii, 112 p.: ill. *Notes*: Includes bibliographies.

Katashiro kugutsu ningyo. Shohan. Tokyo: Heibonsha, 1991. – 245 p.: ill.; 1 videocassette. Puppet theatre. Japan.

Kawajiri, Taiji. **Nihon ningyogeki hattatsushi ko**. Tokyo: Bansei Shobo, 1986. – 320 p.: ill. *Notes*: In Japanese. Includes index. Bibliography: p. 306–7. Puppets and puppet-plays. Japan. History.

Keene, Donald. **Bunraku; the art of the Japanese puppet theatre**. Rev. paperback edn. Tokyo: Kodansha International, 1973. – 88 p. illus. Kaneko, Hiroshi. illus. *Notes*: Distributed in the United States by Harper & Row, New York. 'List of plays': p. 78–81. Bibliography: p. 82–83.

Kelly, Catriona. **Petrushka: the Russian carnival puppet theatre**. Cambridge: New York: Cambridge University Press, 1990. – xv, 292 p.: ill. *Notes*: Includes bibliographical references (p. 269–82) and index. Soviet Union/Russian puppet theatre: Petrushka, history.

Kim, Jae-Chel, ed. **Kokdukagsi-nolum**. [Puppet theatre: Kogdogaksi]. Seoul: Korean Traditional Drama Institute, 1986. 165 pp.

Kipsch, Walter. **Bemerkungen zum Puppenspiel: 1936–1990, eine Auswahl**. Frankfurt/Main: Puppen und Masken, 1992. – 204 p.: ill. *Notes*: Includes bibliographical references. Puppet theatre. Germany. History. 20th century.

Knoedgen, Werner. **Das unmögliche Theater: zur Phänomenologie des Figurentheaters**. Stuttgart: Urachhaus, 1990. – 137 p.: 59 ill. *Notes*: Includes bibliographical references (p. 127) and index. *Subjects*: Puppet theatre. Phenomenology.

Kós, Lajos. **A Bóbita: a pécsi bábegyüttes története**. Pécs: Pro Pannonia Kiadói Alapítvány, 1993. – 202 p.: ill. *Subjects*: Puppet theatres. Hungary. Pécs. History/Bóbita (Puppet theatre).

Kourilsky, Françoise. **Le Bread and Puppet Theatre**. Lausanne: 10: Métropole: La Cité-éditeur, 1971. – 279 p. 12 plates. *Notes*: Bibliography: p. 265–8. Bread and Puppet Theatre.

Kulish, A.P. **Kukol'niki v Peterburge**. St Petersburg: Sankt-Peterburgskaia akademiia teatral'nogo iskusstva, 1995. – 136 p.: ill. *Notes*: Includes bibliographical references. Puppet theatre. Russia (Federation). History/Puppeteers.

Kumar, Sunil. **Puppetry: a tool of mass communication**. Varanasi: National Council for Development Communication, 1989. 77 p.

Kurata, Yoshihiro. **Tokyo no ningyo joruri**. Tokyo: Nihon Geijutsu Bunka Shinkokai, 1991. – xi, 385, p.: ill. (some col.). *Notes*: Includes index. Puppet theatre. Japan. History. Sources/Bunraku.

Law, Jane Marie. **Puppets of nostalgia: the life, death, and rebirth of the Japanese Awaji ningyo tradition**. Princeton, N.J.: Princeton University Press, 1997. – xiii, 322 p.: ill., maps. *Notes*: Includes bibliographical references (p. [301]–11) and index. Awaji Island/Performing arts. Religious aspects/Japan.

Lê, Bá Sinh. **Marionnettes sur eau**. [Water puppetry]. Ho Chí Minh City: Øoànroi nuc dân toc, 1993. – 139 p.: col. ill. *Notes*: French, English and Vietnamese. Water puppetry. Vietnam's unique art form in words and photos.

Leach, Robert. **The Punch and Judy show: history, tradition and meaning**. London: Batsford Academic and Educational, 1985. – 192 p.: ill. *Notes*: Includes index. Bibliography: p. 185–8. Punch and Judy. History/English puppet theatre.

Lee, Miles. **Puppet theatre: production and manipulation**. North Vancouver, B.C.: Charlemagne Press, 1991. – xiv, 226 p.: ill. *Notes*: Includes bibliographical references and index.

Lee, Sang-lan. **Funktionen des koreanischen Puppenspiels Kkoktugaksi-norûm**. Frankfurt am Main and New York: P. Lang, 1993. – x, 172 p.: ill. *Notes*: Originally presented as the author's thesis (doctoral)–Universität Bochum, 1992. Includes bibliographical references (p. 167–72). Puppet theatre. Korea.

Lenz, Johannes. **Figurentheater Jahrbuch**. Frankfurt: Puppen und Masken, 1990. – 405 p.: ill. *Subjects*: Puppet theatres. Directories.

Li, Ch'ang-min. **Chung-kuo min chien k'ui lei i shu**. Nanjing: Chiang-hsi chiao yü ch'u pan she: Chiang-hsi sheng hsin hua shu tien fa hsing,

1989. – 3, 4, 2, 264 p.: ill. *Notes*: Puppet theatre. China.

Liu, Chi. **Chung-kuo mu ou i shu**. Beijing: Chung-kuo shih chieh yü ch'u pan she, 1993. – 284 p.: ill. (some col.). *Notes*: Includes bibliographical references (p. 267–82). Puppet theatre. China.

Liu, Huan-yüeh. **Feng hua chüeh tai chang chung i: Taiwan ti pu tai hsi**. Taipei: T'ai yüan ch'u pan she: Tsung ching hsiao Wu shih t'u shu kung ssu, 1993. – 223 p.: ill. *Subjects*: Puppet theatre. Taiwan.

Luomala, Katharine. **Hula ki'i, Hawaiian puppetry**. Honolulu: Institute for Polynesian Studies: distributed by the University of Hawaii Press, 1984. – xi, 184 p.: ill. (1 col.). *Notes*: Includes index. Bibliography: p. 173–8. Puppets and puppet-plays. Hawaii.

María y Campos, Armando de. **Teatro mexicano de muñecos. Prólogo y notas: antología de 25 peizas de teatro guiñol**. [Mexican puppet theatre. Prologue and notes: an anthology of 25 puppet shows]. México City: El Nacional, 1941. 362 p.

Marionnettes en territoire brésilien. Charleville-Mézières: Editions Institut international de la marionnette, 1994. – 97 p.: ill. (some col.). *Notes*: Published on the occasion of the 10th Festival mondial des théâtres de marionnettes à Charleville-Mézières, Sept. 23-Oct. 2, 1994. Includes bibliographical references (p. 94–7). Puppet theatre. Brazil.

Mattson, Jean M. **Playwriting for the puppet theatre**. Lanham, Md.: Scarecrow Press, 1997. – vi, 235 p.: ill. *Notes*: Includes index. Puppet plays, American.

McCormick, John and Bennie Pratasik. **Popular puppet theatre in Europe, 1800–1914**. Great Britain: Ray DaSilva, 1998. 272 p.: ill.

McKay, Kenneth B. and Andrew Oxenham. **Puppetry in Canada: an art to enchant**. Willowdale, Ont.: Ontario Puppetry Association Pub. Co., 1980. – 168 p.: ill. *Notes*: Bibliography: p. 168. Puppets and puppet-plays. Canada.

McPharlin, Paul. **The puppet theatre in America: a history: with a list of puppeteers, 1524–1948**. New York: Harper, 1970, 1949. – xi, 506 p.: ill. *Notes*: Based on the author's thesis–Univ. of Michigan. Includes index. Photocopy. Ann Arbor, Mich.: University Microfilms, 1970.

Meschke, Michael and Margareta Sörenson. **In search of aesthetics for the puppet theatre**.

New Delhi: Indira Gandhi National Centre for the Arts: Sterling Publishers, 1992. – 176 p.: ill.

Mignon, Paul-Louis and Jean Mohr. **J'aime les marionnettes**. Paris: Denoël, 1960, 1969, – 249 p.: ill. *Notes*: Includes bibliographical references. Puppet theatre.

Miller, George Bertram, Janet Harris and William E. Hannaford. **Puppetry library: an annotated bibliography based on the Batchelder-McPharlin Collection at the University of New Mexico**. Westport, Conn.: Greenwood Press, 1981. – xxiv, 172 p. *Notes*: Puppets and puppet-plays. Documents on puppetry.

Minuth, Johannes. **Das Kaspertheater und seine Entwicklungsgeschichte: vom Possentreiben zur Puppenspielkunst**. [Kaspertheater]. Frankfurt: Puppen & Masken, 1996. – 195 p.: ill. *Notes*: Originally presented as the author's thesis (doctoral–Albert-Ludwigs-Universität Freiburg, 1994) under the title: **Das Kaspertheater: Geschichte des lustigen Handpuppenspiels als Spiegelbild seiner jeweiligen Zeit**. Includes bibliographical references (p. 185–193). Puppet theatre. Germany.

Nguyen, Huy Hong. **Nghe thucat múa roi Viet Nam**. Hanoi: Van hóa, 1974. – 194 p.: ill. *Notes*: In Vietnamese. Includes bibliographical references. Puppet theatre. Vietnam.

—— and Tran Trung Chinh. **Vietnamese traditional water puppetry**. 2nd edn. Hanoi: The Gioi, 1996. – 79 p.: ill. (some col.).

Niculescu, Margareta. **Teatrul de püapuşi ín lume**. [Puppet theatre in the world]. Berlin: Henschel, and Bucharest: Meridiane, 1966. 230 p.

——, ed. **The puppet theatre of the modern world; an international presentation in word and picture**. [Union internationale des marionnettes]. [1st American edn]. Boston: Plays: inc, 1967. – 228 p. 238 illus. (part col.). *Notes*: Translation of **Puppentheater der Welt**.

Obraztsov, Sergei Vladimirovich. **The Chinese puppet theatre**. Boston: Plays, inc., 1975. – 55 p., 12 p. of plates: ill. *Notes*: Reprint of the edn published by Faber & Faber, London. 'Comprises a chapter… from **The Chinese theatre**, published… 1957'. Describes the various types of Chinese puppet theatre, discusses ancient traditional plays still performed, and speculates on the origin of the gloved puppet.

Paërl, Hetty. **Tegen het decor van de rokende Vesuvius: Pulcinella en de magie van het volkspoppentheater in Zuid-Italië: een reisverhaal**. Abcoude: Uniepers, 1993. – 144 p.: ill. *Notes*: Puppet theatre. Sicily/Punchinello.

Philpott, Alexis Robert. **Dictionary of puppetry**. London: Macdonald & Co., 1969. – 291 p. 24 plates, illus., facsim., ports. *Notes*: Bibliography: p. 287–91.

Poliakova, O. and N.V. Filina. **Chto zhe takoe teatr kukol?: sbornik statei**. Moscow: Soiuz teatral'nykh deiatelei RSFSR, 1990. – 205 p., 40 p. of plates: ill. *Notes*: Puppet theatre. Soviet Union.

Pu tai hsi: Pu tai hsi t'u lu. Taipei shih: Chiao yü pu, 1996. – 2 vols. (393 p.): chiefly col. ill. *Notes*: Includes bibliographical references (vol. 2, p. 383) and index. Puppets. Taiwan.

Puppentheater der DDR: eine Bestandsaufnahme. [The puppet theatre of the GDR: a stocktaking]. Leipzig: UNIMA-Zentrum der DDR, 1984. 60 p.

Puppentheater gestern und heute. [Puppet theatre yesterday and today]. Dresden: Staatliche Kunstsammlungen, 1977. 191 p.

Puppet theatre in India. New Delhi: Ministry of Education and Culture, Govt. of India, 1983. – iv, 39 p.: ill. *Notes*: Bibliography: p. 21–2. Modern puppetry and its contemporary scene/Devi Lal Samar – Shadow play in Kerala/F. Seltmann – Shadow puppets and their iconography/Mel Helstien – Modern puppetry and the contemporary scene/Meher R. Contractor. Contribution.

Purschke, Hans Richard. **The German puppet theatre today: ill. documentation, publ. for the 50th anniversary of UNIMA (Union Internat. de la Marionnette) on the creative work of its members in the Fed. Republic of Germany**. Bonn–Bad Godesberg: Inter Nationes, 1979. – 86 p.: 104 ill.

Ruano y Vargas, María Virginia. **Manipulación de muñecos de funda o guante**. México City: Editorial Avante, 1993. – 128 p.: ill. *Notes*: Includes bibliographical references (p. 127–8). Puppet theatre. Mexico.

Sa'd, Faarouq. **Khayal al-Zhil al-'Arabi**. [The Arab shadow theatre]. Beirut: al-Matbou'aat lit-Tawzee' Wa n-Nashr, 1993.

Schrübbers, Christiane. **Kasper, Karagöz, Karagiosis: politisches Theater auf der Puppenbühne**. Berlin: Ararat, 1985. – 72 p.: ill. (some col.). *Notes*: Published in connection with the exhibition held between November 1985 and April 1986 at Galerie im Körnerpark, Berlin (West) and Internationale Zentrum der Volkshochschule Duisburg. Includes bibliographical references. Puppet theatres. Germany. History.

Schumann, Peter. **Puppen und Masken: das Bread and Puppet Theater: ein Arbeitsbericht**. Frankfurt (am Main): Fischer-Taschenbuch-Verlag, 1973. – 108 p.: numerous ill. (part col.). Greene, Wayne, illus. *Notes*: Includes play, The birdcatcher in hell, in English and German. Bread and Puppet Theatre.

Segel, Harold B. **Pinocchio's progeny: puppets, marionettes, automatons and robots in modernist and avant-garde drama**. Baltimore: Johns Hopkins University Press, 1995. – xii, 372 p.: ill. *Series*: PAJ books. *Notes*: Includes bibliographical references (p. 351–60) and index.

Selmeczi, Elek. **Világhódító bábok**. [World-conquering puppets]. Budapest: Corvina, 1986. 212 p.

Shershow, Scott Cutler. **Puppets and 'popular' culture**. Ithaca: Cornell University Press, 1995. – x, 252 p.: ill. *Notes*: Includes bibliographical references and index. Puppet theatre/Popular culture. History.

Singer, Noel Francis. **Burmese puppets**. Singapore and New York: Oxford University Press, 1992. – xii, 98 p., 16 p. of plates: ill. (some col.), map. *Notes*: Includes bibliographical references (p. 94–5) and index. History/Puppets. Burma.

Soekatno. **Mengenal wayang kulit purwa**. Semarang: Aneka Ilmu, 1992. – xvi, 212 p.: ill. *Notes*: Includes bibliographical references (p. 211). Illustration, character, and history of leather shadow puppet Surakarta version, Jawa Tengah Province. Shadow puppets. Indonesia. Java.

Speaight, George. **The history of the English puppet theatre**. 2nd edn. London: Hale, 1990. – 366 p.: ill. *Notes*: Previous edn: London: Harrap, 1955. Includes index.

Suib, Leonard and Muriel Broadman. **Marionettes: how to make and perform with them**. New York: Dover, 1988. – viii, 182 p.: ill. *Notes*: 'A corrected and abridged republication of **Marionettes onstage!**, first published by Harper & Row, New York, in 1975'–. Includes index. Bibliography: p. 171–2.

Sumandi, I Nyoman. **Serba neka wayang kulit Bali**. [Denpasar]: Departemen Pendidikan dan Kebudayaan, Direktorat Jendral Kebudayaan, Proyek Pengembangan Kesenian Bali, 1984. – vii, 71 p.: ill. *Notes*: Wayang/Puppet theater. Indonesia. Bali (Province).

Szilágyi, Dezso. **Die Welt des Puppenspielers**. Berlin: Henschel, 1989. – 245 p.: ill. (some col.). *Notes*: English and German.

Sztaudynger, Jan, Henryk Jurkowski and Henryk Ryl. **Od szopki do teatru lalek**. Lódz:

Wydawnictwo Lódzkie, 1961. (unpaged): ill. *Notes*: Summaries in Russian, English, and French. Puppet theatre. Poland.

Taiwan hsi chü kuan chuan chi. Ch'u pan. [I-lan hsien]: I-lan hsien li wen hua chung hsin, 1993. – 92 p.: ill. (some col.). *Subjects*: Puppet theatre. Taiwan.

Tilakasiri, J. **Puppetry in Sri Lanka**. [Colombo]: Dept. of Cultural Affairs, 1976. – 29 p., 16 p. of plates: ill. (some col.). *Notes*: Includes bibliographical references. Puppets and puppet-plays. Sri Lanka.

Tillis, Steve. **Toward an aesthetics of the puppet: puppetry as a theatrical art**. New York: Greenwood Press, 1992. – xii, 181 p. *Notes*: Includes bibliographical references (p. 171–6) and index. Puppet theatre. Aesthetics.

Tô Sanh. **Nghe thucat múa roi nuc**. Hanoi: Van Hóa, 1976. – 179 p.: ill. *Notes*: Water puppetry.

Universidade de São Paulo. Escola de Comunicações e Artes. Biblioteca. **Teatro de bonecos: bibliografia**. São Paulo: ECA/USP, 1986. – 38 p. *Notes*: Puppet theatre. Bibliography.

Vella, Maeve and Helen Rickards. **Theatre of the impossible: puppet theatre in Australia**. Roseville, NSW: Craftsman House, 1989. – 167 p.: ill. (some col.). *Notes*: Includes bibliographical references (p. 160). Puppet theatre. Australia.

Venkatesvarlu, Bittu. **Tolubommalata pradarsanam**. Hyderabad [India]: 1993. – xviii, 163, 1 p.: ill. *Notes*: In Telugu. Includes bibliographical references (p. 164). Performance of leather puppet show in Andhra Pradesh; a study. Puppet theatre. India. Andhra Pradesh.

Venu, Ji. **Puppetry and lesser known dance traditions of Kerala**. Irinjalakuda, Trichur District, Kerala, India: Natana Kairali, Research and Performing Centre for Traditional Arts, 1990. – xii, 149 p.: ill. *Notes*: Study of folk theatre and dancing. Includes index. Includes bibliographical references (p. 141–2). Performing arts. India. Kerala/Puppet theatre.

Whanslaw, Harry William. **A bench book of puppetry; containing useful references in alphabetical order**. Redhill: Surrey: Wells Gardner: Darton, 1957. – xii, 216 p. illus. (part col.). *Notes*: Bibliography: p. 204–13. An encyclopedia of puppetry containing alphabetically arranged references on the construction and manipulation of puppets.

Wright, John. **Rod, shadow and love: puppets from the Little Angel Theatre**. London: Robert Hale Ltd, 1986.

Yehezkely, Yehoudith. **Teatron bubot**. [Tel-Aviv]: Reshafim, 1988. – xvi, 439 p., 16 p. of plates: ill. *Notes*: Bibliography: p. 433–9. Puppet theatres. Israel.

L2. Masks

Bernolles, Jacques. **Permanence de la parure et du masque africains**. [Permanent ornamentation and African mask]. Paris: G.-P. Maisonneuve et Larose, 1966. 632 p.

Cole, Herbert M., ed. **I am not myself: the art of African masquerade**. Los Angeles: Museum of Cultural History, UCLA, 1985. 112 p.

Enekw, Osmond Onuora. **Igbo masks: the oneness of ritual and theatre**. New York: Columbia University, 1982. 268 p.
Fotopoulos, Dionysis. **Masks Theatre**. Athens: Kastaniotis, 1980.

Janney, Kay Print. **A bibliography on the mask**. Blacksburg, VA; New Orleans, La.: American Alliance for Theatre and Education, Theatre Arts Dept., Virginia Tech; Distributed by Anchorage Press, 1989. – 11 p. *Notes*: Masks. Bibliography.

Obuh, Sulvanus Onwukaike Stanley. **The theatrical use of masks in Igbo areas of Nigeria**. New York: New York University, 1984. 294 p.

Smith, Susan Valeria Harris. **Masks in modern drama**. Berkeley: University of California Press, 1984. – ix, 237 p.: ill. *Notes*: Includes index. Bibliography: p. 201–24. Drama in European languages, 1896–1984. Use of masks.

Vanni Menichi, Carlo, ed. **Le maschere dell 'uomo. Segni plastici de oriente ad occidente**. [The masks of man: plastic signs from east to west]. Pistola: Tellini, 1986. 80 p.

M. Musical Theatre

Alpert, Hollis. **Broadway!: 125 years of musical theatre**. New York: Arcade Pub., 1991. – viii, 248 p.: ill. (some col.). *Notes*: Companion text for the IBM-sponsored show drawn from the collections of the Museum of the City of New York and opening at the IBM Gallery of Science and Art in New York City in May, 1991. Includes index.

Appel, Wolf. **Café Wahn-Sinn: musikalisch-literarische Revue**. St Gallen: Stadttheater, 1993. (unpaged): ill. *Notes*: Revues/Musical theatre.

Appia, Adolphe. **Attore, musica e scena**. Milan: Feltrinelli, 1975. – 252 p., 16 p. of plates: ill. *Notes*: Translation of: **La mise en scène du drame wagnérien**/translated by Delia

Gambelli; **La musique et la mise en scène**/ translated by Delia Gambelli; **L'oeuvre d'art vivant**/translated by Marco De Marinis. Bibliography: p. 237–50. Stage-setting and scenery. Dramaturgy/Wagner, Richard, 1813–83.

Balk, H. Wesley. **The complete singer-actor: training for music theater**. 2nd edn. Minneapolis: University of Minnesota Press, 1985. – xix, 251 p. *Notes*: Includes index. Bibliography: p. 231–9.

Basso, Alberto. **Musica in scena: storia dello spettacolo musicale**. Turin: UTET, 1995. 5 vols. *Notes*: Includes bibliographical references. vol. 1. Il teatro musicale dalle origini al primo Settecento – vol. 4. Altri generi di teatro musicale – vol. 5. L'arte della danza e del balletto. Dramatic music. History and criticism/ Musical theatre. History.

Bawtree, Michael. **The new singing theatre: a charter for the music theatre movement**. New York and Bristol: Oxford University Press and Bristol Press, 1991. – viii, 232 p.: ill. *Notes*: Includes bibliographical references (p. 220–1) and index.

Bell, Marty. **Backstage on Broadway: musicals and their makers**. London: Nick Hern, 1994 1993. – xiv, 288 p. *Notes*: First published in the United States of America under the title **Broadway Stories** in 1993. Includes index. Musicals.

——. **Broadway stories: a backstage journey through musical theatre**. New York: Limelight Editions, 1993. – xiv, 288 p.: ill. *Notes*: Includes index. History and criticism.

Betsuyaku, Minoru and Akihiro Komori. **Akazukin-chan no mori no okamitachi no kurisumasu: Ongaku geki**. Tokyo: Shinsuisha, 1993. – 94 p., 4 p. of plates: ill. *Notes*: Musical theatre. Japan.

Bloom, Ken. **American song: the complete musical theatre companion**. 2nd edn, 1877–1995. New York; London: Schirmer Books; Prentice Hall International, 1996. – 2 vols. (xiii, 2093 p.). *Notes*: vol. 1. A–S – vol. 2. T–Z and indexes.

Bordman, Gerald Martin. **American musical comedy**. New York: Oxford University Press, 1982. 244 p.

——. **American musical theatre: a chronicle**. 2nd edn. New York: Oxford University Press, 1992. – 821 p. *Notes*: Includes index. Musicals. United States. History and criticism.

Bowers, Dwight Blocker. **American musical theater: shows, songs, and stars**. Washington, D.C.: Smithsonian Collection of Recordings, 1989. – 132 p.: ill. *Notes*: Text accompanies four compact discs (SMITH 036) with the same title. Includes index. Bibliography: p. 128. Musical revues. United States.

Citron, Stephen. **The wordsmiths: Oscar Hammerstein 2nd and Alan Jay Lerner**. London: Sinclair-Stevenson, 1996 1995. – xii, 446 p.: ill., ports., music. *Notes*: Originally published: Oxford University Press, 1995. Includes index. Bibliography: p. 415–6. Musical theatre. United States/Hammerstein, Oscar.

Dalhaus, Carl. **Pipers Enzyklopädia des Musiktheaters**. [Piper's encyclopedia of music theatre].

Directory of contemporary operas and music theater works and North American premieres 1980–1989. New York: Central Opera Service, 1990. – viii, 325 p. *Notes*: Includes indexes.

Dizikes, John. **Opera in America: a cultural history**. New Haven, CT: Yale University Press, 1993. 611 p.

Dnepropetrovskii Gosudarstvenyi teatr opery i baleta. [Dnipropetrovsk State Theatre of Opera and Ballet]. Dnipropetrovsk: Oblpoligrafizdat, 1980. 72 p.

Dunham, Katherine. **Dances of Haiti**. Los Angeles: Center for Afro-American Studies, University of California at Los Angeles, 1983.

Ely, Norbert and Stefan Jaeger, eds. **Regie heute. Musiktheater in unserer Zeit**. [Directing today: contemporary music theatre]. Berlin: Quadriga, 1984. 248 p.

Engel, Lehman. **The American musical theatre**. Rev. edn. New York: Macmillan, 1975. – xx, 266 p. *Notes*: Includes index. Discography: p. 229–45. Bibliography: p. 252–3.

Felsenstein, Walter and Siegfried Melchinger. **Musiktheater**. [Music theatre]. Bremen: Schunemann, 1961. 106 p.

Fetterman, William. **John Cage's theatre pieces: notations and performances**. Amsterdam, Netherlands: Harwood Academic Publishers, 1996. – xviii, 282 p.: ill. *Notes*: Includes bibliographical reference and indexes. History and criticism.

Gamo, Satoaki, ed. **Nihon no Ongaku Asia no ongaku**. [A study of Japanese music and Asian music]. Tokyo: Iwanami shoten, 1989. 314 p.

Gänzl, Kurt. **The Blackwell guide to the musical theatre on record**. Oxford: Basil Blackwell, 1990. – 350 p. *Notes*: Includes index. Musical shows.

——. **The British musical theatre**. Basingstoke: Macmillan, 1986. – 2 vols. *Notes*: Includes index. vol. 1. 1865–1914 – vol. 2. 1915–84.

Musical revues, comedies, etc. History and criticism/Musical shows in English, 1866–1979.

——. **The encyclopedia of the musical theatre**. Oxford: Blackwell Reference, 1994. 2 v.xiv., 1,610 p: ill.

—— and Andrew Lamb. **Gänzl's book of the musical theatre**. London: Bodley Head, 1988. – xv, 1353 p., [32] p. of plates: ill. *Notes*: Includes index. Musical shows.

Giannaris, George. **Music and theatre**. Athens: Efstathiadis Group, 1983. – 180 p.: ill. *Notes*: My artistic credo – The ballad of the dead brother: a musical tragedy – Exodus: a dramatic fantasy – The music to the songs of The ballad of the dead brother: accompanied by the Greek texts and their transliteration – Mikis Theodorakis, approaches to music for ancient drama/by George Giannaris. Photocopy. Austin, [Tex.]: BookLab, Inc., 1996. Musical theatre. Greece. Theodorakis, Mikos. Criticism and interpretation.

Glikman, Isaak. **Meyerhold i muzykal'nyi teatr**. Leningrad: Vses. izd-vo 'Sov. kompozitor', Leningradskoe otd-nie, 1989. – 349 p.: ill. *Notes*: At head of title: Leningradskaia gosudarstvennaia konservatoriia imeni N.A. Rimskogo-Korsakova. Includes bibliographical references. Musical theatre. Soviet Union. Meyerhold, 1874–1940.

Glushakov, Igor Valerevich. **Muzychny teatr Belarusi, 1917–1959**. Minsk: Navuka i tekhnika, 1993. – 430 p.: ill. *Notes*: Includes bibliographical references and index. Musical theatre. Belarus. History.

Gottfried, Martin. **More Broadway musicals since 1980**. New York: Harry N. Abrams, 1991. 224 p.

Greek Opera. Athens: Ministry of Culture, 1988.

Green, Stanley. **Encyclopedia of the musical theatre: an updated reference guide to over 2000 performers, writers, directors, productions, and songs of the musical stage, both in New York and London**. New York: Da Capo Press, 1980. – vi, 492 p., [8] p. of plates: ill. *Notes*: Original title: **Encyclopaedia of the musical theatre**. Reprint of the edn published by Dodd, Mead, New York; 'supplemented with photographs and addenda'. Bibliography: p. 472–7. Discography: p. 478–88.

Guernsey, Otis L. **Curtain times: the New York theater, 1965–1987**. New York, NY: Applause, 1987. – viii, 613 p.: ill. *Notes*: Includes index.

Hapgood, Elizabeth Reynolds, ed. **Stanislavski on opera**. New York: Theatre Arts Books:

c1975, – x, 374 p.ill. *Notes*: Based on the teachings of Stanislavski with Pavel Rumyantsev. Translated by Hapgood from the Russian.

Harburg, Ernest and Bernard Rosenberg. **The Broadway musical: collaboration in commerce and art**. New York: New York University Press, 1993. 356 p.

Herrmannová, E., E. Illingová and M. Kuna. 'České hudební divadlo v letech 1945–1960'. [Czech musical theatre 1945–60]. In **Příspěvky k dějinám české hudby II** [Contributors to the history of Czech music II], ed. Milan Kun, 155–232. Prague: Academia, 1972.

Hirsch, Foster. **Harold Prince and the American musical theatre**. Cambridge: Cambridge University Press, 1989. *Series*: Directors in perspective. *Notes*: Includes bibliography and index. Prince, Harold. Directing.

Hischak, Thomas S. **Word crazy: Broadway lyricists from Cohan to Sondheim**. Praeger Publishers, 1991. – 256 p.

——. **Stage it with music: an encyclopedic guide to the American musical theatre**. Westport, Conn.: Greenwood Press, 1993. – viii, 341 p. *Notes*: Includes bibliographical references (p. 293–5) and index.

——. **The theatregoer's almanac: a collection of lists, people, history, and commentary on the American theatre**. Westport, Conn.: Greenwood Press, 1997. – x, 287 p. *Notes*: Includes index. Bibliography: p. 239–44.

Horn, Barbara Lee. **The age of Hair. Evolution and impact of Broadway's first rock musical**. New York: Greenwood Press, 1991. – xvii, 166 p. *Notes*: Includes bibliographical references (p. 151–61) and index. Musicals. History and criticism.

Huertas Vázquez, Eduardo. **Teatro musical español en el Madrid ilustrado**. Madrid: Avapiés, 1989. – 245 p.: ill. *Notes*: Includes bibliographical references. Musical theatre. Spain.

Hummel, David. **The collector's guide to the American musical theatre**. Metuchen, N.J.: Scarecrow Press, 1984. – 2 vols. *Notes*: Discography. Bibliography: vol. 1, p. xvii–xviii. Vol. 1. The shows – vol. 2. Index.

Ilson, Carol. **Harold Prince: from Pajama game to Phantom of the opera, and beyond**. 1st Limelight edn. New York: Limelight Editions, 1992 1989. – xiii, 461 p.: ill. *Notes*: Originally published: Ann Arbor, Mich.: UMI Research Press, c1989. With new postscript. Includes bibliographical references (p. 427–45) and index. A study of one of the masters of musical theatre direction.

Istoria ukrainskoi radianskoi muzyky. Uchbovyi posibnyk. [The history of Ukrainian Soviet music. A teaching guide]. Kiev: Muzychna Ukraina, 1990. 296 p.

Jones, Tom. **Making musicals: an informal introduction to the world of musical theatre**. New York: Limelight Editions, 1997. *Notes*: Based on lectures given at Hunter College, New York City. Musicals. Writing and publishing/ Libretto/Lyric writing (Popular music).

Kislan, Richard. **The musical: a look at the American musical theater**. Rev., expanded edn. New York: Applause, 1995. – ix, 310 p.: ill. *Notes*: Includes bibliographical references (p. 301) and index. History and criticism.

Klein, Jean-Claude. **La Chanson à l'affiche: histoire de la chanson française du café-concert à nos jours**. Paris: Du May, 1991. – 167, 1 p.: col. ill. *Notes*: Includes bibliographical references (p. 167–8) and index. France. History.

Klünder, Achim and Christina Voigt. **Lexikon des Musiktheaters im Fernsehen: 1973–1987**. Munich: K.G. Saur, 1991. – xx, 439 p. *Notes*: Pref. and introd. in German and English; catalogue in German. Music theatre on TV: 1973–87. 'Includes more than 1000 productions, from live opera performances in large opera houses to studio productions by broadcasting corporations and large-scale television filmings. ... It also includes operas and ballets written purely for television.'

Kornick, Rebecca H. **Recent American opera: a production guide**. New York: Columbia University Press, 1991. 352 p.

Kraus, Gottfried, ed. **Musik in Österreich: eine Chronik in Daten, Dokumenten, Essays and Bildern**. [Music in Austria: a chronicle of data, documents, essays and pictures]. Vienna: Brandstätter, 1989. 518 p.

Láng, Attila Endre. **Das Theater an der Wien: vom Singspiel zum Musical**. Vienna; Munich: Jugend & Volk, 1977. – 134, 2 p.: ill. *Notes*: Includes index. Bibliography: p. 136. Theater an der Wien. Austria.

Lerner, Alan Jay. **The musical theatre: a celebration**. New York: Da Capo Press, 1989 1986. – 240 p., 16 p. of plates: ill. (some col.). *Notes*: Reprint. Originally published: New York: McGraw-Hill, c1986. Includes index. Includes bibliographical references (p. 237). Musicals. History and criticism.

Lewine, Richard and Alfred Simon, comp. **Encyclopedia of theatre music; a comprehensive listing of more than 4000 songs from Broadway and Hollywood: 1900–1960**. New York: Random House, 1961. – vii, 248 p.

Lucchesi, Joachim and Ronald K. Shull. **Musik bei Brecht**. Frankfurt am Main: Suhrkamp, 1988. – 1082 p. *Notes*: 'Abkürzungen und Siglen' (2 p.) laid in. Includes indexes. Bibliography: p. 1050–1064. Music/Brecht, Bertolt. History and criticism.

Malm, William P. **Music cultures of the Pacific, the Near East and Asia**. Englewood Cliffs, NJ: Prentice Hall, 1967. 169 p.

Mandelbaum, Ken. **A chorus line and the musicals of Michael Bennett**. New York: St. Martin's Press, 1989. – xi, 352 p., 32 p. of plates: ill. *Notes*: Directors.

Marx, Robert. **Contemporary American musical theater, opera, and experimental music theater: an overview of current conditions and future trends**. [Washington, D.C.]: Policy and Planning Division, National Endowment for the Arts, 1985. – 151 p. *Notes*: Bibliography: p. 150.

Mates, Julian. **America's musical stage: two hundred years of musical theatre**. New York; London: Praeger, 1987, 1985. – 264 p.: ill. *Notes*: Originally published: Westport, Conn.: Greenwood, 1985. Includes bibliography and index. Musical revues, comedies, etc. United States. History and criticism.

Mažeika, Vytautas. **Opera 1940–1965**. Vilnius: Mintis, 1964. 255 p.

Mendenhall, Christian. **American musical comedy 1943–64: a theoretical investigation of its ritual function**. Ann Arbor, MI: University of Michigan, 1989. 284 p.

Mensah, Atta Annan. **Music and dance in Zambia**. Lusaka: Zambia Information Services, 1971.

Miller, Scott. **From Assassins to West Side Story: the director's guide to musical theatre**. Portsmouth, NH: Heinemann, 1996. – ix, 242 p. *Notes*: Production and direction/Musicals. History and criticism.

Monographs on music, dance and theatre in South East Asia. New York: Asia Society Performing Arts Program, 1979–.

Morley, Sheridan. **Spread a little happiness: the first hundred years of the British musical**. [London]: Thames & Hudson, 1987. – 221 p.: ill. (some col.). *Notes*: Includes index. Musical revues, comedies, etc. London.

Muggler, Fritz. **Zum Musikleben in der Schweiz**. [On musical life in Switzerland]. Zürich: Schweizer Kulturstiftung Pro Helvetia, 1982.

Music and dance of the Silk Route. Society for Preservation and Propagation of Eastern Arts, 1987. 53 p.

Musiktheater: Schweizer Theaterjahrbuch no. 45. [Swiss theatre yearbook no. 45: music theatre]. Bonstetten: SGTK, 1983.

Neef, Hermann and Sigrid. **Deutsche Oper im 20. Jahrhundert: DDR 1949–1989**. [German opera in the twentieth century: GDR 1949–89]. Berlin: P. Lang-Verlag, 1992. 595 p.

Novak, Elaine Adams and Deborah Novak. **Staging musical theatre**. Cincinnati, Ohio: Betterway Books, 1996. – 186 p.: ill., music. *Notes*: Includes bibliographical references (p. 174–76) and index. Production and direction.

Park, Kwang. **Pansori sosa**. [Short history of Korean musical theatre]. 2nd edn. Seoul: Singumoonhwasa, 1983. 225 p.

Porter, Steven. **The American musical theater: a complete musical theater course**. 2nd edn. Studio City, Calif.: Phantom Publications; in association with Players Press. Distributed by Empire Pub. Service, 1997. – p. cm. *Notes*: Includes bibliographical references and index. Production and direction.

Redford, H.E.D. **Musical theatre bibliography**. Salt Lake City, Utah: Dept. of Theatre, University of Utah, 1981. – 101 p.

Riley, Jo. **Chinese theatre and the actor in performance**. Cambridge and New York: Cambridge University Press, 1997. – xii, 348 p.: ill. *Notes*: Includes bibliographical references (p. 329–43) and index. Acting Study and teaching China. Chinese opera.

Sadie, Stanley, ed. **The new grove dictionary of opera**. 4 vols. London: Macmillan, 1992.

de Saint-Pulgent, M. **Le Syndrome de l'opéra**. [The opera syndrome]. Paris: Laffont, 1991.

Seeger, Horst. **Opernlexicon**. Berlin: Henschel, 1986. 702 p. First edn. 1978.

Seeley, Robert, Rex Bunnett and Brian A.L. Rust. **London musical shows on record, 1889–1989: a hundred years of London's musical theatre**. Harrow, Middlesex, Great Britain: General Gramophon Publications Ltd., 1989. – ii, 457 p. *Notes*: Rev. edn of: London musical shows on record, 1897–1976/Brian Rust. 1977. Includes indexes. Discography.

Sokol, Martin. **The New York City Opera: an American adventure**. New York: Macmillan, 1981. 562 p.

Sovetskii muzykalny teatr. Problemy zhanrov. Sbornik statei. [Soviet music theatre: issues of the genre. A collection of essays]. Moscow: Nauka, 1982.

Sovremennaya sovetskaya opera. Sbornik. [Contemporary Soviet opera. A collection]. Leningrad, 1985.

Stanishevskyi, Yuri. **Barvy ukrainskoi operety**. [The colours of Ukrainian operetta]. Kiev: Muzychna Ukraina, 1970. 140 p.

Stefanovych, M. **Kyivskyi teatr opery ta baletu**. [The Kiev Theatre of Opera and Ballet]. Kiev: Derzhvydav obrazotvorchoho mystetstva i muzychnoi literatury URSR, 1960. 208 p.

Stegmann, Vera Sonja. **Das epische Musiktheater bei Strawinsky und Brecht: Studien zur Geschichte und Theorie**. New York: P. Lang, 1991. 202 p. *Notes*: Includes bibliographical references (p. 189–98) and index. Dramatic music. 20th century. History and criticism. Stravinsky, Igor, 1882–1971. Brecht, Bertolt, 1898–1956. Weill, Kurt, 1900–50. Criticism and interpretation.

Suskin, Steven. **More opening nights on Broadway: a critical quotebook of the musical theatre, 1965 through 1981**. New York; London: Schirmer Books; Prentice Hall International, 1997. – xvii, 1141 p.: ill. *Notes*: Includes bibliographical references (p. 1097–9) and index. Musicals. First performances. New York. Reviews.

Swain, Joseph. **The Broadway musical: a critical and musical survey**. New York: Oxford University Press, 1990. 384 p.

Tereshchenko, Alla. **Lvivskyi derzhavnyi akademichnyi teatr opery ta baletu imeni Ivanan Franka**. [The Ivan Franko National Academic Theatre of Opera and Ballet in Lvov]. Kiev: Muzychna Ukraina, 1989. 207 p.

Tiagranov, G. **The Armenian Musical Theatre**. 3 vols. Yerevan, 1956–75.

Tschulik, Norbert. **Musiktheater in Österreich: die Oper im 20. Jahrhundert**. [Music theatre in Austria: opera in the twentieth century]. Vienna: Österreich. Bundesverlag, 1984.

Ursínyová, Terézia. **Cesty operety**. [The paths of operetta]. Bratislava: Opus, 1982. 198 p.

Winkler, Elizabeth Hale. **The function of song in contemporary British drama**. Newark: University of Delaware Press, 1990. – 363 p.: ill. *Notes*: Includes bibliographical references (p. 331–49) and index. Dramatic song: theoretical and historical considerations – Folk song tradition and theatrical experimentation: the drama of John Arden and Margaretta D'Arcy – 'Men Run Camps of Mass Murder and Sing Carols': the 'Rational Theatre' of Edward Bond – Dominance of popular song: music hall to rock

– Other musical forms: from religious ritual to political song. Incidental music. History and criticism/English drama.

Woll, Allen L. **Black musical theatre: from Coontown to Dreamgirls**. New York, N.Y.: Da Capo, 1991 1989. – xiv, 301 p.: ill. *Notes:* Reprint. Originally published: Baton Rouge: Louisiana State University Press, c1989. Includes bibliographical references (p. 279–85) and index. United States. History and criticism. Afro-American musical theatre.

Zanetti, R. **La musica italiana nel '900**. [Italian music in the twentieth century]. Busto Arsizio: Bramante, 1989.

Zentgraf, Christiane and Isolde Schmid-Reiter. **Musiktheater-Management**. Thurnau: Europäische Musiktheater-Akademie in Zusammenarbeit mit dem Forschungsinstitut für Musiktheater der Universität Bayreuth: Institut für Theaterwissenschaft der Universität Wien, 1993. 3 vols.: ill. *Notes:* Vol. 2 edited by Isolde Schmid-Reiter and Christiane Zentgraf, vol. 3 by Christiane Zentgraf. Includes bibliographical references. 1. Betriebsformen, Personal- und Finanzmanagement, Planung und Kontrolle – 2. Musiktheater-Marketing – 3. Musiktheater und Recht. Musical theatre management.

N. Dance Theatre

N1. History and Criticism, Dance Studies

Acogny, Germaine. **Danse africaine**. [African Dance]. Frankfurt am Main: Fricke, 1988.

And, Metin. **A Pictorial History of Turkish Dancing**. Ankara: Dost Yayınevi, 1976.

Anderson, Jack. **Ballet and modern dance**. Princeton, NJ: Princeton Book Company, 1987.

Ahye, Molly. **Cradle of Caribbean dance: Beryl McBurnie and the Little Carib Theatre**. Petit Valley, Trinidad: Heritage Culture, 1983. 166 p.

——. **Golden heritage: the dance in Trinidad and Tobago**. Petit Valley, Trinidad: Heritage Culture, 1978. 176 p.

Balet Entziklopediya. [Ballet encyclopedia]. Moscow: Sovetskaya entziklopediya, 1981.

Banes, Sally. **Dancing Women**. London: Routledge, 1998. 208 p.: ill. *Notes:* Dance history. Choreography. Female identity.

——. **Terpischore in sneakers: post-modern dance**. Middletown, CT: Wesleyan University Press, 1987. 271 p.

——. **Writing dancing in the age of post-modernism**. Hanover, NH: Wesleyan University Press, 1994. 412 p.

Bentivoglio, L. **La danza contemporanea**. [Contemporary dance]. Milan: Longanesi, 1985.

Berkson, Robert. **Musical theater choreography: a practical method for preparing and staging dance in a musical show**. New York: Back Stage Books, 1990. – vii, 199 p.: ill. *Notes:* Production and direction.

Bharatha, Iyer K. **Dance dramas of India and the east**. Bombay: Taraporevala, 1980. 73 p.

Bloch, Stella. **Dancing and the drama east and west**. New York: Orientalia, 1992. 13 p.

Boissard, C. **Danse: dix ans de développement de l'art chorégraphique**. [Dance: ten years of development of choreographic art]. Paris: Réunion des Musées Nationaux, 1993. 197 p.

Bowers, Faubian. **Theatre in the east: a survey of Asian dance and drama**. New York: Thomas Nelson & Sons, 1956. 374 p.

Brelsford, W.V. 'African dances of Northern Rhodesia'. In **The Occasional Papers of the Rhodes-Livingstone Museum**, University of Lusaka/University of Manchester, 1974.

Bremser, Martha. **International dictionary of ballet**. Detroit: St James Press, 1993. *Notes:* In two volumes.

Brinson, Peter and Clement Grisp. **The Pan book of ballet and dance**. London: Pan Books, 1981.

Brinson, Peter and Andy Ormston. **The dancer and the dance: developing theatre dance in Ireland**. Dublin: Arts Council, 1985. 79 p.

Buckle, Richard. **Diaghilev**. London: Weidenfeld & Nicolson, 1993 1979. – xxiv, 616 p., 24 p. of plates. *Notes:* Biography/Diaghilev, Serge/ Ballet.

Burt, Ramsay. **Alien bodies: representations of modernity, 'race' and nation in early modern dance**. London: Routledge, 1998. 224 p. *Notes:* German, French and US dance of 1920's and 30's. Explores work of European, American and Afro-American artists. Includes ballet, modern dance, cinema dance and revue.

Calendoli, G. **Storia universale della danza**. [Dance world history]. Milan: Mondadori, 1985.

Carell, Beht Dean. **Three dances of Oceania**. Sydney: Sydney Opera House Trust, 1976. 96 p.

——. **South Pacific Dance**. Sydney: Pacific Publications, 1978. 108 p.

CENAM. **La Danse en France/Dance in France**. Paris: CENAM, 1988.

Cheney, Gay. **Basic concepts in modern dance: a creative approach**. 3rd edn. Pennington, N.J.: Princeton Book Co., 1989. – x, 115 p.: ill. *Notes*: Rev. edn. of: **Modern dance**, 1975. 'A Dance Horizons book'. Includes index. Bibliography: p. 109–12.

Chodorow, Joan. **Dance therapy and depth psychology: the moving imagination**. London and New York: Routledge, 1991. 176 p.: ill.

Cohan, Robert and Stephanie Jordan. **Choreographers, composers, collaboration**. Chur [Switzerland]; Philadelphia: Harwood Academic Publishers, 1992. – 98 p.: ill. *Notes*: Published as **Choreography and dance**, vol. 1, pt. 4 (1992). Includes bibliographical references and index. Music and dance.

Cohen, Selma Jeanne. **International encyclopedia of dance**. New York: Oxford University Press, 1998. 6 vols: ill. *Notes*: Includes bibliographical references and index. A project of Dance Perspectives Foundation, Inc.

——. **The modern dance: seven statements of belief**. Middletown, CT: Wesleyan University Press, 1966. 106 p.

—— and Katy Matheson. **Dance as a theatre art: source readings in dance history from 1581 to the present**. 2nd edn. Princeton, NJ: Princeton Book Co., 1992. – ix, 271 p.: ill. *Notes*: 'A Dance Horizons book'. Includes bibliographical references (p. 257–71). Dance. History. Sources.

Cohen-Stratyner, Barbara Naomi. **Biographical dictionary of dance**. New York: London: Schirmer Books; Collier Macmillan, 1982. – vi, 970 p. *Notes*: 'A Dance Horizons book'. Includes bibliographical references.

Cooper, Susan. **Staging dance**. New York: Routledge/Theatre Arts Books, 1998. *Notes*: Includes bibliographical references and index. Choreography.

Craig, Edward Gordon. **Gordon Craig on movement and dance**. London: Dance Books, 1978. – xxiii, 263 p.: ill. Ed. by Arnold Rood. *Notes*: Includes bibliographical references and index.

——. **Craig on theatre**. London: Methuen Drama, 1991, 1983. – 192 p.: ill. Ed. by J. Michael Walton. *Notes*: Reprint. Originally published: London: Methuen, 1983. Includes bibliographical references (p. 188–90). Craig, Edward Gordon, 1872–1966. Views on theatre.

——. **Going to the dance**. New York: Knopf, 1982. 427 p. *Notes*: Includes index. Articles previously published in the **New Yorker**.

Cristofori, Marilyn, ed. **Hanya Holm: a pioneer in American dance**. Chur [Switzerland]; Philadelphia: Harwood Academic Publishers, 1992. – 118 p.: ill. *Notes*: Includes bibliographical references and index. Hanya Holm: a pioneer in American dance – The 'original' Hanya Holm company/Eve Gentry – The Hanya Holm New York studio in the early 1940s/Mary Anthony – Hanya: mentor, friend, muse/Glen Tetley – Hanya Holm/Alwin Nikolais – Hanya: the Colorado summers and beyond/Margery J. Turner – My fair lady and other Broadway memories/Crandall Diehl – Hanya Holm in the 1980's/Kathryn Appleby – Reflections and memories: comments about Hanya Holm/Martha Hill, Selma Tamber, Julie Andrews. Choreographers. United States.

Devi, Ragini. **Dance dialects of India**. Delhi: Vikas, 1972.

Dienes, Gedeon. **A színpadi tánc története Magyarországon**. [The art of theatrical dance in Hungary]. Budapest: Múzsák, 1989.

Dossier: metteur en scène et chorégraphe. 1995. *Notes*: Discussions of the collaboration between the theatrical director and choreographer and the relationship of theatre and dance. L'exemple Molière/Marie-Françoise Christout – Noir corbeau: Joseph Nadj [L'anatomie du fauve]/Delphine Goater – Claudel et la danse/Katia Bogopolskaia – Rêve poétique: Théâtre du Radeau/Thierry Voisin – Mi figue, mi théâtre: Gilles Nicolas [Tutu]/Philippe Verrièle – Dialogue autour d'une idée utopique mais importante [Lumière 1 et Lumière 2]/Jean-François, Georges Lavaudant – Manutentionnaires du rêve: ALIS [Numéro 7]/Martin C.

Edwards, Harvey. **The art of dance**. Boston: Little, Brown, 1989. – 144 p.: ill. (some col.). *Notes*: Dance photography.

Engdahl, Horace. **Swedish ballet and dance. A contemporary view**. Stockholm: Svenska Institutet, 1984. 32 p.

Febvre, Michèle. **Danse contemporaine et théâtralité**. Paris: Chiron, 1995. – 163 p.: ill. *Notes*: Includes bibliographical references and index. Modern dance/Choreography/Production and direction.

Foster, Susan Leigh. **Reading dancing: bodies and subjects in contemporary American dance**. Berkeley: University of California Press, 1986. – xxi, 307 p.: ill. *Notes*: Includes index. Bibliography: p. 263–85. History/United States. Modern dance.

Friedler, Sharon E. and Susan Glazer. **Dancing female: lives and issues of women in contemporary dance**. Amsterdam: Harwood Academic, 1997. *Notes*: Includes bibliographical references and index. Women dancers/Choreographers.

Ginn, Victoria. **The spirited earth: dance, myth and ritual from South Asia to the South Pacific**. New York: Rizzoli, 1990. 191 p.

Gorskii, Aleksandr Alekseevich. **Two essays on Stepanov dance notation**. New York: CORD, 1978. – xix, 78 p.: ill. *Notes*: Translation of **Tablitsa znakov dlia zapisyvaniia dvizhenii chelovecheskogo tela** and **Khoreografiia, primery dlia chteniia**. Bibliography: p. 74–6. Table of signs for the notation of the movements of the human body.–Choreography, examples for reading. Dance notation/Stepanov, Vladimir Ivanovich, 1866–96.

Graff, Ellen. **Dancers, workers and bees in the choreography of Doris Humphrey**. 1996. *Notes*: Includes bibliographical references (p. 33–4). Humphrey, Doris, 1895–1958/Life of the bee (Choreographic work: Humphrey)/New dance.

Gruen, John. **People who dance: 22 dancers tell their own stories**. Pennington, N.J.: Princeton Book Co., 1988. – ix, 176 p. *Notes*: 'A Dance Horizons book'. Dancers. United States. Biography.

Guest, Ann Hutchinson. **A history of the development of the Laban notation system**. London: Cevera, 1995. – 64 p.: ill., music. *Notes*: Includes index. Cover title. Bibliography: p. 63. History.

Gunji, Masakatsu. **Nihon buyo jiten**. Tokyo: Tokyodo Shuppan, 1977. – 4, 517 p.: ill. *Notes*: Includes indexes. Bibliography: p. 468–76. Japanese dance encyclopedia.

Guy, J.M. **Les Publics de la danse**. [The dance-going public]. Paris: Documentation Française, 1991. 479 p.

Hanraths, Ulrike and Hubert Winkels. **Tanz-Legenden: essays zu Pina Bauschs' Tanztheater**. Frankfurt/M.: Tende, 1984. – 165 p.: ill. *Notes*: Choreography/Dance companies. Bausch, Pina/Tanztheater (Wuppertal, Germany). History.

Haskins, James. **Black dance in America: a history through its people**. New York: HarperTrophy, 1992, 1990. – 232 p.: ill. *Notes*: Includes index. Bibliography: p. 216–17. Videography: p. 218–22.

Hay, Deborah. **Lamb at the altar: the story of a dance**. Durham, [N.C.]: Duke University Press, 1994. – xii, 120: ill. *Notes*: Modern dance. Choreography.

Herbison-Evans, Don. **Dance and computers**. Waterloo, Ontario, Canada: University of Waterloo, Department of Computer Science, 1985. – 12 p. *Series*: Research report. University of Waterloo. Department of Computer Science. 86–51. University of Waterloo. Dept. of Computer Science. Research report. 86–51. *Notes*: Cover title. Bibliography: p. 11–12. Choreography/Electronic data processing.

Highwater, Jamake. **Dance: rituals of experience**. 3rd edn. New York: Oxford University Press, 1996 1992. – 224 p.: ill. *Notes*: Originally published: Pennington, NJ: Princeton Book Co., c1992. Includes bibliographical references (p. 220) and index. Religious dance, Modern. History.

Hodgins, Paul. **Relationships between score and choreography in twentieth-century dance: music, movement, and metaphor**. Lewiston, N.Y.: E. Mellen Press, 1992. – vi, 227 p.: ill. *Notes*: Includes bibliographical references and index.

Hodson, Millicent. **Nijinsky's crime against grace: reconstruction score of the original choreography for Le sacre du printemps**. Stuyvesant, NY: Pendragon Press, 1996. – xxvii, 205 p., 9 p. of plates: ill. (some col.). *Notes*: Includes bibliographical references (p. 203–5). Rite of spring (Choreographic work: Nijinsky).

Hofmeister, Eleni Bookis and Muriel Topaz. **Balanchine, new approaches**. Yverdon, Switzerland: Harwood Academic Publishers, 1993. – 83 p.: ill. *Notes*: Cover title. Includes bibliographical references and index. United States/Modern dance/Balanchine, George.

Honore, Jasmine. **Towards a transcription system for Xhosa Umtshotsho dances**. Stellenbosch: Department of Physical Education, University of Stellenbosch, 1986.

Horst, Louis and Carroll Russell. **Modern dance forms in relation to the other modern arts**. Princeton, N.J.: Princeton Book Co., 1987 1961. – 151 p.: ill. *Notes*: 'A Dance Horizons book'. Reprint. Originally published: San Francisco: Impulse Publications, 1961. 'Suggested musical accompaniments': p. 146–8. Includes index.

Huet, Michel. **The dance, art and ritual of Africa**. Intro. by Jean Laude. Text by Jean-Louis Paudrat. New York: Pantheon Books, 1978.

Humphrey, Doris and Selma Jeanne Cohen. **Doris Humphrey, an artist first: an autobiography**. Centennial edn. Pennington, N.J.: Princeton Book Co., 1995, 1972. – xiv, 305 p.:

ill. *Notes*: 'A Dance Horizons book'. Originally published: Middletown, Conn.: Wesleyan University Press, 1972. Includes bibliographical references and index. Modern dance. History/Humphrey, Doris, 1895–1958.

Humphrey, Doris and Odette Blum. **Doris Humphrey, the collected works**. [Selections. 1978]. New York: Dance Notation Bureau Press, 1978. – 2 vols.: ill. *Notes*: Notations by Odette Blum and others. Includes bibliographical references. vol. 1. Water study. Shakers. Partita V. – vol. 2. Air for the G string. Two ecstatic themes. Day on earth. Choreography/Dance notation/Humphrey, Doris, 1895–1958.

Humphrey, Doris and Barabara Pollack. **The art of making dances**. New York: Grove Weidenfeld, 1991, 1959. *Notes*: Originally published. New York: Rinehart, 1959. Includes index. Choreography/Modern dance.

Jacobson, John. **Gotta sing, gotta dance: basics of choreography and staging**. Milwaukee: H. Leonard Pub. Corp., 1993. – 125 p.: ill. *Notes*: Choreography/Dance.

Jeschke, Claudia. **Representing the body: strategies of dramaturgy and choreography in dance**. 1996. *Notes*: Provides a typology of the phenomenological body in dance in relation to strategies of dramaturgy and choreography from the sixteenth century to the present. Choreography. History/Dance.

Johnston, Jill. **Marmalade me**. New and expanded edn. Hanover, N.H.: University Press of New England, 1998. *Notes*: Most of the essays in this book originally appeared in *The Village Voice*. Dance. Reviews/Modern dance. United States.

Jowitt, Deborah. **Dance beat: selected views and reviews 1967–76**. New York: M. Dekker, 1977. 211 p.

——. **The dance in mind: profiles and reviews, 1976–83**. Boston, MA. 307 p.

Jowitt, Glenn. **Dance in the Pacific**. John Hart and Kath Joblin, eds. Auckland: Longman Paul, 1990.

Kaposi, Edit and Ernő Pesovár, eds. **Magyar Táncművészet**. [The art of dance in Hungary]. Budapest: Corvina, 1983. Published in English, 1985.

Klosty, James. **Merce Cunningham**. New York: Limelight Editions, 1986 1975. – 217 p.: ill. *Notes*: Reprint. Originally published: New York: Saturday Review Press, 1975. Choreographers. United States. Biography.

Kirstein, Lincoln. **Dance: a short history of classic theatrical dancing**. Anniversary edn. Princeton, N.J.: Princeton Book Co., 1987. – xi, 398 p., 48 p. of plates: ill. *Notes*: 'A Dance horizon book'. Includes index. Bibliography: p. 359–64. Dance. History.

Koegler, Horst. **The concise Oxford dictionary of ballet**. Oxford: Oxford University Press, 1988.

Kreemer, Connie. **Further steps: fifteen choreographers on modern dance**. New York: Harper & Row, 1987. – vii, 270 p.: ill. *Notes*: Bibliography: p. 267–70.

Lalham, Peter. **Black theatre, dance and ritual in South Africa**. Ann Arbor: UMI Research Press, 1985. 172 p.

Lavelli, Lucinda and Kavita Hosali-Syed. **A discussion of plagiarism and copyright in relation to dance**. 1996. *Notes*: Provides basic insight into the problem of unlawful use of ideas, teaching the ethical achievement of creative results, what constitutes fair use, and the acceptable parameters for use of material in the public domain. Includes bibliographical references (p. 72).

Leeuwe, Hans H. and J.E. Uitman. **Toneel en dans**. Utrecht: A. Oosthoek, 1966. – 219 p. with illus. (1 fold.). *Series*: Oosthoeks lexicons. *Notes*: Bibliography: p. 215–18. Dutch dance dictionary. In Dutch.

Lloyd, Margaret. **The Borzoi book of modern dance**. [New York]: Dance Horizons (Princeton Book Co.), 1987 1949. – xxiii, 356, xxvi, p.: ill. *Notes*: Dance Horizons book. Include indexes. Bibliography: p. 355–6.

Love, Paul Van Derveer. **Modern dance terminology**. Princeton, N.J.: Princeton Book Co., 1997. – 96 p. *Notes*: Includes bibliographical references (p. 96).

Malone, Jacqui. **Steppin' on the blues: the visible rhythms of African American dance**. Urbana: University of Illinois Press, 1996. – xiii, 272 p.: ill. *Series*: Folklore and society. *Notes*: Includes bibliographical references (p. 215–51) and index. 'Gimme de kneebone bent': music and dance in Africa – 'Keep to the rhythm and you'll keep to life': the style of African American vernacular dance – Overture to vocal choreography: vernacular dance on 'stage' (slavery 1950) – 'Let the punishment fit the crime': the vocal choreography of Cholly Atkins – The history of bands: from African rituals to New Orleans: second lines: the FAMU marching 100: historical overview–colonial America to World War I – The FAMU marching 100: from ballpark bleachers to national TV – African American secret societies: remembering the past and facing the future fraternities and sororities: 'a way of remembering' – Stepping: regeneration through dance in African-American fraternities and sororities: regeneration through dance. Afro-American dance. History.

Maris, Laura. **Jooss' The green table: musical forms and devices as choreographic tools**. 1996. *Notes*: Originally written in 1953 when the author was teaching at the Jooss school in Essen and the Jooss company was preparing to tour England. Includes bibliographical references (p. 169). Choreography/Music and dance/Jooss, Kurt, 1901–79/Green table (Choreographic work: Jooss).

Martin, John Joseph. **The modern dance**. Princeton, N.J.: Princeton Book Co., 1989. – 123 p. *Notes*: 'Unabridged republication of the original edition, first published in 1933, by A.S. Barnes & Co., New York.'–T.p. verso. 'A Dance Horizons book'. Includes index.

Mas i Garcia, Carles. **Aproximació a la tècnica coreogràfica del contrapàs**. Barcelona: Institut del Teatre, Diputació de Barcelona, 1988. – 295 p.: ill. *Notes*: Includes bibliographical references (p. 293). (Dance)/Dance notation/Choreography.

Massine, Leonide. **Massine on choreography: theory and exercises in composition**. London: Faber, 1976. – 221 p.: ill. *Notes*: Includes index. Choreography/Dance notation.

Matheson, Katy. **Dance as a theatre art: source readings in dance history from 1851 to the present**. [2nd edn]. Princeton, NJ: Princeton Book Company, Publishers, 1992. – ix, 271 p.: ill. *Notes*: Includes bibliographical references (p. 257–71). History. Sources.

McDonagh, Don. **George Balanchine**. Boston, Mass.: Twayne Publishers, 1983. – 201 p.: ill. *Series*: Twayne's dance series. *Notes*: Includes index. Bibliography: p. 175. Choreographers. United States. Biography.

Mensah, Atta Annan. **Music and dance in Zambia**. Lusaka: Zambia Information Services, 1971. 22 p.

Miettinch, Jukka O. **Classical dance and theatre in Southeast Asia**. Singapore/Oxford/New York: Oxford University Press, 1992. 175 p.

Moore, Carol-Lynne and Kaoru Yamamoto. **Beyond words: movement observation and analysis**. New York: Gordon & Breach, 1988. – xv, 305 p.: ill. *Notes*: Includes bibliographical references and index. Dance/Choreography/Movement, Aesthetics.

Nettleford, Rex. **Dance Jamaica: cultural definition and artistic discovery. The National Dance Theatre Company of Jamaica, 1962–83**. New York: Grove Press, 1986. 317 p.

——. **Roots and rhythms: Jamaica's National Dance Theatre**. Photographs by María La Yacona. London: André Deutsch, 1969. 127 p.

Newlove, Jean. **Laban for actors and dancers: putting Laban's movement theory into practice: a step-by-step guide**. London: Nick Hern Books, 1993. – 158 p.: ill. *Notes*: Includes bibliographical references (p. 158). Movement (Acting). Movement notation/Modern dance. Choreography.

Novack, Cynthia. **Sharing the dance: contact improvisation and American culture**. Madison, WI: University of Wisconsin Press, 1990. 258 p. Officer, Jill. **The encyclopedia of theatre dance in Canada**. Toronto: Dance Collection Danse, 1990. (Electronic publication).

Ottolenghi, V. **La danza contemporanea**. [Contemporary dance]. Rome: Gremiese, 1990.

Palmer, Bruce and Beth Dean. **South Pacific: islands art and dance**. Suva, Fiji: Fiji Times and Herald, 1972.

Partsch-Bergsohn, Isa. **Modern dance in Germany and the United States: cross currents and influences**. Chur: Harwood Academic Publishers, 1994. – xix, 167 p.: ill. *Notes*: Includes bibliographical references (p. 157–67) and index. Modern dance. Germany. Modern dance. United States. History. Cross-cultural studies.

Pastori, Jean-Pierre. **Tanz und Ballett in der Schweiz**. [Dance and ballet in Switzerland]. Zürich: Schweizer Kulturstiftung Pro Helvetia, 1985.

Payne, Helen. **Dance movement therapy: theory and practice**. London and New York: Routledge, 1992. 269 p.

Percival, John. **Theatre in my blood: a biography of John Cranko**. New York: F. Watts, 1983. – vii, 248 p., 32 p. of plates: ill. *Notes*: Includes index. Choreographers. Biography.

Pollack, Barbara and Charles Humphrey Woodford. **Dance is a moment: a portrait of José Limón in words and pictures**. Pennington, NJ: Princeton Book Co., 1993. – xv, 93 p.: ill. *Notes*: 'A Dance Horizons book'. Biography/Choreographers.

Preston-Dunlop, Valerie Monthland. **Dance words**. Chur, Switzerland; [Philadelphia, Pa.]: Harwood Academic Publishers, 1995. – xx, 718 p. *Notes*: Includes bibliographical references (p. 617–640) and indexes. The dance domain – Dance people – The performer – The performer and the movement – Technique – Costume –

Movement and the moving body – Dynamics and timing of movement – Space-in-the-body and the dancer in space – Notation – Choreographic form – Some ensemble, group, duo and solo dance concerns – Choreographic processes – The dance sound – The sound and the movement – The dance space – Repertory, revival, and tradition – The nexus and the emergence of style – Communication – Dance research.

——. **Point of departure: the dancer's space**. London: V. Preston-Dunlop, 1984. – xi, 129 p.: ill.; 21 x. *Notes*: Bibliography: p. 128–9. Movement notation/Dance notation/Laban, Rudolf von, 1879–1958/Choreography – Manuals.

Ranger, T.O. **Dance and Society in Eastern Africa, 1890–1970: The Beni Ngoma**. London: Heinemann, 1975.

Robinson, Jacqueline. **L'Aventure de la danse moderne en France, 1920–1970**. [The adventure of modern dance in France, 1920–70]. Bouge, 1990. 380 p.

Rogosin, Elinor. **The dance makers: conversations with American choreographers**. New York: Walker, 1980. – 186 p. *Notes*: Includes index. Interviews.

Royce, Anya Peterson. **The anthropology of dance**. Bloomington; London: Indiana University Press, 1980, 1977. – xv, 238 p.: ill., 1 form, music. *Notes*: Originally published: 1977. Includes index. Bibliography: p. 220–7. Dance and society/Anthropological perspectives.

Ruth Page video archives. A collection of 129 videotape cassettes containing dance footage and on-camera interviews which detail the life, career and choreography of American dance pioneer, Ruth Page. Chicago, Ill.: Thea Flaum Productions, 1990. – vi, 545 p. *Notes*: Printed text to accompany the videotape series. Includes index. Choreographers. United States. Biography/Modern dance. Page, Ruth.

Ryan, Allan James. **Early history of dance medicine**. 1997. *Notes*: Historical review of the early scientific articles on dance injuries, the first use of the term 'dance medicine', the beginnings of book publications, and the concept of a comprehensive dance health programme. Includes bibliographical references (p. 33–4).

—— and Robert E. Stephens. **The healthy dancer: dance medicine for dancers: selected articles from Dance medicine: a comprehensive guide**. Abridged edn. Princeton, NJ: Princeton Book Co., 1989 1987. – xiv, 267 p.: ill. *Notes*: Abridged edn. of: **Dance medicine**. c1987. Includes bibliographies and index.

Sakakibara, Kiitsu. **Dances of Asia**. Chandigarh, India: Abishek, 1992. 218 p.

Sandomir, Larry. **Isadora Duncan: revolutionary dancer**. Austin, Tex.: Raintree Steck-Vaughn, 1995. – 128 p.: ill. *Notes*: Includes bibliographical references (p. 122) and index. Modern dance/Duncan, Isadora, 1877–1927.

Schmidt, Jochen and Gert Weigelt. **Tanztheater in Deutschland**. Frankfurt am Main: Propyläen, 1992. – 259 p.: ill. *Notes*: Includes bibliographical references (p. 240) and index. Dance in Germany.

Servos, Norbert, Gert Weigelt and Hedwig Müller. **Pina Bausch–Wuppertal Dance Theatre, or, The art of training a goldfish: excursions into dance**. Cologne: Ballett-Bühnen-Verlag, 1984. – 249 p.: ill. *Notes*: Rev. translation of: **Pina Bausch, Wuppertaler Tanztheater**/Hedwig Müller. 1979. Bibliography: p. 247–8. Choreography/Bausch, Pina/Tanztheater (Wuppertal, Germany).

Shawn, Ted. **Gods who dance**. New York: E.P. Dutton & Co., 1929. 208 p.

Siegel, Marcia B. **Days on earth: the dance of Doris Humphrey**. Durham; London: Duke University Press, 1993, 1987. – xv, 333 p.: ill. *Notes*: Originally published: Yale University Press, 1987. Bibliography: p. 321–4. Includes index. Humphrey, Doris, 1895–1958/Choreography.

——. **The shapes of change: images of American dance**. Boston, MA: Houghton Mifflin, 1979. 386 p.

Smith-Autard, Jacqueline Mary. **Dance composition**. 3rd edn. London: A & C Black, 1996. – vi, 186 p.: ill.; c. *Notes*: Includes bibliographical references and index. Choreography.

Sorell, Walter, ed. **The Dance has many faces**. 3rd rev. edn. Chicago: A Capella Books, 1992. – xii, 273 p.: ill. *Notes*: Includes bibliographical references (p. 257–263). Religious manifestations in the dance/Ruth St. Denis – Dance drama/Doris Humphrey – The Mary Wigman I know/Hanya Holm – Random remarks/Charles Weidman – Notes on choreography/Frederick Ashton – Marginal notes on the dance/George Balanchine – The educational and therapeutic value of the dance/Rudolf von Laban – The dance and pantomime: mimesis and image/ Angna Enters – The Negro dancer in our time/ Donald McKayle – Favorable balance of trade/ Walter Terry – Present problems and possibilities/Helen Tamiris – Comedy in dance/Clive Barnes – Pauline Koner speaking/Pauline Koner – Avant-garde choreography/Selma Jeanne

Cohen – The living dolls/George Jackson – Growth of a theme/Alwin Nikolais – What is the most beautiful dance?/Erick Hawkins – Dance on film/John Martin – Television ballet/Birgit Cullberg – In defense of the future/Walter Sorell – About Balanchine/George Jackson – La nouvelle danse française/Jean-Marc Adolphe – The British scene/Dorothy Madden and Valerie Preston-Dunlop – Reconstruction/deconstruction: currents in contemporary German dance/Claudia Jeschke – A private view of dance criticism/Deborah Jowitt – A very serious thesis and other notions/Gus Solomons Jr – Music for dance: an overview/Greg Steinke – Videamos/Stuart Hodes – Capturing the evanescent/Earl Ubell – 100 years of dance/Murray Louis – By way of conclusion/Walter Sorell.

——. **Dance in its time**. New York: Columbia University Press, 1986, 1981. – ix, 469 p.: ill. *Notes*: Includes index. Bibliography: p. 438–47. History/Dance. Social aspects.

Stanton-Jones, Kristina. **Introduction to dance movement therapy in psychiatry**. New York and London: Routledge, 1992. 288 p.

Stodelle, Ernestine. **Deep song: the dance story of Martha Graham**. New York: London: Schirmer Books; Collier Macmillan, 1984. – xxi, 329 p., 48 p. of plates: ill. *Notes*: 'A Dance Horizons book'. Includes index. Bibliography: p. 291–6. Modern dance. Graham, Martha. Biographies.

Tanz: 20. Jahrhundert in Wien. [Dance: twentieth century in Vienna]. Exhibition catalogue. Vienna: Österreich Theatermuseum, 1979.

Teck, Katherine. **Ear training for the body: a dancer's guide to music**. Pennington, NJ: Princeton Book Co., 1994. – ix, 321 p.: ill. *Notes*: 'A Dance Horizons book'. Includes bibliographical references (p. 307–16) and index.

Theodores, Diana. **First we take Manhattan: four American women and the New York school of dance criticism**. Amsterdam: Harwood Academic Publishers, 1996. – xiv, 180 p.: ill. *Notes*: Includes bibliographical references (p. 163–71) and index. Dance criticism. Croce, Arlene/Siegel, Marcia B/Jowitt, Deborah/Goldner, Nancy.

Thomas, Helen. **Dance, modernity and culture: explorations in the sociology of dance**. London: Routledge, 1995. 232 p.: ill. *Notes*: US modern dance. St Denis, Ted Shawn and Martha Graham.

Tiérou, Alphonse. **Dooplé: the eternal law of African dance**. Chur, Switzerland; Philadelphia,

Pa.: Harwood Academic Publishers, 1992. – xii, 88 p.: ill. *Notes*: Translated from the French. Includes bibliographical references. Dance. Africa, Sub-Saharan.

Topaz, Muriel. **Alvin Ailey: an American visionary**. Netherlands: Langhorne, PA: Harwood Academic Publishers GmbH; International Publishers Distributor, 1996. – 70 p.: ill. (some col.). *Series*: Choreography and dance: an international journal, 8091–6381; vol. 4, pt. 1. *Notes*: Includes index. United States/Choreographers.

Tormis, Lea. **Eesti balletist**. [On the Estonian ballet]. Tallinn: Eesti Raamat, 1967. 228 p.

Van Zile, Judy. **Dance in Africa, Asia and the Pacific: selected readings**. New York: MSS Information Corp., 1976. 177 p.

Vaughan, David and Melissa Harris. **Merce Cunningham: fifty years**. New York, NY: Aperture, 1997. – 315, 4 p.: ill. (some col.). *Notes*: Includes bibliographical references (p. 305–6) and index. Choreography. Pictorial works/Dance photography/Cunningham, Merce.

Vega de Triana, Rita. **Antonio Triana and the Spanish dance: a personal recollection**. Chur, Switzerland; Langhorne, Pa., USA: Harwood Academic Publishers, 1993. – xii, 112 p.: ill. *Notes*: Includes bibliographical references and index. Dancers. Spain. Biography/Flamenco/Triana, Antonio, 1906–89.

Viala, Jean and Nourit Masson-Sekine. **Butoh: shades of darkness**. Tokyo: Shufunotomo, 1988. – 207 p.: ill. *Notes*: 'This book is the first comprehensive study in English of this new dance form' – Jacket. Includes index. Japan.

Watkins, Andrea and Priscilla M. Clarkson. **Dancing longer dancing stronger: a dancer's guide to improving technique and preventing injury**. Princeton, N.J.: Princeton Book Co., 1990. – xii, 281 p.: ill. *Notes*: 'A Dance Horizon Book'. Includes bibliographical references (p. 267–74) and index.

Welsh-Asante, Kariamu. **Zimbabwean dance: an aesthetic analysis of the Jerusarema and Muchongoyo dances**. New York.

White, Joan W. **Twentieth-century dance in Britain: a history of major dance companies in Britain**. London: Princeton, N.J.: Dance Books; Distributed in the USA by Princeton Book Co., 1985. – 191 p.: ill. *Notes*: Cover title: 20th century dance in Britain. Includes index. Bibliography: p. 179. Ballet Rambert/Jenny Mann – The Royal Ballet and Sadler's Wells Royal Ballet/Werdon Anglin – London Festival Ballet/Claire Teverson – London Contemporary

Dance Theatre/Richard Mansfield – The Scottish Ballet/Robin Anderson.

Wigman, Mary. **Le Langage de la danse**. Paris: Papiers, 1986. – 101, 43 p.: ill.; 21 x. Notes: 'L'oeuvre de Mary Wigman. Chorégraphies représentées en public, 1914–1961' – P. 102–105. Translation of: **Die Sprache des Tanzes**. Philosophy/Choreography/Modern dance/Wigman, Mary, 1886–1973.

Wyman, Max. **Dance Canada: an illustrated history**. Vancouver: Douglas & McIntyre, 1991. 224 p.

Zahaikevych, M.P. **Dramaturhiia baletu**. [The dramaturgy of ballet]. Kiev: Naukova dumka, 1978. 259 p.

Zarina, Xenia. **Classical dances of the Orient**. New York: Crown, 1967. 232 p.

Zorn, Friedrich Albert. **Grammar of the art of dancing, theoretical and practical: lessons in the arts of dancing and dance writing (choreography) with drawings, musical examples, choreographic symbols, and special music scores**. New York: B. Franklin, 1977. – xviii, 302 p.: ill. Notes: 'An Artemis book'. Translation of Granimatile der Tanzkunst. Reprint of the 1905 edn. published by Heintzemann Press, Boston. Includes index. Dancing/Dance notation.

N2. Mime Studies

Broadbent, R.J. **A history of pantomime**. New York: Arno Press, 1977. – 226 p. Notes: First published 1901.

Davies, Gill. **Staging a pantomime**. London: A & C Black, 1995. – 144 p.: ill. Notes: Includes bibliographical references (p. 141) and index. Production and direction.

De Marinis, Marco. **Mimo e teatro nel novecento**. Florence: Casa Usher, 1993. – 390 p.: ill. Notes: Includes bibliographical references and index. Mime. History. 20th century.

Decroux, Etienne. **Words on mime**. 2nd edn./ translated by Mark Piper. Claremont, Calif.: Pomona College Theatre Dept., 1985 1977. – iii, 160 p.: ill. Series: Mime Journal, 0145–787X; 1985. Notes: Reprint. Originally published: **Paroles sur le mime**. Paris: Gallimard, 1963. 'A revised and augmented edn was published by Librairie Théâtrale, Paris, 1977. **Words on mime** is a translation of the 2nd edn., 1977 Librairie Théâtrale.' – Mime/Gesture.

Diamon, Mario. **Le Mime**. Montréal: Éditions Logiques, 1997. – 93 p.: ill. Notes: Technique.

Dorcy, Jean. **A la rencontre de la mime et des mimes: Decroux, Barrault, Marceau**. Neuilly-sur-Seine: Cahiers de danse et culture, 1958. – 152 p., 23 p. of plates: ill., ports. Notes: Jean Dorcy – Pour le pire et pour le meilleur/Etienne Decroux – La mime tragique/Jean-Louis Barrault – Le halo poétique/Marcel Marceau.

——, ed. **The mime**. London: White Lion Publishers, 1975 1961. – xxvii, 116 p., 24 p. of plates: ill. Essays by Etienne Decroux, Jean-Louis Barrault, and Marcel Marceau. Translations by Robert Speller Jr. and Pierre de Fontnouvelle. This translation originally published: New York: R. Speller, 1961. – Translation of: **A la rencontre de la mime et des mimes**. Neuilly-sur-Seine: Cahiers de danse et culture, 1958. Includes index. Mime. France, c1920–c1960.

Enters, Angna. **On mime**. 1st paperback edn. Middletown, Conn.: Wesleyan University Press, 1978, 1965. – 132 p.: ill.

Falckenberg, Bettina and Günter Titt. **Die Kunst der Pantomime: Abenteuer und Herausforderung**. Cologne: Prometh, 1987. – 175 p.: ill. Notes: Bibliography: p. 172–3.

Fialka, Ladislav and Eva Soukupová. **Ladislav Fialka: Knoflík. Rozbor inscenace pantomimy L. Fialky v Divadle Na zábradlí v Praze. Premiéra 3. dubna 1968**. Prague: Divadelní ústav: t. SCT 31: Kladno, 1972. – 127, 1 p. illus. (part col.). Notes: Summary in English, Russian, French, and German (30 p.) inserted. Fialka, Ladislav. Czech mime.

Frow, Gerald. **'Oh, yes it is'!: a history of pantomime**. London: British Broadcasting Corp., 1985. – 192 p., xx p. of plates: ill. Notes: Includes index. Bibliography: p. 187–8. Pantomime (Christmas entertainment). History.

Gerber, Anke and Clement de Wroblewsky. **Anatomie der Pantomime: das Buch über die stumme Kunst, oder, Der Leitfaden, an dem die Pantomime hängt**. Hamburg: Rasch & Röhring, 1985. – 197 p., 12 p. of plates: ill.

Hamblin, Kay and Andrew Fluegelman. **Mime: a playbook of silent fantasy**. Garden City, N.Y.: Dolphin Books, 1978. – 191 p.: ill. Notes: Includes index. Bibliography: p. 189–90. Filmography: p. 190. Essays introduce mime as an expressive and recreational activity and instructions are given for many exercises and gestures of this art form. Mime.

Harris, Paul. **The pantomime book: the only known collection of pantomime jokes and sketches in captivity**. London; Chester Springs, PA: Peter Owen; U.S. distributor Dufour Editions, 1996. – 140 p. Pantomime (Christmas entertainment)/English.

Hausbrandt, Andrzej. **Das Pantomimentheater Tomaszewskis**. [Tomaszewski's Mime Theatre]. Warsaw: Verlag Interpress, 1975. – 172 p.: chiefly ill. (some col.). *Notes*: 'Deutsch [von] Barbara Ostrowska'.

Hera, Janina. **Der verzauberte Palast: aus der Geschichte der Pantomime**. Berlin: Henschel, 1981. – 326 p.: ill. *Notes*: Translation of: Z dziejów pantomimy, czyli palac zaczarowany. Includes bibliographical references and index. Mime. History.

——. **Z dziejów pantomimy, czyli palac zaczarowany**. Warsaw: Panstwowy Instytu Wydawniczy, 1975. – 409 p., 64 p. of plates: ill. *Notes*: Summaries in English, French, and Russian. Includes bibliographical references and indexes. Mime. History.

Hunt, Douglas and Kari Hunt. **Pantomime: the silent theater**. New York: Atheneum, 1966, 1964. – xii, 114 p.: ill. *Notes*: Bibliography: p. 111–14. Mime.

Ihering, Herbert and Marcel Marceau. **Die Weltkunst der Pantomime: ein Gespräch**. Berlin: Aufbau Verlag, 1956. – 61 p., 44 p. of plates, 6 p.: ill. *Notes*: Mime.

Kipnis, Claude and Neil Kleinman. **The mime book**. 2nd edn. Colorado Springs, Colo.: Meriwether Pub., 1988, 1974. – 202 p.: ill. *Notes*: Originally published: New York: Harper & Row, 1974. Bibliography: p. 195. Mime.

Kramer, Michael. **Pantomime und Clownerie: Geschichte der Clownerie von der Commedia dell'Arte bis zu den Festivals of Fools: mit Anleitungen und Vorschlägen zur Übung und zum Spiel**. Offenbach/M.: Burckhardthaus-Leatare Verlag, 1986. – 119 p.: ill. *Notes*: Includes bibliographical references (p. 118).

Leabhart, Thomas. **Modern and post-modern mime**. New York: St Martin's Press, 1989. – xii, 157 p., 32 p. of plates: ill. *Notes*: Includes index. Bibliography: p. 148–53. Biography/Mime. History. 20th century.

Lecoq, Jacques. **Le Théâtre du geste: mimes et acteurs**. Paris: Bordas, 1987. – 152 p.: ill. (some col.). *Notes*: Includes index. Bibliography: p. 504.

Loeschke, Maravene Sheppard. **All about mime: understanding and performing the expressive silence**. Englewood Cliffs, N.J.: Prentice-Hall, 1982. – 184 p.: ill. *Notes*: Includes index. Bibliography: p. 177–8.

Marceau, Marcel. **Ronald A. Wilford presents Marcel Marceau and his partner Pierre Verry**. [New York]: Dunetz & Lovett, 1973. – [24 p.]: ill. *Notes*: Drawings by Marcel Marceau. Marceau, Marcel/Verry, Pierre.

——. **The story of Bip**. 1st edn. New York: Harper & Row, 1976. – [30] p.: chiefly ill. (some col.). *Notes*: Bip wants to be a magician who can show people the magic of their world. Mime. Fiction.

—— and Herbert Ihering. **Die Weltkunst der Pantomime**. Zürich: Die Arche, 1961. – 116 p. illus.

——. **Weltkunst der Pantomime**. Zürich: Verlag der Arche, 1972. – 103 p.: ill.

Markova, Elena Viktorovna. **Sovremennaia zarubezhnaia pantomima**. Moscow: Iskusstvo, 1985. – 190, 2 p.: ill. *Notes*: Bibliography: p. 190–1. Biography/Decroux, Etienne.

Martin, Ben. **Marcel Marceau, master of mime**. Montreal: Optimum Pub. Co., 1978. – c150 p.: chiefly ill. (some col.). *Notes*: Mime. Ouvrages illustrés/Marceau, Marcel.

Mawer, Irene. **The art of mime; its history and technique in education and the theatre**. London: Methuen, 1955. – xii, 244 p. front. *Notes*: First published in 1932. Bibliography: p. 235–6.

Meffert, Barbara and Janina Hera. **Welt der Pantomime**. Wilhelmshaven: Heinrichshofen, 1984. – 280 p., 6 p. of plates: chiefly ill. Mimes. Portraits.

Pardoe, T. Earl. **Pantomimes for stage and study**. New York: Arno Press, 1976. – viii, 394 p. *Series*: The Drama League library of the theatre arts. *Notes*: Reprint of the 1931 ed. Includes bibliographies and index.

Pickering, David. **Encyclopaedia of pantomime**. Andover: Gale Research, 1993. – xxxvi, 240 p. *Notes*: Includes index. Bibliography: p. 229–30.

Radler, Friedrich von. **Der wienerische Hanswurst: mit 'Hanswursts Geburt – Pantomime in einem Akt' und einem kurzweiligen Hanswurstspiel in zwei Abteilungen**. Frankfurt/M.: Puppen und Masken, 1987. – 79 p.: ill.

Rosenberg, Christiana. **Praxis für das Bewegungstheater**. Aachen: Meyer & Meyer, 1990. – 102 p.: ill. Mime/Theatre of movement.

Sládek, Milan, Kurt Peters and Frank Meyer. **Milan Sládek Pantomimentheater**. Cologne: Bund, 1985. – 169 p.: ill. (some col.). *Notes*: Mime. Czechoslovakia. Biography/Sládek, Milan.

Smuzniak, Karol. **Wroclawski Teatr Pantomimy, 1956–1978: kronika, dokumentacja**. Wroclaw: Wydawn. Uniwersytetu Wroclawskiego, 1985. – 114 p., 32 p. of plates: ill. *Notes*:

Bibliography: p. 82–114. Pantomime. Poland. Wroclaw. History.

——. **Wroclawski Teatr Pantomimy: mit w teatrze Henryka Tomaszewskiego**. Wroclaw: Zaklad Narodowy im. Ossolinskich, 1991. – 147 p., 32 p. of plates: ill. *Notes*: Summary in English. Includes bibliographical references. Pantomime. Poland. Wroclaw/Myth/Dramatic criticism. Tomaszewski, Henryk.

Svehla, Jaroslav. **Tisícileté umení pantomimy: ukázky z dejin pantomimy**. Prague: Melantrich, 1989. – 210 p.: 95 ill. *Notes*: Includes bibliographical references (p. 197) and index. Pantomime. History.

Tomaszewski, Henryk. **Le Théâtre de pantomime**. Warsaw: Interpress, 1975. – 172 p.

—— and Andrzej Hausbrandt. **Tomaszewski's mime theatre**. Warsaw: Interpress, 1975. – ca. 150 p.: chiefly ill. (some col.). *Notes*: Translation of **Pantomima**. Poland.

Wylie, Kathryn. **Satyric and heroic mimes: attitude as the way of the mime in ritual and beyond**. Jefferson, N.C.: McFarland, 1994. – ix, 254 p.: ill. *Notes*: Includes bibliographical references (p. 223–48) and index.

Yanci, Heinatz, Joachim. **Le Mime: idées et figures, pantomimes, acteurs et danseurs**. Paris: Fischbacher, 1990. – 231 p.: chiefly ill. *Notes*: Mime/Pantomime/Gesture.

——. **Movement and gesture: the illustrated technics and basics of pantomime: a guidebook**. Wilhelmshaven: Noetzel, 1990. – 160 p.: ill.

Zwiefka, Hans Jürgen. **Slapstick, Pantomime, Maskenspiel**. Moers: Edition Aragon, 1988. – 102 p.: ill.; 15 x. *Notes*: Includes bibliographical references (p. 102). Handbooks, manuals, etc/mime.

O. Cultural Policy, Demographics

Abah, O.S. **Popular theatre as a strategy for education and development: the example of some African countries**. Leeds: University of Leeds, 1987.

Abirached, Robert. **Le Théâtre et le prince: 1981–1991**. Paris: Plon, 1992. – 205 p. *Notes*: Includes bibliographical references (p. 203–4). Federal aid to the theatre. France.

Acevedo, Patricia, Clemente Lizana and Carlos Ochsenius. **Cuerpo y cultura autoritaria: dos experiencias de expresión corporal en grupos de base**. Santiago, Chile: Centro de Indagación y Expresión Cultural y Artística, 1984. – 74 p. *Notes*: Includes bibliographical references. Theatre and state. Chile and Brazil.

Aquino, J.L. and J.J. Kitney. **Statistical analysis of subsidised dance, drama, and puppetry companies, 1974–78: activity and financial statistics for twenty-eight performing arts companies receiving general grants from the Theatre Board of the Australia Council**. North Sydney [N.S.W.]: Published for the Theatre Board by the Arts Information Program of the Australia Council, 1980. – 140, 15 p. *Notes*: Theatre and state. Australia.

Aznar Soler, Manuel. **Veinte años de teatro y democracia en España (1975–1995)**. Barcelona: Cop d'Idees: Seminari de Literatura Espanyola Contemporània, Cía Investigadora del Teatro Espanol Contemporáneo, Departament de Filologia Espanyola, 1996. – 239 p. *Notes*: Includes bibliographical references. History. 20th century/Spanish drama. Theatre and state. Spain.

Bain, Reginald Frank. **The federal government and theatre: a history of federal involvement in theatre from the end of the Federal Theatre Project in 1939 to the establishment of the National Foundation on the Arts and Humanities in 1965**. 1972. – iv, 329 l. *Notes*: Bibliography: p. 308–29. Thesis (Ph. D.) –University of Minnesota. Theatre and state. United States.

Bammer, Armin. **Bundestheater und Verfassung: eine historisch-systematische Untersuchung der (verfassungs)rechtlichen Stellung der Bundestheater unter besonderer Berücksichtigung der Kunstfreiheit und der Kompetenzverteilung**. Vienna: Verlag der Österreichischen Staatsdruckerei, 1992. – 387 p. *Notes*: Includes bibliographical references (p. 359–368) and index. Theatre and state. Austria.

Bharucha, Rustom, **Rehearsals of revolution: Political theatre of Bengal**. Honolulu: University of Hawaii Press, 1983. 276 p.

Bradley, David and Roy Wilkie. **Conflict in publicly subsidised theatres: an organisational analysis**. Glasgow: Centre for the Study of Public Policy, University of Strathclyde, 1980. – ii, 51 p. *Notes*: Includes bibliographical references. Theatre and state. Great Britain.

British Information Services. **Entertainment and the arts in Great Britain, the story of Government encouragement**. Rev. New York: [British Information Services], 1956. – 32, 1 p. *Notes*: Cover title. At head of title: British Information Services. Reference Division. I.D.

1024. 'March 1956'. Bibliography: p. 31–3. Theatre and state. Great Britain.

Capelin, Steve. **Challenging the centre: Two decades of political theatre**. Brisbane: Playlab, 1995.

Cavallo, Pietro. **Immaginario e rappresentazione: il teatro fascista di propaganda**. Rome: Bonacci, 1990. – 290 p. *Notes*: Includes bibliographical references (p. 209–76) and index. Theatre and state. Fascism and theatre.

Clottu, Bericht, *et al.* **Beiträge für eine Kulturpolitik in der Schweiz. Bericht der eidgenössischen Expertenkommission für Fragen einer schweizerischen Kulturpolitik**. [Proposals for a cultural policy in Switzerland. Report of the Federal Commission of Experts on a Swiss policy for the arts]. Berne: Swiss Federal Government, 1975. p. 47–94.

Colloque sur le théâtre africain. **Théâtre africain, théâtres africains?: actes du Colloque sur le théâtre africain, Ecole normale supérieure, Bamako, 14–18 novembre 1988**. Paris: Editions Silex, 1988. – 246 p. *Notes*: Includes bibliographical references. Theatre and state. Africa.

Cramsie, Hilde F. **Teatro y censura en la España franquista: Sartre, Muñiz y Ruibal**. New York: P. Lang, 1984. – 205 p. *Notes*: Bibliography: p. 189–205. Theatre and state. Spain.

Dace, Wallace. **National theaters in the larger German and Austrian cities**. New York: Richards Rosen Press, 1980 1981. – xix, 468 p.: ill. *Notes*: Includes index. Bibliography: p. 437–443. Theatre and state. Germany and Austria.

Denmark. Udvalget vedrørende revision af Teaterloven. **Teaterloven: betænkning**. Copenhagen: Statens informationstjeneste, 1988. – 328 p. *Notes*: Includes bibliographical references (p. 277–80). Theatre and state. Denmark.

Drugge, Ulf and Dag Nordmark. **I periferin: en förberedande undersökning av teaterförhållanden och publikreaktioner i Kalix kommun**. Umeå: Sociologiska institutionen, Umeå universitet, 1985. – 136 p.: ill. *Notes*: Bibliography: p. 133–6. Theatre and state. Sweden.

Dux, Pierre. **Le Développement des activités théâtrales: avis adopté par le Conseil économique et social au cours de sa séance du 25 octobre 1977. Annexe à l'avis (scrutin). Déclaration des groupes. Rapport**. [Paris]: Le Conseil, 1977. – 152 p. in various pagings. *Notes*: Includes bibliographical references. Theatre and state. France.

Eyoh, Hansel Ndumbe and Bole Butake. **Beyond the theatre**. Bonn: German Foundation for International Development: Education, Science and Documentation Centre, 1991. – viii, 206 p., 14 p. of plates: ill. *Notes*: Includes bibliographical references (p. 180–205). Interviews/ Theatre and society. Theatre and state. Africa, Sub-Saharan.

Féral, Josette. **La Culture contre l'art**. Sillery: Presses de l'Université du Québec, 1990. – xxvii, 341 p.: ill. *Notes*: Federal aid to the theatre. Québec and Canada. Cultural policy. Canada.

Flotats, Josep Maria. **Un projecte per al Teatre Nacional**. Barcelona: Edicions de la Revista de Catalunya, 1989. – 143 p., 8 p. of plates: ill. (some col.). Theatre and state. Spain. Catalonia.

Frisvold, Ðivind. **Teatret i norsk kulturpolitikk: bakgrunn og tendenser fra 1850 til 1970-årene**. Oslo: Universitetsforl. Edgard Høgfeldt, 1980. – 244 p.: ill. *Notes*: Includes index and bibliography. Theatre and state. Norway.

Galán, Eduardo and Juan Carlos Pérez de la Fuente. **Reflexiones en torno a una política teatral**. Madrid: Fundación para el Análisis y los Estudios Sociales, 1995. – 214 p. *Notes*: Includes bibliographical references. Theatre and state. Spain.

Gallina, Mimma. **Teatro d'impresa, teatro di stato?: storia e cronaca della scena italiana contemporanea**. Turin: Rosenberg & Sellier, 1990. – 141 p.: ill. *Notes*: Theatre and state. Italy.

Gourdon, Anne-Marie. **Théâtre, public, perception**. [Theatre and its perception by the public]. Paris: CNRS, 1982. 253 p.

Gruslin, Adrien. **Le Théâtre et l'État au Québec: essai**. Montréal: VLB, 1981. – 413 p.: ill. *Notes*: Bibliography: p. 401–8. Theatre and state. Québec.

Guy, J.M. and L. Mironer. **Les Publics du théâtre**. [The theatregoing public]. Paris: Documentation française, 1988. 238 p.

Hankins, Dilys R. **Toward a national theatre: the Canada Council, 1957–1982**. 1987 1984. – ix, 109 p. *Notes*: Bibliography: p. 105–9. Thesis (M.A.)–American University, 1984. Photocopy. Ann Arbor, Mich.: University Microfilms, 1987. Theatre and state. Canada.

Herdlein, Hans. **Theaterpolitik: Aufsätze und Reden zur Theaterpolitik 1961–1980**. Hamburg: Bühnenschriften-Vertriebs-GmbH, 1981. – 427 p., viii p. of plates: ill. *Notes*: Includes index. Bibliography: p. 420–4. Theatre and state. Germany (West).

Hình tung Bác Ho trên sân khau. Hanoi: Vicen sân khau, 1993. – 298 p., 5 p. of plates: col.

ill. *Notes*: Theatre and state. Vietnam. 20th century/Ho Chí Minh, 1890–1969. Views on drama.

Howey, Nicholas. **Who's afraid of Franz Kafka. An introduction to theatre activity in Czechoslovakia, 1969**. 1970. – xiii, 414 p.: ill. *Notes*: Bibliography: p. 404–12. Thesis (Ph. D.) –Wayne State University, 1970. Microfilm. Ann Arbor, MI: University Microfilms International, 1971. 1 microfilm reel; 35 mm. Theatre and state. Czechoslovakia.

Hübner, Zygmunt and Jadwiga Kosicka. **Theater and politics**. Evanston, Ill.: Northwestern University Press, 1992. – xvi, 222 p. *Notes*: Includes bibliographical references (p. 218–22). Theatre and state. Censorship. Poland.

Hurtado, María de la Luz and María Elena Moreno. **El público del teatro independiente**. [Audiences of the independent theatre]. Santiago: CENECA, 1982. 89 p. *Notes*: Chilean theatre.

Institute of Jamaica. **A guide to cultural policy development in the Caribbean**. Wahington, DC: Organization of American States, 1984–.

Khéde, Sonia Salomão. **Censores de pincênê e gravata: dois momentos da censura teatral no Brasil**. [Censors with pince-nez and necktie: two periods of censorship in Brazilian theatre]. Rio de Janeiro: Codecri, 1981. 204 p.

Kulturpolitikk i 1980-arene. [Cultural policy in the 1980s]. Stortingsmelding [White paper] no. 23. Oslo: 1981.

Langsted, Jørn. **Teater i lokalpolitik: tre teater-politiske kronikker, 1980**. Århus: Institut for Dramaturgi, 1980. – 36 p. *Notes*: Theatre and state. Denmark.

Macdonnell, Justin. **Arts, Minister? Government and the arts in Australia**. Sydney: Currency, 1992.

Magaldi, Sábato. **Um palco brasileiro: o Arena de São Paulo**. [Brazilian audiences and the Teatro de Arena in São Paulo]. São Paulo: Brasiliense, 1984. 100 p.

——. **O teatro sob pressão: uma frente de resistência**. [Theatre under oppression: a front of resistance]. Rio de Janeiro: Jorge Hazar, 1985. 96 p.

—— and Rosyanne Trotta. **Teatro e estado: as companhias oficiais de teatro no Brasil**. [Theatre and state: Brazil's official theatre companies]. São Paulo: Editora Hucitec/IBAC, 1992. 262 p.

Mbowa, Rose. **Artists under siege: theatre and the dictatorial regimes in Uganda**. Kampala: Makerere University, 1994. *Notes*: Serumaga, Robert. Political aspects. Theatre and state. Uganda.

Netherlands. Ministerie van Cultuur, Recreatie en Maatschappelijk Werk. **Nota toneelbeleid**. The Hague: Staatsuitgeverij, 1977. – 89 p. *Notes*: Theatre and state. Netherlands.

Nielsen, Frank and Pia Knudsen. **Teater i samfundet: kultur og socialt arbejde: rapport fra et miljøproyekt**. [Aalborg]: Aalborg universitetsforlag, 1984. – 128 p.: ill. *Notes*: Theatre and state. Denmark.

Ny kulturpolitikk 1974. [New cultural policy 1974]. Stortingsmelding [White paper] no. 52. Oslo, 1974.

Orkin, Martin. **Drama and the South African state**. Manchester, New York and Johannesburg: Manchester University Press and Witwatersrand University Press, Distributed in the USA and Canada by St Martin's Press, 1991. – 263 p. *Notes*: Includes bibliographical references and index. Theatre and state. South Africa.

Peixoto, Fernando. **Teatro Oficina 1958–82: trajetória de uma rebeldia cultural**. [Teatro Oficina 1958–82: a path of cultural rebellion]. São Paulo: Brasiliense, 1982. 126 p.

Québec (Province). Ministère des affaires culturelles. **La politique du théâtre au Québec**. Québec: Ministry of Culture, 1984. – viii, 79 p.: ill. *Notes*: Includes bibliographical references. Theatre and state. Québec.

Raszewski, Zbigniew. **Raptularz 1967/1968**. Warsaw: Oficyna Wydawnicza Interim, 1993. – 175 p.: ill. *Notes*: Politics and government. Teatr Narodowy (Warsaw).

Reinelt, Janelle G. **Crucibles of crisis: performing social change**. Ann Arbor: University of Michigan Press, 1996. – vi, 250 p.: ill. *Notes*: Includes bibliographical references. Theatre and society/Drama. Social aspects.

Riess, Curt. **Theater gegen das Publikum: Aida als Putzfrau und andere Missetaten**. München: Langen Müller, 1985. – 256 p. *Notes*: Includes index. Theatre audiences. Germany.

Ronfani, Ugo and Antonio Attisani. **Buongoverno del teatro: per una rifondazione della società teatrale**. [Paris?]: Shakespeare & Company, 1994. – 309 p. *Notes*: Includes bibliographical references. Theatre and state. Italy.

Schmidt-Mühlisch, Lothar. **Affentheater: Bühnenkrise ohne Ende?** Erlangen: Straube, 1989. – 159 p. *Notes*: Theatre. Germany (West). Theatre audiences. German-speaking.

Shevtsova, Maria and Robert Abirached. **Theatre and the new cultural policy of France's socialist government**. Devon, England: Dept. of Theatre, Dartington College of Arts, 1982. – 40 p. *Notes*: Includes bibliographical references. Theatre and state. France.

Slawson, Richard Jacobson. **The Peruvian revolution on stage: the rise and fall of the Teatro Nacional Popular of Peru, 1971–1979**. 1991. – x, 184 p. *Notes*: Includes bibliographical references (p. 170–84). Thesis (Ph. D.)–University of Texas at Austin, 1991. Theatre and state. Peru.

So' Jan', U. **Pra jat' sa muin'-**. Rangoon: Ca pe lo ka, 1965. – 240 p. *Notes*: In Burmese. History/Theatre and state. Burma.

Soda, Hidehiko. **Minshu gekijo: mo hitotsu no Taisho demokurashi**. Tokyo: Shozansha, 1995. – 326 p.: ill. *Notes*: Theatre and state. Japan. History.

Solf, Günter. **Theatersubventionierung: Möglichkeiten einer Legitimation aus wirtschaftstheoretischer Sicht**. Bergisch Gladbach: J. Eul, 1993. – ix, 326 p.: ill. *Notes*: Includes bibliographical references (p. 300–26). Theatre and state. Germany.

South Africa. Commission of Inquiry into the Performing Arts. **Report of the Commission of Inquiry into the Performing Arts**. Pretoria: Govt. Printer, 1978. – viii, 122 p. *Notes*: Theatre and state. South Africa.

Suharyoso Sk. **Penyebaran teater tradisional di Kabupaten Sleman: (sebuah laporan penelitian)**. Yogyakarta: Universitas Gadjah Mada, Lembaga Pengkajian Kebudayaan Indonesia, 1979. – x, 99 p.: charts. *Notes*: Indonesia. Theatre and state.

Teatro: plan nacional para su desarrollo. Buenos Aires: Asociación Peronista de Actores Independientes, 1984. – 93 p. *Notes*: Theatre and state. Law and legislation. Argentina.

Temkine, Raymonde. **Le Théâtre en l'état**. Paris: Editions Théâtrales, 1992. – 253 p. *Notes*: Includes index. Theatre and state. France.

Torres Cárdenas, Edgar Guillermo. **Praxis artística y vida políticas del teatro en Colombia, 1955–1980**. 1. edn. Tunja, Boyacá, Colombia: Magister en Historia, Escuela de Posgrado de la Facultad de Educación, Universidad Pedagógica y Tecnológica de Colombia, 1990. – 96 p.: ill. *Series*: Nuevas lecturas de historia, 0121–165X; 11. *Notes*: 'Anexos documentales': p. 83–96. Includes bibliographical references. Theatre and state. Colombia/Theatre and society. Colombia.

Traditions revitalized: essays on the use of selected ASEAN CTM for development communication. Manila, Philippines: ASEAN, 1991. – 231 p. 16 p. of plates: ill. (some col.). *Notes*: Includes index. 'A project of the ASEAN Committee on Culture and Information'. Theatre and state. Asia, Southeastern.

Trezzini, Lamberto. **Geografia del teatro: rapporto sul teatro italiano d'oggi**. Rome: Bulzoni, 1977. – 234 p.: ill. *Notes*: Theatre and state. Italy.

Twenty-fifth Street House Theatre. **Towards a Canadian cultural policy: an indigenous perspective**. Saskatoon: The Theatre, 1981. – 9, [13] p.: ill. *Notes*: Letter of transmittal and brief to the Federal Cultural Policy Review Committee. Cover title. Theatre and state. Canada/Twenty-fifth Street House Theatre.

Una gran revolución en el frente de la cultura. Beijing: Ediciones en Lenguas Extranjeras, 1965. – 119 p. *Notes*: Theatre and state. China/Chinese drama. History and criticism/Communism and literature/Operas, Chinese/Cultural policy.

van Erben, Eugène. **The playful revolution: theatre and liberation in Asia**. Bloomington, IN: Indiana University Press, 1992. 304 p.

Vaughn, Robert Francis. **A historical study of the influence of the House Committee on Un-American Activities on the American theatre, 1938–1958**. 1970. – iv, 591 p. *Notes*: Microfilm. Ann Arbor, Mich.: Xerox University Microfilms, 1978. – 1 reel; 35 mm. Bibliography: p. 573–91. Thesis–University of Southern California. Theatre and state. United States. House Committee on Un-American Activities.

Views of theatre in Ireland 1995: report of the Arts Council theatre review. Dublin: Arts Council, 1995. – 269 p. *Notes*: 20th century Theatre and state. Drama in education. Ireland.

Wardetzky, Jutta. **Theaterpolitik im faschistischen Deutschland: Studien und Dokumente**. Berlin: Henschel, 1983. – 398 p. *Notes*: Includes bibliographical references and index. National socialism/Theatre. Germany.

Washburn, John Nelson. **Soviet theatrical repertory organization and the 'anti-American' propaganda campaign of 1946–1953**. 1981 1970. – x, 455 p. *Notes*: Bibliography: p. 384–455. Thesis (Ph. D.)–Columbia University, 1970. Photocopy. Ann Arbor, Mich.: University Microfilms International, 1981. Theatre and state. Soviet Union.

Wilkie, Roy and David Bradley. **The subsidised theatre: its organisation and audience**. Glasgow: MacLellan, 1970. – 65 p. *Notes*:

Includes bibliographical references. Theatre and state/Glasgow Citizens Theatre.

Zhidkov, Vladimir Prokhorovich. **Teatr i vremia: ot Oktiabria do perestroiki**. Moscow: Soiuz teatral'nykh deiatelei RSFSR, 1990 1991. – v. *Notes*: Includes bibliographical references. History/Theatre and state. Soviet Union.

Zhidkov, Vladimir Sergeevich. **Kul'turnaia politika i teatr**. [Cultural policy and the theatre]. Moscow: IzdAT, 1995. – 320 p. *Notes*: Includes bibliographical references. Theatre and state. Russia (Federation). Cultural policy.

P. Theatre For Young Audiences, Developmental/ Social Action Theatre, Theatre In Education, Careers

Alphandery, Helene Gratiot. **Le Théâtre pour enfants**. Paris: Laboratoire de Psycho-biologie de l'Enfant, 1974. – 276 p. diagrs. *Notes*: 1. Situation du théâtre pour enfants en France. 2. Les créateurs et leurs créations. 3. L'enfant spectateur. – Analyse de la compréhension d'un spectacle, par F. Rosemberg et M. Reinert.- Annexes: 1. L'analyse factorielle des correspondences. 2. Sources d'information utilisées pour établir le recensement des troupes. 3. Liste des troupes. 4. Liste des créateurs. Liste des pièces.- Bibliographie commentée sur le théâtre pour enfants. Theatre. France. Children's plays. In French. Bibliography.

Ambjörnsson, Gunilla and Annika Holm, eds. **Barnteater – en klassfråga**. [Children's theatre – a matter of class]. Stockholm: Rabén & Sjögren, 1970. 144 pp.

Barter, Nicholas. **Playing with plays**. London: Macdonald Educational, 1979. – 96 p.: ill. *Notes*: 'This book is produced with the help of Unicorn Theatre children's workshops'. Acting/ Children's plays.

Beauchamp, Hélène. **Bibliographie annotée sur le théâtre québécois pour l'enfance et la jeunesse, 1970–1983; suivie d'une liste sélective d'articles de presse portant sur les productions de théâtre québécois pour l'enfance et la jeunesse, 1950–1980**. Montréal: Dép. de théâtre, Université du Québec à Montréal, 1984. – 39 f. *Notes*: Children's plays, Canadian (French). Quebec (Province). History and criticism. Bibliography.

——. **Le Théâtre pour enfants au Québec, 1950–80**. [Children's theatre in Québec, 1950–80]. Cahiers du Québec, Collection Littérature. Montréal: Hurtubise-HMH, 1985. 306 p.

Bedard, Roger L. and C. John Tolch, eds. **Spotlight on the child: studies in the history of American children's theatre**. New York: Greenwood Press, 1989. 203 p.

Breitinger, Eckhard, ed. **Theatre for development**. Bayreuth African Studies Series 36. Bayreuth, Germany: University of Bayreuth, 80 p.

Centre de Sociologie du Théâtre. **Théâtres et jeunes publics, 1970–1980**. [Theatre and young audiences, 1970–1980]. Brussels: Direction générale de la Jeunesse et des Loisirs, 1981. 335 p.

Chicorel, Marietta. **Chicorel theater index to plays for young people in periodicals**. New York: Chicorel Library Pub. Corp., 1974. Bibliography.

Cossa, Mario. **Acting out: the workbook: a guide to the development and presentation of issue-oriented, audience-interactive, improvisational theatre**. Washington, DC: Accelerated Development, 1996. – x, 142 p.: ports. *Notes*: Includes bibliographical references (p. 139). Psychodrama/Group psychotherapy for teenagers/Theatre and youth/Drama in education/ Psychodrama in adolescence/Drama/Drama therapy.

Courtney, Richard. **Dictionary of developmental drama: the use of terminology in educational drama, theater education, creative dramatics, children's theater, drama therapy, and related areas**. Springfield, Ill., USA: C.C. Thomas, 1987. – ix, 153 p.: ill. *Notes*: Bibliography: p. 151–3.

——. **Drama education Canada: a bibliography of Canadian publications in drama and theatre education**. Sharon, Ontario: Bison Books, 1987. – 42 p.

——. **Drama and feeling: an aesthetic theory**. Montreal: McGill-Queen's University Press, 1995. – 230 p.: ill. *Notes*: Includes bibliographical references (p. 195–222) and index. Drama in education.

——. **Drama and intelligence: a cognitive theory**. Montreal; Buffalo: McGill-Queen's University Press, 1990. – x, 190 p. *Notes*: Includes bibliographical references (p. 165–82) and index. Cognition.

Crothers, J. Frances. **The puppeteer's library guide; the bibliographic index to the literature of the world puppet theatre**. Metuchen: N.J.:

Scarecrow Press, 1971, 1983. – 2 vols. *Notes*: Vol. 2 includes index. vol. 1. The historical background of puppetry and its related fields.–vol. 2. The puppet as an educator.

Duvanel, Blaise. **Théâtre pour les jeunes en Suisse: Annuaire du Théâtre Suisse** no. 42. [Swiss theatre yearbook no. 42: theatre for young audiences in Switzerland]. Zürich: SGTK, 1979.

England, Alan. **Theatre for the young**. London: Macmillan, 1990.

Erenstein, Robert. **Jeugdtheater geen kinderspel**. [Children's theatre not child's play]. Amsterdam: International Theatre Bookshop, 1981. 115 p.

Fridell, Lena, ed. **Children's theatre in Sweden**. Stockholm: Swedish Centre of the International Theatre Institute, 1979. 96 p.

Gabnai, Katalin. **Gyermekszínház Magyarországon**. [Children's theatre in Hungary]. Budapest: Múzsák, 1984.

Gesell, Izzy. **Playing along: 37 learning activities borrowed from improvisational theater**. Duluth, Minn.: Whole Person Associates, 1997. – xviii, 136 p. *Notes*: Includes bibliographical references (p. 136). Group relations. Problems, exercises, etc.

Hägglund, Kent. **Theatre for children in Sweden. A contemporary view**. Stockholm: Svenska Institutet, 1986. 32 p.

Hodgson, John Reed, ed. **The uses of drama: acting as a social and educational force: an anthology**. 1st Evergreen edn. New York: Grove Press: distributed by Random House, 1979. *Notes*: Reprint of the edn published by Eyre Methuen, London. Includes bibliographical references. Theatre and society/Drama in education.

Hoffmann, Christel, ed. **Kinder- und Jugendtheater der Welt**. [Children's and youth theatre of the world]. 2nd edn. Berlin: Henschel, 1984. 276 p.

Hornbrook, David. **Education and dramatic art**. London: Routledge, 1997. 176 p. *Notes*: New edition brings Hornbrook's classic critique of drama education in schools up-to-date.

Institut Culturel Africain. **Quel théâtre pour le developpement en Afrique?** [Which theatre for development in Africa?] Dakar: Nouvelles Editions Africaines, 1985. 149 p.

Izzo, Gary. **Acting interactive theater: a handbook**. Portsmouth, NH: Heinemann, 1998. Production and direction/Improvisation (Acting)/ Participatory theatre.

——. **The art of play: the new genre of interactive theater**. Portsmouth, NH: Heinemann, 1997. – x, 262 p.: ill. Improvisation. Participatory. Theatre audiences.

Jackson, Tony, ed. **Learning through theatre: new perspectives on theatre in education**. 2nd edition. London/New York: Routledge, 1993. 295 p.

Kamlongera, Christopher. **Theatre for Development in Africa with case studies from Malawi and Zambia**. Bonn: DSE, 1989.

Kemp, David. **A different drummer: an ideas book for drama**. Rev. edn. Toronto: McClelland & Stewart, 1990. – 185 p. *Notes*: Drama in education/Improvisation (Acting). Study and teaching.

Khamis, Shawqi. **Children's theatre**. Cairo: Egyptian Book Organization, 1995. *Notes*: In Arabic.

Kidd, Ross. **The popular performing arts: non-formal education and social change in the Third World**. The Hague: CESO, 1982.

Kitson, Neil and Ian Spiby. **Drama 7–11: developing primary teaching skills**. London: Routledge, 1997. 120 p.: ill. *Notes*: Includes bibliography. Guide to teaching drama.

McCaslin, Nellie. ed. **Children and drama**. 2nd edn. Lanham, MD: University Press of America, 1987. 348 p.

——. **Historical guide to children's theatre in America**. New York: London: Greenwood, 1987. – 352 p. *Notes*: Includes bibliography and index. Children's plays. Children's theatre, 1900–85.

Mda, Zakes. **When people play people: development of communication through theatre**. London: ZED, 1993.

Michaels, Wendy and Peter Newham. **Inside drama**. Melbourne: Pitman, 1987. – 122 p.: ill. *Notes*: Includes index. For secondary school students. Acting and direction.

Minotis, Alexis. **Empirical theatre education**. 2nd edn. Athens: I Ekdosis ton Filon, 1988.

Mlama, Penina Muhando. **Culture and development: the popular theatre approach in Africa**. Uppsala: Nordiska Afrikainstitutet, 1991.

Moreira, Amélia Maria and Irati Antônio. **Bibliografia da dramaturgia brasileira. Teatro infantil e juvenil**. [São Paulo]: Associação Cultural de Amigos do Museu Lasar Segall: Secretaria Municipal de Cultura de São Paulo, 1991. – vii, 110 p. *Notes*: Includes indexes. Children's plays, Brazilian. Bibliography.

Morgan, Bradley J. and Joseph M. Palmisano, eds. **Performing arts career directory: a practical, one-stop guide to getting a job in performing arts**. Detroit: Gale Research, 1994. – xviii, 306 p. *Series*: Career advisor series. *Notes*: Includes index. So you want to be an actor?/ Dick Moore and Helaine Feldman – In the trenches: working as a professional actor/John Keith Miller – There's more to stage acting than Broadway/Robert J. Bruyr – So you think you're funny?/Angela Shelton – Access to the arts: career opportunities for actors with disabilities/ William E. Rickert – The Broadway musical: a performer's perspective/Duane Bodin – Preparing for a career as a general director in opera/ Richard Marshall – Choreographers: who are they? What do they do? How can you become one?/Norman Walker – So you want to be a ballet dancer?/Jan Hanniford Goetz – Careers in dance: working as an artistic director, instructor, or choreographer/Debra Jean White-Hunt – Composing concert music: the joys and hardships/David Cleary – Working as a designer in the performing arts/Donna E. Brady – Setting the stage: careers in theatre design and technology/Konrad Winters – Getting started in the cruise industry/Jim Coston – The business of performing arts/Johanna Humbert – Internships: the pathway to a job in arts administration/Darrell Ayers.

al-Mufraji, Ahmad Fiyyaad. **Masrah at-Tifl Fi l-'Iraaq**. [The children's theatre in Iraq]. Baghdad, 1978.

Norsk Kulturråd. **Utredning om barneteaterarbeid i Norge**. [Report on children's theatre in Norway]. Oslo: Norsk Kulturråd, 1974.

Rioux, Monique, Diane Bilz and Jean-Marie Boisvert. **L'Enfant et l'expression dramatique**. [Dramatic expression and the child]. Montréal: Editions de l'Aurore, 1976. 185 p.

Sats, Nataliia. **Sketches from my life**. Moscow: Raduga, 1985. – 435 p., 80 p. of plates: ill. (some col.). *Notes*: Translation of: **Novelly moei zhizni**. Soviet Union. Autobiography of one of the world's leading children's theatre directors.

Schneider, Wolfgang, ed. **Kinder- und Jugendtheater in der DDR**. [Theatre for children and young audiences in the GDR]. Frankfurt: Dipa, 1990. 110 p.

Shah, Anupama. **Puppetry and folk dramas for non-formal education**. New Delhi: Sterling, 1992. 174 p.

Sparby, Monica, ed. **Unga Klara. Barnteater som konst**. [Unga Klara. Children's theatre as art]. Stockholm: Gidlunds, 1986. 208 p.

Swortzell, Lowell, ed. **International guide to children's theatre and educational theatre**. A Historical and Geographical Source Book. Westport, CT: Greenwood Press, 1990. 360 p.

Theaterwerkstatt in Halle. Die Werkstatt-Tage des Kinder- und Jugendtheaters von 1977 bis 1990. [Theatre workshop in Halle: workshops for theatre for children and young audiences from 1977 to 1990]. Berlin: Ostdeutsche Sektion der ASSITEJ, 1991. 110 p.

Van Tassel, Wesley Harvey. **Theory and practice in theater for children: an annotated bibliography of comment in English circulated in the United States from 1900 through 1968**. 1982 1969. – v, 310 p. *Notes*: Includes indexes. Bibliography: 273–82. Thesis (Ph. D.)– University of Denver, 1969. Photocopy. Ann Arbor, Mich.: University Microfilms International, 1982.

Viktorov, Viktor Iezekiilevich. **The Nataliia Sats Children's Musical Theatre**. Moscow: Raduga Publishers, 1986. – 141 p., 76 p. of plates: ill. (some col.). *Notes*: Includes bibliographical references. Soviet Union. Biography/Children's plays.

Waack, William L. **Career and career education in the performing arts: an annotated bibliography**. Washington: American Theatre Association, 1981. – [50] p. *Notes*: Includes indexes. Performing arts as a profession. Bibliography.

Wisniewski, David. **Teaching with shadow puppetry**. Englewood, CO: Teacher Ideas Press, 1997. 225 p.

Yendt, Maurice. **Les Ravisseurs d'enfants: du théâtre et des jeunes spectateurs**. [Wonder for children: theatre and young audiences]. Arles: Actes-Sud, 1989. 179 p.

Zernitskaia, E.I. **Sovetskii teatr dlia detei, 1918–1972: Ukazatel' literatury**. [Soviet theatre for children. An index of literature]. Moscow: GBL, 1978 1979. – 4 vols. *Notes*: Theatre. Soviet Union. Children's plays. Bibliography.

CUMULATIVE INDEX